# SIGNAL

## Communication Tools for the

## Information Age

## EDITED BY KEVIN KELLY

## A Whole Earth Catalog

### HARMONY BOOKS

Staff gathered on deck, with two weeks to go 'till deadline. Starting with the front row, left to right: Sally, office dog; Don Ryan, usually at the other end of the camera; Susan Erkel Ryan, resting for a change; Laura Benne, paste-up freelancer; Corinne Cullen Hawkins, researcher on loan from Whole Earth Review; Richard Kadrey, with sunglasses and smirk. In the back row, same direction: Kevin Kelly, smiling foolishly (the book is late); Sally, a.k.a. Sarah, Vandershaf, smiling happily (she's done); Sarah Satterlee, chief of the early morning shift; Lori Woolpert, general purpose aide; Kathleen O'Neill, sole designer of book. Not present here, but shown elsewhere: John Chan, paste-upper; David Burnor, master indexer; Jeanne Carstensen, midwife of the preliminary book.

# SIGNAL

*Editor in Chief*
**Kevin Kelly**

*Editors*
**Richard Kadrey**
**Sarah Satterlee**
**Sarah Vandershaf**

*Signal Special Issue Editor*
**Jeanne Carstensen**

*Designer*
**Kathleen O'Neill**

*Production Manager*
**Susan Erkel Ryan**

*Camerawork*
**Don Ryan**

*Pasteup*
**Laura Benne**
**John Chan**

*Proofreaders*
**Hank Roberts**
**Lori Woolpert**

*Indexer*
**David Burnor**

*Researchers*
**David Finacom**
**Corinne Cullen Hawkins**

*Special thanks to*
**Jay Kinney**

*Stats and Halftones*
**Marinstat**

*Literary Agent*
**John Brockman Associates**

*Harmony Books*
**Michael Pietsch**

# POINT

*Bookkeeper*
**Cindy Fugett**

*Subscriptions*
**Paul Davis**

*Office Manager*
**Susan Rosberg**

*Assistant Editor*
**Richard Nilsen**

*Far-Ranging Factotum*
**Dick Fugett**

*Typesetter*
**James Donnelly**

*Circulation*
**Keith Jordan**

*Promotion*
**Richard Schauffler**

*EWEC Editor*
**J. Baldwin**

## Point Board

**Stewart Brand**
**Doug Carlston**
**Robert Fuller**
**Huey Johnson**
**Kevin Kelly**

SIGNAL
**Communication Tools for the Information Age**

Copyright © 1988 by Point Foundation

Published by Harmony Books, a division of Crown Publishers, Inc., 225 Park Avenue South, New York, New York 10003 and represented in Canada by the Canadian MANDA Group.

HARMONY and colophon are trademarks of Crown Publishers, Inc.

Manufactured in the United States of America

Library of Congress Cataloging-in-Publication Data
Signal : a whole earth catalog.
    Includes index.
    1. Telecommunication—Apparatus and supplies—Catalogs.    I. Kelly, Kevin, 1948–
TK5103.S49   1988      621.38'0294      88-13165

BOMC offers recordings and compact discs, cassettes and records. For information and catalog write to BOMR, Camp Hill, PA 17012.

# TABLE OF CONTENTS

# PURPOSE

W E ARE AS GODS and might as well get good at it. So far remotely done power and glory — as via government, big business, formal education, church — has succeeded to the point where gross defects obscure actual gains. In response to this dilemma and to these gains, a realm of intimate, personal power is developing — the power of individuals to conduct their own education, find their own inspiration, shape their own envirnonment, and share the adventure with whoever is interested. Tools that aid this process are sought and promoted by this version of the Whole Earth Catalog.

# FUNCTION

S IGNAL IS AN EVALUATION and access device. It can help a user discover what is worth getting and how to get it. We're here to point, not to sell. We have no financial obligation to any of the suppliers listed. Our only obligation is accuracy for the reader. We only review stuff we think is great. Why waste your time with anything else?

An item is listed in *Signal* if it is deemed:

1. Useful as a tool,
2. Relevant to independent education,
3. High quality or low cost,
4. Easily available, preferably by mail.

The listings are continually revised and updated according to the experience and suggestions of *Whole Earth Catalog* users and staff. Latest news can be found in our magazine, *Whole Earth Review* (see p. 53).

# RANGE

T HIS BOOK LIMITS its investigation to all possible tools having information at one end and a grasp at the other. It considers any idea that can amplify the reach of personal communication, any science which can intercept the power of larger circuits to redirect its flow toward individuals, and any art that can nurture data into information, information into knowledge, and knowledge into wisdom.

# PROCEDURE

O RDER ITEMS from *Signal* directly from the supplier or publisher. Do not order from us. We sell nothing but information. Books can also be ordered from the independent Whole Earth Access Company if marked "or Whole Earth Access" below the book's ordering information.

Consider these points of mail order etiquette; they'll make shopping by mail more pleasant for you and the companies you are dealing with.

1. Write legibly. Say what you want on the outside of the envelope. Writing "mail order" or "catalog request" or "subscription order" will speed your transaction. You can usually request free information with an inexpensive post card.

2. Expect prices to rise. The prices shown here are accurate as of June, 1988. All prices will be greater if you are ordering outside of the U.S.

3. Don't order from the excerpts of the catalogs we've reviewed. Catalog prices go out of date quickly. Request their latest brochure to get the latest specifications and prices.

4. Include sales tax if the supplier is in the state you are ordering from.

5. Use the phone. Most companies will be happy to bill your credit card if you need something quickly. Even if you aren't in a hurry it's worth a phone call to check prices or make sure what you want is in stock. Don't be shy to make use of a company's 800 toll-free number; they have bought one because it increases their business.

6. Use International Money Orders (IMOs) to send money abroad. You can get them at the post office. Don't send a personal check.

7. Be patient. It takes at least two weeks for your goods to arrive; four to six weeks is normal. Make a photocopy of your order before you send it.

8. Be gentle. If you need to complain, remember your goal is resolution, not revenge. If you are polite and specific, the person at the other end will likely deal with your problem sooner. Include your name and full address (with zip code) every time you write or call.

9. Be considerate. Don't send away for stuff just to keep your mailbox full. If something free is worth your writing for, it's probably worth including a stamped, self-addressed envelope (SASE). It guarantees a fast response.

10. You don't have to buy it. Don't forget libraries, user groups, and schools. Libraries can get you most any book in the world if you are willing to wait for the inter-library loan network to do its magic. They also have growing collections of videos, CDs, and tape cassettes. User groups have massive libraries of public domain software. Many schools have inexpensive adult education classes that afford you a chance to use and try out expensive equipment. And then there are friends...

# ORDERING FROM WHOLE EARTH ACCESS

T HE PHRASE "or Whole Earth Access" that appears under most book ordering information in *Signal* means that you can order the book or item from the Whole Earth Access Company in Berkeley, California, an outfit inspired by the *Whole Earth Catalog* but not financially connected with us. We list them as a convenience to our readers, who may want to order multiple books from a single source instead of dealing with various publishers. To order from them:

1. Start with the list price (not the postpaid price). Total the prices of the book(s). Add $3 to each order up to five books, and 50 cents for each additional book for postage. Orders over 20 books will be charged actual UPS shipping rate.

2. Beside listing the title and quantity of books you want, it is helpful to indicate the page number they appear on in *Signal*.

3. Include your street address. All orders are shipped UPS, and UPS does not deliver to P.O. box numbers.

4. For foreign orders, shipping is $4 for the first two books and 50 cents for each additional book, shipped via post office book rate. For orders to developing countries, International Registry Insurance is recommended. That costs an extra $3.60 per order. Remit a bank draft in U.S. dollars.

Send orders, or call in with a credit card, to:

Whole Earth Access
2990 Seventh Street
Berkeley, CA 94710
800/845-2000; 415/845-3000

# INTRODUCING A REALM WITHOUT DISTANCE

*by Stewart Brand*

**B**ACK WHEN the original **Whole Earth Catalog** was having a heyday in the mid-70s, two products were introduced which we recommended heartily. One was the Vermont Castings wood stove, the other was the Apple personal computer. Both cost a few hundred dollars, both were made by and for revolutionaries who wanted to de-institutionalize society and empower the individual, both embodied clever design ideas and good business sense, and both became famous successes.

Stewart works in his boat office, a dry-docked shrimp trawler grounded in our waterfront courtyard.

tion frontiers as one meta-domain—intricately and subversively interconnected. Any tool or skill from one of them may inform or transfigure any other one. With over half of the American workforce now managing information for a living, any apparent drone drudging away on mainstream information chores might be recruited, via some handy outlaw technique or tool, into the holy disorder of hackerdom. A hacker takes nothing as given, everything as worth creatively fiddling with, and the variety which proceeds from that enricheth the adaptivity, resilience, and delight of us all.

In the summer of 1988 Vermont Castings cast its last "Defiant" stove in response to increasing air-quality regulation and struggled to keep its competitive position in a static market. Apple, that summer, was the design leader of America's prime "meta-industry" of personal computers, its revolution still advancing full tilt, and was sitting on a vast cash horde which it employed for basic research on equipping a learning world.

Pretty obvious lesson: the Vermont Castings tool manipulated heat, the Apple tool manipulated information. (So did the **Whole Earth Catalog**, and that's why we're still around too, probably.)

The Whole Earth operation in Sausalito these days is in the hands of a new generation, led by Kevin Kelly (age 36). Some of the old geezers are still on hand—J. Baldwin, Kathleen O'Neill, Don Ryan, Dick Fugett, Richard Nilsen, David Burnor, and me (enjoying a dignified role as editor emeritus)—but the torch has decidedly passed to a fresh band of outlaw-appreciators.

Society is led, Buckminster Fuller used to tell us geezers, by design ideas which emerge in the "outlaw area." That became Whole Earth's domain. Some of the outlaw areas we reported on, such as communes and psychedelic research, were inventive and significant, but short-lived. Some, such as solar energy and environmentalist concerns, eventually went mainstream. And one major area, communication technology, simultaneously went mainstream and expanded its outlaw edge.

Information technology is a self-accelerating fine-grained global industry that sprints ahead of laws and diffuses beyond them. It has done so for twenty-five years and shows every sign of being able to keep dodging for another twenty-five, if not indefinitely. Hence Whole Earth's abiding, and now focussed, interest.

Kevin and crew wish to consider the full gamut of explosively diverging informa-

(Pause for an important distinction . There is a subspecies of computer hacker called "crackers" who use their skills to vandalize systems or steal information for profit. They belong in jail without a keyboard.)

A "hacker," in the emerging definition, is anyone who pushes the edges of the possible and permissible. In **Signal** are techniques for hacking English, music, audio cassettes, postcards, rubber stamps, video, diagrams, robots, and the nervous system, to name a fraction of the myriad represented here. In all of these realms the distance to the edge is not far, and the distance from one to another is no distance at all.

The information world is inherently global, in both senses—all-encompassing and planetary. Welcome to a new whole Earth, whose true-blue image in space we are no longer just viewing, but beginning to live.

## Man and His Symbols

Carl G. Jung
1964; 320 pp.
**$5.95**
($7.95 postpaid) from:
Dell Reader Service
P.O. Box 5057
Des Plaines, IL
60017-5057
or Whole Earth Access

*Carl Jung did a nice thing just before he died. He helped with a British effort to bring all of his work together in one richly illustrated introduction to the breadth of his realm. This book covers his concepts of the unconscious, myths, individuation, the visual arts, dreams, and analysis. Why aren't all psychology books illustrated?*

—Stewart Brand

◆

I vividly recall the case of a professor who had had a sudden vision and thought he was insane. He came to see me in a state of complete panic. I simply took a 400-year-old book from the shelf and showed him an old woodcut depicting his very vision. "There's no reason for you to believe that you're insane," I said to him. "They knew about your vision 400 years ago." Whereupon he sat down entirely deflated, but once more normal.

◆

What we properly call instincts are physiological urges, and are perceived by the sense. But at the same time, they also manifest themselves in fantasies and often reveal their presence only by symbolic images. These

Wild horses often symbolize the uncontrollable instinctive drives that can erupt from the un-conscious—and that many people try to repress.

The "fairy godmother" of many tales is also a symbolic personification of the female Self.

manifestations are what I call the archetypes. They are without known origin; and they reproduce themselves in any time or in any part of the world—even where transmission by direct descent or "cross fertilization" through migration must be ruled out.

## An Illustrated Encyclopaedia of Traditional Symbols

J.C. Cooper
1978; 208 pp.
**$12.95** postpaid from:
Thames & Hudson, Inc.
500 Fifth Avenue
New York, NY 10010
1-800-233-4830
or Whole Earth Access

*Often I've seen religious or ceremonial art and wondered what a particular element stood for. This fascinating reference will, most likely, provide an answer—or several. Each entry guides you from the symbol's generally accepted interpretation to its more specific cultural or geographic meaning. The illustrations are rich and varied, crossing time and continent.*

—Sarah Satterlee

◆

**Parrot** Imitation; unintelligent repetition. *Chinese:* Brilliance; a warning to unfaithful wives. *Hindu:* An attribute of Kama, god of love. An oracular and rain-bringing bird. It had these qualities also in pre-Columbian America.

[Above] Shou-lao, Chinese God of Longevity, holds the **peach** of immortality, long life and prosperity in this late 18th-century soapstone carving. [Right]"Lady with an **Ermine**' by Leonardo. The ermine stands for chastity and purity—but here the symbolism may have been double-edged, for the lady is thought to be the mistress of Lodovico il Moro, of the Sforza family, and the ermine was their emblem.

The Egyptian **sky** goddess Nut bends over the world of creation, ordering all things and creating them, while maintaining her position of transcendence.

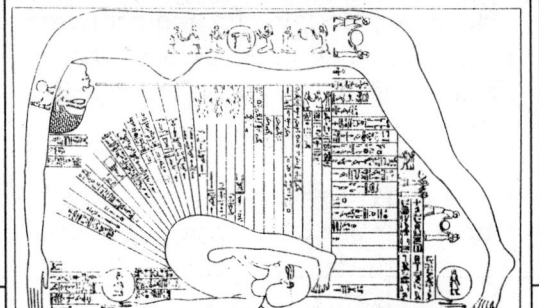

## Number Words and Number Symbols

(A Cultural History
of Numbers)
Karl Menninger
MIT Press
Out of print

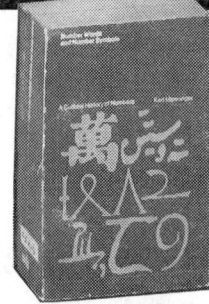

*Suppose you want to help human communication to re-understand itself. So much of that under-standing is wrapped up in numbers that if you penetrate the one you may have a foothold to tweak the other one onto a new course. Invent language and you invent humans.*

*This book penetrates numbers.*

—Stewart Brand

A bundle of Alpine number billets, small flat sticks some 20 cm long on which are carved the cow-rights to which their owner is entitled; the owner's name or symbol is on the reverse side. The most ornate of these sticks, the one at the extreme right showing the number 122, gives the total.

◆

With Three a new element appears in the concept of numbers. I — You: The I is still in a state of juxtaposition toward the You, but what lies beyond them, the It, is the Third, the Many, the Universe. . . . An old Sakai in Malacca, on being asked his age, replied, "Sir, I am three years old." To him 2 was the You, the near and familiar with which he lives, to which he feels related and with which he interacts, but this is no longer true of the It, the 3; for him that is the Many, the Alien, the Unknow-able.

Three as the plural in Egyptian: (1) flood = heaven with 3 water jugs; (2) water = 3 x wave; (3) "many" plants = 3 x plant; (4) hair = 3 hairs; (5) weep = eye with "many" (= 3) tears; (6) fear = dead goose with 3 vertical strokes, the general plural sign, next to the ideogram.

Three as the plural in Chinese: (1) forest = 3 x tree; (2) fur = 3 x hair; (3) all = 3 x man; (4) speak endlessly ("much") = 3 x speak (mouth from which words emerge); (5) rape = 3 x woman; (6) gallop (ride "much") = 3 x horse.

## Gödel, Escher, Bach

Douglas Hofstadter
1979; 777 pp.
**$14.95**
($15.95 postpaid) from:
Vintage Books
Random House
400 Hahn Road
Westminster, MD 21157
1-800-492-0782 (in MD.)
1-800-638-6460
or Whole Earth Access

## The Mind's I

Douglas R. Hofstadter
and Daniel C. Dennett
1981; 501 pp.
**$12.95**
($14.45 postpaid) from:
Bantam Books
2451 South Wolf Road
Des Plaines, IL 60018
1-800-223-6834
or Whole Earth Access

*Hofstadter's second volume,* **The Mind's I,** *as an anthology of essays he co-edits that circles through the apparent paradoxes of consciousness. Round it goes through children, ant colonies, and large computers. Parable and fiction lurk in the book, about the only animals that can keep a tentative grip on the circulating elusiveness of self-consciousness.* —Kevin Kelly

*The subject of the first book—and the frequent preoccupation of its deities, mathematician Kurt Gödel, artist M.C. Escher, composer J.S. Bach, and writer Lewis Carroll—is self-reference, what the author calls* "strange loops" or "tangled hierarchies." It is the domain of extreme paradox, where math, art, religion (lots of zen in the book, honestly employed), and epistemology collide. It is the fearless exploration of black holes of the mind.

*Hofstadter set out to make Gödel's Incompleteness Theorem accessible to the lay thinker, and happily he succeeds in that. Along the way he illuminates a world of music, mathematics, computer intelligence (and gossip), and philosophy. The book confirms the suspicion I've had for years that perhaps the most adventurous and fruitful human frontier we have these days is the hall of mirrors, Lewis Carroll's looking glass.*
—Stewart Brand

◆

Here is a short section of one of the Crab's Genes, turning round and round. When the two DNA strands are unraveled and laid out side by side, they read this way:
... TTTTTTTTTCGAAAAAAAAA ...
... AAAAAAAAAGCTTTTTTTTT ...
Notice that they are the same, only one goes forwards while the other goes backwards. This is the defining property of the form called "crab canon" in music. It is reminiscent of, though a little different from, a palindrome, which is a sentence that reads the same backwards and forwards. In molecular biology, such segments of DNA are called "palindromes"—a slight misnomer, since "crab canon" would be more accurate.
—*Gödel, Escher, Bach*

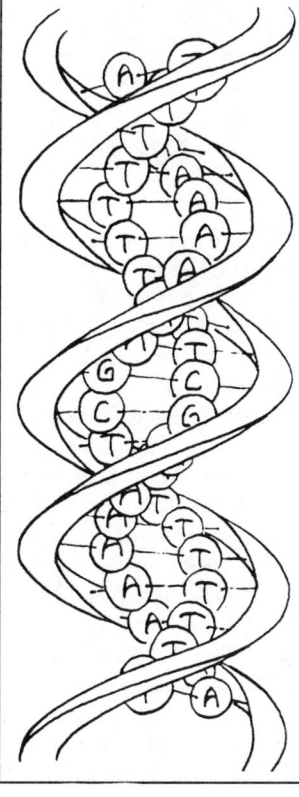

Of course, you can make yourself hear a familiar language as pure uninterpreted sound if you try very hard, just as you can look at a windowpane if you want; but you can't have your cake and eat it too—you can't hear the sounds both *with* and *without* their meanings. And so most of the time people hear mainly meaning. For those people who learn a language because of enchantment with its sounds, this is a bit disappointing—and yet mastery of those sounds, even if one no longer hears them naively, is a beautiful, exhilarating experience. (It would be an interesting thing to try to apply this same kind of analysis to the hearing of music, where the distinction between hearing bare sounds and hearing their "meanings" is far less well understood, yet seems very real.)
—*The Mind's Eye*

## Grammatical Man

(Information, Entropy, Language, and Life)
Jeremy Campbell
1982; 319 pp.
**$9.95** postpaid from:
Simon & Schuster/Mail Order Sales
200 Old Tappan Road
Old Tappan, NJ 07675
1-800-223-2348

*In the age of information it is shocking that there is so little useful information about information — how it behaves, what its economics are, indeed, what it is. A good book on the subject would have to talk about the primary domains of information: Evolution, genetics, computer programming, entropy, whole systems, and human language. This book does. It is the only one to encompass the whole natural ecology of information in a readable way.*
—Kevin Kelly

◆

There are probably more than a thousand billion synapses in the brain, and each one is a kind of coding station, where signals arrive in the form of bursts of electrical pulses, so many a second, and are translated into chemical signals in the form of very small, separate packets. Only if a sufficient number of packets accumulates is a critical threshold reached and information sent across the synaptic gap. The nerve cell on the other side of the gap computes the frequency of the arriving packets and, if the frequency is high enough, fires off a signal of its own. This is the means of transmission along the basic communications channels of the brain. The code of the message is changed from electrical to chemical and then back again to electrical as it moves from one nerve cell to another. Such a procedure allows plenty of room for chance to enter, and shows how misleading it is to compare the essential processes of the brain with those of a computer.

◆

Indeed, Gregory thinks the perceptual system of the brain, so active in testing possible answers to a puzzle set by what the eye sees, is more "intellectually honest" than the supposedly rational parts of the cerebral cortex. Faced with an ambiguous object or drawing, it will not fasten on one interpretation and stick to it, unlike the rational mind, which will often espouse a particular dogma in politics or religion and refuse to relinquish it, no matter how impressive the countervailing evidence may be.

◆

"How can machines reproduce themselves?" Queen Christina of Sweden asked her tutor, Descartes, after he informed her that the human body, though not the soul, could be explained in mechanical terms. Good question. Three centuries after the Queen asked it, John von Neumann suggested an answer. He proposed that in living organisms, and even in machines, there exists a "complexity barrier." Beyond this barrier, where systems are of a very high complexity, entirely new principles come into play. It is possible, von Neumann said, for a machine to make another machine more elaborate than itself once it attains a certain level of organization—once it breaks through the complexity barrier. Complexity is a decisive property. Below the critical level, the power of synthesis decays, giving rise to ever simpler systems. Above that level, however, the synthesis of more elaborate systems, under the right conditions, becomes explosive.

## Cybernetic

American Society for
Cybernetics, Eds.
**$50/year** for 2 issues
and membership
Back issues worth ordering:
**$10**; Vol. 1, Issue 1;
1985; 147 pp.
**$15**; Vol.. 2, Issue 1;
1986; 80 pp.
American Society for
Cybernetics
c/o Department of
Engineering Management
Old Dominion University
Norfolk, VA  23529-0248

*Cybernetics is a very loose approach to an even looser subject: the understanding of whole systems. The closer one comes to the core of a large system, the more it appears to be a hall of mirrors, vanishing into self-reference. Nothing governs it, everything governs it.*

*This infrequent magazine stalks whole understanding through a path of the heart. Contributors have no idea what they are hunting for, only that it is as large and  ungraspable as spirit.*

*— Kevin Kelly*

◆

A subtle thing happens when everything is visible: the display becomes reality. — David Canfield Smith
—Cybernetic I

◆

The old idea of treating a psychiatric symptom was based on the medical notion of curing a part of the body. The illness was in some spatially-defined, out there, unit. We can no longer say that it is in the family, nor is it in the individual. It is in the heads or nervous systems of everyone who has a part in specifying it.

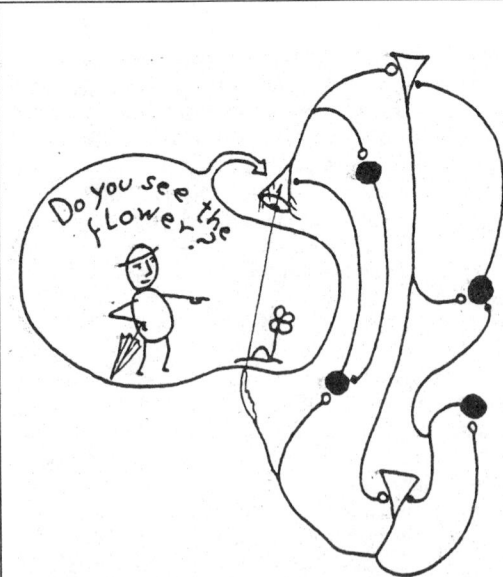

*Figure 3:* The observer by stepping in the synaptic gap defines his or her domains of distinctions as the environment of the nervous system. For the observer there is a flower in the environment; for the dynamics of states of the nervous system as a closed neuronal network there is no flower, only a synaptic gap that is not a gap. The structures of the environment that the observer sees constitute only orthogonal perturbations for the sensors, not an input to the dynamics of states of the nervous system. Arrows like in Fig. A.

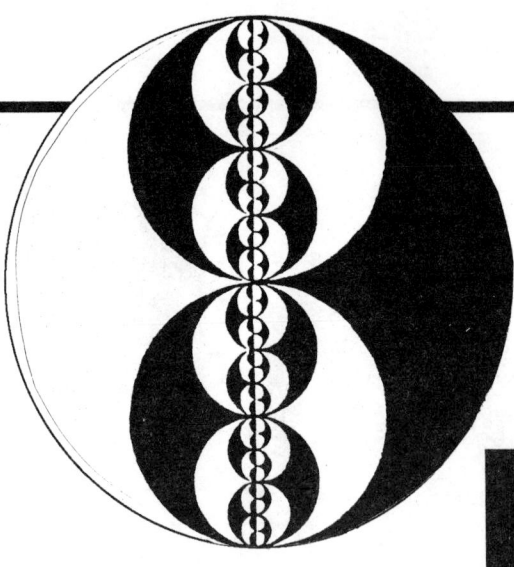

The old epistemology implies that the system, psyche, family structure, the gene — what have you, contains or creates the problem. The new epistemology implies that the problem creates the system. Repeat that, underline that. The problem creates the system. The problem is whatever the origional distress consisted of, plus whatever the distress, on its merry way through the world, has managed to stick to itself. The problem is the meaning system created by the distress, and the treatment unit is everyone who is contributing to that meaning system.
—Cybernetic II

Have a psychotic experience; have another psychotic experience, and get over one of them.

## Cybernetics of Cybernetics

Heinz Von Foerster, Editor
1974, 1986; 523 pp.
**$17.50**
($20.50 postpaid) from:
Spartan Book Store
Customer Service
San Jose State University
San Jose, CA  95191
408/924-1800

*This book was originally made possible through a grant from the Point Foundation, and like most of the things which are influenced by the Whole Earth folks it's eclectic, interesting, not as polished as it might be and a trifle uneven. In other words, human and exciting. It started as a year long (1973-74) class project at the Biological Computer Lab at the University of Illinois at Urbana. The students  collected articles, definitions, word pictures called "conceptual entailment structures" and lumped them together with pictures, and photographs and called it a book.  Articles range from classics to student pieces, but the  author index reads like a who's who in information and cybernetics: Ross Ashby, Gregory Bateson, Stafford Beer,  Stewart Brand, Jurgen Habermas, Garrett Hardin, Ivan Illich,  John Lilly, Humberto Maturana, Warren Mcculloch, Gordon Pask, Bill Powers, G. Spencer-Brown, Francisco Varela, Heinz  Von Foerster and Norbert Wiener to name a few. Unfortunately  the students were experimenting and placed the Table of  Contents and the Index in the center of the book making it  hard to use. I've marked my pages with a marker which eases  but doesn't solve the problem. The new*

◆

GRELLING'S PARADOX. Call an adjective "autological" if it describes itself. "Short" is short, and polysyllabic" is polysyllabic, so "short" and "polysyllabic" are autological. Let "heterological" mean "not autological". "Long and "monosyllabic" are heterological. Is "heterological" heterological?

*—Cybernetic I*

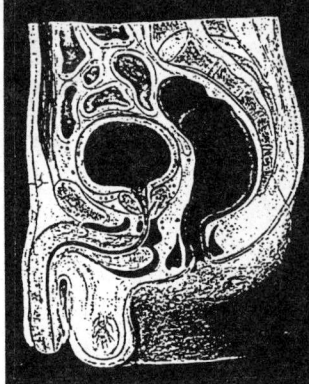

When the penis is simply a means of pleasure among men alone, the exalted worth of the standard of value, the phallus, is devaluated.

*edition was brought  out for the Cybernetic Systems Program at SJSU in a reduced  size format but is still readable.*

*—Elin Whitney Smith*
*[Suggested by Rodney Donaldson]*

◆

Q. What is Cybernetics?
A. I would like to call Cybernetics an offer.
Q. What does Cybernetics offer?
A. Cybernetics offers access to and interaction with complex  systems in order that they may appear simple; to and with  apparently simple systems in order that their complexity may  be revealed. (B. Rebitzer)

◆

The gentleman with the bowler hat insists that he is the sole reality, while every-thing else appears only in his imagination. However, he cannot deny that his imaginary universe is populated with apparitions that are not unlike himself. Hence, he has to concede that they them-selves may insist that they are the sole reality and everything else is only a concoction of their imagination. In that case their imaginary universe will be populated with apparitions, one of which may be *he*, the gentleman with the bowler hat. (Heinz Von Foerster)

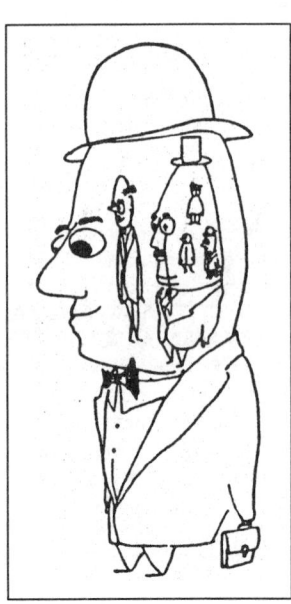

## Understanding Computers and Cognition

Terry Winograd and
Fernando Flores
1987; 207 pp.
**$12.95** postpaid from:
Addison-Wesley
Publishing Co. Inc.
1 Jacob Way
Redding, MA 01867
1-800-447-2226

*What does it mean to understand something?*
*This books tries to understand understanding.*
— Kevin Kelly
*[Suggested by Joel Trachtenberg]*

◆

Living systems are cognitive systems, and living, as a process, is a process of cognition. This statement is valid for all organisms, with and without a nervous system.

◆

If we turn to computer systems, we see that for different people, engaged in different activities, the existence of objects and properties emerges in different kinds of breaking down. As I sit here typing a draft on a word processor, I think of words and they appear on my screen. There is a network of equipment that includes my arms and hands, a keyboard, and many complex devices that mediate between it and a screen. None of this equipment is present for me except when there is a breaking down.

◆

Reflective thought is impossible without the kind of abstraction that produces blindness. The program is forever limited to working within the world determined by the programmer's explicit articulation of possible objects,

---

## Continuing the Conversation

Greg and Pat Williams, Editors. $8/year (4 issues) from:
Hortideas, Route 1,Box 302, Gravel Switch, KY 40328
606/332-7606.

*Continuing the conversation begun by the late*
*Gregory Bateson, biologist, anthropologist,*
*psychologist, epistemologist, and teacher. To him,*
*these thickets of knowledge were sub-circuits in a*
*larger loop which he helped identify—cybernetics.*
*His finished work is frozen in books (see p. 205);*
*his unfinished cybernetics is warmly pursued in this*
*chummy, and sometimes academic, newsletter.*
— Kevin Kelly

◆

DOLPHINS HAVE NO HANDS. Having no hands, they have not been able to change the world around them, so perhaps the effort that humans beings have put into civilization and the "taming" of the natural world has been put by dolphins into changing themselves. If something is amiss the human urge has been to fix something else, not oneself. This is a lot more difficult if you have no hands to do the fixing, so when something is amiss in the dolphin world . . . do dolphins "fix" themselves instead? Might dolphin language provide a contrasting mode of communication to set up against the subject/predicate structure of human language?
—Janie Matrisciano

---

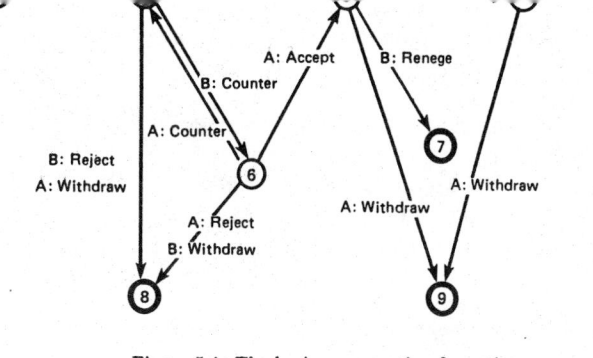

A: Accept    B: Renege
B: Counter
A: Counter
B: Reject
A: Withdraw
A: Withdraw    A: Withdraw
A: Reject
B: Withdraw

Figure 5.1: The basic conversation for action

properties, and relations among them. It therefore embodies the blindness that goes with this articulation.

If we look at intelligence in a broader context, however, the inadequacies of a program with built-in permanent blindness begin to emerge. The essence of intelligence is to act appropriately when there is no simple pre-definition of the problem or the space of states in which to search for a solution.

---

## Systemantics

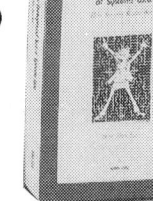

(The Underground Text
of Systems Lore: How Systems
Really Work and How They Fail)
John Gall
1986; 319 pp.
**$14.95** postpaid from:
General Systemantics Press
3200 W. Liberty Road
Ann Arbor, MI 48103
or Whole Earth Access

*The pun in the title carries the important message*
*that systems have "antics"—they act up, misbe-*
*have, and have their own mind. The author is*
*having fun with a serious subject, deciding rightly*
*that a sense of humor and paradox are the only*
*means to approach large systems. His insights*
*come in the form of marvelously succinct rules of*
*thumb, in the spirit of Murphy's Law and the Peter*
*Principle. This book made me 1) not worry about*

WHEN BIG SYSTEMS FAIL, THE FAILURE IS OFTEN BIG.

---

It should be no surprise, then, that the area in which artificial intelligence has had the greatest difficulty is in the programming of common sense. It has long been recognized that it is much easier to write a program to carry out abstruse formal operations than to capture the common sense of a dog. This is an obvious consequence of Heidegger's realization that it is precisely is our "ordinary everydayness" that we are immersed in readiness-to-hand. A methodology by which formally defined tasks can be performed with carefully designed representations (making things present-at-hand) does not touch on the problem of blindness. We accuse people of lacking common sense precisely when some representation of the situation has blinded them to a space of potentially relevant actions.

◆

A major goal of frame formalisms was to represent 'defaults': the way things are typically, but not always. For example we might want to include the fact "Dogs bark" without precluding the possibility of a mute dog.

*understanding a colossal system—you can't, 2)*
*realize you CAN change a system—by starting a*
*new one, and 3) flee from starting new systems—*
*they don't go away.*
—Kevin Kelly

IT BEACHED ITSELF.

COMPLEX SYSTEMS EXHIBIT UNEXPECTED BEHAVIOR.

◆

We begin at the beginning, with the Fundamental Theorem: New systems mean new problems.

◆

The system always kicks back—Systems get in the way—or, in slightly more elegant language: Systems tend to oppose their own proper functions.

◆

Systems tend to malfunction conspicuously just after their greatest triumph. Toynbee explains this effect by pointing out the strong tendency to apply a previously successful strategy to the new challenge. The army is now fully prepared to fight the previous war.

◆

A complex system that works is invariably found to have evolved from a simple system that worked. The parallel proposition also appears to be true: A complex system designed from scratch never works and cannot be made to work. You have to start over, beginning with a working simple system.

## The Blind Watchmaker

Richard Dawkins
1986; 332 pp.
$7.95 postpaid
(order #3448) from:
W.W. Norton
500 5th Avenue
New York, NY 10110
212/345-5500
or Whole Earth Access

The Blind Watchmaker software program is available for $10.95 postpaid with a coupon from the paperback's appendix, which also constitutes the program's manual. It requires a Fat Macintosh or larger to run.

*The Holy Grail of desktop engineering is Richard Dawkins's (author of **The Selfish Gene** and **The Extended Phenotype**) addictive software program, "The Blind Watchmaker." This Macintosh program breeds creatures by asexual genesis. It produces offspring with slight to severe changes from the original. You select which of those offspring you prefer, and let it breed again. In a couple of generations you have a critter you could have never imagined. The mutation rate can be adjusted, as well as 15 other genes which control the image, such as height, scale, segmentation, and branching. Echoing nature, the genes can be set with gradients, or turned off and on by other genes.*

*You can start with a tiny stick and begin breeding that, or as Dawkins put it, "you can put the program on genetic drift, and when you see a nice one, you can go for a little breed." Human intervention is allowed by genetic-engineering mode; you alter the image on the screen by manipulating it with an icon of a hypodermic needle. Genealogy of your work is easy to look up. You can draw out the pedigree from the fossil record in chart form.*

*Dawkins calls his creatures biomorphs, and their domain Biomorph Land. Buried deep in a remote corner of the Land, Dawkins discovered a tiny jewel figure, an image of the Holy Grail. Its genetic formula is "lost." Dawkins has offered a prize of $1,000 to the first person who can dictate the biomorph gene code that will exactly match the bit-map picture of the Holy Grail. Entries for the Holy Grail search should be sent to W.W. Norton at the above address.*

*— Kevin Kelly*

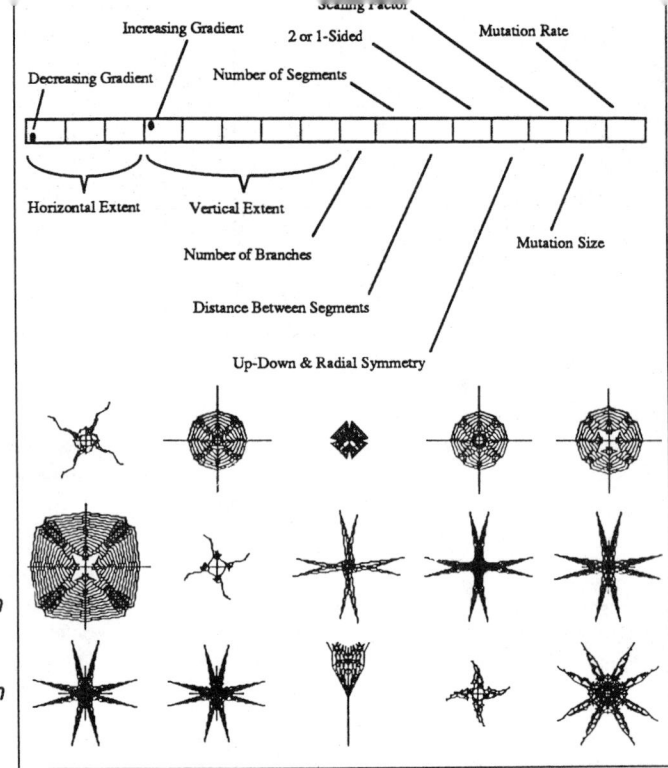

None of the forms found in Richard Dawkins's albums were preconceived. Among his trophies is this page: a collection of animals vaguely resembling those of the Echinoderm phylum (sea urchins, etc.)

---

## The Recursive Universe

William Poundstone
1985; 252 pp.
**$7.95**
($8.95 postpaid; California, New Jersey, and New York residents must pay sales tax.)
from:
William Morrow and Co.
105 Madison Avenue
New York, NY 10016
800/843-9389
or Whole Earth Access

## Life

Public Domain; Macintosh. $3 from: Berkeley Macintosh User Group (BMUG),1442A Walnut St., #62, Berkeley, CA 94709; 415/849-9114

Public Domain; IBM PC. $8 from: Software Copying Company, 33 Gold Street, #13, New York, NY,10038

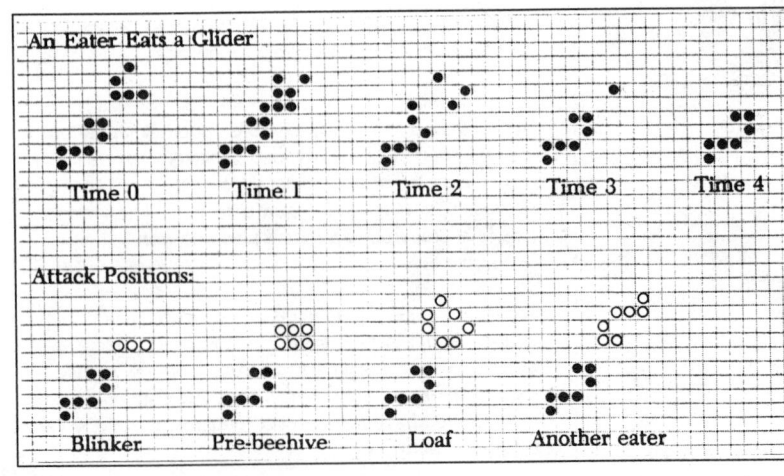

*You are God in the game of **Life,** a computer game. And you create all in it. You design not only the creatures, but the rules of their universe. Let the cells live (a black dot) or die (emptiness) in each generation. And then there is time, a thousand generations a minute. Let there be graphic patterns of your cells' growth, as they pulse in expansion, flicker into extinction. Their destiny is fixed by the original premises that you, God, choose. Mathematically there is no way to tell where the system is going until you try it. That you can TRY it is heavenly.*

*Invented in 1970 by mathematician John Conway, **Life** is no longer played as a mere game. Run on large mainframe computers, this game, and others like it, have proved to be a fertile field of scientific research, the first hands-on cybernetics laboratory. (The discipline is called Cellular Automata.) Some of the curious results and startling implications of running these simple worlds are clearly presented in **The Recursive Universe**. To be a part-time God yourself, you need only a home version of **Life**, which is available in the public domain for IBM and Macintosh computers.*

*— Kevin Kelly*

◆

[Left] The gliders is one of the commonest LIFE objects. When a LIFE screen starts with a random pattern of on and off pixels, gliders form naturally out of the chaos. Yet Conway did not "put" the gliders into LIFE. The designers of ordinary video games have to sit down, draw the graphics, figure out how to animate them, and write it all up as a complicated program. LIFE's program is simple and seems to say nothing about gliders (or blinkers, blocks, beehives...). Everything you see, no matter how unexpected, is the inevitable consequence of Conway's rules.

◆

When LIFE was first introduced, three of the biggest questions LIFE players wondered about were these: Is there any general way of telling what a pattern will do? Can any pattern grow without limit (so the number of live cells keeps getting bigger and bigger)? Do all patterns eventually settle down into a stable object or group of objects?

◆

[Right] One kind of pattern does not even have itself for a predecessor. It is an unstable pattern with no predecessors. The only way it can possibly turn up on the LIFE screen is for someone to use it as a starting configuration. The name for such a configuration is a "Garden-of-Eden" pattern... This is a pattern with no past. It can never appear in LIFE except in the initial state.

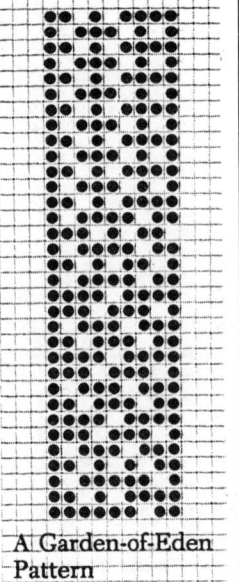

A Garden-of-Eden Pattern

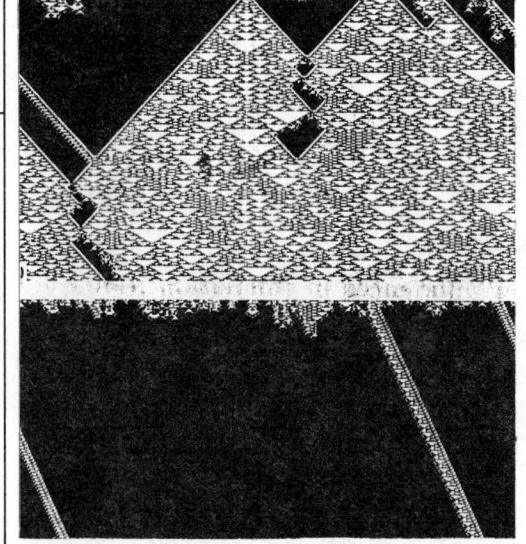

Rules whose dominance is affected by the master rule. The upper and lower examples represent different master rules.

## Cell Systems

**(Versions One and Two)**; IBM PC. **$17**; **$28** for both from: Charles Platt, 594 Broadway, Room 1208, New York, NY 10012

## Freestyle CAs

IBM PC. **$10** from: Rudy Rucker, Math Dept., S.J. State Univ. San Jose, CA 95192

*Charles Platt's* **Cell Systems** *versions One and Two are clever extensions of the game of Life concept. By changing the simple onscreen parameters, you can create cell patterns that scroll up your screen like moving ice mountains, strange caverns and cityscapes. Cell Systems One lets you create patterns using 4 of 8 available colors.* **Cell Systems Two** *doesn't use color graphics, but gives you much more flexibility in creating cell patterns, allowing you to enter parameters graphically, with decimals, or hexadecimals.*

*Freestyle CAs are based on different sets of rules and so look very different. Patterns like Brian's Brain send blocks of "living" creatures skimming across the screen to confront other creatures moving up from the bottom. Sometimes they merge; sometimes they wipe each other out. Interference patterns emerge, like stylized ripples in a cybernetic pool. This is how a computer sees the physical world. Only this is a world where you set up the rules.*

— *Richard Kadrey*

Since this Freestyle CA is a closed-system and never loses any information, the white square acts as a "hole" to remove excess data from the screen.

A few hundred generations into a Cell Systems CA. With the right formula, the CA can live for tens of thousands of generations.

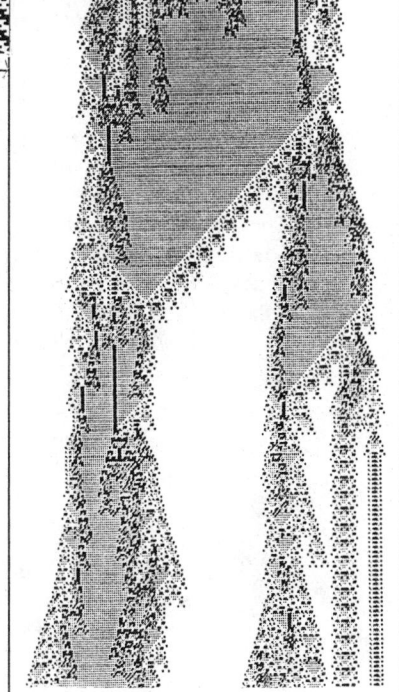

## Complex Systems

Stephen Wolfram, Editor
**$75**/year
(6 issues) from:
Complex Systems
Publications, Inc.
P.O. Box 6149
Champaign, IL 61821-8149
217/244-4250

*A bonafide academic journal, it requires high mathematical understanding. However, occasional articles are comprehendable by plain-English layfolk, and merit attention. The complexity in question permeates key concepts like distributed learning (honey bees co-operating in a hive), fault-tolerant networks (a downed powerline doesn't topple the electric grid), and local politics in cellular automata worlds (local rules, rather than global order, determine the ecology).*

— *Kevin Kelly*
*[Suggested by Steven Levy]*

## Cellular Automata Machines

Tommaso Toffoli
and Norman Margolus
**$30.00**
($32.50 postpaid) from:
The MIT Press
c/o Uniserv Inc.
P.O. Box 1034
524 Great Road (Route 119)
Littleton, MA 01460
617/253-2884
or Whole Earth Access

## CAM6 Board

Cellular Automata Machines, version 6 (CAM 6) are add-on boards which slip into IBM PC clones (PC, XT, and AT). They go for **$1,500.** Call or write Systems Concepts, 55 Francisco St., San Francisco, CA 94133; 415/984-1000.

*One of the reasons CAs may be really important is that they provide a paradigm for the kind of parallel computers (such as the Connection Machine) which we are now just starting to build. Another reason why CAs are important is their essential properties of 1) parallelism, 2) homogeneity, and 3)*

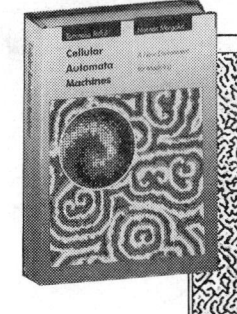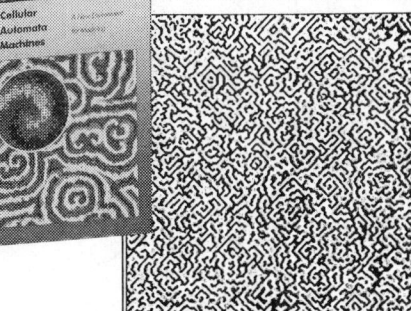

Figure 9.2: Spatial reactions: (a) and (b) use different values of a feedback parameter, while (c) is a non-monotonic threshold version of (b).

*locality make them natural models of all physical processes.*

*Working together in the Information Mechanics Group at MIT, Toffoli and Margolus developed a piece of hardware — the CAM6 — and the software to drive it.* **Cellular Automata Machines** *describes how to use the CAM6 to generate a wide range of CA patterns — including the familiar game of Life, reversible color mandalas, accretion fractals, crystalization processes, colonies of*

*things like insects, billiard-ball computers, and much more. If you really understand some physical process, there is a good chance that you can model it as a cellular automaton rule on the CAM6.*

— *Rudy Rucker*

◆

Cellular Automata are stylized universes defined by simple rules much like those of a board game. They have their own kind of matter which whirls around in a space and a time of their own. One can think of an astounding variety of them. One can actually construct them, and watch them evolve. As inexperienced creators, we are not likely to get a very interesting universe on our first try; as individuals, we may have different ideas of what makes a universe interesting, or of what we might want to do with it. In any case, once we've been shown a cellular-automaton universe we'll want to make one ourselves; once we've made one, we will want to try another one. After having a few, we'll be able to custom tailor one for a particular purpose with a certain confidence.

## Chaos

James Gleick
1987; 352 pp.
**$19.95**
($22.95 postpaid) from:
Viking-Penguin
299 Murray Hill Parkway
East Rutherford, NJ 07073
800/631-3577
or Whole Earth Access

*I hadn't realized that the titillating talk one hears about "fractals," "strange attractors," and such was linking all the systems sciences to each other and linking the most arcane math and physics not only to each other but to the familiar world of clouds and stock markets. The new mathematics of turbulence is fascinating and beautiful enough in its own right. That it gives all of us a fresh handle on understanding everything is the real reward.*

*James Gleick does an excellent job of making highly subtle work so understandable it feels obvious. You'll realize how a butterfly sneeze in China redirects the jet stream in North America, how Jupiter's red spot emerges stably from violent chaos, and how the recent stock market crash was nobody's fault. There's almost nothing you can think about that isn't served with some of the tools of chaos theory. Best of all, the theory is still emerging, and the practical applications have only begun to be explored.*

—Stewart Brand

◆

"Fifteen years ago, science was heading for a crisis of increasing specialization," a Navy official in charge of scientific financing remarked to an audience of mathematicians, biologists, physicists, and medical doctors. "Dramatically, that specialization has reversed because of chaos." Chaos poses problems that defy accepted ways of working in science. It makes strong claims about the universal behavior of complexity. The first chaos theorists, the scientists who set the discipline in motion, shared certain sensibilities. They had an eye for pattern, especially pattern that appeared on different scales at the same time. They had a taste for randomness and complexity, for jagged edges and sudden leaps. Believers in chaos — and they sometimes call themselves believers, or converts, or evangelists — speculate about determinism and free will, about evolution, about the nature of conscious intelligence. They feel that they are turning back a trend in science toward reductionism, the analysis of systems in terms of their constituent parts: quarks, chromosomes, or neurons. They believe that they are looking for the whole.

The chaos game. Each new point falls randomly, but gradually the image of a fern emerges. All the necessary information is encoded in a few simple rules.

## The Journal of Chaos and Graphics

Clifford A. Pickover, Editor
Published irregularly;
subscriptions **free** from:
Clifford A. Pickover
Journal of Chaos
and Graphics
IBM Thomas J. Watson
Research Center
Yorktown Heights, NJ 10598

*A new occasional journal covering all sorts of mathematically based visual wildness, edited by one of the leading researchers. Brief, inspiring reports with barely adequate black-and-white graphics. The seed of future glory.*

—Robert Horvitz

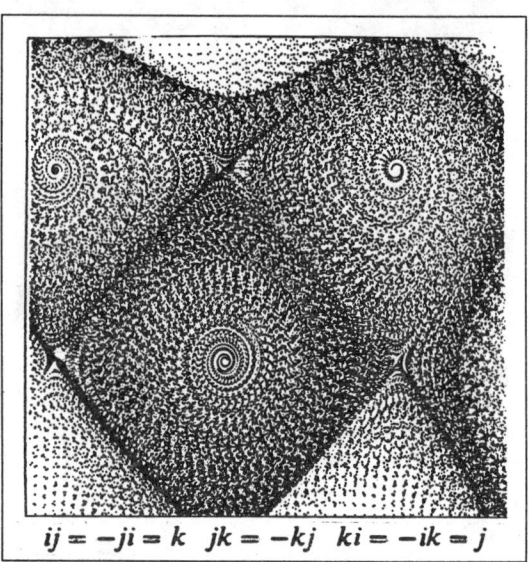

$$ij = -ji = k \quad jk = -kj \quad ki = -ik = j$$

## An Album of Fluid Motion

Milton Van Dyke
1982; 176 pp.
**$10**
postpaid from:
Parabolic Press
P.O. Box 3032
Stanford, CA 94305-0030

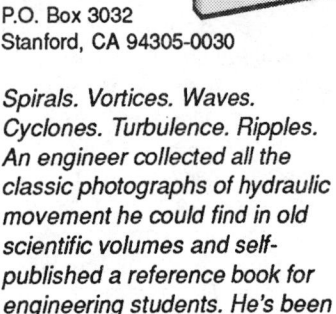

*Spirals. Vortices. Waves. Cyclones. Turbulence. Ripples. An engineer collected all the classic photographs of hydraulic movement he could find in old scientific volumes and self-published a reference book for engineering students. He's been surprised that mostly artists have been buying it. I'm not surprised.*

—Kevin Kelly

[Right] *Diffraction of a shock wave by a finite wedge.*
As the shock wave passes the base, the flow separates and vortex sheets are generated. Further interaction produces an increasingly elaborate pattern of shock waves, slip lines, and vortices.

[Below] A shadowgraph shows the mixing of two streams of the same density at a pressure of 8 atmospheres and a Reynolds number of 850,000. Two vortices have become a single larger vortex in this photograph.

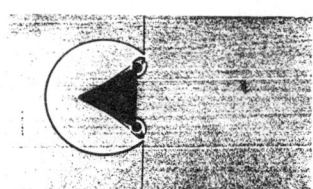

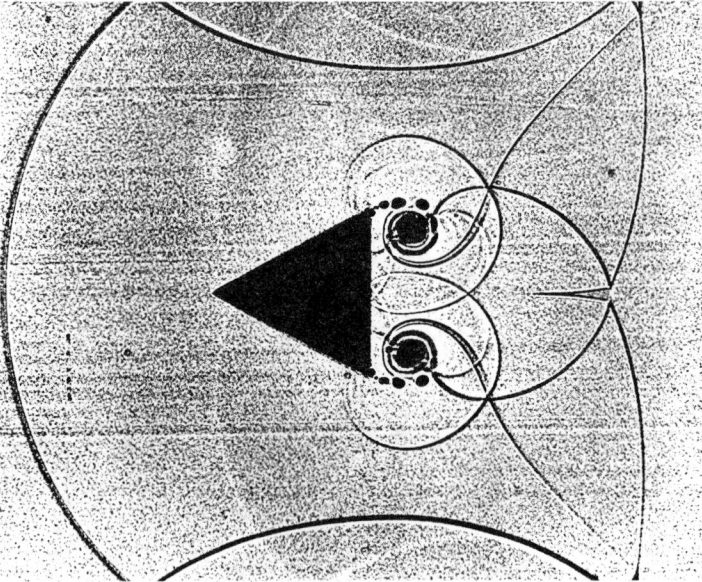

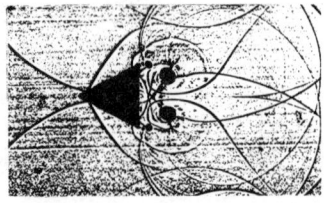

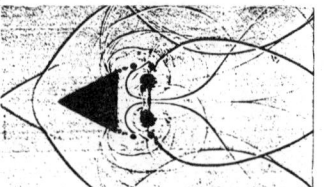

# Fractals & Such

*by Robert Horvitz*

The August 1985 **Scientific American** had a gorgeous, mysterious picture on its cover: a black disk rimmed with smaller disks, surrounded by Kirlian halos of multicolored flame. A. K. Dewdney explained, in that issue's "Computer Recreations" column, that the image represented part of the edge of the Mandelbrot Set, one of the most complex mathematical forms ever devised. His article was illuminated with close-ups of other regions on the edge of the M-Set. Deliriously detailed, all were generated on a computer by repeating a simple calculation on a field of real and imaginary numbers. When this is done many times, the plane around the Mandelbrot Set erupts in convoluted symmetries and fluid-crystal swirls, as the algorithm drives points outside the set to infinity. This explosive turbulence can be made visible by assigning colors to the speed at which each coordinate "flees." The resulting image is mathematically rigorous yet shamelessly psychedelic — wilder but more highly ordered than any manmade design. Since making the cover of **Scientific American**, the Mandelbrot Set has acquired something of a cult following, as people explore the minute worlds-within-worlds at its margin.

The M-Set is a particularly spectacular example of a "fractal" — that is, a form with edges that are unsmooth at any magnification. (Perhaps not surprisingly, the set's discoverer, Benoit Mandelbrot, was the primary developer of fractal geometry.) Fractals are not just an eye-tickling family of irregular shapes; they are a new

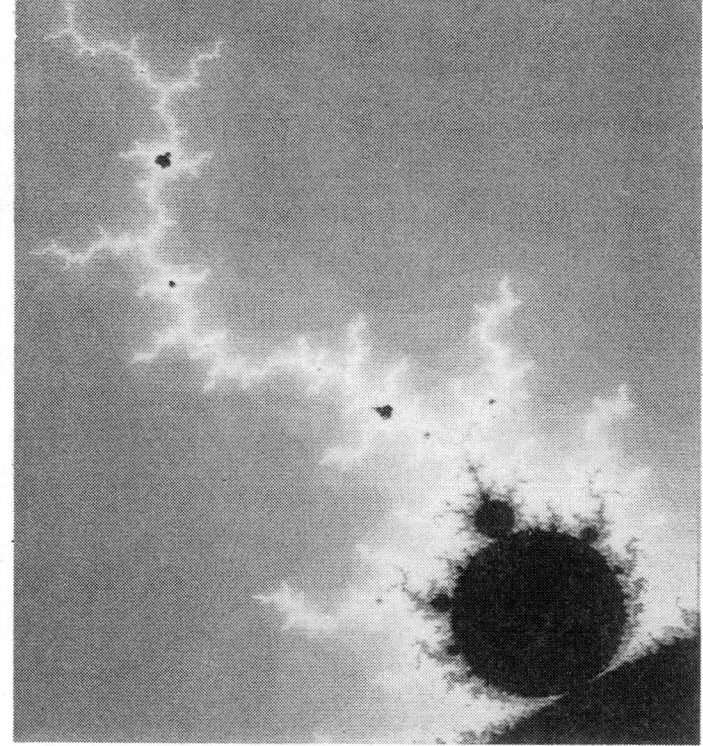

tool for analyzing and modeling natural phenomena that have eluded description in more traditional terms. In addition, the technique used to generate the M-Set, "iterative mapping," has applications in the simulation of "chaotic" processes that have only begun to be tapped.

The beauty, versatility and descriptive power of fractals and iterative mapping have inspired a new kind of graphic research flourishing between art and science. Here are a few gateways into this field:

## Art Matrix

catalog **free** from Art Matrix, P.O. Box 880, Ithaca, NY 14851

*The leading vendor of high-resolution M-Set color graphics — videos, slides, photoprints, and postcards. You gotta love a company whose motto is "A Fractal in Every Paw." Also produces work on commission, and develops and sells software.*

*—RH*

## Amygdala

Rollo Silver, Editor
**$15**/year
(10 issues or 25 color slides); **$30**/year (both) from: Amygdala, Box 219, San Cristobal, NM 87564

*Newsletter for people interested in the Mandelbrot Set. Short articles (including some "math-fi," a new fiction genre related to sci-fi); reviews of fractal-generating software and algorithmic shortcuts; and a running bibliography of important fractal publications. Two kinds of subscriptions are offered: you get either 10 issues of the newsletter, or 25 color slides of the M-Set released over the same time period. Or you can get both the slides and the newsletter.*

*By the way, "Amygdala" is Latin for "almond;" "Mandelbrot" is Yiddish for "almond bread;" and "amygdaloid" is an igneous rock with rounded cavities filled with mineral crystals.* *—RH*

## The Beauty of Fractals

Heinz-Otto Peitgen and Peter H. Richter
1986; 199 pp.
**$35**
($37.50 postpaid) from:
Springer-Verlag New York, Inc.
44 Hartz Way
Secaucus, NJ 07094
or Whole Earth Access

*Some seventy dazzling color pictures, and many more in black and white, make this a seductive introduction for those not mathematically inclined. At the same time, it's packed with enough advanced mathematics to keep a grad student busy for years. Capping it off, there are thoughtful essays on the impact of fractals on the way we view nature, science and art, as well as a personal account of the discovery of the M-Set and a review of the evolution of fractal geometry by Mandelbrot himself.* *—RH*

◆

Why is geometry often described as cold and dry? One reason lies in its inability to describe the shape of a cloud, a mountain, a coastline, or a tree. Clouds are not spheres, mountains are not cones, coastlines are not circles, and bark is not smooth, nor does lightning travel in a straight line. . . . Nature exhibits not simply a higher degree but an altogether different level of complexity.

The number of distinct scales of length of patterns is for all purposes infinite.

The existence of these patterns challenges us to study those forms that Euclid leaves aside as being formless, to investigate the morphology of the amorphous. Mathematicians have disdained this challenge, however, and have increasingly chosen to flee from nature by devising theories unrelated to anything we can see or feel.

At any given place, the sea-horse motif is taken through an infinite number of variations. This is shown in the enlargement series in the "sea-horse valley," which up to a magnification of one million shows ever new constellations of "tail" and "eye" of the sea-horse.

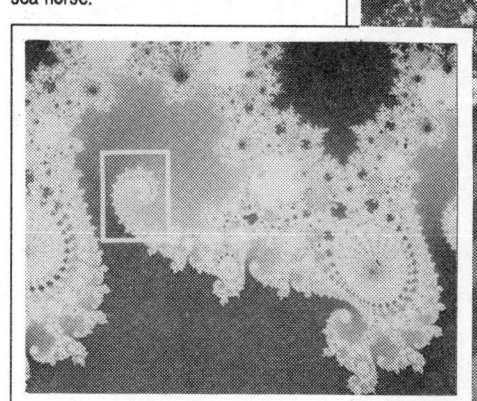

## The Fractal Geometry of Nature

Benoit Mandelbrot
1982; 468 pp.
**$34.95**
($38.45 postpaid) from:
W.H. Freeman & Co.
4419 West 1980 South
Salt Lake City, UT 84104
801/973-4660
or Whole Earth Access

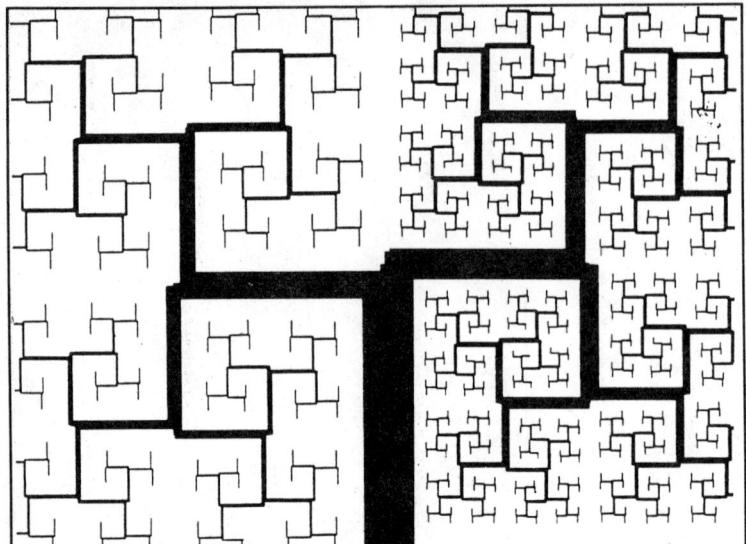

*Fractals, and other members of a growing family of mathematical works of art, are quite well known by now; Lucasfilm employs them for special effects and videogames, and the Mandelbrot set has made the cover of **Scientific American**. But I remember the first time I saw a fractal, a hand-drawn snowflake curve somebody had left around our common workspace. Later, the concepts of self-similarity and recursion would help unlock the secrets of what mathematicians of the last century used to call "monsters"; but back then, I had a hard time wrapping my mind around this simple, complex picture/idea. A fractal is something like a snapshot of a never-ending procedure, an instruction which calls itself over and over; computer graphics are used to reveal the complex beauty of these creations.*

*Mandelbrot's book can be experienced at many levels. The illustrations are breathtaking, from the maze-like black and white plots which show how fractals are "grown," to color-enhanced computer images of dreamscapes and planets that never were. The details of the mathematics are all here, too, and are interwoven with Mandelbrot's very human stories about the mathematicians and scientists (and even the computer programs) who contributed to the growth of the field. I find these works as inspiring as any cathedral's stained glass, and Mandelbrot's book will offer its treasures to me for a long time to come.*

—*Laurie Edwards*

◆

In Koch recursion, every straight interval in a finite approximation is eventually broken up into shorter pieces. In many applications, it is useful to generalize this procedure by allowing certain intervals to be "infertile," so that in later stages they remain untouched.

Here, this generalized procedure is used to grow a "tree." One starts with a trunk having barren sides and a fertile "bud." The bud generates two "branches," on which again only two terminal "buds" are fertile. And so on ad infinitum. The growth is asymmetric to insure that the tree fills a roughly rectangular portion of the plane with no gap and no overlap. However, asymptotic self-contact is not avoided, and indeed every point on the "bark" line can also be obtained as a limit branch tip.

The "subtrees" constructed starting with the main leaders are similar to the whole tree in two different similarity ratios, r1 and r2. . . . This composite Figure results from a Koch tree construction in which the generator is changed at each stage, so that the ratio of width to length decreases to 0. On the left side of the compostie Figure, this ratio decreases even faster than on the right side. The result is that the branch tips are no longer self-similar.

## Growth Morphogenesis

Yoichiro Kawaguchi
1985; 212 pp.
**$29.95**
($32.95 postpaid) from:
JICC USA
3540 Wilshire Boulevard
Suite 406
Los Angeles, CA 90010

*Yoichiro Kawaguchi's work makes use of fractals, but he's not just a finder of fruitful equations, he's a brilliant inventor of visual worlds. Colorfully patterned biomorphs, resembling sea creatures from another planet, grow, writhe, float and evolve in his video animations, while the surroundings, the observer's viewpoint and the light source all move. The dynamism of these forms is partly captured in sequences of stills in this amply illustrated book, with texts in Japanese and English. Some of the chapters seem to be transcribed lectures by Kawaguchi; the hallucinogenic flavor of his thinking is somewhat heightened by the difficulty of translation.*

*Other chapters are descriptions of method and purpose by some of his collaborators, interspersed with short testimonials from his fans. The computer system (64 minis linked in parallel) and the programming concepts he uses are described in the appendix. This is some of the most exciting computer-graphic work I've ever seen.*

—*Robert Horvitz*

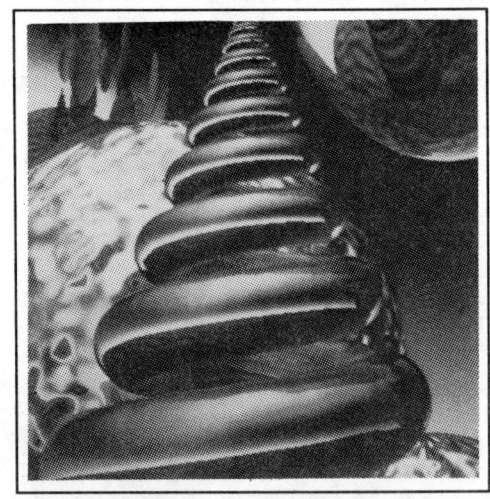

Self-terminating hereditary information takes a completely autonomous shape as the spiral covering the outer skin — the ascending and descending spiral completely covers the outer skin with a firm husk. That is, futhermore, like the properties of a highly acid creature.

◆

The original character which is dispatched and harmonized — the cell-like trait, which grows while sent out in liquid-state from a husk closed within a kernel, self-materializes a definitely hereditary character within a movement combining a semiorganic ionized colloid personality with the arbitrariness of the living body.

◆

Topological paradise — a resonance with intricacy and confrontation between influence and assertion fuse, so that an emotional perspective appears. This is the emergence of a world of words polished through living body rhythms and the weaving of brocade. This is probably reflected screen in the human mental world. It forms a celestial image surpassing the pain of existence bespoken by colors and common sayings.

This may well be the most sublime image that computer graphics can achieve now.

The mimesis in the level of transparency — the mimesis which has melted invisibly within the light, seems to be an art of seclusion within the bounds of human visibility. The living body is purified, and its transparency is gauged at the point at which it can no longer hold impurities inside the body cavity even by using all its might.

# Artificial Life 4-H Show

*by Kevin Kelly*

Some snapshots I took at the First Artificial Life 4-H Show, held September 1987, at the Center for Nonlinear Studies, Los Alamos National Laboratory, New Mexico. This landmark conference brought together an eclectic band of biologists, computer scientists, nano-technology advocates, and mathematical geneticists. For an entire week the workshop showcased primeval organisms infused with a touch of artificial life.

**Lessons of the unreal.** Dutch mathematician and biologist Aristid Lindenmayer (right) waves a fall aster plant he pulled up from the parking lot perimeter. Lindenmayer is one of the grandfathers of biological mathematics — tracing the mathematical patterns in natural growth. Using computers primed with very simple rules, he has reconstructed the complex growth of wildflowers. He determined that exactly three distinct signals traveling up and down a plant stem will produce nearly all observable budding patterns. Interestingly, although there is an extraordinary visual match between real blossom sequences and artificial ones, there's been no botanical chemical signals discovered yet.

The dance of leaf growth and blossoms opening and fading in Ivy-leaved wild lettuce (Mycelis muralis) is governed by "two signals and accumulated delay" in Lindenmayer's color computer graphic display (top).

**The power of one gene** can be seen in the botanical work of Przemyslaw Prusinkiewicz. Prusinkiewicz,

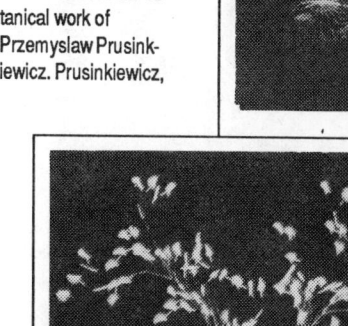

working at the University of Regina in Canada, won the Blue Ribbon prize at the first annual Artificial Life 4-H Show for his colorful garden of artificial flowers grown in a computer. His plants had the individual dignity and distinction you find in real plants — each sample of a species looks similar, but individually different. The laws of their growth are complex simplicity. A few principals, governed by a few numbers, develop this complex artificial plant (above). The same formula, with only one single number accidentally altered late one evening, produced this radically transfigured mutation (above right).

**Emergent behavior** was THE keyword at the conference. Craig Reynolds of Symbolics, Inc., a high-powered graphic computer developer, points out the flocking behavior of winged creatures (called boids) in a film sketch for the color video "Breaking the Ice." The black and white line drawings in the clips are later rendered in color and in volume for the final version.

The flight of individual boids are not pre-calculated. Each boid is set flying with only a few instructions: look out for obstacles and don't bump into your neighbor, but don't stray too far away, either. Everything else that happens is "emergent" — not pre-planned, not fixed, and not expected. The boids fly as a flock on a pre-ordained route, yet each boid can do what it wants, and does. In one trial episode (below), a flock of boids divides to fly around a pillar. One boid conks into the pillar, flutters monetarily, than straggles behind. Nobody ever plotted that.

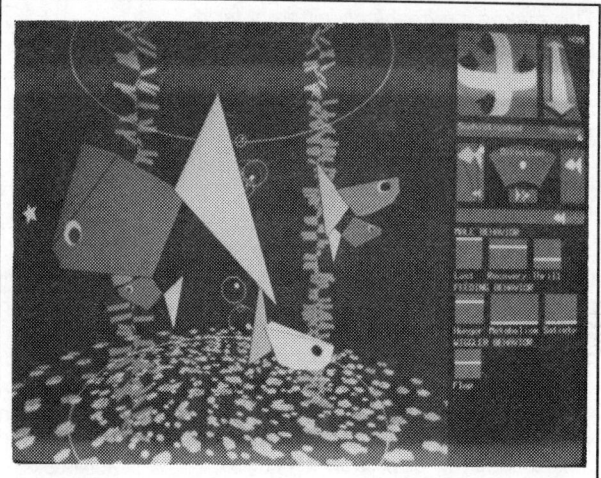

**Learning how to school.** Peter Broadwell had a story to tell about the fishes in his Fishbowl Project, "Plasm: A Fish Sample." He designed the two different color fishes in his computer aquarium to swim round and round in invisible glass bowl. The fishes would eat others of a different color, grow larger, mate to produce offspring of the same color, and die after a certain duration of time. He could alter the rates by tweaking the parameters on the side of the screen. Usually the aquarium would stabilize to a half dozen adult fishes, as shown here. Once, at a computer graphics show, he set the machine up as a visual soother in room where computer artists were resting. During the evening when he was gone, they fiddled with the parameters and left it on overnight. The next morning he came in to see unanticipated evolution: sixty very tiny fish, all of one species, crammed into the bowl like sardines. They were swimming round in circles as a school, a behavior he had never designed into the system.

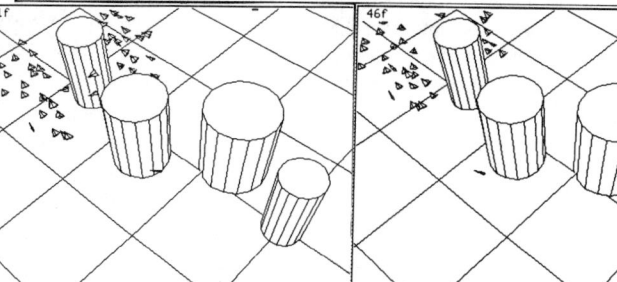

## Cryptologia

Cipher A. Deavours,
David Kahn, Louis Kruh,
Greg Mellen and Brian J.
Winkel, Editors
$28/year
(4 issues) from:
Cryptologia
Rose-Hulman Institute of
Technology
Terre Haute, IN 47803

A quarterly journal for people interested in security codes and ciphers — their history, how they work, and how they're used. With each issue, the magazine's focus shifts more toward the present: new revelations about the Enigma and Ultra codes of World War 2 are down to a trickle; meanwhile, modern cryptography is becoming ever more sophisticated, more widely applied, and more politically sensitive. At the same time, the spread of personal computers gives lots of new people the ability to experiment with code construction and deconstruction.

*Cryptologia*'s writing is often at an advanced level (mathphobes beware), but there's a nice noncommercial feel to it — amateur in the positive sense of being motivated by love of the subject.
This makes it refreshingly different from the coverage data protection gets in the business press: Cryptologians are just as turned on by clever codebreaking as they are by break resistance.

—Robert Horvitz

◆

The WordPerfect encryption algorithm has, however, a fatal weakness which permits the recovery of the key for even quite short plaintexts. The weakness is that the commonly occurring 'space' character is not treated specially. Since this character occurs approximately once in every five characters for a wide variety of languages and other text sources it is trivial to simply try all possible keylengths, testing for the space character in each subtext, and then verifying the resulting key against the checksum stored in the file. Using the methods outlined above a short Pascal program was written using the popular Turbo Pascal by Borland International. When run on an IBM AT computer, a key of 20 characters in length can be found in less than 20 seconds when decrypting a document of about 1500 words.

Copies of the program may be obtained by sending a disk to the author (IBM PC/AT format only) with a note explaining your interest.

◆

Japanese was the greatest difficulty. Ordinary W.T. [wireless telegraph] operators were faced with a number of Morse signs which were new to them and early intercepts from H.M. ships in Eastern waters (which of course took a long time to reach London) were quite unintelligible. A new set of symbols had to be invented and learnt by the operators. However once the interest of some of the officers was aroused rapid progress was made and a number of Japanese ciphers were duly broken.

## Sentinel

Not copy-protected; Macintosh 512K, Enhanced, Plus, SE, II. $295 from Ingram Software, 800/456-8000

*In their zeal to create a computer that was wide open and transparent to the user, the creators of the Macintosh didn't put in any closets. So there's no place to hide a private file. Anyone using a Macintosh had to expect that their laundry would be on view. That often prevented a single Mac from becoming a group tool.*

*Sentinel* safely locks up sensitive files with a heavy-duty encryption code. (Comes in two flavors — regular/fast, and government level DES/not as fast). The system is not as elegant as it should be. For instance, files which you keep locked don't lock themselves again after you leave — you have to encrypt them again. But it does the job. Don't loose your password or you'll never get your data back. (Keep a backup!)

—Kevin Kelly

**Document**

*A locked document's icon as it appears on the desktop*

## The Cartoon Guide to Genetics

Larry Gonick
and Mark Wheelis
1983; 214 pp.
$6.95
($7.30 postpaid) from:
Harper & Row
2350 Virginia Avenue
Hagerstown, MD 21740
800/638-3030
or Whole Earth Access

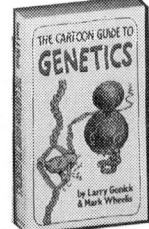

*The stickiest, most wrenching paradoxes we have known are being handed to us by the science of genetics (it's now possible to have five parents).*

*There's no better way to quickly come to grips with things like recombinant DNA than to chortle your way through this cartoon book. It makes genetics hilariously simple. Starts out uncovering the basic territory of chromosomes and hybrids, and ends up in the most current research on protein folding and genetic surgery. Dumb jokes and brilliant cartooning make it easy all the way —* MAD *magazine style.*

—Kevin Kelly

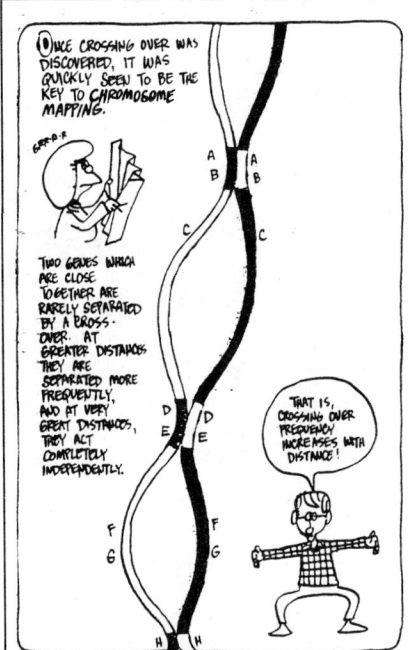

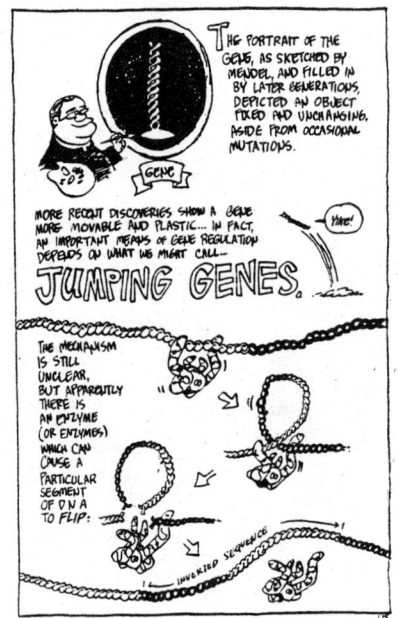

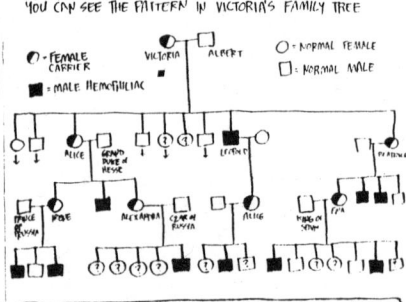

## Structure in Nature Is a Strategy for Design

Peter Pearce
1978; 245 pp.
**$12.50**
MIT Press
Recently out of print.

*Get this book back in print!*

*The similarity among organic and manufactured structures, particularly between crystalline objects and buildings, suggests structures are governed by a common language. The most common expression, made by say a snow flake or a skyscraper, is that function is maximized when material is minimized. Discovering the fundamental vocabulary of spatial organization is the theme of this graphic book.*

— Kevin Kelly

Twelve spheres packed around a point form the icosahedron (a); and twenty planar triangular arrays of spheres around a point form the 20 faces of the icosahedron shell (b,c).

◆

Systems can be envisaged which consist of some minimum inventory of component types which can be alternatively combined to yield a great diversity of efficient structural form. We call these minimum inventory/maximum diversity systems. . . .

The snowflake is a most graphic example in nature of the minimum inventory/maximum diversity principle. . . . All planar snow crystals are found to have star-like forms with six corners (or subsets thereof). More specifically, they have the symmetry of a regular hexagon. However, within this six-fold form, no two snowflakes have ever been known to be exactly alike.

Symmetrical view of a cubic labyrinth section assembled from 90, 120 degree saddle hexagons, comparing continuous surface modules to triangulated modules.

◆

The formative processes in natural structure are characteristically governed by least-energy responses. Perhaps the simplest expression of this is found in the principle of closest packing, a principle which even in its most elementary form is common in both animate and inanimate worlds.

## Art Forms in Nature

Ernst Haeckel
1974; 100 pp.
**$7.95**
($9.20 postpaid) from:
Dover Publications
Attn.: CRX
31 East 2nd Street
Mineola, NY 11501
516/294-7000
or Whole Earth Access

*The possibilities of structure in nature. Exemplified by marine and micro-organisms rendered in nearly hallucinogenic vividness by a turn-of-the-century German biologist. There's no science fiction fan-tasy that has yet approached the baroque abundance of (extra)terrestrial life forms shown here.*

— Kevin Kelly

[Right] Various species of sea-lilies (animals related to starfishes and sea-urchins).

[Far right] Various species of fungi of the class Basidiomycetes.

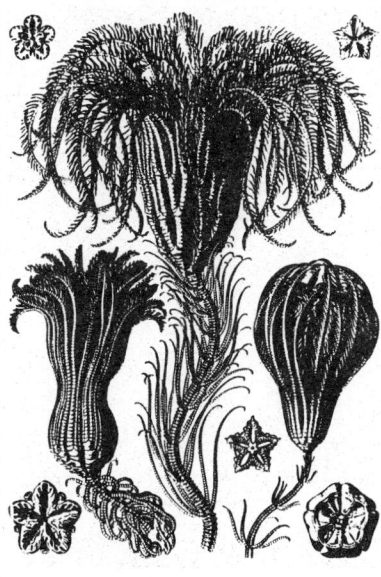

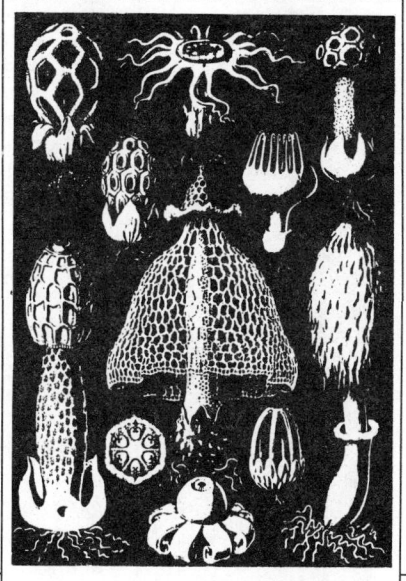

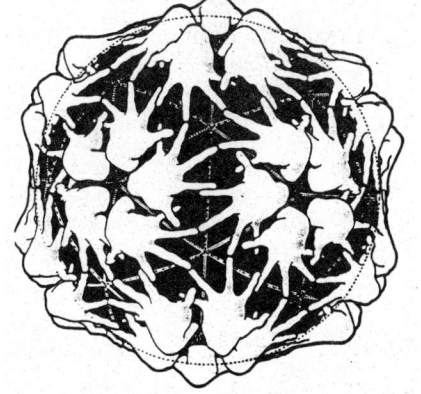

**Fig. 9-10.** A drawing by D. L. D. Caspar illustrating strict equivalence in a shell with icosahedral symmetry constructed from sixty identical left-handed units. The three classes of connections in this surface lattice are represented by the specific bonding relations: thumb-to-pinkie = pentamer bond; ring finger-to-middle finger = trimer bond; and index finger-to-index finger = dimer bond. Any two of these classes of bonds would hold the structure together. The triangles drawn under the hands define equivalent subdivisions defined by the three- and fivefold axes at their intersections.

## Shaping Space: A Polyhedral Approach

Marjorie Senechal and
George Flack, Editors
1987; 284 pp.
**$49.95**
($52.45 postpaid) from:
Springer Verlag NY Inc.
175 Fifth Avenue
New York, NY 10010
212/460-1500
or Whole Earth Access

*Remember solid geometry? The younger of you may not; computer programming has largely displaced that discipline as a teacher of logic. Nonetheless, the field seethes today as biologists and chemists seek geometric keys to understanding complex physical structure, and mathematicians seek improved methods of modeling.*

*This book is a look at some recent action, the 1984*

*Shaping Space conference at Smith College. Like many conference-based books, this one is a bit of a potpourri. Instructions for easily gluing paper models in grade school are right in there with abstruse theoretical dissertations riddled with techno-jargon. Also typical of conference-based books is the feeling of excitement as sometimes messy explorations are presented complete with surprises and controversy. Enough introductory geometry has been added to make much of the fun accessible to the motivated newcomer. Unfortunately, accessibility denied by the outrageous price is another matter. Have your library get it for you.*

—J. Baldwin

◆

In nature where there is regularity, with structures built of identical parts, there are likely to be regular plans. Geometric considerations are always important in these plans, and sometimes they predominate. However, satisfactory a priori predictions about what in fact happens in nature cannot be made. The only way to find out is to look.

## On Growth and Form

D'Arcy Wentworth Thompson
(Edited by John Tyler Bonner)
1917; 1961; 346 pp.

**$20.95** postpaid from:
Cambridge University Press
510 North Avenue
New Rochelle, NY 10801
800/872-7423
or Whole Earth Access

*A paradigm classic. Everyone dealing with growth of form in any manner can use the book. We've seen worn copies on the shelves of artists, inventors, engineers, computer systems designers, biologists.*

—Stewart Brand

◆

A great engineer, Professor Culmann of Zürich . . . happened (in the year 1866) to come into his colleague

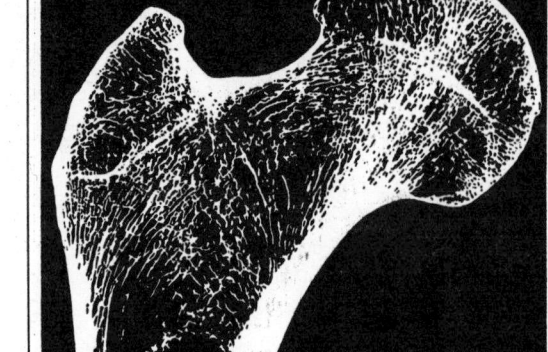

Head of the human femur in section.

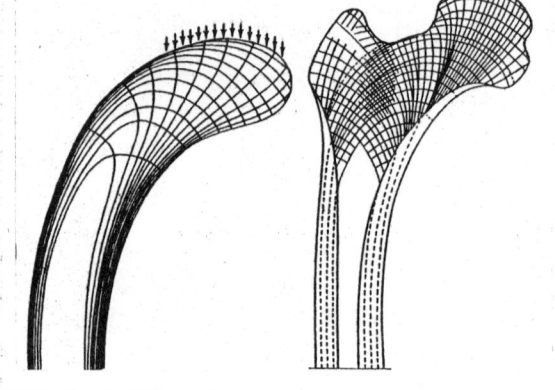

Crane-head and femur.

Meyer's dissecting-room, where the anatomist was contemplating the section of a bone. The engineer, who had been busy designing a new and powerful crane, saw in a moment that the arrangement of the bony trabeculae was nothing more or less than a diagram of the lines of stress, or directions of tension and compression, in the loaded structure: in short, that Nature was strengthening the bone in precisely the manner and direction in which strength was required; and he is said to have cried out, 'That's my crane!'

---

## Form, Function and Design

Paul Jacques Grillo
1960; 1975; 238 pp.

**$9.95** postpaid from:
Dover Publications
31 East 2nd Street
Mineola, NY 11501
or Whole Earth Access

*This book is wonderful. Here is a man trying to tell the truth about design and about our lives and civilization. I never heard of him. When I read his book I can't understand why not.* —Steve Baer

*There really is no better introduction to all that is admirable in design. Baer had to remind me of the book; I had forgotten how much I owe to it. It is full of the kind of lore and wisdom that you immediately take for your own.*

—Stewart Brand

◆

The squid — the only truly jet-propelled animal — is the archetype of the rocket missile of our time, with its gravity-free vertical soar, totally free from the use of wind resistance in take-off.

Acanthoteuthis antiquus.

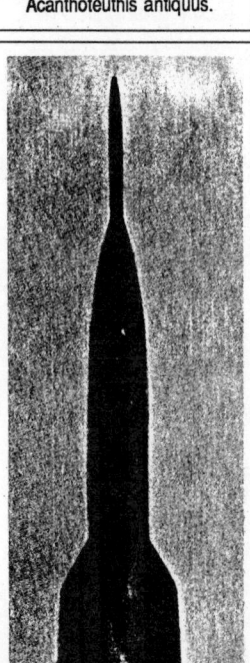

V-2 rocket, WAC-Corporal, Feb. 24, 1949.

Cretaceous echinoid.

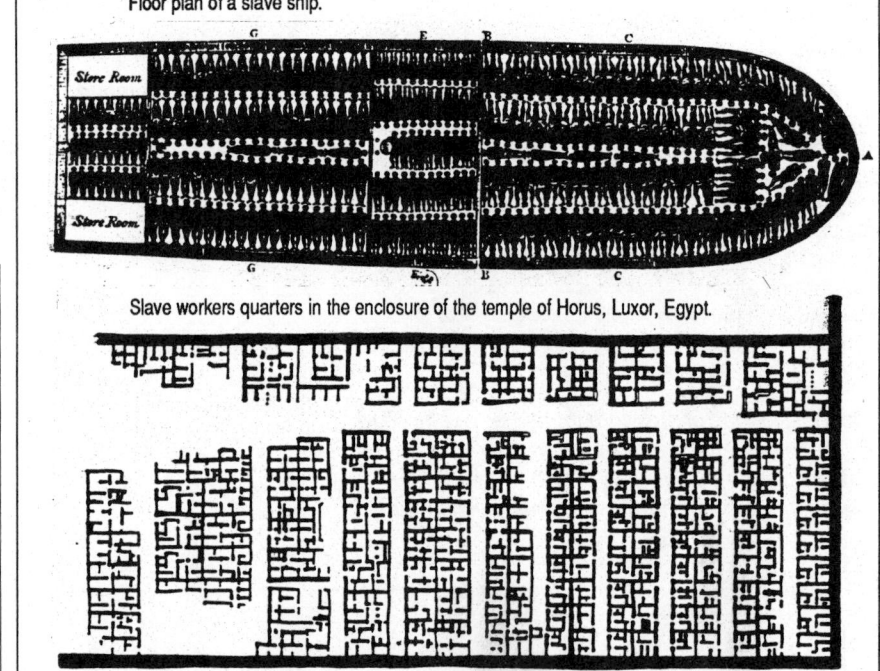

Floor plan of a slave ship.

Slave workers quarters in the enclosure of the temple of Horus, Luxor, Egypt.

◆

Whether in the hull of a slave trader ship or in an Egyptian village compound, slaves are packed in a military right-angle discipline. The gridiron plan here, typical of the military camp, is made of a rectangular lattice of dead-end lanes, symbolic of the dead-end life of the slave. How can we call ourselves free when the very pattern of our streets today is such a sad manifestation of our slavery to routine and reflects such a desperate lack of freedom?

◆

Ever since Greek architecture was rediscovered during the Renaissance, architects have tried in vain to find a mathematical curve that the Greeks might have used for their Doric capitals. It was finally found out that no curve of analytic geometry could be used, for the good reason that the curve which inspired the Greek architects was not a perfect curve, but the living forms of the common sea urchins, so abundant in the Mediterranean.

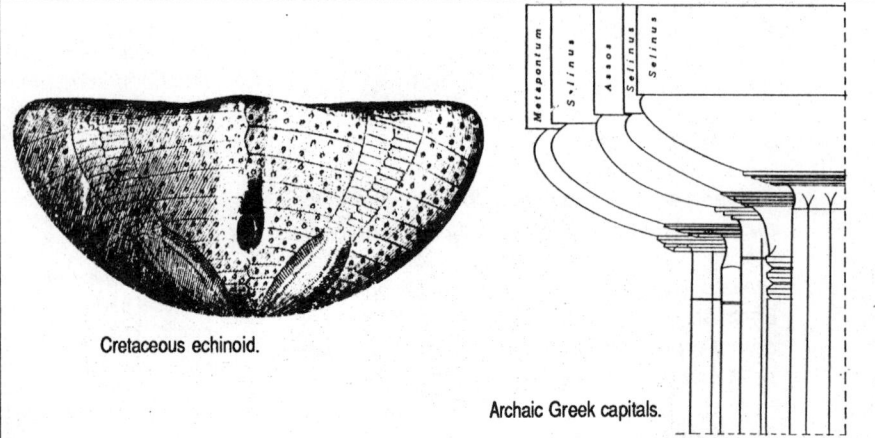

Archaic Greek capitals.

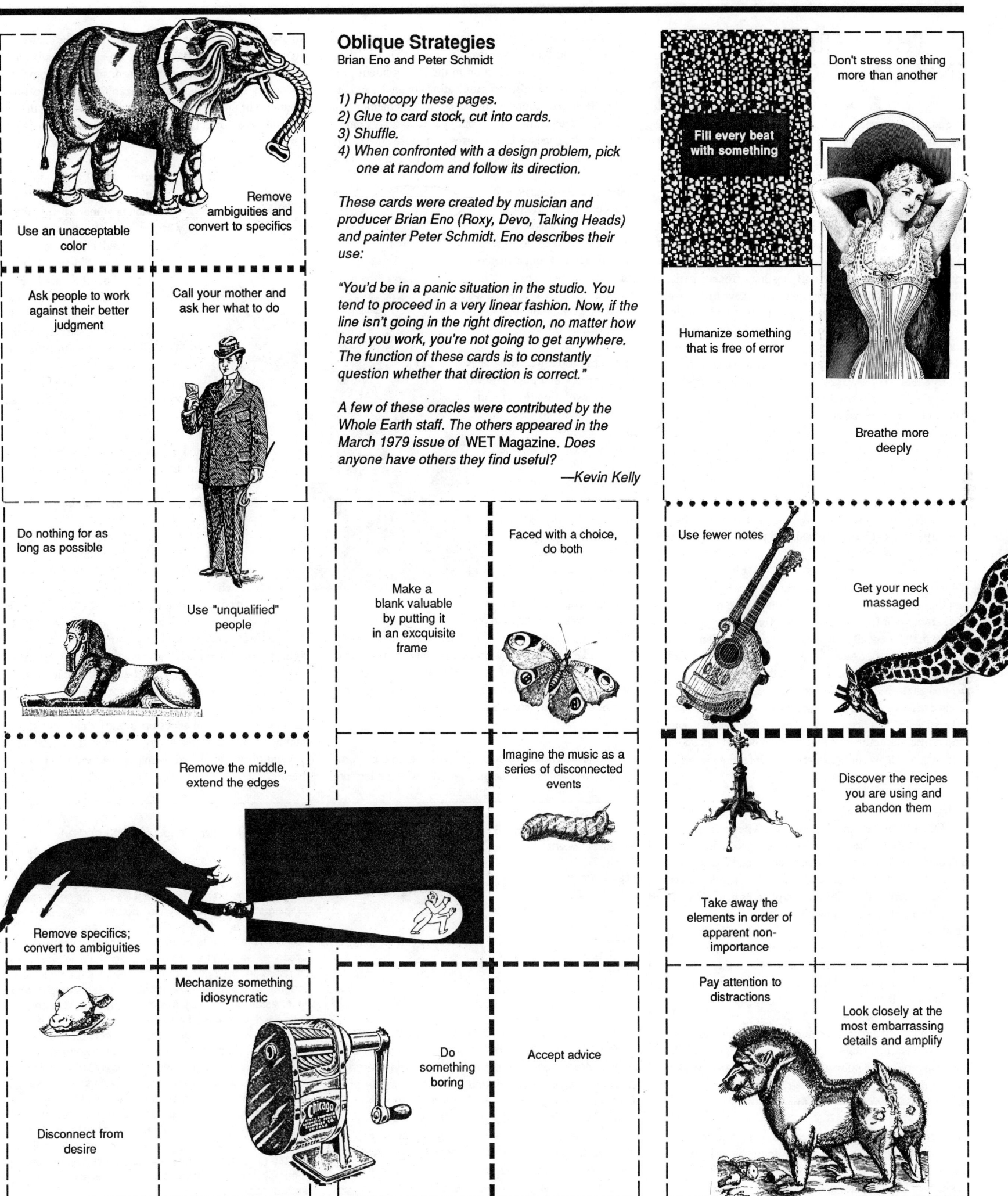

## Oblique Strategies
Brian Eno and Peter Schmidt

1) Photocopy these pages.
2) Glue to card stock, cut into cards.
3) Shuffle.
4) When confronted with a design problem, pick one at random and follow its direction.

These cards were created by musician and producer Brian Eno (Roxy, Devo, Talking Heads) and painter Peter Schmidt. Eno describes their use:

"You'd be in a panic situation in the studio. You tend to proceed in a very linear fashion. Now, if the line isn't going in the right direction, no matter how hard you work, you're not going to get anywhere. The function of these cards is to constantly question whether that direction is correct."

A few of these oracles were contributed by the Whole Earth staff. The others appeared in the March 1979 issue of WET Magazine. Does anyone have others they find useful?

—Kevin Kelly

Use an unacceptable color

Remove ambiguities and convert to specifics

Don't stress one thing more than another

Fill every beat with something

Ask people to work against their better judgment

Call your mother and ask her what to do

Humanize something that is free of error

Do nothing for as long as possible

Use "unqualified" people

Make a blank valuable by putting it in an excquisite frame

Faced with a choice, do both

Use fewer notes

Get your neck massaged

Breathe more deeply

Remove the middle, extend the edges

Imagine the music as a series of disconnected events

Discover the recipes you are using and abandon them

Remove specifics; convert to ambiguities

Take away the elements in order of apparent non-importance

Pay attention to distractions

Mechanize something idiosyncratic

Do something boring

Accept advice

Look closely at the most embarrassing details and amplify

Disconnect from desire

# ✳ THE SCIENCE OF ✳ INFORMATION VIRUSES

*by Keith Henson*

We don't have a science of social prediction. Until recently we haven't even had much in the way of theories. Our continual surprise at the development of cults, religions, wars, fads, and other social movements is a notable exception to the steady progress humans have made in building better models of our environment. Our lack of good models must be considered a major deficiency.

A successful theory for the development of social movements will have to provide a unifying theory for events that make up much of the evening news. It will have to discover common features that lie behind the diverse trends causing problems in Nicaragua, South Africa, Northern Ireland and the Middle East. It should be able to produce a plausible model for the breakup of the Rajneesh cult. The theory should be able to predict the conditions under which Turkey will be subverted by a fundamentalist version of Islam similar to that which has led to so much grief in Iran.

Tentative answers to these questions are beginning to emerge from the new field of memetics. Memetics (from meme, which rhymes with cream) is an outgrowth of evolutionary biology. It takes the age-old saying "ideas have a life of their own" literally, and applies models from biology to the evolution, spread, and persistence of ideas (memes) in human culture.

One aspect of memetics can be thought of as "germ theory applied to ideas." Social movements can be modeled as side effects of infectious ideas that spread among people in a way mathematically identical to the way epidemic disease spreads. Drug fads, for example, have closely followed epidemic-like curves. I don't think it can be demonstrated that civil authority has any more effect on the course of these "epidemics" than it had on the course of the Black Death. At a deeper level, research in neuro-science and artificial intelligence is starting to develop an understanding of why we are susceptible to "infectious information," both the benign and the deadly.

"Meme" is a word coined in purposeful analogy to "gene" by Richard Dawkins in his 1976 book, **The Selfish Gene**. To understand memes, you must have a good understanding of the modern concepts of evolution, and this is a good source. In the last chapter of Dawkins' book memes were defined as replicating information patterns that use minds to get themselves copied much as a virus uses cells to get itself copied. (Dawkins credits several others for developing the concepts, especially the anthropologist F. T. Cloak.) Like genes, memes are pure information, whether the sequence is coded in DNA, printed on paper, or written on magnetic tape.

Humans are not the only creatures that pass memes about. Birds can learn variations of songs. The songs of whales are also replicating information patterns that fit the model of a meme. So is the termite-catching technique that chimps pass from generation to generation.

Meme is similar to "idea," but not all ideas are memes. A passing idea which you do not communicate to others, or one which fails to take root in others, falls short of being a meme. The important part of the "meme about memes"

is that memes are subject to adaptive evolutionary forces very similar to those that select for genes. That is, their variation is subject to selection in the environment provided by human minds, communication channels, and the vast collection of cooperating and competing memes that make up human culture. The analogy is remarkably close. For example, genes in cold viruses that cause sneezes by irritating noses spread themselves by this route to new hosts and become more common in the gene pool of a cold virus. Memes cause those they have successfully infected to spread the meme by both direct methods (proselytizing) and indirect methods (such as writing). Such memes become more common in the culture pool.

The entire topic would be academic except that there are two levels of evolution (genes and memes) involved and the memetic level is only loosely coupled to the genetic. Memes which override genetic survival, such as those which induce young Lebanese Shiites to blow themselves "into the next world" from the front seat of a truck loaded with high explosives, or induce untrained Iranians to volunteer to charge Iraqi machine guns, or the WWII Kamikaze "social movement" in Japan are all too well known. I have proposed the term "memeoid" for people whose behavior is so strongly influenced by a replicating information pattern (meme) that their survival becomes inconsequential in their own minds.

Given that memes have been interfering with our reproduction for a long time, one must wonder why humans are

still so susceptible to information diseases. The answers to such questions are starting to come from research in artificial intelligence, neuroscience, and archeology. It is becoming apparent that our vulnerabilities are a direct consequence of the way our minds are organized, and that organization is a direct consequence of our evolutionary history.

Marvin Minsky (a principal founder of AI) and Michael Gazzaniga (one of the major workers in split brain research) have independently come to a virtually identical model of the mind. Both view minds as vast collections of interacting, largely parallel (co-conscious) modules or "agents," or a "Society of Mind." The lowest level of such a society of agents consists of a small number of nerve cells that innervate a section of muscle. A few of the higher-level modules have been isolated in clever experiments by Gazzaniga, some of them on patients whose right and left hemispheres had been divided by trauma or surgery.

One surprise from this work is that we seem to have our mental modules arranged in a way that guarantees we will form beliefs. What we believe in depends, at least in part, on what we are exposed to and the order in which we are exposed. Gazzaniga argues that we slowly evolved the ability to form beliefs because the ability provides a major advantage in surviving. Being able to infer, that is to form new beliefs, and to learn, in the sense of acquiring such beliefs from others, was a major advance over learning by trial and error. Being able to pass the rare new ways our ancestors found for chipping rock or making pots from person to person and generation to generation was vital in allowing humans to spread over the Earth.

---

### The Selfish Gene

Richard Dawkins
**$7.95**
postpaid from:
Oxford University
Press
Attn: Order Dept.
16-00 Pollitt Drive
Fair Lawn, NJ 07410
201/796-8000

*This book contains the first mention of memes as tools of evolutionary change. Just as a gene is a unit of information in the DNA molecule, a meme is a unit of information (an idea, a song, a notion of fashion or politics, etc.) that lodges in our minds and is capable of changing us. And just like any living organism, a meme's basic goal is to reproduce itself. By writing this review, I have passed a meme on to you. If you are receptive, you will read the book and tell your friends about it. They, in turn, will tell other friends. And on and on.*
*— Richard Kadrey*

◆

Just as genes propagate themselves in the gene pool by leaping from body to body via sperms or eggs, so memes propagate themselves in the meme pool by leaping from brain to brain via a process which, in the broad sense, can be called imitation. If a scientist hears, or reads about, a good idea, he passes it on to his colleagues and students. He mentions it in his articles and lectures. If the idea catches on, it can be said to propagate itself, spreading from brain to brain. As my colleague N. K. Humphrey neatly summed up an earlier draft of this chapter: ". . . memes should be regarded as living structures, not just metaphorically but technically. When you plant a fertile meme in my mind you literally parasitize my brain, turning it into a vehicle for the meme's propagation in just the way that a virus may parasitize the genetic mechanism of a host cell. And this isn't just a way of talking — the meme for, say, 'belief in life after death' is actually realized physically, millions of times over, as a structure in the nervous system of individual men the world over."

## COMPUTER VIRUSES

*by Corinne Cullen Hawkins*

Computer viruses, like their biological counterparts, trick the host into reproducing copies of the invading organism. They spread from computer to computer through electronic bulletin boards, telecommunication systems, and shared floppy disks. Viruses are created by human programmers, for fun or malice, but once they begin to spread, they take on a life of their own, creating disruption, dismay, and paranoia in their wake. Here are some of the more notorious and virulent viruses to date.

**(C) Brain Virus** — First sighted Fall, 1987 at University of Delaware. It changes the volume label (the name you give it) of a floppy or hard disk to (C) Brain. The boot record contains a message: "Welcome to the dungeon . . . Beware of this VIRUS. Contact us for vaccination." The message includes an address and phone number of Brain Computer Services, a computer company in Lahore, Pakistan, and the names of two brothers, Basit and Amjad.

The virus marks some disk sectors as bad. It modifies several command files, maybe all of them eventually, without changing file sizes or dates. Even if the boot sector is rewritten, the virus remains active through the command files it modified. No known cure. (comp.risks, April 5, 1988) This is the first virus to infect an American newspaper's computer system (The Providence Journal-Bulletin). When the phone number in Pakistan was called, the person who answered expressed surprise that the virus had travelled so far — and refused to give his last name. (New York Times May 25, 1988).

**Israeli Virus** — First sighted by Yuval Rakavy, a student at Hebrew University; first mentioned publically in "Maariv," one of Israel's daily newspapers, Jan. 8, 1988. Designed to begin destroying files on May 13, and to slow computer response on the 13th of any month. What called attention to the virus was an error in the virus code itself, which caused it to mistake previously infected programs as uninfected. In error, it would add another copy of itself to the program. Some programs were infected as many as 400 times and the growth in size of the program was noticeable. This one was discovered before D-day, but it had infected home, university, and military computers before it was detected.

**LeHigh Virus** — First sighted on November 25, 1987 by Jeffrey Carpenter. It attaches itself to a few lines of the operating system used on the IBM PC's that LeHigh University provides for student use. It is a corruption of a legitimate program, Command.Com, the basic boot-up file of MS-DOS and PC-Dos. The virus doesn't change the length of Command.Com, which makes it more difficult to detect. The virus destroys data on floppies and hard disks by writing zeros to the first thirty-two sectors of a disk (which erases the directory), making the data unrecoverable. The virus waits until it has been copied four times before it wipes out the data on the disk on which it resides.

**MacMag Virus** — First sighted by Chris Borton March 8, 1988. The virus was launched in December 1987 by Richard Brandow, publisher of MacMag magazine in

Montreal, Canada. The virus was designed to pop up a message of peace on Macintosh screens on March 2, the anniversary of the introduction of the Apple Macintosh SE and Macintosh II. After March 2, the virus erased itself. Although this virus was designed to be benign, it had some nasty side effects: it played havoc with users' System folders, resulting in thousands of hours of lost work.

The virus spread to Europe and the west coast and it is the first virus to infect a commercial personal computer product. It was inadvertently passed to Aldus by Marc Canter, president of MacroMind Inc. of Chicago. Mr. Canter's personal machine caught the virus, which was transfered to training software he was writing for Aldus. Aldus admits that the infected disk was copied for three days. Half of the infected disks were distributed to retailers; the other half are in Aldus' warehouse.

MacMag Virus display.

Richard Brandow, Publisher of MacMag, and its entire staff would like to take this opportunity to convey their **Universal Message of Peace** to all macintosh users around the world.

Written by : **Drew Davidson**          Click to continue

**Bell Labs Virus** — A compiler program (which translates a programmer's instructions into numbers that a computer can read) had been altered so that it embedded a hidden "trapdoor" each time it created a new version of the operating system. The trapdoor altered the system so that, in addition to normal users' passwords, it would recognize a secret password known only to one person. The instructions never showed up in the program listing — it was undetectable through normal means. The virus never escaped Bell Labs.

**MacInVirus** — First known encounter by David Spector; this virus was written by a West German and posted to CompuServe in a HyperCard stack. It's a very simple virus, easily defeated, just a few pages of Pascal and fifty lines of assembly code. The virus is disguised as a resource that inserts itself in a system trap handler (the place where the computer catches errors so they won't cause system crashes). The virus destroys hard disks and the applications that run on them.

**Atari ST Virus** — First dissected March 22, 1988 by Martin Minow. Once installed, this virus will copy itself onto every non-write protected disk used. It tests an uninfected disk to see if it contains the virus, replicates, then it keeps count of how many times the disk is used after that. When a certain limit is reached, the virus writes random data across the central directory and file allocation tables — which contain the map of unused sectors for the disk, making it unusable. The virus then removes itself from the damaged disk. The current virus doesn't affect hard disks. This virus may survive a reset.

As viruses have proliferated, so have vaccines, disinfectents, and other remedies.

**Protec ($195** from Sophco. Inc., P. O. Box 7430, Boulder, CO, 80306). A system of programs that includes Vaccinate — a virus, itself, which infects the host via the Syringe program. It warns the user if a virus infection has occurred. It also includes Canary — a quarantine program. When new files are imported from an unknown source, a user places the Canary program on a diskette with the suspect files. If the Canary dies, a virus program is present.

**Ferret** — created by Larry Nedry and Scott Winders. Notifies an infected user of the date that the Scores virus installed itself. It's helpful in determining where/how the virus was picked up. Ferret is available on electronic bulletin boards such as CompuServe and MacNET.

**Vaccine** — by Don Brown at CE Software. It enables your computer's operating system to detect alterations to the code of your system files and applications. Warning: If your system is already infected when you install Vaccine, there will be no warning from Vaccine of the viruses existence. If Vaccine is installed on a sterile system and the Scores virus is introduced later, Vaccine will warn of the virus attack but it will not prevent infection. Vaccine is available on electronic bulletin boards.

**Interferon** — written by Robert Woodhead. A shareware program that detects and claims to recognize "signals" that viruses give off when they are present, **Interferon** was intended to complement the **Vaccine** program. Interferon is available on electronic bulletin boards.

**Data Physician** — the grandaddy of virus remedies ($199 from Digital Dispatch, Fridley, Minnesota). It detects and in some cases eliminates viruses. It includes: Data MD — creates a list of computer data files to be protected and watches them while the computer is in operation; Antigen — attaches itself to an individual computer program and checks it for viruses each time it's used. Padlock — prevents anything from being written on a storage disk unless the computer operator pushes a button to give permission; Data Physician works on IBM PC and UNIX systems.

**Disk Defender** — (Director Technologies, Inc., Technology Innovation Center, 906 University Place, Evanston, IL, 60201; 312/491-2334). This is a product which write protects in hardware all or part of a personal computer hard disk. This protects the operating system and commonly used programs from viruses.

**Virus RX** — developed by Apple, this is a detection tool to determine whether a system has been infected by the Scores virus, and if so, which applications have been affected. It lists damaged applications, invisible files, altered system files, and altered applications. Virus Rx reports different levels of concern from simple comments to "dangerous," and finally to "fatal." This program is available through Apple dealers, AppleLink, and through some users-group bulletin boards.

# Programming Language Books

*by Richard Kadrey*

What follows is a list of computer language books that we think will help you in that eternal quest for tight code. We've listed two books, one beginner and one advanced, for the four most popular languages currently in use. This list is by no means comprehensive, but is just something to get you started. If you have questions about books we didn't list or languages we didn't mention, try calling your public library or Computer Literacy Bookshops (see review on this page). This list was put together with Laurie Hahn of the Computer Literacy Bookshop in San Jose.

### Basic: Getting Started
William S. Davis;1981; 69 pp., **$7.95**; Addison-Wesley

### Basic Handbook: Encyclopedia of the BASIC Computer Language, 3rd edition
David A. Lien;1986; 826 pp., **$24.95**; Compusoft

### Proficient C: The Microsoft Guide to Advanced C Programming
Augie Hansen;1987; 512 pp., **$22.95**; Microsoft

### C Programming Language, Second Edition
Brian W. Kernighan and Dennis M. Ritchie; 1978; 272 pp., **$28.00**; Prentice Hall

### Oh! Pascal, Second Editon
Doug Cooper and Michael Clancy; 1985; 607 pp., **$24.95**; Norton

### Mastering Turbo Pascal Files
Tom Swan; 1987; 327 pp., **$18.95**; Sams

### Complete Book of Macintosh Asembly Language Programming
Dan Weston; 1986; 568 pp., **$25.95**; Scott F.

### Assembly Language Primer for the IBM PC & XT
Waite Group and R. La Fore; 1984; 501 pp., **$24.95**; NAL

---

**File Copying**

Given getchar and putchar, you can write a surprising amount of useful code without knowing anything more about I/O. The simplest example is a program which copies its input to its output one character at a time. In outline.

```
    get a character
    while (character is not end of file signal)
        output the character just read
        get a new character
```

Converting this into C gives

```
    main()      /* copy input to output; 1st version */
    {
        int c;

        c = getchar();
        while (c != EOF) {
            putchar(c);
            c = getchar();
        }
    }
```

— From C Programming Language, Second Edition

## Computer Books By Mail

Newsletter **free** from: Computer Literacy Bookshops, 2590 North First Street, San Jose, CA 95131; 408/435-1118

*All of the computer and software books discussed in **Signal** are available through the Computer Literacy Bookshops. They carry pretty much every computer book available (over 20,000 titles), as well as 150 different computer and computer-related magazines. If you aren't sure of the book or magazine you want, they can research the subject and suggest the one that might be best for you. And they're willing to ship your merchandise anywhere in the world. Good people to have on your side.*
— *Richard Kadrey*

---

**Beginners' BASIC** explains all the fundamentals of BASIC programming, from flowcharting to subroutines, string handling to graphics, PEEKs and POKEs.

## Beginners' BASIC
Peter Lear
$5.95
($7.95 postpaid) from:
Hayes Publishing, Ltd.
3312 Mainway
Burlington,
Ontario L7M 1A7
Canada
416/335-0393
or Whole Earth Access

*My new favorite instruction book presents the concepts of BASIC programming in only 64 pages. The colors and pictures are comfortable and friendly. Explanations are quick and easy to grasp. Written for children, great for adults, here is simple material, simply presented, without muddying the waters. An excellent book.* — *James Stockford*

---

## Using QuickBASIC
Don Inman and Bob Albrecht
1988; 436 pp.
$19.95 postpaid from:
McGraw-Hill Book Company
Princeton Road
Hightstown, NJ 08520
609/426-5254
or Whole Earth Access

*QuickBASIC is to ordinary BASIC what the Indy 500 is to roller derby. By using the tools presented in this book, BASIC can be transformed into a powerful, professional level language with the modular characteristics of, say, Pascal, without giving up the interactive qualities of BASIC. Quick-BASIC also lets you write, compile, debug, and run programs in one environment.*

***Using QuickBASIC** is written primarily for people with some programming experience, but it does contain a quick intro to BASIC. From there, the book moves onto to QuickBASIC, providing a clear, structured overview of the language with sections on building a toolkit, editing your pro-*

*grams, writing sub-programs, creating sequential structured and unstructured files, debugging, and writing executable files for a MS-DOS environment.*

*If you started out in BASIC and moved on to other languages because you couldn't find the power you needed, this book could have you looking at BASIC code in a whole new way. Inman and Albrecht also have a diskette available with all the programs discussed in the book, and then some. They have a teachers' guide, too, for educators who want to start their kids off right.* — *Richard Kadrey*

When you first load QuickBASIC, at the right end of the menu bar you will see F1=HELP. Press the F1 key and a Help screen appears, as shown in Figure 1. The keyboard combinations used to perform specified functions are listed in separate boxes. You can return to the editing screen any time by pressing the ESC key.

From the Help screen, you can use the TAB key to move the cursor to the Keywords box and press ENTER. A list of BASIC keywords (words which have specific programmatic meanings in the BASIC environment) appears, as shown in Figure 2. To see information on a given keyword, use the arrow keys to move the highlight to the desired keyword and press ENTER.

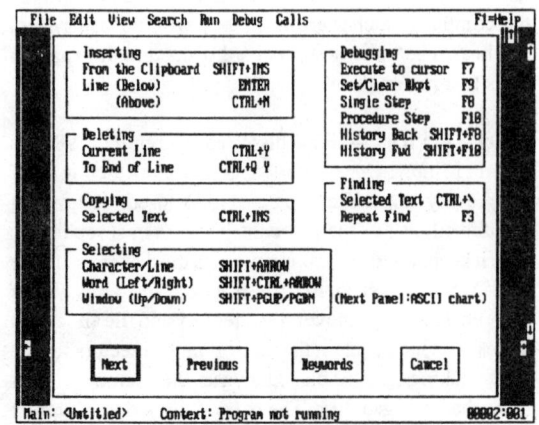

Figure 1

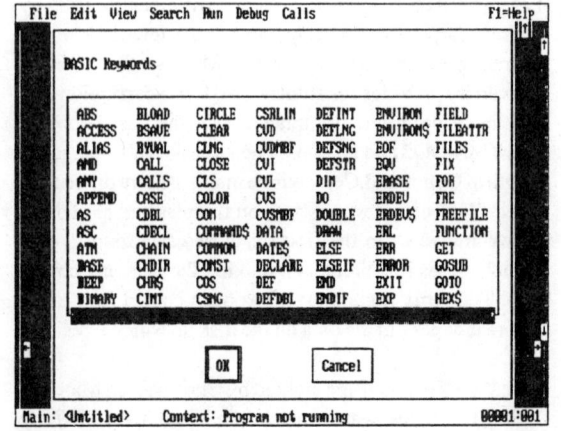

Figure 2

## Dr. Dobb's Journal

(of Software Tools for the
Professional Programmer)
$25/year
(12 issues) from:
Dr. Dobb's Journal
P. O. Box 27809
San Diego, CA 92128
415/424-0600

*Where **InfoWorld** is my meat and potatoes, I find **Dr. Dobb's Journal** is my monthly visit to a trade show "hospitality suite." Some months it is chips and dip and a **Coke** while other months it is cracked crab, caviar, and champagne.*

Harold applies algorithmic logic
to everyday situations

*Dr. Dobb's is very much a "hacker's" magazine and makes no bones about it. Until recently contributors were not paid for their efforts. Even now submitted articles and programs are placed into the public domain.*

*Dr. Dobb's seems to have its finger on the pulse of the proletariat of the computer world. This steady-handed approach in a computer magazine is welcome relief from the blowin'-in-the-wind feeling I get from most other mags every time a new computer comes onto the market.*

*I will probably never trash-can my Dr. Dobb's back issues, because they make excellent reference materials. Being that I am a **programmer** (software engineer?) by trade, I find back issues invaluable for finding tricks-of-the-trade subroutines.*
*—Thomas Spence*

## MacTutor

David E. Smith, Editor
$30/year
(12 issues) from:
MacTutor
P. O. Box 400
Placentia, CA 92670
714/630-3730

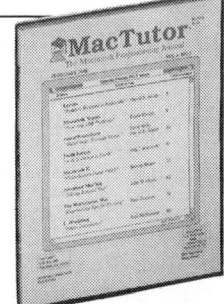

*This journal is recommended for programmers interested in learning how to program for the Macintosh. It's better than pretty good, especially for the intermediate programmer. As a professional Mac programmer, I still pick up some tips here. I enjoy the rumors and gossip that the magazine picks up from their bulletin board. For the best in Mac programming tips, get their **Complete MacTutor, Volume II**, which was published at the peak of their being the center for Macintosh information.*
*— Mike Coffey*
*[Suggested by Bob Murphy]*

◆

As most of you know, the Mac II has six expansion slots. Each of these slots can have something really neat plugged into it, like additional processors, data acquisi-

tion boards, and other stuff like that. But, if you don't have a video card and monitor plugged in, you won't be able to see what's going on. I ought to know. My monitor took about a month longer to arrive than my CPU did. The Mac made a nice sound when I turned it on, but that really got boring after the first couple of hundred times. Anyway, with six slots available, enterprising (and loaded) people can plug in six video cards to use with many monitors of various shapes and sizes

So, with lots of screens putting quite a load on your table, what would you expect to see? Several identical copies of your desktop? Sounds interesting, but not very practical. **Quickdraw** treats all the video devices collectively as a single, possibly irregular, display. Windows may be placed anywhere on the desktop, and as a result a single window can extend over several monitors. The effect is especially impressive when adjacent monitors have different color environments, or

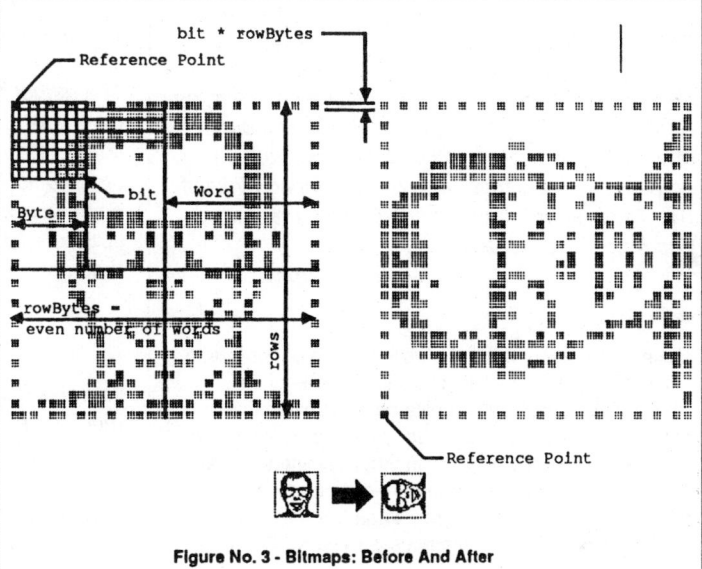

Figure No. 3 - Bitmaps: Before And After

one is color and the other b/w. This spectacular feat is accomplished through careful management of graphics devices.

## Numerical Recipes

(The Art of Scientific Computing)
William Press et al.
1986; 700 pp.
$44.50 postpaid from:
Cambridge University Press
510 North Avenue
New Rochelle, NY 10801
800/872-7423
or Whole Earth Access

*Numerical algorithms are the tools used for "number-crunching." Unfortunately, they're under-utilized because they have an aura of magic to many programmers.*

***Numerical Recipes** is a cookbook for when you want to get a job done, not wade through abstract discussions. When you need to find out how to do a Fast Fourier Transform for the job due yesterday, you'll get a basic grounding in the topic, discussion of the alternative techniques, and best of all, tested source code you can adapt for your own use. The authors' frequent opinions on when and where to*

use each technique are mostly right on the mark.

*The original **Numerical Recipes** had examples in Fortran and Pascal, and thanks to demand, there's now a C version as well. You can also buy all the example code on IBM PC or Macintosh-compatible disks.*
*— Bob Murphy*
*[Suggested by James Guilbeau]*

◆

Hamming's motto, "the purpose of computing is insight, not numbers," is particularly apt in the area of finding roots. You should say this motto aloud whenever your program converges, with ten digit accuracy, to the wrong root of a problem, or whenever it fails to converge because there is actually no root, or because there is a root but your initial estimate was not sufficiently close to it.

◆

Where would any book on numerical analysis be without Mr. Simpson and his "rule"? The classical formulas for integrating a function whose value is known at equally-spaced steps have a certain elegance about them, and they are redolent with historical association. Through them, the modern numerical analyst communes with the spirits of his or her predeces-

sors back across the centuries, as far as the time of Newton, if not farther. Alas, times do change; with the exception of two of the most modest formulas. . . the classical formulas are almost entirely useless. They are museum pieces, but beautiful ones.

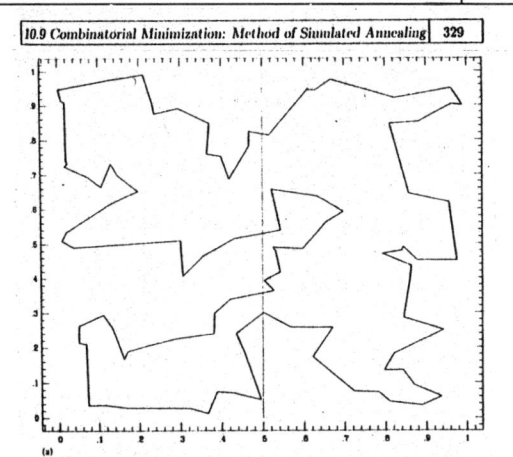

10.9 Combinatorial Minimization: Method of Simulated Annealing | 329

Figure 10.9.1. Traveling salesman problem solved by simulated annealing. The (nearly) shortest path among 100 randomly positioned cities is shown in (a). The dotted line is a river, but there is no penalty in crossing. In (b) the river-crossing penalty is made large, and the solution restricts itself to the minimum number of crossings, two. In (c) the penalty has been made negative: the salesman is actually a smuggler who crosses the river on the flimsiest excuse!

## Programming Pearls
Jon Bentley; 1986; 200 pp.; **$16.25**
($17.88 postpaid)

## More Programming Pearls
Jon Bentley; 1988; 200 pp.; **$16.25** ($17.88 postpaid)
both from: Addison-Wesley Publishing Company, 1
Jacob Way, Reading, MA 01867; 800/447-2226 or
Whole Earth Access

*Two of the keys to good programming are creativity and a playful approach to problem-solving. Bentley's collections of brief essays and magazine columns encourage these traits in a mildly mind-bending manner.*

*I expected to skim through these books, snag a few flashy new insights about programming, and be on my way. Bentley, however, draws you in like a fly fisherman. He proposes a simple problem, and encourages you to approach it in a workman-like manner. When you return with your answer, he replies, "Did you consider this?" No, you took the obvious approach, so you go back and work on it some more. Little that he says is profound by itself, but as you keep returning and being corrected, suddenly. . . enlightenment!*
— Bob Murphy

The moral of each of the stories is the same: don't write a big program when a little one will do. Most of the structures exemplify what Polya calls the Inventor's Paradox in his How To Solve It: "the more general problem may be easier to solve". In programming this means that it may be harder to solve a 73-case problem directly than to write a general program to handle the N-case version, and then apply it to the case that N=73.

## Using the Structured Techniques
(A Case Study)
Audrey M. Weaver
1987; 247 pp.
**$27** postpaid from:
Prentice Hall
200 Old Tappan Road
Old Tappan, NJ 07675
201/767-5937
or Whole Earth Access

*This book will help you build software that you won't later regret. Structured program design, and the design of structured code, are taught in schools all over the world today. If you're unfamiliar with these concepts, this book is an invaluable introduction; if you've studied these in courses, this manual will you show you how to actually put them into practice.*

*The author brings information modeling to life as we follow Alan, a young programmer at International Telewidgets Corporation through every step of a project from conception to maintenance. At each juncture, Alan applied the techniques from structured design, making clear thinking almost automatic.*

*We learn best by doing, and watching Alan break a complex problem into manageable parts gives us a much richer understanding of structured programming than a mere exposition of technique. We have the comfortable illusion of watching real people figure out how to use the techniques to solve real problems, and it's almost as good as*

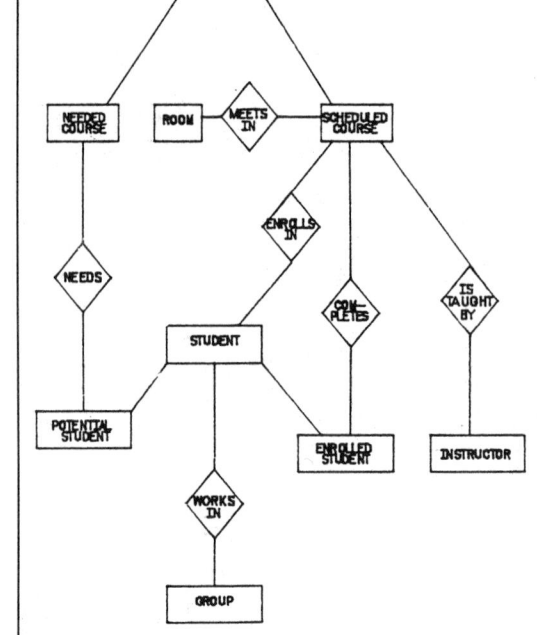

An information model consists of an object-relationship diagram, object definitions and relationship definitions. Objects are the things that a business stores information about. An object can be something tangible, such as a person or a place, or it can be something intangible such as a concept, agreement, or event. For example, an object can be an employee, a customer, a contract, or a ballgame. In an information model, you define the objects that your system records data about and how these objects are related to each other. The illustration shows an object-relationship diagram naming the relationships someone needs to take a course.

*solving them ourselves. I highly recommend this book, and wish I had read it many years ago when I started writing programs.*
— Matthew McClure

## The Elements of Programming Style
Brian W. Kernighan
and Dennis Plauger
1978; 160 pp.
**$22.50** postpaid from:
McGraw-Hill Book Company
Princeton Road
Hightstown, NJ 08520
609/426-5254
or Whole Earth Access

*For programmers, this is the one book to have if you're only having one. Like its namesake, Strunk and White's* **Elements of Style**, *the book concentrates on the essential practical aspects of style by example.*

*Collected into chapters under such names as "Expression," "Control Structure," "Common Blunders," and "Efficiency and Instrumentation" are real programs, not toys made up to illustrate a point. These bad examples serve as springboards for incisive discussions of the best ways to write correct and readable programs. Sad to say, these programs come primarily from programming textbooks, where our next generation of programmers is turning for guidance. Each of the examples gets rewritten, sometimes in more than one way, to*

*illustrate the principles the authors espouse. The examples are in FORTRAN or PL/I, but are nonetheless valuable in BASIC, COBOL, Pascal or any other common language. As the authors prove, "The principles of style are applicable in all languages, including assembly codes."*

*Each example is followed by an aphorism that captures the point: "Write clearly — don't be too clever"; "Choose a date representation that makes your program simple"; "Make it right before you make it faster"; The rules are listed together at the end of the book. A programmer could do worse than paste the list on the wall.*

*This book could be used as a textbook for a programming course, yet the examples are sufficiently self-contained to allow you to open the book at random, read a few pages, and come away a better programmer. In fact, that's not a bad way to work with the book on your second or third reading.*

*One of the strongest messages in the book is that programming is a holistic task. The error in the sine function is not with the formula or the numerical analysis — the first place many programmers would look — but arises from the simplest of all*

*blunders, an uninitialized variable. Time and again, using subtle or surprising examples, Kernighan and Plauger lead us to sharpen our sharpen both our reading and writing skills by discussing what is wrong in a given instance, how to correct it, and, most important, how to avoid it.*
— Dennis Geller

**SUMMARY OF RULES**

Write clearly — don't be too clever.

Avoid temporary variables.

Write clearly — don't sacrifice clarity for efficiency.

Let the machine do the dirty work.

Use uniform input formats.

Use the good features of a language; avoid the bad ones.

Make your programs read from top to bottom.

Don't stop with your first draft.

Let the data structure the program.

Each module should do one thing well.

Make input easy and output self-explanatory.

## Programmers at Work

Susan Lammers
1986; 385 pp.
**$14.95**
($16.95 postpaid) from:
Microsoft Press
Attn.: Consumer Sales
16011 NE 36th Way,
Box 97017
Redmond, WA 98073-9717
206/882-8080
or Whole Earth Access

*One of the most impressive things about computer hackers is that, in their drive to get more out of their hardware, they exploit fresh ways of viewing problems. This outlook is frequently enlightening on subjects that have nothing to do with computers. So in a sense, each of the 19 interviews that Susan Lammers has conducted with some of the major pioneers in microcomputing is more than just a story of how code-hackers actually program. Each is like a kind of Crackerjack box — the Utterly Disarming, Frequently Astonishing Insight is the prize. There's also a fascinating appendix where we see actual code, worksheets, etc. of these wizards.*

— *Steven Levy*

◆

Interviewer: What do you perceive as aesthetically beautiful or pleasing in either the listing or the structure of the algorithms when you look at a particular program?

Simonyi: I think the listing gives the same pleasure that you get from a clean home. You can just tell with a glance if things are messy — if garbage and unwashed dishes are lying about — or if things are really clean. It may not mean much. Just because a house is clean, it might still be a den of iniquity! But it is an important first impression and does say something about the program. I'll bet you that from ten feet away I can tell if a program is bad. I might not guarantee that it is good, but if it looks bad from ten feet, I can guarantee that it wasn't written with care. And if it wasn't written with care, it's probably not beautiful in the logical sense.

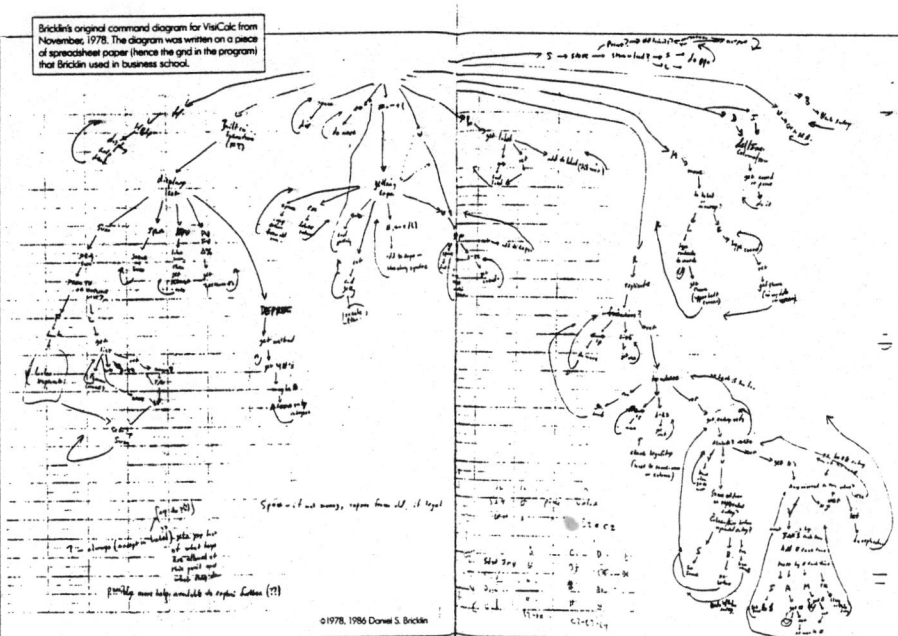

Bricklin's original command diagram for VisiCalc (the original electronic spreadsheet) from November, 1978. The diagram was written on a piece of spreadsheet paper (hence the grid in the program) that Bricklin used in business school.

◆

Interviewer: What did you intend the character of Pac Man to be like?

Itwani: Pac Man's character is difficult to explain even to the Japanese — he is an innocent character. He hasn't been educated to discern between good and evil. He acts more like a small child than a grown-up person. Think of him as a child learning in the course of his daily activities. If someone tells him guns are evil, he would be the type to rush out and eat guns, even the pistols of policemen who need them. He's indiscriminate because he's naive. But he learns from experience that some people, like policemen, should have pistols and he can't eat just any pistols in sight.

◆

Interviewer: What goals and work rules did you set when you were working on Framework?

Carr: One piece of advice I had been given was to hold off programming for as long as possible. Once you've got a corpus of code building up, it's hard to change direction. It sets like concrete. So I held off for as long as I could, but I couldn't hold the design in my head forever.

◆

Frankston: . . . If you cannot explain a program to yourself, the chance of a computer getting it right is pretty small.

◆

Simonyi: The first step in programming is imagining. Just making it crystal clear in my own mind what is going to happen. In this initial stage, I use paper and pencil. I just doodle, I don't write code. I might draw a few boxes or a few arrows, but it's just mostly doodles, because the real picture is in my mind. I like to imagine the structures that represent the reality I want to code.

Once I have the structure fairly firm and clear in my mind, then I write the code. I sit down at my terminal — or with a piece of paper in the old days — and write it.

◆

Interviewer: You seem to scorn complexity. When you design a system, do you strive for simplicity?

Lampson: Right. Right everything should be made as simple as possible. But to do that you have to master complexity.

Interviewer: In practical terms, how do you achieve that?

Lampson: There are some basic techniques to control complexity. Fundamentally, I divide and conquer, break things down, and try to write reasonably precise descriptions of what each piece is supposed to do. That becomes a sketch of how to proceed. When you can't figure out how to write a spec, it's because you don't understand what's going on. Then you have two choices: Either back off to some other program you do understand, or think harder.

Also, the description of the system shouldn't be too big. You may have to think about a big system in smaller pieces. It's somewhat like solving problems in mathematics: You can write books that are full of useful hints, but you can't give an algorithm.

## Hackers

Steven Levy
1984; 448 pp.
**$4.50**
($5.25 postpaid) from:
Dell Books
P. O. Box 1000
Pinebrook, NJ 07058-01000
800/932-0070
or Whole Earth Access

*Steven Levy is to computer history what Barbara Tuchman is to the 14th Century. He tells how programming changes people, how programmers created a subculture, and how that subculture changed the whole culture.*

— *Art Kleiner*

◆

Something new was coalescing around the TX-0: a new way of life, with a philosophy, an ethic, and a dream.

The Hacker Ethic:

Access to computers — and anything which might teach you something about the way the world works — should

be unlimited and total. Always yield to the Hands-on Imperative!

Hackers believe that essential lessons can be learned about the systems — about the world — from taking things apart, seeing how they work, and using this knowledge to create new and even more interesting things. They resent any person, physical barrier, or law that tries to keep them from doing this.

All information should be free.

Mistrust Authority — Promote Decentralization.

The best way to promote this free exchange of information is to have an open system, something which presents no boundaries between a hacker and a piece of information or an item of equipment that he needs in his quest for knowledge, improvement, and time on-line. The last thing you need is a bureaucracy.

Hackers should be judged by their hacking, not bogus criteria such as degrees, age, race, or position.

You can create art and beauty on a computer.

Computers can change your life for the better.

## Mathematical Snapshots

H. Steinhaus
1950, 1983; 311 pp.
**$8.95**
($10.95 postpaid) from:
Oxford University Press
Attn.: Order Department
16-00 Pollitt Drive
Fair Lawn, NJ 07410
800/451-7556
or Whole Earth Access

*The most graphically insightful math book in print. Most math feeds proof; this lovely stuff feeds understanding and is no less rigorous. If someone were going to see only one mathematics book in their life, this would be the best.*

—Stewart Brand

◆

To determine the centroid of a stick, we place it

horizontally on the edges of our palms and then we bring our hands closer together; finally they meet in the center of gravity. The stick never loses its equilibrium because when the centroid, which is initially between the palms, approaches one of them, the pressure on the nearer palm becomes many times greater than the pressure on the other palm; its product by the coefficient of friction must finally surpass the analogous product for the other palm; when this happens, the relative movement of the other one starts. This play continues alternatively until both palms meet; the centroid is always between them and it is there at the final stage. The trick is done automatically without any conscious effort.

[Below] When we cut a cylinder by a plane, we get an ellipse.

---

## Understanding Calculator Math

Texas Instruments Learning Center
1976, 1978; 224 pp.
**$4.95**
($7.95 postpaid) from:
Texas Instruments
Attn.: Accessories Department
P.O. Box 53
Lubbock, TX 79408
806/747-1882
or Whole Earth Access

*This book explains the basic keys and then takes you through some common business, home and scientific problems that make you itchy to work out your own problems. It's the only good introduction to calculator use we've seen. Though originally published by electronics manufacturer Texas Instruments, you can use it with anybody's calculator. T.I. published a whole series of such books, on the sly premise that if you give people well-crafted, enthusiastic introductory manuals to calculator/computer/communications technology, they'll get hooked.*

—Art Kleiner

◆

**Balancing Your Checkbook.** Here's a trick to help find mistakes — if your checkbook balance and statement balance differ by an amount that is evenly divisible by 9, chances are that your error is one of transposing two numbers (i.e., recording 54 instead of 45, or 329 instead of 239).

---

BASIC KEYS

### $\boxed{1/x}$ — Inverse Function or "Reciprocal" Key

The $\boxed{1/x}$ key just takes the number in the display and divides it *into* 1. (By the way — the letter "x", used in calculator keys just means "any number that may be in the display.") The $\boxed{1/x}$ key can be used at any time: it acts immediately on whatever number is in the display, and doesn't affect other calculations in progress.

*Example:*
You're trying to fill a swimming pool and want to speed up the process. You turn on a main fill faucet that would fill the pool by itself in 10 hours, set up a garden hose that would do it in 28 hours, and a fire hose that would take 6 hours on its own. How long does it take with all three working?

*Solution:*
$$\frac{1}{\text{Time Total}} = \frac{1}{T_1} + \frac{1}{T_2} + \frac{1}{T_3}$$
where $T_1$, $T_2$, and $T_3$ are the times for the faucet, garden hose and fire hose, respectively.

| Press | Display/Comments |
|---|---|
| 10 $\boxed{1/x}$ $\boxed{+}$ 28 $\boxed{1/x}$ $\boxed{+}$ | |
| 6 $\boxed{1/x}$ $\boxed{=}$ $\boxed{1/x}$ | **3.3070866** hours, or about 3 hours, 18 minutes. |

Note that the $\boxed{1/x}$ key "inverts" or flips over fractions; and this process can be useful in evaluating expressions you'll find in many situations — especially in basic science (see *Physics* section).

---

## Overhead Calculator

**$42** postpaid from:
Stokes Publishing
1125 Robin Way
Sunnyvale, CA 94087
408/736-4637

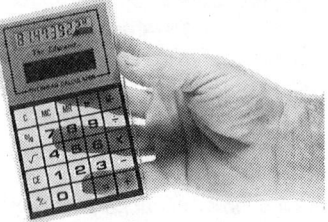

*Calculator math, that is teaching math using calculators, is so effective that it is becoming mandatory in progressive elementary schools. This transparent glass (and solar powered!) calculator lets the teacher go through the steps projected overhead while the rest of the class fingerbutton their own. Two, four, six, eight, this is how we calculate.*

—Kevin Kelly
[Suggested by Bob Albrecht]

---

## Math Aids

Catalog **free** from P.O. Box 64, San Carlos, CA 94070
415/593-2839.

*Looking through this catalog of books and sundries, you would think that mathematics was something that anyone could enjoy.*
—Kevin Kelly

**THE TANGRAM In wood $5.00**
•made from stained wood 1" thick
•assembles to the traditional tangram square measuring 11"x11"
•for classroom, desk, or coffee table
•discover how to form over 1000 tangram figures

**THE EIGHTH BOOK OF TAN $3.25**
by Sam Loyd •A treasure trove of tangram puzzles, history and solutions by America's foremost puzzler.

**THE FUN WITH TANGRAMS KIT $2.95**
by S. Johnson•120 tangram puzzles with two complete sets of tangram pieces.

---

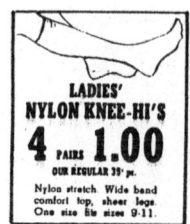

---

## Survival Mathematics

(Basic Math to Help You Cope)
Edward Williams
1983; 364 pp.
**$9.95**
($11.55 postpaid) from:
Barron's Educational Series, 250 Wireless
Boulevard, Hauppauge, NY 11788
800/645-3476
or Whole Earth Access

SURVIVAL MATHEMATICS

*Somebody you know might need some help in basic arithmetic. Have them try this exercise book which employs figures from everyday life for practicing math. Adding up a bill, determining if you're gonna save money on a sale, calculating what kind of insurance costs less. Just as the title says: survival mathematics.*

—Kevin Kelly

## How to Lie with Statistics

Darrell Huff
1954, 1973; 142 pp.
**$2.95**
postpaid from:
National Book Company
Keystone Industrial Park
Scranton, PA 18512
800/233-4830
or Whole Earth Access

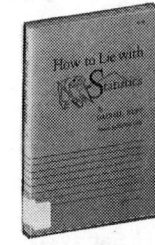

*In these days of polls and "proof" furnished by testing by "independent laboratories," it might be well to bear in mind the lessons given by this simple book. It's been around a long time, but it's still deadly.*   —*J. Baldwin*

◆

We'll let our graph show how national income increased ten per cent in a year.

Begin with paper ruled into squares. Name the months along the bottom. Indicate billions of dollars up the side. Plot your points and draw your line, and your graph will look like this: (fig. 1).

Now that's clear enough. It shows what happened during the year and it shows it month by month. He who runs may see and understand, because the whole graph is in proportion and there

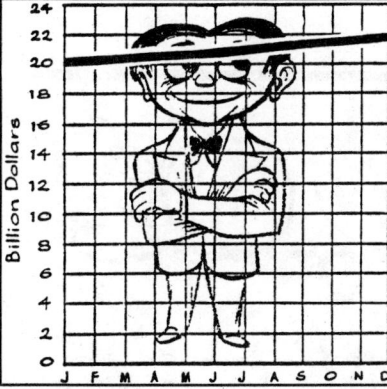

Fig. 1

Fig. 2

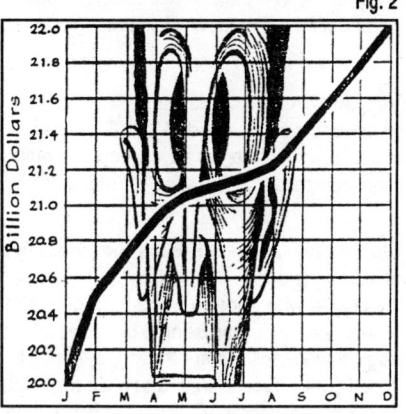

Fig. 3

is a zero line at the bottom for comparison. Your ten per cent looks like ten per cent — an upward trend that is substantial but perhaps not overwhelming.

That is very well if all you want to do is convey information. But suppose you wish to win an argument, shock a reader, move him to action, sell him something. For that, this chart lacks schmaltz. Chop off the bottom (fig. 2).

Now that's more like it. (You've saved paper, too, something to point out if any carping fellow objects to your misleading graphics.) The figures are the same and so is the curve. It is the same graph. Nothing has been falsified — except the impression that it gives. But what the hasty reader sees now is a national-income line that has climbed halfway up the paper in twelve months . . . .

Now that you have practiced to deceive, why stop with truncating? You have a further trick available that's worth a dozen of that. It will make your modest rise of ten per cent look livelier than one hundred per cent is entitled to look. Simply change the proportion between the ordinate and the abscissa (fig. 3). There's no rule against it, and it does give your graph a prettier shape. All you have to do is let each mark up the side stand for only one-tenth as many dollars as before. That is impressive, isn't it? Anyone looking at it can just feel prosperity throbbing in the arteries of the country. It is a subtler equivalent of editing "National income rose ten per cent" into ". . . climbed a whopping ten per cent." It is vastly more effective, however, because it contains no adjectives or adverbs to spoil the illusion of objectivity. There's nothing anyone can pin on you.

## Statgraphics

Version 2.6. Not copy-protected; IBM/PC/XT/AT and compatibles (384K; 2 disk drives or hard disk required). **$895** complete ($325 or $125 for upgrades) from STSC, Inc. 2115 East Jefferson Street, Rockville, MD 20852, 301/984-5123.

*Statgraphics has made my day. Finally a complete statistics program with built-in graphics, and it's not copy protected at that. Statgraphics is the best statistics package I've found.*

*The plotting capabilities are superb! They include three-dimensional graphic and bar charts as well as 3-D surface plots, which makes the display and interpretation of statistical data almost easy.*

*Statgraphics does the following: smoothing (9 kinds), time series (16 kinds), categorical analysis (4 kinds), multivariate matrices and plots (15 kinds), and nonparametric tests (12 kinds).*   —*Woody Liswood*

One unique feature of Statgraphics is its ability to display data in three dimensions, as seen in this floating three-dimensional plot showing gas economy for cars of differing weights and horsepower.

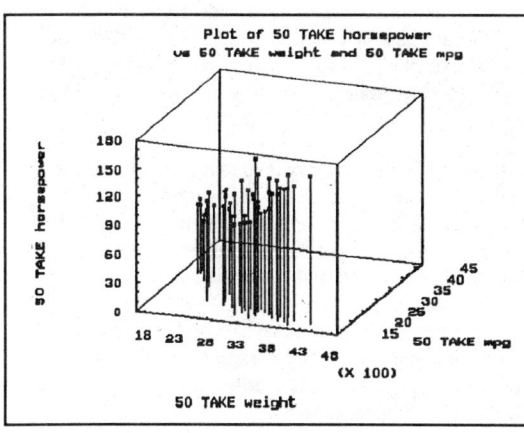

## StatView II

**$495** (for the Mac II); **$399** (for the SE+) from Abacus Concepts, P.O. Box 3086, Berkeley, CA 94703; 415/540-1949

*Egad. I've got all this data and I need to make sense of it. StatView II on the Macintosh is probably the most non-mathematical way of applying mathematics to your problem. Using the Mac's visual point-and-pick method, choose a variable, or two, and chart the data from that point of view. What's the divorce rate among left-handed males over six feet in height named Bob? Does this rate correlate with beer drinking? StatView likes those kinds of jobs. It's also handy with super-sophisticated double-twist backhanded regression analysis (and serious stuff like Wilcoxon signed-rank, Wald-Wolfowitz runs, Pearson correlations, t-Tests, harmonic means, skewness and kurtosis, among the easier ones to pronounce).*

*StatView II needs a Mac II (or souped up SE) to run on. This combination nears the statistical power of today's corporate mini-computer and surpasses yesterday's Fortune 500 mainframe. But it's thousands of times easier to use, and considerably easier to pick up on than the best IBM PC stat program. A background in statistics still helps. Market researchers, chemists, psychologists, medical agencies, sociologists — any one trying to clarify data — will find this tool essential. I'd love to see a course using this to teach statistics.*   —*Kevin Kelly*

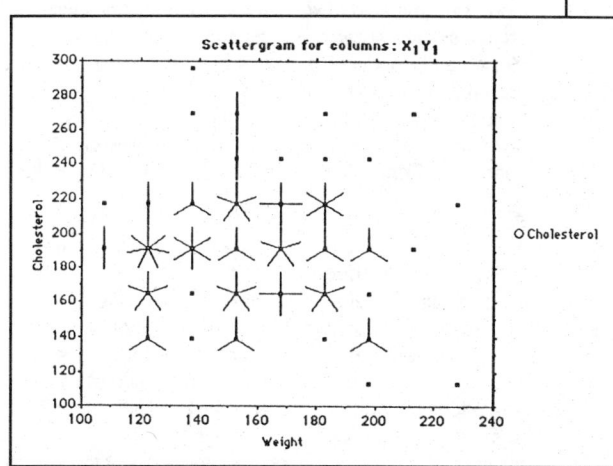

One view of the variable "Cholesterol."

|  | Name | Gender | Age | Weight | Cholesterol | Trigly |
|---|---|---|---|---|---|---|
| 1 | J. Suds | male | 22 | 138 | 197 | |
| 2 | T. Wilson | female | 22 | 115 | 181 | |
| 3 | D.S. Quintent | male | 22 | 190 | 190 | |
| 4 | R. Beal | female | 22 | 115 | 131 | |
| 5 | R. James | male | 25 | 160 | 172 | |
| 6 | S. Kaufman | male | 22 | 150 | 233 | |
| 7 | M. Mubrold | male | 23 | 154 | 194 | |
| 8 | L. Phote | male | 24 | 185 | 155 | |
| 9 | C. Norman | male | 23 | 178 | 234 | |
| 10 | R.S. Smith Jr. | male | 22 | 158 | 201 | |
| 11 | Walker | male | 26 | 188 | 258 | |
| 12 | W. Rogers | male | 22 | 150 | 212 | |
| 13 | M. Lumpole | male | 22 | 123 | 137 | |
| 14 | D. Fineman | female | 27 | 138 | 285 | |
| 15 | R. Smith | male | 22 | 143 | 218 | |

The raw data, in columns. Each column heading can be considered a variable.

## They Have A Word for It

Howard Rheingold
1988; 224 pp.
**$7.95**
($9.45 postpaid) from:
Jeremy P. Tarcher, Inc.
9110 Sunset Boulevard
Suite 250
Los Angeles, CA 90069
213/273-3274;
or St. Martin's Press
800/221-7945

People who learn a second language often experience a new part of themselves, a personality or set of perceptions coaxed out of them by the inner nature of the new language. Howard Rheingold's collection of untranslatable words from 44 different languages shifts our perceptions from as many perspectives.

His is a dictionary of both words and ideas. It works to reveal the cultural blinders with which we experience the world.

—Jeanne Carstensen

◆

*Bol* (Mayan): Stupid in-laws. [noun/adjective]
The Apaches have the *sitike* relationship, which is a very positive kind of in-law-ship. In Poland, there is a similar kind of kinship obligation, which can be regarded in a more grudging kind of way, in regard to relations who are considered *swojak*. But the Mayans of southern Mexico and Honduras use the same word—*bol* (BOWL)—to serve for in-laws as well as stupidity! Variations of this root word also indicate the kind of dazed befuddlement that accompanies a blow on the head, or the kind of stupor that can be induced by drugs.

◆

*Biritilulo* (Kiriwina, New Guinea): Comparing yams to settle disputes. [noun]
When a member of a group makes the mistake of saying the irrevocable "hard words" . . . to a member of another group, the individuals and their associates have the choice of combat or the ritualistic comparison of yams. The offending individual's clansmen quickly organize a *buritilulo*; as soon as the loud and frightening but ultimately harmless exchange of boasts about the size of the opposing clan's yams is under way, fighting is

*Palatyi* (Bantu): A mythical monster that scratches at the door. [noun]

*Bricoleur* (French): A person who constructs things by random messing around without following an explicit plan. [noun]

averted.
In contemporary American business . . . . a ritual for averting conflict is badly needed. . . . Gather at the local bar and select a ritual object for clamorous comparison: A personal computer? Briefcases? Watches?

◆

*Wabi* (Japanese): A flawed detail that creates an elegant whole. [noun]
To many people who see the world through modern sensibilities, beauty is represented by the kind of technological sleekness, smoothness, symmetry, and mass-produced perfection that is usually associated with a sports car or a skyscraper. A highly prized Japanese teacup, which might fetch tens of thousands of dollars from a collector, might be very simple, roughly fashioned, asymmetrical, and plainly colored. It would not be uncommon to find a crack. The crack—*the beautiful, distinctive, aesthetic flaw that distinguishes the spirit of the moment in which this object was created from all other moments in eternity*—might indeed be the very feature that would cause a connoisseur to remark: "This pot has *wabi*."

## Standing by Words

Wendell Berry
1983; 213 pp.
**$10.50**
($12 postpaid) from:
North Point Press
850 Talbot Avenue
Berkeley, CA 94706
415/527-6260
or Whole Earth Access

I cannot imagine a better English teacher than farmer, essayist, poet, novelist Wendell Berry. His writing and his thinking are hard liquor, the kind that makes you go "whooh!" with savor and respect. His subject this time is language, and the model is not far off. His writing (and speaking, if you get the chance to hear it) is his own best example.

More even than his works on agriculture (**The Unsettling of America**), this book of essays goes to the center of a wide and terrible malaise that is obscured from our view by its very size. When the land weakens, when the use of language weakens, nothing else can be truly strong.

## The Synonym Finder

J.I. Rodale
1978; 1361 pp.
**$21.95**
($24.89) postpaid from:
Rodale Press, Inc.
33 East Minor Street
Emmaus, PA 18049
or Whole Earth Access

*The word you have in your head is usually not the word you need on the page. A thesaurus takes you from here to there. Ideally every dictionary would incorporate a thesaurus, but since they don't, the best we've seen (thousand of entries, 1.5 million synonyms, organized alphabetically, easiest to use) is not Roget's, not Webster's, not even Random House's, but Rodale's.*

—Art Kleiner

◆

**signal**, n. **1.** sign, marker, guidepost, milepost, milestone, landmark, seamark; beacon, light, flag, warning light, caution light, flare, rocket; monitor, pilot, gauge, meter, instrument; alert, warning, siren, whistle, alarm, *Archaic.* alarum, horn, toot, tocsin, bell; cry, call, yell, scream. . . .
**7.** significant, historic, landmark, important, meaningful, momentous, weighty, big, consequential; outstanding, extraordinary, extraordinaire, glorious, grand, fantastic, fabulous, splended, *Inf.* super, *Sl.* bang-up; unparalleled, nonpareil, unequaled, unprecedented; striking, impressive, breathtaking, brilliant; unbelievable, amazing, astonishing, *Inf.* unreal; notable, noteworthy, remarkable, unforgettable; exceptional, special, unusual, uncommon, unfamiliar, out of the ordinary, unheard of; rare, unique, singular, one of a kind.

Berry wrote elsewhere once, "I stand for what I stand on." This book is about that kind of precision.

—Stewart Brand

◆

Two epidemic illnesses of our time—upon both of which virtual industries of cures have been founded—are the disintegration of communities and the disintegration of persons. That these two are related (that private loneliness, for instance, will necessarily accompany public confusion) is clear enough. And I take for granted that most people have explored in themselves and their surroundings some of the intricacies of the practical causes and effects; most of us, for example, have understood that the results are usually bad when people act in social or moral isolation, and also when, because of such isolation, they fail to act.

◆

One of the uses of poetry is to reveal and articulate and make and preserve the necessary connections between the domestic and the wild. It is one of the ways we may, with the hope of return, get out of our minds (our own and other people's) into the world of creatures, forms, and powers that we did not make. Access to that world is sanity. To be trapped in one's own mind is insanity. To be trapped in another person's mind—by political or technological tyranny—is imprisonment.

## Et cetera

Russell Joyner,
Editor
$25/year
(4 issues, includes
membership) from:
International Society
for General Semantics
P.O. Box 2469
San Francisco, CA 94126
415/543-1747

*General Semantics is the art and science of thinking about symbols instead of swallowing them whole and unexamined. **Et cetera** is the quarterly magazine put out by the International Society for General Semantics, and it prints smart, scholarly articles about the dangers of loose thinking and fuzzy talk. It's a good antidote for face value. Your subscription also gets you a monthly collection of additions called **Glimpse**.*

*—Anne Herbert*

◆

The answering machine reverses the whole history of the telephone by restoring the rights of the receiver to initiate communication. A dimension of privacy that had virtually disappeared from daily life has been put back: to be interrupted by the anonymous ring of the telephone is no longer the price one must pay for membership in a communication network. The extraordinary ability to call any number at any time from almost anywhere still exists, but has lost much of its meaning. For the answering machine gives everyone the protective status once reserved for the executive by his secretary. In this sense the new device is a democratizing instrument, but the kind of democracy that results is a rather odd one—a democracy in which everyone has an equal right not to participate.

"Somehow obscenities don't seem so bad when they're not the same old tired expressions everybody else uses."

◆

How many Ethiopians can you stuff into a phone booth?

*—All of them.*

◆

Three proofs that Christ was a Puerto Rican:
—(1) His first name was Jesus; (2) He was always in trouble with the law; (3) His mother didn't know who His father was.

## Maledicta

Reinhold Aman, Editor
**$19**
(1 issue) from:
Maledicta Press
331 South Greenfield Avenue
Waukesha, WI 53186
414/542-5853
or Whole Earth Access

*The last taboos of our culture—obscenity, insults, and completely tasteless ethnic and racial slurs— are boldly investigated by these forbidden-word connoisseurs, basking in the thrill of the verboten. If the language in this journal was any filthier you would have to scrub it out with Comet. For you halfwit gutter throats with a deficient vocabulary, we're not only talking about four-letter words. Recent issues of **Maledicta** compare a list of obscenities printed or left out in 20 different dictionaries, then go on to explore all the euphemisms for farting, report on colorful verbal abuse by the rich and famous, track down bathroom graffiti, dirty jokes, and kakologia, categorize high school sex slang, and so on. Much of it is legitimate academic studies, although always done tongue-in-toilet.*

*—Kevin Kelly*

◆

Little Jimmy, four years old, was bugging his mother. So she told him to go across the street to watch the construction workers and learn something. After two hours he came back inside, and mother asked him what he had learned.

"Well, first you take a goddamn door and you try to fit it into the fucking doorway. But if the son-of-a-bitch doesn't fit, you have to take the cocksucker down again. Then you take a cunt-hair off on both sides and put the motherfucker back up again."

Jimmy's mother was shocked by his language. "You just wait till your father comes home! I want you to repeat that for your father!"

When Jimmy's dad came home, mother told him to ask Jimmy what he had learned acress the street.

Jimmy told dad the whole story. His dad was furious and told him, "Son, go outside and get me a switch!"

"Fuck you!" replied Jimmy. "That's the fucking electrician's job!"

## The Best of Maledicta

Reinhold Aman, Editor
1987; 200 pp.
**$9.95**
($10.95 postpaid) from:
Running Press
125 South 22nd Street
Philadelphia, PA 19103
or Whole Earth Access

*Technically, this book should have been called **The Worst of Maledicta**. Quibbles aside, this compilation of 8 years of **Maledic-tion** is entertaining and even educational—reading it will extend your vocabulary in ways that **Reader's Digest**'s "Word Power" quizzes never could.*

*—Sarah Vandershaf*

THANK YOU FOR NOT FARTING

## A Writer's Time

Kenneth Atchity
1986; 194 pp.
**$12.95** postpaid from:
W.W. Norton
500 5th Avenue
New York, NY 10110
or Whole Earth Access

*There I was with a nice advance from a New York publisher to write a book, and there was only one tiny problem, which I did not discuss with the publisher. I'd never written a book and didn't know how. I knew how to write, to edit, even to publish, but authoring? Help!*

*Help came in the form of a little book (read it in an evening; read it again the next evening) that spelled out precisely the task at hand: how to write a book. I got innumerable good things from Atchity's counsel, but the main three probably were these:*

• *Time is everything in the labor of writing. Organize your time, and the writing will have a chance to organize itself. I used most of Atchity's tips except the taking of many mini-vacations (I didn't have time).*

• *Use 5 x 8 cards! Salvation. Every idea, every separable quote, every item from the literature I was researching, each went onto its own card. Organizing the eventual 1,800 cards into piles was defining the chapters; subpiles defined the sections; sequences within the subpiles defined the sequence of the day's writing. This was THE handle without which I would have floundered for months.*

• *Define in a sentence what the book is about. Searching for that sentence organizes your thinking; using it organizes your writing. Revising consists of removing everything that isn't in support of*

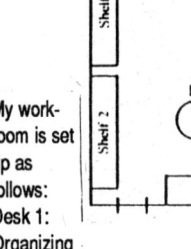

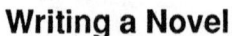

My workroom is set up as follows: Desk 1: Organizing and work desk. Desk 2: Printer, just-printed material, compact edition of the *Unabridged Oxford English Dictionary.* Desk 3: Less used reference books, projects that need to remain out between work sessions. Shelf 1: My published writing. Shelf 2: Scrapbooks and *The Encyclopedia Britannica.* Shelves 3 and 4: Frequently consulted books and records. Shelves 5 and 6: Dictionaries, literary encyclopedias, notebooks containing projects temporarily on hold. File 1: Correspondence. File 2: Drawers of research and ideas.

*that sentence. In my case (**The Media Lab**, 1987, Viking) the sentence was a quote, "How will we directly connect our nervous systems to the global computer?"*

*If this review sounds like a burble of gratitude, that's because it is.*          —*Stewart Brand*

◆

Always head for drama at this point in the process (first draft): choose the more dramatic alternative at every crossroads. Writing yourself "into a corner" guarantees drama as much as it does anxiety; the reader will relish watching you write yourself out of the corner.

◆

You can edit objectively after three days have passed and you cannot edit objectively after three minutes have passed. So the attempt to edit instantly is negating the natural process, not allowing time to do its job.

◆

No time is more important than the time used to examine and schedule your time.

## Writing a Novel

(Some Hints for Beginners)
Dorothy Bryant
1979; 122 pp.
**$6.95**
($7.95 postpaid) from:
Ata Books
1928 Stuart Street
Berkeley, CA 94703
415/841-9613
or Whole Earth Access

*Neither Bryant's title nor her subtitle ("Some hints for beginners") really gives a sense of this slim book's power. While it is chock-full of practical ideas and suggestions that are as useful for nonfiction as fiction, what makes **Writing a Novel** so special is its expression of the writer's experience of writing, in simple, transparent prose. Bryant writes the way a good teacher speaks: with firm authority and light-hearted understanding, all in the same sentence. A few well-chosen paragraphs can get me started when nothing else works.*

—*Sallie Tisdale*

◆

Ideas that are likely to turn into novels are magnetic; they attract other ideas, other scribbles about them on more cards. When I begin to accumulate many note cards on one subject, I segregate these cards and give them their own little box. I usually have three or four card boxes labeled with limp working titles like "Girl With Cat." These collections of cards might turn into novels.

◆

"Don't save anything!" Put everything you've got into the rough draft of this one book, as if it's the only book you'll ever write. . . . Within the scope of what this novel of yours can do, put in everything you know, everything, so that by the end of the rough draft, you feel as if you have said everything you'll ever have to say, are empty, and done.

## On Writing Well

(An informal guide to writing nonfiction)
William Zinsser
1976 (rev. enlarged 1988); 246 pp.
**$7.95**
($9.45 postpaid) from:
J.B. Lippincott Co.
Downsville Pike, Route 3, Box 20B
Hagerstown, Md 21740
800/638-3030

*The fact that William Zinsser revised his excellent **On Writing Well** a mere four years after its first publication (and it's now in its third edition) says more about writing well than anything I can think of. Writing, to be good, cannot be writ as if in stone, not even by a professor of it. It's got to be honest, responsive, current, and above all mindful of the reader's impatient intelligence.*

*If you are serious about communicating with your readers, this book belongs on your shelf right next to Strunk and White's **Elements of Style** and the*

dictionary of your choice.
—*Stephanie Mills*

◆

As for what point you want to make, I'll state as a rule of thumb that every successful piece of nonfiction should leave the reader with one provocative thought that he didn't have before. Not two thoughts, or five—just one.

◆

If a phrase comes to you easily, look at it with deep suspicion—it's probably one of the innumerable cliches that have woven their way so tightly into the fabric of travel writing that it takes a special effort *not* to use them. . . . Strive for fresh words and images. Leave "myriad" and their ilk to the poets. Leave "ilk" to anyone who will take it away.

From a manuscript which had already been rewritten and retyped four or five times.

The writer must therefore constantly ask himself: What am I trying to say? ~~in this sentence?~~ Surprisingly often, he doesn't know. ~~And~~ Then he must look at what he has ~~just~~ written and ask: Have I said it? Is it clear to someone encountering ~~who is coming upon~~ the subject for the first time? If it's not ~~clear,~~ it is because some fuzz has worked its way into the machinery. The clear writer is a person ~~who is~~ clear-headed enough to see this stuff for what it is: fuzz.

I don't mean ~~to suggest~~ that some people are born clear-headed and are therefore natural writers, whereas others ~~other people~~ are naturally fuzzy and will ~~therefore~~ never write well. Thinking clearly is ~~an entirely~~ conscious act that the writer must force ~~keep forcing~~ upon himself, just as if he were embarking ~~starting~~ out on any other ~~kind of~~ project that requires ~~calls for~~ logic: adding up a laundry list or doing an algebra problem ~~or playing chess.~~ Good writing doesn't ~~just~~ come naturally, though most people obviously think it does ~~it's as easy as walking.~~ The professional

## Elements of Style

William Strunk, Jr.
and E. B. White
1979; 92 pp.
**$3.50** postpaid from:
Macmillan Publishing Co.
Order Dept.
Front and Brown Streets
Riverside, NJ 08075
or Whole Earth Access

*A thin volume that teaches and demonstrates the virtues of brevity. And clarity. And how good writing is inseparable from common sense. "Strunk and White," as everyone calls it, is fewer than 100 pages, but those pages last a lifetime.*
—Steven Levy

◆

Use the active voice. The active voice is usually more direct and vigorous than the passive:

I shall always remember my first visit to Boston.

This is much better than

My first visit to Boston will always be remembered by me.

The latter sentence is less direct, less bold, and less concise.

◆

Write with nouns and verbs. . . . not with adjectives and adverbs. The adjective hasn't been built that can pull a weak or inaccurate noun out of a tight place.

◆

Use definite, specific, concrete language. Prefer the specific to the general, the definite to the vague, the concrete to the abstract.

A period of unfavorable weather set in.

It rained every day for a week.

He showed satisfaction as he took possession of his well-earned reward.

He grinned as he pocketed the coin.

◆

Keep related words together. The position of the words in a sentence is the principal means of showing their relationship. Confusion and ambiguity result when words are badly placed. The writer must, therefore, bring together the words and groups of words that are related in thought and keep apart those that are not so related.

He noticed a large stain in the rug that was right in the center.

He noticed a large stain right in the center of the rug.

◆

Do not overstate. When you overstate, the reader will be instantly on guard, and everything that has preceded your overstatement as well as everything that follows it will be suspect in his mind because he has lost confidence in your judgement or your poise.

## mehitabel s catalog

(Books & Supplies for Writers,
Editors, & Publishers)
P.O. Box 60357
460 California Avenue, Suite 15
Palo Alto, CA 94306
415/326-6530

*expression is the need of my soul types* archy *the cockroach. If you have the same need,* mehitabel s *will help satisfy it.* archy *and his feline friend* mehitabel *first appeared in 1916 in Don Marquis' New York Sun column. (Because* archy s *typing method — hurling himself onto the keys, one at a time — prohibited the use of the shift key, all his writing was in lower case.) Here are over 300 titles, discriminatively selected and reviewed, to aid and inspire writers, publishers, editors, filmmakers, graphic artists, photographers — anyone with a needy soul like* archy s.
—Sarah Satterlee

Copyright 1930
by Doubleday &
Company, Inc.

READS IT AND SNIFFS AT IT.

How to Write Computer Manuals for Users
Susan J. Grimm
$21.00  hc 211pp  1982
The author's stated main purpose is "to eliminate the costly trial and error process in the writing of user's manuals." The book does just that, with a rigorous, step-by-step method for analyzing needs, structuring material and writing and editing the manual for use.

Media Are American:
Anglo-American Journalism in the World
Jeremy Tunstall
$16.50x pb 352pp  1977
A well-documented account of our news media exports and the astonishing effects on Europe and the third world countries. United Stated government policy, advertising throughout the world and the alternatives to American-dominated news media are covered, and the situation is much worse today.

Dictionary of Foreign Terms
C.O. Sylvester Mawson; revised by Charles Berlitz
$5.95  pb 368pp  1979
This wide-ranging reference book contains definitions of more than 15,000 words and phrases from every major foreign language, from ancient Greek to modern Russian and Swahili. Included are terms encountered in literature, law, science, politics and other areas.

## Webster's Professional Thesaurus

Version 1.0. Not copy-protected. IBM PC, PC/XT, PC AT, PS/2; hard disk; DOS 2.0 or higher; 1,208,576 bytes disk storage. **$129.95** ($132.45 postpaid) from: Simon & Schuster, 200 Old Tappan Road, Old Tappan, NJ 07675. 800/624-0023; (within N.J.) 800/624-0024

or Whole Earth Access

*Too often, the word you need on the page is not the word you entered on the screen. An onscreen thesaurus helps you scan through possible synonyms and automatically replaces the old word with the better word. Quality in an onscreen thesaurus depends on the number of synonyms available; this one puts the equivalent of a page or two of* **Roget's** *on your screen for every word you look up. I actually stopped using one word processor —Framework II— because I couldn't get* **Webster's Thesaurus** *to work with it.*
—Art Kleiner

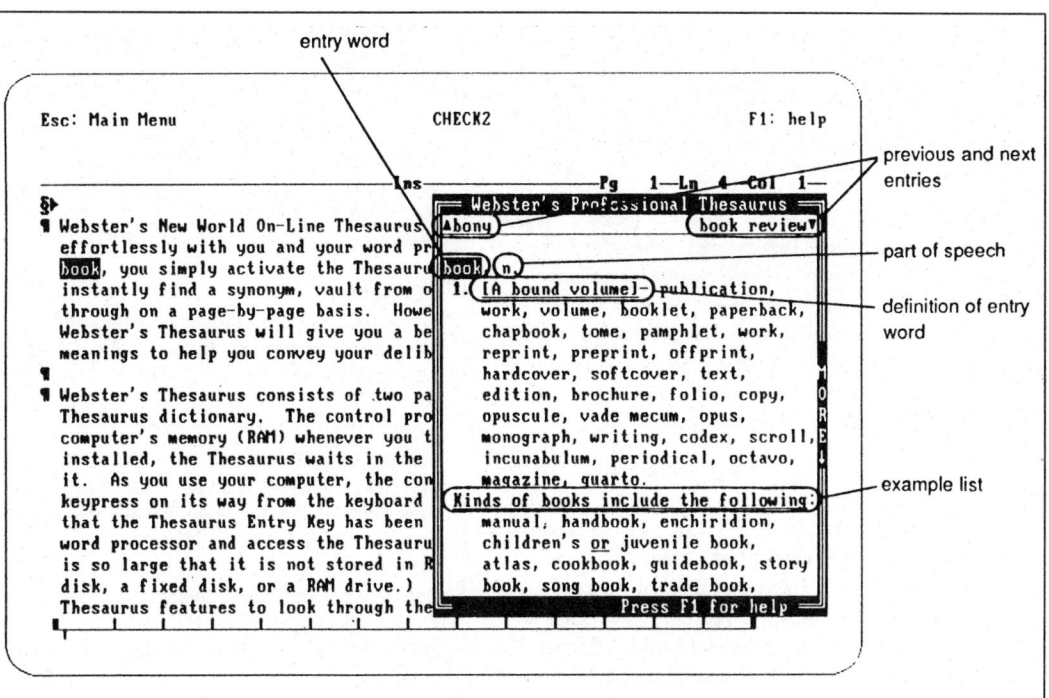

A Thesaurus entry page.

# Writing on a Computer

*by Art Kleiner*

A WRITING PROGRAM — or "word processor," as IBM dubbed it back in the early 1960s — is essentially a compromise. It mediates between the staid, two-dimensional, printed page, and the wigged-out, evanescent, multi-dimensional world behind your computer screen. Most word processing newcomers are so dazzled by the freedom of shuffling words around, that they forget the real task of a word processor is formatting — making sure the word looks exactly the way you want it on the printed page. You'll realize how hard that is the first time you try to word-process your resume.

Because the Macintosh is so rigidly and cleverly designed to control the look of the printed page, it (along with a laser printer) excels at formatting, which makes it the best affordable word processing machine. But MS-DOS computers are cheaper, quicker, and far more prevalent. Whatever you get, make sure it contains a hard disk — so that your written work and notes can live, semi-permanently, as a sort of landscape you travel through, inside your machine.

Choosing a word processing program is a personal decision. No other program is melded as intimately to the structure of your thoughts. Of the word processing programs I've tried, these are the ones I recommend for different types of people. Oddly enough, I find myself (sigh) using them all:

**WordPerfect** (5.0 for MS-DOS, Macintosh, Amiga, and other computers) — best all round. On the Mac and MS-DOS machines, it surpasses its equally quirky rival, Microsoft Word. Generally, I prefer WordPerfect's crypticness to Word's cumbersomeness. The "clean screen" WordPerfect presents is its best-known feature, but it excels at subtleties — like the way each line reformats itself as soon as you move to the next line. Version 5.0 is a much better formatter, especially for laser printers, than its still-available predecessor, version 4.1. Though 5.0's newness makes it (by definition) buggy, WordPerfect's support is well-reputed, and everywhere you go you'll find people who know it. I use this program whenever I'm on a strange computer, or need to create files that will travel from one computer to another.

**PC-Write** (MS-DOS) — Far and away the best bargain — a full-fledged word processing program for $75. Great formatting control, especially on inexpensive printers which other programs can't always master. But shareware author Bob Wallace has tacked on so many features over the years, that this is somewhat hard to learn. It uses only plain text, and handles only short files; I use it for much of my quick, short work.

**Nota Bene** (MS-DOS) — A group of graduate students adapted an extremely versatile professional-level word processing program called XYWrite, added a superb set of extra features (different types of footnoting and bibliographies, for starters), and linked with a groundbreaking "text base" facility. You enter, say, notes and interview transcripts, or material downloaded from computer networks. Then, while writing, say, a piece on

superconductivity, you can browse through all segments that contain the phrase "maglev", and import any into your document, for further juggling. Nota Bene is somewhat hackerish — for many tasks, you must type in commands — and its onscreen help is execrable. But I find myself using it for all my serious writing.

**Framework II** (MS-DOS) — Probably the most intuitively correct word processing program ever designed, in a package that also includes spreadsheets, data management, and telecommunications. Most importantly, Framework frees you from what Ted Nelson calls "the tyranny of the file;" you can work with as many documents as you wish at once, and switch rapidly back and forth between them. Tradeoff: formatting is not so versatile. Framework users live in this program and never leave. Expanded memory boards are highly recommended. I use it for complex jobs involving many interrelated documents.

**Q&A** (MS-DOS) — Best simple-to-use word processing program I've seen for MS-DOS computers, with enough features so you'll hardly grow out of it. For a

little extra, you get a version with a built-in file manager for easily making mailing lists. I use it to introduce other people to word processing.

**Fullwrite Professional** (Mac) — The kitchen sink and then some, including the ability to wrap text around graphics. Somehow, they designed all these complex features so that non-computer people can control them without twisting our brains through hoops. Only trouble: it requires 2 megabytes or more of memory, which effectively adds $800 (as I write this) to the cost of your Macintosh. This is the hands-down best word processing program, though, on every level, that I have ever used. I use it whenever I can.

**WriteNow** (Mac) — Easy to learn, effective, and fast; best choice for a beginning word processing program. I use it for quick stuff on the Mac. A forthcoming version (2.0) is supposed to be more versatile.

Another tool:

**Typing Tutor.** Writing on a computer without knowing how to touchtype is like being a concert violinist without knowing how to read music. But anyone can touchtype: all you need is this tool and maybe a dozen hours, scattered over a few weeks.

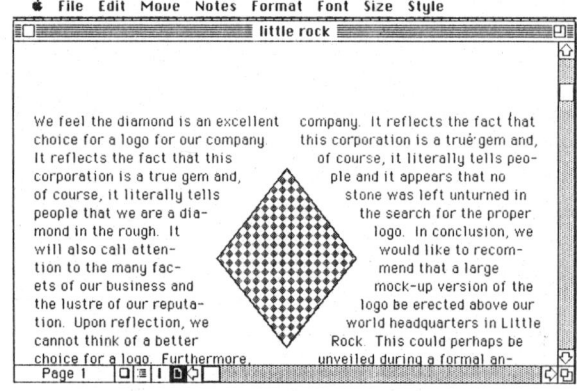

— PC-Write for IBM PCs and compatibles

— Fullwrite for the Macintosh

Two ends of the word processing spectrum: PC-Write for the IBM and Fullwrite for the Macintosh. PC-Write is the best bargain around for IBM and IBM-compatible users — a professional quality word processing system for $75. It's formatting controls are extremely flexible, and it runs well on inexpensive printers, something many more expensive software can't do. It isn't the easiest program to master, however, being somewhat "hackerish" in its structure. Fullwrite for the Macintosh is like a combination word processing/desktop publishing system. The illustration shows one of its best features — the ability to automatically wrap text around graphics.

**WordPerfect**
Version 5.0; not copy-protected; IBM PC **$495**; Macintosh **$395**; from: WordPerfect Corporation, 1515 Technology Way, Orem, UT 84057; 800/321-4566

**PC-Write**
Version 2.5; not copy-protected. **$75**. from: Quicksoft, 219 First Avenue North, #224, Seattle, WA 98109; 206/282-0452

**Nota Bene**
Version 3.0; not copy-protected; IBM PC **$495**; from: Dragonfly Software, 285 West Broadway, Suite #600, New York, NY 10013; 212/334-0445

**Framework II**
Copy-protected; IBM PC **$695**; from: Ashton-Tate; 10150 Jefferson Boulevard, Culver City, CA 90230; 800/437-4329, ext. 2240 or, in CO, 303/799-4900, ext. 2240

**Q&A**
Version 3.0; not copy-protected; IBM PC **$349**; from: Symantec Corporation, 10201 Torre Avenue, Cupertino, CA 95014; 408/253-9600

**FullWrite Professional**
Version 1.0; not copy-protected; Macintosh **$295**; from: Ann Arbor Softworks, 9852 Teller Road, #106, Newbury Park, CA 91320; 805/498-4844

**WriteNow**
Version 2.0; not copy-protected; Macintosh **$175**; from: T/Maker; 1390 Villa Street; Mountain View 94041; 415/962-0195

**Typing Tutor**
Not copy-protected. Macintosh **$59.95**; IBM PC **$49.95**; from: Simon & Schuster, Electronic Publishing Group, 1230 Avenue of the Americas, New York, NY 10020; 212/698-7000

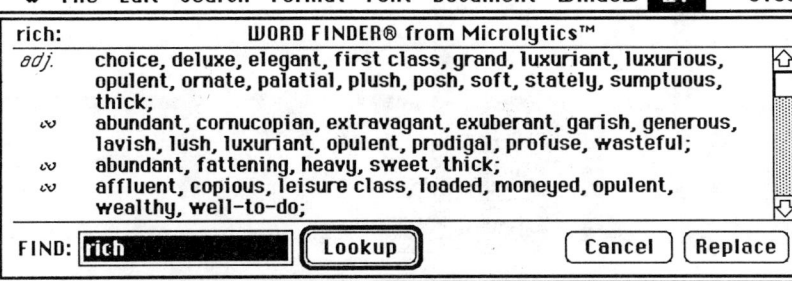

```
 File  Edit  Search  Format  Font  Document  Window  WF        3:53
```
```
rich:                WORD FINDER® from Microlytics™
adj.    choice, deluxe, elegant, first class, grand, luxuriant, luxurious,
        opulent, ornate, palatial, plush, posh, soft, stately, sumptuous,
        thick;
  ∞     abundant, cornucopian, extravagant, exuberant, garish, generous,
        lavish, lush, luxuriant, opulent, prodigal, profuse, wasteful;
  ∞     abundant, fattening, heavy, sweet, thick;
  ∞     affluent, copious, leisure class, loaded, moneyed, opulent,
        wealthy, well-to-do;

FIND: [rich          ]  ( Lookup )        ( Cancel )  ( Replace )

is just as good as Rodale's, maybe better, and I can check it in mid-stride, as
it's a "desk accessory" for the machine I'm writing on.  That means I can
"select" any word that's giving me pause, invoke the WORD FINDER desk
accessory by grabbing it from the pull-down "Apple" menu always available
on screen, and instantly a rich array of related words appears in a window
(carefully placed not to cover the text being worked with), organized into
nouns, verbs, adjectives, etc.  If I like one of the words better, or just want to
```

## Word Finder

Not copy-protected. Macintosh version 1.0. $59.95; PC
MS-DOS version 4.0 $79.95 from: Microlytics, Inc., 300
Main Street, East Rochester, NY 14445; 800/828-6293

*Often in writing it's important not to break stride as an idea leads you down an eloquent path. If you stumble on a wrong word or stupidly repeated word, that self-consciousness can throw you off, and stopping to grab a thesaurus for help can make you lose the thought's momentum entirely. Till now I've found Rodale's book* The Synonym Finder *($19.95, Rodale Press) to be the least disruptive word fixer.*

*I've converted to Word Finder because its selec-tion of alternate words is just as good as Rodale's, maybe better, and I can check it in mid-stride, as it's a "desk accessory" for the machine I'm writing on. That means I can "select" any word that's giving me pause, invoke the Word Finder desk accessory by grabbing it from the pull-down Apple menu always available on screen, and instantly a rich array of related words appears in a window (carefully placed not to cover the text being worked with), organized into nouns, verbs, adjectives, etc. If I like one of the words better, or just want to try it in the sentence, I double-click on the word, and Word Finder replaces my original word with the new one, and the window vanishes. (It can do this with any text-making program — word processing, telecom, outlining, or whatever.)*

*Not only haven't I lost the chain of thought, the quick glance at alternative words may have clarified the thought itself. I find I use the tool even more than a spelling checker. For now, Word Finder is the best word finder on the market for the Mac.*
— *Stewart Brand*

## Language Technology

Louis Rossetto, Editor
$50/year
(6 issues) from:
Language Technology
P. O. Box 624
Norwell, MA 02061-0624

*This thrilling periodical began with a seemingly dull mission: to explore machine (computer) translation of one language into another. The editors use that query as an excuse to follow their curiosity into overlapping concepts such as Controlled English (a simplified vocabulary to force clear technical writing), automatic lip syncing, bilingual word processors, synthetic grammars, hyper-linked text, and re-newed Pidgin languages. Each issue expands the border-less territory of their search.*

*Language is so easily employed without gadgetry, that as in the case of arithmetic and mathematics, when technology does bear down upon it, it is pressed into self-discovery. In this awakening lies the germ of universal language calculators.*
— *Kevin Kelly*

◆

Machine translation research has received a boost as an indirect result of legislation enacted last year by the U.S.Congress. The Japanese Tehnical Literature Act calls for coordinating federal and industry of translation activities, cataloging more Japanese re-search reports and translating many more technical documents. But a major problem has been the United States' lack of competent trans-lators; according to the Government Computer News, only 500 Ameri-cans are qualified for the job.

Machine-assisted translation (MAT) seems the only so-lution. The United States Air Force is trying to develop advanced computer systems that can determine the appropriate meaning of a character by reading characters in context, GCN reports.

### SPEECH RECOGNI-TION SYSTEM FOR ABNORMAL SPEECH

*Ryu Tajiri*

**B**iophysicist Elliot Davis, a research asso-ciate with the State University of New York's Health Instrument Devices Insti-tute in Buffalo, New York, has devel-oped a computer speech recognition system that he says can recognize and respond to a wider range of pronunciations and sounds than current systems.
The system, now in a patent application process, can consistently respond to words and sounds that have wide varieties of pronunciation through accent or speech impediment. Davis hopes the system can be developed for use by persons who suffer speech dis-orders associated with paralysis.

An ergonomic keyboard designed by Marquardt GmbH, in collaboration with the Stuttgart-based Institute for Industrial Economy and Organization. Marquardt has left unvaried the arrangement of keys. What's so obviously new is the shape of the keyboard. Instead of confronting the user with straight rows — as if human beings had arms growing out of their chests — the Marquardt ergonomic key-board is divided into two "keyblocks," fanning out at 30 degrees from each other, facing the user's shoulders.

## ForComment

Version 1.16; Not copy-protected. For IBM compatibles.
$295 from: Broderbund Software Inc., 17 Paul Drive,
San Rafael, CA 94903-2101; 415/492-3200

```
Options: Select Jump Print Collate Window Size Export
Press ENTER to view comments or revisions by reviewer, date or type
                                              Line  11   of 21
• Eighty-seven years ago, our fathers brought forth on this
• continent a new nation dedicated to the proposition that all men are
  created equal.◄
    Now we are engaged in a great civil war, testing whether that
• nation can long endure. We are met on a great battle-field of that
  war. We have come to dedicate a portion of that field, as a final
  resting place for those who here gave their lives that that nation
• might live.◄
    But in a larger sense, we can not dedicate this ground.  The
  brave men, living and dead who struggled here, have consecrated it,

┌ Abe, this is too abrupt. My suggested revision adds a few words to
│ slow the pace and make it more stately.
└─────── aj  11-11-1987
    But in a larger sense, we can not dedicate--we can not
  consecrate--we can not hallow--this ground. The
  ─────── aj  11-11-1987

──── F1 for help ────
```
ForComments' Review menu screen

*Organizations write important stuff in groups. If you want to change a company policy, say, everyone will want to get into the act: one person drafts a proposal, then herds of interested parties will re-view the draft, scrawling marginal notes and sug-gested changes all over the original. ForComment controls that group writing/approval process ele-gantly. Each comment is carefully stored by con-tributor, recording each person's suggestions by date and initials in an audit/edit trail file, so you can go back later and reconstruct how the final docu-ment was put together. You even get to try out suggested changes without modifying the original to see how well that suggestion might work. ForComment is particularly useful when all parties are linked together by a local area network, but works quite well passing the annotated document around on a floppy disk.*
— *Richard Dalton*

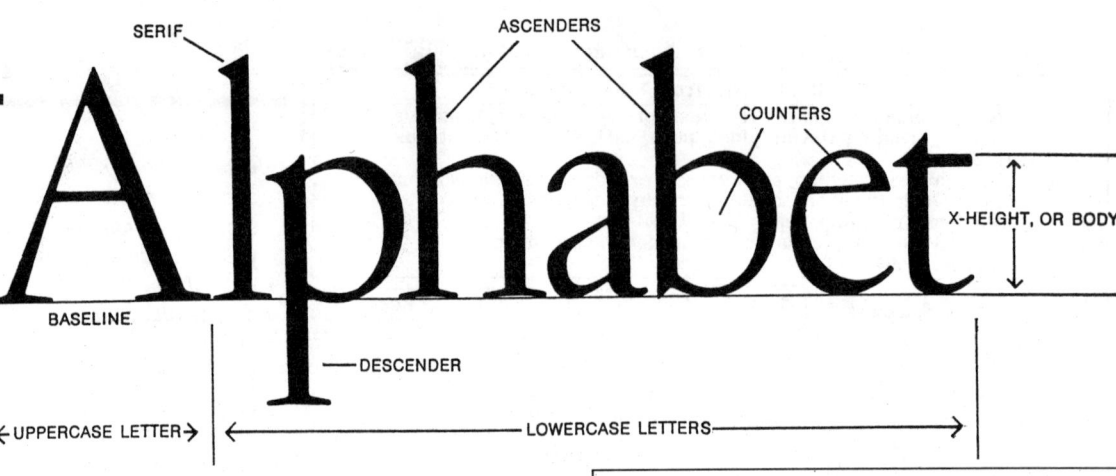

Roman uppercase and lowercase letterforms.

SERIF · ASCENDERS · COUNTERS · X-HEIGHT, OR BODY · BASELINE · DESCENDER · UPPERCASE LETTER · LOWERCASE LETTERS

### Designing with Type
(A Basic Course in Typography)
James Craig
1971, 1980; 175 pp.
**$24.95**
($26.95 postpaid) from:
Watson-Guptill Publications
1695 Oak Street
Lakewood, NJ 08701

*Whether it's a poster or a book, designers have to work with words. Letters come in all shapes and sizes, each with its own personality and charm. But they all have the same purpose — transferring ideas and information.*

*Legibility and impact are not accidental. Starting*

*with alphabetical history, families of type and units of measurements, and finishing up with leading and copy fitting, the clear examples in this book will add new meaning to the words you see.*
—Kathleen O'Neill

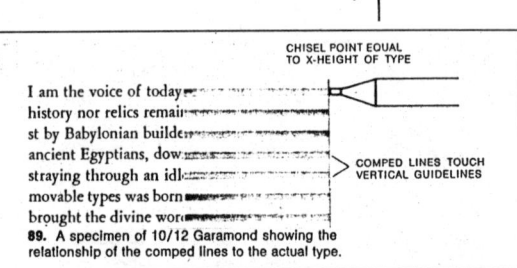

I am the voice of today
history nor relics remain
st by Babylonian builder
ancient Egyptians, dow
straying through an idl
movable types was born
brought the divine wor

CHISEL POINT EQUAL TO X-HEIGHT OF TYPE

COMPED LINES TOUCH VERTICAL GUIDELINES

**89.** A specimen of 10/12 Garamond showing the relationship of the comped lines to the actual type.

### Twentieth Century Type Designers
Sebastian Carter
1987; 168 pp.
**$24.95**
($26.20 postpaid) from:
Taplinger Publishing
Co., Inc.
132 West 32nd Street
New York, NY 10011
212/741-0801

*Typography is as invisible to most readers as molecules are in daily life. Yet it's subtly crucial to the underlying structure of anything we read. As a writer, typesetter, magazine editor, design dabbler, and (recently) desktop publishing aficionado, I sought to understand typography for years: why did the same page change so much just from changing between Century, say, and Helvetica? Why did Palatino feel so regal, and Souvenir so clunky? I leafed through dozens of dreary type spec books in vain, never finding the soul of this intensely personal craft form. Finally, Sebastian*

*Carter's tribal history educated me — partly about letterforms, partly about the dedicated madmen who designed them, and mostly about the sense of civilization which letterforms evoke.*

*For anyone who uses type — designers, desktop publishers, typesetters, maybe even readers — this otherwise readable group biography become-magnificently practical.*
—Art Kleiner

Types by Ernst Schneidler. Schneidler Mediäval (1936) with Amalthea italic (1956), and Legend (1937).

*Theodor Heuss* Das Buch
ist der Bote, der zum Gespräch
einlädt. *Wir wissen: das gilt schon unter uns.*

A A B C C D D E E F f G G H H I J J
O P Q R R S S T T C U V W X
abcdefghijklmnopqrstuvwxyz

### Poster Maker Plus
Version 2.5, not copy-protected, Macintosh. **$59.95**
($63.45 postpaid) from Broderbund, P.O. Box 12947, San Rafael, CA 94913; 800/527-6263.

*For bending type as if it were rubber, this neat program for the Macintosh can't be passed over. You can enlarge the text to any size when you print it on a Laserwriter, which means that it can later be reduced for reproduction with impeccable resolution. And you can print out both type and graphics in sheets to assemble it as a gigantic poster.*
— Kevin Kelly

SIGNAL SIGNAL

### Postscript Type Sampler
1988; 300+ pp. (more as new fonts added). **$49.95**
($53.95 postpaid) from: MacTography, 702 Twinbrook Parkway, Rockville, MD 20851. 301/424-3942.

*"Good reference tool for desktop typesetters,"* says Kathleen. Catalog of over 800 type samples from 17 manufacturers of Postscript fonts.
—Sarah Satterlee

Georg Trump (1896-1985).

| Character |
|---|
| ✓ Plain text |
| **Bold** |
| *Italic* |
| Underline |
| Outline |
| Shadow |

**Fat Los Angeles Bold**
Bold–Modified
PostScript Face

**Los Angeles Bold 10/12 Left Justified**
Bold–Macintosh Text Style

ABCD
YZab
z123

*My time is developme further p I shall hav over the s*

## The Calligrapher's Handbook

Heather Child, Editor
1986; 260 pp.
**$12.95**
($13.95 postpaid) from:
Taplinger Publishing Company
132 West 22nd Street
New York, NY 10011
212/741-0801
or Whole Earth Access

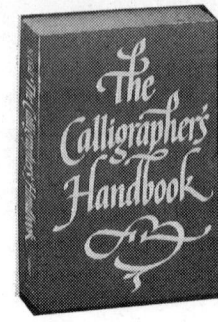

The original edition of **The Calligrapher's Handbook,** published in 1956, consisted of a series of essays on various aspects of the craft of calligraphy and illumination by students of Edward Johnston. These students not only worked in the tradition he revived, but also developed and refined certain aspects of practical technique long after the initial publication of his **Writing and Illuminating and Lettering** in 1906.

This new version reflects more than just a simple expansion of the repertory of techniques and craft methods. Heather Child, who edited the new **Handbook,** says in her preface:

"The motivation for work has moved away from the functional making of manuscripts into the more in-

novative sphere of individual expression and experiment where mood, colour, texture and dynamic use of space often take precedence over legibility."

The new **Calligrapher's Handbook** has been completely redesigned, for the most part successfully. It is larger in format, and contains many new

*Illus.* 3: The pen angle will, however, be a higher one for italic and 'Rustic' alphabets.

*Illus.* 4: A formal roman letter with arch form requires, for strength of construction, that the arch be upright and symmetrical. If the pen is allowed to slide away on its thin stroke, a weak asymmetrical shape can result.

illustrations, excellent technical drawings by Alison Urwick, and many examples of calligraphy by members of the Society of Scribes and Iluminators.
—John Prestianni

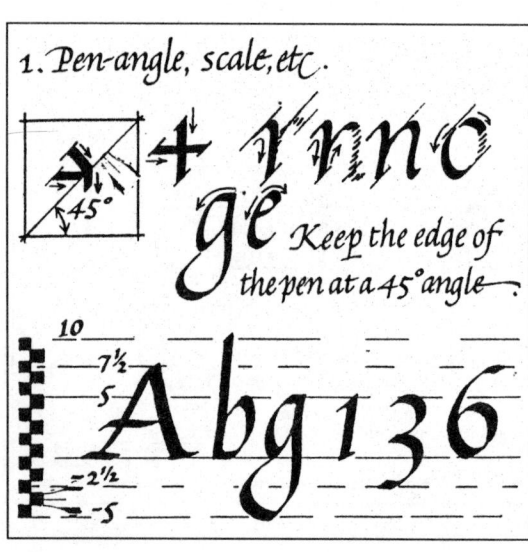

## Italic Calligraphy & Handwriting

(Exercises & Text)
Lloyd J. Reynolds
1969; 64 pp.
**$4.50**
($5.50 postpaid) from:
Taplinger Publishing Company
132 West 22nd Street
New York, NY 10011
212/741-0801
or Whole Earth Access

This little book contains concise and precise instruction on attaining a classic "hand." Master these teachings and you will be a calligrapher. Don't master them and you will still learn to honor the process.
—Sarah Satterlee
[Suggested by Susie Taylor]

## John Neal, Bookseller

**Free** catalog of calligraphy books and supplies;1833 Spring Garden Street, Greensboro, NC 27403
919/272-7604

*Just browsing through this catalog makes me wish I had continued with that calligraphy class I started 5 years ago and didn't. John Neal carries and reviews a wide assortment of books on letter arts—instruction, history, reference, inspiration—as well as supplies.*
—Sarah Satterlee
[Suggested by John Prestianni]

**The Farnese Hours.** Introduction and commentaries by Webster Smith. 167 pp. 4¾x7. 63 full-page, full color illustrations, reproduced in actual size. Tooled, simulated suede binding, slipcased $45.00.
Once the most admired of all illuminated manuscripts, the Farnese Hours is again rising in the estimation of critics fascinated with mannerism. By "the Raphael of miniaturists," Giulio Clovio, these illuminations show the influence of Durer and especially Michaelangelo. Stunning double-page color spreads with elaborate borders. A beautiful volume.

**Mitchell Poster Nibs.** Slightly oblique square cut points. Each point fitted with large capacity ink reservoir. Specify: L13, L14, L15, L16, L17, L18, L19, L20. Set of 8 $9.95. $1.40 ea.

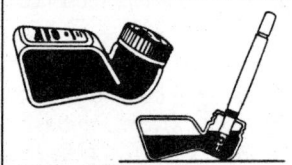

**Pelikan 1931 Ink Well.** 2 oz. Glass Bottle. Pelikan 4001 ink. Specify Blue or Black. $3.98
A decorative & useful reproduction of their 1931 bottle. The low design makes spills less likely & you can always see the ink level when dipping or filling. The plastic cap won't rust - use the bottle again & again.

## MacCalligraphy

Version 2.0; for Macintosh. 512K. Not copy-protected. **$149.95** from: Qualitas Trading Co., 6907 Norfolk Road, Berkeley, CA 94705

*This Japanese-style calligraphy package is a class act from start to finish.*

*Start with the packaging—a simple wooden box—and a nicely designed manual, then into the easily used software that lets you make brushstrokes that look like brushstrokes and not like ruled lines.*

*Different brush sizes, styles of stroke (Son, Gyou, Ten and Kai), touch and Washi (paper absorbency) give a great diversity of shape. Shades of grey, mixed on an inkstone with ink*

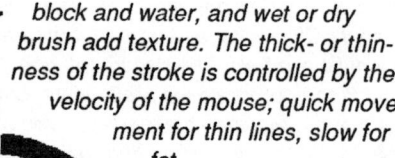

*block and water, and wet or dry brush add texture. The thick- or thinness of the stroke is controlled by the velocity of the mouse; quick movement for thin lines, slow for fat.*

*There's even some rice paper to print out your finished work. If painting should become too stressful, click the teacup icon and be transported to the subtly changing garden scene for a moment's meditation.*
—Kathleen O'Neill

## Chinese Word Processors

**Kuo Chiao Chinese Characters:** Version 1.0. **$174** postpaid from Key International, 834 Henderson Ave., Sunnyvale, CA 94056; 408/247-6220

**TianMa:** Version 2.06. **$615** postpaid from Pacific Rim Connections, 3030 Atwater Drive, Burlingame, CA 94010; 415/699-0911

**FeiMa:** S version $200; regular version $400; SE version $590, all postpaid from Unisource Software, 23 East Street, Cambridge, MA 02141; 617/477-8383

*The complexities of Chinese have been married to the conveniences of personal computers. Of several Chinese software programs I know about, the Kuo Chiao program is the most affordable ($174). It allows four methods of entering words as characters: 1) by Pinyin (Roman letters); 2) by Chinese phonetics; 3) by radical and stroke order; and 4) by creating your own. Each way gives you 10,000 full-blooded Chinese characters (or newfangled simplified ones) ready to be word processed, left to right*

*or up to down. Runs on an IBM compatible with a graphics card.*

*Far more elegant is the program TianMa (Heavenly Horse). It has similar input methods, but does sophisticated word analysis in which it will select the proper character based on the other words in a phrase. This semi-intelligence requires massive memory, so it comes with a dedicated RAM card for the IBM PC. You'll still need a graphics card. It will manipulate 9,000 characters, traditional or simplified. Costs $615.*

*The most graphic heavyweight Chinese word processor runs on the Macintosh. Called FeiMa (Flying Horse), the program boasts the usual way of entering characters as well as two others: pick one out of a scrolling dictionary, or type in the English word and it will translate. The graphic superiority comes at the price of a smaller glossary. The Mac Plus version ($400) comes with 2,400 words (enough to write a newspaper story), with an additional 3,080 words in the hard-disc version ($590). You can get*

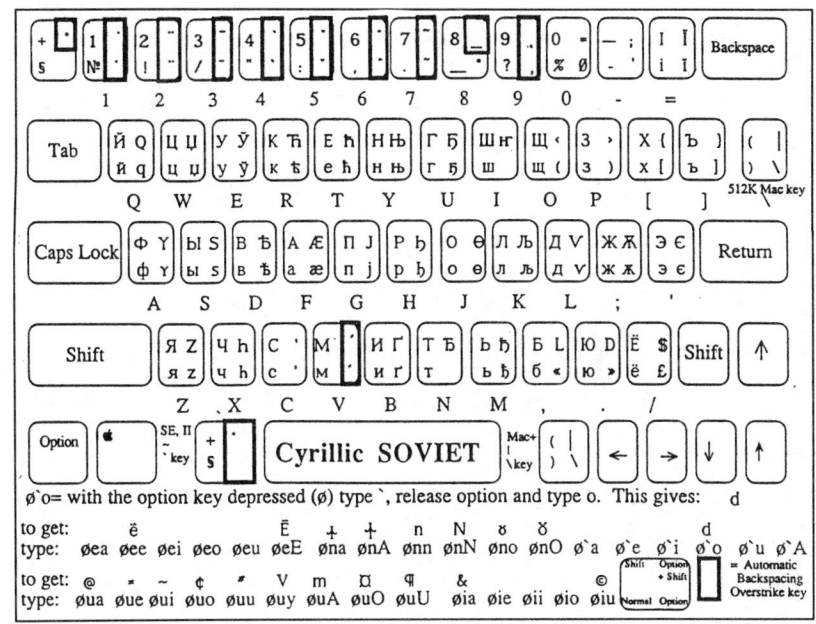

子曰：「有朋自遠方來，不亦悅乎．
學而時習之，不亦悅乎．」

Confucius said:
'When friends come from afar,
it is a pleasant thing.
When you review what you have learned,
it is also a pleasant thing."

An original Confucian proverb and its English translation using the TianMa program. Surrounding this review is the desktop screen of the ZhongWen Chinese operating system on the Macintosh.

*a limited version that allows only Pinyin entry of 2,400 words for $200.*

*Apple has recently written a Chinese operating system for the Macintosh. It serves as a foundation for any kind of software program (spreadsheets, file managers, games and, of course, word processors) that might want to speak Chinese. Called ZhongWen (Chinese for "Chinese"), it is currently available only from Hong Kong or Taiwan Apple distributors.*

*— Kevin Kelly*

## Linguists' Software
Catalog **free** from: Linguists' Software, 925 Hendley Lane, Edmonds, WA 98020; 206-775-1130

## Japanese Language Services
Catalog free from: Japanese Language Services, Software Department, 186 Lincoln Street, Boston, MA 02111; 617/338-2211

*If you've been beating your head against the wall trying to find Macintosh-based word processing software in languages like Russian, Arabic, or Korean, here are two companies that will save a lot of wear and tear on your skull.* **Linguists' Software** *specializes in European, Russian, Near and Far Eastern languages. Besides common tongues like Spanish, German, and French,* **Linguists' Software** *carries modern and ancient Greek, Coptic, Hebrew, Egyptian Hieroglyphics, Arabic and Farsi, Akkadian, Cyrillic, Chinese, Kanji, Kana, Korean, and Thai. Their TECH and LaserTECH packages feature mathematical and scientific symbols. The documentation that accompanies their programs is pretty lame, but if you have some Macintosh experience you should be able to get the system up and running quickly anyway. Most of their software average between $80 and $100.*

*Japanese Language Services carries a number of Linguists' Software packages. They also offer online Japanese clip art and calligraphy programs, as well as Japanese language-based computers and software such as the Japanese version of Lotus 1-2-3 and JAM, a text program that lets you create Japanese characters in many Macintosh applications. Software prices range from $50 to $400, but most packages are between $80 and $100.*

*— Richard Kadrey*

A standard Soviet Cyrillic keyboard layout in **Linguists' Software**'s LaserCyrillic program. With LaserCyrillic, you can also work in other Cyrillic-based keyboard layouts, including Serbian/Macedonian and Ukranian.

Examples of fonts in Linguists' Software's MacSemitic Coptic Devanagari.

## Audio-Forum

Catalog **free** from: Audio-Forum,
96 Broad Street, Suite A-30, Guilford,
CT 06437; 800/243-1234

*Don't expect to learn a language by listening to tapes. The best you can expect from cassettes is tireless practice, at your convenience, of what you learn from a class or tutor. Audio-Forum has the best selection of courses, including a well respected crash course called "Language/30." Some of the full-length courses were originally developed by the U.S. Foreign Service Institute. All come with a text book (essential) in a cacophonous selection of languages: Zulu, Xhosa, Serbo-Croation, eight dialects of Arabic, Urdu, Khmer, and of course, good ole Spanish and French.*

— Kevin Kelly

## Berlitz Video for Travellers

**$59.95** (VHS only)
($62.95 postpaid) from:
Berlitz Publications
900 Chester Ave.
Delran, NJ 08075
800/257-8345
or Whole Earth Access

*This series of videos is not designed to teach you a foreign language, but to give you the basics you'll need to survive in most "tourist" situations. First, you watch and listen as the couple in the video acts out a typical vacation scenario (exchanging money, renting a room, ordering a meal, etc.); then, the scene repeats, and you take the place of the vacationers, replying to the actors on the screen using the vocabulary you just learned. This is definitely language minimalism, but if, like most of us, your first concern is finding out when the train leaves or if you can get a room with a bath, then these tapes are an excellent supplement to "phrase-book" French, German, Italian or Spanish. Each tape comes with an audio*

Buying clothes in Germany: The Berlitz Video for Travellers gives you the phrase in German and the English translation ("No, that's not quite my taste. Can I see another blouse?").

*cassette, so you can practice in the car, and a Berlitz phrase book, so you can keep adding to your vocabulary.* — Richard Kadrey

## Language Acquisition Made Practical

E. Thomas Brewster and
Elizabeth Brewster
1976; 384 pp.
**$13** ($16 for book and
instructional cassette)
postpaid from:
Lingua House
135 North Oakland
Pasadena, CA 91182
818/584-5276
or Whole Earth Access

*This superb handbook trains you to learn any language in the world on your own, in the language's home turf.*

*The trick is to teach native speakers to teach you to learn their language. Comprende? It's done slowly, naturally, and playfully — the way you learned English. Your assistant doesn't even have to dig your jive. You begin conversing with one word, trying to make as many mistakes as you possibly can, entertaining the folks in the marketplace or anywhere else they'll put up with your blabberings. This well-tested program shows you how to con-*

Raise the sides
of the tongue

*struct your own exercises that fit the language you are after and later how to discover its grammar by yourself. The goal is multicultural-ism, inseparable from multilingual-ism. Like realizing that you don't need a degree in anything to build your own house, learning that you can become fluent in another language without schools is deliciously radical.*

— Kevin Kelly

Associate the word
with the thing

◆

By using these sentence patterns you can get extra drill on new vocabulary while talking with people. You can touch an object and ask "What is this?" They may answer, "This is Kefala." You can then touch a similar object and ask "Is this Kefala?" and they will answer positively or negatively.

If you are talking with children, this can become quite a game and give you lots of practice with new words. Children will often catch on, and participate with you in the game. First, you can ask the questions while they answer. Then you can trade roles and let them ask the

questions while you try to answer. If you enter into the spirit of the game, everybody can have fun while you practice vocabulary.

◆

To prepare for a Comprehension drill, you need to plan a list of related activities and have Kino make up a 3 x 5 card with activities written in his language. The activities for the first day might include sit, stand, squat down, clap your hands, scratch your leg, stretch your arms. In the drill, Kino will instruct you in his language to do an activity; for example, "stand up." He will stand up and you observe and then mimic the action by standing yourself. Do not say what he says. Kino then introduces the second item, performing the activity while giving you the verbal instructions. You mimic the activity — for example, "sit down." Kino then again gives the first instruction, "stand up," and you respond by standing. Then Kino can give the instructions without acting them out himself — "sit down," "stand up," and you respond to his verbal directions. When doing comprehension drills, respond rapidly without hesitation and make a distinct robust response with your body.

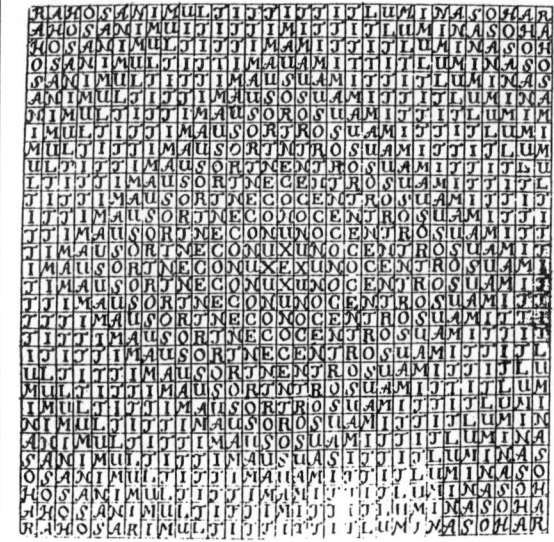

### The Classical Wizard
(Magus Mirabilis in Oz)
L. Frank Baum
Hinke & Van Buren, Translators
MCMLXXXVII; 259 pp.
**$19.95** postpaid from:
Scolar Press
2430 Bancroft Way
Berkeley, CA 94704
415/548-0585
or Whole Earth Access

*Mrs. Rose in 8th and 9th grades and Mrs. Jaeger in the next two were the scariest, hardest, most exacting teachers I ever had. They both taught Latin. And not because I want my children to suffer as I once did but because I wish for them at least one of the two unambiguous, enduring gifts of my formal education, I now implore them to take Latin.*

*Latin may have disciplined my mind. That's said to be one of its virtues. But what gives me daily pleasure is the thrill of the chase, the treasure hunt, finding my way to the heart of the maze, uncovering the mystery. Language is the setting for this adventure — many words I hear and see are actually composites and mini-histories waiting for me to unravel. With a syllabic clue or two I can*

*even piece together an unknown word's meaning from its Latin roots, archly snubbing the dictionary's monodimensional definition.*

*To wander through Oz in Latin seems the ultimate linguistic adventure: as you follow Dorothy from Kansas to the Emerald City, you also trace your language's passage from ancient Rome to the midwest, and then both returning to their roots, home again. And as we all know, "Nullus est locus instar domus."*
—Sarah Satterlee

*P.S. Thank you, Mrs. Rose and Mrs. Jaeger.*

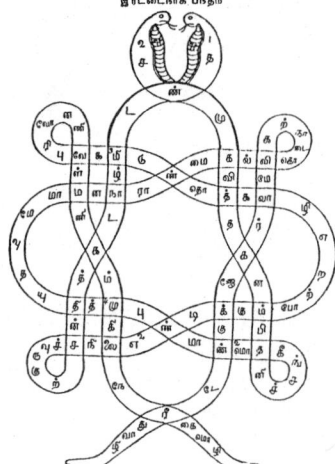

A letter labyrinth where the first letter of the written text is placed in the center and is the first to be read.

A pair of snakes in Tamil, probably from the 18th century. Printed from the Sithira Kavi malai ("Pictorial garland of poems") of P.V. Abdul Catoor Sahib Pulavar.

### A Basic Course in American Sign Language
Humphries, Padden & O'Rourke
1980; 280 pp.
**$17.95**
($19.95 postpaid) from:
T.J. Publishers
817 Silver Spring Avenue,
Suite 206
Silver Spring, MD 20910
301/585-4440
or Whole Earth Access

### American Culture: A Deaf Perspective
Susan Rutherford, Producer; videos, 30 minutes each (specify VHS or Beta) 1. Heritage; 2. Folklore; 3 Literature; 4. Minorities. Sale: **$125** each, **$400** series; rent: **$25** each, **$100** series; sample reel, 12 minutes, **free** from: Friends of the San Francisco Public Library, Special Media Services, San Francisco Public Library, Civic Center, San Francisco, CA 94102; 415/558-5634

*ASL must be seen to be understood. Its grammar is movement, shape, orientation, and location. Shoulder shrugs are adverbs, eyebrows conditional statements. It is 3-dimensional, visual, gestural.*

*As with other languages, ASL shapes and is shaped by its own culture. A 4-part video series from Friends of the San Francisco Library, **American Culture: A Deaf Perspective**, graciously tenders the key to the Deaf community which defines itself not by degree of hearing loss but by use of "the sign." (There are people who are deaf who are not part of this community, striving to be part of the hearing world.) All the interactions are signed with voice-overs: after a few minutes you're as unaware of the spoken words as you are of the*

### Visible Language
Sharon Poggenpohl, Editor
**$27**/4 issues from:
Wayne State University Press
5959 Woodward Avenue
Detroit, MI 48202

*A marvelous little journal "concerned with all that is involved in our being literate," as it says on the cover, and reminding us that "writing/reading form an autonomous system of language expression."*

*Each issue is guest edited. The entire Winter 86 issue was devoted the world-wide tradition of pattern poems (or concrete poetry). Another issue poked around the visible language of spelling. A third grappled with the enforced strictness of legally mandated Plain English.*

*The journal as a whole illuminates the mystical*

*subtitles in a foreign film. Parts 2 and 3 on folklore and literature are the most intriguing to me — tall tales, puns, haiku, and poems are transmitted directly from fingers to funny bone, hand to heart.*

*ASL can't be learned from a book alone, although you can get the fundamentals of syntax and vocabulary from a good one, such as **A Basic Course . . . .** Even deaf signers rarely learn it from their families, where most people acquire their native tongue: 90% of deaf children are born*

*relation between what is said and its visible representation.*
— Kevin Kelly

◆

Colloquial contractions are now an integral part of American written English, conventionalized by common practice. . . . In extended prose texts it is possible to indicate tones by setting the context and describing the manner of speaking. But in the brief words that we meet in jokes, advertisements, and greeting cards, spelling can serve the function of suggesting tone directly.

*to hearing parents. Because so much of its expression is dependent on the signer's self — intention, facial and body movement, eye contact — you really need a teacher.*

*As communication gets increasingly high tech and potentially more anonymous (networks and virtual communities notwithstanding), there's beauty to me in a language that requires you to look into each other's eyes.*
—Sarah Satterlee

A. I WALK, WRONG RAIN. 'As I was walking, it suddenly started raining.'

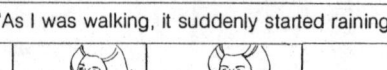

The sign WRONG can be used as a conjunction, meaning 'without warning, suddenly'.

## At a Journal Workshop

(The Basic Text and Guide for Using
the Intensive Journal)
Ira Progoff
1975; 320 pp.
**$11.95**
($15.45 postpaid) from:
Dialogue House Library
45 West Tenth Street
New York, NY 10011
212/673-5880
or Whole Earth Access

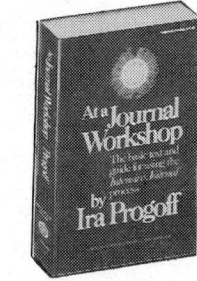

*Progoff, a former protege of psychologist Carl
Jung, has devised an innovative way of keeping a
psychological journal.*

*Like most Jungian psychologists, Progoff feels that
each of us possess self-directing, self-healing
capacities which are not always accessible to our
day-to-day consciousness. Persons seeking to get
in touch with these capabilities have usually required professional guidance. The Intensive Journal method was developed to allow people to use
journal-writing to gain entry to those capacities.
(Progoff and his associates also teach his journal
method through a series of weekend and week-*

long workshops. For information about workshops
in your area, write to the address above.)*

*My own experiences with the exercises were deep
and surprising. When people asked Anaïs Nin how
to keep a diary, she referred them to this book.*
—Tom Ferguson, M.D.

◆

Because time has passed them by, we assume that the
choices we rejected or waived are now dead, and that
there is no longer any potentiality in them. We have, on
the other hand, many indications that projects which we
planned but could not carry through at an early point in
our life became ripe for fulfillment at a later time. As the
author of *The Cloud of Unknowing* states it, "We grow by
delays," and for this reason the later expressions of our
plans are often more productive and meaningful than
they could possibly have been at the earlier time.

◆

We remain in the quietness with our eyes closed, now
progressively feeling the presence of a person, a being
who personifies the inner continuity of the life of our
body. We feel the presence of the person within the
process of our physical life, and we speak to it. We greet
it as a person. We address it, saying what comes to us
to be spoken. Whatever we say, we write in the Journal.

## Diarist's Journal

$2 from 102 W. Water St., Lansford, PA 18232

*Would you believe something new under the sun?
This is solely devoted to diaries, new and old,
published and unpublished, and primarily consists
of diary excerpts. These brief glimpses into other
lives are mainly fascinating and certainly never
boring. There are also reviews of a few books on
diary-writing and some thoughts on the genre.
Open to submissions from any diarist.*
—Mike Gunderloy
FACTSHEET FIVE (see p. 40)

It requires no artistic talent to make maps of consciousness. They
can be stick figures or shapeless blobs. Their purpose is your own
enjoyment and self-awareness, not accuracy or beauty. Sometimes
when I am particularly confused I draw a map of all my conflicting
parts. Often friends and family members will appear, my work, my
ambitions, the house I live in or wish to live in. I try to put them on the
page to represent graphically my relative psychic distance to each
element and their relationship to each other in my mind.

◆

Some people use catharsis so skillfully that they have
made an art of it. After all, great literature has often
served as a purgation for the writer. Most of us, though,
just have to get it out in raw, primitive form. If you dump
anger, greed, lust, and grief into your diary remember
that the diary isn't you — it's all the things you've purged
yourself of for your own well-being.

## The New Diary

(How to use a journal for
self-guidance and
expanded creativity)
Tristine Rainer
1978; 323 pp.
**$8.95**
($10.45 postpaid) from:
Jeremy Tarcher, Inc.
St. Martin's Press Cash Sales
175 Fifth Avenue
New York, NY 10010

*A diary, a journal really, is less a product than a
process. It is more verb than noun. The verb is
secret, special, yours. The noun can be anything,
found anywhere. Maybe it's a three-ring binder of
lined paper, maybe a blank sketchbook you paste
dreams into, maybe a map you accumulate so you
can circle a place and say "I am here."*

*I have not met a great scientist, artist, or creative
instigator who didn't rely on a journal or notebook
as a fundamental tool. If schools were wise they'd
teach this. If they were perfect they would use this
near perfect book.*

*Based on the author's 12 year study of her own
and other people's diaries, it's alive and real and
wonderful. Help eradicate dullness. Give a blank
book and this to a friend.*

— Kevin Kelly
[Suggested by Scott Kim]

◆

Paul Gauguin, the painter, began his intimate journal
with the phrase, "This is not a book." He repeated the
line frequently throughout the journal to remind himself
that writing a diary is not like writing a book or any other
form of literature. Gaugin wanted to write his diary as he
painted his pictures, dabbing a few experimental colors

Some diarists write in different directions over the page. They treat
the page as free space that can be divided in innumerable ways, not
simply with imaginary lines that run from left to right and top to
bottom.

at first, adding more as his intuition told him, following
his fancy, "following the moon," discovering the pattern
from what had occurred by chance.

◆

When asked how to write a diary by those just beginning, I generally respond: "Write fast, write everything,
include everything, write from your feelings, write from
your body, accept whatever comes." That is often all the
guidance they need.

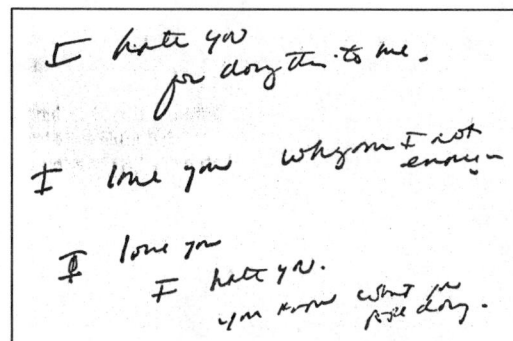

The physical energy that sometimes goes into cathartic writing is itself a release of emotion for the diarist.

## Screenplay

(The Foundations of Screenwriting)
Syd Field
1979, 1982; 246 pp.
**$8.95**
($10.95 postpaid)

## The Screenwriter's Workbook

Syd Field
1984; 211 pp.
**$8.95**
($10.95 postpaid)

Both from:
Dell Reader Service
P.O. Box 5057
Des Plaines, IL 60017
800/932-0070
or Whole Earth Access

*A nuts-and-bolts approach to creating a screenplay. The book benefits greatly by its detailed references to successful examples — particularly Robert Towne's script for* **Chinatown.** *Author Syd Field is a Hollywood insider who doesn't question the system, but frankly explains how a movie is structured and why. At times he sounds like an old-school mogul knocking sense into some artsy-fartsy literary type. This quality makes* **Screenplay** *not only a valuable writing resource, but an instructive volume for film buffs, too.*

—Stephen Levy

*There's also a companion volume, set up as a workbook. You'll probably want to read both.*

—J. Baldwin

---

### The Paradigm Structured

*The Story:*

| Act I (pp. 1–30) | Act II (pp. 30–90) | Act III (pp. 90–120) |
|---|---|---|

mp
60

setup

resolution

Plot Point I
(pp. 25–27)

confrontation

Plot Point II
(pp. 85–90)

© 1980 Syd Field

---

◆

The function and purpose of a plot point is simply to *move the story forward.* It is an incident, episode, or event that hooks into the action and spins the story around into another direction.

Do all films have plot points? All films that "work" have a strong, organic structure with plot points clearly defined.
—*The Screenwriter's Workbook*

◆

The standard screenplay is approximately 120 pages long, or two hours long. It is measured at one page per minute. It does not matter whether your script is all dialogue, all action, or both.

The rule holds firm — one page of screenplay equals one minute of screen time. The beginning is Act I, referred to as the *setup,* because you have approximately 30 pages to set up your story. If you go to a movie, you will usually make a decision — either consciously or below the level of awareness — about whether you "like" the movie or "dis-like" the movie. The next time you go to a movie, find out how long it takes you to make a decision about whether you like the film or not. It takes about ten minutes. That's ten pages of your screenplay. You've got to hook your reader immediately.

—*Screenplay*

## Script City

Catalog $2 from:
Script City
1765 North Highland
 Avenue
Suite 760-WE
Hollywood, CA 90028
213/871-0707

*Script City is the company to go to for the original scripts of hundreds of movies, TV movies, TV episodes, as well as books about how to write scrips, how to sell scripts, and the movie biz in general.*

*I bought a copy of the script for my favorite movie,* **Red Dawn,** *from them. Looking through the script, I almost had a spasm. The original script held together a lot better and told a far more coherent story than the final product. If nothing else, I reappraised John Milius, the director, pretty thoroughly.*

*If you want to write a movie script on a subject that has had several movies made about it already, procuring copies of the scripts of these movies might save your brainchild from being bounced for being too like a previous effort.*

*Script City also sells pictures of stars, movie posters and lobby cards for the fanatical film fans out there.*

—Eric Oppen

## The Corporate Scriptwriting Book

(A Step-by-Step Guide to Writing Business Films, Videotapes and Slide Shows)
Donna Matrazzo
1980, 1986; 207 pp.
**$14.95**
($16.45 postpaid) from:
Communication Publishing Co.
548 NE 43rd Avenue
Portland, OR 97213
503/239-5141
or Whole Earth Access

*For the Roxie, it's not. Short and sweet for a captive audience, it is. Ten minutes at the most, aimed at increased sales, morale improvement, skill training, or stockholder joy. Might be a slide show, video, or film. Here's how it's done. Judging by the awful presentations I've seen, the skills involved must be elusive. This book should help.*

—J. Baldwin

◆

The "Talking Head," which is a shot of a person talking directly to the camera, is perhaps the most misused and over-used of all frameworks. Talking heads should only be used for significance — of the person, the message, or both. More important, they should only be used for very brief periods. Fifteen seconds or less is fine, 30 seconds gets to be boring and 60 seconds (or more!) is inexcusable.

◆

Length is another critical area. It's been said that there ought to be a "10 Minute Rule" for in-house productions, that no program should be longer than ten minutes. About that time, audiences begin to squirm in their seats. If your show lasts much longer than that, it must be very powerful or snappy to hold their attention.

Ten minutes is a long time. It's equivalent to *twenty* television commercials and one-third of the evening news. Handled well, almost anything can, and often should, fit into ten minutes.

# Interactive Literature

*By David Shaw*

*While Stewart Brand was lecturing at MIT, he came across a recent innovation: interactive literature. His accounts of this new participatory drama prompted me to contact the creators. I called Dave Shaw, a graduate of MIT and now a research biochemist, who is president of the Society of Interactive Literature. We met in the lounge of the Lafayette Hotel in Boston. I taped our conversation, which I abridged severely, and Dave confirmed for accuracy.*

*—Kevin Kelly*

**M**Y FRIENDS and I will play almost any kind of game. The games we love have a certain amount of diplomatic negotiation going on. A player tries to influence the outcome of the game by interacting with other players. That's why chess doesn't interest us much. Chess is one of those games where the better player will always beat the worse player, no matter how hard one tries to talk him out of it.

In most games there's only one correct way to do anything. You may have choices, or decisions, to make, but they will lead up a decision tree to the same ends, game after game. We became interested in role-playing games like Dungeons and Dragons because you can decide exactly what you want to happen. But we wanted a better role-playing system, where characters could interact face to face in some sort of real space, in real time, where they could actually put a lot of depth into the portrayal of the characters. There are groups all over the country now that stage murder-mystery weekends. It's almost interactive literature but not quite. You go and you watch a bunch of people act something out for you, which is not much different from watching a play. Or, you get sort of written into the game, but either way, what you do is very channeled. We wanted a game where you decide reality.

I found the beginning of what we were looking for while I was working at a biology lab. One week during a critical lab experiment my co-worker, Walt Freitag, disappeared for an entire weekend. I asked where he was, and someone said he's turning a hotel into another planet. When he came back, by way of explanation he dropped a compendium on my desk. In a hundred pages or so it outlined a scenario, rules and characters for a whole other world—a process now called interactive literature. I jumped in.

A good example of a successful interactive literature game is called Shadows of Sundown. The scenario is a post-nuclear-holocaust gathering in which all the characters meet at the World Trade Center, or what is left of it, to decide what they are going to do about putting the country back together again. Different factions of players plan, scheme, and plot for very different goals. The object of the game is to see where it ends up. The largest single game we played had two hundred people in it. The games tend to run in hotels small enough where we can take over the whole hotel.

By encouraging characters to wear costumes, it becomes immensely involving. Past games have had thieves who wore black with leather gloves, and a king with red cape and jewelled crown. For a game called Watergate, everybody was running around in three-piece suits, except the character Hunter Thompson, who had the Hawaiian shirt and the bag of drugs. In Sundown, we've had mutant characters who went so far as to create prosthetic makeup. One guy had bits of wires and chips hanging out of his jaw; another one painted half of his face green, and had stuff rotting off his hands. Costumes help enforce a sense of reality. You tend to forget that you're in the lobby of the Best Western Inn in Danvers, Massachusetts.

What we try to do, as game masters, is provide detailed information as to what kind of character you are—your abilities, power, and goals—but then allow you as much freedom as you want as to how you portray yourself. You're given a character packet that has a sheet or two describing who you are, what you know, and what you have. These "blue sheets" contain the background you should know pertinent to your character, the history of your particular neighborhood, and what's going on in your planet, political faction, or corporation. This is where the literature aspect of interactive literature

Games at RECON 3, a fantasy scenario in Boston.

comes in. The beginnings of these games derive from writers interested in storytelling. The literature is in writing characters creatively, something that you would delight in reading as well as playing. Instead of just saying you are X, we put a convincing, even enjoyable, story behind it.

Every character starts out with "items," which are usually represented by index cards. These are powers, instruments, or resources. You may have an index card that says "one .45-caliber automatic, two shots spent already." Real-world physical combat is against most of our principles, so in combat you don't actually touch the person at all. It's all conceptual. If you're shooting at a person, bullet and laser beam wounds are represented by a little stick-on dot which you put on the opponent's shoulder.

Information exchanging is really what happens in these games. You use information to manipulate events toward your particular end. Every character has a series of goals. Maybe your goal is to find who has two ounces of platinum. Sooner or later you'll find the guy with two ounces of platinum, but then you have to cut some sort of deal to get him to give it to you. Sometimes it's a simple exchange of one thing for the other. But there are other, more exciting levels. You can be double-crossed, or encounter any of the cliches that you see in detective or suspense movies.

We have no real idea how a game is going to end up. All we know is at what point the game will stop. A game may be designed to conclude after players have elected the new hierarchy for the local galaxy. But up until then what happens is only hinted at in the character sheets. The characters have a life of their own. To keep things from getting completely chaotic, there are game masters who act as arbiters. When things are getting a little out of hand, then they step in and tweak the game.

We're writing a new game called Fast Forward. It's based within the cyberpunk science fiction genre. In that scenario everybody is at some indeterminate time in the future in a small chunk of what's left of the metropolitan axis on the East Coast called the Sprawl. There are youth gangs, there are companies doing corporate warfare, and there's a bunch of kids hacking a big computer network. In the game we'll have our own PC computerized bank in the hotel, a kind of a credit-card system, where all the credit transfers for the game will occur. It'll be very susceptible to players' hacking. In fact some players will HAVE to hack around, if their characters are hackers. Some characters will play artificial intelligences, devoted solely to a particular corporation's interest.

There's a book by Larry Niven and Steve Barnes, called **Dream Park**, which envisions a giant fantasy park. When you fight the monster in its lair, sure enough this giant dragon comes out of the cave. And if you're going to shoot it with energy bolts, well, energy bolts come out of your gun. We don't have that kind of technology yet. But we do have a friend in Connecticut who's been experimenting with running interactive literature outdoors in big parks, and that's something we'd like to explore next. Contact us at the Society for Interactive Literature, 130 Morrison Avenue, Somerville, MA 02144; 617/623-0133.

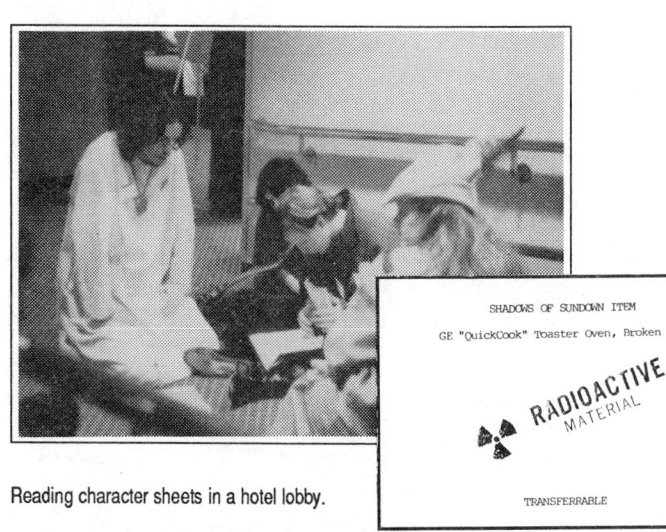

Reading character sheets in a hotel lobby.

SHADOWS OF SUNDOWN ITEM

GE "QuickCook" Toaster Oven, Broken

RADIOACTIVE MATERIAL

TRANSFERRABLE

*by Jeanne Carstensen*

DEEP DOWN, I think we all believe we're the smartest hunks of flesh to ever walk the planet.

Admit it. You know the real truth and want to publish it. You are destined to write, edit, design, draw, and cartoon your ideas into the psyche of this raging nation (this nation's raging psyche?). If only you had access to the presses . . .

So start your own magazine. Engage the best writers and artists (you and your friends) and distribute it to the most influential opinion leaders (you and your friends). Exercise your right to rave. After all, that's what professional writers do. They just get paid for it. You can do it too.

"'Zines" are wildly partisan small magazines of the fanatic, or devoted, depending on your view of the subject matter. They're unabashedly non-commercial — true labors of love — and don't seem to conform to any standard of quality except their own. 'Zines rave about special interests: hobbies like play-by-mail games, science fiction, "fringe" political groups, punk bands, comics, mail and xerox art, underground cassette music distribution, or that most special of special interests — the writing and art of one editor/writer/artist/designer.

Sometimes the raving is obnoxious, petty, or mediocre. Self-importance and incompetence can come together with unfortunate results in a 'zine with no criticism to monitor it. The art can be bad, the writing worse. But at least it's the raving of people who are dedicated to their concerns. It could also be called "passion." And sometimes passion joins with competence in an unusual way no mainstream publication would publish.

The thousands of (mostly xeroxed) 'zines published in this country constitute a raucous wave of underground exploratory publishing: highly personal and idiosyncratic expressions, visual and/or written, distributed for free or very cheaply to small but loyal groups of "subscribers." It's a world of staggering diversity and varying quality.

'Zines are highly specialized, that's the point; their audience may be only 25 people. So if the following reviews don't happen to interest you, don't give up. There are thousands of 'zines out there on every topic imaginable. I just happen to like the art-oriented 'zines; they bring nonlinear relief to my work as an editor. Subscribe to FACTSHEET FIVE and order 'zines in your particular area of interest. Or, of course, start your own.

**NOTHING** is the way things are.

—WOO-WOO

## AFM

*Probably my favorite, though it can hardly be considered a 'zine. There is no front or back cover, and no pages in between. A postcard will get you an envelope of some kind of art; each mailing is unique.*

*My first AFM was an envelope full of lacy paper art, color cardboard shapes, and collages. There's nothing like receiving an AFM package, because it's not every day that you receive a colorful pile of whimsical pieces of art. My latest AFM package drew even more attention than usual around the office. It was a large box plastered with stamps and decorations. Inside was an original drawing which I now have on my wall: sort of eighties psychedelic.*

*For me, AFM (which stands for Alterial Facial Mandala) is kind of a shared dream. I send them a little drawing. AFM sends it back weeks later pasted on the outside of an envelope. "It got lonely," they tell me. I have never been to Florida or met the AFMers, but we share the drawings and bits of color back and forth just for fun. AFM explains them-selves like this: "This package contains the residue of a process known as AFM. We do not wish to profit from this; rather we are recycling our personal resources to communicate our found freedom."*

*Part of the AFM process is exchange. You have to participate and that's the price. —Jeanne Carstensen*

## WOO-WOO

*Woo-Woo brought the office to a stand-still when it arrived. Well, not quite — Wow! Chortle! Hey, listen to this! Billing itself as "a linguistic cattle prod, a visual alarm clock," its gentle, transcendental anarchism is aimed at those of us who drowse from time to time. Wake up, get real, relax. Definitely my favorite 'zine.*
*—Sarah Satterlee*

*Mike Gunderloy's alternative/underground 'zine review is the best single source of 'zine information. Mike somehow manages to write hundreds of short, helpful, funny reviews each issue on 'zines of confounding variety. He calls FACTSHEET FIVE "the 'zine of crosscurrents and cross-pollination." One 30-minute browse of the anarchistic, evangelical, xerox- and mail-art, bioregional, libertarian, animal-rights, and music 'zine reviews (to name only a few kinds) spreads around a lot of strange pollen. Don't miss this 'zine of 'zines.*
*—Jeanne Carstensen*

## FACTSHEET FIVE

# Magazine Frontiers

*by Kevin Kelly*

At every phase in the natural history of magazines there has been small, brave publications that see their business as re-defining the medium. In the last 50 years there has been a strong subculture of "literary" magazines. In the 60s this exploded into the politically radical underground press, and in the late 70s into the New Wave in print. These days the magazine frontier is conspicuous by its large, oversize format and a (self) conscious emphasis on style and design, in part brought about by new technology — accessible computers and copy machines.

This bunch differs from 'zines in that 'zines are generally one-person-published with no intention of pleasing anyone, while these are group-published with aims of being liked. I watch both currents. Like 'zines, magazine frontiers appear and disappear too rapidly to keep track of. The ones featured here were handy and representative of the edge. I wouldn't pretend to guess where they will take us, but I'll bet that mainstream magazines will eventually follow, again.

## FAD
$15/6 issues. P.O. Box 656, San Francisco, CA 94101

*They're into sex and rock'n'roll as an oversize excuse for getting decked out in avant garde fashions. Raw style.*

## BOMB
$22/4 issues. New Art Publications, P.O. Box 2003, New York, NY 10013

*An unpredictable barrage of experimental interviews, photography, art, new writing emanating from the gut of New York City. Bold and BOMBastic.*

I was born in America. It was somewhere inland. At the junction of two dirt roads about three hundred yards from my house was a black telephone in a yellow booth; sometimes walking by you could hear it ringing. Sometimes walking by you'd answer but no one ever spoke; there'd either be the buzz of disconnection or no sound at all. By the time I was eighteen I thought I had outgrown the sound of telephone calls that weren't for me.

◆

He existed in a state of limitless possibility — which is not good for the soul.

## Mississippi Mud
$15/4 issues. 1336 S.E. Marion Street, Portland, OR 97202

*Not from Mississippi. Standard "little magazine" content — poetry, drawings, odd ball short stories — spilled playfully onto an "extra big magazine" format.*

## Emigre
$6.95/current issue. Emigre Graphics, 48 Shattuck Square #175, Berkeley, CA 94704

*The message is in the medium: innovative, unorthodox Macintosh-designed pages of personal writing.*

## A Critique of America
$18/6 issues. 405 W. Washington Street, Suite 418, San Diego, CA 92103-9832

*Unlike most mentioned here, this one has hard-toothed reporting and a reality-bound sensibility. Feels like a firery underground mag in a stylish new robe.*

## Arrival
$10/4 issues. 48 Shattuck Square, Berkeley, CA 94704

*A class act. Highly selected writing, lots of picture stories for thinking people (one issue had an intelligently captioned documentary on Mexicans crossing the border) and quirky excerpts from unusual books and correspondents.*

There are several cemeteries in L.A. where you can visit famous dead

BOMB: Willem Dafoe in the Wooster Group's Route 1 & 9.

people. Ever want to be all alone with a movie star? Well, at one of these cemeteries you can be all alone with the likes of Tyrone Power, Douglas Fairbanks, and Rudolph Valentino. There won't be much conversation, but on the other hand, they can't have you thrown out, either. Think of it: people who would never have had anything to do with you while they were alive have to put up with you now, like it or not!

## Clinton St. Quarterly
$16/8 issues. (2-yr. subscription only). P.O. Box 3588, Portland, OR 97208. 503/222-6093

*Sort of a regional (Northwest) tabloid that got so good it's worth perusing anywhere. Printed on newsprint; follow them for content, not design.*

◆

What made American farmers the most productive in the world is now threatening to put them out of business: abundant energy. From a labor-intensive livelihood, farming has become a capital- and energy-intensive industry that requires the investment of large amounts of capital and energy into the land and obtains high yields in return. But, like big industry, farmers have been fooled.

## Impulse
$18/4 issues. 16 Skey Lane, Toronto, CANADA M6J3S4

*One from Canada that manages to shake off American presuppositions of what a magazine should cover. Loose, futuristic (they're subtitled "The Magazine of Next Week"), it has a European patina of high-brow punk: intellectualism and rock videos, for instance. Supported by a pantheon of Canadian Arts Councils, it's well crafted.*

FAD: When choosing a hat, one should evaluate the effect in terms of: line, shape, mass, position, diversity, texture, & color.

## The Reader's Adviser

(13th Edition). Volume 1: The Best in American and British Fiction, Poetry, Essays, Literary Biography, Bibliography and Reference. Volume 2: The Best in American and British Drama and World Literature in English Translation. Volume 3: The Best in General Reference Literature, the Social Sciences, History and the Arts. Volume 4: The Best in the Literature of Philosophy and World Religions. Volume 5: The Best in the Literature of Science, Technology and Medicine. Volume 6: Indexes. **$75** each ($78.50 postpaid); **$195**/3-volume set ($204.75 postpaid); **$375**/6-volume set ($393.75 postpaid)

All from:
R.R. Bowker Co.
Order Department
P.O. Box 762
New York, NY 10011
800/521-8110
or Whole Earth Access

*If you throw darts at a world map and go where they point, you'll have a much more interesting vacation than anything the travel bureau can offer. Likewise if you throw one of these hefty volumes at a bed, examine the open pages and read in the direction indicated, your mind will meet minds a bookstore dare not carry. Every goddamn page has fascinating people and works that I've never heard of in my high rent liberal education, warmly and searchingly remarked upon, with all the access information you need to waltz cheerfully through library procedures to the goods.*
—Stewart Brand

◆

KING, MARTIN LUTHER, JR. 1929—1968 (Nobel Peace Prize 1964)

## ABC of Reading

Ezra Pound
1934, 1960; 206 pp.
**$6.95**
($8.64 postpaid) from:
New Directions Books
W.W. Norton & Co.
500 Fifth Avenue
New York, NY 10110
800/233-4830
or Whole Earth Access

*In grade and high school I was taught how to hate Shakespeare, most novelists, and all poetry. College merely burnished my ignorance, adding the ability to hate in French. Ezra Pound, where were you when I needed you? Through Pound, literature becomes a place to revel, confirm, maybe even grow.*
—Stewart Brand

◆

It doesn't, in our contemporary world, so much matter where you begin the examination of a subject, so long as you keep on until you get round again to your starting-point.

◆

"Literature is news that STAYS news."

---

Son and grandson of Baptist preachers, King was born into a middle-class black family in Atlanta, Georgia. At Morehouse College his early concerns for social justice for blacks were deepened by reading Thoreau's (see Vol. 1) essay "Civil Disobedience." He enrolled in Crozer Theological Seminary and there became acquainted with the Social Gospel movement and the works of its chief spokesman, Walter Rauschenbusch. Mahatma Gandhi's practice of nonviolent resistance (*ahimsa*) became for him later a tactic for transforming love into social change.

After seminary, he postponed his ministry vocation by first earning a doctorate at Boston University School of Theology. There he discovered the works of Reinhold Niebuhr and was especially struck by Niebuhr's insistence that the powerless must somehow gain power if they are to achieve what is theirs by right. In the Montgomery bus boycott it was by economic clout that the blacks broke down the walls separating the races, for without black riders, the city's transportation system nearly collapsed. . . .

Book by King
**A Testament of Hope: The Essential Writings of Martin Luther King, Jr.** Ed. by James M. Washington, Harper 1986 $22.00. This really does have most of the essential writings: King's **Strength to Love** and **Stride toward Freedom** appear to be intact in this recent collection.
—*Volume 4, The Best in the Literature of Philosophy and World Religions*

## The Read-Aloud Handbook

Jim Trelease
1979, 1987; 243 pp.
**$10.95**
($12.95 postpaid) from:
Penguin Books
299 Murray Hill Parkway
East Rutherford, NJ 07073
201/933-1460
or Whole Earth Access

*The value of this book is in its practical and simple approach — if we want to we can have children who want to learn to read, and to think. We need only give them our time. Trelease makes convincing and hopeful arguments on how to reverse the increasing illiteracy in America. His chapter about television's effects on kids is downright scary, but he gives parents workable suggestions on how to control its influence. From picture books to novels, more than 300 titles are synopsized, and there are references to hundreds of other good books.*
—Lindi Wood

◆

More than half a century ago there was a poor Quaker woman who took in a foundling child and began reading Dickens to him every night. Surely she could not have dreamed the words and stories would have such an enormous impact; the boy, James Michener, would write his first book at age 39 and his thirty-second at 78. In between there would be bestsellers translated into fifty-two languages, selling more than 60 million copies, and enjoyed by countless millions of readers.

Reading aloud to a child is a good way to inspire a love of reading in adulthood

---

## How to Read a Book

(The Classic Guide to Intelligent Reading)
Mortimer J. Adler and
Charles Van Doren
1940, 1972; 426 pp.
**$9.95**
($11.95 postpaid) from:
Simon & Schuster
200 Old Tappan Road
Old Tappan, NJ 07675
800/223-2348
or Whole Earth Access

*Adler and Van Doren propose a reexamination of the much-overlooked idea that there are techniques for reading books, just as there are techniques for driving in the rain and playing soccer. They've resurrected and present here a collection of rules and instructions of the sort used in the Middle Ages as part of the trivium of logic, grammar, and rhetoric. Few people could read then, but the ones who could usually read very well. The authors believe that with this rhetorical tool kit and a lot of hard work, most people can learn to do the same.*

*I spent 6 1/2 years in college. My best intellectual happening there was coming across this book.*
—T. Durso

*I spent 1 year in college. I dropped out after reading this book. Under its tutorship I read a fair chunk of classic literature with more enthusiasm, insight, and reward than came with university classes.*
—Kevin Kelly

◆

Analytical reading is thorough reading, complete reading, or good reading — the best reading you can do. If inspectional reading is the best and most complete reading that is possible given a limited time, then analytical reading is the best and most complete reading that is possible given unlimited time.

The analytical reader must ask many, and organized, questions of what he is reading. We do not want to state these questions here, since this book is mainly about reading at this level: Part Two gives its rules and tells you how to do it. We do want to emphasize here that analytical reading is always intensely active. On this level of reading, the reader grasps a book — the metaphor is apt — and works at it until the book becomes his own. Francis Bacon once remarked that "some books are to be tasted, others to be swallowed, and some few to be chewed and digested." Reading a book analytically is chewing and digesting it.

# OUT-OF-PRINT BOOK SOURCES

### by Kevin Kelly

The average lifespan of a book these days is about 18 months, and decreasing yearly. Because of a new tax law, publishers are penalized for keeping books in stock, and so they don't print more than they think will sell in a year or so. After the second year most books, even truly great ones, go out of print, which means that you or your bookstore cannot order it from the publisher.

Where can you buy a book that's gone out of print? (If all you want to do is borrow it, you need go no further than your library.) Your local used-book bookstore can usually list the book you are searching for in the professional journal of book collectors, *A B Bookman's Weekly*. It'll cost a one-time fee of $1 per book. Collectors read the magazine and contact the bookstore owner if they have the title you want; the bookstore owner then notifies you. It can take several months to hear a nibble.

A little quicker way is to employ one of several out-of-print book finders. You notify them (by phone or letter) of the title you want, and they will notify their own private network of collectors, who then report back to the finder, who then sends you a price quote for the book. If you agree to the price/condition, the finder will request physical delivery of the book and inspect it before shipping to you.

It costs you nothing to have them send a query out for you; in order to pay their bills, finders add a percentage to the cost of the book. Most finders won't deal with a book selling for less than $15. The average cost of an out-of-print book they find is about $20 — the same that an average new hardcover book goes for. The whole transaction from query to book-in-hand takes about a full month.

As an example, I simultaneously notified the five services below that I was searching for three books: a volume of photographic natural history, a short story anthology, and an obscure early novel by the now-popular British science fiction author J.G. Ballard. Three weeks later, Out-of-State Book Service notified me that they found the photographic book. My cost: $30 for a hard bound copy "in excellent condition." The last time it was in print, it was as a $28 paperback, so it was a good buy. One week after that I got a computerized postcard from Culpin's saying that they found the novel I was after. Their source wanted $73 for it, I guess because of Ballard's new-found popularity. I never heard anything about the other book. No guarantees, but since it costs me nothing to search, it's worth it for the hit now and then.

**Out-of-State Book Service**, Box 3253, San Clemente, CA 92672-1053; 714/492-2976

**Culpin's Booksearch**, 3827 West 32nd Avenue, Denver, CO 80211; 800/545-2665

**Avoniea Books**, Box 74, Main Station, White Plains, NY 10602; 914/946-5923

**Greenmantle**, Box 1178A, Culpepper, VA 22701-7324

**Continental Book Service**, Box 1163-B, New York, NY 10009

## Directory of Specialized American Bookdealers
The Staff of American Book Collector
1987; 520 pp.
**$47.50**
($49.50 postpaid) from:
Moretus Press, Inc.
P.O. Box 1080
Ossining, NY 10562
914/941-0409

## Buy Books Where Sell Books Where
(A Directory of Out of Print Booksellers and their Author-Subject Specialties)
Ruth E. Robinson and Daryush Farudi
1988; 274 pp.
**$29.75**
postpaid from:
Ruth E. Robinson Books
Route 7
P.O. Box 162A
Morgantown, WV 26505
304/594-3140

*Both these reference volumes list stores and dealers who sell out-of-print books. Total sources, Specialized: 3000; Buy Books Where: 2100. But gross body count isn't a fair comparison, since each volume includes sources the other doesn't. Between the two, you stand a good chance of finding someone who sells the book you're looking for.*
*—Sarah Vandershaf*

## The Buckley-Little Book Catalogue
$15 from:
Buckley-Little Book
Catalogue Co., Inc.
Kraus Building
Route 100
Millwood, NY 10546

*However you feel about William F. Buckley, Jr.'s opinions, you gotta admit he had a good idea when he and Stuart Little formed a company to distribute those out-of-print books that authors hoard in their basements, attics, and garages. Although many of the titles are now stored in a central warehouse, some books are still available directly from authors, who often will autograph copies before sending them out.*

*The catalog's standards are more egalitarian than you might expect — for $50, any author with "a serious committment to authorship" can list any OOP title, giving any description he or she likes. But what the catalog may lack in objectivity it more than makes up in offering books, from the famous to the obscure, that you can't get anyplace else.*
*—Sarah Vandershaf*

## UMI Author Guide to Out-of-Print Books
Catalog on microfiche **free** from UMI, P.O. Box 1467, Ann Arbor, MI 48106; 800/521-0600

*I once spent several frustrating hours searching for a copy of **The Realm of the Nebulæ**, astronomer Edwin Hubble's 1924 proof that galaxies exist beyond our own. I finally found the thing after collaring a librarian to help me. And that was at the Library of Congress! Imagine the difficulty of finding such important-but-obscure historical works at your local library.*

*If you are in this position and are willing to buy the book, the **UMI Guide** might be able to help. Over 100,000 out-of-print books and dissertations — including the elusive **Nebulæ** — are indexed on 12 microfiche slides. UMI reprints the books on order and delivers them within 30 days. Out-of-print books cost 26¢ per page, with a minimum price of $20 per book and a maximum of $150; dissertation prices vary. Some of the books are seriously out-of-print (i.e., since the 19th Century), and the collection as a whole leans towards academic and historical publications — for those times in life when only the primary source will do.*
*—Sarah Vandershaf*

71266
JIGGS IS BACK
George McManus. Celtic Book (pap) 12.95 2.98

## Daedalus Books
Catalog **free** from Daedalus Books, 2260 25th Place, NE, Washington, D.C. 20018; 202/526-0564

*Here's a new and welcome twist on "remaindered" books (the heavily discounted hardbacks often found at bookstores). As Daedalus' owners point out, "remainders are not books that don't sell, but simply books (whether bestseller, classic, or disappointment) whose remaining stock at publishers' warehouses is larger than their projected sales." That often happens to good books.*

*Daedalus selects what it considers the best of the lot, with an eye towards literary bargains, then sells them via mail order at tremendous savings. Prices average $3-$5 a book, which means you can buy a hardcover that is cheaper than the paperback.*
*—Joe Kane*

## Finding Facts Fast

Alden Todd
1972, 1979; 123 pp.
**$3.95**
($4.95 postpaid) from:
Ten Speed Press
P. O. Box 7123
Berkeley, CA 94707
415/845-8414
or Whole Earth Access

*A basic handbook for laypeople. It has beautiful two- and three-page descriptions of how to treat hundreds of problems in research from very elemental to very advanced levels. From "finding the right library" to "government as an information source" to "oral history collections" and "obtaining out-of-print books." Every time I get lost in the world of information I use Todd to ground me.*
*—Richard Green*

*Yup. Still unsurpassed after 16 years. This is where you learn research common sense.*
*—Art Kleiner*

---

# How to learn things: A handy tip

*by Anne Herbert*

If you're starting to learn about a field that you know nothing about, go to the children's library and get some fifth, sixth, seventh grade books about it before you go on into grownup books. Basic books for grownups tend to be aimed at college freshmen taking required courses — and everyone knows that they're supposed to suffer, including the people who write the books. Basic books for kids are aimed at kids browsing in libraries who don't have to be there and could leave anytime. The books have colors and pictures and a will to sell the subject; the good ones assume you know nothing without being condescending. You can get some vocabulary and feel for the shape of the subject before you get into the stuck-up real books. Kids' books can also help if you are one of those freshmen in one of those required courses.

---

# Libraries

*by Art Kleiner*

Just as churches can be sanctuaries for live human bodies, libraries should be revered as sanctuaries for live human thoughts and feelings. Libraries also provide a free way to read any book in this catalog — if it isn't in that branch, most libraries have excellent interlibrary loan methods for finding just about anything (given enough time). As Anne Herbert wrote, "I've known people who would call 17 bookstores to find a book and never go down the street to the library. At the library, it doesn't matter if the books are out of print. They're there, and the price is right."

*"Libraries will get you through times of no money better than money will get you through times of no libraries."*
*—Anne Herbert*

---

◆

Another starting point is with companies, organizations and associations, through which you can find the specialists who would know their own trade press. The researcher can then go directly to his target by asking the specialized craftsman, or professional, or businessman:

"What trade journals do you read? Which ones do your colleagues read? Which are your best printed sources of information?" and, "Do you have copies of them?"

> **NEW NATIONAL HEALTH INSUR-ANCE PROGRAM**
>
> Mr. KENNEDY. Mr. President, today I am pleased to make public an outline of a significant new national health insurance program, prepared by the Committee for National Health Insurance in collaboration with my office.
>
> It is nearly 10 years since CNHI was formed. Its goal was and is to achieve high quality health care for all Americans as a matter of right, within a system that brings runaway health costs under control.
>
> Many aspects of American life have changed since CNHI was formed in 1968. Many of these changes have been positive and have enriched the quality of life for millions of Americans. But in one area—the health area—the crisis which was just emerging in 1968 has grown seriously worse. The major reason has been the runaway escalation of health care costs.
>
> This rampant inflation takes its toll everywhere—on Federal budgets where the percentage of the Federal dollar spent on health has risen from 4.3 percent in 1963 to 12.7 percent this year; on State budgets where Medicaid costs have become the single most rapidly escalating cost; on corporations which pay more and more each year for health benefits; on the American family which must pay $2,115 today, and $3,590 in 1983 for benefits which cost $533 in 1963; on the elderly, who pay more for their care today out of their own pocket than the year Medicare was implemented.
>
> Hospital costs are so out of control that usually rational people talk about

---

## Knowing Where to Look

(The Ultimate Guide
to Research)
Lois Horowitz
1984, 1988; 440 pp.
**$19.95**
($22.45 postpaid) from:
Writer's Digest Books
1507 Dana Avenue
Cincinnati, OH 45207
513/531-2222
or Whole Earth Access

*Information is everywhere — in public libraries, universities, government organizations, the memories of experts, historical societies, museums, computer databases, churches, etc., etc. The problem is knowing how to access the specific information you need. That's called research, and here's a well-organized manual for conducting all kinds of information searches, written by Lois Horowitz, a University of California/San Diego reference librarian and newspaper columnist. She points us wisely to a wide range of reference tools, well-known and obscure directories, indexes, bibliographies, microfilm subject sets, and registers. And she introduces research strategies.*

---

◆

The **Congressional Record**, printed daily when Congress is in session, is a highly useful source of information on matters of current interest as well as a gold mine for historians and biographers. The main body of the **Congressional Record** is a verbatim transcript (sometimes edited) of the words spoken on the floor of the U.S. Senate and House of Representatives. In addition, the Appendix to the record includes all kinds of papers which members of Congress arrange to have inserted into the record as "extensions" of their remarks, without reading them aloud. . . .

What makes the **Congressional Record** so valuable in research is its index, which is compiled fortnightly during the annual sessions of Congress, and is cumulated after the session adjourns into one alphabetical index for the session. The index covers both floor action and the Extension of Remarks, and is meticulously maintained by name and subject.

This makes it possible for you to find quickly the page references to every speech or passing remark made by any Member of Congress, every paper introduced into the **Record**, and every bill he sponsored. Under a given subject (such as "narcotics" or "income taxes") you can find who discussed it on the floor; what bills concerning it were introduced, or acted on by either house or by committees; and what articles and speeches touching on it were inserted into the **Record** in the Extension of Remarks.

The **Congressional Record** includes every word spoken on the floor of the Senate or House of Representatives.

---

*Dry and boring? Nope, because the pointers are illustrated with scores of fun examples for the author's newspaper column, "The Reference Librarian," helping plain folks with research problems about everything from movie stars to missing persons to UFOs.* —*Ted Schultz*

*This is the book to use after **Finding Facts Fast**.*
*—Art Kleiner*

◆

Let's say you're *not* an expert in criminology, but you want either to write a detective novel or to find out more about your legal rights. How can you learn the techniques of police interrogation, the tricks used in questioning to get the truth, the things a police officer can and cannot legally do, the procedure for a polygraph test, or the components of a written report? Spending time with a police department representative might be one way to find out. But what happens if you doubt the objectivity of his information? Must you visit the local police station for many weeks and take copious notes on police routines? That's another possibility — if you have weeks to spend.

You don't have to abandon your research, or as a novelist, avoid certain episodes at the expense of realism. You might try textbooks. Check Subject Guide to Books in Print where you'll find an inventory of police officers' textbooks.

# Eight Sneaky Ways To Get Information About Groups You're Investigating

*by Art Kleiner*

1. Make up wildly exaggerated lies. Call the people in charge and ask if this rumor you've heard is true. When they correct it, they may inadvertently tell you something less extreme which you needed to know.

2. Ask their competitors and critics about their sins. Ask the people in charge about what their critics said, without mentioning the critics by name.

3. Find as many people as you can who work in the organization, and talk to them all, even those who annoy or intimidate you. Ask all your friends if they know anyone. Ask each person if they know others. Be honest but mild about who you are and why you're there. Ask each person about what the others said.

4. Consider the feelings of the people whom you interview. If your consideration shows, they will tell you more. Keep sensitive stuff secret if they specifically ask you to, but ask someone else to confirm it, without saying who told you originally.

5. Read everything you can about the organization — especially in-house newsletters or magazines, if you can get them, and trade journals. Then call the writer, or other sources, and specifically ask about what was hinted at in the articles.

6. Ask questions that require lengthy answers no matter what the answer is.

7. Hang around a place during its daily business and observe. Be genuinely interested in the day-to-day affairs, or pretend to be, while you're there. Gossip.

8. Assume that all your starting assumptions will be wrong.

## The Reporter's Handbook

(An Investigator's Guide to Documents and Techniques)
Investigative Reporters and Editors, Inc.
1983; 504 pp.
**$14**
($15.25 postpaid) from:
St. Martin's Press
College Division
175 Fifth Avenue
New York, NY 10010
800/221-7945
or Whole Earth Access

*Most good reporting starts when a reporter smells that something's wrong. But you don't have to be a professional reporter to follow your nose. Anyone can help stop a local abuse by tracking down the facts, but it often means an extended hunt down a trail of paper and interviews. This manual for following that trail is an encyclopedic directory in itself, listing dozens of documents, agencies, and reports that you might never hear about any other way. Put together by a group of experienced investigative journalists, it's one of the few college textbooks that's fun to read.*

—*Art Kleiner*

◆

You're methodically researching your project on the ridiculously expensive monorail the county wants to build at the new zoo when your editor starts flailing his arms and hollering at you. The police desk has an update on a bust at a disco last night. It turns out they found in the back room 10 bales of marijuana, 20 kilos of cocaine and 100,000 Quaaludes. A Columbian citizen was among those arrested.

The cops are cooperating with the Drug Enforcement Administration, not with you. They're giving out nothing beyond the arrest sheets.

There are a hundred unanswered questions: Who owns the disco? What else does this person own — land, buildings, cars, boats, airplanes? What's the disco owner's economic background? Has the owner ever been accused of a crime? Does the owner use corporations to hide behind? Is there a limited partnership involved? Who are its investors? How much did they invest? Who's in business with this person?

Public records will answer every one of those questions for you in a few hours.

## Competitor Intelligence

Leonard M. Fuld
1985; 479 pp.
**$24.95**
($29.90 postpaid) from:
John Wiley & Sons, Inc.
1 Wiley Drive
Somerset, NJ 08873
201/469-4400
or Whole Earth Access

*A comprehensive guide to sources and methods of gathering intelligence when the target is a business. Designed to help corporations forecast and X-ray their competition, this manual would be just as helpful to environmental groups investigating polluters, unions estimating employer profits, or peace activists studying military contractors. Countless lists of references and information contacts, with addresses and phone numbers. Tips on creative investigation techniques (nothing illegal). Illuminating discussion of how economic activity produces information that flows, pools, leaks and decays. More tools and ideas than you can shake a corporate structure at.*

—*Robert Horvitz*

◆

*Dynamism.* This factor states that the more dynamic and actively growing an industry, the easier it is to get the intelligence you are looking for. Yet you will also find that along with the information you receive, you also encounter accuracy problems. . . .

*Regulation.* The more regulated the industry, the higher the intelligence access for any one company. Translated into more basic terms: The more companies have to account for their actions to a government authority, the more information they will disclose about their activities.

◆

Public data does not necessarily mean published data. There are other sources [of intelligence] that are also publicly available, yet are not found in published form. They include telephone interviews, counting the number of parking spaces in a parking lot, and attending a trade show. All the intelligence you discover about your competitor through these nonpublished sources is still valid intelligence and is very much in the public arena.

◆

Check to see if your target company uses an independent trucking fleet. Many smaller manufacturers cannot afford to maintain an entire fleet of trucks. Here is where truck leasing can play an important role in your search. Like corrugated boxes, rented trucks are another incidental intelligence source. Find the leasing company and you may have found a source of production and shipping information on your target company.

## Center for Investigative Reporting

530 Howard Street, 2nd Floor, San Francisco, CA 94105; 415/543-1200. Bureau at 309 Pennsylvania Avenue, SE, Washington, DC 20003; 202/546-1880.

*So you suspect wrongdoing and want to investigate and do a story. Who do you call first? Maybe you should start with the Center for Investigative Reporting. A loose association of freelance journalists, CIR keeps in touch with information sources — public interest groups, concerned officials, news media — that could have the lead you're looking for.*

—*Sarah Vandershaf*

One of over 100 investigative stories produced by CIR reporters and collected in **Investigative Reports**, available for $6.

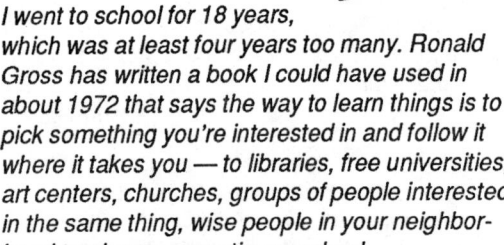

Y OU MAY notice that two of the three books on this page are out of print. Well, there are two reasons for this. *One*: inasmuch as the library is an indispensable part of the life and livelihood of the independent scholar, you can think of finding these two books on the shelves of your local library as practice. *Two*: (the real reason) we couldn't find any good replacements for Ronald Gross' books. Have fun tracking them down.
—Sarah Vandershaf

## The Lifelong Learner

Ronald Gross
1977; 190 pp.
Simon and Schuster

OUT OF PRINT

*Get this book back in print!*

*I went to school for 18 years,*
*which was at least four years too many. Ronald Gross has written a book I could have used in about 1972 that says the way to learn things is to pick something you're interested in and follow it where it takes you — to libraries, free universities, art centers, churches, groups of people interested in the same thing, wise people in your neighborhood, and even, sometimes, school.*

*The best part is the stories of particular lifelong learners like Ted Marchi, who learned to build roads because his part of Nebraska needed some; Helen Baker, who became a leading expert on juvenile rights with persistence and without a law degree or college education; and Malcolm X, who taught himself a lot of what he knew in the prison library. The key, as Helen Baker said, is, "When I want to know something, I go and find out." That's a faster and simpler process than wanting to know something and figuring out how to get accredited as an expert in it — a process that takes much time and money and doesn't necessarily teach you what you wanted to know in the first place.*

*That's the message of this book. When I read it I thought, "Yeah, I know that." Then I remembered it took me 18 years of schooling to figure it out. If you think that you're only a serious learner when you're in school and that you have to stay there or go back to be serious, read this book. It might save you some boredom and wasted effort and yield you some fun and good work.* —Anne Herbert

◆

"With a shock I realized the way I ran my business was anti-learning. I had no tolerance for mistakes. I wanted everything done right the first time — including the solutions to problems nobody had faced before.

◆

The most important tool of free learning is a log — or journal, diary, notebook, whatever you choose to call it. Always have a pad and pencil on hand for jotting down ideas, thoughts, feelings, and even dreams. (It's also useful for keeping track of reminders and random information.)

## Bear's Guide to Non-Traditional College Degrees

John Bear, Ph.D.
1985; 265 pp.
**$9.95**
($10.95 postpaid) from:
Ten Speed Press
P.O. Box 7123
Berkeley, CA 94707
415/845-8414
or Whole Earth Access

*Education and accreditation have parted ways. For job opportunity, get some easy degrees. For an interesting life, get some hard education. I can see good arguments for getting them separately — you don't cross your purposes or narrow your possibilities so much. This intelligent, practical book will tutor you in the non-traditional course.*
—Stewart Brand

◆

The philosophy behind "credit for life experience" can be expressed very simply: Academic credit is given for what you know, without regard for how, when, or where the learning was acquired. . . .

The most common error people make when thinking about getting credit for life experience is to confuse time spent with learning. Being a regular church-goer for thirty years is not worth any college credit, in and of itself. But the regular church-goer who can document that he or she has taught Sunday school classes, worked with youth groups, participated in leadership programs, organized community drives, studied Latin or Greek, taken tours to the Holy Land, or engaged in lengthy

## The Independent Scholar's Handbook

Ronald Gross
1982; 261 pp.
Addison-Wesley

OUT OF PRINT

*Get this book back in print!*

*Ever talk about Plato at four*
*in the morning in a doughnut shop with a well-read blue-collar stranger? That's the feeling this book evokes. The author doesn't describe the ways to get accreditation, academic legitimacy, or even intellectual power. He tells how to find out the things that would change your life if you took the trouble to learn them, how to tell other people about them, and how to support yourself meanwhile. The methods include reporting and cultivating experts, but mainly forming the kind of relationship with libraries that master chefs have with their food suppliers. The book is full of anecdotes about independent researchers like Eric Hoffer that make you want to follow up everything they ever wrote; but more important, it's full of solid advice, the kind that will be news even to people who have pursued this particular path with a heart for years. This catalog's best contributors always seem to work this way.* —Art Kleiner

"It is my wish that this be the most educated country in the world, and toward that end I hereby ordain that each and every one of my people be given a diploma."

philosophical discussions with a clergyman, is likely to get credit for those experiences.

◆

In my counseling practice, I regularly hear from people who are distressed, often devastated, to have discovered that some project on which they have been working for many months was really not what their faculty advisor or school had in mind, so they are getting little or no credit for it.

Indeed, I went through a similar sort of event myself. After I had worked nearly two years on my Doctorate, one key member of my faculty guidance committee died, and a second transferred to another school. No one else on the faculty seemed interested in working with me, and without a binding agreement of any sort, there was no way I could make it happen. I simply dropped out.

◆

As your interests, feelings, curiosity, enthusiasm, and concerns begin to converge on a particular topic, it will be well to draft, purely for your own use at first, a brief statement of your plans. I have never known an independent scholar who did not discover, at the end of an hour or two of work on such a one-page statement, that he or she had sharper goals.

◆

By making the process of browsing a bit more self-conscious, you can conduct your own informal "reconnaissance" of the terrain of learning. All you have to do is follow these three rules: (1) Pick the best places. (2) Keep moving. (3) Keep a list.

◆

Eric Hoffer said: Listen, suppose you come to San Francisco looking for a person whose address you don't know. You can trace him by research. You look in the telephone directory, you go to City Hall; if he's a workman, you go to the unions; if he's a doctor, you go to the medical associations, and so on. This is not my way! My way is to stand on the corner of Powell and Market and wait for him to come by. And if you have all the time in the world and you are interested in the passing scene, this is as good a way as any; and if you don't meet him, you are going to meet someone else. That's how I do research. I go to the library, I pick up the things that interest me, I use whatever comes my way. And I believe that if you have a good theory, the things you need will come your way. You'll be lucky. You know what Pasteur said: Chance favors the prepared mind.

## Magazine Index and Newspaper Index on Microfilm

*By far the best method for finding magazine or newspaper articles are these self-contained microfilm displays available for use in most libraries (one is for magazines one for major national newspapers). Each is the size of a regular microfiche reader but with only one filmstrip roll, which the libraries update monthly or bi-monthly. Unlike the awkward multi-volume **Reader's Guide to Periodical Literature** that you were introduced to in grade school, these are a one-stop index — you don't have to keep going from volume to volume. In a single fell swoop, you can check 400 different magazines since 1977, and the major national newspapers for your topic — and without a computer.* — Kevin Kelly

## Thomas' Register of American Manufacturers

*Who manufactures those odd things (like watch springs, egg packers, or cement burial vaults) you never see for sale in the Sears catalog, and where do you get the parts and equipment to make them?*

DON'T BUY THESE
USE THEM AT A LIBRARY

*Thomas' tells you where to locate any and all. Twenty-one volumes, 30,000 pages of fine print, zillions of products and tools, it's the great American catalog of everyday technology and production.* — Kevin Kelly

## Encyclopedia of Associations

*First stop for finding any organization or group. These are, by and large, accessible groups willing to help you research thousands of fast-moving topics that books can't keep up with. Plus hilariously obscure pursuits like barbed wire collecting.* — Art Kleiner

## Prompt
(Predicasts Overview of Markets and Technology)

*Beneath the feathery glamor of newsstand magazines and newspapers there is a larger substrata world of dreary, factual industry and trade journals. They form the bulk of all magazines printed, but are ignored by anyone outside their specialty (and are difficult to find). **Prompt** tracks thousands of these technical journals, presenting the news of industry and commerce in digestible abstracts, indexed by field, and referenced to original sources. And what sources! There's no other way I would run into: **Armor: the Magazine of Mobile Warfare; American Dyestuff Reporter; Yugoslavian Electric Power Systems; Drug Store News; Meat Outlook; Middle East & African Economist; Experimental Vehicle Newsletter; World Oil**; and so on. Without having to read any*

*of them, one gets an informed world view of material use and trade by scanning **Prompt**.* — Kevin Kelly

## Statistical Abstract of the United States

*Tells how many of who's doing what where this year. How many unemployed teachers, National Park visitors, or new housing projects. Exhaustive and inexpensive.* — Art Kleiner

## Current Biography Yearbook

*They rewrite news stories into biographical sketches of anyone who's been important in the news. Especially good for historical biographies, back to 1940.* — Art Kleiner

## Personal Name Index
(to the New **York Times Index**)
Volume 1 (1851-1974)
Volume 2 (1975-1984, but is completed only up to the E's)

*In two volumes, here's the easiest way to begin a search for contemporary accounts of a notable person. The listings will lead you to every **New York Times'** mention of a person, grouped into a single entry under that person's name, instead of under multiple entries for every year. Note that the listings refer to references in the **NYT Index**, and not to the pages of the paper itself, so you need to use this in conjunction with the **NYT Index**. Nonetheless, it beats hunting through a whole century of indices to find references to a by-gone person of note.* — Kevin Kelly

THESE MAKE HANDY PERSONAL
REFERENCE TOOLS

## The World Almanac
Mark S. Hoffman, Editor. **$5.45** ($6.45 postpaid) from World Almanac Education, 1278 West Ninth Street, Cleveland, OH 44113; 800/521-6600 or Whole Earth Access

*When I was ten I remember being given two thick paperbacks: the **Johnson Smith Novelty Catalog** full of spy code rings and x-ray glasses, and the **1952 World Almanac**. I spent a long time leafing through each of them, but the **World Almanac** had more staying power. Now as librarian, I find it one of the most useful reference works available. The print is a bit small, and the maps are just so-so. Published each November, current through October. Use the detailed index in the front, or the one-page Quick Reference index in the back.* —Steve Cisler

## Brewer's Dictionary of Phrase and Fable
E. Cobham Brewer; revised by Ivor H. Evans, 1981; 1248 pp. **$34.70** ($36.44 postpaid) from Harper & Row, Keystone Industrial Park, Scranton, PA 18512; 800/242-7737 or Whole Earth Access

*A dangerously seductive encyclopedic reference to the maddening obscure phrase, the curiously opaque line, and the abstruse story. **Brewer's** is a*

*necessity for reading books your grandfather read, explaining the vernacular that was part of his language but is, alas, lost to us poor solemn birds. This book is guaranteed to bring color to your language and whimsy to your correspondence.* — Jan Adkins

## Bartlett's Familiar Quotations
John Bartlett, Editor, 1980; 1540 pp. **$29.95** ($31.70 postpaid) from Little, Brown and Company, 200 West Street, Waltham, MA 02254; 617/227-0730 or Whole Earth Access

*Endlessly and instantly entertaining. Its chronological format gives it an order of contemporaries, and its brief entries remind a writer of the power in the short, terse statement. It has a truly useful index and the best cast of characters in publishing.* —Jan Adkins

## Word Finder
(The Phonic Key to the Dictionary), Marvin Morrison, 1987; 386 pp. **$11.95** postpaid from Pilot Light, P.O. Box 305, Stone Mountain, GA 30086-0305; 404/296-3294 or Whole Earth Access

*Forever solves the problem "how can I look it up*

*when I don't know how to spell it?" An ingenious book, well-conceived and executed. Arranged phonetically, and easy to use with a little getting used to. Great for writers and those with literacy problems.* — Cliff Martin

*Also forever solves the maddeningly persistent problem of deciphering other people's personalized license plates.* — Sarah Satterlee

## The National Directory of Addresses and Telephone Numbers
Geri Hardy, Editor, 1988. **$45** ($49.50 postpaid) from General Information, 401 Park Place, Kirkland, WA 98033; 800/722-3244 or Whole Earth Access

*The only one-volume, inexpensive, handy desktop directory of national addresses and phone numbers I know of. It's for those daily small hassles like when you want to look up the address for the Quaker Oats Company and you have no idea where they are headquartered. Or you need the department of tourism in New Mexico, and don't know what city it's in. They're all here with 150,000 other significant address numbers. If you research by phone a lot you'll save its price in directory assistance charges.* — Kevin Kelly

# Citation Indexing

*by Kevin Kelly*

JUST AS footnotes and a bibliography trace an idea's ancestors, citation indexing traces an idea's offspring.

Where did an idea come from? By weaving back through a chain of footnotes, one can get a pretty good notion of all the sources that were the origin of a particular idea. Citation indexing answers a converse question: What are the ideas afterward that this particular idea influenced? As an example, with traditional references you can track all the influences on Richard Dawkins's writings about "memes." Citation indexing would allow you to track all later papers that then cite Dawkin's writings, or in other words, all the other writers who found Dawkin's ideas important. For some ideas, the number of citations will dwindle with every year; for others it will increase.

Citation indexing could, in theory, make a list of any book or paper in the future that acknowledges this article of mine as a source of ideas. A year from now you could follow all the divergent paths these ideas have led to, probably weird offbeat corners you would have never found otherwise. It's always a fair bet that someone else lured by the same idea you find important may have something to tell you.

While simple in concept, citation indexing is murderously complex in logistics. It's the perfect job for an overeducated computer. A very large one at the Institute of Scientific Information (ISI) in Philadelphia keeps track of all the millions of connections in all the scholarly publications in English and generates the index as a printed annual mammoth 14 volumes wide, each volume bigger than the Manhattan Yellow Pages. The awesome series, known as the **Science Citation Index** usually lives on its own table in research libraries. Or, these days, as a vaporous thin electronic database service that can be searched online via Dialog.

Citation indexing, and the **Science Citation Index** in particular, have turned out to be useful in several other unique ways. Once all this information was burned inside a massive computer memory, information scientists tried to visually map the pattern of citations. What they saw was a display of link clusters that corresponded to the way information flowed from lab to lab, scientist to scientist. Overall it portrayed the behavior of information as a communicable disease (see Memes, page 18).

Researchers new to a field could look at a citation cluster map and get a good hint of where the godfathers were. An investigator could begin his research exploring the flock at the center and gather the most pertinent ideas there. Sweeping outward from the nucleus he would have to cast his net wider and wider over more and more papers to haul in the same catch of useful news. Paying attention to citations is a way to filter out so much extraneous material.

Citation indexing has proved so useful in pinpointing erupting activity in science that it is used many times as a measure to decide where to fund research. Just pour your money into the hub of an expanding cluster. It also quickly became evident that it could be used to measure the significance of a scientist's work. Rather than just count up how many papers he published, count up how many times someone else cited his work. This has been a boon to those

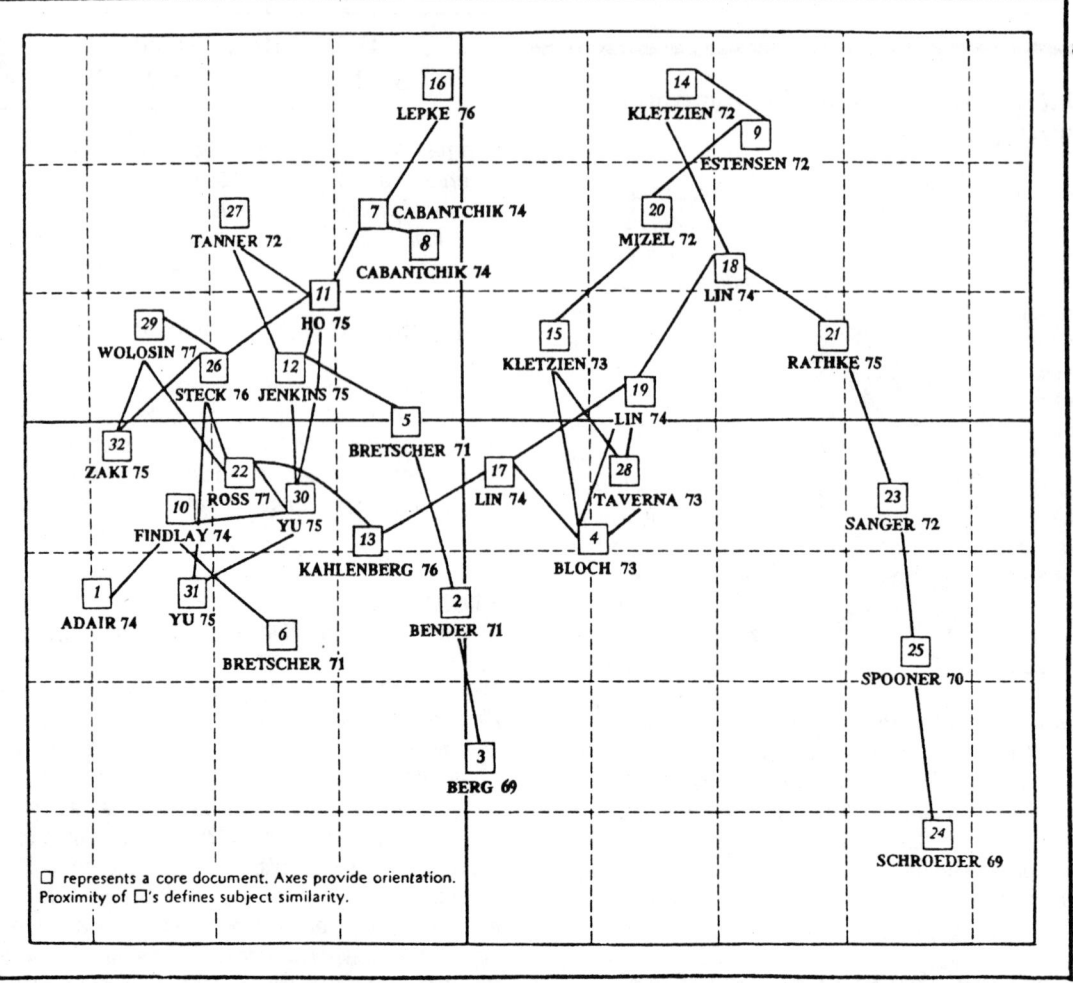

ERYTHROCYTE MEMBRANE-PROTEINS

A map showing the progression of ideas from one scientist to another. The most concentrated clumps of citations are likely to be the most rewarding spots to begin research on a subject. This chart tracks biomedical documents dealing with red blood cell membranes in vertebrates. From the *Institute of Scientific Information Atlas of Science — Biochemistry and Molecular Biology 78/80*, 1981.

who make a few key contributions, and a bane to those churning out mediocre reports that no one pays much attention to. Citation levels as a factor in academic promotions is a very touchy subject.

The same can be said of counting citations of various scholarly journals. Some journal's papers are cited more often than others, and citation indexing easily ranks them from the most often "quoted" to the least. Like other measurements (circulation, number of pages) numbers aren't everything. Nonetheless, information trackers who know which journals are consistently producing articles that other people find noteworthy can quickly narrow the scope of a search in an impossibly wide thicket of data. In fact a small core of about 200 journals out of the 80,000 published produce the majority of cited articles.

You'll find this tracking in the **Journal Citation Reports** published by ISI, available wherever the **Science Citation Index** is. They have developed two measurements to evaluate optimum publications: 1) The Immediacy Index — a measure of how quickly the average article in a particular journal is cited; 2) Impact Factor — a measure of the frequency with which the average article in a particular journal has been cited in a particular year. As in citation indexing for authors, citation analysis of journals can depict the flow of information and indicate areas of particular restlessness.

This peculiar brand of investigation is able to map the structure of investigative information. The father of this information mirror, Eugene Garfield, reports his experi-

| JOURNALS RANKED BY CATEGORY | | |
|---|---|---|
| CANCER | Impact Factor | Cited Half-life |
| 1 ADV CANCER RES | 7.000 | 6.2 |
| 2 CANCER METAST REV | 4.750 | 2.0 |
| 3 CANCER RES | 4.003 | 5.5 |
| 4 INT J CANCER | 3.368 | 5.5 |
| 5 J CLIN ONCOL | 2.935 | 1.3 |
| 6 CARCINOGENESIS | 2.650 | 2.8 |
| 7 J NATL CANCER I | 2.648 | 7.7 |
| 8 CANCER | 2.595 | 6.8 |
| 9 CANCER TREAT REP | 2.548 | 5.1 |
| 10 BRIT J CANCER | 2.535 | 6.2 |
| 11 EXP CELL RES | 2.455 | 7.6 |
| 12 CANCER GENET CYTOGEN | 2.398 | 2.9 |
| 13 LEUKEMIA RES | 2.261 | 3.2 |
| 14 BREAST CANCER RES TR | 1.843 | 2.6 |
| 15 CANCER TREAT REV | 1.835 | 5.3 |
| 16 GANN | 1.794 | 5.2 |
| 17 CANCER IMMUNOL IMMUN | 1.763 | 3.7 |

Journal rankings by category indicate the impact of articles published in the literature of a particular field. From *Journal Citation Reports*.

ments and conclusions with citation index in his very readable text **Citation Indexing — Its Theory and Application in Science, Technology, and Humanities**. Since it measures what has so long been only hunched at, Garfield rightly sees it as the science of science, at best, and the science of scientific information, at least.

**Citation Indexing**: Eugene Garfield, 1979; 274 pp. **$18.95** ($20.95 postpaid). **Current Contents: $298**/yr (52 issues). **Science Citation Index** and **Journal Citation Reports** are found at most research libraries. All from Institute for Scientific Information, 3501 Market Street, Philadelphia, PA 19104; 800/523-1850

# How to Use Your Library

*by Steve Cisler, Librarian*

Your local library is your main link to a tax-paid information network. Here's what you should do when you visit or call the library. First, ask if there is a reference desk. The people working in this area have great experience dealing with complex questions. A librarian can especially help you when you are not sure what information you need, or even what questions to ask. Librarians are professionals at clarifying unsure questions.

Assuming that there are not five or six people waiting to be helped, you will be asked a number of questions about your request. If you have thought about these beforehand, let the librarian know the following, even if he or she does not ask you:

1. Your deadline. Some questions, even seemingly difficult ones, can be answered in a minute. Many libraries have a "tickler file" of requests and queries that have been answered over the years. A surprising number of people request the comedy routine "Who's on First?" so we have it handy for quoting or copying. Some libraries even have the audio cassette version available. Other questions may take hours, days, weeks, or months to answer. The more time you have, the more information can be gathered.

2. The reason you need the information. A few times a month someone will approach my desk and blurt out, "Birds" or "Egypt" or "AIDS" and figure that the keyword

is enough for me to read their mind. Give us a hint. When someone asks, "Where are your bird books?" they really want to know something else. So I ask them a series of questions to find out what they really want: material on endangered condors, how to raise parakeets, or how to identify a hummingbird that has used a neighbor's birdfeeder. We aren't being nosy (though a good librarian is always curious yet discreet); we just want to focus on your needs and not just give you the first thing on the shelf.

3. How technical can the material be? Some can use material in foreign languages; others have a good understanding of the subject and don't need introductory texts.

4. How much you will be willing to pay for the information? There may be a charge for reproducing magazine articles, for borrowing some books or microforms, for requesting books that are not on the shelf, or for conducting an online information search in your behalf. Ask what the library policy is, but try to gauge what your own financial limits are. The problem of paying for services has never been resolved in many public libraries. Because we usually refer to public libraries as "free" instead of tax-supported, many libraries will not provide some services if they have to charge. Thus, you may not be able to have online searches of expensive databases in those systems where all services are free but whose tax support is minimal.

In short, if you can state your needs clearly, you are a lot more likely to get better service. We don't think there is such a thing as a stupid question.

## Directory of Special Libraries and Information Centers

11th Edition
Brigitte T. Darnay, Editor
1988; 1974 pp., 2 vols.
**$350** postpaid from:
Gale Research Company
Book Tower
Department 77748
Detroit, MI 48277-0748
800/223-4253

*You'll find this two-volume work in larger public and academic libraries. It serves as a guide to more than 18,500 "special libraries, research libraries, information centers, archives, and data centers maintained by government agencies, business, industry, newspapers, educational institutions, nonprofit organizations, and societies" in various fields. Of particular interest to information junkies is the 80-page subject index which lists 6 sources for fairy tale research; 7 sites that house information on propaganda; 6 libraries on terrorism. Each entry lists the name, address, phone, chief librarian, and information about the staff, subjects, size of collection, the actual holdings, the number of subscriptions, and any special services such as reference service for the public — which the U.S. National Oceanic & Atmospheric Administration National Hurricane Center Library offer. Because of the expense few individuals will consider buying this work, but if you are making a telephone inquiry to find more information on a particular subject, ask the reference librarian if she or he has access to this work. It can save a lot of time. If there are numerous references, you'll do best if you search through it yourself. Most librarians I know don't use it a great deal, but it is invaluable when you do need it.*
— Steve Cisler

# Yellow Pages: Portable Reference Libraries

## Local Yellow Pages

*No reference book matches the practical currency of the Yellow Pages in your local telephone directory. On any subject you can browse, call, inquire, ask who else would have information, and proceed to the heart of any matter.* — Stewart Brand

## Manhattan Yellow Pages

*About once a year, I check out a Manhattan Yellow Pages from the local university library (you can order one for yourself for about $13 from your local phone company). Just about everything in the world is there, including useful listings not found in other Yellow Pages: for instance Factors. For example, let's say I need 10,000 used gallon jugs for a solar storage unit. Someplace there is somebody with 10,000 used bottles to sell. The Factor gets us together and takes a small cut as his fee. If you're the man with the bottles to sell, you also call a Factor.* — J. Baldwin

## International Yellow Pages

*I'm not sure how often you'll need this, but it's great to know that you can find the yellow pages for major cities throughout the world in some large libraries. I looked up Pizzerias in the Rome (Italy) Yellow Pages. There were nearly 600 listed. I*

*called il Boscaiolo Pizzeria, on Via degli Artisti to see if they delivered. . . . "Click." Oh, well, someday I know that just what I need will be listed in one of these international directories, perhaps the Hong Kong Yellow Pages (it's half in English).*
— Kevin Kelly

## Research Center Directory

Peter D. Dresser, Editor
1988; 1741 pp.
**$365**
($379.60 postpaid) from:
Gale Research
Book Tower
Department 77748
Detroit, MI 48227-0748
313/961-2242

*In your quest for information you are not alone.
A hundred to one, whatever you are looking for has a specialist dedicated to it or its domain. Here are contacts to 9700 university-related and nonprofit centers that conduct on-going research programs on nearly everything under the sun. By and large, they have excellent specialized libraries and information specialists on hand. Without exception, I have found these experts anxious to share their fascination and love of subject.*
— Kevin Kelly

**★8468★**
**FLAG RESEARCH CENTER**
3 Edgehill Road
Winchester, MA 01890
Dr. Whitney Smith, Executive Director
Phone: (617) 729-9410
Founded: 1962
**Organizational Notes:** Independent research organization. *Sources of Support:* Consultant fees. *Staff:* 2 research professionals, 1 other. *Memberships:* Serves as secretariat-general of International Federation of Vexillological Associations.
**Research Activities and Fields:** Vexillology, state heraldry, and sphragistics. Collects data on design and history of flags of all types, coordinates similar work carried on by individuals and institutions elsewhere, and disseminates this material through correspondence, publications, and consultant work. Maintains close relations with organizations and individuals interested in flags and provides flag information service to governments, encyclopedia publishers, flag manufacturers, and others. *Special Resources:* Maintains a collection of 1,000 flags of all nations.
**Publications and Services:** Research results published in books, magazines, flag charts, and bibliographies. *Publications:* Monographs; Flag Bulletin (bimonthly). *Meetings/Educational Activities:* Holds an international vexillological congress biennially, attendance by invitation. *Library:* 8,000 volumes and 60,000 documents and microfilms on vexillology, heraldry, sphragistics, and symbology, with emphasis on developing a complete library on flags and flag history.

**★8953★**
**INDIANA UNIVERSITY**
**LATIN AMERICAN MUSIC CENTER**
School of Music
Bloomington, IN 47405
Dr. Juan A. Orrego-Salas, Director
Phone: (812) 335-2991
Founded: 1961
**Organizational Notes:** Integral unit of School of Music at Indiana University, but with its own board of control. *Sources of Support:* Parent institution. *Staff:* 2 research professionals, 1 graduate assistant, 1 other. *Affiliated Centers:* Archives of Traditional Music and Black Music Center (at the University).
**Research Activities and Fields:** Folk and popular music, and art music repertory of Latin America, including history, composition, performance, and literature.
**Publications and Services:** Some research results published in monographs. *Publications:* Music in Latin America (irregularly); Music in the Americas (irregularly). *Meetings/Educational Activities:* Provides instruction in Latin American music. Holds festivals of Latin America music; periodic inter-American composer's seminars; inter-American conferences on ethnomusicology. *Public Services:* Provides information, advice, and counseling services. *Library:* 6,500 scores and microfilms of Latin America music and 5,000 tapes of art and traditional music; David Fenske, librarian.

## How to Make Money Doing Research with Your Computer

Paul & Sarah Edwards
1984; 40 pp.
**$29.95**
($31.95 postpaid) from:
The Rugge Group
1626 Chestnut Street
Berkeley, CA 94702
415/524-3212
or Whole Earth Access

*Sue Rugge invented the occupation of information brokering in 1971 when she began what later became Information On Demand, the original company that sold you whatever kind of information you wanted. Her business became the model for a whole economy. I find it significant that Sue Rugge was not a librarian, and that the founder of the archetypical Information-Age business did not even graduate from high school. She drew on what she calls her "eclectic generalism."*

*Paul and Sarah Edwards, authors of* **Working From Home** *(see page 174), interviewed Sue Rugge and produced a spiral bound monograph of the transcript. It's an excellent, clear overview of what an information broker does and assumes the*

*reader is not a librarian yet is enticed by this curious new profession. It's also an example of the business: an interview packaged into a not-cheap book — but that's what it's all about.*

— *Kevin Kelly*

◆

What are some of the types of problems that people bring to you which they hope to solve by getting information?

They run everywhere from avalanches to zeolites. That's what one of our ads says. It's really so varied. It's amazing. They might ask what the market for Christmas trees in Hawaii is, what the latest information is on curing cancer by vitamin C injections, or what is the latest technology in charged coupled devices. Every time the phone rings you have to be totally alert to a new subject that you've never heard of before.

◆

Confidentiality is extremely important. I mean we have actually worked on a lawsuit where we were doing work for both sides of the case. And, of course, the other side didn't know we were working on it, but we did because we knew what the case was. The fastest way I know of to go out of business would be to mention even the general topic that you were doing for somebody. The fact that a particular company is getting into a new field is extremely confidential information.

## Mind Your Own Business

(A Guide for the Information Entrepreneur)
Alice Warner
1987; 165 pp.
**$24.95**
($27.95 postpaid) from:
Neal-Schuman Publishers, Inc.
23 Leonard Street
New York, NY 10013
212/925-8650
or Whole Earth Access

*The economics of information flow is still awaiting its Keynes, yet the micro-economics of information brokering is clearer: it's a marginal operation.*

*Information wants to be free . . . , says Stewart Brand. Which means making a living by brokering information is like trying to get rich selling refrigerators to Eskimos. You're selling features.*

*. . . But information also wants to be expensive, finishes Stewart. That means you need marketing strategies, business plans, and capitalization for a service with no tangible product, no inventory, and no price. (Let's see. Should this be free or $1000?)*

*The advice in this book assumes you are a librarian or entrepreneur-to-be who already knows how to tap information. Check out this source for a concise lesson in the strange business of selling customers stuff you don't own.* —*Kevin Kelly*

◆

Online searching can be done for a flat fee. This can be perilous, but it is a good deal easier to sell for a flat fee than to sell by the we-can't-tell-until-we-get-into-it method. Also there is no penalty for being fast and smart; as one searcher says, "It may take only five minutes of my time, but it saves the client hundreds and he or she should pay for it."

◆

"We are expanding into other wide open areas. We haven't done much database searching because someone else up here does it well and I refer. But there are other areas, such as document delivery (we're near the state capital), which could work for us. The number of opportunities are endless; this did not appear so when I began."

## The Information Brokers

(How to Start and Operate Your Own Fee-Based Service)
Kelly Warnken
1981; 154 pp.
**$15.95**
($19.25 postpaid) from:
R.R. Bowker Company
Order Department
P.O. Box 762
New York, NY 10011
or Whole Earth Access

*What with the blooming of computerized data bases and the information economy, independent*

*research is becoming a promising new self-employment opportunity for liberal-arts educatees. The people who search data bases now will have an inside track into strange new information-shepherding jobs in computer networks to come. How to get started? This book tells how. It also tells where to learn the skills and sell them once you've got them.* — *Art Kleiner*

◆

Neither the client nor the fee-based information service owns the information. Information belongs to the public and is not "sold" by the fee-based information service to the client. What is sold is the expertise required to gather information for a client.

## Information Broker

Helen Burwell, Editor
**$35/year** (6 issues)

## Directory of Fee-Based Information Services

Helen Burwell, Editor
1987; 238 pp.
**$30.95** postpaid

Both from: Burwell Enterprises, 5106 FM1960 West Suite 349, Houston, TX 77069; 713/537-9051

*The* **Information Broker** *is a thin newsletter serving up tips for the task of free-lance researching as well as recent additions to the* **Directory**, *which lists all known information brokers and independent librarians in the US and 33 other countries (600 in total). The* **Directory** *is a good place to get a handle on what this small industry (and your com-*

*petition) is doing. It would also be a good place to shop for brokers if you need the following kinds of help: locating documents, tracking votes, compiling bibliographies, uncovering technical research, indexing a book, or translating text. It's indexed by subject, service, and state.* — *Kevin Kelly*

◆

Many magazines have a letters to the editor column containing comments and corrections from readers, as well as errata from past issues. These columns are a rich and little-recognized source of additional and hard-to-find information. Because they go unrecorded by some indexing firms, it's worthwhile to leaf through the next several issues following the issue(s) containing pertinent articles uncovered in your research.

—*Information Broker*

# My Favorite Online Databases
*by Alfred Glossbrenner*

The databases and online systems I like best include the following: NewsNet, ABI/INFORM, and PTS PROMT, and the many user-created databases on BIX, Compu-Serve, Delphi, GEnie, People/Link, The Source, and similar systems. Because they have no concept of how *much* information is out there, new and amateur online searchers who venture forth in search of one particular fact inevitably find themselves drowning in a sea of irrelevant — and expensive — information.

In the hands of an information professional, several of the databases and systems on the above list will yield very precise information on a staggering number of topics. But because of its unique feel, each is also well-suited for the properly coached non-professional as well. Proper coaching is simply this: Don't go into a database looking for a specific fact, figure, or statistic. Instead, use these resources to get a feel for a situation, an industry, a problem, or whatever.

Think of electronic information as a wonderful source of *starting* points for additional research — names, companies, consulting firms, addresses, phone numbers, books, and contacts — not as the source of the ultimate answer to life, the universe, and everything. After all, the point is getting the information you need, not how to get it. And given a contact or two, the telephone and the typewriter can be as mighty as the communicating personal computer.

### NewsNet

I don't think I've ever signed onto NewsNet and not found what I was looking for, something I wish I could say about DIALOG, BRS, and other major systems. NewsNet has a clean, quick feel to it, with readily available help menus.

To grasp what NewsNet offers, imagine yourself at the podium of a room filled with over 300 men and women, each of whom is an expert in a particular industry or field: Advertising and Marketing, Aerospace, Automotive, Banking, Chemicals, Education, Electronics and Computers, Energy, Environment, Government and Regulatory, Health and Hospitals, Politics, Public Relations, Social Sciences, Travel and Tourism. You can ask these people anything about their respective fields and receive an informed answer. That's NewsNet.

In reality, the database consists of over 350 industry and professional newsletters, the type that carry annual print edition subscription fees ranging from $150 to $500. The publication schedules vary (daily, weekly, or monthly), but each newsletter is available online within hours of leaving its creator's personal computer or word processor. And, of course, several years' worth of past issues is available for searching as well.

The key thing about NewsNet is that each newsletter is produced by a single individual or small staff of people who spend all their working hours focusing on a particular field. So if you want to know what's going on with, say, PCBs, dioxin, or other hazardous wastes in Ohio, the newsletter called *State Regulation Report: Toxics* in the "Chemical" section can probably tell you. Notice that this example fits with what I've called getting a "feel" for a situation. The toxics report could tell you the number of tons of dioxin spread in Cuyahoga County, Ohio in the last ten years. But it is more likely that it will be able to tell you whom to contact in Ohio or in Washington, DC to get that information.

### ABI/INFORM and PTS PROMT

Certainly no single database is appropriate for every information need, but the ones that come closest are those that deal with magazines. Magazines fill a very special role in documenting the life and times of the twentieth century. Each issue is like a new volume in a never-ending encyclopedia.

Magazine articles also tend to involve more research and consequently offer greater depth than most newspaper articles. So if you want to get a feel for, say, how American families are coping with the shortage of adequate day care facilities, a list of every magazine article done on the subject in the past three years would be an ideal source.

You can whip up such a list in about 90 seconds for magazines on ABI/INFORM or PTS PROMT. Better still, when you use one of these databases, you can request an informative, fact-packed abstract of each article, in addition to its publication particulars. IN-FORM covers some 680 publications; PROMT, about 1500 (with far less overlap between the two than you might imagine). But even where both databases cover

the same publication, it can pay you to look at both, since their abstracts may offer a slightly different angle.

Between them they cover all of the major consumer magazines (**Time, Nation's Business, Newsweek,** etc.). But they also cover such publications as **PC Tech Journal** and **Byte, Public Finance** and **Plastics World, Solar Age** and the **Yale Law Journal.** In most cases, the abstracts are so informative that you won't need to look up the source article.

**NewsNet, Inc.:** 945 Haverford Road, Bryn Mawr, PA 19010; 800/345-1301; 215/527-8030.

**ABI/INFORM:** UMI Data Courier, Inc., 620 South Fifth Street, Louisville, KY 40202; 800/626-2823 or 502/582-4111.

**PTS PROMT:** Predicasts, Inc., 11001 Cedar Avenue, Cleveland, OH 44106; 800/321-6388 or 216/795-3000.

## Online
Helen Gordon, Editor
$85/year
(six issues)

## Database
Nancy Garman, Editor
$85/year
(six issues)

Both from:
Online, Inc.
11 Tannery Lane
Weston, CT 06883
203/227-8466

*Unlike the other publications about information brokering on these pages, this pair of professional journals tells you how and where to find information.* **Online** *is the more general, discussing developments in hardware and on-line information services.* **Database** *delves into the minute particulars of specific databanks. Both are the stomping grounds for the new breed of electronic librarians.*
*— Kevin Kelly*

◆

The power of the single terminal user to acquire and manipulate information will be increased to an astonishing degree. The mere ability to do it will be far overshadowed by the skill needed to sift, condense, organize, and ultimately to present information in ways that add value to it without diminishing its impact.   *— Online*

## How To Look It Up Online
Alfred Glossbrenner
1987; 486 pp.
**$14.95**
($16.45 postpaid) from:
St. Martin's Press
Cash Sales Department
175 Fifth Avenue
New York, NY 10010
212/674-5151
or Whole Earth Access

*There's a slippery ocean of online information services out there. We recommend that you hire Sir Alfred, the wisest old salt sailing on the sea of information, to guide you to fruit-laden islands. He knows all the shortcuts for navigating through the invisible realm of databases, what you'll find when you land, how to set your course, and how to*

*unravel the knotty question of how much it costs. He has earned his medals (previous books of his we've recommended:* **How to Buy Software, The Complete Handbook of Personal Computer Communications**), *and is uncommonly trustworthy.*              *—Kevin Kelly*

◆

"Document delivery" is the industry's term for the service of sending you a photocopy, facsimile, or actual copy of the source document from which an online abstract or bibcite was derived. It is no exaggeration to say that if you are willing to pay for it, you can obtain a copy of anything that is referenced online. That includes magazine articles, conference papers and proceedings, video and audio tapes, patents, complete books, chapters from books, maps, monographs, charts, architectural diagrams — if it exists anywhere in North America, you can have it in your hands tomorrow morning.

## Information Providers

```
No more than
18,000 feet to
       ┌──────────┐
  🏠    │          │────── Dow Jones
  🏠 ╱200╲         │
  🏠(Residences)   │────── Bay Area Teleguide
  🏠    │          │
  🏠    │PacBell   │────── MCI Mail
  🏠   Danville    │
                   │────── PGE
                   │
                   │────── Danville
                   │       Bulletin Board
                   │
                   │────── Bank
                           of America
```

Six primary information providers participated in Project Victoria.

# Press Clippings

*by Richard Kadrey*

Press clipping services have been around for almost as long as the press itself, and like the press, they've had to change with the times. Luce and Burrelle's, two of the biggest and oldest services, still call themselves "press clipping" companies, but both offer far more than that. As basic services, they use topics or key words that you provide to pull clips from thousands of daily newspapers, magazines, the Dow Jones News Service, AP, UPI, and Reuters wire services. The cost of these services isn't cheap. Both companies work on three month-minimum contracts, with Luce starting at **$179** a month, and Burrelle's at **$181** (Burrelle's does have a special one-month contract available for **$260**). Besides the price of the service, each clip will cost you between **95** and **97** cents. Burrelle's has other options that can effect the total price: for instance, monitoring periodicals east or west of the Mississippi exclusively is cheaper than nationwide coverage; they also have special magazine-only, wire service-only, and Black Press-only options. Both companies mail clippings to you twice a week, so you can expect them from 10 to 14 days after publication. Luce's IMPACT service compiles information from periodicals and puts them in management reports that can cover any topic or region of the country, and can even check your publicity costs by comparing the ad prices on a publication-by-publication basis. Burrelle's has a service called NewsExpress, which pulls stories from the morning editions of 24 major city daily newspapers, and promises to have the stories on your desk by 9 A.M. that same morning.

One service that was not available in the early days of clipping services is video monitoring. Both Luce and Burrelle's offer a variety of video information, from videotapes of shows and topics (**$75** each from Luce in Beta, VHS, and U-MATIC formats) to transcripts of specific television shows (Burrelle's also offers radio transcription services at **$40** a month.).

If you need national periodical clipping or video monitoring, these are the big kids on the block. But if you check your local Yellow Pages, you can usually find local clipping services that can handle regional news much cheaper than either of these companies.

## Luce Press Clippings

Information **free** from: Luce Press Clippings, 420 Lexington Avenue, New York, NY 10170; 800/528-8226

## Burrelle's Press Clippings

Information **free** from: Burrelle's Press Clippings, 75 East Northfield Road, Livingston, NJ 07039; 201/992-6600

## Executive News Service

Information **free** from: CompuServe Information Service, 5000 Arlington Centre Boulevard, Columbus, OH 43220; 800/848-8990 (in Ohio, 614/457-8650)

*If you use CompuServe a minimum of $10 per month you can sign up for their ENS, Executive News Service. It allows you to have "file folders" with key words. You then have your choice of news services to do the search from. I get news all the time about the Grateful Dead and their members culled from local, state and national news services, keyed to their names, the Dead, etc. It's a neat way to just have your key words, check in a few times a week and download all the info. Very case specific. For instance, I have "Jerry Garcia" as one of my key words. I got back a listing of high school all-state football players in some state in the Northeast, one of which was Jerry Garcia.*
— Bernie Bildman

## Automatic Subject Citation Alert

Information **free** from: ISI, 3501 Market Street, Philadelphia, PA 19104; 800/523-1850

*The company behind the Science Citation Index and Current Contents service (see page 48), the Institute for Scientific Information (ISI), uses citations to provide personal information filtering. Let's say you have an ongoing research project. You provide ISI with a list of specific papers you have already found to be invaluable, along with names of authors whose work is generally useful to you, as well as key words you are always on the lookout for. They will construct an "information profile" which they apply across the ceaseless river of scientific information surging through their computers. Each week they mail you the abstracts or titles of what they caught. You can go hunt for the full article in a research library, or if you're far from one, you can check off the papers you want them to send you. A customized service goes for about $225 per year. Less tailored, but less expensive ($195/year), are*

## NewsNet

Rates start at **$24**/hour (8 A.M. to 8 P.M. Eastern time) 300 bps; Information from: NewsNet, Inc., 945 Haverford Road, Bryn Mawr, PA 19019; 800/345-1301; Pennsylvania 215/527-8030

*Imagine over 300 full-text newsletters combined with three hard news wire services delivered to your door step every day and you've got a good image of NewsNet. This is an information junkie's paradise.*

*This is not the place to log on and while away a few hours; it's the place you go to for up-to-the-minute information on several hundred topics. The specialized newsletters often carry news stories well before the newspapers.*

*The specialized "news clipping" service allows you to define 10 sets of "keywords" of particular interest to you; a kind of personalized electronic research assistant. For example, you can specify "biotechnology" and anytime a new piece of information is stored on NewsNet, the service scans it for the word "biotechnology." If that word appears anywhere in the article, it is automatically clipped to your special "news flash" section. When you log on, it's waiting for you to download. No hunting, no searching. Just open your copy buffer and save it to disk.*

*However, if you decide you need to search through "old issues" of the newsletters, NewsNet allows you to search through all its back issues. NewsNet claims that 75 percent of its information is unavailable anywhere else online.*

*The service is expensive, but it beats toiling away for hours in a library, searching through the stacks, only to find the article you need was "clipped" by an unthinking individual.*
— Brock N. Meeks

*one of the 300 pre-modeled filters that will deliver that week's absolute latest scientific abstracts on hot topics such as AIDS, superconductors, solar energy, Biofeedback, or artificial intelligence. They even offer a 90-day free trial.*

*Finally, for those independent scholars working in remote electronic cottages, or under rapid time pressure, ISI offers a service which will fax a copy of any scientific article in the world to you within 30 minutes of your phone request. My goodness! I can't wait for the rest of the world information economy to begin.*
— Kevin Kelly

---

RECORDER PROGRESS

BURLINGAME, CA
WEEKLY    10,840

OCT 15 1986
*BURRELLE'S*

From Burrelle's: a mention of the Whole Earth Review in the **Recorder Progess**, a newspaper published in Burlingame, California.

# Soviet flag in church photo, priest sees red

By Janet Parker Beck    *4262A*

The Rev. Stefan Pavlenko is "seeing red" over a photograph that links his Church of All Russian Saints in Burlingame with the hammer and sickle of the Soviet Union's flag.

While the photograph, staged by the <u>Whole Earth Review</u> without Pavlenko's permission, apparently won't be published, a similar picture taken at the Russian Orthodox Church headquarters in San Francisco will be, according to the magazine's editor.

Pavlenko says that any picture associating the Russian Orthodox

blue field with a yellow hammer and sickle.

"At first, I thought it was some kind of communist demonstration against the church," the archpriest recalled. But the photographer told Pavlenko he was hired by Whole Earth Review to take a picture depicting the idea of "peace and love among people of the world."

Pavlenko was furious. It is, he said, extremely detrimental to depict his church in the same context as the Soviet Union. Most members of the church, he said, have suffered in some way from Soviet tyranny and many of his 200

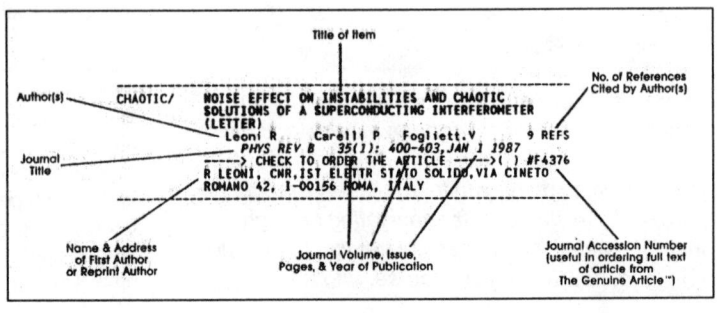

Example of an ISI report listing

# Real News Sources

*by Kevin Kelly*

Where did all the news in this book come from? From the recommendations of a informal circle of friends who are, more or less, information junkies. I was curious what sources these intelligence agents found to keep them nourished with real news — dispatches that report on a new pattern of things, rather than on new variations of old news. I polled them as we gathered:

I read anything and everything. For business purposes I read *Locus* (see p. 181) - the Business Week of the science fiction world. My favorite 'zine is *Science Fiction Guide* (see p. 181), published by Charles Platt — juicy stuff. The place I get my most news from is *High Technology*, which I love. I read *Science*, too, and *Fact Sheet Five* (see p. 40), a really bizzare under-ground 'zine. I pay attention to *Inquiry* (see p. 55) for a radical Islamic view of the world, and I subscribe to *Soviet Life*, which you can't beat. Now that I think about it I get an awful lot of my quirky news from friends who send me clippings. And recently I started my own BBS called *Cheap Truth*. People all over the country call in on it, and so I collect weird news that way.

> — Bruce Sterling
> Cyberpunk author

For straight news I read the English paper *Manchester Guardian* (see p. 55). My favorite mag is the fashionable *Vanity Fair*, and the English life style magazine *Face*. I don't read much science news other than *New Scientist*. I get most of that kind of science stuff from clippings that Bruce Sterling sends me.

> — William Gibson
> Author of **Neuromancer**

I start each day reading the *Washington Post* - every article but sports. Trade journals and specialized news-letters come in every day, most dealing with communications. Just started getting *Automatic ID News* (journal of the bar-code industry) and *EMI and Compatibility* (control of electromagnetic interference). Also subscribe to several radio hobby publications (especially recommend the *W5YI Report, Monitoring Times & Review of International Broadcasting*. WTOP-AM is the local news-radio station. When that's not on, usually my scanner is, listening to DC police and federal land mobile channels (one of the special benefits of living downtown). At night, always listen to BBC World Service, Radio France International (esp. for African

news) and Radio Netherlands (esp. for media news). Usually try to hear All Things Considered and MacNeil-Lehrer, occasionally one of the commercial TV net newses. But I find I get the best news from friends with common interests, most of them journalists or audio-visual production techies. I still haven't learned to control this flood for maximum utility. Often my news-sources tend to run my time.

Once a month I spend a weekend at the Library of Congress devouring reports from the Joint Publications Research Service (JPRS) and the Foreign Broadcast Information Service (FBIS). These are the CIA's two public translation services covering foreign newsmedia. The latter are primarily short-shelf-life news monitored from foreign broadcasts and daily newspapers. The JPRS reports tend to deal with longer-term developments, trends, think-pieces, science news. These two services are gold-mines, unequaled by anything else I've ever seen. Issued monthly, no mortal can afford a subscription, but most places that archive FBIS/JPRS do subscribe.

> — Robert Horvitz
> Communication artist

Every evening I run with All Things Considered on my Walkman headphones. Between daily perusal of the *New York Times* and *USA Today*, I get the long and short of it. Both of them have many (10% or more) health related items. For more medical related news I get *The Sieve* from Rodale, which monitors medical literature, and every so often I go to the library and read back issues of the main medical journals.

> — Tom Ferguson
> M.D. and co-publisher of *Medical Self-Care*

I watch no TV. No radio either. I read *Science* and

*Science News*. Lots of newsletters and xeroxed papers.

> — Eric Drexler
> Nanotechnology visionary

I use the telephone. Get lots of trade journals. My favorite is a Japanese electronics trade magazine — a real peek at the future. I read the *Wall Street Journal, New York Times*, and almost all of *Whole Earth Review*. And I catch All Things Considered when I can. I also videotape Pee-Wee Herman's show on Saturday morning to keep up on the pop culture.

> — Mike Liebhold
> Special projects director at Apple Computer

*Whole Earth Review* (I even read CoEvolution)
*The Spectator*
*New Scientist*
*Vogue*
*Louie M Vogue* (Italian men's Vogue)
*Wall Street Journal*
*International Herald Tribune*
*Music Technology* (see page 125)
World service of the BBC
National Public Radio
*West Africa Today*
*Hi-Fi Sound*
*Aviation Week & Space Technology*

> — Brian Eno
> Musician and visual artist

## Pacific News Service

Sandy Close, Editor; **$100**/year (52 packets) from: Pacific News Service, 604 Mission Street, San Francisco, CA 94105; 415/986-5690

*This international news service reported about El Salvador four or five months before any American news people. Their reporters were the only Americans to ask Iranian students why they were rioting. They consistently asked the brutal questions about topical issues like the Miami riots, housing shortages, low quality in public schools, effects of microelectronics on the workplace — issues that normal news services like AP/UPI cover in **People** magazine style or not at all.*

*When I was a typesetter at a community newspaper, we used to fight over who got to do the PNS stories. As a freelance science writer I was treated by PNS with an editorial grace I've experienced nowhere else (low pay, though; they're struggling). Now they're making their weekly reports (about six stories a week) available to individuals at $100 a year. Expensive but worth it, especially if your local paper doesn't carry them. I'm planning on finding some friends to share a subscription with.*

> — Art Kleiner

◆

WORLD'S SIXTH DIVIDED COUNTRY? — BEHIND-THE-SCENES TALK OF AFGHAN PARTITION, By Batuk Vora. Smoke from inside the diplomatic volcano indicate that one of the options being considered for Afghanistan's future is partition. While some argue that this would enable the anti-Soviet rebels to set up a provisional government and eventually secure control over the entire country, they are underestimating the ability of the Kabul government to survive.

## Whole Earth Review

Kevin Kelly, Editor
$20/year
(4 issues) from:
Whole Earth Review
P.O. Box 38
Sausalito, CA 94965
415/332-1716

*All the wonderful things we don't have room to explore here we print in our magazine of unorthodox cultural and technical news. See page 226 for more explanation.* —Kevin Kelly

## Utne Reader

Eric Utne, Editor
$18/year
(6 issues) from:
Utne Reader
Subscriber Services
P. O. Box 1974
Marion, OH 43306-1974
612/929-2670

*Handy idea, handy result. A magazine offering "The best of the alternative press" — a **Reader's Digest** for New Age types. The press represented varies in its alternativity from **Esquire, Savvy**, and **Harper's**, to **In These Times, ChurchWorld, The Progressive** (some good stuff, makes me want to check out the source publication), **The Guardian**, and **Dissent**. (Those and more in one issue.) There're full articles, edited articles, glosses, and magazine reviews by subject area (a bunch on renewable energy, a bunch on American Indians).*

*By and large any issue is bound to stop scanners and force them to read two to six times — that's better than **Esquire** or **New Age Journal** are managing these days. If you're cutting back on your magazine exposure, probably a healthy practice in the excessively pop culture going on, the **Utne Reader** might be a good tool for tapering off.*

> — Stewart Brand

# FEC Direct Access Program

*by Robert Horvitz*

All campaigns, parties and political action committees (PACs) must file regular reports with the Federal Election Commission disclosing their expenditures and sources of income. Most of this information is quickly released to the public; it can be politically useful and *very* revealing. Want to know which candidates are getting money from tobacco companies or the National Rifle Association? Who's renting whose mailing lists? How much your opponent is spending on advertising, or accumulating in debt? The FEC will gladly share that with you.

To make their disclosure reports even more accessible, the FEC has set up a Direct Access Program — basically, an online computer service you can dial into 24 hours/day, 7 days/week. To get into DAP, you first send a letter to the FEC Press Office (999 E Street, NW, Washington, DC 20463) requesting enrollment in the Direct Access Program. Enclose a check for $25 or more, made out to the subcontractor, Digital Equipment Corp. Access costs $25/hour, payable in advance. A customer service rep from the FEC will call back in a few days to give you the phone number and a password. That's basically all there is to it. No special software is needed — just whatever communications program you normally use.

The data available online is much the same as is found at the FEC's Public Records office in Washington. But being electronic, it can be sorted, filtered and merged by computer in ways that would be much harder to do manually. However, an important data-set not available online — which is available at the FEC office — is the names of individuals who've given more than $500 to a campaign. The FEC prohibits use of their campaign contributors lists for commercial purposes or for solicitations. That's why they don't give them out electronically. Note that some contributors lists contain pseudonyms to make that ban enforceable.

To save connect-time, FEC publishes a series of indexes that are available free on request in small quantities. Candidates are identified by name, but PACs have ID numbers. You can find the ID for a particular PAC online, but it's faster and much cheaper to look it up in the index ahead of time. Write to the FEC Press Office for descriptions of the indexes available.

## The Congressional Record

Published each day either House or Senate is in session. **$1.50** per issue at US Government Bookstores. **$225**/year (**$112.50**/six months) on paper or **$118**/year on microfiche from Superintendent of Documents, Government Printing Office, Washington, DC 20402.

*This is probably the single most useful tool for monitoring Congress' activities. With only a few days' lag, it provides the full text of bills and amendments, transcripts of floor debates, tabulations of votes, conference reports, notice of committee and subcommittee meetings, and the upcoming legislative calendar. Congressmembers can also add "extensions of remarks" — things*

## Information U.S.A.
Matthew Lesko
1986; 1253 pp.
**$22.95**
($25.95 postpaid) from:
Viking-Penguin
299 Murray Hill Parkway
East Rutherford, NJ 07072
800/631-3577
or Whole Earth Access

*This mammoth directory is dedicated to "all federal bureaucrats" and makes the point that 710,000 members of this much maligned profession are actually information specialists. The premise at the heart of the book is simple: "somewhere in the federal government there is a free source of information on almost any topic you can think of." A book that opens doors and gives the name, address, phone number and price list behind each one.* —Richard Nilsen

*they want on the public record even though they weren't said in Congress. While often pretty trivial, there are some surprising gems in those pages. The **Record** also regularly lists the office addresses and phone numbers of all Senators and Representatives, as well as their current committee assignments.*

*The big problem with the Record is finding something in particular. The sequence of topics dealt with is apparently arbitrary: a debate on military funding can be interrupted for a proclamation on Cholesterol Awareness Week, votes on shoe import duties and an obscure water project, followed by a speech countering something the President said the previous day. For help in locating the particular page where a subject was discussed, check the **CR Index** ($1 per issue from the Government Printing Office). These "semi-monthly" indices are consolidated at the end of each Congressional session, then published as hardbound references. For things too recent to have found their way into the **Index,** you can call 202/275-9009, and ask the people compiling it for help.*

—Robert Horvitz

## Federal Register

Published Monday-Friday (except Federal holidays). **$1.50** per issue at US Government Bookstores. Subscriptions **$340**/year (**$170**/6 months) on paper or **$188**/year or (**$94**/6 months) on microfiche from Superintendent of Documents, Government Printing Office, Washington, DC 20402.

*This is where you find out about new federal regulations, Executive Orders and proclamations, announcements of public meetings, project authorizations, licensing decisions, etc.*

*Twice each year, in April and October, the "Unified Agenda of Federal Regulations" is published in the Register. This is to inform people about significant rule-making proceedings underway, or scheduled for coming months, at all federal agencies. There's also a Cumulative Monthly Index to the Federal*

## The Federal Database Finder
(A Directory of Free & Fee-Based Databases & Files Available from the Federal Government)
**$125** postpaid from:
Information USA
P.O. Box 15700
Chevy Chase, MD 20815
301/657-01200

*Did you know there are thousands of computerized databases of government information, some of them free? If you didn't, it's not surprising; the government spends billions on maintaining the databases, and practically nothing on advertising them. **The Federal Database Finder** lists 4200 of these information sources and tells you how to use them (you don't need to have a computer yourself). Matthew Lesko, who wrote **Information U.S.A.** (reviewed next door), is also responsible for this book, which shares his philosophy that government information should be accessible to all — that is, all who can afford **The Federal Database Finder**'s steep price.* —Sarah Vandershaf

*Register. Subscriptions are $22/year from the Superintendent of Documents, and I highly recommend getting it — in preference to subscribing to the **Register** itself. Most libraries get the **Register**, so if you read about something in the index that you want to look up, you should have no trouble finding a copy. Meanwhile, the daily issues fill up the library's shelves, not yours.*

*Or, if you're familiar with the structure of the Code of Federal Regulations or need to track changes in particular rule-parts, you can subscribe to the **List of CFR Sections Affected**. This is $24/year for 12 cumulative monthly issues, from the GPO.*

*It used to be that any agency decision with legal effect had to be published in the **Register**. However, under the Reagan Administration, agencies have been given some discretion in what they can withhold. The rationale — ostensibly — is to save money, staff-time and paperwork; the effect is to keep the public uninformed about bureaucratic decisions. Any Presidential candidate who'll change this anti-public policy gets my vote.*

—Robert Horvitz

## Weekly Compilation of Presidential Documents

Published each Monday. **$1.75** per issue at US Government Bookstores. Subscriptions **$64**/year domestic (**$105**/year by first-class mail) or **$80**/year foreign from Superintendent of Documents, Government Printing Office, Washington, DC 20402.

*This is the official record of Presidential statements: transcripts of speeches and press conferences, nominations and appointments, proclamations, etc. Also includes some details about the President's daily schedule, and a cumulative index of topics addressed in his public statements (very handy).* —Robert Horvitz

## Manchester Guardian Weekly

**$58/year**
(52 issues) from:
Manchester Guardian
Weekly
20 East 53rd Street
New York, NY 10022
212/688-1330

*The only good
English-language newsweekly is the **Manchester
Guardian Weekly**. It is 32 pages/week with heavy
emphasis on international news. The articles are
culled from the previous week's editions of **The
Guardian**, **Le Monde**, and **The Washington Post**,
so that France and the U.S. are well covered. As a
British paper, **The Guardian** pays special attention
to nations in the Commonwealth and in the Common Market.*              —Avery Hart

# America baffles Europe ...
# ... Europe baffles America

◆

Armenian demonstrators in their hundreds of thousands
are the most spectacular reminder so far that the Soviet
Union is also the Russian Empire, and that the USSR 71
years after Lenin's revolution is no more a monolith that
it was under the Tsars. Kazakhs, Crimean Tatars, and
Balts have already shown that many decades of Communist centralism have failed to extinguish nationalism in
the outlying regions, any more than they have in the satellite states of eastern Europe. . . .

The vast civic protest of the last fortnight dramatically re-
vives an issue dormant for 65 years. A significant minority (one in three) clearly does not wish to remain under
Azerbaijan, populated mostly by Shi'ite Moslems, even
though all are officially equal under Communism.

## Inquiry

Mohamed Iqbal Asaria,
Editor
**$30/year**
(12 issues) from:
Critique
P.O. Box 11368
Santa Rosa, CA 95406

*If I had to restrict my
recommendations to
only one Muslim magazine, it would un-
doubtedly be **Inquiry**. Published in London, this "Magazine of Events and
Ideas" is of unfailing interest month after
month in its coverage of the intellectual
ferment in the Islamic world. This is the
place to find deep critiques of Moderni-
zation, High Technology, and Multina-
tionals along with self-critiques of Muslim
intellectuals' idealism. **Inquiry** also provides news of Islamic countries and reviews of books and cultural events.*
                        —Jay Kinney

◆

Following the Makkah violence, the Saudis
quickly managed to score propaganda
points. The relative isolation of Makkah (no

## Pravda

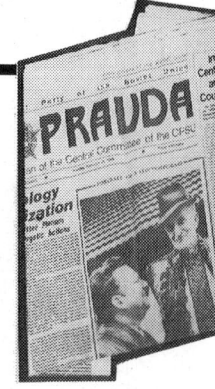

**$630/year**
(365 issues)
or **$99.50/year**
(52 issues) from:
Context Corp.
2233 University Avenue
Suite 225
St. Paul, MN 55114
612/646-2548

***Pravda**, the official newspaper of the Communist
Party of the Soviet Union, used to be the less-than-
informative official version of Soviet reality. Now, in
the context of the radical reform movement in the
USSR, **Pravda**, like most of the rest of the Soviet
media, is hot stuff — a place where you can follow
the latest political battles between reformers and
conservatives, read about the latest exposé of
corruption among officials, and laugh at satirical
political cartoons lampooning bureaucrats. The
regular features remain as well: TV and radio
program listings (Pushkin's poetry is prime time
fare), highly opinionated and critical letters to the
editor (usually criticizing the newspaper for either
going too far or not going far enough!) and texts of
important speeches and documents. If the English-
language daily dose is more than you need, the
weekly summary of the most topical items might be
your best bet.*              —Richard Schauffler

◆

G. Gulyuk, head of the Vologdamelioratsia Association,
repeatedly assured the residents that he would meet
their basic demands with regard to their living conditions.
But he didn't have time to accomplish this — he was
promoted. And this occurred after the province people's
control committee brought him to account for figure
padding and unsatisfactory construction work on social,
cultural, and other public facilities. I attempted to find out

non-Muslim Western journalist is allowed in) and the fact
that the riot took place during the peak of the pilgrimage
helped Saudis to doctor the facts. They released their
own casualty figures and doctored a documentary, which
was crudely one-sided.

In Malaysia, massive investment has gone into heavy industry. The
returns from these are questionable.

from him why he hadn't kept the promise he made to the
residents of Priluki.

"According to the calculations, there should be enough
heat," G. Gulyuk answered. "I don't see any particular
problems."

Meanwhile, houses continue to be built in the settlement,
and the new leadership of the association, in the person
of P. Sery, isn't racking its brains over where to get heat
from them.
                        —from an article titled "We're Freezing"

## Third World Week

Peter B. Martin, Editor
**$49.50/year**
(52 issues) from:
South-North News Service
4 West Wheelock Street
Hanover, NH 03755
603/643-5071

***Third World Week** has a
two-part function — diffusion
of grass-roots reporting from seldom-represented
parts of the planet and an active sponsorship and
training of local newspeople to perpetuate same.
Available on-line and in hard copy.*

***TWW** often shocks both left and right — a pro-Iran,
pro-Contra report in one issue! Good reading.*
                        —John Benecki

◆

KATHMANDU, Nepal — Here in the capital of Nepal,
Govinda Ghimere, a 21-year-old invalid with a useless
right hand, earns his living with the help of an old
bathroom scale.

Every morning, Ghimere sits with other bathroom-scale
proprietors on the ground along a footpath inside the
Sundhara bazaar in downtown Kathmandu. Sundhara is
a busy flea market with rows of vendors and four-
wheeled carts where delicacies are cooked before your
very eyes.

A French tourist with a large carton steps on Dari's
scale, writes down the weight and gets off. He puts down
the carton, weighs himself again. He hands the boy 50-
paisa coin, and walks off toward the nearby post office.
The tourist now has a good idea of how much the carton
he is mailing to France will weigh.

A scale imported from nearby India costs about 550
Nepalese rupees (U.S. $24). Used scales are available
at half that price.

A scale keeper can earn about 20-25 rupees a day. That
comes to U.S. $27-34 a month, or an average annual
income of about U.S. $366 — much higher than that of
most Nepalese, which averages only about U.S. $140.

## Editing Your Newsletter

(How to Produce an Effective Publication Using Traditional Tools and Computers)
Mark Beach
1988; 169 pp.
**$18.50**
($20.50 postpaid) from:
Coast to Coast Books
2934 NE 16th Avenue
Portland, OR 97212
503/282-5891
or Whole Earth Access

*Now in its third, revised edition, this book has no competitors. Beach is a perfectionist, and his recommendations are contagious. Major selling points: its visual approach—short on preaching, long on actual examples; a superb glossary; forms that can be photocopied and used; wonderful examples of photo processes and how they compare.*

—Cliff Martin

**Elements of a newsletter.** Control over cost, quality, and schedule requires clear communication among every one responsible for the production process. Precise language for newsletter elements reduces mistakes caused by confusion. This book uses the basic terms shown above with their meanings illustrated. These meanings are standard among graphic arts professionals.

## How to Do Leaflets, Newsletters and Newspapers

Nancy Brigham with
Ann Raszmann and
Dick Cluster
1982; 144 pp.
**$14.95**
($15.95 postpaid) from:
Kampmann and Company
9 East 40th Street
New York, NY 10016
or Whole Earth Access

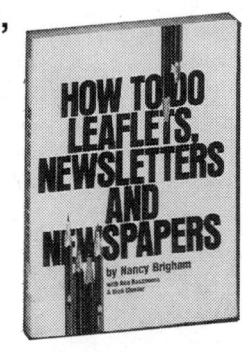

*There's no leverage like local publishing—it's cheap, fast, relatively easy, and outrageously effective if done well. In this manual are all the instructions you need to do it well. (Technically, at least; the rest is character.) The book is its own best demonstration. I wish I'd had it when we started.*

—Stewart Brand

◆

Granted, the substitutes for sexist grammar aren't as natural-sounding as the original version. But when inequality is built into our language, speaking naturally takes a back seat to speaking so that large groups in your audience won't be offended or left out.

◆

Using photos: Whoever's looking at you will end up looking into the eyes of the reader browsing through your paper. Suppose you snap a furious tenant ranting

and shouting about how his rent is too high and his landlord is terrible. If the tenant's looking right at the camera, he'll be ranting at the reader. Instead of sympathizing with him, your reader will feel threatened and unjustly accused.

Start pasting up from the bottom

Distribute type onto each page

Getting the line spacing right

type sample used as guide

## Publishing Newsletters

Howard Hudson
1982, 1988; 224 pp.
**$12.95**
($14.45 postpaid) from:
Macmillan Publishing Co.
Order Department
Front and Brown Streets
Riverside, N.J. 08075
1-800-257-5755

*The best book to cover the whole business of starting, managing, and succeeding at newsletter publishing. From a legend in the newsletter world (founder of the Newsletter Association and publisher of the "Newsletter on Newsletters"). Best selling point is his effort to show how hard it is to succeed at newsletter publishing, to get renewals and keep costs to a minimum. No one should think about doing a newsletter without consulting this book!*

—Cliff Martin

◆

Whatever their physical appearance, there is one unifying characteristic of newsletters: *they provide specialized information.* They are informal publications, created to service designated audiences or universes rather than a mass audience.

◆

Much government material is written in infuriating gobbledygook. As one Washington newsletter publisher said, "Our position is secure until the government learns to write in English. But that will not happen in our lifetime, if ever."

◆

As I have stressed, even if you can afford it, don't make your decision to use type rather than typewriter composition on the basis of printing appearance. . . . I've noted that often the most expensive newsletters in printing quality are put out by nonprofit groups or sell for $5 a year, while the $300 and up subscription letters are typewriter composition. Whatever the sponsorship of the newsletter, it's the content that comes first.

## The Newsletter on Newsletters

$96/year (bi-weekly) from 44 West Market Street, P.O. Box 311, Rhinebeck, NY 12572; 914/876-2081.

*The hard-nose approach to making a high-priced high value newsletter your livelihood. Delivered to you in a high-priced newsletter format, of course. As Ivan Levison, a newsletter producer himself, said, "In a world of broadcasting, newsletters represent the victory of narrow-casting." Yep.*

—Kevin Kelly
[Suggested by Ivan Levison]

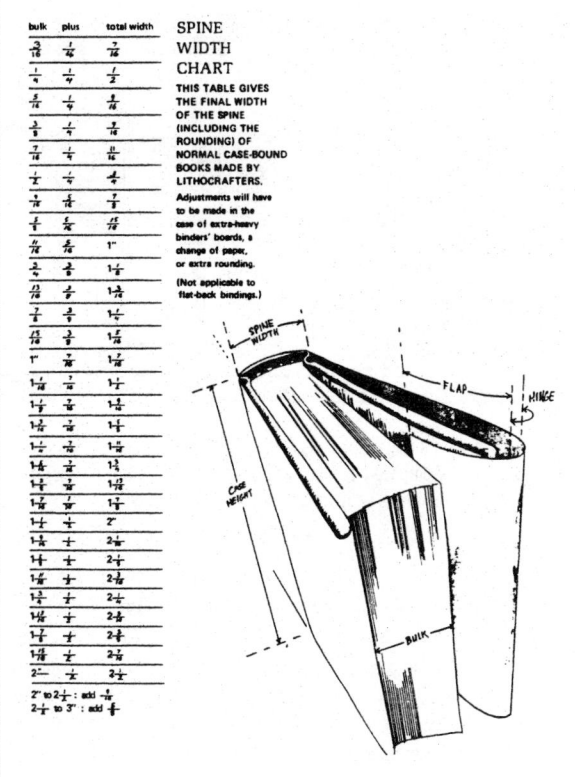

SPINE WIDTH CHART

THIS TABLE GIVES THE FINAL WIDTH OF THE SPINE (INCLUDING THE ROUNDING) OF NORMAL CASE-BOUND BOOKS MADE BY LITHOCRAFTERS.

Adjustments will have to be made in the case of extra-heavy binders' boards, a change of paper, or extra rounding.

(Not applicable to flat-back bindings.)

## The Complete Guide to Self-Publishing

(Everything You Need to Know to Write, Publish, Promote, and Sell Your Own Book)
Tom & Marilyn Ross
1985; 399 pp.
**$19.95**
($21.95 postpaid) from:
Writer's Digest Books
1507 Dana Avenue
Cincinnati, OH 45207
1-800-543-4644
1-800-551-0884 (in Ohio)
or Whole Earth Access

*For once the title doesn't lie. This one will stand long after a dozen other books have come and gone. The hard-won experience (including failures) of their own self-publishing comes through in this practical and intelligent book. Holds no secrets about the full-time job it becomes (mail clerk, accountant, collection agency, shipping department, editor, and janitor). Helps make the self-publishing process profitable and fun.*

—Cliff Martin

◆

Not every book is suitable for a one-title mail-order campaign. Bookstore shoppers go browsing with the idea that they'll buy a book when they find the right one. The mail-order buyer typically has no thought of buying until motivated by your ad. Whereas the browser may shop for several minutes, the mail-order counterpart is usually won or lost in seconds.

◆

PRICING A BOOK:

| | | |
|---|---|---|
| $300 | | Three months' overhead expenses |
| 0 | | Manuscript typing (you typed it, so your labor is included in overhead figure) |
| 100 | | Editing |
| 200 | | Design |
| 600 | | Typesetting |
| 2,800 | | Printing |
| $4,000 | | TOTAL |

The $4,000 divided by two thousand books equals $2 per book. Multiplying by five yields a $10 suggested retail sales price. Take a tip from major retailers and set the price at $9.95.

## The Self-Publishing Manual

(How to Write, Print & Sell Your Own Book)
Dan Poynter
1979, 1984, 1986; 346 pp.
4th edition, revised
**$14.95**
($15.95 postpaid) from:
Para Publishing
P.O. Box 4232
Santa Barbara,
CA 93140-4232
805/968-7277

*No other book tells you how to print, copyright and sell your own book with as much practical experience as this one. Heed what it says. Heed what it does as well — it is profitably self-published, along with another ten books, by the author.*

—Kevin Kelly

◆

If you receive an inquiry from a market you never thought would be interested in your book, draft a letter to similar groups saying "this group ordered the book and we thought you might be interested too." The mailing may be just 100 pieces — no great investment — and there is a good chance of a payoff.

◆

Before you go to press, obtain your resale permit so you won't have to pay sales taxes on your books when you pick them up from the printer. Check the posted resale permit at a nearby store, the name of the controlling agency will be on it.

◆

Don't hesitate to stop an ad that isn't paying its own way. Advertise only in the best months. Books sell best in February through April because people are confined to their homes by the weather.

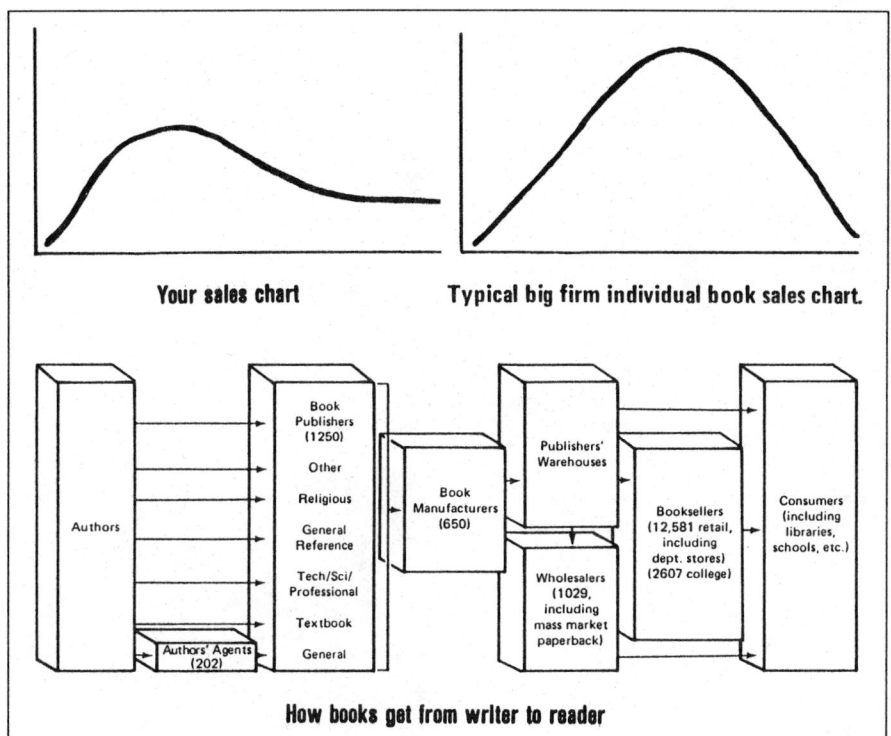

**Your sales chart**          **Typical big firm individual book sales chart.**

**How books get from writer to reader**

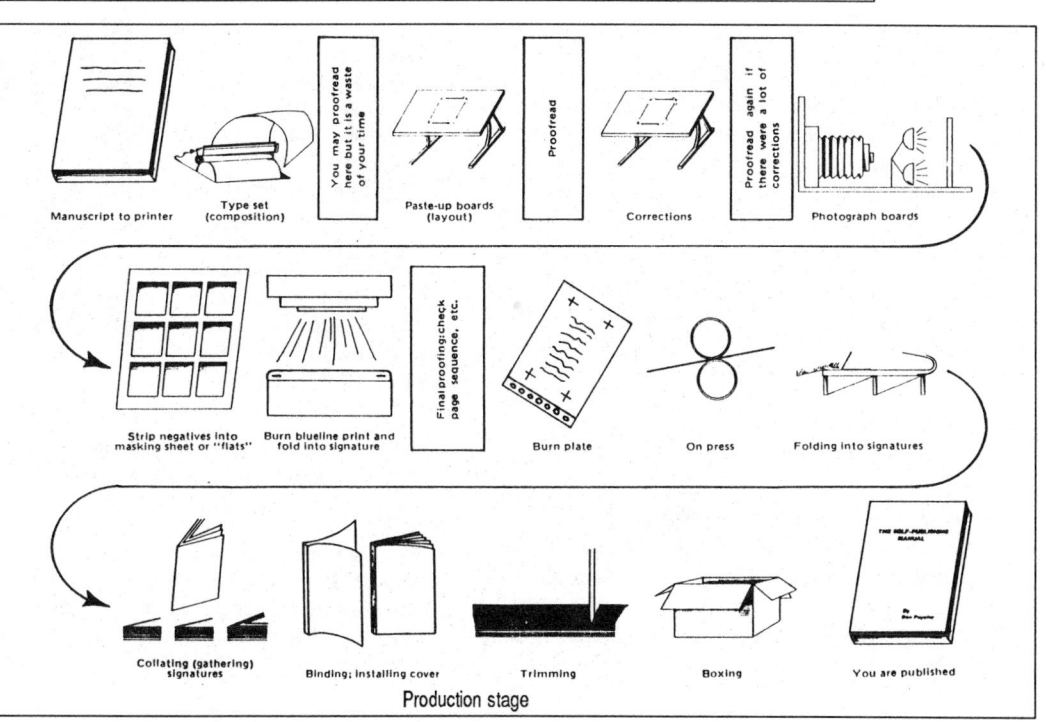

Production stage

# THIS DESKTOP PUBLISHED BOOK

*by Kevin Kelly*

This page you are reading began as notes jotted into a Macintosh word processor. Like the other pages in **Signal**, they are writ in the heavy duty hand of Microsoft Word 3.01. We make use of Word's nifty style

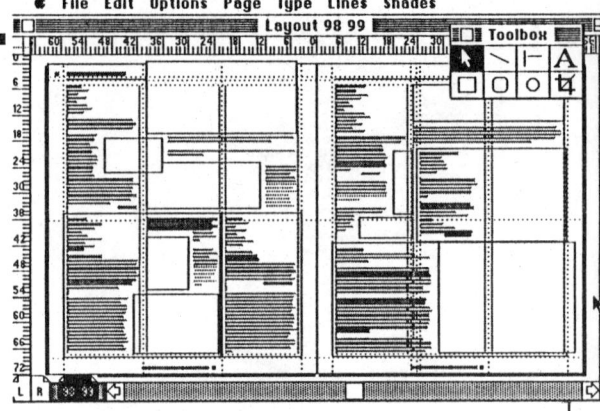

This is what a page looks like on the Mac screen after it's been designed. Compare this miniature image of pages 98-99 (Cinematography & Animation) with the actual spread in this book.

[Above] Richard Kadrey checks proof sheets that churn out the Laserwriter's exit tray. A dependable and quiet robot, it is essentially a small copy machine grafted onto the brain of a personal computer.

sheets, which allow a single code to activate a particular text format. For instance, the typeface, column width, line spacing, and character size of this sentence are all invoked by the single name we assigned on the Mac menu, "article body." That means that as we are writing we can see what the text will look like on paper. The finished writing is spell-checked with Word's built-in speller (handy, but not infallible), and printed out for a second proofreading by one of our human proofers, either Lori Woolpert or Hank Roberts.

At this stage the copy is in many small pieces, each review in its own file, and often times on different editor's machines (Macintosh SE's). The editor in charge of a page will round up the files and gather them into a second software program, the engine of desktop publishing, PageMaker 3.0. The editor of this page was Sarah Vandershaf. She loads the files onto her machine then prints out a proof page on our sole Laserwriter, which is at the apex of a bird's nest of cables coming into it from every Mac in the office. To conserve expensive cartridges ($100 new) we feed it cheaper refilled ones for proofs (about $50 per refill).

The oversize pages of **Signal** come out of the Laserwriter in two half sideways pages (thanks to a trick taught us by Jay Kinney), are taped together, and empty spaces filled out with xeroxed illustrations. This proof page, along with a floppy disk containing the file, are sent over to art director Kathleen O'Neill's desk.

Kathleen then lays out the pages on her Mac Plus using PageMaker 3.0. It takes about one hour per page to

arrange the text and picture boxes to fit. The illustration boxes can be enlarged or elongated very easily, and the 3.0 version of PageMaker allows Kathleen to run text around an odd-shape illustration, so that the end of the text snuggles up to a custom fit along the edge of the illustration. This was a backbreaker on standard typesetting equipment.

Don Ryan shoots the book covers with a 4 x 5 view camera loaded with Polaroid 52 black and white film. The pics are later ganged for group half-toning. He uses a Polaroid MP-4 industrial copy camera to shoot pictures excerpted from books that have grey half-tones. Any strictly black and white "line" drawings are merely xeroxed using our fabulous Mita copy machine and a special clay-coated paper to increase its already fine resolution. The xerox will then be pasted down with wax.

The completely designed layout pages are proofed a second time, then sent back to the editors for correc-

[Left] Sarah Vandershaf pours finished writing into the Page-Maker template in her Mac SE. Her screen displays the full spread as two teeny pages. Even from where she is sitting it's impossible to read; the text shows as flexible blocks of gray — enough to get a rough idea of placement.

[Above] Kathleen O'Neill parked her Mac near a window overlooking her courtyard flower garden. Where papers used to cover her desk, a spinning hard disk now does. Kathleen's sketching hand finds the square stationary pointing gadget (Felix) to be superior to the usual mouse. It takes up less desk space and in marathon design sessions it's less tiring on the forearm, preventing "Macintosh elbow."

[Above right] Don Ryan aims the Polaroid MP-4 at a book illustration to transform it into the right sized half-tone for its new home in **Signal**

[Right] John Chan inspects a nearly completed paste-up, in this case pages 32-33. Everything except the pictures comes already drawn out on the raw pages. His chief task is to paste down the xerox illos and photographs in the designated places. The job is made a bit more challenging because things frequently don't quite fit.

tions, and finally printed out by production manager Susan Erkel Ryan on clay-coated paper (Pro-Tech 94180) in the Laserwriter. Paster-uppers John Chan and Laura Benne apply a thin coat of hot wax to the back of the laserprinted pages and stick them down on posterboard "flats." There the additional gingerbread goodies of photographs and xeroxed drawings are added.

A copy of the layout pages go to David Burnor, who indexes each one on a Compaq computer (IBM compatible) compiled in Smart Database.

By a true blessing we had no major equipment breakdowns and thus no chance to test our backup system, which may or may not have been adequate. Although we relied heavily on Macintoshes and PageMaker, the real complexity of producing an illustrated book mocks the casualness which "desktop published" conveys. It's not something you do while watching TV. Our usual typesetter didn't have anything to do, but the editors typed far more, and while the paste-up folks had it easier, Kathleen had twice the burden of both designing and electronically pasting-up for them. We still don't know yet if this is a net gain. It certainly made everything happen in a shorter time period, which is not always a good thing.

**PageMaker** 3.0, **$595** from Aldus Corporation, 411 First Avenue South, Suite 200, Seattle, WA 98104; 206/628-2375

**Pro-Tech Laser Ultra** 94180 paper from James River Corporation, P.O. Box Z, Ludlow, MA 01056; 800/521-5035

# Cheap(er) Desktop Publishing on the IBM

*by Ted Nace*

Using cheap IBM clones as the starting point, tens of thousands of people have set up desktop publishing systems that cost about half as much and in many ways outperform their Macintosh counterparts.

The overall hardware and software budget for such a system runs to about $4000 (about the same as a good used car). The bare hardware essentials are an AT clone with a hard disk (around $12,000 in late 1988), an HP LaserJet II printer (around $1650), a mouse, and software. Software means PageMaker (easiest to learn), or Xerox Ventura Publisher (faster than PageMaker and more popular), or WordPerfect 5.0 (the first word processor with enough graphic and typographic capabilities to compete against PageMaker and Ventura).

The main ingredient is type. Previously, you needed a $5000 PostScript laser printer if you wanted access to commercial quality fonts in a wide range of sizes. Now, a medley of hardware and software products are avail-

able that generate equally good fonts for the cheaper HP LaserJet. The most widely used of these new type generators is Fontware from Bitstream, which is now being given away with WordPerfect, PageMaker, and many other products.

Desktop publishing systems built around IBM clones have two drawbacks. The first is the quality of graphics software, which still lags behind the Macintosh. The second is the fact that it takes more time and effort to find and assemble the parts of such a system, sort out incompatibilities among components, and master programs which — unlike those for the Macintosh — don't conform to a single consistent design. But for those on a tight budget, the clone route is the obvious choice.

Two useful books:

**LaserJet Unlimited, Edition II,** Ted Nace and Michael Gardner, 1988; 212 pp., **$28.45** postpaid

**Ventura Tips and Tricks (2nd Edition),** Ted Nace, 1988; 286 pp., **$26.45** postpaid

Both from Peachpit Press, 1085 Keith Avenue, Berkeley, CA 94708; 415/527-8555

## The Illustrated Handbook of Desktop Publishing and Typesetting

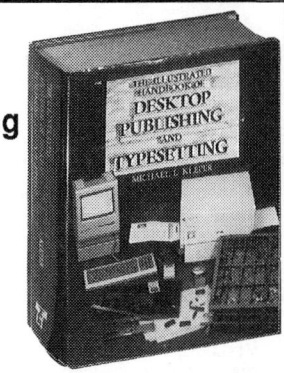

Michael L. Kleper
1987; 770 pp.
**$29.95**
($33.95 postpaid) from:
Graphic Dimensions
134 Caversham Woods
Pittsford, NY 14534-2834
716/381-3428
or Whole Earth Access

*What is erroneously called desktop publishing is actually desktop* typesetting. *Much of traditional publishing has always been done at a desk, and much of the rest still can not be. The only new aspect of publishing now taking place at table height is the job of formatting text into tiny hard-edged letters. It's an ancient craft with timeless principles. For that reason an old-fashioned encyclopedic tome like this one continues to be useful in a field that outdates books so fast that normally anything this big and heavy would be a dinosaur the day it was printed. There's probably more here than the average reader wants to know. I'd guess the book's niche is as a library reference for the typesetting regular who needs to know how to encapsulate typesetting technology into the vernacular of desktop appliances. Not for the uninitiated.*
*— Kevin Kelly*

*A diagram of the innerworkings of the HP LaserJet printer. In many respects, it resembles a tabletop plain paper copier*

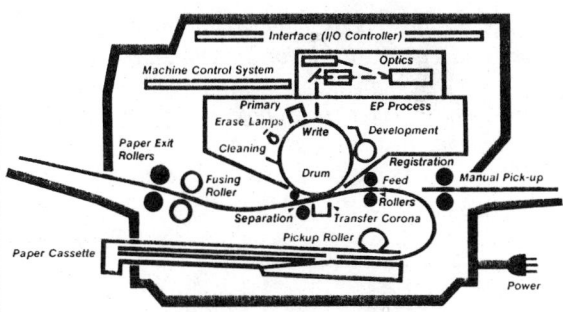

## Unibind 11 Desktop Binding

Information **free** from Unibind, 2213 Birch Street, Vancouver, BC Canada V6H 2S9; 800/663-6807

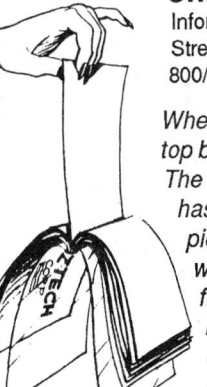

*Where's desktop publishing without desktop binding? At loose ends, that's where. The big desktop publishing revolution has created all sorts of needs to hold pieces of paper together. What you want is a cheap way to bind the pages from laser printing into a saleable book. What most commercial binding companies want to sell you is outrageously overpriced equipment.*

*I have sorted through dozens of different binding systems from $5 staplers to $5000 industrial machines. A couple are real jokes. One or two are passable. The winner, which I use to bind my self-published books, is the new Unibind 11 system.*

*This is a perfect binding system that consists of 11 x 17 clear vinyl covers with a colored backing strip. Hot glue is*

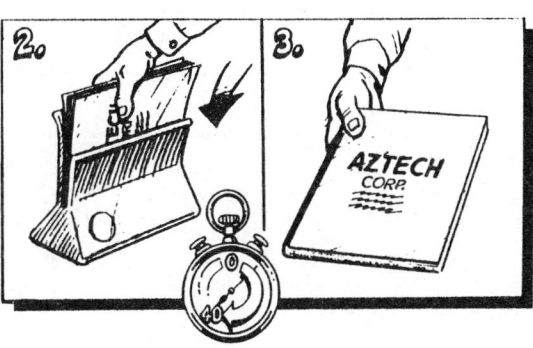

*pre-applied to the cover spine. You put the pages into the cover and then pop the works into a toaster-style machine for half a minute or so. Then you whop the cover onto a cooling plate and set it aside to cool.*

*Unibind will lend you the Unibind toaster ($270) for free if you buy enough covers over a one year period. The cost of a cover per book is in the 60 cents to dollar range.*
*— Don Lancaster*

## Personal Publishing

Terry Ulick, Editor
$24/year
(12 issues) from:
Hitchcock Publishing Company
25W550 Geneva Road
Wheaton, IL 60188-2292
312/665-1000

## Publish!

David Bunnell, Editor
**$39.39**/year
(12 issues) from:
PCW Communications, Inc.
501 Second Street
San Francisco, CA 94107
800/222-2990

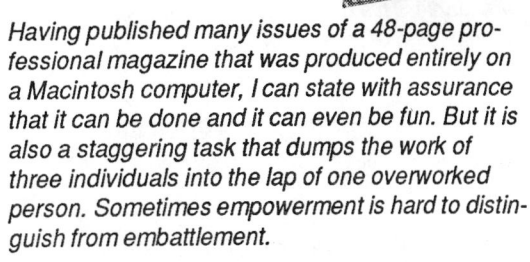

*Having published many issues of a 48-page professional magazine that was produced entirely on a Macintosh computer, I can state with assurance that it can be done and it can even be fun. But it is also a staggering task that dumps the work of three individuals into the lap of one overworked person. Sometimes empowerment is hard to distinguish from embattlement.*

*Two magazines keep things in perspective.*

***Personal Publishing*** *is the better of the two,*

*devoted to helping low-end do-it-yourselfers. It's put out by three people in a Chicago suburb, and is itself a Macintosh and Laserwriter production — one of the better-looking such publications I've seen. It's geared to those who are just starting out in personal publishing and is strong on explaining and illustrating the fundamentals of the field. Almost entirely staff-written, the magazine is opinionated, partisan (it favors the Mac over any other PC), and inspirational.*

***Publish!*** *comes from the publishers of **MacWorld** and **PC World** and follows in their successfully slick footsteps. I almost let my subscription lapse recently because it is very geared to individuals who are responsible for publications and presentations in corporate settings, and are far more IBM-oriented than I am. But on my last issue they revamped its design, and there was enough valuable information peppered throughout that I renewed.*
*— Jay Kinney*

## Getting It Printed

(How to Work with Printers and Graphic Arts Services to Assure Quality, Stay on Schedule, and Control Costs)
Beach, Shepro & Russon
1986; 236 pp.
**$29.50**
($31.50 postpaid) from:
Coast to Coast Books
2934 NE 16th Avenue
Portland, OR 97212
503/282-5891
or Whole Earth Access

*Hard to imagine we ever got by for so long without this book! A landmark both in content and design, a great combination of a nice book to look at, plus every page has useful information. From the "idiot" stage to fairly advanced technical printing information. Like getting a $300 course for thirty bucks! A must for any book publisher.*

—Cliff Martin

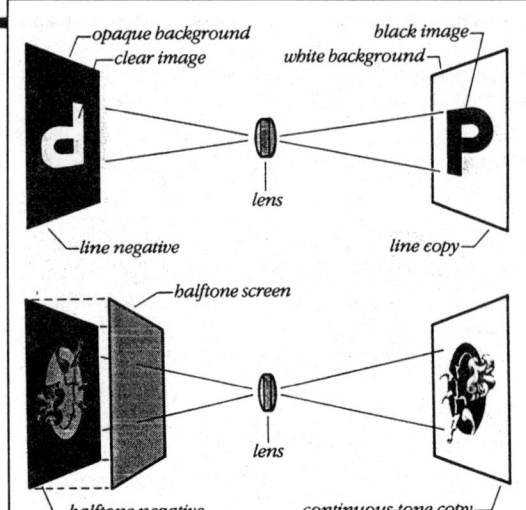

Line copy, such as type and clip art, is photographed in a process camera to make either a quick printing plate or a line negative for commercial printing. Continuous-tone copy, such as photographs and watercolor illustrations, is exposed through a screen in contact with the film to make halftone negatives.

The ball and background are coarsely screened at 40 lines per inch. Even these large dots create the illusion of the original continuous-tone image.

## Perma-Bound Binding

(for paperback books)
Hertzberg-New Method, Inc. Vandalia Road
Jacksonville, IL 62650; 800-637-6581; (217) 243-5451

*A library bindery, this company will "Perma-Bound" your paperbacks for as little as $3.00 apiece ($25 minimum order). After removing the original paper cover, they reinforce the binding and then rebind, sandwiching the paper cover between binder board and clear polyester film. Voila! Cheaper than hardbound,\* more durable than paperback, and a great way to save that treasured book whose pages are beginning to fall out and whose cover is getting ratty. (If too ratty, the pages can still be rebound but with a solid-color cover imprinted with title and author.) Your favorite might be bound already—call for their catalog of over 6,000 titles.*

*\*Cost comparison: **Lake Wobegon Days** by Garrison Keillor is $17.95 in hard cover, $4.95 in paper, and $8.40 Perma-Bound.*

—Sarah Satterlee

## The Practical Guide to Craft Bookbinding

Arthur W. Johnson
1985; 96 pp.
**$9.95** postpaid from:
W.W. Norton
Keystone Industrial Park
Scranton, PA 18512
1-800-233-4830
or Whole Earth Access

*A well designed book intended for the novice. It provides a good foundation in the craft with inviting clarity. I was immediately drawn to the fine illustrations, which I find of great help in understanding unfamiliar procedures. The last section of the book has step-by-step procedures for a number of different styles of binding.*

—David Jouris

Cut two strips 100 x 12mm at right angles from one corner of a sheet, and mark one to identify its original position. Hold them together by the ends and dampen them with the mouth. One strip will remain upright and the other will collapse in a curve. The grain direction runs the length of the one that is erect.

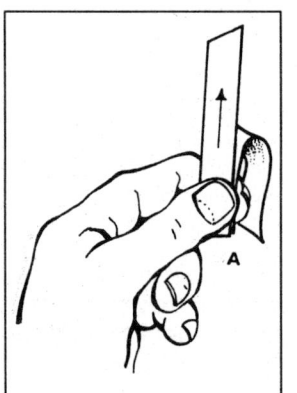

Establishing the grain

◆

No binding operations are successful unless the grain in paper, cloth, board, mull and jaconette all run the same way, from the top of the book to the bottom. If conflicting energies occur, boards will warp, endpapers crinkle, joints will split and the book will not close.

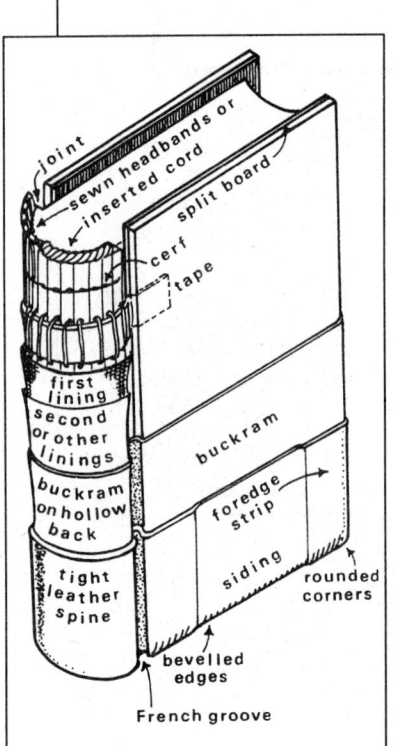

French groove

Library-style binding in whole buckram, with a hollow back, hidden cloth-joined endpapers, sewn on four tapes, rounded and backed.

## Editing by Design

Jan V. White
1982; 248 pp.
**$34.95**
($38.45 postpaid) from:
R.R. Bowker Company
Book Order Department
201 East 42nd Avenue
New York, NY 10017
800/521-8110
or Whole Earth Access

*Outstanding book on design — using the image and images of the page to carry a message with pure clarity. This one book, heeded, could cure the rotten design of most amateur publishing.*

—Stewart Brand

Top: The size of each picture does not reflect the relative importance of each in the story. So the reader has to discover it through thought and analysis and hard, slow work.

Bottom: There can be no question in anyone's mind about which picture the editors deemed most important. Not only does the spread communicate more clearly and faster, but it looks better and more dynamic. Yet all the type is in this scheme that was shown in the scheme above.

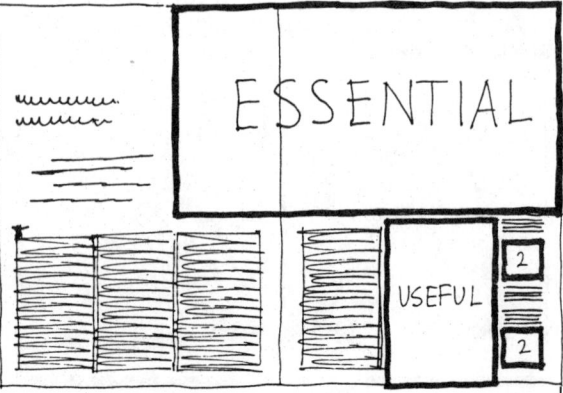

## Is There a Book Inside You?

(How to Successfully Author
a Book Alone or Through
Collaboration)
Dan Poynter and Mindy Bingham
1985, 1987; 229 pp.
**$9.95**
($11.20 postpaid) from:
Para Publishing
P.O. Box 4232
Santa Barbara, CA 93140-4232
805/968-7277
or Whole Earth Access

*A rare combination of inspiration and "how-to." I am particularly impressed by the chapters on choosing your topic and co-authoring (a tricky relationship at best). Throughout the book are very short, but contemplative quotes for writers, publishers, and others, plus "checklists" to self-assess your progress or suitability for special projects. One of the best books on getting started, planning, and finishing your book idea.*

*—Cliff Martin*

◆

If you cannot afford to take time from your career to become an expert writer, it may be more practical and cost effective to leave the writing of the manuscript to a writing professional. If, for example, your "other" work pays you $50 to $100 per hour, it does not make economic sense to spend time doing work you can buy for $10 or $15 per hour. You may decide to hire a typist, editor, co-author, ghostwriter or other collaborator.

## How to Get Happily Published

Judith Applebaum &
Nancy Evans
1978, 1981, 1982; 271 pp.
**$8.95**
($10.45 postpaid) from:
New American Library
P.O. Box 999
Bergenfield, NJ 07621

*The most human and truthful book on the good, bad and ugly of being commercially published. Written by a couple of "insiders" (who now run a very successful New York marketing firm). Outstanding are the sections on working with an editor (and its effect on the success of your published book), and the "getting yours" portion—contractual obligations, full royalty disclosures, etc. Recently revised and updated.*

*—Cliff Martin*

◆

Remembering that a query must do double duty — by selling your idea to the editor it's addressed to and then by helping him sell his colleagues — makes it easier to compose a good one.

1. State your specifics.
2. Explain your approach.
3. Cite your sources.
4. Estimate length.
5. Provide a tentative delivery date for your manuscript.
6. Mention your connections and qualifications.
7. Convey some sense of your enthusiasm for the project.

## University Press of America, Inc.

4720 Boston Way, Lanham, MD 20706, 301/459-3366

*Several months ago I received the letter that many authors recognize: "Due to shitty sales, we ain't gonna publish your book anymore." Mine was a textbook and it had a long run and two editions so I can't complain. Yesterday, I received this letter from an outfit called University Press of America:*

"It has come to our attention that your book, **Life Styles**, will no longer be available from Little, Brown and Company. If you are interested in having your book reprinted, we would encourage you to send us a copy for our consideration according to the following scale:

| | |
|---|---|
| 0-500 copies: | 5% |
| 501-1000: | 7 1/2% |
| 1001-1500: | 10% |
| 1501-2000: | 12 1/2% |

The UPA reprint is a facsimile reproduction of the original volume with a new cover, title page, and copyright page indicating both the original and the current copyright holder. Our contract specifies a five year reprint arrangement with royalties paid on net sales. Our marketing efforts include an extensive direct mail program, book exhibits at 45 annual meetings, review copies, and "on approval" copies to prospective adopters."

## How To Be Your Own Literary Agent

(The Business of Getting
Your Book Published)
Richard Curtis
1983, 1984; 257 pp.
**$8.95**
($9.95 postpaid) from:
Houghton Mifflin Company
Wayside Road
Burlington, MA 01803
800/225-3362
or Whole Earth Access

*A goldmine of information and mostly inside advice (from a successful literary agent) on the structure of publisher's contracts.*

*—Cliff Martin*

◆

Suppose you have a contract with a mass-market publisher that calls for a 6 percent royalty on your $3.00 book, or $0.18 per copy, but the contract says that if your book is sold at more than 50 percent discount your royalty will be reduced by half, to 3 percent, or $0.09 per copy. Well, a few years ago such a reduction was only a marginal possibility. Today, however, it's more like a probability. You may therefore find yourself getting $0.09 a copy when you were expecting twice that amount! That's a loss of $9000 for every 100,000 copies sold.

◆

There is an odd and perverse species of author who says, "Hell, I hope I *am* sued! Think of the publicity that'll create for my book!" . . . The book sales thus stimulated seldom do the author much good, for by virtue of the warranty and indemnity provisions of the publisher's contract with the author, *the publisher has the right to freeze all those royalties and use them to defray legal expenses and/or pay damages or settlements.*

*I called them today and was expecting that they wanted me to pay some reprint fee. Instead I discovered that they pay all fees and even pay a "small" advance. It's found money for me; however, Life Styles includes readings from other sources and would involve seeking permissions again. It's not worth it but they may be interested in reprinting another book.*

*This is vulture publishing in many respects but one which is a good idea.*

*—Saul Feldman*

*UPA publishes about 600 titles a year, mainly social science graduate and undergraduate texts and references, 45 of them reprints. They consider books from three sources: interested third parties, authors, and out-of-print lists from publishers. I begged their reprint person to consider Peter Stevens' Patterns in Nature—she said they probably wouldn't do it because of the photos. (No permissions, no photos.)*

*—Sarah Satterlee*

**Shirley Burke Agency**
370 East 76th Street, B-704
New York, NY 10021
**Tel:** (212) 861-2309
**Year Established:** 1948
**Agent:** Shirley Burke.
**Agency Commission:** 10%, domestic; 20%, foreign.
**Foreign Representatives:** Mori-Tuttle, Japan; Hughes Mossey, Ltd., U.K.; Agence Hoffman, France; Dagmar Henne, Germany; A/S Bookman, Scandinavia; Carmen Balsells, Spain.
**Agency Policies:** Does read unsolicited queries; provide editorial services at no charge. Does not read unsolicited MSS; return material without SASE; supply ghostwriters/collaborators; charge a reading/evaluation fee. Recently placed titles include: MOZART (McGraw-Hill); OUR FATHER'S HOUSE (Putnam); WILD ORCHIDS (Warner).
**MS Categories:** novel-length fiction; trade nonfiction; how-to books.
**Specialities:** art; biography, autobiography; celebrity books; crafts & hobbies; foreign affairs; military; music; mysteries; philosophy; romances (women's); young adult romances.
**Comments:** Current clients: 15. Among agency clients, 85% are published authors. Half of MSS represented are fiction, half nonfiction. Reports: 2 weeks, queries.
**Professional Listings:** LMP, FWM, WM, CB.

## Literary Agents of North America

3rd edition
1988; 204 pp.
**$19.95**
($22.45 postpaid) from:
Author Aid/Research Associates
340 East 52nd Street
New York, NY 10022
212/758-4213
or Whole Earth Access

*Much more comprehensive than the listing in Literary Market Place and more meaty entries. Wonderful cross-indexes by subject specialty, policies, size of agency, geographic listing and listing by names. Not seen at many libraries. Please recommend that they own a copy!*

*—Cliff Martin*

## Publishing Short Run Books

Dan Poynter
1987; 121 pp.
**$5.95**
($7.20 postpaid) from:
Para Publishing
P.O. Box 4232
Santa Barbara, CA 93140-4232
805/968-7277

*The subtitle says its all: "How to Paste Up and Reproduce Books Instantly Using Your Quick Print Shop." A quick-fix printing book—how to produce small quantities of books fast. Ideal for testing a market, or for small businesses wishing to make an impression.* —Cliff Martin

◆

For short-run book production the Xerox Models 9200 and 9400 are good while the 8200 and 9500 produce better copy. The 8200 and 9500 are the top of the line and do the best on solid areas and photographs up to

To center elements on the layout, measure and mark the center of the element with non-repro blue pen. This is most easily done with a center finding rule: one with the zero in the middle. Then mark the center line of the board and match up the two marks. This is much faster than measuring from the edges.

LEADERSHIP

100 line.... The best copies are often made right after a service call.

◆

Coordinate your print run in advance with your copy shop. The end of the month is often their busiest time because that is when all the small community newsletters are being printed.

◆

To divide an area into equal parts, place a ruler on an angle to any number of the ruler that is easily divisible by the number you wish to divide the area by. In the example, we want to make six equal columns so we angle the ruler to twelve. Mark off every two inches, remove the ruler and draw the vertical columns with the T square and triangle.

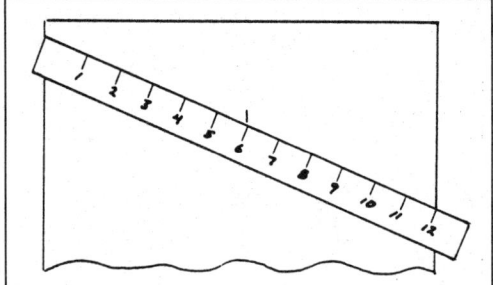

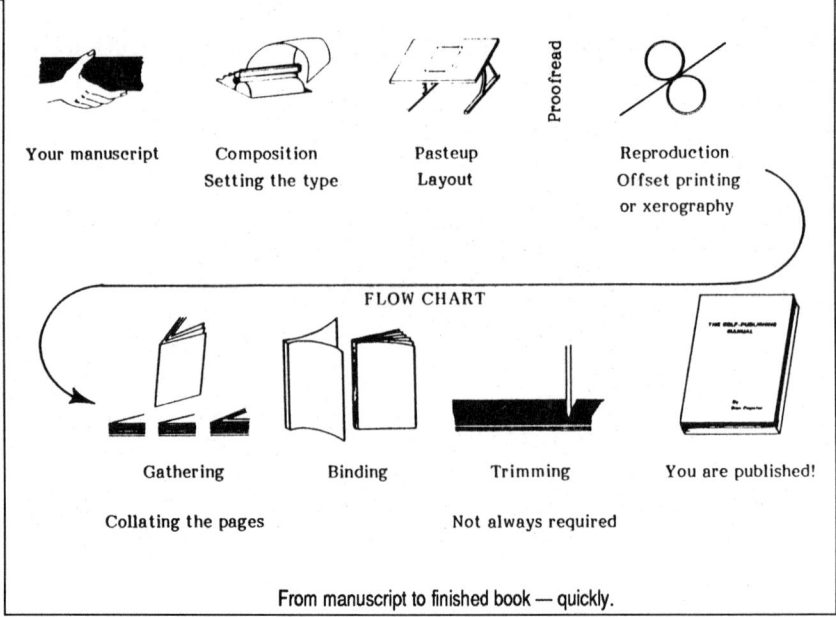

Your manuscript | Composition Setting the type | Pasteup Layout | Proofread | Reproduction Offset printing or xerography

**FLOW CHART**

Gathering
Collating the pages | Binding | Trimming
Not always required | You are published!

*From manuscript to finished book — quickly.*

## COSMEP

(The International Association of Independent Publishers); **$45**/year; include your publishing genre, such as General Trade, Cookbooks, Poetry, etc.; P.O. Box 703, San Francisco, CA 94101; 415/922-9490

*The oldest, largest and wisest association for small presses. Membership benefits include monthly newsletter (full of useful networking ideas and resources), group insurance, annual meetings, workshops, discounts, etc. Also has displays at major book trade conventions.*
—Cliff Martin

◆

Bingham recommends finding a printing broker (an agent who will help you find an overseas printer). Such a broker will know which printers are overworked at the moment, which ones are offering the best prices, which ones are the most reliable and which ones favor dealing with Americans.

◆

Poste Restante International Ltd., 366 Coral Circle, El Segundo, CA 90245 (phone: 213-640-1306) offers services to both book and magazine publishers. They will ship magazines overseas and remail them in foreign countries to that country's subscribers, reducing costs and transit times. They also offer overseas bulk dropshipment distribution.

## Small Press

(The Magazine & Book Review of Independent Publishing)
Michael Coffey, Editor
**$29.50**/year (6 issues) from:
Meckler Publishing
P.O. Box 3000
Denville, NJ 07834

*New York is not publishing. Small presses are. Most of the hundreds of thousands of books published each year are put out by thriving small-time publishers, not by Madison Avenue. Most of these folks are new and specialized. They produce technical books, how-to manuals, slim volumes of poetry, large gorgeous handmade tomes, corporate reports, or regional guides and cookbooks. **Small Press** is for them. Done with the graphic care a fine book would be, this magazine profiles successful small presses, and it stresses both fine bookmaking and fine bookkeeping—the details of publishing as a small business and craft. Computers make small-time publishing sensible and powerful, and this journal wisely tracks that gigantic revolution.*
—Kevin Kelly

◆

**About Books, Inc.** (PO Box 538, Saguache, CO 81149) is accepting applications for a year-round internship program. Those selected will receive hands-on experience in all phases of consumer book publishing and marketing with this well-known writing, publishing, and marketing firm. Internships run from three to six months at About Books' headquarters, a 320-acre horse ranch in the Colorado Rockies. Those invited receive room, board, and a stipend. Bright, eager, non-smokers are invited to apply.

◆

As a small publisher, you may want to hire an agent for Frankfurt. The agent finds a publisher for your book, does the footwork and research, and has the advantage of already knowing a lot of the publishers. Usually the agent takes care of the negotiations for contracts, and a good agent gets the advance money for you and does the ongoing accounting.

## Directory of Book, Catalog, and Magazine Printers

John Kremer, 4th edition, 1988, 192 pp., **$12** ($13 postpaid) from: Ad-Lib Publications, P.O. Box 1102, Fairfield, IA 52556-1102; 800/624-5893.

*Comprehensive listing of printers of books, booklets, catalogs, magazines, journals, manuals, directories, or other bound publications, by quantity, size, binding and price.*
—Sarah Satterlee

This book is a 320 page, 6 x 9 inch perfectbound book printed black ink on 375-400 ppi (cheapest house stock) paper with a 10 pt C1S cover printed with 2 colors plus film lamination (negatives provided for text, camera-ready copy for cover). Shrinkwrap in groups of four. This quote was requested in late fall of 1986.

| Printers | 5000 | 10,000 | 15,000 | 20,000 |
|---|---|---|---|---|
| Webcom | $5680 | $ 8,680 | $11,685 | $14,680 |
| Thomson-Shore | $6145 | $11,175 | $16,205 | $21,235 |
| Braun-Brumfield | $6155 | $11,382 | $16,609 | $21,836 |
| McNaughton | $6198 | $11,331 | $16,485 | $21,638 |
| Cushing-Malloy | $6793 | $11,502 | $16,343 | $21,057 |
| Bookcrafters | $6971 | $12,722 | $18,450 | $24,178 |
| John Deyell | $6979 | $11,879 | $16,729 | $21,279 |
| Edwards Brothers | $9078 | $16,387 | $23,759 | $31,114 |
| Aprinco | $10,825 | $19,100 | $27375 | $35,625 |
| Average Price | $6903 | $12,340 | $18,226 | $23,191 |

## Immediately

* Select a company name . . . . . . . . . . . _____ _____ _____
* Plan your first list of books . . . . . . . _____ _____ _____
* Send for copyright forms and information _____ _____ _____
* Contact the Library of Congress for CIP info _____ _____ _____
* Apply for ISBN number and SAN number . . . . _____ _____ _____
* Get listed in Intl Directory of Small Presses _____ _____ _____
* Get listed in Gale Publishers Directory . . . _____ _____ _____
* Join one or more trade associations . . . _____ _____ _____
* Subscribe to one or more trade journals . . . _____ _____ _____
* Study books on publishing . . . . . . . . . _____ _____ _____
* Obtain appropriate business permits . . . . . _____ _____ _____
* Register with tax offices (especially sales) _____ _____ _____
* Apply for post office box (permanent address) _____ _____ _____
* Open a business checking account . . . . . _____ _____ _____
* Print letterhead, envelopes, business cards . _____ _____ _____
* Organize fulfillment and distribution of books _____ _____ _____
* Notify wholesalers of new business . . . . _____ _____ _____
* Send news releases to Publisher's Weekly, etc. _____ _____ _____

## Later

* Get listed in Writer's Market . . . . . . . _____ _____ _____
* Get listed in Literary Market Place . . . . . _____ _____ _____
* Offer MC/VISA charge card privileges . . . . _____ _____ _____
* Establish an 800 toll-free phone number . . . _____ _____ _____

## Yearly

* Plan publishing calendar . . . . . . . . . . _____ _____ _____
* Re-evaluate long-term goals and plans . . . . _____ _____ _____
* Design, produce, and distribute catalogs . . _____ _____ _____
* Update customer mailing list (twice/year) . . _____ _____ _____
* Update key contact mailing list . . . . . . . _____ _____ _____
* Update reviewer mailing list . . . . . . . . _____ _____ _____
* Advertise in Publisher's Trade List Annual . _____ _____ _____
* Update listings in LMP and other directories _____ _____ _____
* Attend ABA, ALA, and other trade conventions _____ _____ _____
* Send author royalty statements (twice/year) . _____ _____ _____
* Celebrate your anniversary in the business . _____ _____ _____

## Book Marketing Made Easier

John Kremer
1986; 156 pp.
**$14.95**
($16.95 postpaid) from:
Ad-Lib Publications
P.O. Box 1102
Fairfield, IA 52556-1102
800/724-5893
or Whole Earth Access

*A do-it-yourself kit for new publishers. Biggest selling points are its excellent planning forms—how to figure a budget for book production, promotion, marketing. Plus great sample letters, forms, charts and a whole host of other goodies. I particularly like the "Publisher's Marketing Timetable"—a well thought out and invaluable checklist from the manuscript stage to post-publication sales. Essential.*

—Cliff Martin

◆

As part of your financial calculations, you will want to calculate the breakeven point for each book. The breakeven point is the number of copies you have to sell in order to cover your basic costs in publishing a particular book. The formula for calculating breakeven is as follows:

$$\frac{production + promotional + miscellaneous\ costs}{net\ price\ minus\ unit\ royalty\ costs}$$

## 101 Ways to Market Your Book

(For Publishers and Authors)
John Kremer
1986; 303 pp.
**$14.95** ($16.95 postpaid)

## Book Marketing Update

John Kremer, Editor
**$48**/year, 6 issues. Both from: Ad-Lib Publications, P.O. Box 1102, Fairfield, IA 52556-1102; 800/624-5893.

*I have personally worn out two copies of this superlative book! I wish this was required reading for any small publisher—it would put the big New York publishers out of business. Insights into the obvious markets (libraries, bookstores, reviews) plus great advice on the weird markets (premium sales, mail order catalogs, foreign markets, spinoffs for more income)—the list is endless.*

—Cliff Martin

*Some of the specifics are outdated—for instance, Armed Forces Radio Network no longer interviews interesting authors over the phone, the "free" listing in **Broadcast Interview Source** is now $135, there have been some personnel and phone number changes—but there are still more valuable suggestions per square inch of type than I've seen elsewhere. Besides, if you get the Update, you'll get these changes as they happen as well as up-to-the-minute marketing info.*

—Sarah Satterlee

◆

SPOTTING NEW MARKETS: 90% of all teenage girls have bought something by mail. 70% have bought magazines, 25% books and records. Their average annual spendable income is $900.

◆

Dan Poynter, author/publisher of *The Self-Publishing Manual,* has just started a new co-op mailing service to 800 of the top radio stations which do telephone interviews. This mailing currently goes out twice a year. For more information, write to Radio Interviews Mailing, Para Publishing, P.O. Box 4232, Santa Barbara, CA 93140-4232; (805) 968-7277.

◆

Many readers will buy a book despite a bad review—if for no other reason than to prove the reviewer wrong. Others buy out of curiosity. Still others buy because they remember reading about the book but do not remember whether the review was good or bad.

---

**14:03 Alternative Retail Outlets: A Checklist**

[ ] art supply stores—graphics, art, architecture
[ ] appliance stores—house & home, how-to, cookbooks
[ ] automobile dealerships—automobiles, how-to, travel
[ ] barber shops—sports, recreation, novelty, humor
[ ] beauty shops—beauty care, fashion
[ ] camera shops—photography, art, travel, coffee-table books
[ ] campgrounds—recreation, sports, travel, novelty
[ ] candy shops—cookbooks, diets
[ ] chain stores—general, mass-market, novelty, celebrity bios
[ ] children's stores—juveniles, games, humor, child care
[ ] Christmas stores—Christmas titles, juveniles, crafts
[ ] churches—religious, family life, inspirational
[ ] clothing stores—fashion, beauty care, diet, exercise
[ ] coffee shops—cookbooks, poetry, general
[ ] college stores—textbooks, general, literature, novelty
[ ] cookware stores—cookbooks, diets, health
[ ] computer stores—computers, business
[ ] craft stores—crafts, how-to, hobbies
[ ] discount stores—general, remainers, mass-market
[ ] doctor's offices—health, diet, cookbooks, recreation
[ ] dress shops—fashion, beauty care, sewing
[ ] drug stores—general, mass-market, novelty, beauty care
[ ] fabric shop—sewing, crafts, fashion, beauty care
[ ] fish markets—seafood cookbooks, recreation, sports
[ ] fitness centers—health, diet, recreation, cookbooks
[ ] florists—gardening, how-to, crafts
[ ] food stands—cookbooks, gardening, how-to
[ ] garden supply stores—gardening, crafts, cookbooks
[ ] gas stations—travel, atlases, humor, novelty
[ ] gift stores—coffee-table books, humor, novelty, hobbies
[ ] golf clubs—sports, recreation
[ ] gourmet shops—food, cookbooks, diet, crafts
[ ] grocery stores—food, cookbooks, diet, crafts
[ ] gun shops—sports, recreation
[ ] hardware stores—crafts, how-to, sports, recreation
[ ] health food stores—cookbooks, health, alternative lifestyles
[ ] hobby shops—crafts, hobbies, how-to
[ ] home improvement—house & home, how-to, crafts, design
[ ] hotel gift shops—travel, novelty, coffee-table books
[ ] hospital gift shops—cookbooks, diets, humor, health
[ ] houseware shops—cookbooks, crafts, how-to
[ ] law offices—business, law, politics, social issues
[ ] marinas—seafood cookbooks, recreation, sports
[ ] maternity shops—juveniles, child care, education
[ ] military PX's—general, military, adventure, recreation
[ ] movie theaters—celebrity biographies, movies, entertainment
[ ] museum shops—coffee table books, art, literature, juveniles
[ ] music stores—music, celebrity biographies
[ ] newsstands—local titles, general, novelty
[ ] novelty shops—humor, games, novelty, recreation
[ ] office supply stores—business, humor, novelty, computers
[ ] print shops—graphics, art, novelty, business
[ ] prison commissaries—general, literature
[ ] record shops—music, celebrity biographies, novelty
[ ] religious stores—religion, family life, general
[ ] school supply stores—education, juveniles, crafts, how-to
[ ] shoe stores—fashion, beauty care, running, exercise

## Book Marketing Opportunities Database

IBM PC and Macintosh. **$249** for full database; **$150** for PR-Flash (publicity resources); **$10** demo disk from Ad-Lib Publications, P.O. Box 1102, Fairfield IA 52556-1102; 800/624-5893.

*Easy-to-use database program with thousands of marketing and media contacts—wholesalers, chains, specialty booksellers, syndicated columnists, editors and reviewers, etc.; updated every 3 months; does labels, customized reports; interfaces with word processors to create personalized form letters; includes a promotional cycle database to help you keep track of who you sent what about which. I've only played with the demo disk and it looks like an an incredibly useful tool for the self- or small publisher.*

—Sarah Satterlee

## National Stampagraphics

**$14**/year (4 issues) from: Taylor'D Graphics, 1952 Everett Street, N. Valley Stream, NY 11580

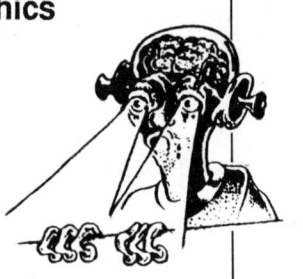

*There is a parallel universe, y'know, but — SURPRISE — it's rubber! The masters and mistresses of this vulcanized vastness have summoned into being the heavens,*

—BIZZARO

*the seas, every realm in between, and all that dwells therein.*

***National Stampagraphic** is a good transporter. A stampaholic's quarterly, its articles about stamps and stampers will inspire and instruct. (A recent issue gave directions for fashion stamping, including pantyhose!) But its real value is in the ads: each catalog offered is your ticket to a new rubber reality — images arcane to trite, styles cute to cosmic.*

—Sarah Satterlee

—ALL NIGHT MEDIA

—INKLING STAMP CO

### Rubber Stample

*Here's a small sampling of companies to get you stamping:*

**All Night Media Inc.** Catalog **$2** from Box 2666, San Anselmo, CA 94960; 415/459-3013

**Bizzaro, Inc.** Catalog **$1** from P.O. Box 16160, Rumford, RI 02916; 401/728-9560

—BIZZARO

**A Stamp in the Hand.** Catalog **$2** from P.O. Box 5160, Long Beach, CA 90805

**Inkling Stamp Co.** Catalog **$3** from P.O. Box 40195, Santa Barbara, CA 93140

—A STAMP IN THE HAND

WHEN YOU ARE UP TO YOUR ASS IN ALLIGATORS, IT IS OFTEN DIFFICULT TO REMEMBER YOUR INITIAL ASSIGNMENT WAS TO DRAIN THE SWAMP.

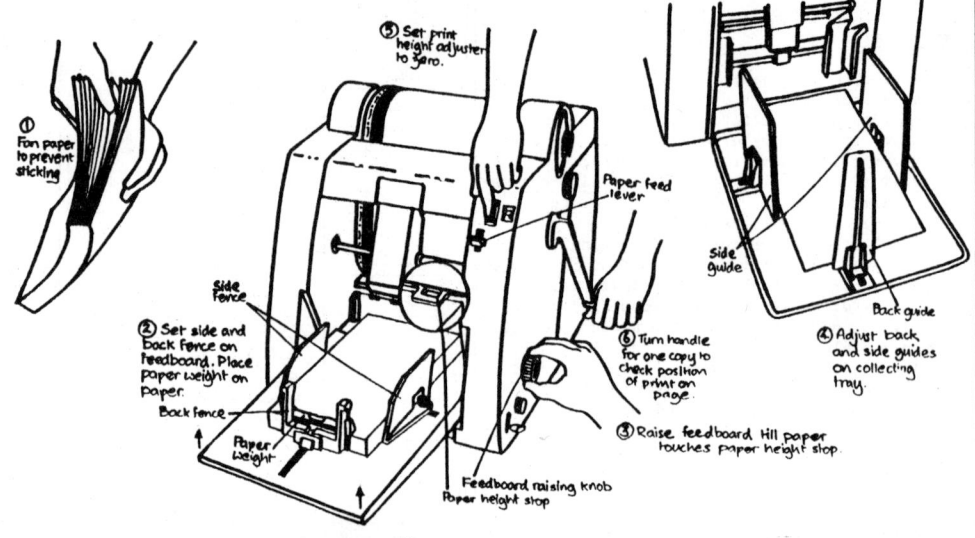

Stencil Duplicating: Loading the paper and printing trial copies.

## The Alternative Printing Handbook

Chris Treweek and Jonathan Zeitlyn
1983; 110 pp.
£7 (about $13) postpaid from:
Islington Bus Co.
Palmer Place
London N7 8DH ENGLAND
or Whole Earth Access

*If you don't have a community printing resource center nearby, here's second best. This book tells*

*you how to get something into print, explaining method, advantages, limitations, equipment, cost, number of copies, and print quality in a straightforward, friendly manner. There are sections on design, production and distribution as well. The "how-to" illustrations are well-drawn and -captioned; examples of leaflets, flyers and posters show what you can produce with a little time and the know-how you'll glean from between these covers.*

—Sarah Satterlee
[Suggested by Cliff Martin]

## The Printer's Devil

(Graphic Arts for the Small Press)
Joe M. Singer, Editor
**Free** upon request
Mother of Ashes Press
P.O. Box 135
Harrison, ID 83833-0135

## The Samisdat Method

(A Do-It-Yourself Guide to Printing)
Merritt Clifton
56 pp.
**$5** postpaid from:
Merritt Clifton
Box 129
Ridgeford, VT 05476

*Joe Singer runs a small press, both as publisher and printer. He puts out a great little newsletter, **The Printer's Devil**, filled with friendly advice and pointers, from him and his correspondents. Merritt Clifton publishes **The Samisdat Method**, an incredibly shoddily (for the subject matter) printed handbook of incredibly useful information.*

*This is outlaw printing at its finest. Actually, there's nothing illegal about it at all. It's just that folks who are in it sound like inky desperados, riding the range on their sinewy mimeos and Multiliths, outside the citified laws of Desktop Publishing. These people are opinionated and passionately defensive of your, their, and everyone's right to say whatever. By running their own presses, they insure that freedom. And by disseminating printing advice, they'll help you do it, too.*

*If you've got more ink in your veins than blood, link up with these guys.* —Sarah Satterlee

◆

My mimeograph is an A.B. Dick model 420 named Errata. This is a hand-crank, open-cylinder machine which I bought used (of course) about three years ago for $30. Open cylinder machines are obsolete and use a paste ink rather than the more modern, and faster drying, liquid inks closed-cylinder machines use. Since the only pink paper available in Coeur d'Alene, a city of about 20,000 population, was not a "true" mimeo stock but a multi-use paper which recommended mimeo printing be done with fast drying ink I had some problems caused by the paper's failure to absorb the paste ink fast enough. On the other hand, I cut the stencils for this job with an electric typewriter, rather than with a manual machine as I have had to do in the past.

—Printer's Devil

◆

Let's assume you're a hardcore do-it-yourselfer, living in the ass end of nowhere, determined to get absolutely first-quality repro even if you don't have a nickel for equipment. Can you do it? I did for about five years, after Fred Merkel, Bill Robinson, and P.J. Kemp combined talents to discover the contact exposure method of both negative-making and plate-burning.

—The Samisdat Method

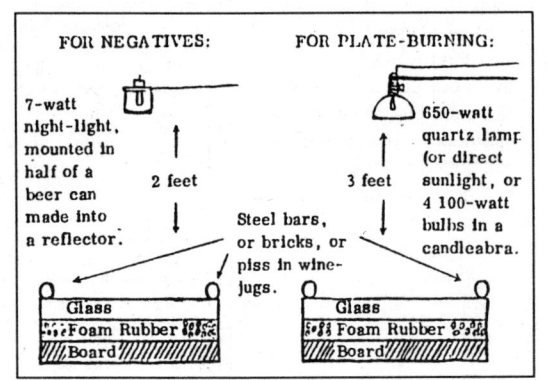

## Printmaking

(History and Process)
Saff and Sacilotto
1978; 436 pp.
**$36** postpaid from:
Holt, Rinehart and Winston
6277 Sea Harbor Drive
Orlando, FL 32887
800/782-4479
or Whole Earth Access

*I was about to say that this is the best book that gathers all of the printmaking media under one cover, but that's not it. This is the best book on printmaking, period.* **Printmaking: History and Process** *includes sections of relief (e.g. woodcuts), intaglio (etching and engraving), silkscreen and lithography; and the treatment of each of these media is better than in any books I've seen on just one of them.*

*I learned many of the basic procedures of printmaking from this book. Now, years later, I am a full-time printmaker and I still use it.*
—Turner McGehee

Register guides for screen printing include three-point register tabs (a), register buttons (b), and the T-bar method (c).

Four intaglio techniques: Drypoint (a), engraving (b), etching (c), and collagraph (d). Each column shows a plate close-up, detail of a print, and plate cross-section.

## The Artist's Silkscreen Manual

Andrew B. Gardner
1976; 160 pp.
**$9.95**
($11.45 postpaid) from:
Putnam Publishing
#3995085
P.O. Box 506 — Dept. B.
E. Rutherford, NJ 07073
or Whole Earth Access

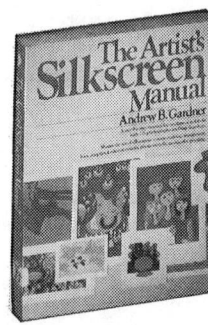

*With clear line drawings and numerous photos, Mr. Gardner leads the reader step by step from selecting materials and assembling the frame, through stretching and preparing the screen, to choosing a squeegee and deciding upon the method for creating the stencil. There is a complete description of possible inks and chemicals involved and the use of same. Knife-cut stencils and photo stencil techniques are thoroughly explained with ample illustrations and an invaluable troubleshooting guide. Likewise for printing plus a glossary of terms and index. This is the only book on silkscreening that has taught me more than I picked up in a five-day workshop.*

—Susan Edwards

Use of the swivel knife, showing how the blade rotates as the hand changes direction.

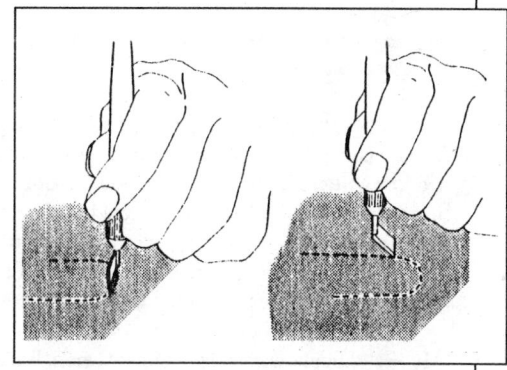

## Gocco Printer

B-6 image size 4" x 5 3/4", **$98** ($103 postpaid); B-5 image size 5" x 9", **$320** ($328 postpaid); each comes with enough supplies to get started.

## The Gocco Guide

Claire Russell and Mary Worthington
1983; 129 pp.
**$10** ($11 postpaid)
All from: Think Ink, 1452 NW 185
Seattle, WA 98177

*"Gocco" means "child's play," accurately descriptive of the level of expertise required to operate this nifty little gadget. And certainly any child in your household would be happy to prove it, if only the adult inhabitants would quit monopolizing it!*

*Essentially the Gocco is a photo screen printer. You use flash bulbs to make the screen. The original art needs to contain carbon (most inks and all photocopies are carbon-based). There's a little flash bulb housing that sits on top of the press's upper half. When you press it shut, flash bulb light passes through a light-transparent film, over the artwork, hits the carbon of the artwork, is re-radiated as infra-red light, which melts the film, thereby making the print master. Lift off the flash bulb housing, and lift up a clear acetate sheet which sits*

*on top of the print master. Squish ink from a tube onto the master, lower the acetate, put a piece of paper on the bed, press down — there's Print. No. 1.*

*You can get from 50 to 250 prints from one inking, depending on how fine-lined your original art is. When prints become unacceptably faint, simply lift the acetate sheet and re-ink. And by all means squish different inks on different areas of the master for multi-colored prints.*

*Lazann Ryle, a piano teacher, showed me a Gocco in action; she was printing a 10-point type logo on envelopes for her students. Each came out clearly with no smudges or featheriness. Quite impressive.*

*You can print on just about anything that will lie flat on the Gocco's bed: Lazann showed me napkins,*

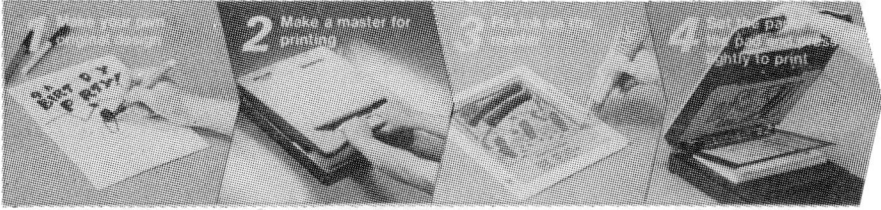

**PRINT GOCCO B5 SET CONTENTS**
① Printer main unit ② Lamp housing ③ PRINT GOCCO B5 MASTER (STENCIL) ④ PRINT GOCCO INK 100cc per tube (white, black, red, blue, brown, yellow, green) 7 colors ⑤ PRINT GOCCO LAMP ⑥ RISO Pen (fine) ⑦ RISO Pen (medium) ⑧ RISO Pen (bold) ⑨ Ink blocking ⑩ Separating tape ⑪ Drawing paper B5 ⑫ Owner's guide

**SPECIFICATIONS:**
●Printing area: 160 × 230mm ●Dimensions: 310(W) × 430(D) × 170(H)mm (including lamp housing) ●Weight: 5kg ●Power supply: Three "C" size batteries (1.5V)

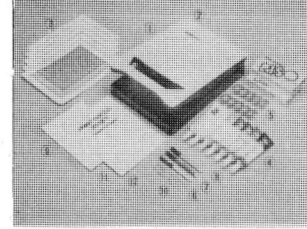

●One set only is required from making a PRINT GOCCO MASTER to printing ●Cut illustrations, printed materials and your own graphics can all be used as an original ●Can be used by everyone: just press the handle ●One touch, multicolor printing: you can even mix the 7 supplied colors to produce your own favorite shades ●No worry about ink-soiled hands ●80—100 prints can be made from one ink filling ●30—50 sheets of paper can be set at one time to increase printing speed

*wedding invitations, postcards, tea towels, even a mirror. Although the image area is fairly small, you can feed a larger piece of paper or cloth through and print a bit at a time.*

*Do get* **The Gocco Guide** *with your printer (the original instructions are translated somewhat idiosyncratically from Japanese). Its step-by-step directions are very clear and it's loaded with tips and hints culled from two experienced users.*

—Sarah Satterlee

## Why I Love My Used Copy Machine

*by Tom Ferguson*

I relied on an outside copy service for my first ten years as a full time writer. I didn't really think I needed my own copier — I only averaged 30-50 copies per week, and that only meant a trip or two to my local copy shop.

Then about a year ago my wife Meredith received a small Canon Personal Copier as a present, and we suddenly found dozens of new ways to use it: Meredith used it for her archeology research. I brought my "to copy" file home each night. Our daughter Adrienne made copies of her notes for for her friends at school. And friends began dropping over regularly "to use your copy machine." It was small, convenient, and quite nice to have around. I once overheard my wife, on the phone, telling a friend that her new copier was "even cuter than my husband."

We didn't know how we'd managed without it. Since it was now much more convenient to make copies, I soon found myself averaging 60-100 copies per week. And I began to think of how convenient it would be if I had another machine at the office.

It wasn't just laziness. Sometimes I'd be sending out a letter, and would want to enclose a copy of the article I'd just written. But it wasn't important enough to make it worth holding the letter until I could get home to make a copy. I realized that there would be even more uses for a copier if I had one at the office. So finally the day came when I began to shop for an office copier.

My first thought was to get another Canon. But in talking to friends and salespeople, I realized that the Canon, wonderful as it was, was a light-duty model. Maximum recommended use was 400-500 copies per month. You were not supposed to leave it on between copies. That meant you had to wait for it to warm up each time you used it. I began looking at some of the small office

models you could leave on all day. They held three or four times as much paper. And they turned out to be a good deal less expensive — half a cent a copy vs. two to three cents per copy for the Canon.

After visiting several local copier stores, I fell in love with a small Toshiba. There was only one problem — it listed for $1695. The Canon had been around $700.

I decided to ask about used models. Now copier salespeople do not like to talk about used copiers. They would much prefer to sell you a new one. The used copier department is considered a step down in status, like the used car section at an auto dealer. But I finally found found a young saleswoman who seemed to know what I was talking about.

She took me into a back room with an impressive selection of old war-horses. They were slow and boxy, but they all produced beautiful copies, and the price was more than reasonable. I would have been happy to buy one, but I knew they simply would not fit in the small space I had available.

I was about to leave, when the saleswomen "remembered" that they did have a small copier coming in on trade the following week. If I liked, she would give me first shot at it. It would be selling for $800.

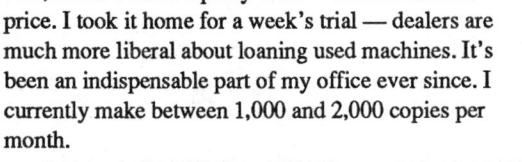

It turned out to be the little Toshiba I liked — in a older-model case they had made for 3M. It was not quite as cute, but it worked equally well — and for half the price. I took it home for a week's trial — dealers are much more liberal about loaning used machines. It's been an indispensable part of my office ever since. I currently make between 1,000 and 2,000 copies per month.

## Copier Half-tone Alternatives

Copyscreen is available at most art supply stores, or for **$3.25** from Dot Pasteup Supplies, 1612 California St., P.O. Box 369, Omaha, NE 68101; 800/228-7272.

*A half-tone is a photo that has been rephotographed behind a black dot matrix; this breaks the image into individual dots so that it can later be reproduced in newspapers and magazines. Copyscreen is a clever variation on this idea, using a white dot matrix to simulate the half-tone process. Just place a Copyscreen onto the glass surface of any good copying machine and voila! — near half-tone quality for the five to fifteen cents it costs you for a regular copy. This is a great tool for making quick xeroxes for friends, and for little magazines that would like to run photos, but can't afford photostats.*

*— Richard Kadrey*

The top smile was copied unscreened, the middle using Copyscreen-1, a 65-line screen, and the bottom with Copyscreen-2, an 85-line screen.

## Canon PC-20 Personal Copier

Suggested retail **$1,095**; actually available for far less (down to about **$700**). Check local Canon dealers and discount office-supply outfits. Cartridges containing toner in assorted colors, drum and developer are about **$80**.

*I've come to believe that a personal copier is as important as a personal computer for doing research, writing, almost any intellectual activity. Having one vastly accelerated a book project for me — I copied notes from my notebooks and quotes from books and taped them onto 5 x 8 cards, and those cards became the handy coin of the book's realm. I share information more now, because it's so easy to knock out a copy for someone, and I file stuff more reliably in multiple versions. A copier is even invaluable around the home — copy the recipe from a bulky cookbook, copy the portion of the map you're driving on today, make a copy of Auntie's postcard or Junior's theme for Mom.*

*The great thing about the small copiers that have much of their high-tech in disposable cartridges is that they so seldom break down or even need fiddling with. In over a year of intense use I've had zero problems with my Canon. Limitation for artists and jokers: because the platen moves, it's hard to make copies of your body parts. The machine doesn't enlarge or reduce or collate or work at high speed, but who cares? I can cart it around (with a little puffing), and its feed tray eliminates hand-feeding of paper. Not a cheap appliance, but its value is enormous, way more than I expected.*

*— Stewart Brand*

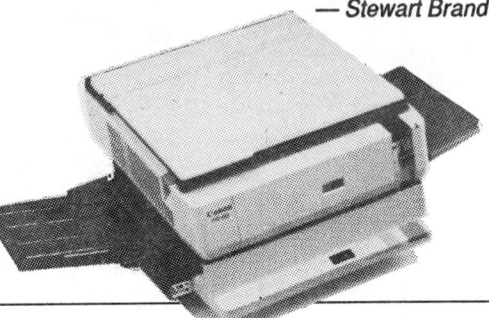

## XEROX ART MAGAZINES

*Look at xerox art magazines for art and design ideas and for a dreamlike glimpse into the events of the artist's unconscious, love life, or neighborhood. Here is ample inspiration for your own xerox publishing efforts — on a one-time or ongoing basis. These highly eclectic personal expressions are difficult to evaluate for an audience greater than one. So when reading through the reviews in* **Fact Sheet Five**, **Sound Choice**, *or other magazines, take note of what sounds fun and order away. Experimentation is the rule here, for readers and publishers alike. Here are three I like:*

*Box of Water: Distinct, bold images, many of them xeroxed drawings rather than the ubiquitous collages, on heavy grey paper. Also with "textual experimentations." Contact addresses for all contributors, 'zine reviews, and information on current xerox art compilations and mail art catalogs. More elegant than the usual fare.*

**Box of Water**: Stephen Perkins, Editor. **$5** (2 issues) from 135 Cole Street, San Francisco, CA 94117.

*False Positive: Editor Donna Kossy uses a high-quality copier and takes full advantage of it with good paper and superb color-xerox covers. This mix of Kossy's collages and "black humor, off-beat ideologies, and anomalous art" is actually coherent, unlike many other 'zines that might be described the same way. Oh she's sarcastic. I love it.*

**False Positive:** Donna Kossy, Editor. **$10** (4 issues) from Out-of-Control Data Korporation, PO Box 432, Boston, MA 02258.

*PhotoStatic Magazine: A collection of xerox art broadsides of every possible style with short notes about the artists. Vaguely related by theme.*

**PhotoStatic Magazine**: Lloyd Dunn, Editor. **$6**/year (6 issues) from 330 South Linn Street, Iowa City, IA 52240.

— *Jeanne Carstensen*

## Instant Litter

(Concert Posters from Seattle Punk Culture)
Art Chantry
1985; 112 pp.
**$10**
($11 postpaid) from:
The Real Comet Press
3131 Western Ave. 410
Seattle, WA 98121
206/283-7827

*The ultimate disposable art: xerox posters for garage bands, stapled to telephone poles. Art Chantry of Seattle was so struck by a phenomenon he calls "more a community primal scream than advertising" that he began to collect and research the posters of the Seattle punk music scene.*

*The result,* **Instant Litter**, *is strange and wonderful and disturbing, filled with the manipulation of innocent middle-class images to display the frank and explosive energy of middle-class fugitives. Whenever possible the posters are deciphered by source and the history of the band; over 150 reproductions.*

— *Sallie Tisdale*

## Work Hard and You Shall Be Rewarded

Alan Dundes
and Carl R. Pagter
1978; 223 pp.
**$6.95**
($8.45 postpaid) from:
Indiana University Press
10th and Morton Streets
Bloomington, IN 47405
812/335-5429
or Whole Earth Access

## When You're Up To Your Ass in Alligators

Alan Dundes
and Carl R. Pagter
1987; 272 pp.
**$9.95**
($11.95 postpaid) from:
Wayne State
University Press
Detroit, MI 48202
313/577-4603
or Whole Earth Access

*Every office I have ever been in has at least one corner plastered with cartoons, doggerel, and folk art made possible by the xerox machine. Taped on walls and bulletin boards, circulated by friends, these half-serious postings are galleries for a national communications channel that touches nearly everyone. Like all folklore, they are unexamined messages from the culture's subconscious. The material which gets passed around the most is often racist, pornographic, or anti-bureaucratic — socially acceptable ways of confronting the tabooed and the feared. These two collections, accurately subtitled "Urban Folklore from the Paperwork Empire," relay the quiet shift from an oral folklore to an inked folklore, driven by the inventions of typewriters, copy machines, and instant printers.*

— *Kevin Kelly*

Performance, xerox, and mail artist Tom Patrick
— he says "posturban artist" — has taught
xerox art at U.C. Berkeley. —Jeanne Carstensen

## XEROGRAPHY BY TOM PATRICK

**BLACK AND WHITE**
1. Making letterhead stationery in exactly the quantities needed.
2. Copying careworn phone lists onto strong paper.
3. Moving and editing text without a computer (cut and paste!).

4. Copying my kid's best drawing before he mails it away.
5. Cheaply enlarging or reducing (Kodak copier recommended).
6. Culling images I need for art projects without having to tear up large numbers of books and magazines.

7. Experimenting! For instance, by making acetate xeroxes of drawings and laying them over either the original or another design, moires and delightful juxtapositions can be generated. Or, combine several sizes of the same image.

A Thermofax copier (at many schools) with special coated cloth can make small silk screens of these xeroxes.
COLOR (Canon copier recommended)
8. Sharing a sketch with a friend — even if it's a watercolor.
9. Instant photography of small treasures.

10. Outrageous art! like collage, yet it allows 3-D objects and manipulations while the machine slowly scans each color.
11. Copying old color photos before they fade.

12. Giving each of my children a copy of the childhood photo album. Expensive, but invaluable.
All this, without the computer user's up-front capital expense.

## XEROX ART

It's a quick way of visual thinking, and your inspiration need only last seconds. As a reproductive tool, the xerox machine is fast, cheap, and versatile, making freedom of expression possible instantaneously. It's creativity at the push of a button.

You can make posters, books, magazines, postcards, to name just a few possibilities, and multiply your original designs to unlimited quantities.

## MATERIALS

Pictures from magazines, photographs, cloth, feathers, paper scraps, found objects, your elbow; any material you want to arrange on the copier window.

## BLACK AND WHITE

My favorite B&W copiers are the Kodak 9400 and 9500; they are efficient and give bold, clean copies. But sometimes I want my copies softer and grayish — that's when I seek out an old, funky Savin copier or one of its equivalents. These machines still use the original "wet" process to make copies, which produces the softer look.

Many black & white copiers let you reduce (down to about 40 percent of the original size) or enlarge (up to 400 percent) in one shot.

Panels, posters, and even billboards are possible with multiple enlargements. Doing enlargements can be expensive, though, anywhere from 50¢ to $7 per copy. Reduction costs about 20¢ per copy and regular copies range from 2.5 to 15¢ each. Shop around.

## SOME TECHNIQUES

After you arrange your materials on the copier glass, experiment with different ways of reproducing what's lying on the glass.
CHOICE OF COPIER — As mentioned above, some copiers produce crisp, bold images while others come out soft and grey. Know your machines.
ONE-OF-A-KIND COPIES — Unpredictable "actions" and events may leave you with an original, the image that only you have a copy of. "Mistakes" often lead to new techniques and discoveries about the machine.

**COPY MOTION** — Moving the image on the screen while the camera is working. Older machines with a slow-scanning light bar work particularly well, humorously elongating the image. Also works with color machines since they use the same scanning light bar technology.

**DEGENERATION** — Simply degenerating the sharpness of an image by making copies of the preceding copy, ad infinitum. Or first reducing, then enlarging.

**FOCAL DISTANCE** — Play with holding items you're copying at different distances from the glass. The glass is the focal plane, so items flush against it are in perfect focus. They get blurrier the farther away from the glass they are. ►

# Mail Art

*by Jeanne Carstensen*

*Of all the things I've lost I miss my mind the most.*

The mail art network, or just "The Network" as it's often referred to, is a grassroots, global association of artists who communicate via the post. If the medium is mailable, it can be mail art; xerox art, artist's books, postcards, audio and video art, original postage stamps, language art, recycling art and "zines" all qualify. Every mail artist has a LIST, the canvas of geographically remote names and addresses upon which she or he works. They're culled from mail art 'zines, friends, and from the mail art the artist receives from being on someone else's list.

Why do talented artists, incessant communicators, and nice people flood the post with their mailable art? Because mail art satisfies a basic need for communication. Mail art is the flowering of the postal system, its creative fulfillment. And who doesn't lust after mail?

To get involved in the mail art network all you need is names of mail artists and time to send out your work and keep corresponding. The quarterly **Fact Sheet Five** (page 40) has hundreds of "zine" reviews in each issue. If you're going to subscribe to one publication, that's the one.

Here's a list of mail art magazines compiled by San Francisco mail, xerox, and performance artist Stephen Perkins; it's by no means comprehensive.

## ND
**$5/year (3 issues) from:**
P. O. Box 4144, Austin, TX 78765

## Foist
**$5/year (2 issues) from:**
Collective Foist, P. O. Box 44, Penfield, NY 14526

## Spiegelman's Mail Art Rag
Send SASE for information:
Lon Spiegelman,1556 Elevado Street, Los Angeles, CA 90026

## Kaldron
**$5/year (1 issue per year) from:**
Kaldron, P. O. Box 7036, Halcyon, CA 93420

## Compilation magazines:
Write to the individual magazines for deadlines, themes, etc.; include SASE, or an International Reply Coupon (available at your local post office).

## Alto
Cas, Post-74, I-37066 Sommacampagna, Verona, Italy

## Level
P. O. Box 50164, Indianapolis, IN 46256

## Mani Art
Pascal Lenoir, Rue Dumage, 60570 Andeville, France

*Using a house shape for an accordian book, artist Sheril Cunning rubber-stamped a visual story inside.*

Ed Varney, *2nd International Intermedia Artists' Stamp Edition*, Canada, 1978. Artists' stamps.

## Rubberstampmadness
RSM Enterprises, P. O. Box 6585, Ithaca, NY 14851. **$15**/year (6 issues)

*A few years ago, artists realized the value of being able to produce single images over and over and started designing their own rubber stamps. Since then, they have become a mainstay of mail art. **Rubberstampmadness** is the best the single source for all things rubber and stampable. Their how-to articles inspire you to new heights of stamping artistry, while their ads hawk stamps with images of everything from teddy bears and rainbows to Balinese masks and computer terminals.*
— *Richard Kadrey*

## Correspondence Art
Michael Crane and Mary Stofflet, Editors.
**$15.95**
($17.95 postpaid) from:
Contemporary Arts Press,
P. O. Box 3123,
Rincon Annex,
San Francisco, CA 94119
415/431-7672
or Whole Earth Access

*Should you want to gaze back on Network activity through 1983 expertly frozen in an anthology of primary documents, **Correspondence Art** is more than just competent. Here is the international art-scene view of mail art in DETAIL, as told by the Network's more famous participants in manifestos, short art-history-type articles, and examples of their mail art.*
— *Jeanne Carstensen*

# Unhurried Communication: A Conferencing System Without Computers

*by Ann Weiser*

Discussion groups that meet by mail are a cheap, accessible means of group communication. They're computer conferences without the computer, available for the price of a postage stamp. We call them many-to-manys. The simple recipe goes like this: a many-to-many usually has from twenty to fifty members. One person is the "Organizing Editor." By a given deadline, each person writes a letter about the same topic and sends it to the editor. The editor adds his/her own letter and a cover page listing the members and setting the next deadline, copies the letters, and sends a set to each member.

Now comes the fun part: by the next deadline, each member writes another letter that includes comments and responses to the letters people wrote before. So it becomes an ongoing, participatory, interactive group conversation by mail. And each person appears in their own typeface — even in their own handwriting if they want — because the pages are copied as is, no editing. It's easy to add pictures, sketches, diagrams.

Who pays for this? Each person sends the editor a deposit, usually $5 at a time, to be used for their own postage and copying costs. The editor keeps track of the money and lets the participants know when they need to send more. Depending on the number of people who write each time, and how cheaply the editor can get copying done where he or she lives, many-to-manys can range in cost from 50¢ to $1.50 per person per issue. A lot cheaper than computer conferences!

But other than cost, how do many-to-manys compare with computer conferencing? We've found that a lot of people still don't have computers, or if they have computers they don't have modems. If even one person in a group doesn't have a modem, that group can't communicate by computer. But it can communicate by many-to-many.

Other advantages of a many-to-many compared to a computer: it's easier to send "right brain stuff": pictures, diagrams, sketches, handwriting. Not everyone's page looks alike. You can even pick up a sense of personality from typewriter styles!

Also, there are advantages (and disadvantages) to the monthly rhythm of a many-to-many. A computer conference is continuous. Any time you look there may be more of it. But a many-to-many has one deadline that everybody writes by. Then you get one packet in the mail and that's all of it for the month. You can hold it in your hand, get a feel of the whole of it, respond to that wholeness. ("The June pages felt very interconnected.") Computer conferences are praised for being asynchronous: one person can write in the afternoon, and another at 3:00 a.m., and it's all part of the same thing. Well, many-to-manys are asynchronous, too. You can write your page in your own time, in your own way, as long as it shows up in the editor's mailbox by the deadline.

Many-to-manys grew out of APAs, the amateur press

associations used by science fiction fans to trade amateur magazines and discuss every subject under the sun. I had been a science fiction fan and had belonged to several APAs when I went to a conference led by Robert Theobald called "Values and the Future." Fifty of us were frustrated to find that at the end of two days there was so much left to say about the subject. I described the APA format and talked about how, unlike a newsletter, it would allow "many-to-many" communication rather than "one-to-many." Someone seized on that phrase and that's how the many-to-many (M2M for short) got its name.

Futurist Robert Theobald joined and participated in that first M2M. When he saw the results, he asked me to help start more M2Ms as part of his fledgling organization Linkage, now called Action Linkage.

One thing I love about many-to-manys is their variety. They come in all kinds and sizes, with all kinds of social structures, almost like miniature societies. In one, the editor sets a question each time for the members to respond to the next time. In another, the editor spends two or three pages at the beginning of every issue summarizing the contents, which gives a sense of orientation. The editor also writes personal notes in red ink on each person's copy, another way of encouraging involvement.

We even have a Computer Many-to-Many, showing that computers and M2Ms can coexist peaceably. Many of the participants are involved in computer conferencing elsewhere, but contribute to the Computer M2M for the benefit of those who want to talk about the impact of computers on society, but don't yet have computers and modems. We also have The M2M on M2Ms, which discusses ways to improve the M2M form. There are lots of ideas for improving the ability of M2M groups to focus on tasks together, develop topics, and create consensus on issues. And we're just beginning.

Altogether, Action Linkage has about fourteen M2Ms. I've heard that at the time of the American Revolution there were Committees of Correspondence, which operated through the mail in round-robin letter format. I'd like to think of us as their communicational heirs.

---

*Ann Weiser is the coordinator for Action Linkage, a network of activists teasing out ways to enhance group brainstorming. You can get the booklet **Letter Groups** for $5 postpaid from Action Linkage, 5825 Telegraph Ave. #45, Oakland, CA 94609.*

—Kevin Kelly

# The Circle Letter

*by Rhoda Weber Mack*

The circle letter is a traveling salon, a soft-tech conference session, a recall of a lost art form — the well-written letter. It is useful for keeping community with scattered friends and colleagues, for keeping lives current, or for playing mental handball with ideas. We use this one for our eight-sibling family, to keep the common conversation intact, and to take the heat off the homeplace as bulletin board.

Here's the starter: write your own letter, and mail it with a list of mail stops to the next in line, who inserts his/her own letter along with yours, to the next stop. Etcetera all the way back to you. Now, read the fat contents with relish, withdraw your old letter, add a new one, and mail it on. Full circle.

My old circle letters add up to a diary of our days, forgotten moments with our children, moods of summer afternoons or wintry mornings long ago when I sat down to add my commentary to the family circle letter.

---

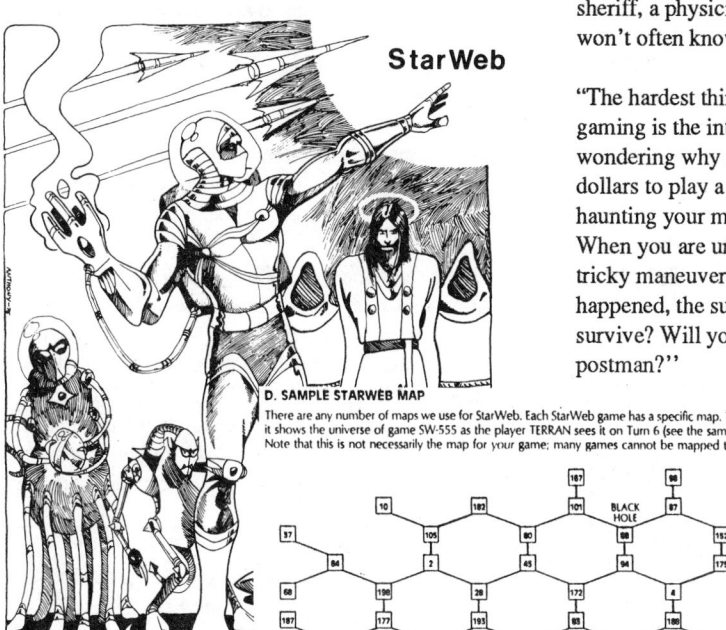

# Play-by-Mail Games

*by Kevin Kelly*

These were my instructions: "You are a religious fanatic. Your purpose is to convert the entire galaxy to your particular point of view. Each of your converts has a 10-percent chance of converting the whole of that planet. Other players may win back your converts by unloading consumer goods on them." There were 200 other characters battling for the same worlds I was, and I had to have my next move in the mail, postmarked by tomorrow.

Play-by-mail games are widespread, but hidden by the privacy of first class envelopes. The first play-by-mail games were probably unfinished games of Chess or Go extended by messages between two players. Then as other strategy games came along, ones which demanded careful moves that could be easily relayed on paper, it was natural to try them by post. By the seventies, entire stores were devoted to room-size strategy board games, a few of which might be played by mail. The stores were also incubators for the peculiar teenage phenomenon of role-playing games, like Dungeons and Dragons.

Games-by-mail today combine the logical challenge of the computer with the intrigue of role playing. Rick Loomis, who invented this genre of game-by-mail in 1970 and now runs Flying Buffalo, the most reliable play-by-mail commercial service, describes the general procedure:

"The concept is simple: you send written instructions for each turn to the game company. The company processes and plots out the results. It reports back your new position, and acts as moderator and referee.

"Your role in the game will vary according to the game setting. Thus, you might be a feudal baron, a chieftain of a nomadic tribe, or—in the case of Illuminati—the wise and crafty leader of a great conspiracy to take over the world.

"For $2 or so, you get a rulebook, background materials, and instructions for filling out your turn sheets. At this point, games begin to differ in what they demand of you. There are games where you have to remember lots of codes to enter on your turn-sheet, and games where you write out long essays detailing what you want your character to do.

"After processing your turn, the game company will send you between one-half and ten pages of information about your turn. Most likely it will come back as a computer printout that will tell you what happened, either in code, in English, or something in between. Then you fill out another turnsheet based on these results, and send it back to the game company for another round. The usual cycle is every two weeks, or

every month if you live overseas. (You also can request slow or fast modes of the games.) The company charges about $3 for each turn. Many have a credit accounting system, and debit you each play. You can also buy a lifetime "play" for about $500, which allows you to keep scheming forever.

"Games vary a great deal in terms of the amount of inter-player communication. Players in 'no-diplomacy' (or 'anonymous') games compete, but are not allowed to communicate or make deals with each other outside the game. At the other extreme, the biggest 'full-diplomacy' games have elaborate alliances, player-run

organizations, and often their own newsletters. Many play-by-mail alliances span continents, and occasionally generations, and last for years. The games have their own histories as well. StarWeb, one of the most successful play-by-mail games, has completed over a thousand cycles of its interstellar contest.

"There are about 10,000 players involved in games at the moment. Although there has been a big push for the last five years urging people to send their turns via computer networks like CompuServe or MCI Mail, only about 10 percent do so. The computers which run the games are invisible, and don't interest players. Play-by-mail gamers like mail. They can forward a message to other players with their move, swapping addresses. Pretty soon they have a mailbox full of personal, passionate mail.

"One of the fascinating things about play-by-mail games is that the backgrounds of the players are so diverse. Your allies may include a student, a county sheriff, a physicist, and a Shakespearean actor, but you won't often know, or care.

"The hardest thing to describe about play-by-mail gaming is the intensity of the experience. You start out wondering why any sensible person would pay three dollars to play a game, but within weeks you are haunting your mailbox, waiting for your next turn. When you are under attack, or you have just sent off a tricky maneuver, and you are waiting to see what happened, the suspense is tremendous. Will you survive? Will your plan work? Where's that lazy postman?''

**StarWeb**

**D. SAMPLE STARWEB MAP**

There are any number of maps we use for StarWeb. Each StarWeb game has a specific map. The map below is only a sample; it shows the universe of game SW-555 as the player TERRAN sees it on Turn 6 (see the sample printout on the facing page). Note that this is not necessarily the map for *your* game; many games cannot be mapped this neatly.

## Access to Play-By-Mail Games

*It takes a long time to play a PBM game: months, years. I have played in three games, each very different from another, and recommend all of them.*

*Feudal Lords (Graaf Simulations) is a game of economic development, diplomatic intrigue, and military adventuring set in England, A.D. 801. You begin as a Baron of one of 46 fiefdoms and as one of 15 players. The computer controls the other 31 fiefs. Your job is to build up your fief and acquire control over other fiefs. Each fiefdom has basic economic resources; you must carefully develop your economy while building your military and political strength. Diplomacy is essential if you want to survive and thrive in this excellent simulation of a feudal society. Cost: rules $2.50. Setup $10 (includes three turns). Turn fee $3. Turn frequency every three weeks. Graaf Simulations, 27530 Harper, St. Clair Shores, MI 48081.*

*Heroic Fantasy (Flying Buffalo): Design a team of adventurers and send them into the labyrinth. Guide them as they explore, overcome adversity, contend with the labyrinthian guardians, search for fame, glory, and treasure, treasure, treasure. HF has a little of the flavor of a "kill and loot" role-playing game, but without the social interaction. Cost: rules $2.50. Setup $5. Turn fee $2.50. Turn frequency every two weeks, once a month, or once a week (electronic mail).*

*The classic PBM game, StarWeb (Flying Buffalo) is a strategic space game in a network of 255 star systems. You begin knowing only one, build spaceship fleets, explore connecting systems, capture worlds, locate other players and negotiate with them. Try a slow game and you will probably meet people worldwide. Cost: rules $2. Setup $5. Deposit $5. Turn fee $4. Turn frequency every three weeks, once a month (slow game), or once a week (electronic mail). Flying Buffalo, Inc., P.O. Box 1467, Scottsdale, AZ 85252-1467.*

*Play-by-mail game masters come and go with great irregularity. For a list of reliable companies, send a self-addressed, stamped envelope to Play-By-Mail Association (PBMA), 8149 E. Thomas Road, Scottsdale, AZ 85252.* —Bob Albretch

## Computer Adventure Games

*by Sarah Vandershaf*

The first time I ever played a computer game was at a MacWorld show in San Francisco. I wandered aimlessly from booth to booth and finally stopped at a Mac with an odd picture on its screen: trees, a door, a skull mounted above the door. Immediately a sales rep in a three-piece suit (who had probably seen too many potential customers walk away from the game in frustration) flew to my side. He grabbed the mouse, aimed the pointer, and double-clicked on the skull. The skull rose, revealing a key underneath. *Things move!* "Now you can go in," the sales rep said.

And I never came out. That first one (which you game mavens no doubt recognize as *Shadowgate*) hooked me on computer games forever. I solved it, got two other games developed by *Shadowgate's* creators, solved them, and then started sniffing around for still more games to devour. But I was far from omnivorous; I ignored arcade-type games, computer versions of familiar board games (chess, bridge, Monopoly), and flight simulators. Adventure games. All I wanted was the adventure games.

Adventure games usually fall into one of three categories: text-only games (no pictures); games that, like *Shadowgate*, combine text and pictures with a single, unseen actor (you); and advanced role-playing games with text, pictures, and multiple on-screen characters. For those of you who have never played a computer game, the text-only games are like reading a novel that talks back to you; the text-picture games are like watching an animated cartoon that you can,

to some extent, control.

Computer games do tend to usurp other media. I have cut down on my fiction reading (bad) and completely forgotten about television (good!) since becoming a computer-game addict. Most of the games imitate — or parody — familiar literary genres. In my short gaming career, I have been a hard-boiled detective, a traveler stranded in a haunted mansion, a brave knight battling the minions of an evil wizard, and the heroine of a historical romance set on a pirate-infested Caribbean isle.

Game addictions are strictly a matter of personal taste. Since I started with a text-picture game on a black and white Mac monitor, I'll probably prefer that combination forever after. You can get *Shadowgate* and other games in color if you have an Amiga (games often come in multiple versions to accommodate different types of computers). And, of course, you could forget graphics altogether and go for the all-text games.

I admit I don't understand why anyone would prefer a game without pictures to one with — there's something about the graphics-text games that draws you into their little worlds more completely than words alone can.

For instance, in the scene above from *Uninvited* (the aforementioned haunted-house game and sister to *Shadowgate*), the immediate challenge is to get past the odd creature blocking your path to the middle door. Above the scene is a menu of actions ("examine," "operate," etc.) you can perform on the creature using the objects in the inventory or anything you can find lying around the room. You could try "hitting" the creature with the

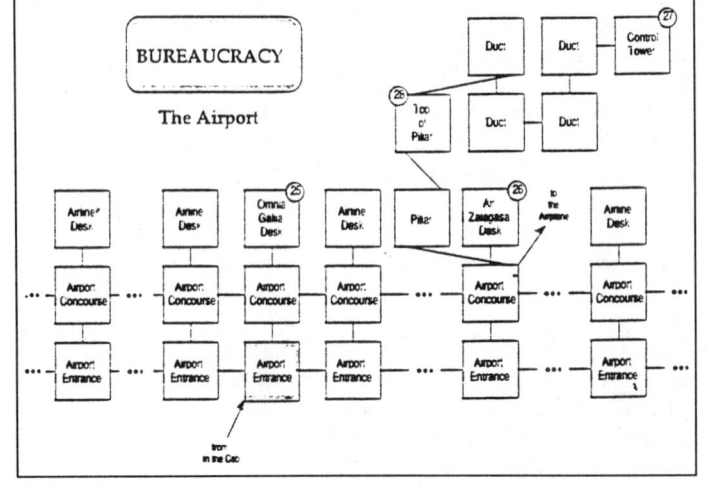

This elongated room contains three doorways.

A strange, hideous creature stares at you.

Mr. Wigglewort is just one of many helpful and good-natured creatures you will encounter in *Uninvited*. He likes the music of Rudy Vallee.

axe. Or perhaps "operating" the Victrola will work (music hath charms . . . ?). If the beast remains unfazed, you can explore other rooms, dropping old things from the inventory and bringing back new things until you hit upon the right combination (the creature's behavior gives you a hint). It seems silly, but when you do get through that door at last, you feel like you've really *accomplished* something.

So, whether you want to explore an emerging new entertainment medium or simply have thousands of hours of your life to waste, here are several great adventure games with which to begin your own addiction:

Text-only games: *Zork I & II, Moonmist, The Hitchhiker's Guide to the Galaxy, Bureaucracy.* Catalog **free** from Infocom, Inc., P.O. Box 478, Cresskill, NJ 07626; 800/262-6868

Graphics-text games: *Uninvited, Shadowgate.* Catalog **free** from Mindscape, Inc., 3444 Dundee Road, Northbrook, IL 60062; 800/221-9884

---

## Keys to Solving Computer Adventure Games

M.K. Simon
Book I
1987; 286 pp.
Book II
1988; 292 pp.
**$19.95**
($23.95 postpaid)
Each from:
Prentice-Hall
Attn.: Mail Order Sales
200 Old Tappan Road
Old Tappan, NJ 07675
201/767-5937
or Whole Earth Access

*You buy a brand new game, play it for a while with no serious problems, and then it happens. YOU'RE STUCK! Really stuck. You try everything you can think of, but the answer eludes you. After a week of frustration, you're willing to do anything to get the solution. Even willing to buy the hint book produced by the game's manufacturer — for $10 or so.*

*Or you can buy these books, which give you maps and exact solutions to nearly four dozen recently-released games (as solved by the author, who*

*apparently plays these games a lot). If you, too, play adventure games a lot, these volumes can save you quite a bit of cash. However, be forewarned! Unlike some manufacturer's hint books, which provide levels of solutions from vague clues on up to "Do this, stupid," these books tell you the answers outright. Use only when your desperation exceeds your desire to figure the game out for yourself.*

—SV

◆

*Book I*: A View to a Kill, Ballyhoo, Black Cauldron, Borrowed Time, Brimstone, Chalice of Mostania, Crimson Crown, Destiny, Fantastic Four, Forbidden Castle, Fraktured Faebles, King's Quest II, Leather Goddesses of Phobos, Lost Ark of the Covenant, Mickey's Space Adventure, Neverending Story, Oo-Topos (New Version), Rambo, Real Life, Spellbreaker, Tass Times in Tonetown, The Mist, Transylvania (New Version), Trinity, Voodoo Island.

*Book II*: Arazok's Tomb, Breakers, Bureaucracy, Deja Vu, Enchanted Scepters, Essex, Fellowship of the Ring (Parts I & II), Goldfinger, Gunslinger, High Stakes,

Hollywood Hijinx, Indiana Jones, Moonmist (Blue, Green, Red & Yellow Variations), Shadowgate, Space Quest, Stationfall, The Lurking Horror, The Pawn, Uninvited.

You've slain dragons and vanquished villains, but are you ready to do battle with the ultimate Forces of Evil in *Bureaucracy*? It's based on the real-life experiences of the game's author, Douglas Adams, so it could be tougher than you think. This map, from *Keys to Solving Computer Adventure Games: Book II*, may save your life or at least get you waited on faster at the reservations desk.

# The WELL

*by John Coate*

I WORK AT THE WELL, Whole Earth's online computer conferencing network. The WELL itself sits in an air-conditioned closet at the Whole Earth office. A bunch of phone lines come into the building. There's a modem for each phone line. These modems in turn are wired up to a Vax computer. The Vax is about the size of a large dishwasher. We can handle up to 23 callers at a time, which we often do with over a thousand people logging in each month. When people visit us they like to go in and look at the equipment. When you see the lights on the modems flickering you know that conversations are happening. Minds are meeting.

Personal computers are amazing communication tools. Put a computer together with a modem and you can converse simultaneously with several people, collaborate on writing projects, find work, gather and refine ideas, get technical updates, swap some stories, argue politics, and get a recommendation on a good restaurant and movie without getting up from your desk. Online conferencing networks can be both a place where you meet people — like a neighborhood pub — and a tool for gathering and storing information.

As I sit at my desk in the WELL office shuttling between conferences, doing mail, writing pieces like this one, and talking online as well as on the phone to new users, I check to see who is logged in every few minutes. I know most of the names. Because we have had a lot of social gatherings I know many faces to go along with the names. Many have become my good friends.

Sometimes when I'm working I feel like I'm in the wheelhouse of a big Mississippi riverboat. On the decks people are strolling and talking as they lean against the rail. There's a casino and parlors and places to eat. Way down below they're talking shop with the machinists. There are regulars and newcomers. Everyone has a unique point of view. Sometimes it's choppy, but usually it's steady as she goes.

WELL stands for Whole Earth 'Lectronic Link. It's the collaborative brainchild of Whole Earth's Stewart Brand and Larry Brilliant, best known for his work with the SEVA Foundation and head of Network Technologies (NETI). Whole Earth and NETI each own half of the WELL. After spending time working on projects through the EIES network, Stewart and Larry conceived the WELL as a place where a variety of people could meet online without spending an arm and a leg. Early on Stewart said the WELL is the "kind of thing coffee shops were supposed to be about, but are pretty hard to find these days."

Although there is a lot of useful information stored on the WELL like in a library, it is through conversing in conferences, electronic mail (email) and real-time that the fabric of the community is knit.

There are over ninety WELL conferences. Some are computer specific, some are technical, and some consist

John Coate [left], on-line party host and Welcome Wagon Chairman; Cliff Figallo [right], WELLville Town Supervisor. Respectively, "tex" and "fig" on the WELL.

of people throwing out their ideas, telling their stories or arguing social and political issues. After talking with people about all kinds of different things over time you get the feeling that you know that person even if you have never met face to face.

So you cruise around to different conferences and you find out what people think about things. The information moves "horizontally" among the peer group of the participants. Anyone can start a discussion topic in a conference. Topics can be linked between different conferences. After awhile I think the word "community" begins to describe what goes on better than does "network." In a community, the interactions are ongoing. You run into some of the same people every day. Over time, professional and personal interaction can overlap. There becomes a sense of place to it. It often reminds me of an electronic Greenwich Village. Logging in can be like going down to the street to check the action.

We don't have a lot of rules; we manage the WELL in a very low key style. It really can't be done any other way. The keystone of the WELL organization is the conference hosts. Every conference has a host. That word was very deliberately chosen. Public online conferences are a lot like ongoing parties and someone has to make sure there's ice in the cooler, food on the table, continuity in the discussions, and good general organization.

Online conferencing is talking by writing. You set up your context, get to the point, and get out. Because it's a conversation between sometimes fairly large groups, you don't want to "dominate the rap" and you don't want to be repetitive. You have to remember that people are looking at computer screens, which seem to put unique demands on people's ability to focus on long-winded pieces. If your "posting" runs longer than one or two screen lengths, it had better be pretty interesting. And you will hear from people if they think you ramble too much.

The flip side of that, though, is if you have a good story to tell or enjoy quality repartee, or can lay out and quickly back up an argument or insight, then the chemistry can be there for a kind of ad hoc think tank that has soul and is fun. We talk about everything from war and law, music, work, birth, death, where this "info age" is

going, and AIDS to online talk shows, tales of past experiences and exploits, online gift notifications (better known as Pokeybux), your thoughts on human relationships, bugs in the latest version of PageMaker, reports of WELL weather, the Maddog Improvement Society, and critiques of the latest Grateful Dead show.

Ah yes, the Deadheads. There's plenty of action around the Grateful Dead. The Grateful Dead Conference is the WELL's largest, with people logging in from all over the country. It's mostly good talk, but some online collaboration happens too. Once we designed a WELL T-shirt together. We chose the design, had someone take the money and another person got them printed up.

The WELL is a confluence of social and cultural elements. Similar to Chesapeake Bay, where nine different rivers merge, the WELL's character comes from hackers, writers, artists, Deadheads, knowledge workers, fugitives from the counter-culture, educators, programmers, lawyers, musicians, and many more.

The Info conference, for example, is regularly visited by a magazine editor, a college journalism teacher, an author, a consultant to a state assembly committee, an info age muckraker, a retired Army colonel turned info age pioneer, a manager from Pacific Bell, a librarian, and members of the Congressional Office of Technology Assessment. We evaluate news, laws, discuss government hearings, and theorize about the forces at play that are attempting to capture their piece of the action as these new information tools become more widespread. It's exciting, relevant stuff because it has to do with basic Constitutional freedoms. In these discussions, age, race, or culture don't matter. Your contribution to the discussion is the only thing that counts.

I think if the WELL establishes one thing it is that meeting through computers doesn't have to be a step in some inexorable march toward an Orwellian society with people droning away at isolated terminals. There is a kind of magic to the fact that real human emotions, "vibes" if you will, can carry through the chips and wires.

If you can get your computer and modem to dial a phone number, you can log in to the WELL. Usually the default settings that come with the communications program work fine. The WELL does cost money to use, but at $8/month + $3/hour the rates are among the lowest in the country for comparable facilities.

Actually, the phone company makes more on this than we do. But we have ways of tipping the balance sheet more in your favor on the cost of the phone call. If you live outside of the San Francisco Bay Area you can save substantial money on the phone call by reaching the WELL via Tymnet. If you live in the Bay Area call us and we'll give you tips on cheaper phone access through special local lines. In addition, the WELL is one of the few places where an individual account has full access the the worldwide UNIX community through USENET and UUCP mail.

To sign up just call 415/332-6106 with your modem and type **newuser** <cr> at the Login: prompt. Or call us at 415/332-4335 if you'd like more information.

# Minitel Report

*by Robert Horvitz*

WHEN THE FRENCH GOVERNMENT said it intended to set up an electronic text and graphical information system accessible nationwide through phonelines by giving a free terminal to anyone willing to do without a yearly paper phonebook, experts snickered. The French had a reputation for art, topless beaches, formal gardens, and poodles — not for high-tech innovation. Attempts to mass-market such systems in more "advanced" countries had all gone sour, and the data format France adopted was incompatible with those used elsewhere. It looked like a sure fiasco.

But now that Le Minitel has grown into the most successful videotex system anywhere, the snickering's stopped: everyone's too busy trying to figure out how to adapt its winning ways.

The free terminals, the handiness of a free electronic "phonebook" with automated search and list capabilities, and the convenience of centralized billing for all Minitel services that aren't free, led to quick and wide acceptance, even by those with no taste for technology. The fact that the first-generation terminals had virtually no memory encouraged news sources and businesses to put information online, because users had to call back each time they needed to look something up, getting billed each time.

Then, sexy-chat "messageries" caught on in a big way, with strangers flirting pseudonymously with each other in the privacy of their own homes. These are still popular, but they really just paved the way for more diverse and practical services, such as teleconferencing, electronic publishing and banking, teleshopping, electronic mail, travel reservations, etc. Over 5,000 services are now available, with more being added every day. More sophisticated (and costly) terminals with memory and color screens, and Minitel emulation packages for personal computers, are rapidly replacing the little freebies that primed the pump. With over 3 million registered users in France, Minitel is now spreading to other countries — though nearly all the services offered still assume fluency in French.

For information on access from the US, call MinitelNet Service at 800/822-6638; from Canada, call 212/307-5510. As of mid-1988, six hours of access from the US costs **$150** ($25/hour). MinitelNet also sells terminal emulation software for Macintosh and PC-type computers ($49 - $99).

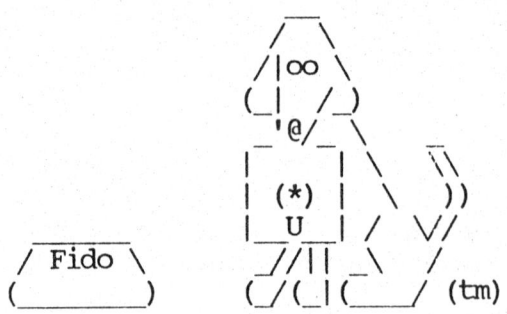

## FidoNet

Information **free** from: IFNA (International FidoNet Association, P. O. Box 41142, St. Louis, MO 63141; 314/576-4067 (voice)

*FidoNet is sort of a poorman's/homegrown Usenet, a loose network of bulletin boards that use Fido compatible software to download data from one system to another. The downloading is usually done at night when phone rates are low; afterwards a user on any BBS connected to FidoNet can read messages from other users on other BBSs. A user can also send messages to any other user on the larger network. It's a way to connect many local community networks into an ad hoc meta-network. The process is called echomail, and besides sending individual messages, there are always several echomail conferences to participate in. FidoNet isn't the prettiest system in the world, but the emphasis here is on information exchange, not techno-flash.*

*— Richard Kadrey*

## Link-Up

Loraine Page, Editor
$22/year
(11 issues) from:
Learned Information, Inc.
143 Old Marlton Pike
Medford, NJ 08055
609/654-6266

*A tabloid with personal writing that keeps track of new computer networks, information services, terminal software, and anything else you need to telecommunicate effectively via personal computer. Some articles pick a topic (investing, psychology, detective work, religion) and describe everything online that's related. Link-Up is also beginning to cover some of the legal and social ramifications of the new telecom technology.*

*— Art Kleiner*

◆

The University of the Pacific's School of Pharmacy offers doctors and psychiatrists drug information via a private service, Drug.Info, on Source Telecomputing. The University's staff reviews most major publications to provide an up-to-the-minute digest of important drug developments. You can quickly scan articles and choose those that appear most significant to your practice. You can then forward the article to your associates via electronic mail.

Before you decide to meet a CompuServer or attend a CompuServe CB party in some faraway city, check out the pix in the CB database. If you are using Compu-Serve's Vidtex communications software, you can download and print digitized pictures of other CompuServers. To get into the database, you send CompuServe a good, sharp 5" x 7" or 8" x 10" black and white photo of your head and shoulders.

## The Complete Handbook of Personal Computer Communications

Alfred Glossbrenner
1985; 512 pp.
**$14.95**
($16.45 postpaid) from:
St. Martin's Press
175 Fifth Avenue
New York, NY 10010
800/221-7945
or Whole Earth Access

*Only book you need. All the lore on how to set up your computer for networking, find the particular networks you need, and connect your computer to someone else's typesetting equipment or directly into another computer. Now in its extensively revised second edition, this book resounds with enthusiasm and clarity.*

*— Art Kleiner*

Industry newsletters of the sort found on NewsNet are really more like private, expert consultations. Most contain "the inside dope" on what's going on in a particular field. And most can tell you what's likely to take place six months from now, what your competition is doing, how national and world events are likely to affect the industry as a whole, and so on. In many cases there will also be commentary and analysis, interviews with key people, advice, tips, and other information — all of it gathered, selected, and filtered through the expertise and experience of the newsletter's creator or editor.

This is the kind of information the general press will never carry. . . . More than 80 percent of all newsletters on the NewsNet system are transmitted directly to the company's Prime computers from the personal computers and communicating word processors of their creators. As a result, you can be reading a newsletter within hours of the time it left its creator's floppy disk.

◆

One of the important features offered by a system like MCI Mail is the option to have your message printed out and delivered by U. S. mail. This is important because it lets you send letters to people who do not have access to a personal computer.

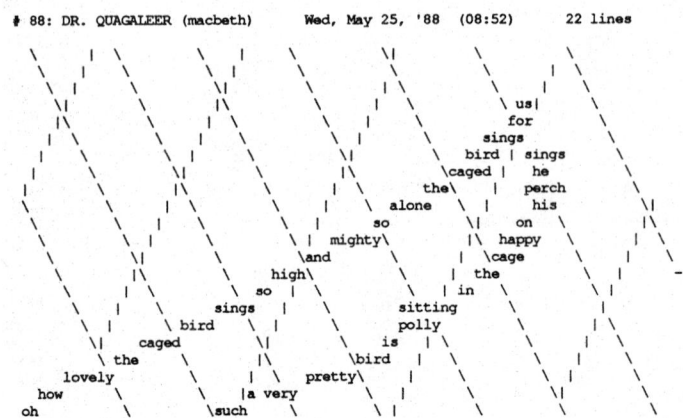

Visual poetry from the WELL's online poetry conference.

# THE ELECTRONIC LANDSCAPE

*by Brock N. Meeks*

With over 3,000 electronic services available to anyone with a modem, personal computer and telephone line, the question of "which one do I use?" often narrows down to "which service most appeals to me on a personal level?"

Below is a "personality sketch," if you will, of several different online services; the sketch is done with a broad brush rather than a detailed pen and ink rendering. You'll find some of these services resemble a large metropolitan city. Others can be likened to a country club atmosphere, and some are strictly business resources.

## CompuServe
Columbus, Ohio; 614/457-8650; **$11.75**/hour

CompuServe is the biggest online service in the nation. With more than 500 different services and forums, and more than 250,000 subscribers, CompuServe is like New York City complete with its ethnic barrios, eclectic culture, and high brow tastes. It is Manhattan, the Bronx and Central Park all rolled into one, 24 hours a day, 365 days a year.

Special Interest Groups (SIGs) draw like minded people together in an electronic meeting place to discuss their personal common denominator, be that Rock Music, Telecommunications, or Assembly Language programming. Each SIG contains a database with a wealth of information and computer programs focusing on the particular special interest.

The most popular service on CompuServe is the "CB Simulator" where hundreds of people "type talk" at each other via their keyboards, from all corners of the world. Participation here is like being in the midst of one giant cocktail party; you can be "vocal" or simply "listen in" by watching the lines of conversation scroll past your screen.

If you're into big cities, CompuServe offers you just that: an impersonal metropolis where you have to ferret out your own comfortable niche.

## The Source
McLean, Virginia; 703/734-7500; **$8.40**/hour for SIGs

If CompuServe is the Hertz of online services, The Source is Avis; they're number two, but they try harder. The Source has SIGs, like CompuServe, but they've never attained the popularity of those on CompuServe. The big drawing point for The Source is the conferencing system structure itself, called Participate, or simply Parti.

Parti allows users to create their own conferences, and here you'll find conferences on every subject imaginable. Because these conferences are run by the users, their stability is often quirky; one week they're flourishing with activity, the next they are silent. At any particular time, Parti is like fraternity party on a Friday night.

The Source also offers organizations the opportunity to set up private conferences for their own private use. This combination of a party like atmosphere and a serious business use gives The Source a "split personality." Because of this, The Source has struggled to really define itself, and maybe why, after all these years, they're still "trying harder."

## Delphi
Cambridge, Massachusetts; 617/491-3393; **$6.60**/hour, direct dial-in after 6 P.M.

Delphi, for a long time, was the only "alternative" online service for those disenchanted with both The Source and CompuServe; a kind of online refugee's retreat. As a result, Delphi developed a very close and loyal following. You either love or hate Delphi, there's not much middle ground.

Delphi's user base has never grown much, topping out at less than 10,000. You'll find SIGs here, but because the user base is smaller, there's definitely more of a "home town" feel to the system.

Easy to use, easy to get used to. You won't find an overwhelming list of services here; but you might just find your electronic home.

## Byte Information Exchange
Peterborough, New Hampshire; 603/924-7323; **$9**/hour, direct dial-in after 6 P.M.

This service is a direct outgrowth from one of the computer industry's most popular publications, BYTE magazine. Byte Information Exchange, or BIX for short, is high tech stomping ground that boasts some of the nation's most brilliant (and outspoken) computer personalities. It is also the home of an award winning online news service called Microbytes Daily, a daily news wire focusing on the computer industry.

If you've got a technical question—about anything—you'll find the answer in any of BIX's freewheeling conferences. This is the computer industry as it used to be: people sharing ideas and solutions without the greed and grit associated with today's corporate driven, litigation-laced industry.

Despite the technical prowess displayed online, the feel of BIX is more like an informal gathering rather than the stuffy academic air that is usually associated with technical discussions.

In addition, BIX has perhaps the largest active group of international users. And BIX isn't just all technical bits and bytes. Like the quirky personalities that made the emerging computer industry one of the most colorful groups around, you'll find conferences here dedicated to anything from cats to current events.

## Whole Earth 'Lectronic Link
Sausalito, California; 415/332-4335; **$8**/month membership, plus **$2**/hour connect charge

Established as an outgrowth of the Whole Earth Catalog, the WELL is a mirror image of the iconoclastic publication. (See page 73 for details).

The WELL's personality is "people first, technology a distant third or fourth." Just how "people-like" is the WELL? A good example are the WELL parties held at regular intervals where members get together face-to-face and carry on the discussions and relationships cultivated online.

WELL users are affectionately referred to as "Wellbeings"; conference moderators are "Fair Witnesses." The system is heavily infused with intellect and compassion; ideology and idealism.

Authors, artists, Silicon Valley hi-tech experts, political activists, all gather here in a passionate give and take of daily debate that makes the WELL one of the most unique systems available.

If you're looking for a stimulating conversation, among an extremely accepting and intelligent populace, this is the place. If you're looking for online shopping, computer programs, or online game playing, you'll have to look elsewhere.

## Chariot
Old Colorado Springs, Colorado; Office 303/632-4848; Online 303/632-4111

Like the WELL, Chariot is a regional-type of system, reflecting the atmosphere of its surrounding area. Based in Old Colorado Springs, CO, this system was spearheaded by one of the legends in the electronic community, Dave Hughes.

Hughes' longstanding passion for the potential of online communications has led to Chariot being the focus of everything from local government to a segment on the McNeil-Lehrer News Hour.

Like the WELL, Chariot has a personality of "home folks" passionately involved in life; the fact that they happen to own a modem is almost an afterthought.

If Chariot is known for anything, it must be the several avenues of "leading edge" applications supported on the system. Packet Radio communications, electronic democracy, and NAPLPS, a sophisticated computer graphics standard that enables the combination of text and graphics to be combined on the same screen, are just a few of the applications promoted. For these applications, and others like them, Chariot is a virtual nationwide clearinghouse of information.

## GEnie
Rockville, Maryland; 301/340-4494; **$5**/hour 6 P.M. - 8 A.M. Monday - Friday, weekends, and holidays

The youngest of the systems noted here, GEnie is quickly emerging as a sophisticated and well respected online service.

It contains a well-rounded offering of services, including SIGs, online news services, and a CB Simulator like CompuServe's.

Because the system is still relatively new, the system has a more friendly feel to it than either The Source or CompuServe. You won't be overwhelmed by esoteric commands needed to navigate the system. The SIGs are small enough so that members know each other and discussions are lively and well attended.

If you're looking for a lot of features, and still want a friendly atmosphere, at a good price, GEnie is a good choice. You won't find the personal level of interaction found on a system like the WELL, but the range of features may draw you into GEnie over a system like the WELL.

## People/Link
Chicago, Illinois; 312/870-4260; **$4.95**/hour 6 P.M. - 8 A.M. Monday - Friday, weekends, and holidays

"Love at first byte" is the motto of People/Link, or Plink, as it is known among its loyal users. It's been called the electronic version of New York's famous Studio 54; on any one night you might find Tom Selleck, Robert Redford, Madonna and Whitney Houston online—all electronic alter-egos, of course.

The system promotes an atmosphere of mirth and myth; advertisements for the system have depicted a nerdy looking accountant transforming himself into an electronic version of Indiana Jones for a foray into Plink's Partyline CB simulator-type service.

There's not much substance here, SIGs are called Club-Links and tend to be superficial, at best, superfluous at worst. However, the system doesn't attempt to camouflage this image. This system is strictly for fun; don't log on here expecting to enter into a serious dialog on SDI.

## Quantum Link
Vienna, Virginia; 703/448-8700; **$9.95**/month for basic services

Quantum Link is somewhat narrow in scope; you have to have a Commodore 64 or 128 computer to log on here. Other machines are locked out due to the way the software is set up. Given that, the system draws from the largest group of Commodore owners: kids. This gives Quantum Link the personality of eternal youth, complete with youths zest for life, and its accompanying foibles and follies.

Online game playing, both solitary and interactive with other members, is a big draw here. Although it's a good source of information for the Commodore computer, it's not much use to anyone over the age of 18.

# The Bulletin Board Proletariat

*by Kevin Kelly*

A VOLUNTEER PROLETARIAT maintains one of the most invisible communication undergrounds going. Linked by phone lines, a web of computer bulletin board systems (BBSs) work night-duty collating messages and electronic mail for free. Regulars patronize small-time BBSs because they can feast on immediate gossip about very specialized subjects. Name a topic and there is almost certainly a BBS dedicated to it somewhere.

To get onto a BBS, you dial a phone number with your computer, and after reading the welcome message, you follow a menu of choices until you arrive at a topic you like. You can then read messages left by others (the bulletin board aspect) and post some of your own by typing them in. The result is a public answering machine, on which anyone can read all messages. Comments are served to you intelligently so that you read only the ones posted since you last checked in, no matter how long that's been. If you've been gone two weeks, you read two weeks' worth, and then you're caught up to the center of what is being said. It'll seem to the other callers that you were there all along, keeping quiet. The sum is a collective conversation that continues for weeks or months, and which happens at your convenience. In theory they stick to one topic. In practice there's enough continuity to keep it informative, and enough diversity to keep it alive.

Any old computer will let you in. You fit it out with a telephone adapter, called a modem (about $100), and plug it into the phone jack. You'll find listings of public BBSs in the back of Computer Shopper ($18/year from Patch Publishing, P.O. Box F, Titusville, FL 32781), in regional tabloids like California's Computer Currents and Microtimes, and at user-group meetings. Once you find one, it'll lead you to many others, board hopping as long-distance as you care to. Pirate boards, the truly underground BBSs where teenage hackers boast of their exploits, appear and disappear so fast they can only be found by hopping.

Propelling much of the drive in regular use of BBSs is the superhighway of PC Pursuit (800/336-0437). Run by Telenet, PC Pursuit lets anyone call BBSs located in most cities for a flat $25-per-month fee, unlimited time, as long as it's in the evening. Without PC Pursuit many notable BBSs would be out of reach for half the country.

No one knows exactly how many bulletin board systems there are. The best guess is that there are about 7,000 operating at one particular time. They come and go with the irregularity of phone line static. Immensely easy to start, a BBS usually be-

comes a hassle to maintain over the long stretch. While it's up and running, though, it's promoting a new brand of conversation. BBS sysops (system operators) keep them going because of the unsurpassed advantages of having people from all over the country calling in at their own expense to post amazing messages on the very subject one cares about.

BBSs are a gathering medium, not a broadcasting channel. The ones that work sculpt a comfortable visiting space to welcome comments. Dave Hughes, the pioneer tele-communications visionary, says the acid test for a BBS is if it averages one posted message for every two calls in. Any fewer messages and it will fade rapidly.

To start your own home-based BBS, you'll need a computer, modem, and one of these recommended software packages. For the Apple, we suggest GBBS. It's easy to set up in less than an hour, takes customized modifications superbly, and tends to be crash-proof. Consensus in the Macintosh world is that Red Ryder Host is the ticket for a home-based Mac BBS. Since it doesn't matter too much what computer you use, the most efficient way is to run your BBS on an IBM clone. The choice for IBM and compatible is TBBS. It's programmable by amateurs, and has been around a long time. Release 2.1 comes in three flavors. Single phone line (still about $300); Eight and sixteen line, which will take up to eight and sixteen phone lines, respectively ($895 for 8 lines; $1495 for 16 lines). Another option allows you to send mail to the free-forwarding FIDO service linking up BBSs at night ($100). With both FIDO mail and 8 or 16 lines in, a souped-up BBS approaches the capabilities of a local tele-conferencing system like the WELL. In fact, having both public and private access to your personal answering machine is the innovation brewing here. A BBS may be part of the household furniture someday.

**TBBS:** Version 2.0. For IBM and compatibles; needs 384K and hard disk for single line. Not copy-protected. **$300** for single line, **$895** for 8 line, **$1495** for 16 line, **$100** for FIDO mail; from: eSoft, 4100 South Parker Road/Box 305, Aurora, CO 80014; 303/699-6565.

**GBBS:** Version 1.3. For Apple family; needs two drives. Not copy-protected. **$128** postpaid from: L & L Productions, P. O. Box 5354, Arvada, CO 80005; 303/420-3156.

**Red Ryder Host:** Version 1.4A. For Macintosh, Mac Plus, and Macintosh SE; needs 512K. Not copy-protected. **$60** postpaid from: FreeSoft, 150 Hickory Drive, Beaver Falls, PA 15010; 412/846-2700.

---

**Uncle Tim's Hot Tub BBS.** (916) 689-4670. 8-N-1, 300/1200 baud. 24 hours. A optional experience coming live from Almost-Elk-Grove, California. Features: Main Hot Tub, Amiga Tub, Naturism/Nudism Tub, C Language Tub, Politics Tub, Tasteless Tub and Other Boards Tubs. No fees. System is as open as the software will allow. Registration unnecessary but nice. We're new and growing! Give us a call, we'd love to hear from you! Sysop: Tim Beckwith.

**The Dead Board** (717) 677-9573, 24 hrs., 8 bit word, 1 stop bit, no parity, 300/1200 baud. Grateful Dead tape trading and info; space for bulletins, ads and public mail.

**Cold Moon On A Single Star.** (415) 668-6101, San Francisco. 24 hours, Fido board. Chinese culture, history, language, Chinese cooking, discussion, etc. Asian community events. Sysops: Joseph Puig and Susan Chen.

**Musician's Network BBS.** Musician's information exchange. Space for want ads, bulletins, and public mail. Uploading and downloading available. BBS operates on Fido Software. 8 bits, no parity, 1 Weekends only, 6pm Fri-(415) 893-1618. Sysop:

**Lynzie's Motherboard** (818) 508-6482/(213) 650-0519. 24 hours, 300/1200/2400 baud, 8-N-1. Private E-mail, download library, dating matchup, interactive chat between users, 4 phone lines on rotary. Public boards include emkloyment, food and restaurant reviews, sci-fi, political, debate, for sale and many more. Monthly social happenings for local users. Sysop: Lynzie Flynn.

**The Shark's Head BBS** - Something for everyone, from serious to ridiculous. No-fee, membership system. We're not only user friendly, we're friendly users. Member SVSE. Dusty & Candy Van, (408) 247-4810.

**Photobytes,** a photography oriented BBS, features product information, help files, photo contest listings, plus much more. Sponsored by Wentling C___ Shops. 300 ba___ 2515, 24 h___

**Dial-Your-Match #1.** (818) 842-6900. 24 hours, 7 days, 300/1200 baud. Meet new friends! The original and most unique friendship BBS. Online since October 1981. DYM network allows you to send messages across the USA.

**Vietnam Vets-The LooneyBin.** Nancy and Todd Looney, sysops. Dedicated to 'Nam vets, their wives, lovers, and friends. Good friendly conversation plus referrals and counseling. Online 23 hours 3/12/2400. (408) 293-___ooNet #143/27.

**Earth-Rite RBBS.** We specialize in Earth Religion and related topics. We are not a software exchange. (415) 651-9496. 24 hrs., 300/1200 baud.

**Humor & Wisdom.** A board dedicated to the exchange of comic relief and things to ponder in a new age of consciousness. Free, as all things should be. 300/1200 baud, (415) 937-2508.

---

**The Live Wire.** (415) 540-0529. 300/1200, 24 hours. A digital magazine for the graphic-arts community (printers, typesetters, self-publishers, artists). Free. Sysop: Rick Hepting.

**Feminist BBS.** (312) 225-9138. 8-N-1, 24 hours, 300/1200 baud. Feminism, women's issues, general talk. Sysop: Susan B. ___ony.

**Bulletin Board System.** BBS devoted to handicappers and racing fans in So. Cal. On line every weekend. Log-on: race data for Santa Anita, Hollywood Park and Del Mar. (213) 934-6026.

**Videodrome BBS.** Where computers and video meet. (213) 324-5882. Open weekdays 4 pm - 2 am, weekends 12 2 am. A Commodore ___

**The Flying Fido.** Fido network 143, node 23, is now up and running 24 hours per day, except during FidoMail. 300/1200 baud, (408) 946-3183. Special interest in aviation; ul/dl of pd software Free.

**Association of Apple 32 Users BBS.** (408) 263-0299. 24 hrs., 300/1200. Sysop: John Griffith.

**Sofia System.** (408) 244-5055. 300 baud. 24 hours, BBS protocol. Conversations and e-mail. ___lines of multi-user interac-___ ___rked nationally. Sys-

**Jukebox Bulletin Board (JBBS)** (213) 670-8053. 8-N-1, 24 hours, 7 days, 300/1200 baud. Message board for buyers, sellers, and anyone interested in antique jukeboxes. Free. CP/M password available on request. No Fees. sysop: Ray Etchepare.

**Secret Partner** 1. (213) 543-5273. 8-N-1, 24 hour, 300/1200 baud. "Find your long-awaited sweetheart." Walter F. Howard, sysop. **The Wounded Land.** (408) 736-6490. Active fantasy role playing games. 24 hours, 300 baud. Sysop: The Spirit.

**Bay Area Bulletin Board.** (408) 723-7238. 24 hours, world wide net mail, 66 megs of online programs for download, adult message area, several special interest areas. 8-N-1, 300/1200/2400 baud. Sysop: Jim Acker.

**DYM #296.** (408) 720-0724, 300 baud, 8-N-1. A BBS focused on personal e-mail and friendly exchanges of information. Features user match function and ing Public. Current Topics, User Activities. and two Adults Only sections. No fees required. Online registration/verific___ required. Sysop: O__. (408)

**Matchmaker San Jose.** (408) 249-4566. 300/1200 baud, 24 hours, 7 days, 4 lines in hunting. 300 plus calls a day. Matchmaker San Jose is the ultimate pen pal system. Make a date, meet a friend, have the time of your life. Nationally networked. Type "mm" at login. Sysop: The Matchmaker.

**Dragon Flight.** (408) 353-3703. 24 hours. 300/1200 baud. "The Social System." Over 15 theme oriented message bases. Online quizzes. New remotes wanted! No fee. All ages ,and computer types welcomed! Sysop: Bronze Tooth.

## Out of the Inner Circle

(A Hacker's Guide to
Computer Security)
Bill Landreth
with Howard Rheingold
1985; 230 pp.
**$9.95**
($11.95 postpaid) from:
Microsoft Press
10700 Northup Way
Box 97200
Bellevue, WA 98009
800/242-7737
or Whole Earth Access

*The intent of this book is to give an introduction to how crackers (hackers who crack into systems) work. I thoroughly enjoyed it, but since it is not a step-by-step tutorial, it left me wanting more details on nearly everything it covers. But if you're interested in what makes hackers crack, and want a very useful glimpse into the subculture that makes almost everyone in the Establishment nervous, Out of the Inner Circle is excellent.*

*Among the specific methods Landreth outlines are the "hack-Hack"; the decoy; direct access to memory; rapid-fire attacking the computer to trick it into thinking you have legitimate access; becoming a remote sysop; using a trapdoor; the Trojan horse; logic bombs; and worm programs. Anyone with more than a passing interest in computer security should be familiar with all these techniques, and*

*Landreth's explanation's are quite clear, general descriptions of how they work.*
*— Matthew McClure*

◆

Very few people, from the designers and operators of large systems to the investigators and law-enforcement officers who deal with hackers, understand what hackers are trying to do, much less why they're trying to do it. During my own trial, for example, the judge decided to postpone sentence until after I had undergone psychiatric evaluation.

What makes hackers hack? Why are they so dedicated? Why do they spend so much of their own time on other people's computer systems? And just what do they think they are trying to accomplish? It is not rare for a hacker to put in a sixty- or seventy-hour work week (without getting paid, of course). And these are not empty hours, filled by staring out the window. Hacking is a challenge and a game of wits, and during their work sessions, hackers are using all the skills and ingenuity

they have developed. Hackers enjoy what they do.

◆

Normally, two steps are involved in the basic methods hackers use to gain unauthorized access to computers: First the hacker obtains an account. That's the easy part — sometimes it's as easy as calling and asking for one (posing as a university student, perhaps); more usually, it means getting account names from bulletin boards, company phone lists, or trash bins. . . maybe using a friend's or relative's account on The Source. . . .

It is the password that is a secret. Therefore, a hacker's second step involves ways of faking or discovering passwords. This is one of the areas in which lax security makes the hacker's job easier than it need be: Well-chosen passwords that are easy to remember, but difficult for a hacker to guess (yes, there are such things), and educated users who keep their secret passwords secret are a very effective defense at this level of security.

### [Flowchart]

```
CLEAR SCREEN
    ↓
USER HAS ENOUGH MEMORY? → NO → END
    ↓ YES
USER HAS HIGH SECURITY? → NO
    ↓ YES
THE HACKER'S HIDDEN TASKS {
CREATE A SECOND OPERATOR ACCOUNT
    ↓
SET PASSWORD TO "HACK"
    ↓
CALL MEMORY AVAILABLE
    ↓
PRINT RESULTS
    ↓
END
```

---

## 2600

Emmanuel Goldstein,
Editor
**$15/year**
(four issues) from:
2600 Subscription
Department
P.O. Box 752
Middle Island, NY
11953-0752, 516/751-2600

*My favorite newsletter is 2600, which bills itself as "the hacker quarterly." With concrete information and delightful detail, its editors explain the intricacies of the phone system, the VMS operating system, satellite jamming, and other subjects of interest to those who believe information should be free and flow without barrier. Some of the most interesting features are the news roundups whose descriptions are quite inspiring. If you're a phone phreak or a potential hacker, this newsletter is definitely for you. I love it.*

*— Matthew McClure*

◆

AUTOVON is an acronym for "AUTOmatic VOice Network," and is a single system with DCS (Defense Communications System). It is presently mostly based on electro-mechanical switches, and is a world-wide network for "unsecure" voice communication for the DOD and several related agencies. . . .

How to Participate: You can easily alter your touch tone

phone to make it have the extra column that utilizes the 1633 Hz tone. Standard Bell phones have two tone generating coils, each of which can generate four tones. This gives you sixteen possibilities of which you only use twelve. This leaves you with access to the four unexplored tones. A standard way to modify the touch tone phone is to install a switch to tell it whether to use the silver box tones or not. When the switch is in one position, you will get normal tones, in the other you'll get 1633 Hz tones. Bell calls these buttons A, B, C, and D, while the Army named them, from highest to lowest, Flash Override, Flash, Immediate, and Priority. All other calls are called Routine if no precedence button is pushed. . . .

◆

When you enter an authorization code to access a long distance company's network there are a few things that happen. The authorization code number you enter is cross-referenced in a list of codes. When an unassigned code is received the switch will print a report consisting of the authorization code, the date and time, and the incoming trunk number (if known) along with other miscellaneous information.

When an authorization code is found at the end of a billing cycle to have been abused, one of two things is done. Most of the time the code is removed from the database and a new code is assigned. But there are times when the code is flagged "abused" in the switch. This is very dangerous. Your call still goes through, but there is a bad code report printed. (This is similar to an unassigned code report, but it also prints out the number being called.) You have no way to know that this is happening but the IC has plenty of time to have the call traced. This just goes to show that you should switch codes on a regular basis and not use one until it dies.

◆

A couple of years ago while listening to the local voice-paging channel on my scanner, I figured that anybody could just call one of those phone numbers and get their message on the air. So after calling some numbers above and below my friend's voice pager number I found that this was true — I heard myself on the scanner. Problem was, you had to listen to everyone else's messages, too. Some kind of selective tone decoder for the scanner was in order — the cheaper the better. Also, some kind of tone-encoding system was needed that anyone had access to, so why not use the touch tones? After some experimenting, I found that a touch tone decoder chip with two 2N2222 transistors and a few resistors and capacitors (about $10 total at Radio Shack) could be used to decode the * (or any other) touch tone from the scanner's audio section and switch the audio onto the speaker. It all fit quite nicely into a matchbox-sized container taped to the back of my portable scanner, and could be powered by the scanner batteries.

◆

There is one trick which comes in handy. To get free directory assistance (DA) from a Customer Owned Coin Operated Telephone (COCOT), you dial 0-NPA-555-1212. If the NPA is within the New York City area (212, 516, 718), the call speeds straight through to DA. (Note: the caller must also be within that area.) Most COCOTs let you dial 0+ without asking for money, so your DA call would be free. Similar variations of this trick probably work in other parts of the country.

◆

This command creates a file in your account which will subsequently capture all the activity occurring at your terminal. Any keystrokes, any commands, all the actions done at the keyboard will be logged in the file as well as going on at the terminal as normal.

## Teleconnect

Andy Moore, Editor
$15/year
(12 issues) from:
Teleconnect
12 West 21st Street
New York, NY 10010
800/542-7279

## Which Phone System Should I Buy?

1987; 316 pp.
**$39.95**
($43.95 postpaid) from:
Telecom Library, Inc.
12 West 21st Street
New York, NY 10010
800/542-7279

*One of the most viciously, smart, and unpretentious trade magazines around — covering telephones and the telephone industry. They also publish books. If you run a small business, their biannual* **Which Phone System Should I Buy?** *answers exactly that question. No one else will, not even high-priced consultants.* — Art Kleiner

◆

To save money, the White House has changed the Moscow Hot Line to a low-cost long distance carrier.

The White House has discovered an extra benefit. There'll never be another war. The superpowers are spending their time bitching at each other about the quality of the line and whose fault it is.

## Panasonic Answering Machine

Panasonic KX-T1622 **$114.95** (retail); **$84** (street price; $90 postpaid) from Whole Earth Access; information **free** from: Panasonic Company, One Panasonic Way, Secaucus, New Jersey; 800/922-0028

*Instant assistant. Doesn't mop floor, but does take messages, reads them to you when you call in, records conversations on cue, and performs numerous other secretarial duties. No bigger than a paperback book (it uses tiny microcassettes), it's dependable and also cheap.*

—Kevin Kelly

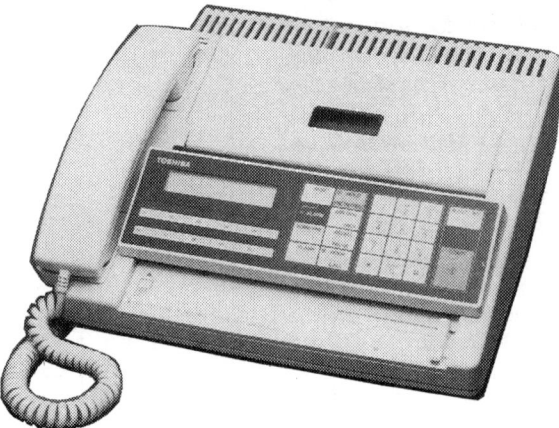

## Toshiba 30100 Phone/Copier/Fax Machine

**$1,795** (retail); information **free** from your local Toshiba copier dealer or: Toshiba America, 9740 Irvine Boulevard, Irvine, CA 92718; 714/583-3700

*An amazing phone for any large or small business. The* **Toshiba 30100** *is not only a fully-decked business phone featuring a 50 telephone number memory (with 10 single-touch numbers), last number redial, on-hook dialing, and message receiving capability, but a fax machine (with a separate 50 number fax memory) and copier as well. A liquid crystal display shows you the time and date, the name and number you're calling (if you're dialing from memory), the feature activated, the length of your call, and a warning if it detects an error in your fax transmission.*

*This phone is the way of the future — each employee can now be his or her own mini-data center and not have to depend on other departments getting information to them.*

— Richard Kadrey
[Suggested by Robert Horvitz]

## Hello Direct

(Catalog of Business
Telephone Accessories)
**Free** from:
Hello Direct
2346 Bering Drive
San Jose, CA 95131-1121
800/444-3556

*A complete business phone catalog. Everything from padded phone rests ($5.95) to call forwarding devices ($335) to portable teleconferencing systems ($1565).* **Hello Direct** *says that "We ship over 90% of our order in 24 hours or less." They offer a 30 day exchange or refund on their equipment, and all their products are guaranteed for one year, parts and labor. We haven't purchased anything from them ourselves, so we can't confirm their claims, but if you're in the market for phone equipment, you'd have to look a long time to find this much quality stuff in one place.* — Richard Kadrey

## Location of Controls

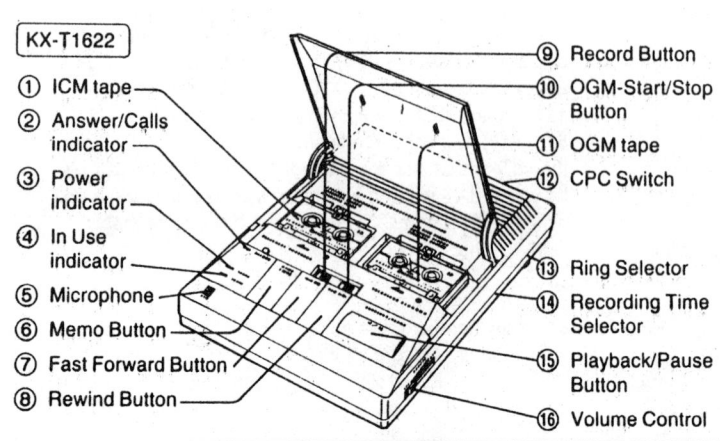

KX-T1622

① ICM tape
② Answer/Calls indicator
③ Power indicator
④ In Use indicator
⑤ Microphone
⑥ Memo Button
⑦ Fast Forward Button
⑧ Rewind Button
⑨ Record Button
⑩ OGM-Start/Stop Button
⑪ OGM tape
⑫ CPC Switch
⑬ Ring Selector
⑭ Recording Time Selector
⑮ Playback/Pause Button
⑯ Volume Control

## The Practical Guide to Voice Mail

Martin F. Parker
1987; 306 pp.
**$24.95** postpaid from:
McGraw Hill Books
Princeton Road
Hightstown, NJ 08520
609/426-5254
or Whole Earth Access

*Voice mail originated in answering machines. The message you hear on your everyday machine is, in a sense, a "voice letter" sent to a particular phone address. The "letter box" for this audio mail quickly developed into the interactive recording you get when you call hot-lines: "If you would like more information, dial a 2, if you would like...." Your voice is "mailed" to the right department.*

*Voice mail is now exemplified by the marriage of keyboard to phone. In one kind of system, you'll see the titles of messages left for you displayed on a screen which you select visually, and then hear audibly. In another you can make a copy of your phone message to forward onto a colleague, or save in a file, or command that acknowledgement of receipt be announced next time the sender calls. The sender also has the choice of hearing his message to edit it before it is "sealed" and sent.*

*In the future, all forms interbreed and hybridize. Currently voice mail is seen primarily in elephantine systems. This book expertly tracks the rapid evolution of voice mail toward rodent-like ubiquitousness, compactness, and domestication.*
— *Kevin Kelly*

◆

Some Voice Mail users check their messages at regular, convenient times; others prefer to have Voice Mail notify them whenever one or more new messages have been sent to their Voice Mail mailbox. In either case, the first step in doing your mail will be to enter your personal password from the touch-tone keys of your telephone. (You can change this password at any time, so that you will always be sure your messages are confidential.) You

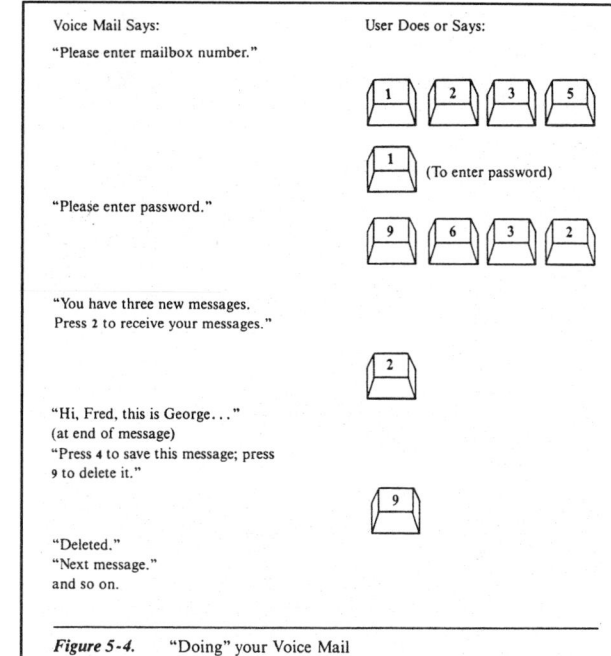

*Figure 5-4.* "Doing" your Voice Mail

Listening to your voice mail. From **The Practical Guide to Voice Mail**.

can then listen to your Voice Mail messages and handle them much as you handle letters in an in-basket. One at a time, you listen to a message, review it if necessary, and then decided what action to take. You can throw the message away; answer it; send it to someone else for action or information; or save it for future action, reference, or reminder. If you are looking for a certain message, you can scan through your Voice Mail without completely listening to each message.

◆

A Voice Mail service bureau makes it possible to have a Voice Mail mailbox without buying a Voice Mail system or installing the system in your company's facilities. A Voice Mail service bureau is a service company that installs a medium-to-large-sized Voice Mail system with the capacity to provide many mailboxes and then rents these mailboxes to subscribers for a monthly fee.

# Pagers

*by Blair Newman*

Over 6 million pagers (aka "beepers") are now in use, because they're the cheapest and most convenient way of "keeping in touch."

There are 4 different kinds of pagers, but all share a common characteristic: every pager is linked by radio to a unique telephone number.

Tone Only: These pagers simply beep or vibrate when someone dials their phone number. To get the message you have to call your office, answering service, or answering machine.

Digital: When a digital pager's phone number is dialed a computer answers with a beep, and waits for the caller to touch tone dial a phone number, which then appears on the digital pager's LCD display. Digital pagers are the most popular type, and typically rent for $17 to $24 a month.

Voice: When you call a voice pager's number the computer answers with a beep and then records a 7 to 10 second voice message. A few moments later the voice pager beeps and plays the voice message. Voice pager rentals run from $25 to $32 a month.

Alphanumeric: Alphanumeric pagers, the newest technology, are like digital pagers except their display shows both letters and numbers — so you get the entire message instantly. They're priced at $35 to $40 a month, but calling the alphanumeric pager's number requires a modem equipped computer to communicate the text message.

The most advanced pager service (the one I use) is provided by Metagram Corp. They've combined a 24 hour answering service with full text paging. Put your phone on call forwarding to your Metagram number and a live operator answers in your name, keyboards the message, and it shows up instantly on your pager. The Metagram pager has a 1,500 character capacity, and remembers messages until you explicitly erase them — it's the electronic equivalent of a stack of pink "While You Were Out" slips. Metagram is now available in many major cities, and they're rapidly expanding nationwide. Pricing is $60 a month, which is less than the combination of an answering service and digital (number only) paging.

For more information check under Paging in your Yellow Pages. To find out if Metagram is available in your area, call (800) 262-6382.

The Metagram pager forwards messages to you via a 24 character LCD display. It has a total memory of 1,500 characters, and remembers messages until you erase them.

# Watson

Version 6.2; **$199**. From: Natural Microsystems
8 Erie Drive, Natick, MA 01760; 617/655-0700

*Watson is a board that fits into your IBM PC or PC-compatible computer and turns it into a flexible voice mail center. Watson's basic function is to answer calls and record messages, but you can also program it to give messages to specific callers when they enter an ID code. If you want to deliver a series of messages to callers (for instance, a list of possible extensions they can dial) Watson can do it, and even change the sequence of messages in response to touch-tone signals from the caller. Watson also has the ability to make stock calls for you, dialing a pre-programmed series of numbers, delivering the message, and recording a voice or touch-tone response. If a number is busy, Watson will automatically call back later. Sort of like having a tiny phone operator in a box.*
— *Richard Kadrey*

## PeaceNet

3228 Sacramento Street,
San Francisco, CA 94115;
415/923-0900

This computer messaging service hosts over a hundred online conferences for peace and social activist groups: EcoNet (ecological issues), HomeoNet (a homeopathic doctor's conference), the National Freeze Campaign, the Christic Institute, the Central America Resource Network, the Center for Innovative Diplomacy, Institute for Security and Cooperation in Outer Space, etc. It's worth joining not just for the news-postings and calendars of events (e.g. American Peace Test's schedule of nuclear blasts at the Nevada test site), but because participating groups often use PeaceNet to administer themselves. It's a treat to follow discussions of internal issues, goals, strategies and tactics, and most times kibitzers can add their two cents. Openness is an important principle for many of these groups; PeaceNet makes that ideal both practicable and involving. (The system has limited-access sections and electronic mail facilities, too.)

Reachable in larger cities through Telenet, after a sign-up fee of $10, the cost is $10 per month, plus $5 per hour (off-peak) and .005 cents per kilobyte for disk storage in excess of 100k. Groups get discounts.
— Robert Horvitz

## Power Structure Research Database

4 floppy disks. $35/$100 from Micro Associates,
P. O. Box 5369, Arlington, VA 22205

For the past ten years, Daniel Brandt has been compiling a "power structure research" database with its own easy-to-use, search-and-sort software designed to run on a microcomputer. It presently contains the names of nearly 30,000 individuals and groups identified in 55,000 citations from books and articles about the intelligence community, big business, the U.S. foreign policy establishment, domestic spying and political infiltration, assassination and conspiracy theories, and right-wing organizations.

Each name-entry is linked to as many as 50 published sources. Names associated with a foreign country at a certain time can be identified by specifying the place and time span of interest. For example, if you want a printout of all the names in the database connected with Chile from 1970 to 1973, along with citations of publications describing their activities, a few simple commands will do it.

The database is available as a set of three double-sided floppy disks, with programs on a fourth

## The National Security Archive

1755 Massachusetts Avenue NW/Ste. 500,
Washington, D.C. 20036; 202/797-0882

Former Washington Post reporter Scott Armstrong's initial idea was to create a public depository for documents concerning U.S. national security, foreign policy, military and intelligence activities obtained via Freedom of Information Act requests. Acquiring documents turned out to be just the start. Most of what the National Security Archive does now is assemble and index topical collections from primary sources to provide "as complete a documentary record of recent and contemporary policymaking as possible within the constraints of security classification."

Current projects range from the history of U.S. military uses of space to the evolution of U.S. policy toward South Africa 1960-87. The Archive sells such collections and their indexes
— Robert Horvitz

## Electronic Information Exchange System

Computerized Conferencing and Communications Center, New Jersey Institute of Technology, Newark, NJ 07102; 201-596-EIES

EIES is a computerized conferencing system designed to facilitate communication among geographically dispersed groups of people. Over the years it has been the site of some of the bravest experiments in this new computer communication medium. CareNet, an active Latin American resource network uses the system (also accessible on PeaceNet), as well as the Whole Earth Review, and Western Behavioral Sciences Institute — that should get the reward for the best experimental educational use of computer conferencing. One aspect of EIES of great interest is the Virtual classroom being developed by Starr Roxanne Hiltz, one of the founders of EIES. Virtual classroom online conferences are being developed to support college level course work, including ongoing dialog, assignments, exams, class discussions, etc.
— Steve Johnson

floppy. The software provides phonetic and leading-letter search capabilities for names whose spelling is uncertain. Purchasers receive update announcements every quarter, and are entitled to buy later editions at discount prices. The cost of a four-disk set is $35 for individuals and nonprofit organizations, $100 for all others. An outstanding example of political/infotech activism. Anyone curious or concerned about the web of influences operating behind the surface of democracy should have a copy. When ordering, be sure to specify the type of computer it'll run on. Versions are currently available for devices running CP/M, DOS 2.0 or 3.0.
— Robert Horvitz

Secret Department of State cable, now declassified, dated November 9, 1978, from Ambassador to Iran William H. Sullivan. Nine weeks before the Shah fell, it is titled "Thinking the Unthinkable" and discusses the first registered, official concern that the Shah might not survive the growing turmoil in Iran.

Secret Department of State cable, now declassified but heavily excised, discusses a conversation with a Salvadoran official which identified "six Salvadoran millionaire emigres in Miami" as responsible for directing and financing right wing death squads and probably the murders of American citizens.

## New York On Line

P.O. Box 829, Brooklyn, NY 11202;
718/852-2662

NYOL is a bulletin board system for progressive groups and individuals who wish to share information and resources locally and nationwide. Some of the information online includes resource lists of groups active on issues such as Central America and Southern Africa; information and analysis of the "Contragate" scandal; articles and essays on the implications of computers for working people; information on desktop publishing and design; calendars of events and newswire services. Southscan is a weekly bulletin of Southern Africa. The will shortly be initiating a similar service directly from Managua, Nicaragua.
— Steve Johnson

## Telecommunications Cooperative Network (TCN)

505 Eighth Avenue, Suite 1805, New York, NY 10018; 212/714-9780

TCN provides low-cost long distance and computer communications exclusively to nonprofit groups. It currently has 1,000 member organizations, including foundations, universities, hospitals, associations, religious and public interest organizations. The TCN computer communications system is run on the Dialcom system. It provides electronic messenging services as well as gateway to other computerized information services including the UPI newswire, and the CITITEX community development program data. Groups that constitute the cooperative vary in range from the American Civil Liberties Union to the Boys Club of America, from the Agricultural Development Center to the American Society for the Prevention of Cruelty to Animals, Columbia University, the Aspen Music Festival and Nuclear Times.
— Steve Johnson

## How to Produce Your Own Videoconference

Georgia A. Mathis
1987; 165 pp.
**$36.95**
($39.95 postpaid) from:
Knowledge Industry
Publications, Inc.
701 Westchester Avenue
White Plains, NY 10604
800/248-5474
or Whole Earth Access

*What a delicious treat a video-teleconference would be if it worked. But, so far it only kind of works.*

*What you want is two-way video and audio, that is, equal communication for any participant. What you get in practice is one-way video via satellite, and two-way voice via phone lines. That means one side sees nothing (in seminars that blind side is the speaker, and in TV news it's the person being interviewed live). Just as bad, both sides share the technical handicap of having one conversation split between a high road/low road transmission.*

*Despite these grim flaws, a videoconference can liberate a far-flung project from stagnation in airport*

Phone room set up to receive questions from remote sites in an area removed from the studio to assure quiet for the operators. A monitor is provided so the operators can watch the program.

*waiting rooms, and enliven a undertaking that depends on the personality of a few people, such as politics. This book is the most concrete and useful one out of a whole lot of theoretical books on the topic.* — *Kevin Kelly*

◆

Hotel sites are most often chosen for videoconference networks. This is true for several reasons:

1. Hotels are equipped with meeting space.

2. Some hotel chains (e.g., Holiday Inns, Inc. and Marriott Corp.) have a great deal of experience with videoconferencing and may even have all the technical equipment you need on site.

There are some things to watch out for, though, when dealing with hotels for your videoconference. In most cases, a videoconference is not an extremely important piece of business for them. They place videoconferencing in the same category as weddings and local club dinners because you will probably use only a limited amount of their space, your attendees will be in and out quickly, and it is unlikely that you will use many overnight rooms or need much food service.

◆

Public television stations, through the PBS system, made up the first real network of videoconference receive sites. This is because the PBS system itself was the first TV network to be delivered by satellite... Here are some positive aspects of using public television stations:

1. The price is often lower than at hotels. You can expect to pay from $500 to $2000 a day to use their facilities.
2. The equipment you need, and qualified technicians to run it, are already at the site.
3. The PBS system has a department in Alexandria, VA called ConferSat (part of PBS Enterprises) to help you book suitable space at stations, thus saving you a lot of legwork.

# Where To Have Your Video-Teleconference

*by Richard Kadrey*

US Sprint's "The Meeting Channel" provides video-teleconferencing facilities in over 300 locations in 25 countries (including mainland China), and the number of locations is growing all the time. When this kind of conferencing was introduced a few

years ago, the first people to take advantage of it were big companies wanting to save on travel expenses — Atlantic Richfield, Xerox, JC Penny, Citibank, etc.; they used corporate "private rooms" hooked right into The Meeting Channels' fiber optic lines. Now, anyone can book time on The Meeting Channel using one of Sprint's "public rooms." Depending on the quality of the transmission you need (e.g., the speed of the transmission over the lines), your location, and the location you want to talk to, you can have a video-teleconference for as little as $60 or as much as $2,400 an hour. Rates for three or more locations tied together start at $120 an hour. However, video conferencing is still primitive enough that hooking up more than 2 locations at once may require you to make some big compromises.

Let's say you want to hold a video conference between 4 locations: San Francisco, Houston, Chicago, and New York. First, you should book this type of conference as early as possible, at least a week in advance. And since

each Sprint public room is different, you will want to ask what kind of equipment is available at each location. Most sites have color video cameras, but some also have VCR's and graphics terminals plugged into The Meeting Channel's lines.

When you make a reservation for a multipoint conference, you will have to designate one of the locations as the Master Site, in this example San Francisco; this location can send audio and video to all the other rooms; another location, say New York, is called the Primary Site. All four locations can hear this site, but the Primary can speak and reply only to the Master Site. The other two sites, Houston and Chicago, cannot broadcast, but only receive sound and images from the Master and Primary sites.

Broadcasting at Sprint's lowest recommended speed (768 kbps), your video conference will cost you $450 per half hour for the transmission, plus $150 per hour for room rental at each site, coming to a total of $3,100 for your 3 hour conference.

A new player in the video-teleconferencing industry, and one that promises to make this kind of meeting commonplace, is Holiday Inn. They now provide "receiving rooms" for video conferences, rooms that can only receive signals, not send one. Prices start at $200 for a half-day (4 hours) room rental, a $100 set-up fee, and $400 - $600 equipment rental (video monitors are cheaper to rent than video projectors, etc.). You can book rooms on relatively short notice, and since you can hardly throw a rock without hitting a Holiday Inn, setting up a video conference is easier than ever. Now if they can only figure out a way for us to see AND talk to each location, you'd have the hottest thing in communications since pink princess phones.

## The Meeting Channel

Further information **free** from: The Meeting Channel, US Sprint, 1815 Century Boulevard, Atlanta, GA 30345; 800/241-8470.

## Holiday Inn

For Holiday Inn information, contact the location nearest you.

# Video-Teleconferencing Magazines

*by Richard Kadrey*

Video teleconferencing is a new enough phenomenon that useful publications about it are still rare. And the ones that are useful tend to be expensive. The following short list of magazines will keep you up to date on what's happening on the video teleconferencing front. Two of them are well over $150 a year, so you might try talking your company or local library (or a nearby business library) into stocking them.

## TeleSpan

Shirley Singletany, Editor; **$207**/year (12 issues) from: TeleSpan, Inc., 50 West Palm Street, Altadena, CA 91001; 818/797-5482

## Telecommunications Policy

Susan Hunter, Editor; **$141**/year (4 issues) from: Butterworth Publishers, 80 Montvale Avenue, Stoneham, MA 02180; 800/548-4001

## Teleconference

Patty Portway, Editor; **$60**/year (6 issues) from: Applied Business Communications, Inc., P. O. Box 5106, San Ramon, CA 94583-0906; 415/820-556

## Worldwide Telecommunications Guide for the Business Manager

Walter L. Vignault
1987; 417 pp.
**$49.95** postpaid from:
John Wiley & Sons, Inc.
Order Department
1 Wiley Drive
Somerset, N.J. 08875
1-800-225-5945

*The wired planet. Expanding subject, shrinking comprehension. Start here for the important very small detail, very big picture. International corporations (not governments) are quickest to grasp this pulse, and therefore are the audience of this technical book. Anyone else plugging in?*

— *Kevin Kelly*

Chapter 3: Worldwide Environment. Can you connect both ends of a telephone line with compatible equipment to any country? No. Some line attachment products may not be allowed in some countries due to telephone company restrictions. How do you get around telephone company restrictions? The key is negotiating. Suggestions will be offered to improve your chances of obtaining the facilities you need.

Chapter 10: International Traffic. Consistent services are important for worldwide communications to simplify the management and control of moving information. New networks and services are available for communicating to other countries. Telex gets your message to more countries than any other means. What are the other alternatives? Private lines and data and packet switched data networks may offer an alternative solution for international data and message exchange.

In many European countries the profits generated by the

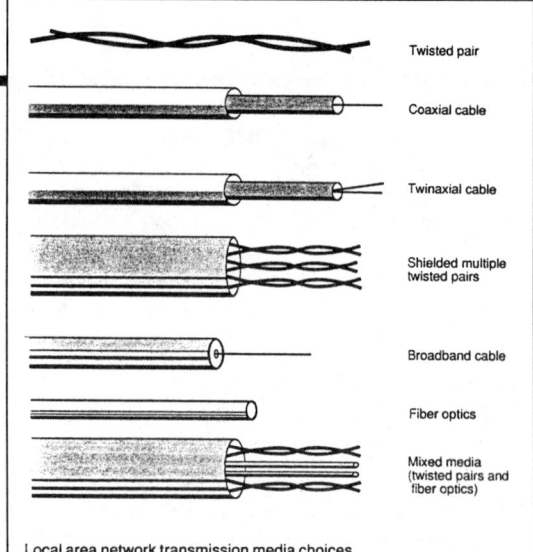

Local area network transmission media choices.

telephone and telegraph activities subsidize the post office branch. In some countries, such as France, the PTT revenue is used to support social programs (officials believe that raising a telephone bill is more palatable to voters than raising taxes).

## The Phenomenon of Man

Teilhard de Chardin
1955; 352 pp.
**$8.95**
($10.45 postpaid) from:
J.B. Lippincott
Rt. 3 Box 20B
Hagerstown, MD 21740
1-800-638-3030

*Written in 1955 by a mystical Catholic priest and noted amateur anthropologist (who also perpetrated a serious anthropological hoax) this is the primeval "cosmic" book.*

*Teilhard de Chardin provides a metaphysical understanding to the ascending global communications network and the modern expansion of infor-*

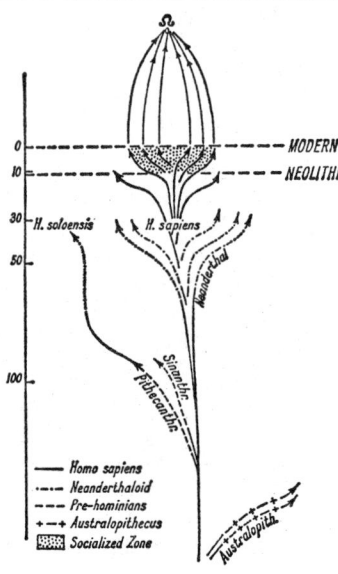

The development of the human Layer. The figures on the left indicate thousands of years. They are a minimum estimate and should probably be at least doubled. The hypothetical zone of coverage on the point Omega is obviously not to scale. By analogy with other living layers, its duration should certainly run into thousands of years.

*mation. He views human culture as the evolutionary advancement from non-life to the "deployment of the noosphere" — Teilhard's coinage for the materialization of a human thought membrane around the earth. His is the ontogeny of a planetary circuit, now in progress.*   — *Kevin Kelly*

Noogenesis rises upwards in us and through us unceasingly. We have pointed to the principal characteristics of that movement: the closer association of the grains of thought; the synthesis of individuals and of nations or races; the need of an autonomous and supreme personal focus to bind elementary personalities together, without deforming them, in an atmosphere of active sympathy. And once again: all this results from the combined action of two curvatures — the roundness of the earth and the cosmic convergence of the mind — in conformity with the law of complexity and consciousness.

## DHL Worldwide Express

Information **free** from: 800/225-5345

*Mail is still the sleepy giant of communications — wide but slow. When your package must absolutely positively get there quick, and "there" is Timbuktoo, Katmandu, the Congo, or any of those other far away places that are now manufacturing our goods, snail mail won't do. You should know about DHL Worldwide Express. DHL has offices in 180 countries (more than the UN does) so it can deliver documents and packages door-to-door to most cities in the world. Sort of like a global Federal Express.*

*For instance, say you live in Blue Eyes, Arkansas. You can have DHL pick up the urgent small package at your door and they'll get it to your partner sweating it out in Moukoundo, Congo (or any of its other 34 large towns) within three days. That'll cost $78 if its contents resemble documents, and $118 otherwise. They'll bill you.*

*Naturally in this complex world, there are foot-*

*notes. Packages other than documents to most communist countries have to be picked up at the airport. DHL will charge $20 extra if you want something delivered in the boonies beyond the main cities of most developing countries. Europe gets your stuff in one day, Hong Kong and India the day after, but the Himalayan kingdom of Nepal won't get it till the fifth day. DHL is supremely helpful sorting all this out by phone on their 800 number.*

*Delivered door-to-door, DHL will cost at least 10 times as much as the post office, but they'll get it there 10 times faster.*

*You'll need their current* **Worldwide Express Guide** *which lists destinations with content guide-*

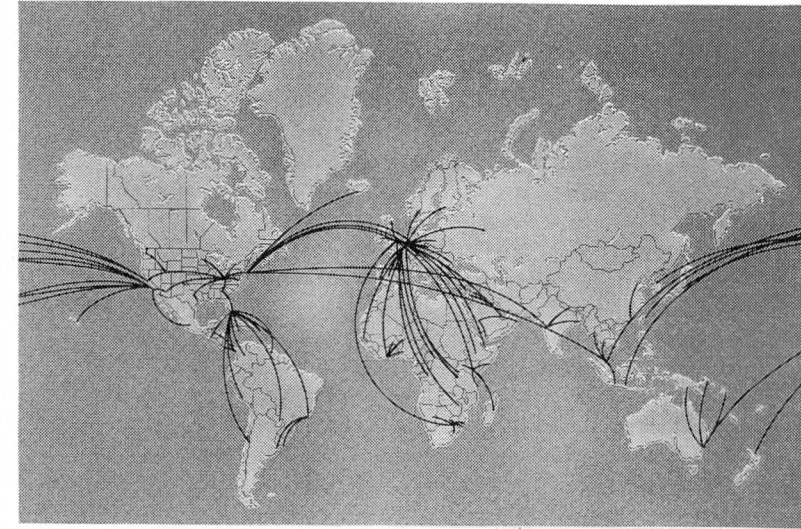

*lines, and you'll need their* **Quick Reference Guide** *which gives transit times and prices. Both are free.*

— *Kevin Kelly*

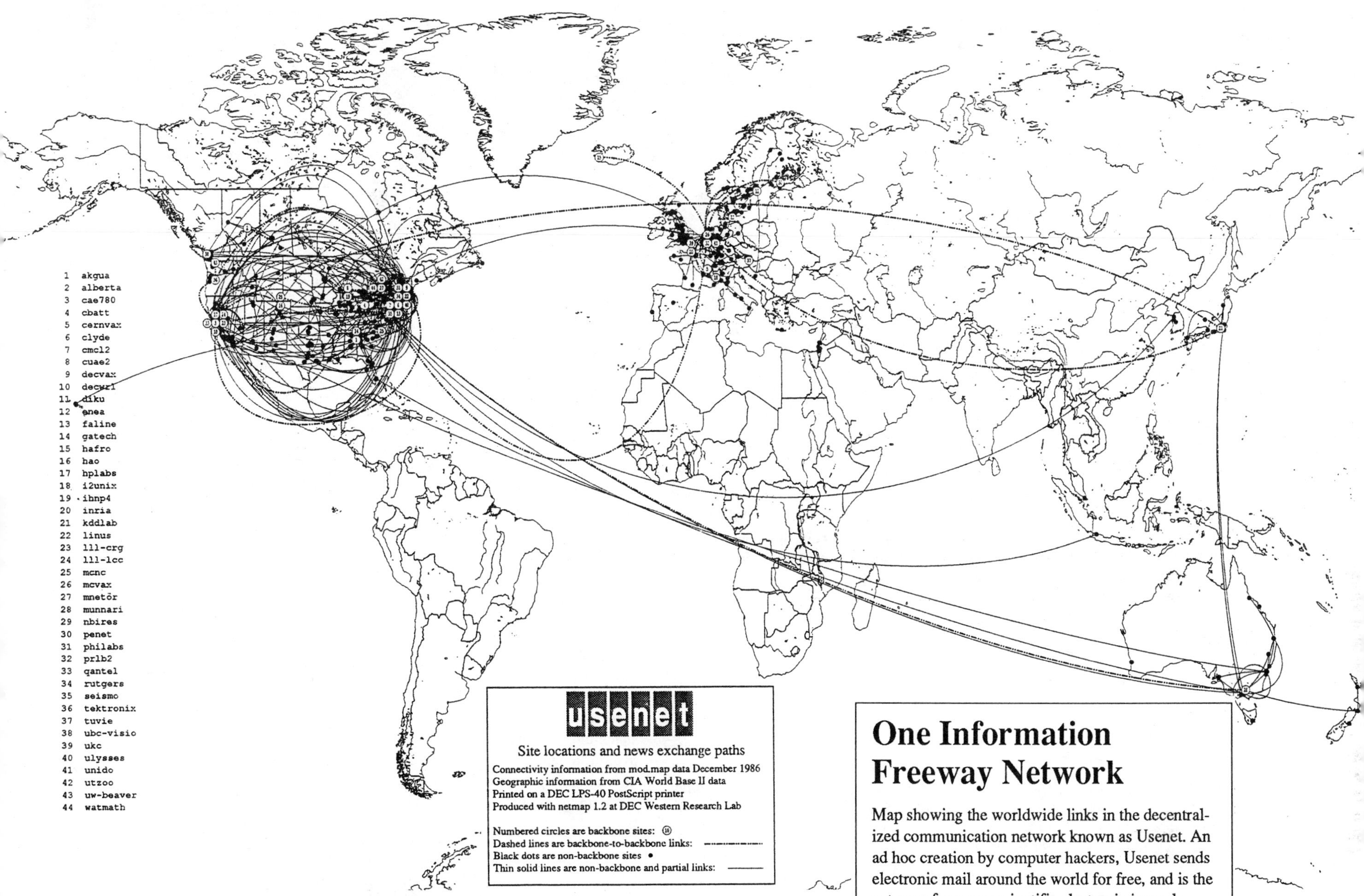

| 1 | akgua |
| 2 | alberta |
| 3 | cae780 |
| 4 | cbatt |
| 5 | cernvax |
| 6 | clyde |
| 7 | cmcl2 |
| 8 | cuae2 |
| 9 | decvax |
| 10 | decwrl |
| 11 | diku |
| 12 | enea |
| 13 | faline |
| 14 | gatech |
| 15 | hafro |
| 16 | hao |
| 17 | hplabs |
| 18 | i2unix |
| 19 | ihnp4 |
| 20 | inria |
| 21 | kddlab |
| 22 | linus |
| 23 | lll-crg |
| 24 | lll-lcc |
| 25 | mcnc |
| 26 | mcvax |
| 27 | mnetor |
| 28 | munnari |
| 29 | nbires |
| 30 | penet |
| 31 | philabs |
| 32 | prlb2 |
| 33 | qantel |
| 34 | rutgers |
| 35 | seismo |
| 36 | tektronix |
| 37 | tuvie |
| 38 | ubc-visio |
| 39 | ukc |
| 40 | ulysses |
| 41 | unido |
| 42 | utzoo |
| 43 | uw-beaver |
| 44 | watmath |

## usenet

Site locations and news exchange paths

Connectivity information from mod.map data December 1986
Geographic information from CIA World Base II data
Printed on a DEC LPS-40 PostScript printer
Produced with netmap 1.2 at DEC Western Research Lab

Numbered circles are backbone sites: ⓑ
Dashed lines are backbone-to-backbone links: - - - - - -
Black dots are non-backbone sites •
Thin solid lines are non-backbone and partial links: ———

# One Information Freeway Network

Map showing the worldwide links in the decentralized communication network known as Usenet. An ad hoc creation by computer hackers, Usenet sends electronic mail around the world for free, and is the gateway for many scientific electronic journals which are "published" daily, thus outpacing printed journals which may delay findings by six months or more. Most Usenet sites are quasi-officially or unofficially located within the computers of universities and large corporations, and are tolerated because of the tremendous amount of technical news they conduct. Persons without access to a university or company account can tap into the global anarchy of Usenet through the WELL gateway (see page 73).

## Information Highways

Lawrence E. Murr,
James B. Williams
and Ruth-Ellen Miller
1985; 78 pp.
**$25** postpaid from:
Hypermap/LIRN
P. O. Box 23452
Portland, OR 97223
503/241-2212

*We know shamefully little about the nature of information. Try to buy a map that shows how information flows in all its varieties around the world. Bet you won't find one.*

*One small corner has been done. Compiled by astute librarians in Oregon, this self-published monograph traces the regional information paths in the Pacific Northwest. The overlapping networks of electronic, transportation, and paper information*

*delivery routes are collated into an atlas of communications. Wisely, the writers include airlines and overnight couriers as communication channels. Emphasis is given to the remarkable freeways of interlibrary loans. (Libraries pass books among themselves, so that patrons can borrow books that a small branch doesn't have on its shelf. In effect you can get nearly any book you want, if you're willing to wait for it.) The larger theme of the book is the cartography of intangibles.*

*—Kevin Kelly*

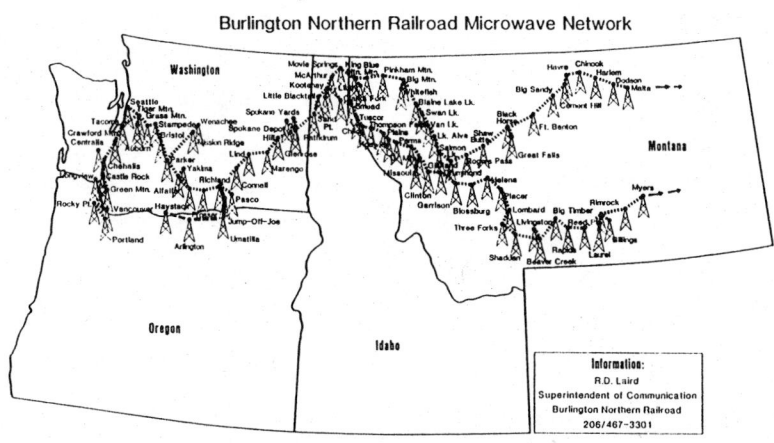

Burlington Northern Railroad Microwave Network

Information:
R.D. Laird
Superintendent of Communication
Burlington Northern Railroad
206/467-3301

# FRAGMENTS OF A WORLD INFORMATION ECONOMY

*by Peter Schwartz*

NOT TOO LONG ago the manufacture of things like textiles and steel and automobiles were the driving structures out of which industrialism emerged. The winners in that game profited from mass production, economics of scale, and low-cost resources. Now, the value added in transforming material is related to our capacity to *understand and use information* in various ways. How are the rules of this new game going to be written?

The principle technologies involved are telecommunications and computing. And the two great systems that will use them predominantly are *finance* and *recorded entertainment*. By recorded entertainment I mean television, movies, music, and so on, on a worldwide scale. I single out these two systems because, in both cases, the markets and products are becoming increasingly global and accelerated by rapidly advancing technology.

In the new game, the linking infrastructure is going to be a function of what finance wants on the one hand, and what the electronic entertainment media wants on the other. Everything else will be piggybacked on that. The rules for satellite allocation or for broadcasting bandwidth allocation or for how one makes money or for how finance is regulated, will be focused around these two industries.

Today no one is thinking about the meaning of the rules being developed in an informal, unpredictable, evolutionary way around the short-term exigencies of those industries. Ultimately they will, quite by chance, evolve into something, and that something will become the organizing paradigm of the next century. That paradigm, inasmuch as we've ambled from the real of the material to the informational, will become a kind of global consciousness. It is the system within which we all begin to think about ourselves collectively.

---
**READING LIST**
---

An economy takes shape as the outcome of a very large number of micro decisions. In his last great masterpiece, the three part **Civilization and Capitalism, 15th-18th Century**, Fernand Braudel describes this process in great detail. The gradual elaboration of markets, the development of trading companies, the creation and application of new technology and so on come together to create the fabric of the capitalist economy.

Gone with the Wind
Information that increases in value as it ages.

Stock prices
Information that diminishes in value as it ages.

During the 19th Century and the early 20th Century the industrial economy was created in a similar array of decisions. Most had to do with the new technologies, first of steam and the railroad and later electricity and the petroleum-fueled internal combustion engine. The shape of the modern world was formed in those decisions. How people would work, where they would live, who would be rich and who would be poor, which skills would count and which would not, which nations would rise and which would fall . . . were more the result of many small choices rather than the apparently momentous decisions of a few great men.

The world economy of the next century is being shaped by a similar set of current decisions mostly having to do with information systems. What standards, if any, will help integrate the disparate information technologies that have emerged from the age of incompatibility as Jay Ogilvy calls it—my Mac won't talk to your IBM. How will the international trading of stocks, bonds, and currencies be regulated? Will cable TV be taken over by the phone companies or will cable companies start offering voice services? Will the office of the future be modeled on the factory of yesterday or does hypertext provide a model for information relationships and hence work flows of tomorrow's office? Will we get it in time that offices are about intelligence and not automation?

Unfortunately little valuable is yet in print that will enable one to see these microdecisions coming into being. Among the best and most interesting is **The Deal of the Century: The Breakup of AT&T** by Steve Coll. It is the story of a political and economic tragedy. Forces are unleashed which once set in motion are uncontrolable. It is a story with no winners and all losers including the American people. In the interplay of technological, business and political decisions the future of American telecommunications is transformed and not for the good of anyone. The events and characters are sufficiently engaging and the writing so good that the book can't be put down.

A more academic and rigorous treatment of the same tale can be found in Peter Temin's **The Breakup of the Bell System.**

A useful though not at all engaging treatment of the many facts of the evolving information system can be found in **Information Technology: the Trillion Dollar Opportunity** by Harvey L. Poppel and Bernard Goldstein. The book is quite comprehensive covering computing, telecommunications, entertainment, how businesses in the industry are competing, regulation and so on. It is rich in data and a useful source book, but not a great read.

How does economics change when the substance is symbols and not physical objects? Rather than chemistry or physics, semiotics and literary criticism may be more appropriate disciplines to understanding economic realities in the information domain. Space and time mean very different things when you have to move a video image rather than tons of steel.

One of the few books that has usefully grasped this concept is **The Alchemy of Finance** by George Soros. In the physical world what we believe usually doesn't matter. The forces of nature are mainly independent of human intentions. That assumption lies behind almost all of the physical and biological sciences. Unfortunately the social sciences like economics

have attempted to base their worldview on the physical science paradigm. Soros rightly argues that markets, which form the integrating system of the economy do not behave like physical systems at all.

Alchemy provides a better model, he suggests. Alchemists failed because wishing won't turn lead into gold. But what investors believe about the value of IBM will drive up (or down) the value of its stock. What traders believe about the future of oil will affect the price of oil and hence how much is found and used. The dynamics of markets are very much a function of what people believe and how they behave as a result. Soros' book is the sort of a natural experiment in applying this idea to anticipate the behavior of financial markets. The subtitle of his book is "reading the mind of the market." It is worth noting that he is one of the most successful investors of our day. His ideas emerge out of the real world experience of the market.

Albert Bressand, a young French economist and leader of a small think tank in Paris called *Promethee* is one of the most perceptive thinkers and writers in the field, but has yet to produce any books in English. His papers are worth getting, but a real theory of the information age has yet to emerge. The Adam Smith or the Marx of the information age are not yet in print. Maybe the ideas have yet to be born. I have often suspected that economics is really history. So we may only read about it long after the information economy has arrived.

**The Structures of Everyday Life**, Vol 1: Civilization and Capitalism 15th-18th Century. Fernand Braudel, 85; 624 pp. **$17.95. The Wheels of Commerce**, Vol. 2: Civilization and Capitalism 15th-18th Century. 1986; 720 pp. **$16.95. The Perspective of the World**, Vol. 3: Civilization and Capitalism 15th-18th Century. 1986; 704 pp. **$34.50.** For postpaid order, add $1.50 for one title, $.50 for each additional: J.B. Lippincott, Rt. 3 Box 20B, Hagerstown, MD 21740; 800/638-3030

**The Deal of the Century: The Breakup of AT&T.** Steve Coll, 1986; 384 pp. **$19.95** postpaid from: Macmillan Publishing Co., Front and Brown Streets, Riverside NJ 08075; 800/257-5755

**The Fall of the Bell System: A Study in Prices & Politics.** Peter Temin and Louis

Galambos, 1988; 305 pp. **$27.95** postpaid from: Cambridge University Press, 510 North Avenue, New Rochelle, NY 10801; 800/872-7423.

**Information Technology: The Trillion Dollar Opportunity.** Harvey L. Poppel and Bernard Goldstein, 1987; 224 pp. **$21.50** ($22.58 postpaid from): McGraw Hill, Princeton Road, Heightstown, NJ 08520; 800/262-4729

**The Alchemy of Finance: Reading the Mind of the Market.** George Soros, 1987; 352 pp. **$10.95.** ($12.05 postpaid) from: Simon & Schuster, 200 Old Tappan Road, Old Tappan, NJ 07675; 800/223-2336

**Promethee.** Albert Bressand, Director. 12 Rue du Havre, Paris 75009 FRANCE. 331-428-52401.

# Bypassing the Phone  Companies

*by Benn Kobb, KC5CW, and Howard Goldstein*

Packet radio is a technique for distributing electronic mail and messages to specific terminals using radio channels. Its significance is that it offers computer users complete bypass of the wired telephone network and their high costs. You can therefore communicate long distances, dependably, without technical knowledge, for free.

The basic elements of a packet station are a cheap computer, a small radio transceiver, and a "terminal node controller (TNC)," the packet equivalent of a modem. A $200 hand-held radio and a $100 Commodore 64 computer work as well as anything.

The distance range of packet radio is around eight miles line-of-sight on open terrain, with an antenna up 30 feet and about 10 watts of power. Devices called digital repeaters (digipeaters) can extend the range of any station by retransmitting the packets. There's a protocol that lets you string up to eight of these digipeater hops together to reach another person. Plus, every TNC including your own is also a potential digipeater (you don't notice if someone "uses you").

Many local and regional ham groups operate digipeaters, collecting dues from their members for upkeep; some are designated "gateways" to local or wide-area networks, or to long-distance paths via satellite or shortwave.

Radio amateurs have been quick to grasp the potential of packet, as it offers a much faster and more efficient way to handle messages than anything they had previously. It's also better suited to an urban environment than shortwave voice communication, the traditional mainstay of amateur traffic distribution. In cities, very little power and antennas that are just inches long are enough to get a packet signal to the next node in the network.

The future of packet radio lies in the heavens, on satellites. The first to be launched is PACSAT, a joint project between radio amateur groups AMSAT in Washington, D.C., and VITA, a 25-year-old organization that provides technical assistance to Third World countries. The idea is to set up an orbiting public mailbox. The satellite's orbit will bring it in view of any point in the world four times a day for several minutes at a time. During each pass it will dump whatever messages it has to packet radio listeners and pick up any new messages and hold them until it can post them. Japanese amateurs are also launching a similar low-orbiting computer mailbox called JAS-1. Both are inexpensive devices built by volunteers and donations.

The ground equipment needed to get satellite mail fits into a briefcase — including the antenna. It runs on batteries. The initial cost is estimated at $1000. However, to use packet radio (via digipeaters or satellites), you need to have a ham license, and your messages cannot be for commercial use.

**Gateway,** Stan Horzepa, Editor; **$6**/25 issues from:

## The Packet Radio Handbook
Jonathan L. Mayo, KR3T
1987; 217 pp.
**$14.95** postpaid from:
TAB Books, Inc.
Blue Ridge Summit,
PA 17294-0550
800/233-1128
or Whole Earth Access

## Your Gateway to Packet Radio
Stan Horzepa, WA1LOU
1987; 239 pp.
**$10**
($12.50 postpaid) from:
American Radio Relay League
225 Main Street
Newington, CN 06111
203/666-1541
or Whole Earth Access

*Talk about dinosaurs! You still need to pass a Morse Code proficiency test to send radio messages via the amateur radio network. A few radio hackers have a better idea: cheap computers hooked up to their ham gear. Instead of a human radio operator laboriously transmitting a rapid series of dots and dashes into the scattered atmosphere to be deciphered by a trained human listener far away (if he can hear it), packet radio hams use computers to do all the coding and relaying. While they are at it, the computers also direct messages to particular areas of the globe depending on the destination address affixed to the message "packet", thus significantly increasing the range and usefulness of ham radio. With this system, shortwave radio messages (they must carry only personal and non-commercial content) become a sort of free radio mail.*

*The good ole boy network of ham radio fans is being revolutionized by these radio hackers. Here's the two books that will bring you up to speed. **Packet Radio Handbook** is a good introduction; **Your Gateway to Packet Radio** gives a thorough grounding in the technical methods.* —Kevin Kelly

◆

In the simplest case, a packet network consists of a few stations within direct communications range from each other on a single frequency. A more complex network involves digipeating (simplex packet repeaters) to extend a station's communication range and gateways for accessing stations with different capabilities (such as

As the Computer Age dawned in Amateur Radio, radio hackers had to be very resourceful. Here, a young radio hacker built a wall of aluminum cylinders to contain the RF generated by his TRS-80 Model 1 computer. —*Your Gateway to Packet Radio*

those on another frequency or using another modem configuration). This is the stage of networking that present day amateur packet radio has reached in the United States. —*The Packet Radio Handbook*

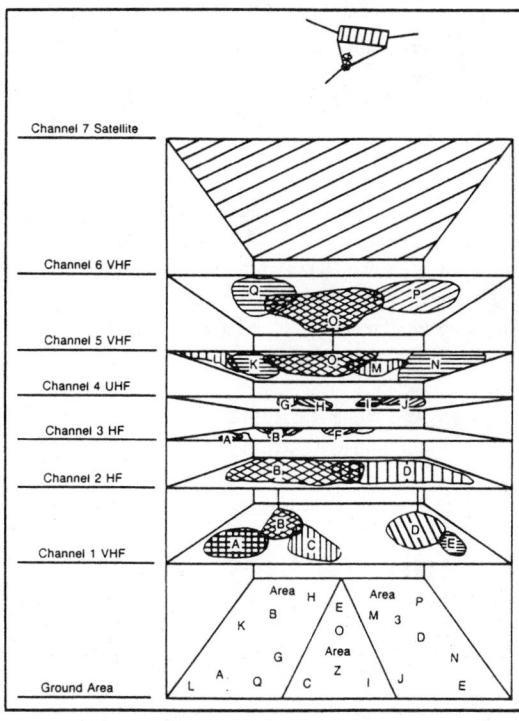

A model representing the present day amateur packet radio multiplexed network. Stations B, D, and O are gateways which allow stations on one layer to communicate on another layer. By spreading the total number of stations over several channels, the congestion on a single channel is reduced. Notice the wide coverage of the satellite channel. —*The Packet Radio Handbook*

**ARRL,** 225 Main Street, Newington, CT 06111

*To hook into the packet radio network we suggest you read Gateway, a newsletter published by the American Radio Relay League. If a "packeteer" could only get one magazine this is the one, and it's not overly technical.*

**CompuServe's HamNet SIG (GO** HAMNET). For information on joining, write or call: CompuServe, P.O. Box 20212, Columbus, OH 43220; 800/848-8199 or 614/457-0802

*HamNet has a section and data library devoted to packet, with at least one introductory on-line document*

on the subject, and an on-line version of **Gateway**, edited by ARRL, that reports significant, fast-breaking news and announcements every two weeks.

**Advanced Electronic Applications, Inc.,** P.O. Box C-2160, Lynwood, WA 98036; 206/775-7373

**Heath Company,** Benton Harbor, MI 49022; 800/253-0570

**Kantronics,** 1202 E. 23rd Street, Lawrence, KS 66046; 913/842-7745

*Each of these companies sells packet radio equipment. Send for their catalogs.*

## Electronic Cottage
# on Wheels

*by Steven K. Roberts*

I am an agent of future shock, frolicking in that strange region where the boundaries between technology and magic blur. I have finally found a job I like: high-tech nomad.

I live in a world that is part bicycle, part computer network, and part kaleidoscopic amalgam of lifestyles that span the full spectrum of human behavior. My office is a computerized, 36-speed, 220-pound, 8-foot-long recumbent bicycle bedecked with solar panels and enough gizmology to re-seed Silicon Valley after the Big One. While traveling full time on this machine, I maintain a freelance writing business—the ideal way to get paid for playing. With occasional layovers for major projects, I have been doing this since late 1983, cranking out some four million pedal strokes, and about the same number of keystrokes.

What are the tools that have allowed me to break the chains that once bound me to my desk and make a living anywhere with virtually no overhead?

During my first 10,000 miles, I carried only one computer. Though it was an astonishingly robust system (the Hewlett-Packard Portable PLUS), I still couldn't write while riding. Since 10,000 miles corresponds to roughly 1,000 hours of pure pedaling time (half a business year), this is no small matter—I had far too many days of good ideas, good intentions, and no work output.

I took a year's sabbatical from the road and dedicated myself to building a different system. The original

Steven Roberts uploads a days worth of writing into the nearest port — a roadside pay phone. Steven can be reached on CompuServe 72757, 15.

intention—being able to type while riding—quickly evolved into a complete bicycle control and communications system.

When I'm on the road, my fingers dance a quiet staccato on the handlebars. They move as if playing the flute, pressing combinations of eight waterproof keys to yield any of 256 binary codes—a convenient handlebar/keyboard that will type both letters and control characters. Up in the console, the bicycle control processor reacts—decoding the incoming data into a modified Radio Shack Model 100. The net effect: smooth, machine-readable text captured while I'm on the road, yielding files that can be downloaded to the HP for fine tuning and subsequent transmission from the first available telephone to my Ohio office via electronic mail on the GEnie computer network.

The solar battery-charging process is now under computer control, as are the security system, self diagnostics, electronic compass, and more. A fourth processor handles speech synthesis (it can read text files out loud and explain itself to curious passers-by); a fifth manages

packet data communication via two-meter ham radio. A CB radio is also on board, culturally useless by comparison, but still valuable enough to justify its weight.

Other radio-related devices include a Sony digital shortwave for international broadcast reception, a Sony Watchman micro-TV, and an FM stereo. Naturally, there is also an audio casette deck, and a compact disc player is planned for under-dash installation soon.

All the equipment described so far, plus behind-the-scenes control circuitry, requires electricity—in six different voltages. A pair of 10-watt Solarex photovoltaic panels serves as the primary source. When too many cloudy days occur back to back, a power supply with line cord allows refueling from house current.

The bike itself was designed for full-time, heavily loaded touring, with thick-wall, chrome-moly tubing, triple rear stays, tandem-style crossover drive, wide-range gearing (later expanded to 36 speeds), and a 48-spoke undished rear wheel with disc brake. The entire machine was fitted with braze-ons to support my unusual needs. I took it from there—using the bike as as substrate for the trappings of my life, changing form every year or so as new technologies become available.

Full-time bicycle touring raises an interesting issue. What, in the words of Alvin Toffler, can a traveler use as an "enclave of stability" while wandering endlessly across the earth's surface? The bike itself, while deeply familiar and "home" in may ways, is not enough to satisfy that basic need.

My enclave of stability is found on the networks—a strange amalgam of satellite and bicycle, cloud and soil, a place that is no place yet is every place at once. Give me a telephone and I'm home: all it takes is connection of the computer and a few typed commands and I cross that familiar threshold, see the GEnie sign-on messages that let me know I'm inside. Beyond those electronic portals I meet my closest friends, keep up with the activities of my Ohio office, publish weekly travel tales, seek help with arcane technical problems, find kindred spirits, and sometimes just hang around bantering with other vaporous denizens of the network—intellectual projections of real humans sitting somewhere on Earth. I wander freely in physical space, returning to my stable home in Dataspace night after night for stability and security.

I'm often asked how far, how fast, how many states, how long. The frequent questions along these goal-oriented numerical lines are hard to answer properly on the streets: I am here. Period. Tomorrow I might be somewhere else but maybe I'll still be here—who knows? If you think too much about where you're going, you lose respect for where you are.

# Handie-Talkies

*by Blair Newman*

Amateur ("ham") radio can be a low cost alternative to cellular phones. With a $250 "handie-talkie" you can make virtually unlimited local telephone calls at an annual cost of about $30.

There are, however, a few catches:

(1) You can only make outgoing calls, and not receive incoming ones.

(2) Only "personal" calls are legal. Business conversations, even ordering a pizza to go, are prohibited by FCC regulations.

(3) You have to join a "repeater club" (a repeater is a base station linked to the phone lines) and pay their dues (the $30/yr.).

(4) You have to get a Technician class ham license from the federal government, which means passing a two part test. The first part has multiple choice questions about electronics and FCC regulations. It's pretty easy be-

cause the entire "pool" of possible questions, and their answers, are published. The second part requires being able to understand Morse code at 5 words per minute. Think of it as learning a foreign language — a language with only 40 "words": the 26 letters of the alphabet, the 10 digits, and 4 punctuation symbols. The easiest way to learn is listening to Morse code practice tapes. It takes 10 to 20 hours.

For more info check your local library for introduction-to-ham-radio- books, check the Yellow pages under Radio for your local ham retailer, or call Ham Radio Outlet (800-854-6064; in CA 415/342-5757) and order **The Technician/General License Manual** (ARRL, $5), plus either **The 21 day Novice Course** (West, $20) or **Tune in the World** (ARRL, $20). The latter two include practice tapes.

A final note: The vast majority of activity on the ham radio bands are recreational discussions, not phone calls. It's kind of the audio equivalent of computer conference, similar to telephone "chat lines" except free. Different groups "hang out" on different frequencies: In San Francisco one channel is mainly Grateful Dead-heads, another is mainly computer hobbyists, etc.

# The General Mobile Radio Service

*by Benn Kobb*

Instantaneous, two-way mobile voice communication can save a lot of time and trouble in daily life, and be very useful in managing group activities.

In the mid-1970s, when truck drivers set up rolling radio networks to warn of speed-traps and help each other find fuel during the oil embargo, Citizens Band (CB) radio boomed. Though still somewhat useful for moni-toring traffic conditions and reporting emergencies, CB today is plagued by interference, technical shortcomings, and a subculture of recreational users. CB is not suitable for many personal communications needs.

However, the General Mobile Radio Service (GMRS), CB's predecessor, offers professional quality, noise-free, two-way communications on frequencies that make smaller hand-held radios practical. GMRS is making a comeback among folks who need radio to coordinate their daily personal, business and family activities.

Unlike amateur, commercial and governmental radio services, where only certain types of information may legally be transmitted, GMRS licensees can use their channels to discuss any personal or business matter, so long as proper station identification is used and messages are relatively brief.

An FCC license is required, but you don't have to learn Morse Code, pass a technical exam, or be a business to get one. You simply have to fill out a license form correctly and be at least 18 years old. The license costs $30 and is good for 5 years. It permits you to operate on one or two of GMRS's eight channels. License forms and instruction guides are available from your local FCC office, or from the Personal Radio Steering Group (see below).

If you own or have access to a scanner, (a radio receiver often used to listen to police and fire communications), program it to scan 462.550 - 462.725 MHz. That will reveal what GMRS activity already exists in your area. You'll want to know who your airwave "neighbors" are before you begin the licensing process, so you can sign up for the least-crowded channels.

A repeater is a relay station located on a tower or tall building. Its purpose is to expand the range of hand-held or vehicular radios, so you can communicate with a family member or friend on the other side of town, even though your small radio cannot reach that distance by itself. Repeaters aren't allowed in CB, and cannot be used by unlicensed "walkie-talkies," either. However, they are one of GMRS's major advantages. Repeaters are usually set up and operated by local user cooperatives or public-service teams (volunteers who provide radio communications in emergencies). They are often open to anyone in the area who obeys GMRS regulations and pays a small usage fee.

GMRS radios are identical to those manufactured for the ultra-high-frequency (UHF) "business" bands. The only difference is that the radio is tuned specifically for

GMRS. Look in the Yellow Pages under "Radio" for dealers in your area. Expect to pay $500-$2000 for a brand new handheld or vehicle-mounted transceiver. Many GMRS users buy used equipment, which is plentiful and usually cheaper than new. Local GMRS user groups are often able to recommend good sources of equipment.

Even though GMRS is classed by federal law as a "personal radio service," the FCC has allowed large commercial operations to usurp channels in many areas.

These fleet-dispatchers, factories, and package-delivery services are often intolerant of nonbusiness users of GMRS. Fortunately, the FCC has proposed major revisions to the rules of GMRS which are expected to take effect in 1989. These should enhance access to the service by individuals and families.

The not-for-profit Personal Radio Steering Group, Inc. (PRSG), was established in 1982 to encourage and assist individuals in getting licensed for and using GMRS, and to fight against further commercial usurpation of GMRS channels. They publish the GMRS National Repeater Guide ($3, 62 pp.); a booklet titled "What is the GMRS?" (free for 45-cent SASE, 12 pp.); and an informative monthly newsletter called the Personal Radio Exchange ($20/year). All are recommended if you think GMRS may be appropriate for your needs.

That's what GMRS offers. While it does have limitations, it's one of the most accessible and functional of all the services that utilize the public airwaves.

**Personal Radio Steering Group, Inc.**, P.O. Box 2851, Ann Arbor, MI 48103; 313/769-1616; Compuserve: 73016, 163.

## Cellular Telephones
(A Layman's Guide)
Stuart Crump, Jr.
1985; 146 pp.
**$9.95 postpaid from:**
TAB Books, Inc.
Blue Ridge Summit, PA 17294-0550
1-800-233-1128

## Cellular Mobile Telephone Guide
A. Seybold & M. Samples
1986; 202 pp.
**$9.95**
($13.45 postpaid) from:
Howard Sams & Co.
4300 West 62nd Street
Indianapolis, IN 46268
1-800-428-7267

*Neither of these two books are definitive, but there's not much else reliable.* **Cellular Telephones** *introduces nicely with lots of diagrams. It will help you determine if you need one.* **Cellular Mobile** *figures you're already sold on the idea but need to demonstrate the cost/benefit ratio to feel good about it. It then helps you choose one to actually install in your car (all cellular radio is car-bound so far). I doubt that anything can save you from the sharks selling the gear.*

*— Kevin Kelly*

◆

In addition to radio energy being absorbed by trees and walls, it also "bounces" around or is reflected by metals, certain types of rock, and even dirt and water. Because of these bouncing, reflecting, and absorbing effects on radio signals, it is not possible to design a system that will provide 100% coverage in any given area. If your vehicle is parked and you find you cannot access the system, perhaps moving the car just a foot or so will make a great difference. When pulling up to a stop light

or moving slowly in traffic, you might notice some "fading" or loss of signal.

◆

The carriers have estimated that the average cellular telephone bill will be in the neighborhood of $125 to $150 per month.

◆

As a general rule, you should remember one thing: Whatever you say on a cellular phone can be heard by other people. *—Cellular Mobile Telephone Guide*

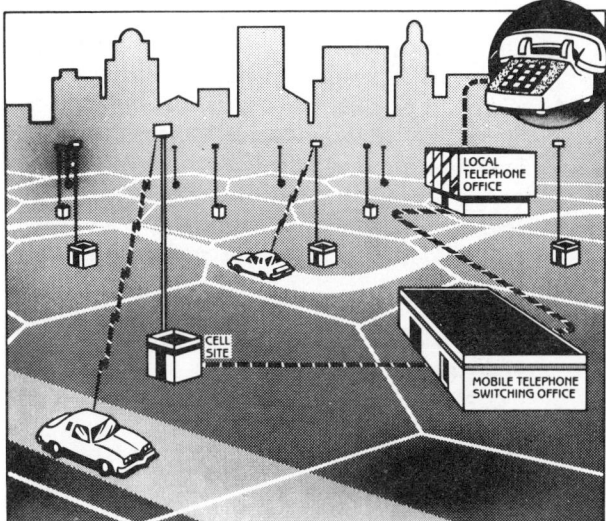

HOW CELLULAR WORKS. Cellular depends on a network of "cells" (indicated on this diagram by the hexagon-shaped segments) that cover a city. A low-powered radio transmitter and control equipment is located near the center of each cell. This cell-site equipment is connected to the "mobile telephone switching office" (MTSO), which is the gateway to the regular landline telephone network. When you place a car-phone call, the MTSO monitors the strength of your phone's signal at each of the cell sites near you. The closest site handles your call. As you move from one cell to another, your signal is automatically "handed off" to the next cell, giving you a clear, strong signal. *—Cellular Telephones*

## The Handbook for the Radio Amateur

Mark Wilson, Editor
$23.50 postpaid from:
ARRL
225 Main Street
Newington, CT 06111
203/666-1541
or Whole Earth Access

The largest and oldest national organization of ham radio operators, the *American Radio Relay League*, publishes a wide variety of excellent books, learning aids, and how-to guides, designed to serve absolute beginners as well as advanced experimenters. Their annual **Handbook** is a comprehensive reference, finely honed over the years to explain radio theory and practice in the clearest, most accurate, hands-on terms. Includes many construction projects.

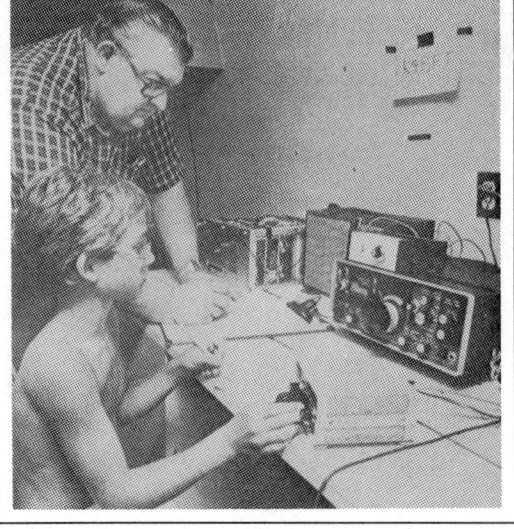

Bill Christian, K4IKR (left) and Tim Dionne, KB4BDG, operate in an annual Field Day, a two-day event where thousands of radio amateurs around the U.S. set up and operate portable, emergency-powered stations.

Don't order it without asking about their other goodies.
—Robert Horvitz

## Monitoring Times

Larry Miller, Editor
$18/12 issues from:
140 Dog Branch Road
Brasstown, NC 28902
704/837-9200

This monthly, aimed at shortwave listeners, scanner enthusiasts, ham operators and satellite dish owners, tells how to tune in virtually any radio signal in the air. (Since no help is needed with local AM and FM broadcasts, those are ignored in favor of more exotic fare.)

**MT**'s core is a current worldwide schedule of English-language shortwave broadcasts. Reviews of new receivers and radio publications, interviews with on-air personalities, and simple do-it-yourself projects fill most of the rest of the page-space. Even if you don't own the kinds of receivers that enable you to tune in hurricane-hunting aircraft, Mississippi barges, or Radio Havana, a subscription to **Monitoring Times** is a cheap way to pre-

| 0100 UTC | | [8:00 PM EST/5:00 PM PST] | | | | |
|---|---|---|---|---|---|---|
| 0100-0103 | S | Port Moresby, Papua New Guinea | 3295 | 4890 | 5960 | 5985 |
| | | | 6020 | 6040 | 6080 | 6140 |
| | | | 9520 | | | |
| 0100-0110 | | Vatican Radio, Vatican City | 6150 | 7315 | 9605 | 11780 |
| 0100-0115 | | All India Radio, New Delhi | 6055 | 7215 | 9535 | 9910 |
| | | | 11715 | 11745 | 15110 | |
| 0100-0120 | | RAI, Rome, Italy | 9575 | 11800 | | |
| 0100-0125 | | Kol Israel, Jerusalem | 7462 | 9435 | 9845 | |
| 0100-0130 | | HCJB, Quito, Ecuador | 9720 | 11775 | 11910 | 15155 |
| 0100-0130 | | Radio Berlin Int'l, E. Germany | 6080 | 9730 | | |
| 0100-0130 | | Radio Canada Int'l, Montreal | 9535 | 11845 | 11940 | |
| 0100-0130 | T-A | Radio Canada Int'l, Montreal | 5960 | 9755 | | |
| 0100-0130 | | Radio Japan, Tokyo | 15280 | 17810 | 17835 | 17845 |
| 0100-0130 | | Laotian National Radio | 7113v | | | |
| 0100-0145 | | WYFR, Oakland, California | 5950 | 7440 | 9555 | 9680 |
| 0100-0150 | | Deutsche Welle, West Germany | 6040 | 6085 | 6145 | 9545 |
| | | | 9565 | 11785 | | |
| 0100-0200 | | (US) Armed Forces Radio and TV | 6030 | 15345 | | |

Broadcast loggings.

view what's available, and make a more informed decision when you do decide to take the plunge.
—Robert Horvitz
◆

Do you remember the old civil rights hymn "We Shall Overcome," made famous by the followers of the Rev. Martin Luther King? Recently it was heard in English on the shortwaves, on the 6220 kHz domestic service of Radio Iran! Apparently, the song has taken on a new meaning for the followers of the Ayatollah: overcoming Iraqis.

## Association of North American Radio Clubs (ANARC)

P.O. Box 462, Northfield, MN 55057

Radio club newsletters are one of the best — and cheapest — ways to get current information about shortwave schedules and frequencies, reviews of new products, tutorials on how to improve reception, and share the fun of probing the radio spectrum. If you want to meet others who share that interest, save money buying used equipment, or get help in identifying a mysterious station or noise-source, that's exactly what clubs are for.

The *Association of North American Radio Clubs (ANARC)* is the umbrella organization for groups whose radio activities don't require a license (as distinguished from ham radio, which does require a

license). Some ANARC clubs specialize in shortwave listening, others in scanners, AM, FM, catching TV broadcasts from distant sites, etc. Some clubs are local (the Michigan Area Radio Enthusiasts, for instance); others are international (e.g., the North American Shortwave Association). To find one that fits your needs, send a self-addressed stamped envelope to ANARC Publications, P.O. Box 462, Northfield, MN 55057 USA. Ask for their Club list, which gives the addresses, membership fees and interests. For a good overview of the whole club scene, write to the same address for a subscription to the **ANARC Newsletter** ($7.50/year, 12 monthly issues). (In the post-Watergate spirit of Full Disclosure, I'm the current head of ANARC, and edit the **Newsletter**.)
—Robert Horvitz

## The Sony ICF-SW1

$339.95.
For dealer nearest you, call 800/222-7669.

During the past 10 years, Sony has revolutionized shortwave radio design, putting superior performance into ever-smaller and easier-to-use packages. Considering how much circuitry is needed to pluck weak signals out of the overcrowded bands for international broadcasting, their latest entry, the ICF-SW1, seems almost miraculous.

About the size of an audio cassette, it has a digital frequency display, keypad tuning, 10 programmable channel pre-selects and a 24-hour clock/timer. In addition to shortwave, the SW1 offers AM, stereo FM, and longwave coverage (longwave is used for broadcasting in Europe). There's a built-in speaker, but the ear pieces supplied with the set provide better sound. An "active" (amplifying) antenna comes with the SW1, as does a power-supply that automatically adapts to whatever voltage comes out of the wall-socket. The set can also operate from two internal AA batteries.

Because of the SW1's extreme compactness, some compromises had to be made. You can only tune through the shortwave band in 5 kHz steps, for example. Since most SW stations are 5 kHz apart, that's usually OK — but stations on offset or oddball frequencies won't be heard as well. It also lacks single-sideband capability, so you can't listen to the aircraft, ships, and ham radio operators that communicate in the bands between the ones used for shortwave broadcasting.

For travellers who need an ultra-small, lightweight radio, there's nothing else in its class. For those who want a good portable, the SW1 should be considered — although larger portables are available that are comparable in performance, and quite a bit cheaper.

—Robert Horvitz

## A*C*E

Keith J. Thibodeaux, Editor
$12/year (12 issues) from:
Keith J. Thibodeaux
P.O. Box 1744
Wilmington, DE 19899

*The Association of Clandestine radio Enthusiasts (A*C*E) is for people interested in pirate and clandestine broadcasting.*

*"Clandestine" in this context means unlicensed stations trying to undermine the political order in a target area. Most are covertly sponsored by governments, or overtly identified with insurgent groups. Radio Venceremos, "official voice of the Farabundo Marti National Liberation Front," is a well-known example in Central America. A less well-known example, closer to home, is "La Voz de Alpha 66," an anti-Castro station based in or near Miami that broadcasts three nights a week in Spanish to Cuba. A*C*E's monthly newsletter publishes reports about such stations, though the primary focus is on "pirates."*

*Pirates aren't trying to overthrow a government; they generally just want to offer an alternative to what licensed stations carry. In Western Europe, where broadcasting has traditionally been monopolized by national governments, pirates went on the air to provide*

The heart of a transmitter is its oscillator which determines the fundamental carrier frequency which can later be amplified and modulated by the rest of the rig. Figure 2 displays the schematic diagram for our transmitter's oscillator.

*local, ethnic, and commercial programming. Their popularity proved the need for such programming and in many cases led to liberalization of broadcasting controls. The pirate scene in North America is quite different. Here it's more in the nature of a prank or a sport, with public service not a typical motive. There are some genuinely bizarre and creative pirates ("The Crooked Man" and "Radio Angeline" are my two favorites), but the majority are lame parodies of legal stations. The FCC cracked down on U.S. pirates last fall, just as the scene was starting to snowball. Since then, only a few stations have made brief appearances (usually on Saturday night around 7425 kHz shortwave).*

*But A*C*E continues to be the best way to track this sort of activity. Membership gets you their monthly newsletter, with loggings, reports of busts, interviews with pirates, technical tips, etc. Also included are extensive listings of recent "numbers" broadcasts — mysterious coded messages believed to be instructions beamed to spies. Some people make a hobby of trying to figure out the codes or locating the transmitters. Most of this work goes on behind the scenes, but the listings in A*C*E will at least help you find the broadcasts.*
*—Robert Horvitz*

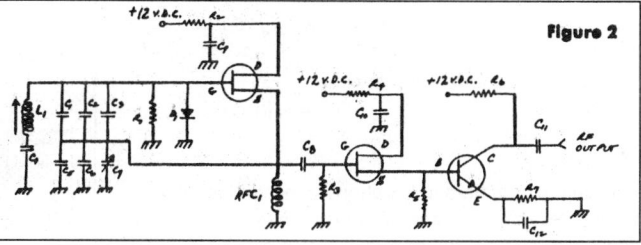

**Figure 2**

◆

*The Crooked Man: 3433, 3/24, 0005-0015*, SIO=454. Rock mx, w/ "telephonic" voice over mx "When I was in S. Carolina he gave me a haircut," "he's afraid of me," "he's on speed," claimed to have invented the ultra violet light, much talk revolved around blue and purple. Sounded like he was either tripping or psychotic. Must be a good actor. Nobody could be that wasted and put such a decent signal, exactly on freq a year after last being reported here and sound* just *as strange! (Provance, OH)*

◆

*Voice of Bob: 7435, 2/15, *2042-2053*, SIO=211-222. Featured "Mr. Science Lecture Series" The Neutron. Some mx and several different air personalities. Hilo address. (Mendyk, IL)*

◆

This month we begin with some QSL address information. Recent QSL reports from several sources indicate that a few addresses have produced verifications from some commonly heard Latin American clandestines. Among these is La Voz de Alpha 66 at P.O. Box 420067, Miami, Florida 33142. In addition, both Radio Miscut and Radio Monimbo have reportedly been verifying and/or quasi-verifying through the UDC-FDN United States office, which is located at 1000 Thomas Jefferson Street, Suite 607, Washington, DC 20007. It is highly recommended that detailed, polite reports, as well as prepared QSL cards, be utilized when corresponding with these addresses. Otherwise, your odds of a reply will go down significantly, and the QSL sources themselves may dry up for other DX-ers in the future.

## Equipment Suppliers

*Although radio equipment is more widely available than it used to be, you may not have a store nearby that carries a good selection. Mail order is still a convenient way to shop, and the prices are generally less than you'd pay in a store. These are some of the leading mail order suppliers of shortwave equipment.*
*—Robert Horvitz*

**EGE:** Catalog $1 from 14803 Build America Drive, Building B, Woodbridge, VA 22191; 703/494-8750 or 800/444-4799 (catalog orders only).

**Universal Shortwave Radio:** Catalog $1 from 1280 Aida Drive, Reynoldsburg, OH 43068; 614/866-4392 or 800/431-3939 (catalog orders only).

**Electronic Equipment Bank:** Catalog **free** from 516 Mill Street, NE, Vienna, VA 22180; 703/938-3350 or 800/368-3270 (catalog orders only).

**Grove Enterprises:** Catalog **free** from P.O. Box 98, 140 Dog Branch Road, Brasstown, NC 28902; 704/837-9200 or 800/438-8155 (catalog orders only).

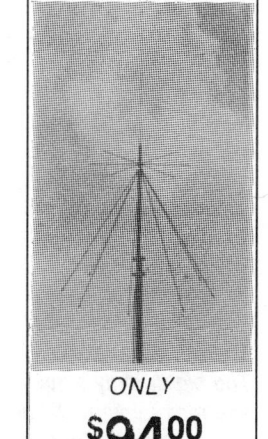

ONLY

$**94**00

plus $3 UPS
$5 U.S. Mail Parcel Post
Canadians: $10 Air Parcel Post

Professional Wideband Discone from Grove Enterprises

## The Complete Manual of Pirate Radio

Zeke Teflon
25 pp.
$2 postpaid from:
Bound Together
Book Collective
1369 Haight Street
San Francisco, CA 94117
415/431-8355

*A cynic once said that freedom of the press belongs to those who are rich enough to own one. The author of this booklet, who goes by the nomme d'aire of Zeke Teflon, feels the same way about freedom of broadcast and the transmitters required for the operation. His refreshingly anarchistic attitude is that the air belongs to everyone, and he gives us a formula for reclaiming it from the media conglomerates.*

*The fact that most of Zeke's schemes are illegal and could land you in the pokey must be kept in mind, but that very risk adds to Zeke's zest for the venture. He gives us an overview of the possibilities — AM, FM, shortwave, availability of used*

*equipment, antenna needs, the pros and cons of fixed, remote and mobile operations, plus cost estimates, which are surprisingly low. A few hundred dollars could launch a small outfit.*
*—Dick Fugett*

◆

Piracy is illegal. If you're busted the government can seize your equipment, drag you through the courts, fine you hundreds or even thousands of dollars, and theoretically, throw you in jail, although I've never heard of that happening to anyone. So, it makes sense to take every possible precaution to avoid The Knock (on your door from the FCC).

The ideal situation — in terms of maximizing listenership — for a radio station is to broadcast 24 hours a day, on a set frequency, with high power, from a fixed location. Attempting such operations as a pirate, however, would be suicidal.

On the other extreme, you could go on the air with an extremely low power (under 100mw) transmitter which would be legal under FCC rules and regulations. If you would be satisfied with a broadcasting radius of a couple of blocks, that would be the route to go. In fact, in cities with high population densities such as San Francisco and New York, such an approach makes a lot of sense.

## Satellite TV Week

John Ponce, Editor
$48/year
(52 issues) from:
Satellite TV Week
P. O. Box 308
Fortuna, CA 95540
800/345-8876

*Decidedly the best listings for figuring out which program to watch when there are 18 satellites, each delivering three channels on average, in four time zones, beaming down 24 hours a day. Many other contenders' listings are muddled and unwieldy (they come out monthly or fortnightly; this arrives weekly). It has the neatest movie index, which notes every place and every time a particular movie will show. Can't miss it.*

— Kevin Kelly

"A SONG IS BORN" ** (1948, Musical) Danny Kaye, Virginia Mayo. A group of academics writing a history of music finds its work interrupted by a nightclub singer on the run from the authorities. (1 hr., 53 min.)
**Mon.** 19 [G1]11:00 am; 23 [F3] 2:00 pm **Thu.** 19 [G1] 3:00 am **Fri.** 19 [G1] 1:00 pm; 23 [F3] 6:00 am, 4:00 pm **Sat.** 10 [F4] 10:00 am, 8:00 pm

"SORCERER" *** (1977, Suspense) Roy Scheider, Bruno Cremer. Four desperate men risk their lives while hauling explosive nitroglycerine through South American jungles to battle an oil-well fire. 'PG' (2 hrs., 2 min.)
**Sat.** 10 [G1]7:30 am; 10 [G1] 6:00 [G1] 10:30 am,

10 [F3] 10:30 am
"TESTAMENT" *** (1983, Drama) Jane Alexander, William Devane. The aftermath of nuclear holocaust - from not knowing who launched the attack or why, to the horrors of slow death b radiation poisoning -- and its effects on a northern California family. 'PG' (Adult Situations) (1 hr., 29 min.)
**Sun.** 10 [G1]3:30 pm; 13 [F3] 11:00 am, 11:55 pm; 14 [G1] 6:30 pm; 23 [G1] 8:00 am, 8:55 pm **Thu.** 13 [F3] 2:00 pm; 23 [G1] 11:00 am **Sat.** 10 [G1] 10:00 am, 11:45 pm; 14 [G1] 1:00 pm, 2:45 am

"TEX" ** (1982, Drama) Matt Dillon, Jim Metzler. With his caring, but important older brother, an Oklahoma [...] experiences the [...] up. 'PG'

## The World of Satellite Television

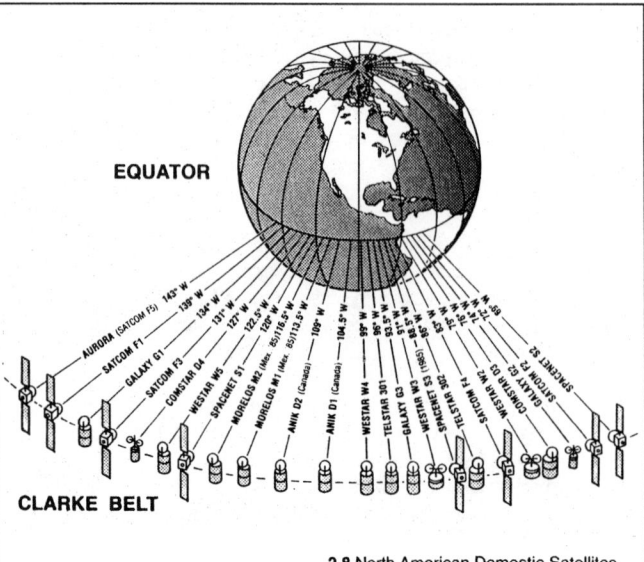

Mark Long and
Jeffrey Keating
1983; 224 pp.
$10.95
($12.95 postpaid) from:
Quantum Publishing, Inc.
P. O. Box 310
Mendocino, CA 95460
707/937-4488
or Whole Earth Access

*The big dummy's guide to installing, operating and maintaining a backyard satellite dish (by the authors of **The Big Dummy's Guide to C. B. Radio**). A basic, sensible, essential initiation to a precision tool.*

— Kevin Kelly

◆

Satellite signals are microwaves that exhibit most

## The Hidden Signals on Satellite TV

Thomas P. Harrington
and Bob Cooper, Jr.
1984; 179 pp.
**$14.95**
($16.70 postpaid) from:
Universal Electronics, Inc.
4555 Groves Road, Suite 3
Columbus, OH 43232
614/866-4605
or Whole Earth Access

*With more satellite-relayed TV programs being scrambled, backyard satellite dish promoters are starting to publicize the fact that your dish enables you to monitor other types of satellite-relayed signals, too. This book tells most of what you need to know to monitor long-distance phone calls, news agency teletype, stock and commodity prices, corporate data communications, audio services, etc. I'm not recommending you use your satellite dish that way; the importance of this book is in showing that it's relatively easy to do, using off-the-shelf equipment.*

*The book has lots of pictures and charts, but is badly copy-edited with many typos. Spelling errors can be seen and discounted at a glance; numerical typos are much harder to pick out, and this book has a lot of numbers. I'd be leery of taking them as gospel, but it's the descriptive passages that really matter, and there is no more explicit and detailed how-to manual currently available.*

— Robert Horvitz

◆

On some pure data and telephone transponders (non-video), you may hear something that sounds like a buzz saw, or something that sounds like musical chimes, or you may hear a telephone circuit ringing or a busy signal. On the active phone channels, you will hear telephone conversations, some radio feeds, communications circuits between satellite control operators, hotel and motel reservation sections, auto rental companies; at any given moment you could find between 600 to 1200 separate carriers in place!

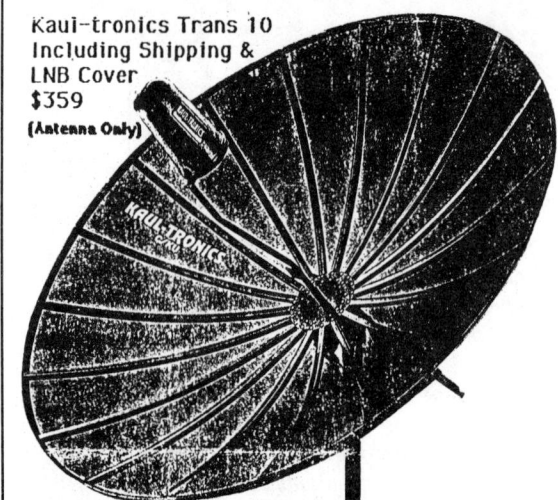

## The Spaceage Electronics Corp.

Catalog **free** from: P. O. Box 15730, New Orleans, LA 70175; 800/624-65909

*Simply the lowest prices on satellite dishes and receivers. Depending on where you live, their hours aren't the most convenient for calling: Monday through Friday, 9 AM to 5 PM Central time, but you can get a complete system package for between $1200 to $1800. The usual mail-order trade-off is in effect — some bargains, some risk. We have no experience with them. It looks dangerous if you have no idea what to buy.*

— Kevin Kelly & Richard Kadrey

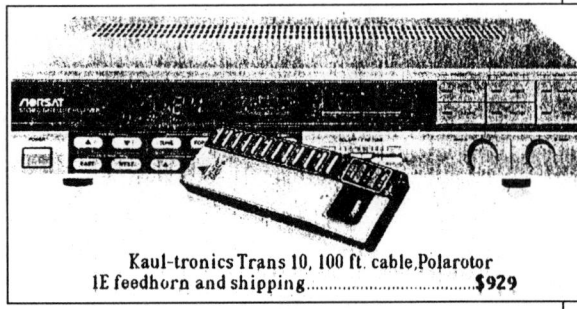

Kaul-tronics Trans 10, 100 ft. cable,Polarotor
1E feedhorn and shipping..................$929

of the characteristics of light, except visibility. Like visible light, they travel in a straight path along the line of sight. Since all geostationary satellites are positioned over the equator, if you want to receive them from the northern hemisphere, your antennae must have an unobstructed view of the southern sky. So, before you go running out and spending several thousand dollars for an earth station, you should be sure there are no tall buildings, trees, powerpoles, or other substantial obstacles to prevent signals from reaching your dish.

◆

*Symptom 11.* Picture looks fuzzy, with the ghost of another picture on top of the channel you want.

*What To Check.* You LNA polarizer is not completely tuning into the correct polarity. This could be caused by a bad power connection between the mechanical rotator and its indoor control mechanism. If electronic polarization is used, a bad cable connection or improper initial setup of the LNA/feedhorn could be the cause.

**2.8** North American Domestic Satellites.

# Satellites: Extraterrestrial Tools

*by Mark Long*

Working overseas helped me step beyond my purely American viewpoint to realize that the world is inhabited by numerous people and cultures with their own unique traditions, values and aspirations. I felt some of these ways were equal or superior to those I acquired while growing up in suburban America. Once I was back in the U.S., however, it was far too easy to get mesmerized by narrow nationalistic concerns which fail to consider how the rest of the world lives. To keep my global perspective honed to a fine edge, I employ a backyard full of dish-shaped antennas, each directed toward one of 40 telecommunications satellites which are accessible from my home in rural Florida. With the aid of my satellite "farm," I gain access to more than 200 television channels from 17 countries.

## Four Arguments for the Elimination of Television

Jerry Mander
1978; 371 pp.
**$7.95**
($9.45 postpaid) from:
William Morrow Publishing
Company
6 Henderson Drive
West Caldwell, NJ 07006
201/227-7200
or Whole Earth Access

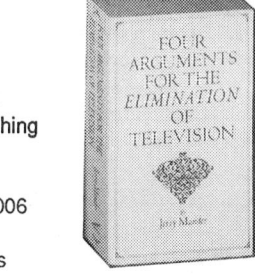

*Former adman Jerry Mander denounces the inherent dangers of a system where information is controlled by commercial interests and distorts our perception of reality. Food for thought if you're trying to kick the TV habit.*

*— Fabrice Florin*

◆

A majority of adults, nearly as high a percentage as children, use television to learn how to handle specific life problems: family routines; relationships with fellow workers; hierarchical values; how to deal with rebellious children; how to understand deviations from the social norm, sexually, politically, socially and interpersonally. The overall fare of television situation-comedies and dramatic programs is taken as valid, useful, informative, and, in the words of the report, "true to life."

Most viewers of television programming give the programming concrete validity, as though it were not fictional. When solving subsequent, similar problems in their own families, people report recalling how the problem was solved in a television version of that situation. They often make similar choices.

◆

Even if a given subtle emotion can be conveyed from time to time on TV, you could never build an entire program on it as you could on violent emotions. In signal-to-noise terms the entire program would become indistinct in comparison with the background of more aggressive, expressive and efficient action shows.

Russian cartoon program.

[Below] Test pattern for a Middle Eastern channel.

[Bottom] Peruvian historical documentary.

To receive foreign TV news programs, I maneuver my dish to catch signals emanating from Satcom F1. Channel 11 carries the early and late evening news from ITN London every day at 12:45 and 5:45 p.m. EST. On the same satellite, Channel 24 transmits the RAI Evening News from Rome weekdays at 1:45 p.m. EST. The daily Visnews and World Television News (WTN) roundups from London also appear on this satellite at other times of the day.

My favorite channel these days is on Telstar 301, which carries Russian News programs from Moscow. An American company known as Worldview receives the Moscow Evening News each day from one of the Soviet satellites and then retransmits it via Telstar 301. The Russian-language soundtrack is translated into English and the Russian TV signal is converted to the NTSC video standard so American TV sets can resolve their programs in full living color.

From watching this and the untranslated Soviet channels I get the clear idea that Russians are human beings just like the rest of us. They don't look any different, and many of their activities, like celebrating the holiday season with Christmas trees, or searching for a good mechanic to fix their automobile, are universal experiences. On the nightly news spots you see them sending their kids off to summer camp. You watch the weather, and you get to see temperatures in Siberia, which kind of freeze you right there.

I see the whole culture of the country, from the programs the kids watch in the mornings to the exercise programs. I can watch documentaries that cover both the present five-year agricultural plan and chess championships. The Russian satellites is not just used by the Russians; it's also shared by the Warsaw Pact countries.

I believe that one of the most significant uses of international TV here in North America is to allow students to really see what's happening culturally and economically in other countries. Recently I installed a satellite station at the Naval Academy in Annapolis that is used by Navy cadets to watch Russian TV in political science classes. Midshipmen who will be our future naval officers can see what is behind the Soviet government. By watching Russian TV everyday, they see the people as they really are, which, I hope, will make our officers better able to relate to them on a more human level.

I discovered from watching international TV that

satellites have a much greater impact on people in South America than they do here in the United States. Most of South America has no cable TV, and in many places they have no more than one or two, if any, broadcast channels. For them, access to programming from other countries via satellite is really very significant.

For example, most North Americans fail to understand the enormous impact and importance of Brazil in South America. We have no concept whatsoever of how sophisticated Brazil is. But if you watch their daily television programming, you immediately get a sense of the culture, significance and sheer magnitude of Brazil (with 135 million people it's the second most populous country in the Americas, after the U.S.). They have a wide variety of well-made programming and news reporting.

Some incredible political changes have been happening in Brazil. From my living room I watched their own TV broadcast demonstrations of hundreds of thousands of people marching in the streets. I could feel people's emotions as they began to have a direct voice in their government. To watch that developing and building up over a month's time, finally culminating in the election of a revisionist candidate was incredibly wakening. Measured by its impact on the world, Brazil is more significant than either France or Italy, but our TV ignores it. On the CBS News, Brazil might get three minutes a month. With my dish and extraterrestrial tools I can watch as much as I want.

# Non-commercial FM and Low-power Television

*by Lorenzo W. Milam*

The most inexpensive way to become a broadcaster is to put a noncommercial FM station on the air. This will only work if you are out in the boondocks (at least 150 miles from the nearest major city). It might cost you $10,000 to begin broadcasting, but it will be less if you are smart, careful, patient, wily, and know how to steal FM transmitters under cover of darkness. Make contact with the National Federation of Community Broadcasters at 1314 14th Street NW, Washington, D.C. 20005; 202/797-8911. They will give you a step-by-step on how to apply for such a station. You will need an engineer, a nonprofit corporation, a transmitter site, a frequency, and lots of time.

In 1980, the FCC opened the door for "low power" television station (LPTV) applications. The rules permitted new television stations in most markets. The Commission was deluged with applications, and has only recently cleared away most of them. Periodically, they open doors — called, naturally, "windows" — for further applications. These are announced in the trade magazines like **Broadcasting** (which is too expensive to subscribe to, but which you can find at your local public or university library).

Channel 2-13 (VHF) LPTV is *really* low power (ten watts maximum, which might not carry more than half a mile). For UHF (Channels 14-69), you are allowed transmitter output power up to 1,000 watts. With a clever antenna system, and multiple transmitters, you might be able to cover a fairly major service area.

The VHS stations are cheap, but the UHF transmitters can cost at least $25,000, and the antennas another $10,000. The rules on the programming and operation are quite lax — the FCC gives you enormous latitude on what you can program.

(We thought of getting an LPTV station on the air, running continuous slides of the kid's birthday party from last summer, footage from NASA [all space shots are public domain], and home movies collected from all the neighbors. We'd play some bizarre and wonderful music on the sound channel—gagaku from Japan, Balkan folk singing, songs of Henry Purcell, Blind Lemon Jefferson. What a way to spend an evening, no? Launching into space with the Monkey Chant, landing on the moon to "Sound of the Trumpets," walking on the Mare Incognito with "The A-to-Z Blues." Under the LPTV programming rules of the FCC, it's all legal.)

What I have told you about Low Power Television is worth a mere pickle. The real kicker is how you can get close to going on the air with little or no effort on your part:

Because of the first application rush, the FCC was forced to set up a lottery system so they could process them all. In the last three years, the Commission has made over 4,000 grants of LPTV stations all over the country, including

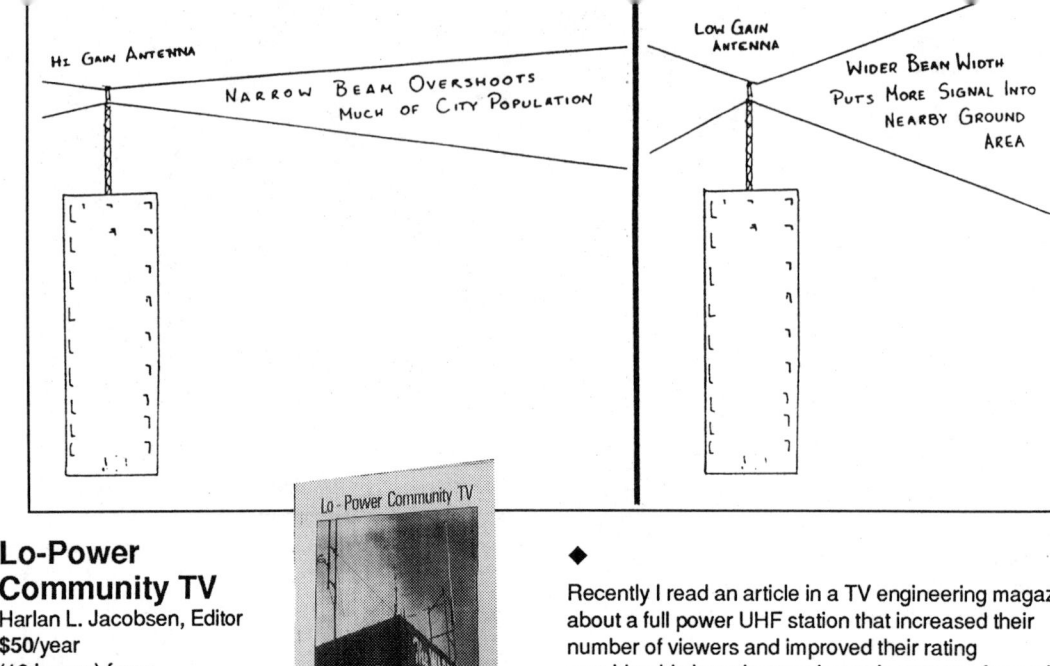

Alaska, Hawaii, Puerto Rico, the Virgin Islands, Guam, and Micronesia. However, many of the people who got permits aren't building. There are no more than 250 LPTV stations on the air right now.

The commission doesn't take kindly to grantees who hold onto the permits and never build. Unless they have very good excuses, they are forced to surrender them a year from the date of the grant. This can be a bonanza for you. What you have to do is to find out what permits have been granted for your area, or the city or cities you're interested in. From this information, you can make contact with the permit holders. If they have lost their permit, you can perhaps pick up the transmitter site option, and file your own application, using some of the information from their (successful) application. If they still have the permit, but are running into difficulties building the station, you might be able to negotiate with them. In return for your helping to get the station on the air, you might be able to share the ownership. At worst, you can learn a great deal by talking with the people involved, and reading over the applications that have been filed, gone onto lottery, and been granted. Even those that have lost out will teach you what is available in the way of equipment and sites. This is basic FCC form school; how to put an application in the hopper and (perhaps) how to win.

(To do all this, you need a copying service in Washington, D.C. that specializes in FCC Releases. A good one is Berry's Best, 1705 DeSales Street NW, Washington, D.C. 20036; 202/293-4964. You can hire them to dig up any

## Lo-Power Community TV

Harlan L. Jacobsen, Editor
$50/year
(12 issues) from:
Lo-Power Community
Television Publishing
7432 West Diamond
Scottsdale, AZ 85257
602/945-6746

*Editor Harlan Jacobsen appears to be a sort of populist hero in low-power TV circles. His no-frills magazine is a good source of detailed, practical advice on running a low-power TV station. Sample copies are $5.*

*—Sarah Vandershaf*

◆

Recently I read an article in a TV engineering magazine about a full power UHF station that increased their number of viewers and improved their rating considerably by going to a low gain antenna from a high gain antenna.

They noted that the theoretical power in the fringes would be way lower, but noted they lost very few viewers in the outlying areas.

The theory behind this is that the high gain antenna has such a narrow beam width that the 80% of their viewers, who were nearby in town, were being overshot in order to put a higher power signal out in the country. With the low gain antenna and wider beam width, they were putting more of the signal in the ground nearby.

## The LPTV Report

Jacquelyn Biel, Editor
$25/year
(12 issues) from:
LPTV Report
P.O. Box 25510
Milwaukee, WI 53225-0510
414/781-0188

*Slicker than **Lo-Power Community TV**, this magazine, "the official information channel of the Community Broadcasters Association," will give you the legal and business angles on low-power TV, as well as some technical insights.*

*—Sarah Vandershaf*

◆

In the rush to apply for LPTV permits, some early applications were not engineered very well, the thought being that they could be easily modified after grant. Also, sites that were available four years ago may no longer be available. Thus, some new CP holders are finding that they need to locate a new antenna site. . . . The new site must be very close to the old one, and the new proposal must not serve any people that the old one didn't. This usually means that you'll need a new site that is less than a mile away from the old one.

filing at the FCC that you might want to see. I would ask for copies of the winners' names from the last two years' worth of lotteries.)

# Interactive Video

*by Fabrice Florin*

Interactive video will give you a good reason to turn your TV back on. Rather than watching passively, slumped in an armchair, you drive this video software like a computer program. At the touch of buttons you scan through a storehouse of images and sounds much as you would flip through the pages of a book. With the help of a microcomputer you can rearrange the display of sound and images in a new order, or have it branch in alternative paths for guided tours, lessons or games. Like a good book, it encourages multiple viewings.

The heart of the new machine is a videodisc, the same glimmering plastic laser videodiscs that play popular movies and, in compact size, music. Each disc becomes an extremely durable visual encyclopedia with up to 54,000 color pages per disc side. A slide collection that large would cost four or five times the price of the disc. It can also contain the equivalent of several 16mm films, which could justify the purchase of both a player and a disc. Some of the better discs have dual sound tracks. The initial one is for beginners; then you graduate and go through the same images with the advanced sound track. The largest drawback so far is that you cannot *record* images or sounds—unless you produce your own videodisc (see below).

# Creating Your Own Videodisc

*by Fabrice Florin*

Producing an interactive videodisc is easier than it sounds. A disc is essentially a half-hour video program containing short clips and still images arranged so that users can find them quickly. Pressing a disc requires special equipment, but it's a pretty straghtforward operation. And with programs like HyperCard, the cost of making your videodisc interactive is mainly a function of how much of your own time you want to invest in creating the links. The most common method involves editing a re-master videotape of up to 30 minutes that will contain both clips and stills.

You edit the clips as you would any other video or TV program, using a 3/4" or 1" videotape editing system. Although professional producers prefer to use high-quality 1" videotape editing facilities ($100-400/hour), it is also possible to rent cheaper 3/4" editing systems for as

low as $20/hour. For most in-house uses, a Sony series 5800 3/4" editing system should do, as long as you know what you're doing. The editing system lets you assemble separate clips from various sources onto a single master videotape, as well as insert new audio or video materials into it.

Recording still pictures one frame at a time is trickier. The most effective way is to send your images to a specialized image transfer facility such as Stokes or Image Pre-Mastering and they'll do the job for you, generally recording it onto 1" tape. If your material is easy to transfer (such as a couple of slide carousels with all slides horizontally oriented), figure between $1 and $2 per picture (under $1 for volume deals), plus incidental costs ($300-500 minimum for set-up fees). You could also have a local video facility shoot all pictures with a professional video camera connected to a Sony 2500 1" videotape recorder that can record single frames (depending on volume, $100-200/hour). Alternatives include buying (or renting from specialized vendors at $500/day) a write-once disc recorder such as the Panasonic TQ-2026F, then transferring the series of frames to your 3/4" or 1" final edited master.

Finally, when you have all your stills and clips on a single edited tape re-master, you send it out to a pressing facility, which will make one or more discs for you. For about $2000, companies such as 3M will press a disc master from which you can order additional copies for around $10/disc. If you only need one or two copies for in-house use, you

could also order plastic or glass "check discs" from such companies as Crawford Communications, pressed overnight for about $300-500 per disc.

**Crawford Communications:** 506 Plasters Avenue, Atlanta, GA 30324; 404/876-8722. Instant "check discs" — 48-hour turn-around.

**Discount Videodisc Players:** Catalog **free** from American Technology Resources, 1245 Providence Road, Media, PA 19063; 215/565-6434. Although this dealer specializes in industrial videodisc equipment, consumers can find some pretty good deals on reconditioned players or brand new models at wholesale prices. Ask for referrals if they don't have what you need.

**Image Pre-Mastering:** 1781 Prior Avenue, St. Paul, MN 55113; 612/644-7802. Transfer 35mm slides directly to 1" tape.

**Panasonic Industrial Corp.:** 2 Panasonic Way, Secaucus, NJ 07094; 201/392-4603. Write-once disc recorders.

**Pioneer Communications:** 600 E. Crescent Avenue, Upper River, NJ 07458; 201/327-6400. Leading manufacturer of consumer and industrial videodisc players.

**Stokes:** 7000 Cameron Road., Austin, TX 78752; 512/458-2201. Transfer 35mm slides to 35mm film, then film to 1" tape.

**3M:** Optical Recording Department, 223-5S 3M Center, St. Paul, MN 55144; 612/733-2142. Leading videodisc pressing facility.

Shuttle Reports (NASA)

King Kong

## Voyager Company
Catalog **free** from: 2139 Manning Avenue, Los Angeles, CA 900215; 213/475-3524.

*Publisher of the **Criterion Collection**, including such cinematic milestones as **King Kong** and **Citizen Kane**, and other videodiscs, reproduced from the finest prints, with production stills, storyboards and rare outtakes, as well as informative text and audio commentaries. HyperCard stacks also available.*

—FF

## Optical Data Corporation
Catalog **free** from: 66 Hanover Road, Florham Park, NJ 07932; 201/377-0302.

*Publisher of videodiscs such as **Space Archives** (NASA Space Discs): Highlights of the Apollo and Space Shuttle missions, with breathtaking spacewalks, spectacular lunar landscapes and some really gorgeous pictures of the Earth from outer space. Half a dozen different discs are available. $45 each postpaid. Optical Data also offers outstanding videodiscs on HyperCard stacks also available for educational applications.*

—FF

## Discount Video Tapes

Catalog **free** from: Discount Video Tapes, Inc.
P.O. Box 7122 Burbank, CA 91510; 818/843-3366

*If you're looking for a novelty video, you're likely to find it here.* **Santa Claus Conquers the Martians, Assassin of Youth,** *(1935 killer weed propaganda flick), and* **The Secret Life of Adolf Hilter** *(including rare footage from der Fuhrer's personal film library) are all here, along with hundreds of classics from the golden age of television, dozens of Saturday matinee serials, and every grade B western you can think of. Better yet, Discount Video Tapes has an amazing collection of films from the short-lived black filmmaking industry of the 30's and 40's. A real find. Sale prices range from $20 to $60; rentals cost $35 for five titles for two weeks. This includes shipping to you. Return shipping is at your own expense. Tapes are formatted in both VHS and Beta.*
— *Corinne Cullen Hawkins*

ATOMIC ACTION!
Blazing out of space!

COMMANDO CODY
SKY MARSHAL OF THE UNIVERSE

RADAR MEN FROM THE MOON

George WALLACE
Aline TOWNE
Roy BARCROFT

## The Knowledge Collection

Catalog $8.95 from:
167 Central Avenue
Pacific Grove, CA 93950
800/345-1441

*How-to books, even the best, only guide you so far. At some point a how-to video tape, even a mediocre one, will open up better visual understanding (oh, so that's how it goes!) so that the skill moves from your head to your hand quicker. Someone has finally rounded up all the how-to video tapes available for sale (about 1500) into a fat mail order catalog. They seem to include everything, poor to fair to excellent: sports coaching, health care material, dancing lessons, and the brightest of the Saturday morning TV do-it-yourself instruction. Self-education rewinds.*
— *Kevin Kelly*

HIS MOST POPULAR PICTURE!

MODERNIZED WITH MUSIC AND SOUND!

GREATEST LOVER!

RUDOLPH VALENTINO
in The EAGLE
with VILMA BANKY

IDOL OF MILLIONS!

---

---

## Facets

Catalog $4 from:
Facets Multimedia Center
1517 West Fullerton Avenue, Chicago, IL 60614
800/331- 6197

*Hop into a foreign filmmaker's mind — see the world in a new way. Seventeen countries are represented in this catalog of 3000 videos, which has a hefty section on independent and classic U.S. films as well. I looked for every off-beat and art film I could think of — and found them all here. This is the catalog for film buffs and anyone else who enjoys films of substance, artistry, and peculiarity of vision. Prices range from $19.95 to $79.95. Both VHS and Beta are for sale; rentals are VHS only and cost $10 per tape.*
— *Corinne Cullen Hawkins*

## Target Video

Catalog **free** from: Target Video,
678 South Van Ness, San Francisco, CA 94110

*Founded by award-winning video artist and director Joe Rees, Target Video is a great source for video recordings of punk bands and underground artists. One of Target's most recent assaults on what it calls "gibbering disco complacency" is a stunning and violently beautiful video documentary of five machine performances by Survival Research Laboratories called Virtues of Negative Fascination. Other Target recordings include performances by Diamanda Galas, Iggy Pop, Throbbing Gristle, the Sex Pistols, Black Flagg, Joanna Went, and the Dead Kennedys, some taped live in Target's own performance space. Many of the performances in Target's catalog are intercut by Rees with existing documentary and industrial footage to create images that are as funny and brutal as they are politically charged. In all, Target has some five hunded hours of video tapes to choose from.*
— *Richard Kadrey*

## A Parent's Guide to Children's Video

Martha Dewing, Editor
$14.97/year
(6 issues) from:
Children's Video
389 Fourth Street
Brooklyn, NY 11215
800/972-5858

*The premiere edition of this magazine is a valuable resource for parents — a buyer's guide to children's videos. It's the most inclusive listing of quality kidvid I've seen. It includes little-known educational and religious videos, shorts (both foreign and domestic), as well as feature films. I disagreed with some of the reviews — you*

Stories and Fables

*probably will too — but they are informative and detailed.*

*This issue sets a high standard. If later issues live up to it the magazine will provide an important service: helping parents monitor and guide their*

*children's media absorption. I hope it suceeds.*
—Corinne Cullen Hawkins

◆

*Walt Disney Home Video*
STORIES AND FABLES Volumes 1-19
*Walt Disney, 50 minutes each, ages 6 and up, live action.*
This is a massive international series of fables, folktales and fiction in 19 volumes originally shot on film and ultimately transferred to videotape. Each tape consists of two complete stories that are well-acted and beautifully narrated (the actors do not ever speak but complement the narrative in a simple and clear manner). . . .

This series may be a well kept secret on a back shelf at your neighborhood home video store or library, but ask for it and try out a couple. The less jaded you and your children are, the better you'll like it. It resembles home cooking—nothing too fancy, just good, honest fare.

Carol Burnett Show sketches featuring Nora Desmond, Burnett's takeoff of the Gloria Swanson role in Sunset Boulevard, are among the best candidates for home taping.

## Video Review

Roy Hemming, Editor
$12/year (12 issues) from:
Video Review, P.O. Box 919
Farmingdale, NY 11737-0001;
800/525-0643

Carol Burnett Show sketches featuring Nora Desmond, Burnett's takeoff of the Gloria Swanson role in Sunset Boulevard, are among the best candidates for home taping.

Identical pictures as seen on conventional TV (top) and high-definition TV (bottom) — increased resolution and nearly filmlike clarity. Someday, every TV picture will be this good; the only question is when.

*Where can the home viewer go for insight into the video market? Well, you might try Video Review. A combo trade journal and critic's corner, this magazine covers both new product technology and new movie releases with the same wry sensibility.*
—Sarah Vandershaf

## The Complete Guide to Videocassette Movies

Steven H. Scheuer, Editor
1987; 671 pp.
$19.95
($22.95 postpaid) from:
Henry Holt & Co.
521 Fifth Avenue
New York, NY 10175
212/886-9200
or Whole Earth Access

*I've rented my share of video dogs — predictable suspense, flat comedies, fizzled action movies. Video rental store catalogs hype all their movies equally — no help there in deciding what movie to take your chances on. And with the staggering array of videos to choose from, a good videocassette guide will save you money and disappointment.*

*In a survey of six videocassette guides, I found this*

*one to be the definitive consumer guide. The others either gave long, in-depth, witty and wonderful reviews of only a few movies or short, dull or unimaginative reviews of thousands of films.*

*This guide, with over 5000 reviews, includes every theatrical and made-for-TV film available by fall 1987 (except for pornography). Reviews include the right kind of honest detail to help decision*

*making and are fun to browse. Movies are listed alphabetically, with icons identifying the genre, and are indexed by genre in the back. The only thing missing is an index by actors and directors.*
—Corinne Cullen Hawkins

---

THE GENERAL ☆☆☆☆
1927, USA
Buster Keaton, Glenn Cavender, Jim Farley, Marian Mack. Directed by Buster Keaton. 81 min.

Buster Keaton's greatest comedy (along with *Sherlock, Jr.*) could be described as a balletic duet between Keaton and a runaway locomotive. Buster plays a would-be Confederate who tries to win his train back from a platoon of Union soldiers. The logistics alone make the film an astounding spectacle. Most of the film was shot aboard and atop a speeding train, with Buster taking more risks per scene than a trapeze artist. Unfortunately, it is impossible to recommend a video version of this film. Badly scratched and horribly washed-out prints strip this masterpiece of its meticulous attention to detail; indeed, oftentimes Buster's facial takes are impossible to read. Further, this movie demands the kind of careful viewing and absolute absorption that are endemic to watching a projected film, and this state of awareness is difficult to achieve in front of a television. Hopefully, Keaton's work will soon be accorded the kind of video transfer provided by the CBS Playhouse Chaplin series.

---

THE CREATURE FROM THE HAUNTED SEA ☆☆
1960, USA
Antony Carbone, Betsy Jones-Moreland, Edward Wain, Edmundo Rivera Álvarez, Robert Beam. Directed by Roger Corman. 60 min.

This is one of those films that you should give thanks to the great god VCR for having resurrected from the dead. If you've seen either Roger Corman's *Little Shop of Horrors* or *A Bucket of Blood* (and if you've seen them, and liked them), then you must get this, because it sort of forms a trilogy with the other two, and it's been all but impossible to see for years. The story goes that Corman was in Puerto Rico making two quickie movies with the same cast and production crew. When he was done he figured, well, why not stay another week, seeing as all the necessary people are here, and make another one? So he called Charles Griffith, author of *Little Shop* and *Bucket*, and asked if he could write another comedy-horror film that afternoon. This is the result. A gangster agrees to use his boat to transport a group of political refugees off a revolution-torn island. When he discovers that they've taken the national treasury with them, he decides to kill them off, blame the deaths on the local sea monster, and keep the loot himself. Of course, there turns out to be a *real* sea monster (not that the thirty-nine-cent costume will fool you for a minute) who claims his revenge; the final shot in the film is the beastie picking his teeth after finishing off the crew. Robert Beam, who plays one of the crew members, was promoted to actor from boom man when Corman, who was supposed to play the role himself, decided that it was too tough.

## The Video Production Guide

Lon McQuillin
1983; 382 pp.
**$28.95**
($31.45 postpaid) from:
Howard W. Sams & Co.
4300 West 62nd Street
Indianapolis, IN 46268
800/428-3602
or Whole Earth Access

*If you're serious about getting involved in the technical side of video production, here is the most up-to-date and comprehensive introduction to the field. This thorough overview of the production process gets down to the nuts and bolts of planning, shooting, and editing a videotape or television program. The book outlines most of what you need to know about video, from how professional equipment works to how to get a job. A definitive textbook of the video craft.*
—Fabrice Florin

◆

Study commercials with the sound turned off, and you'll

The complete audio/video man.

be better able to examine the camera and lighting techniques used without the distraction of the audio. If you have a video tape recorder (VTR) available to you, record some commercials and study them with and without the sound.

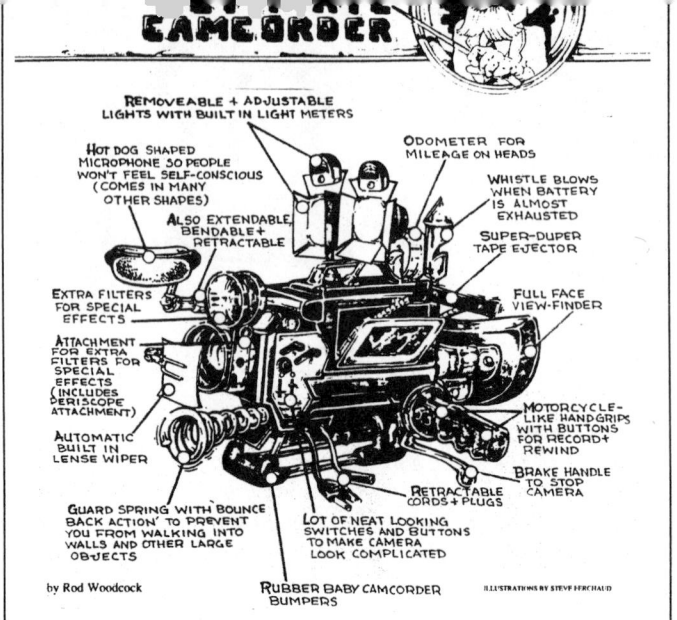

REMOVEABLE + ADJUSTABLE LIGHTS WITH BUILT IN LIGHT METERS

HOT DOG SHAPED MICROPHONE SO PEOPLE WON'T FEEL SELF-CONSCIOUS (COMES IN MANY OTHER SHAPES)

ODOMETER FOR MILEAGE ON HEADS

WHISTLE BLOWS WHEN BATTERY IS ALMOST EXHAUSTED

ALSO EXTENDABLE, BENDABLE + RETRACTABLE

SUPER-DUPER TAPE EJECTOR

EXTRA FILTERS FOR SPECIAL EFFECTS

FULL FACE VIEW-FINDER

ATTACHMENT FOR EXTRA FILTERS FOR SPECIAL EFFECTS (INCLUDES PERISCOPE ATTACHMENT)

MOTORCYCLE-LIKE HANDGRIPS WITH BUTTONS FOR RECORD+ REWIND

AUTOMATIC BUILT IN LENSE WIPER

BRAKE HANDLE TO STOP CAMERA

GUARD SPRING WITH 'BOUNCE BACK ACTION' TO PREVENT YOU FROM WALKING INTO WALLS AND OTHER LARGE OBJECTS

LOT OF NEAT LOOKING SWITCHES AND BUTTONS TO MAKE CAMERA LOOK COMPLICATED

RETRACTABLE CORDS + PLUGS

RUBBER BABY CAMCORDER BUMPERS

by Rod Woodcock          ILLUSTRATIONS BY STEVE FERCHAUD

The ultimate camcorder: many of the features exist already in various models offered under a variety of brand names. Other features are available only on professional camcorders used by TV stations, but could easily be added to a consumer model.

## CNN News Hound

Cable News Network pays **$25-$125** for news footage; 800-544-NEWS.

*An amateur photographer once won the Pulitzer Prize for a photograph taken with a Brownie camera. The photographer just happened to be at the scene of an accident when it happened. Right place plus right time equals instant fame.*

*Amateur videomakers who run across a breaking news story can parlay their luck into a little cash via Cable News Network's "News Hound" program. Call their toll-free number to submit your video of any newsworthy event — rocket explosions, assassinations, acts of war — in your neighborhood or in your travels. Good luck and good shooting!*
—Sarah Vandershaf

## Videomaker

Bradley Kent, Editor
**$10**/year(6 issues) from:
Videomaker
Depot Square
Peterborough, NH 03458
916/891-8410

*A slick yet friendly how-to magazine for amateur videomakers. Tells you what to buy and how to use it. Camcorders, VCRs, home editing units, plus some access to programming sources.*
—Jeanne Carstensen

**VIDEO CAMERA LIGHT**
**DLP-250H          $49.95**

Designed to mount on any video camera shoe, the DLP-250 is a compact 250 watt flood unit featuring a broad, even beam pattern. Light-weight and equipped with an extra long 15-foot cord, the light can be adjusted to a variety of angles to fill a host of camera situations. Use to enhance colors and eliminate undesirable shadows. Complete with 250 watt (EYH) 3200°K, 50 hour quartz lamp, camera shoe mount bracket and a light stand adapter mount.

**DLP-250**

## Universal Video

Catalog **free** from:
Universal Video 195 Bonhomme Street
P. O. Box 488 Hackensack, NJ 07602
201/487-6340

*This impressive catalog of video accessories, supplies, and equipment offers a whole range of useful products, from cable adaptors to VCR cleaning kits. Professionals and amateurs alike will find some nifty gizmos that would be hard to get in a store.*
—Fabrice Florin

## Sony Camcorders

**Sony Pro 8 Camcorder** (CCD-V110): Full-featured professional model. List price **$1995**; available for **$1395** from Whole Earth Access.

**Sony Auto Handycam** (CCD-V3): Low-end version; more compact, with fewer features. List price **$1500**; **$799** from Whole Earth Access.

(Sony dealers are everywhere, and prices vary considerably. Check the Yellow Pages.)

*Continuing the trend to close the gap between professional and hobbyist tools, we now have technology for homemade TV. High-quality, low-cost videos can be taped with a camcorder, a combination of CAMera and video cassette reCORDER bundled into a lightweight unit small enough to wield with one hand. It uses new 8mm cassettes (which, by the way, can also record 24 hours of digital music). The model we have been using is the Sony Pro 8 CCD-V110, not the cheapest one on the shelf, but one with all the features (autofocus, mike options, built-in rechargeable battery) that you'll need to make a*

*respectable documentary or art video.*

*I found the quality of resolution startling. Like Kodachrome film, it seems to enhance the vibrancy of colors. There were very few lighting situations (fluorescent mall light, dim overhead bulb, gray overcast day) where the camcorder didn't perform excellently without auxiliary floodlights. Stewart, who is using one to document his conferences on learning, says he finds the quality better than broadcast TV. I know one filmmaker who sneaks short segments made with the Sony Pro 8 into nationally syndicated TV programs. Viewers don't notice the difference.*

*You don't need a VCR to play back the videos you make. There's a wire that connects the camcorder to your TV so the camcorder itself becomes a VCR. Unfortunately, it's no good for editing. Worse still, there's nothing currently made that will let you edit a camcorder video gracefully and cheaply. Simple on-site editing can be done with the camcorder's fade and dissolve features. But until a reasonable editing machine comes into the consumer market, there will be no commercial desktop 8mm films.*
—Kevin Kelly

## Independent Filmmaking

Lenny Lipton
1972,1983; 445 pp.
**$13.95**
($15.35 postpaid) from:
Simon & Schuster
Mail Order Sales
200 Old Tappan Road
Old Tappan, NJ 07675
800/223-2336
or Whole Earth Access

*My quick survey of film schools shows Lipton's book still the favorite how-to; it's become a kind of institution. Video freaks may find Lipton's views condescending, but he has added a useful section called "Video for the Filmmaker." This book remains technically astute and entertaining to read.*
—Tom Schneider

◆

It's usually quite easy to produce smooth motion on the screen hand-holding a camera with a lens half the normal focal length, say 5 to 7 millimeters for 8mm and super 8, or 10 millimeters for 16mm. Short focal lengths also help to take the place of a tripod you're trying to hold steady, with no intended motion. With practice, it's very nearly possible to reproduce the steadiness of a dolly or tripod mounted camera. Accomplishing this is really no great feat. To help hold a motionless shot steady, you can lean against anything available, a wall for example, but really, this isn't necessary.

Why use a tripod, if it doesn't matter? The traditional

The Steadicam. Expensive and cumbersome, it is the last word in smooth hand-held cinematography, and has been used to good effect on many features. (Cinema Products)

advice for filmmaking is to use a tripod whenever possible. My practice is to avoid using a tripod whenever possible.

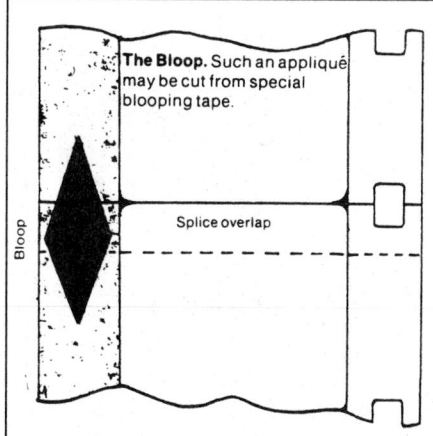

**The Bloop.** Such an appliqué may be cut from special blooping tape.

Bloop

Splice overlap

Spliced optical track often makes a popping sound at the splice point. The way to eliminate this is called blooping. You make a small oval or wedge shape over the splice with ink. This makes an inaudible sound that covers the sound of the splice. You can use especially formulated blooping ink, or you can try metallic blooping tape, cut to the shape of a flat parallelogram, and pressed directly over the splice.

## Feature Filmmaking at Used-Car Prices

Rick Schmidt
**$8.95**
($11.95 postpaid) from:
Viking-Penguin
299 Murray Hill Parkway
East Rutherford, NJ 07073
800/631-3577
or Whole Earth Access

*A painfully honest autobiographical account of the art and emotional adventure of putting out low-budget feature films for about $6000. Surviving his fourth film, author Rick Schmidt eagerly reels off his sobering, trench-hardened advice for the naive hopeful. It's a path for a warrior.*
—Kevin Kelly

◆

My friends and I had discovered early in our filmmaking careers that it seemed as difficult to make a five-minute film as a seventy-minute film, and it was often just as hard to get $200 as $2,000. The difference was that with a feature you had at least a chance to sell it somewhere and make some money back.

◆

If you are still hesitant about trying to write your film, one possible way to break the "block" is to speak about your film into a recorder. Once you have described your concept and talked about the characters, location(s) you envision, and mood you'd like to achieve, remembering to give your story a beginning, middle, and end, spend $50 to have a typist transcribe your words on paper. When the typist hands you twenty pages of rough "scripting," you will realize that you can create a recipe for your feature film.

◆

The benefits of showing your film at in-person shows greatly outweigh the difficulties. You are able to show your film to an interested audience and then hear their feedback during the in-person discussion following the screening.

MY DINNER WITH ANDRE
A New Yorker Films Release © 1981
Available from Grove Press in paperback

## Off-Hollywood

David Rosen
and Peter Hamilton
1987; 298 pp.
**$30**
postpaid from:
The Independent
Feature Project
21 West 86th Street
New York, NY 10024

*Nearly everyone who read the original script for El Norte said the film could not be made. After two years of unsuccessful fundraising, filmmakers Anna Thomas and Greg Nava became totally discouraged and decided their project would never be completed. Weeks later American Playhouse producers opted to back the film. El Norte went on to be the most successful foreign-language film produced and directed by American filmmakers, grossing $5.5 million.*

*Off-Hollywood tells the stories behind the making*

of eleven American independent features, including **El Norte**, with an emphasis on distribution and marketing. Compiled by the Sundance Institute and the Independent Feature Project, it's designed to increase filmmakers' savvy in promoting their films. The documentation of the financing, production, distribution, marketing, and promotion of the films is thorough and specific. Filmmakers tell what worked, what didn't, and why.

*The logistics of making a feature film are daunting.* **Off-Hollywood** *wants independent filmmakers not just to succeed, but to excel. The quality of American filmmaking is at stake.*
—Jeanne Carstensen

◆

**Andre** succeeded despite the minimum amount of predetermination of its future audience. It is an example of a concept which drove its creators and its producer to complete a work because of the power of the idea, rather than of any supposed fit between the idea and the audience. Yet, in a general sense, its expected audience was the art-film moviegoer, particularly one who would be attracted to a work directed by Louis Malle.

The success of **Andre** invites a consideration of the relationship between the great influence of the major critics and the functioning of word-of-mouth. Most of the principals agree that without an accolade from Ebert and Siskel, **My Dinner With Andre** would have failed to attract enough of an audience at its New York opening run to allow word-of-mouth to develop.

## Cinefex

Don Shay, Editor
$17/year
(4 issues) from:
Cinefex
P. O. Box 20027
Riverside, CA 92516
714/242-9704

*It is evidence of film's magic that what happens behind the scenes has always been as entertaining as the show up front, and sometimes more.*

*When monsters slobber and spaceships hurtle across the screen, I believe it. But when the scene is flipped and I'm shown how the most convincing special effects are done, I find it unbelieveable, yet altogether spellbinding.*

*Hundreds of people work years to construct incredibly elaborate illusions out of latex, tiny models and winking computers — each a secret of fine craftsmanship waiting to be told. This amazing magazine (scads of color pictures, no advertising) is what some folks around here sneak off to a corner with and read for hours.*
*—Kevin Kelly*

Above: An army of technicians prepare to orchestrate Falkor's multitudinous cables. The 43-foot-long mechanical creature was capable of various head movements and facial expressions, including the ability to form words.

Left: Atreyu (Noah Hathaway), the young warrior-hero of **The Neverending Story**, rides Falkor the flying luckdragon on his quest to save Fantasia from doom.

For maximum control, "Dream Quest" dismissed the possibility of using actual cloud footage for **The Adventures of Buckaroo Banzai** in favor of creating their own on stage. Experimentation led to the employment of polyester fiber fill glued onto pieces of plexiglass. Here, minor adjustments are made to simulated cloud formations.

---

## American Cinematographer

George Turner, Editor
$17.95/year
(12 issues) from:
American Cinematographer
P.O. Box 2230
Hollywood, CA 90078
213/876-5080

*You can be an insider for the price of a subscription. **American Cinematographer** is where you'll find out how it's done when you can hire ten experts and all the equipment you need to produce three perfect minutes on screen. **Cinematographer** has taken more interest lately in the history of American filmmaking, besides frontline reports on the latest marriages of film and video.*
*—Tom Schneider*

◆

[Bo Welch, production designer for **Beetlejuice**]: "If you envision purgatory as being a never ending visit to the department of motor vehicles to renew your license, it gives you some idea of what we were going for! It was not intended to be scary except in unconventional ways. The main set in the afterlife is a vast secretarial pool where the desks go on and on, into the deep background, lost in a sea of computer printout paper and other kind of flotsam. Corpses are shown being conveyed through the secretarial complex by means of overhead pulley systems. Basically, this is the place where the newly dead go for their assignments to resolve whatever they left unresolved at the time of their demise.

"How does one go about fashioning the look for this kind of thing? Our choice was to make it drab and institutional. The two colors that predominate in this part of the afterlife are a rather sickly green and yellow as seen though a corrugated plastic patio roof."

Left: Winona Ryder floats to a calypso beat in **Beetlejuice**.
Below: To the discomfiture of newly-dead Alec Baldwin, the Char Man (Douglas Turner) can't stop smoking in the afterlife even after being burnt to a crisp in real life.

---

## Premiere

Susan Lyne, Editor
$18/year
(12 issues) from:
Premiere
P.O. Box 11395
Des Moines, IA 50347
212/725-7926

*You'll have to wade through gossipy movie star profiles and graphic design that looks like it wandered off the pages of **Cosmo** to get to the good stuff — unflinching reviews of new film releases and articles that give an insiders-eye-view of the eternally fascinating (if occasionally repellent) Hollywood movie machine.*
*—Sarah Vandershaf*

◆

Though **Cry Freedom** is often a chore to watch, it has a cumulative effect that is unexpectedly involving. Attenborough could have made a soft, conciliatory film, the cinematic equivalent of the song "We Are the World." Instead, his film is a testament to the futility of the liberal position on South Africa. It bluntly demonstrates that there is no reasoning with the proponents of apartheid, no appealing to their finer instincts, no sense in waiting for gradual change. The Woods family became part of the struggle by giving up first its freedom and then its worldly goods. The film offers no less painful alternatives and refuses to let right-minded spectators feel good about themselves. **Cry Freedom** has the lumpish gracelessness of a political pamphlet, and that is part of its power, conveying urgency and the need for commitment. It is neither art nor entertainment, but a call to arms.

## The Animator's Workbook

(Step-by-Step Techniques of Drawn Animation)
Tony White
1986; 160 pp.
**$27.50**
($29.50 postpaid) from:
Watson-Guptill Publications
1695 Oak Street
Lakewood, NJ 08701
201/363-5679
or Whole Earth Access

*This is a big book about drawing animation. I think it's the best book on hand-drawn animation because it stresses the subtleties of natural paths of movement. Subtle and natural equal convincing animation. Animation that isn't convincing is hard to look at. Convincing may be the key operative in film and in media in general.*

*—Bill Ritchey*

When contemplating an action, the animator must first ascertain which body part is leading the action and which part is following through. A classic example of this can be seen in the javelin thrower. Experienced javelin coaches always emphasize that there is more to javelin throwing than just running and throwing. Apart from the fast run up, they emphasize that at the end of the run the feet should be planted in a solid, steady position with the hips driven forward and the javelin arm held well back. From this powerful hip position, the throw unwinds from a series of movements, which bear a strong resemblance to the whip action from the center to the upper tip of an archery bow.

The simplest fire effect is that of a candle flame. A candle flame moves very little, unless it is fanned by a draft from an open door or window, so it can be quickly produced. Basically, there need be only three key positions of the flame, each moving only a little from the others.

When an eye blinks, never draw a straight line in midposition for the breakdown. Either make it curve upward just above the center line, or make it curve downward just below.

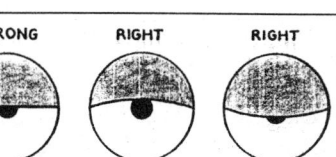

## Cartoon Colour Co.

Catalog **free** from:
Cartoon Colour Co.
9024 Lindblade Street
Culver City, CA 90232
213/838-8467

*This catalog has some tools you'll need to begin, especially if you plan on buidling your own stand or if you want to have your animation shot on a professional stand:*

*1. Heavy mylar 12 field and 16 field.*
*2. A roll of punched background bristol.*
*3. Punched tracing paper.*
*4. Punched 3 field cells and tracing paper.*
*5. Punched cels.*
*6. Tap on punched strips.*
*7. A light box with pin strips (optional).*

*—Bill Ritchey*

**FAX ANIMATION DISCS**
No. 1413 — Fax 12/16 field disc used for either 12 or 16 fields by reversing position of each bar. Disc is rugged aluminum casting, finished in baked enamel, 20" outside diameter, turning guide cast in back for rotation in 16-1/2" hole. Large 15-1/2" x 9-1/2" shatterproof, opalite, plexiglass window diffuses back light. Top and bottom 2" x 18" sliding, scaled, aluminum peg bars slide in milled slots and held in place by magnetic strips. Acme Standard round pegs screw in; flat pegs snap into brass bushings.

## VideoWorks II

Version 1.0. Not copy-protected. Macintosh 512K or larger Mac recommended. **$195** from Brøderbund Software, 17 Paul Drive, San Rafael, CA 94903; 415/492-3200.

*Once upon a time, film animation was a labor-intensive process requiring dozens of worker-elves painting action sequences frame by frame onto acetate "cells." Modern video technology has changed all that, and the advent of high-powered $500,000 computers dedicated to video animation has made for some breath-taking TV commercials and station IDs. Still, it has mostly been the Macintosh that has brought animation techniques within reach of the artist on the street.*

*VideoWorks II is the premiere animation program for the Mac. Not only does it enable you to animate short "movies" that run on the Mac's screen, but it also gives you the ability to set up sequences of MacPaint and PICT documents and animated clips that can be run as "slide shows" for business presentations. Included with the program are some basic animated clips, artwork and sound effects that serve as elements in movies or presentations of your own. VideoWorks II works in both black and white and in color if you have a Mac II with color board and monitor.*

*Given the complexity of the tasks it sets out to accomplish, VideoWorks II's interface is reasonably accessible. The 284-page users' manual is outstanding. If you have a Mac and a desire to create moving pictures, VideoWorks II is the route to take.*
*—Jay Kinney*

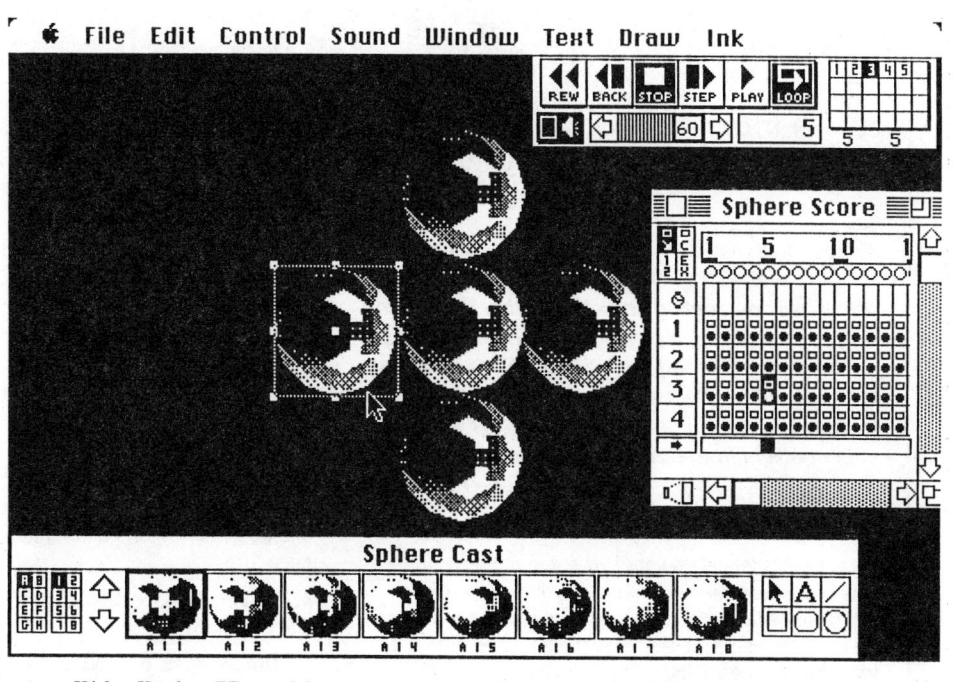

VideoWorks II enables you use up to 512 pieces of art in animated "movies". These movies can then be strung together along with sound effects and screenshots from other programs to produce animated presentations for business and pleasure.

## Multi-Image Design and Production

Phiz Mezey
1988; 163 pp.
**$24.95** postpaid from:
Butterworth Publishers
80 Montvale Avenue
Stoneham, MA 02180
617/438-8464
or Whole Earth Access

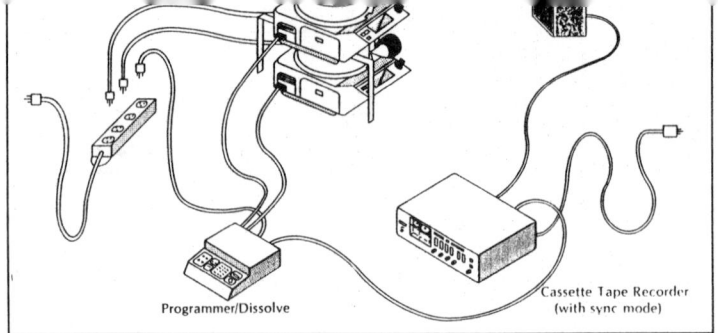

A simple two-projector setup today might include two projectors, a programmer/dissolve, and a monaural tape cassette recorder.

*Programmer/Dissolve*   *Cassette Tape Recorder (with sync mode)*

This storyboard for a three-projector speaker-support series is a preliminary sketch showing different possible introductions for the series. The windows with the Xs show where a photograph (not yet selected) will appear.

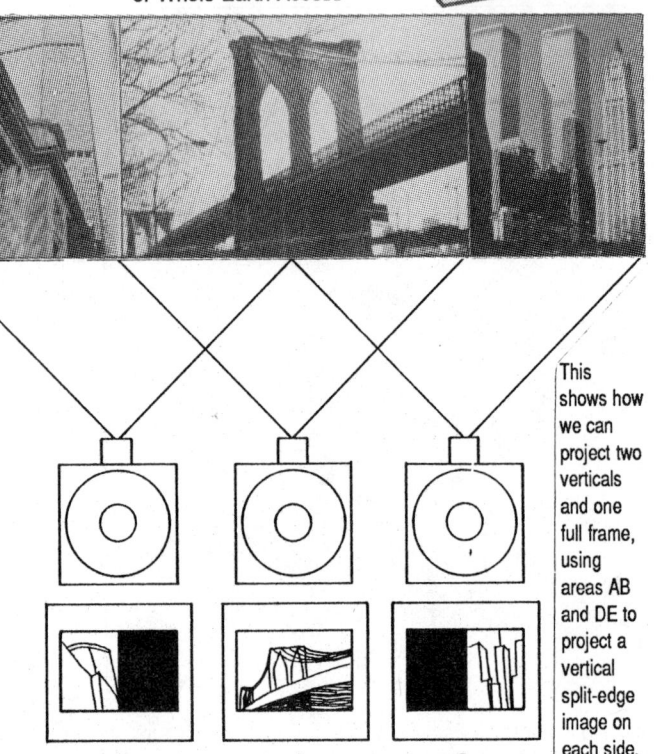

This shows how we can project two verticals and one full frame, using areas AB and DE to project a vertical split-edge image on each side.

L      C      R

*One projector, two projectors, three projectors, wow!*

*For getting your point across, a multi-projector slide show gets the most wows for a buck. It may be a cliché in visitor centers and museums, but a well made multi-image production can easily bring a jaded classroom, conference hall, or traveling show to its feet.*

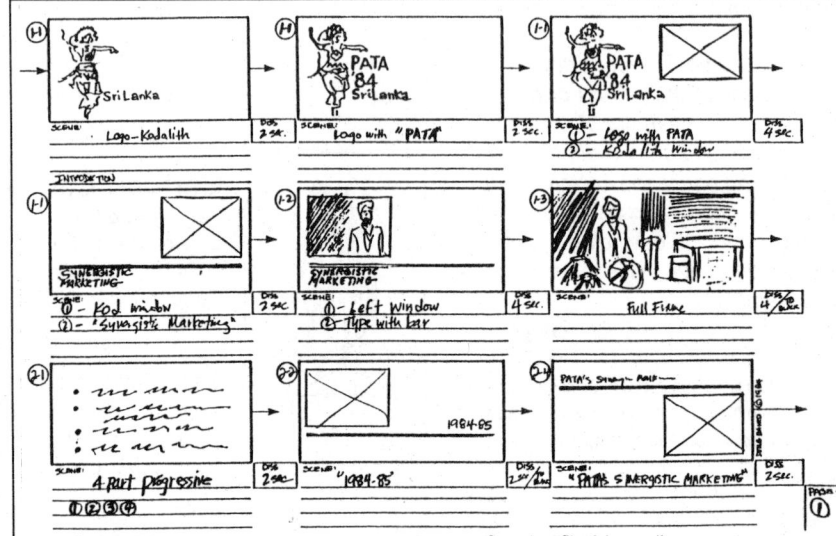

*They are complicated buggers to launch though. I've assembled three different hour-long shows using dissolve units and synchronized sound tracks, and each one took a month to complete. It would have gone a little quicker had I read this book first. And when I'm ready to create my next presentation, I'll check this book again because they have a thorough survey of the latest multi-projection equipment, from the low-cost on up.*
— Kevin Kelly

---

## Presentations Plus

David A. Peoples
1988; 239 pp.
**$12.95** postpaid from:
John Wiley & Sons
1 Wiley Drive
Somerset, NJ 08873
201/469-4400
or Whole Earth Access

*A presentation is a little bit more complicated (and a lot more effective) than an ordinary speech. You are usually presenting something other than words — perhaps slides, a product demonstration, or a complex idea that requires visuals. Speechmaking laws are still in effect (be brief, use stories, keep it to three points), but a few additional tips will keep your spotlight from fading into mumbled oblivion.*
— Kevin Kelly

◆

From the presenter's point of view, the most important part of the presentation is the close. It is at the close where you either accomplish your objective, or you don't. So important is the close, that we plan it and design it from the very beginning.

◆

The Seven Deadly Sins

1. Show an organization chart, tell the history of your

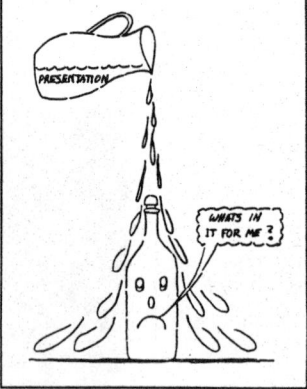

1. The audience must have a selfish reason to pay attention.

2. A reason gets the plug out but most of the material spills on the floor.

3. Adding spice to get attention and interest is like adding a funnel. Now all the presentation goes into the bottle.

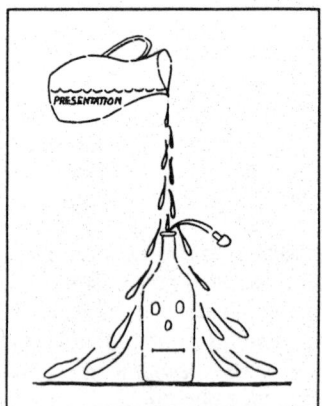

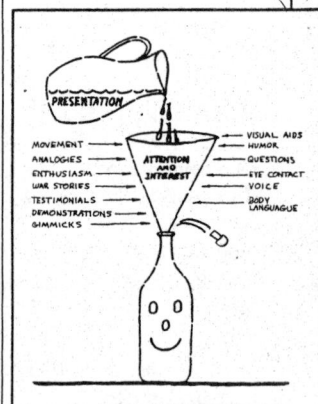

department, and apologize in advance.

2. Do not explain any reason why the subject has any value to the audience.

3. Use a presentation designed for one audience — for a different audience.

4. Tell the audience more than they want to know.

5. Turn the lights out and show slides or foils while reading a script.

6. Read verbatim every word on every visual.

7. Do not rehearse — play it by ear.

If we use the iceberg close we can control what the audience will remember, that our product or service is:
1. Comprehensive
2. Easy to use
3. Easy to maintain

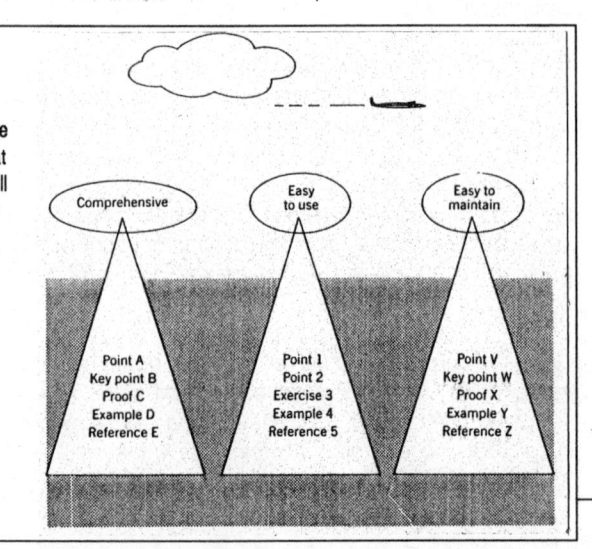

# How to Make Meetings Work

Michael Doyle & David Straus
1976; 301 pp.
**$3.95**
($4.95 postpaid) from:
Berkley Publishing Group
Order Department
P.O. Box 506
E. Rutherford, NJ 07073
800/631-8571 ext. 445

*It always amazes me how a group of otherwise pleasant people can go collectively insane as soon as they get in a meeting together. Anyone who suffers through the wrangling and frustration of poorly run meetings will find this book very useful. I particularly like its emphasis on achieving consensus, a worthy goal that lots of people talk about without knowing much of how it can be achieved.*

—Linda Williams

◆

The very presence of the group memory has many beneficial effects. It provides a physical focus for the group. Rather than siting in a closed circle around a conference table, channeling their energies toward each other, the members sit in a semicircle and automatically focus their energies on the problem as represented by the group memory. This simple change can make a tremendous difference.

A clearly legible record capturing the key ideas of the meeting on large sheets of paper taped or pinned to the walls of the meeting room. We call this record the "group memory."

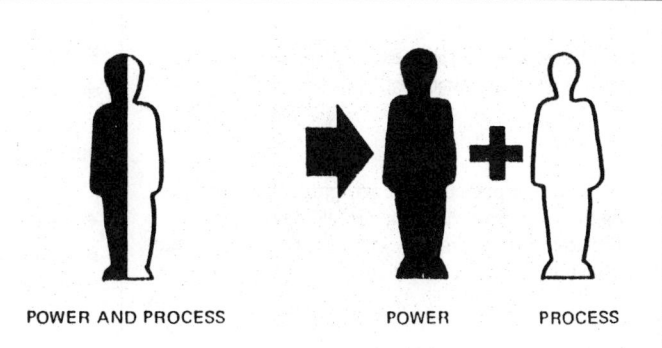

POWER AND PROCESS          POWER          PROCESS

Neutral and nonevaluating, the facilitator is responsible for making sure the participants are using the most effective methods for accomplishing their task in the shortest time. The manager, as decision maker, participates fully in the meeting, fights for his or her ideas, sets constraints, and does not give up any power and responsibility.

# Meetings, Bloody Meetings/ More Bloody Meetings

Each **$155**/3-day rental; **$200**/4-to-7-day rental.
Both **$260**/3-day rental; **$340**/4-to-7-day rental from:
Video Arts, Inc., Northbrook Tech Center
4088 Commercial Avenue, Northbrook, IL 60062
800/553-0091

*And another bloody meeting. Except this meeting is to watch a life-changing twenty minute video by John Cleese, of wacky Monty Python fame. Funny, clever, sobering, and above all, supremely effective, this video will leave you with the indelible five fundamental principles of running a productive meeting. Cleese plays a harried manager who is put on trial in a dream for his crimes of wasting others' time with his ineffective staff meetings. The court is run by his own haphazard rules to hilarious and memorable results. Send your whole organization through this video (and its equally worthwhile follow up, **More Bloody Meetings**), and come out liberated from congregation incompetence.*

—Kevin Kelly
[Suggested by Sarah Vandershaf]

# How to Plan and Book Meetings and Seminars

Judy Williams
1987; 146 pp.
**$7.95**
($8.95 postpaid) from:
Ross Books
P.O. Box 4340
Berkeley, CA 94704
800/537-3338 (in CA)
800/367-0930
or Whole Earth Access

# The Book of Meeting Checklists

Helen Adam
1985; 37 pp.
**$9.95**
($11.95 postpaid) from:
Helen Adam & Associates, Inc.
Benjamin Fox Pavilion
Jenkintown, PA 19046
or Whole Earth Access

*We're talking Serious Meeting here, generally big ones in rented spaces, where logistics are at least as important as content. The larger the meeting, the more harrowing the logistics, the greater the need for careful preparation. Nothing will prevent burst water pipes, a no-show speaker, or a bomb scare, but these books will spare you the catastrophes and embarrassment of poor planning.*

*How to Plan . . . is a good introduction to planning tactics, from booking hotel rooms to scheduling coffee breaks. **Checklists** is just that — items addressing every conceivable contingency are included, many of which you'll probably never need, many more you never would have thought of and are glad they're listed here.*

*Although the orientation is corporate, both books offer valuable information for planning problem-free meetings of any sort.*

—Sarah Satterlee

◆

Hotels will look at the total picture when making a decision on meeting room rental. They will consider revenue from sleeping rooms, planned food and beverages functions, profit from audio-visual equipment rental, incidental income from your attendees, future bookings and referrals from your company. A reduction or complete removal might be possible.

◆

Coffee is sold by the gallon. Sound like an enormous amount? Guess again . . . one gallon of coffee serves approximately eighteen to twenty cups. For a group of ten that's two cups to last two or three hours.

◆

If your group has met all day in a U-shape put them at rounds for their meals.

### PRE-MEETING CHECKLIST

☐ Tables arranged according to diagram?
☐ Chairs arranged according to diagram?
☐ In the numbers ordered?
☐ Projector and table in place?
☐ Flags, signs and banners in place?
☐ Tables draped properly?
☐ Ice water and glasses in place?
☐ Ashtrays distributed properly?
☐ Pads and pencils on tables?
☐ Platform set up correctly?
☐ Lectern correct (floor or table model)?
☐ Lectern lights and controls in working order?
☐ Lighting as ordered?
☐ Light controls located?
☐ Dimmer switch work?
☐ Who will darken the room?
☐ Projectionist at his post?
☐ Has he been cued?
☐ Slides in place?
☐ Screen set up properly?
☐ If overhead projector in use, are acetates and pencils ready?
☐ Extra bulbs available?
☐ Blackboard, chalk and erasers ready if needed?
☐ If flip chart used, extra markers available?
☐ Are all handout materials ready?
☐ Does the microphone work?
☐ Tape recorder set up to begin?
☐ Where are PA controls?
☐ Who will handle them?
☐ Checked room for static or sound problems?

## Workshops & Seminars

(Planning, Producing, and Profiting)
Pat Roessle Materka
1986; 167 pp.
**$10.95**
($12.05 postpaid) from:
Simon & Schuster
Attention: Order Department
200 Old Tappan Road
Old Tappan, NJ 07675
800/223-2336
or Whole Earth Access

*You've done one seminar as a favor, and the attendees kept asking for more. It feels great. Here's how to proceed to hone your workshop-running skills and join the podium circuit.   — Kevin Kelly*

◆

Short written exercises provide a good change of pace from the highly verbal lecture/discussion format. They give participants a chance to process what has been said, to turn their thoughts inward and see how the topic applies to them.

◆

Should you do freebies? Should you charge lower rates for some groups than for others? Absolutely. Especially when you're just starting out in the business.

◆

The tone you set at the beginning of the workshop will cue people on how to conduct themselves. If you allow a steady stream of chatter to go on as you are introducing the subject, the audience will presume talking during the presentation is acceptable. If you pause and wait in silence for the conversation to die down, they'll get the

Many workshops take place in restaurants or hotels where the meeting rooms are set up with round tables, each seating about eight people. This can be conducive to a good learning climate, since the audience is already seated in circles. The disadvantage is that if the tables are full, two or three people have to twist around in their chairs to see you. So if you're planning on this seating arrangement, allow for five people at each table, not eight, so that everyone has an equal vantage point.

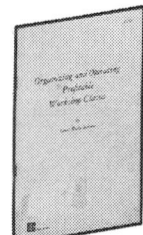

**Horseshoe**

**Banquet Style**

message. If it's a particularly rowdy group, be as aggressive as they are. Say cheerfully, "Hey! I have a lot of important things to share with you, but I can't get started until I have everybody's attention!"

◆

Time-honored advice for organizing any oral presentation:

> Tell them what you're going to say.
> Say it.
> Tell them what you said.

## Organizing and Operating Profitable Workshop Classes

Janet Ruhe-Schoen
1981; 31 pp.
**$2.50**
($3.50 postpaid) from:
Pilot Books
103 Cooper Street
Babylon, NY 11702
or Whole Earth Access

*It's sort of shocking that ALL you need to know to turn your skill into a class can be compressed into so small and blithe a booklet.*
— Stewart Brand

◆

Don't just chat and have coffee at the first class, and assume you are getting acquainted. Your students want to learn; put them to work.

◆

If you explain something, a student may see your point, but if you have the students DO something, they will understand and remember your point.

◆

People generally dislike being part of a very small class; they prefer a class of about 10 participants. Don't let the class become too large either. If there is that much interest, form two units.

◆

It's better not to have the students pay at each session. That means if they are absent, they don't pay. Such a payment policy is unfair to you. You are using your time to prepare and teach classes and you should be paid for your time.

SAMPLE POSTER

Don't give all the details on the poster, people don't read fine print or cramped copy. A successful poster arouses curiosity, but does not satisfy it.

## Project Management Using Micro-computers

Harvey Levine
1986; 416 pp.
**$21.95** postpaid from:
McGraw-Hill
P.O. Box 402
Heightstown, NJ 08520
800/262-4729
or Whole Earth Access

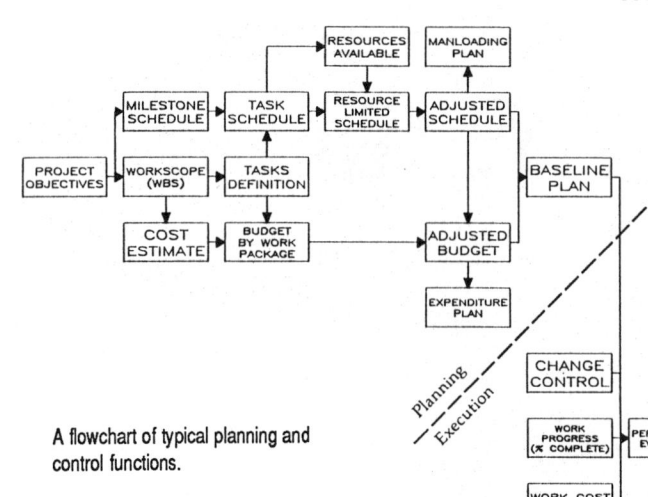

A flowchart of typical planning and control functions.

*Staging a large happening means keeping all the different parts of the projects alive without letting them eat each other. As ringmaster, you need to herd the competing schedules through the center of a "critical path" — the specific series of events that forms the backbone upon which the other events hang. Get the critical path done and the project happens.*

*Project management software assists sorting out this fluid ecology of needs. A sophisticated package will handle the side currents of a large event's sub-projects, and will calculate the metabolism of the parts — the man-hours needed or available, or the rate of other critical resources. The benefit of this kind of tool is felt most on on-going or repeating projects. It's probably overkill for a one time conference. It's probably necessary if you're running a factory.*

*But we have used a simpler project management software package (it was a free review copy) for clarifying the work flow on several of our large one-time projects. We probably didn't need heavy duty scheduling power, but its ability to print out PERT charts of critical chores helped to visualize what seemed a wild and improb-*

*able task. We wouldn't have bought one if we had had to pay for it.*

*Is it worthwhile for your event? If you have more than one to do, or have real need for computerized advice, I would suggest reading* **Project Management Using Microcomputers** *for an understandable introduction to the mechanics, and (dis)advantages of project management software in general and most of the better packages in particular.*
—Kevin Kelly

## A Conference and Workshop Planner's Manual

Lois B. Hart
and J. Gordon Schleicher
1979; 150 pp.
**$16.95** postpaid from:
Leadership Dynamics
3775 Iris Avenue, Suite 3B
Boulder CO 80301
303/440-0909
or Whole Earth Access

*The best conferences are on new subjects by new people. The worst conferences are by new people who don't know what they're doing. This straightforward text — it's basically a well-experienced checklist — can make the difference.*

— *Stewart Brand*

◆

After the resource person [speaker] has confirmed his or her willingness to participate according to the terms of the contract, you should send a follow-up letter. In this letter, you will provide the resource person with the following:

— A current agenda, including names of other speakers and their topics
— Information on housing, meals, airport pickup arrangements, directions, and maps
— Information on the design of the assigned meeting room
— Feedback from the planning committee on information the resource person sent regarding the design, required materials, or other requests
— Information on any pre-event or post-event activities
— Any required registration procedures
— Information on whether a member of program committee or a facilitator has been assigned to him or her and how contact will be made.

◆

Decide on when the exhibits will be open, keeping in mind the following:

— Exhibit hours should be the equivalent of from one-third to one-half of the total conference time.
— At least one-third of the time schedule for exhibits should not compete with other conference or workshop programs.

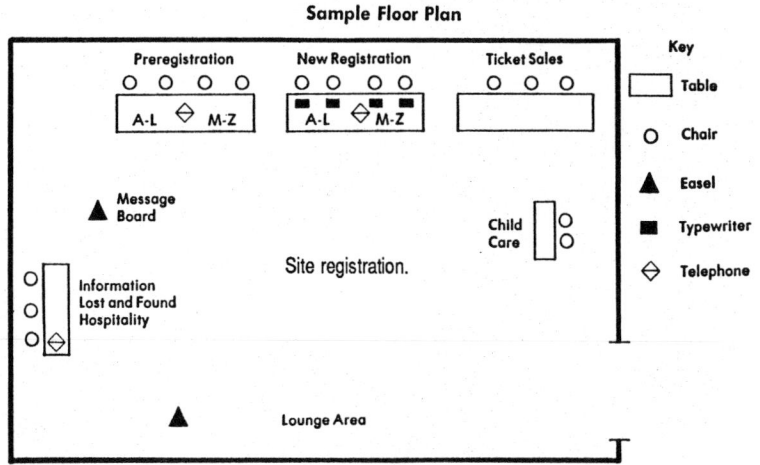

Sample Floor Plan

## Minnesota Western, Inc.

(Visual Presentation Systems)
**Free** catalog from:
800/635-8600
800/682-2424 in southern CA

*If you want what you say to stick, don't just say it — display it. As retention rates are five times greater for verbal information accompanied by visual reinforcement, anything important enough to convene a meeting for calls for spiffy presentation technique and products. Generous dollops of both are contained in this audio-visual catalog: staples (overhead projectors, chalkboards) and high-tech innovations (computer projectors, electronic copyboards) are backed up by a 30-page section on how to hold an effective meeting. Good solid advice applicable to workshops and conferences as well, and yours for a toll-free phone call.*

—*Sarah Satterlee*

## PC-File Plus

Shareware; IBM-PC, 384 Mb RAM **$69.95** ($74.95 postapaid) from ButtonWare, Inc., P.O. Box 96058, Bellevue, WA 98009-4469; 800/454-0479

*You're not still keeping that mailing list on 3X5 cards, are you? PC-File Plus is database software for keeping mailing lists and for many other uses. This long-available shareware champion is inexpensive and it WORKS (when I was first learning my way around an IBM-PC, this was the one program I easily learned to use). Once you have PC-File Plus keeping your list up to date you'll think of many other uses for it. It can easily handle thousands and thousands of names, making such things as conference invitations, workshop announcements, membership newsletters, or other mailings a relatively sane job. And when you start to push the limits, you'll be glad for ButtonWare's efficient phone support.*

— *Keith Jordan*

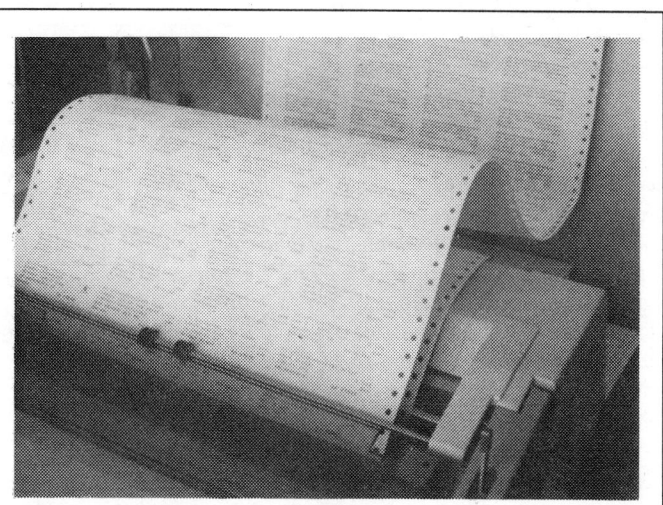

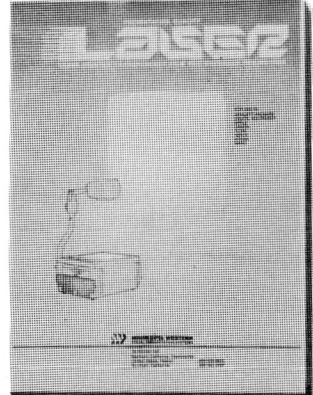

Laser Printer Transparency Film

Caramate Slide Viewer/Projector

◆

If you are creating originals for projected visuals, there are three rules that will serve as guidelines for choosing the correct type size.

A. The smallest image seen on the screen should be one inch high for every thirty feet of viewing distance.
B. The smallest lettering on a visual should be at least one-quarter inch or 18 point.
C. If an overhead transparency is readable by the naked eye at ten feet, it will be able to be read when projected.

The Presenter by Pierce

## Working Prototypes
**$7** postpaid

## Exploratorium Cookbooks
Vol.1, **$78**; Vol. 2, **$58**;
Vol. 3, **$78** postpaid

All from:
The Exploratorium, 3601 Lyon Street,
San Francisco, CA 94123; 415/563-3456

*Hey, keep your hands away from there you kids! Hands-on is what museums traditionally shielded their treasures from. Hands-on is what the unorthodox Exploratorium promotes. Located in San Francisco, this vanguard science museum has revolutionized attitudes about exhibits. They have built hundreds of demonstrations that demand to be handled, mauled, poked, grappled with, and understood in a visceral way. Making the process entirely transparent, the Exploratorium provides explicit construction plans in three volumes for others to imitate or amend. The small booklet, **Working Prototypes** is my favorite. It succinctly conveys the design approach needed to wrestle intelligence into plywood and wire boxes.*
— Kevin Kelly

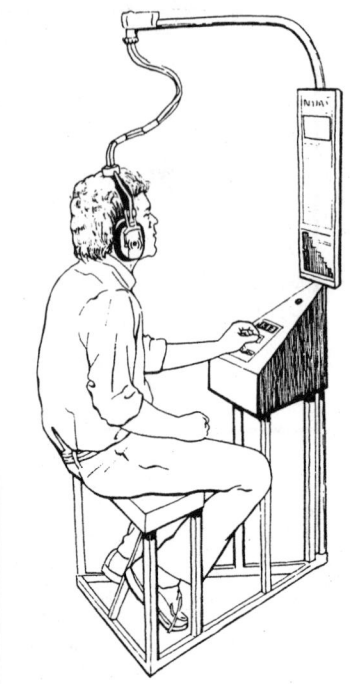

### Description

A tone is played through a set of headphones. The visitor can adjust the frequency of the tone (which is displayed on a digital counter), testing how high or low a frequency he or she can hear. A person's high frequency range varies with age, exposure to loud environments, etc.

## Exhibits for the Small Museum
Arminta Neal
1976, 1978; 169 pp.
**$13.95**
($15.95 postpaid) from:
American Association
for State and Local History
172 2nd Avenue North
Suite 102
Nashville, TN 37201
or Whole Earth Access

*I used to work in exhibit design and can affirm that this is a right handy little book for the friendly task of making stuff visible, interesting, understandable, and protected. Great primer for a first-time museum. (Don't tear down that old building. Do this book to it.)*
—Stewart Brand

A closet with a slide projector, mirrors, and translucent rear-projection screen can be a useful set-up. By "bending" the projector's beam with mirrors, it is possible to get the equivalent of a 6'9" projection distance in a closet that is only 30" deep.

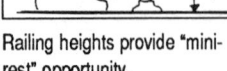

Railing heights provide "mini-rest" opportunity.

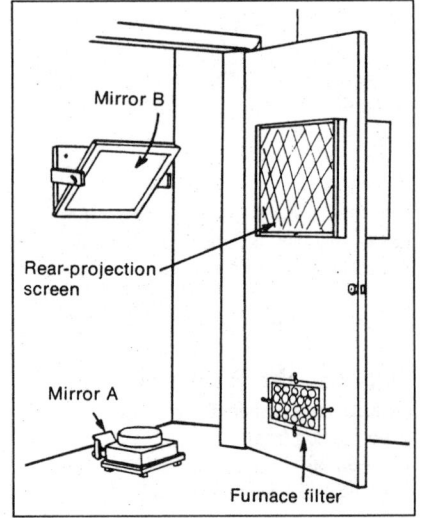

Mirror B

Rear-projection screen

Mirror A

Furnace filter

## Help for the Small Museum
(Handbook of Exhibit Ideas and Methods)
Arminta Neal
1969, 1987; 176 pp.
**$19.95**
($20.95 postpaid) from:
Pruett Publishing Co.
2928 Pearl Street
Boulder, CO 80301
800/247-8224
or Whole Earth Access

*A straightforward, down-home, step-by-step how-to handbook for those interested in building simple, low-cost exhibits and displays. It is what its title says—help for the small museum. Not much news for those concerned with reaching the media-fed audience, the art of storytelling, or imaginative techniques, but maybe that's another book or two. It feels good.*
—Gordon Ashby

## Focused Sound

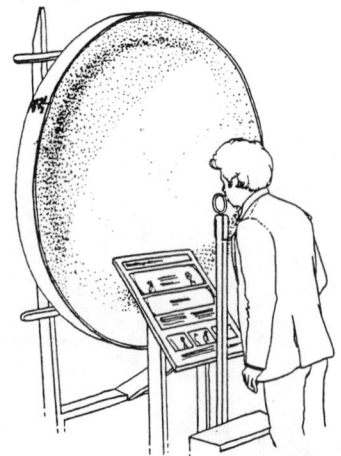

### Description
This exhibit demonstrates the reflection and focusing of sound by two large spherical reflectors. The two reflectors are large plaster "mirrors" facing one another approximately 50 feet apart. When a person at one mirror talks (or even whispers when the museum is quiet) a person at the other mirror can hear him.

### Construction
Our sound mirrors were made by professional statuary builders during a renovation of the Palace of Fine Arts. They first made a negative casting of a large spherical metal searchlight mirror 5 feet in diameter with a 2 foot focal length (used in our "Hot Spot" exhibit). This negative casting was then used as the mold for the two plaster sound mir-

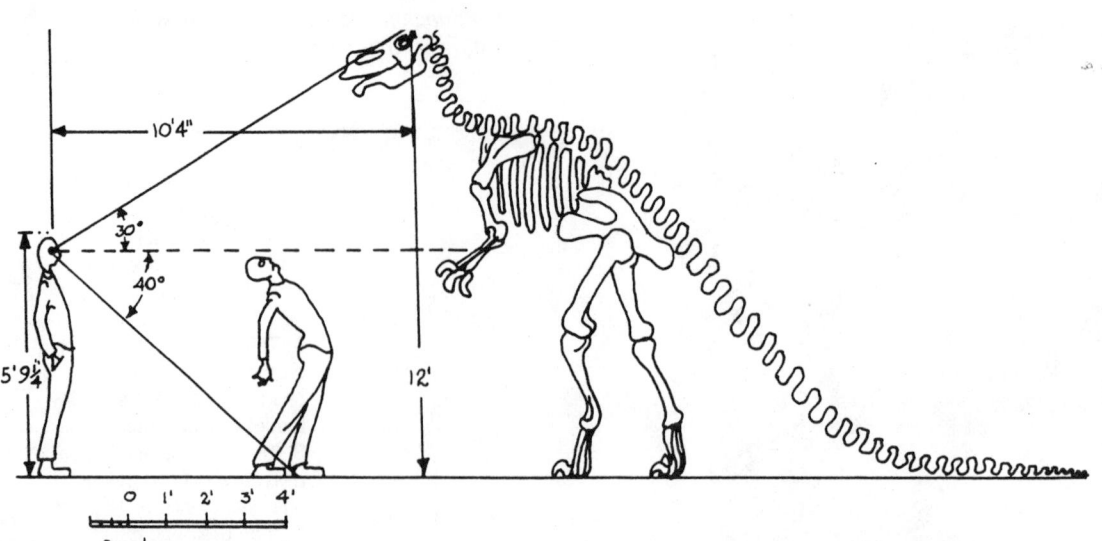

Some quite large objects, such as murals, heroic statues, Greek friezes, Egyptian tomb paintings, totem poles, or dinosaurs, will inevitably soar above the visitor's viewing limits unless there is space to back far enough away from the object to comprehend it without becoming a case for an orthopedic specialist.

## Theatre Crafts How-To (Vol. 1)

The Editors of Theatre Crafts Magazine
1984; 165 pp.
**$10.95** postpaid from:
Theatre Crafts Magazine
135 Fifth Avenue
New York, NY 10010
or Whole Earth Access

## Theatre Crafts Magazine

Patricia MacKay, Editor
**$22.95/year**
(10 issues) from:
Theatre Crafts Magazine
P.O. Box 470; Mt. Morris, IL 61054

*You say you're not a stage set designer? Well, step right this way anyhow and check out this remarkable assortment of clever shop tricks and procedures — you'll probably be able to put many of them to work offstage. There are lots of things you won't find in home-shop magazines: an inexpensive air cylinder with a 20-foot (or less) stroke, for instance, or a simple vacuum-former. How*

British artisan Paul Fowler built Maurice Sendak's "Wild Things" for the opera **Where the Wild Things Are.** Partnered by his wife Gill, Fowler runs his propbuilding business out of a 2,000 sq. ft. workshop in an old converted brewery in Lewis, East Sussex. *—Theatre Crafts Magazine*

*about directions for casting fake stone lions out of foam? Or a method of permanently bending PVC pipe into the frame for a gazebo? As you'd expect, the book is particularly strong on lightweight constructions that can be easily dismounted and rebuilt. It's a way of thinking about things that can be very useful — just the opposite of the fortress-building mentality. The collection is from the respected* **Theatre Crafts Magazine.** *—J. Baldwin*

Fish net woven on a bias (top) does not provide the supportive backing for cut drop sets that square netting does (bottom). *—Theatre Crafts How-To*

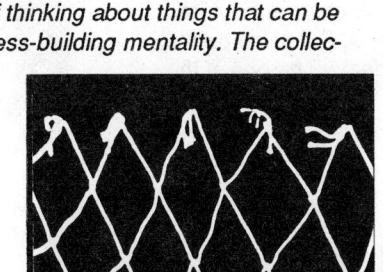

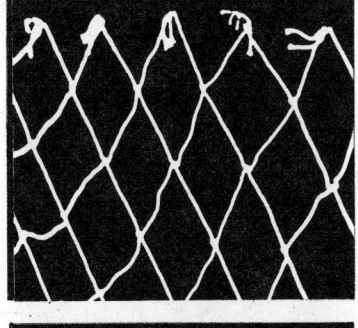

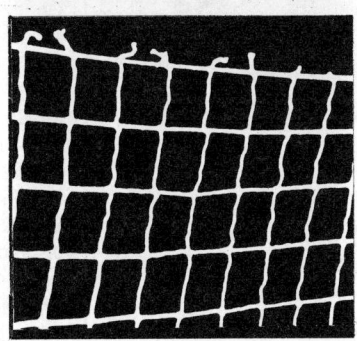

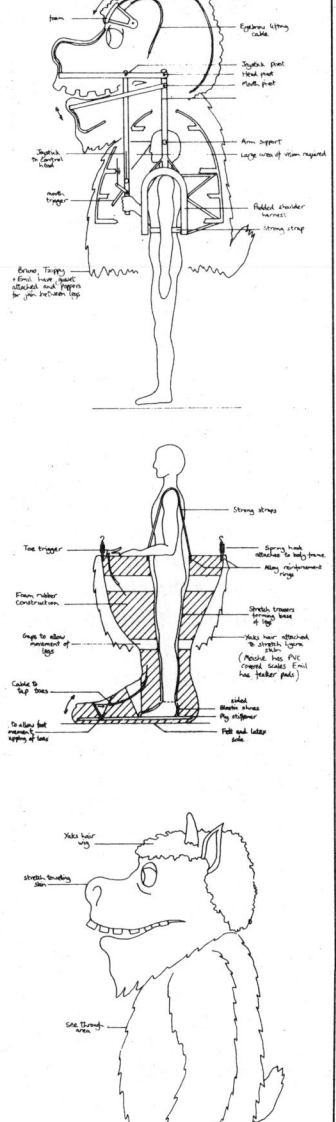

## The Small Theatre Handbook

Joann Green
1981; 163 pp.
**$11.95**
($14.20 postpaid) from:
Kampmann and Company
540 Barnum Avenue
Bridgeport, CT 06608
800/526-7626
or Whole Earth Access

*All the practical steps to take in creating a new theater and maintaining it are covered by this good-humored handbook: from budgets, funding, and legal requirements to choosing plays, managing actors, and touring productions. Written with such love of small theatre, it still points out where stresses are sure to arise and tells how to work through them.*

*Green emphasizes the importance of keeping that critical balance of respect and responsibility between the artistic and administrative staffs.*

*The book should be a little longer in the fundraising area, but there's an excellent bibliography.*
*—Annette Rose, Antenna Theater*

◆

Don't count on selling tickets. Do your best at publicity, and keep your fingers crossed. The price of a ticket should not be so small that the audience feels that it — and the experience of the theatre itself — is inconsequential. Nor should it be so high that the audience fears that nothing could possibly be worth this much money. You may be tempted not to set a price at all, but to ask for "donations at the door." Resist. Accept responsibility for setting, if not a value on the two hours you ask someone to spend with you, than at least a monetary metaphor for it.

## French's Basic Catalogue of Plays

**$1.25** from:
Samuel French, Inc.
45 West 25th Street
New York, NY 10010
212/206-8990

Harkee The Cat..................
Harlequinade, A..................
Harmfulness of Tobacco, The
Harold...........................
Harold and Maude.................
Harrigan 'n' Hart................
Harry, Noon and Night ........
Hatful of Rain, A................
Haunted High School, The....
Haunted Host, The .............

*America's giant of play publishers offers a catalog organized by special interest — Chinese plays, Monologues, Black plays, etc. — and indexed by author and title.*

*—J. Baldwin*

## Norcostco Catalog for the Performing Arts

**$2** from Norcostco, 3203 North Highway #100, Minneapolis, MN 55422; 612/533-2791.

## Theatrical Equipment and Supplies Catalog

**$2** from Mutual Hardware Corp. Ordering Department, 5-45 49th Avenue, Long Island City, NY 11101; 718/361-2480.

*Low-cost theater equipment, costumes, makeup, etc. for school-size productions. I can't imagine opening a new wave nightclub or restaurant without some of these toys.* *—Stewart Brand*

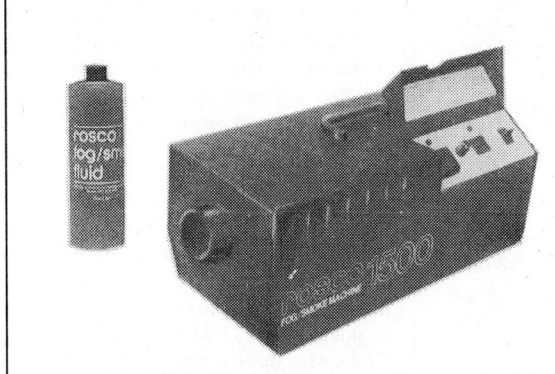

### How to Be a Working Actor

(The Insider's Guide to Finding Jobs in Theater, Film, and Television)
Mari Lyn Henry
and Lynne Rogers
1986; 302 pp.
**$9.66**
($12.16 postpaid) from:
Henry Holt & Co.
115 West 18th Street
New York, NY 10011
800/247-3912
or Whole Earth Access

*Acting is, at best, a chancy way to make one's living. Less than ten percent of professional actors earn a decent wage from acting alone. This book is written for those who aspire to join that ten percent. In their advice to the beginning actor on how to launch a career, the authors are realistic about the chances of success. But never do they lose faith that you, the reader, will be one of the lucky minority who bask in the limelight and get paid for it, too.*

—Sarah Vandershaf

### Respect for Acting

Uta Hagen with
Haskel Frankel
1973; 227 pp.
**$14.95**
($15.70 postpaid) from:
Macmillan Publishing Co.
Order Deptartment
Front and Brown Streets
Riverside, NJ 08075
800/257-5755
or Whole Earth Access

*Uta Hagen's book is an indispensable companion to Stanislavski's. A consummate actress and teacher, she offers precise methodologies for developing one's intuitions, perceptions and responses, and coaxing open the doors of the subconscious as reservoir for solutions to acting problems. (Which are real-life problems, no?)*

*Her style is passionate, and her standards are demandingly high, offered to what is best in world theater.*

—Peter Coyote

◆

A great danger is to take the five senses for granted. Most people do. Once you become aware that the sources which move in on you when you truly touch, taste, smell, see and hear are endless, you must also realize that self-involvement deadens the senses, and vanity slaughters them until you end up playing all alone — and meaninglessly.

◆

Overacting, as it is usually thought of, means that the actor is playing to the gallery instead of with the other characters on stage. Or that he is hanging onto his own sensations or wallowing in false emotion. Underacting is primarily an empty imitation of nature, the actor playing in the "manner" of naturalness, unrelated to the roots of the given reality.

Nick Granito

David K. Varn
as Mr. Jymi
ALL MY CHIL

Donna Svennavik

JOHN ZARCHEN IS IN LOS ANGELES

After your initial interview with an agent or casting person, an effective means of follow-up is the photo-postcard.

### Audition

(Everything an Actor Needs to Know to Get the Part)
Michael Shurtleff
1978, 1987; 264 pp.
**$4.95**
($6.95 postpaid) from:
Bantam Books
414 East Golf Road
Des Plaines, IL 60016
800/223-6834
or Whole Earth Access

*Michael Shurtleff, casting director for such hits as **The Graduate, Beckett, The Sound of Music,** and **Pippin,** offers a montage of useful observation from a life spent discriminating winners from losers. Not as technique-oriented as Stanislavski, but a well-built compass indicating specific direction, and his tone and bits of show-biz lore are honest as a good comedian and quite in tune with the times.*

—Peter Coyote

◆

An actor cannot play boredom or he will be boring. He must find what it is that the character wants instead of the boring condition he's in, and he must fight for that. I use the word *fight* because the actor must find the strongest, most positive goal possible. Nothing less will do.

◆

Humor is not being funny. It is the coin of exchange between human beings that makes it possible for us to get through the day . . . . One would sometimes think actors are trying to reverse the life process by what they do onstage. They take humor out instead of put it in. That's what makes acting unlifelike.

Both of David Varnay's photographs illustrate the imaginative use of accessories. The leading man wears a hat. The character prop is a marvelous comic touch.

◆

Legitimate talent agents and personal managers do not advertise in the Want Ad section of any newspaper or in the trade papers. An ad that solicits "new faces" for commercials, for modeling, or for films and then implies that experience is unnecessary and suggests that high salaries are waiting to be paid to the first people who answer the ad, is a phony.

◆

Almost every actor in New York has worked in one or more of the productions of Plays for Living, a division of the Family Service of America. These productions are original half-hour dramas that illustrate a particular family stress situation: alcoholism, a child's inability to read, stealing, lying, and the like. The plays are presented to parents' associations or similar groups in school auditoriums, churches, or meeting halls throughout New York City. . . . While the payment received is minimal, the experience of adjusting to different theaters and audiences is invaluable. Some of the material is excellent for audition scenes.

To learn more about Plays for Living, contact: Family Service of America, 44 East Twenty-third Street, New York, NY 10016.

### An Actor Prepares

Constantin Stanislavski
1964, 1987; 295 pp.
**$18.95**
($20.45 postpaid) from:
Theatre Arts/Methuen
29 West 35th Street
New York, NY 10001
212/244-3336
or Whole Earth Access

*The Source Text. Stanislavski's studies of the techniques of the best actors of his day are the basis of all subsequent teachings. His dedication and worship of nature are an inspiration.*

—Peter Coyote

◆

Never lose yourself on the stage. Always act in your own person, as an artist. You can never get away from yourself. The moment you lose yourself on the stage marks the departure from truly living your part and the beginning of exaggerated false acting. Therefore, no matter how much you act, how many parts you take, you should never allow yourself any exception to the rule of using your own feelings. To break that rule is the equivalent of killing the person you are portraying, because you deprive him of a palpitating, human soul, which is the real source of life for a part.

◆

When you speak to the person who is playing opposite you, learn to follow through until you are certain your thoughts have penetrated his consciousness. Only after you are convinced of this and have added with your eyes what could not be put into words, should you continue to say the rest of your lines.

## Impro

Keith Johnstone
1979, 1988; 208 pp.
**$14.95**
($16.45 postpaid) from:
Theatre Arts/Methuen
29 West 35th Street
New York, NY 10001
212/244-3336
or Whole Earth Access

*Most theater texts are
like books on learning to ride a bike. Only after you
have the hang of it are they valuable. This book is
a rare peek into genius. Keith Johnstone, associated with George Devine and Tony Richardson of
the Royal Court Theatre in London, creator of the
Theatre Machine, comes across as a true magi-*
cian, an inspired innovator of techniques for
plugging people into the wellsprings of their own
imaginations. One of the most useful and provocative books I have ever read on theater.
—Peter Coyote

◆

There are people who prefer to say "Yes" and there are
people who prefer to say "No." Those who say "Yes" are
rewarded by the adventures they have, and those who
say "No" are rewarded by the safety they attain. There
are far more "No" sayers around than "Yes" sayers, but
you can train one type to behave like the others. . . .
Fred Karno understood this. When he interviewed
aspiring actors he'd poke his pen into an empty inkwell
and pretend to flick ink at them. If they mimed being hit
in the eye, or whatever, he'd engage them. If they looked
baffled and "blocked" him, then he wouldn't.

◆

'Try to get your status just a little above or below your
partner's,' I said, and I insisted that the gap should be
minimal. The actors seemed to know exactly what I
meant and the work was transformed. The scenes
became 'authentic', and actors seemed marvellously
observant. Suddenly we understood that every inflection
and movement implies a status, and that no action is
due to chance, or really 'motiveless'. It was hysterically
funny, but at the same time very alarming. All our secret
manoeuvrings were exposed. If someone asked a
question we didn't bother to answer it, we concentrated
on why it had been asked. No one could make an
'innocuous' remark without everyone instantly grasping
what lay behind it. Normally we are 'forbidden' to see
status transactions except when there's a conflict. In
reality status transactions continue all the time. In the
park we'll notice the ducks squabbling, but not how
carefully they keep their distances when they are not.

## Improvisation for the Theater

(A Handbook of Teaching
and Directing Techniques)
Viola Spolin
1983; 395 pp.
**$10.95**
($11.82 postpaid) from:
Northwestern University Press
625 Colfax Street
Evanston, IL 60201   312/491-5313
or Whole Earth Access

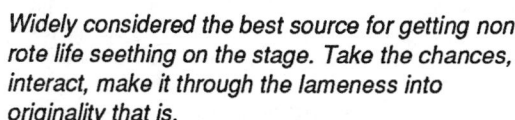

*Widely considered the best source for getting non-
rote life seething on the stage. Take the chances,
interact, make it through the lameness into
originality that is.*
—Stewart Brand

◆

Hidden Conflict

Two or more players.

Where, Who and What agreed upon. Each player takes
a conflict and states it to himself in the first person
without letting the other know what it is.

POINT OF CONCENTRATION: never to verbalize the
problem (conflict).

EXAMPLE: Where — kitchen. Who — husband and
wife. What — breakfast.

Hidden conflict: Husband — I am not going to
work. Wife — I want him to leave. I'm expecting
a visitor.

POINTS OF OBSERVATION

1. Let audience know each player's hidden conflict.
2. When the hidden conflict is stated, the scene is over.
3. Variation of this is to write a series of hidden conflicts
on slips of paper and let actors pick after they have
decided on Where, Who and What.
4. HIDDEN CONFLICT forces use of objects and was
one of the early exercises that started the semantic shift
from "conflict" to "problem," thus opening up new doors
of inquiry.

◆

Set up a large blackboard. Have the class agree on a
Where. Now have each member of the group call out an
item to be placed on the floorplan. Draw them in as they
are called out (illustration 1). When the floorplan is

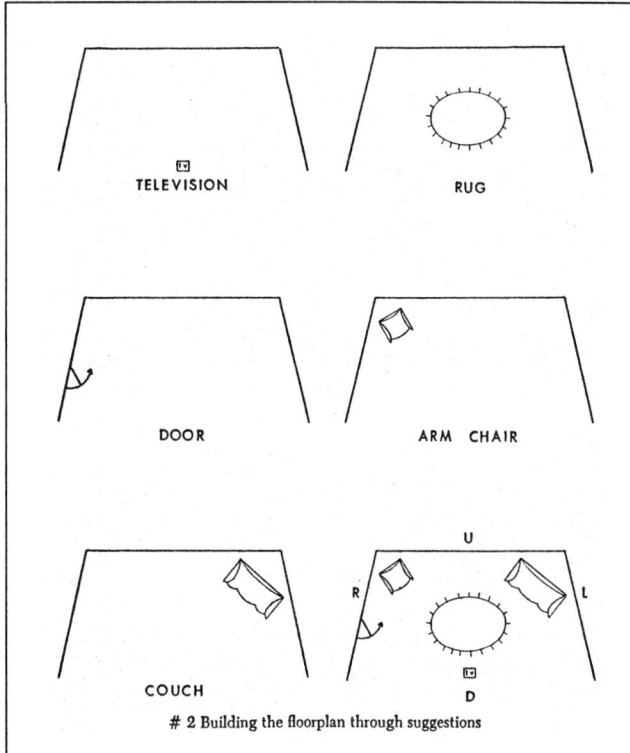

# 2 Building the floorplan through suggestions

completed to everyone's satisfaction, ask the question:
Who shall we have in the Where? When they have
decided, select two players to go on stage and play the
Who. Now ask this question: What are they doing there?
When this has been agreed upon, show the class how
the floorplan works. With the help of the two
players, walking through the scene and using
the props, the exercise should become clear
to them. Encourage the rest of the class to
watch carefully.

Are they sharing what they are doing with the
audience? Are they showing and not telling
us where they are? Do they both handle the
objects in the same way? Did they walk
through tables? When the total class is
involved to the teacher's satisfaction, then it is
time to pass out the individual blackboards or
paper and get to work on the problem.

Evaluation

Was the concentration complete or incomplete? Did the team solve the acting problem?
Did we know Where they were? Did they
handle all the objects? Did they talk about
using the objects ("I think I'll close the
window" etc.), or did they use them?

Check the actors' floorplan against what the
audience observed (illustration 2). In the early
stages of the exercise, the players will often
be confused and will not use all the objects.
As the exercise is repeated, this confusion
will be overcome. Just coach to use *everything* on stage and continue side-coaching to
refer to their
blackboards
as often as
they wish.

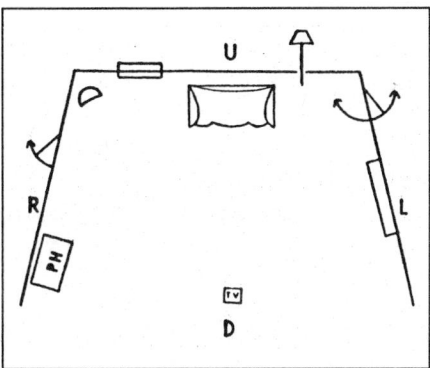

Illustration 1: Building the floorplan through suggestions.

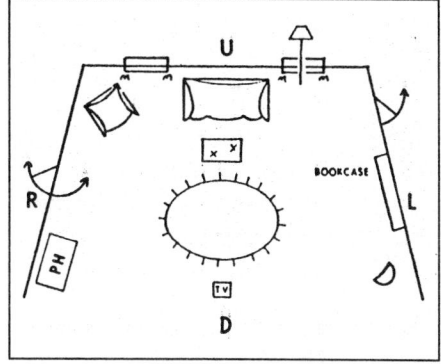

Illustration 2: Audience's floorplan drawn from players' use of Where.

## The Dark Side of Genius

(The Life of
Alfred Hitchcock)
Donald Spoto
1983; 665 pp.

**$4.95**

($5.95 postpaid) from:
Random House
400 Hahn Road
Westminster, MD 21157
800/638-6460
or Whole Earth Access

*There are plenty of powerful directors whose lives and work are documented and worth studying: Huston, Ford, Kurosawa, Truffaut. The advantages of examining Hitchcock are that so much is known about him; that most of his films are available for rental on video cassette; and that his methods are rather obvious. It's no detraction from his genius to observe that Hitchcock was only a few steps ahead of the state of the art; consequently, the world was ready for his innovations and took to them immediately. When you look at one of his films now (try watching it two or three times to get past being taken in by the story), it's like a textbook*

Hitchcock (foreground, pointing) directing **The Mountain Eagle** in Munich (1925).

*demonstration of how to create suspense, develop a story, reveal a character's inner thoughts, etc.*

*Dark as some of his themes were, and much of his*

*life, the man sure knew how to tell a good story.*

*His life would have made one of his most macabre films.*

—Tom Schneider

◆

The fantasies Hitchcock spun and that his screenwriters gave structure to were always geared to cinematic realization. His films depended on the emergence, from deep within him, of mysterious images — images that were often violent, at times tender. From his own secret longings and vivid imagination there came the small germs of stories — sometimes fearful and erotic, sometimes quietly comic or dreamlike. But the plots and the characters would always be subordinate to the power of the images — just as in dreams, the narrative is never quite logical or clear and is always subordinate to the images. Similarly, the residue of feelings left by dreams, like the impression left by Hitchcock's images, is more important than any half-remembered "plot."

## Directing for Film and Television

Christopher Lukas
1985; 193 pp.

**$11.95**

($13.95 postpaid) from:
Doubleday Cash Sales
P.O. Box 5071
Des Plaines, IL 60017
or Whole Earth Access

*You can't learn directing from a book. The author*

*makes this clear from the start, then goes on to bring a remarkable amount of his considerable experience into nearly proving himself wrong. This is not just for beginners. Open the book anywhere and find a generous serving of truth from a working director who has passion, wit, and a rare talent for teaching.*

*Put this on your shelf next to **When the Shooting Stops**. . . . you'll have the core of a very good library on film craft.*

—Tom Schneider

◆

One of the most exciting kinds of script writing is the kind that places us right in the midst of a scene. We see the lovers quarreling, but we don't know why — yet. The scene has reached a point of tension; we have to fight to keep up; they know so much more than we do, but it's exciting precisely because the scene has momentum. Conversely, a script in which dialogue starts as we dissolve to the scene, though we know that the characters have been with each other for two hours, limps along. A script in which every scene crackles with accepted facts that we perceive rather than receive, is a good script. A script that crackles, in general, that leads us from scene to scene, enticing us to want to see more, is a good script.

1.

2.

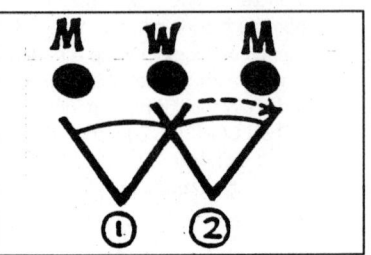

3.

**La Nuit de Varennes:** In a coach, traveling along in the middle of the dusty French countryside are three passengers (Drawing 1). We see a two-shot of the countess and the writer (Drawing 2). She is on the left. We now cut to a two-shot of the countess and the priest (Drawing 3). She is now on the right (because she is sitting between the two of them). This is not supposed to work, because it means that she will "jump" from the left side of the screen to the right side of the screen and it will be distracting. The right way to do the scene (says the "director's handbook") is to use a three-shot of the passengers, then individual shots of each and use the two-shots only if "bridged" by one of those other shots. Or, pan from one two-shot to another (Drawing 4).

The cut described above, the one that isn't supposed to work, why *does* it work? Probably because the editor chose just the right *moment* to make the cut, when the eyes of the audience were on the priest and not the countess; or when the sentence that the writer was saying was so cogent that we just didn't pay attention to that so-called wrong cut.

## Contact Quarterly
Nancy Stark Smith
and Lisa Nelson, Editors
$17/year (4 issues) from:
Contact Quarterly
P.O. Box 603
Northampton, MA 01061
413/586-1181

*Subtitled "a vehicle for moving ideas," this is a magazine by and for dancers interested in improvisation, movement games, the space between athletics and art. Its patron saints are Simone Forti and Steve Paxton. Has a nice, casual spirit, full of shared energy, serious fun and eccentricity.*
*—Robert Horvitz*

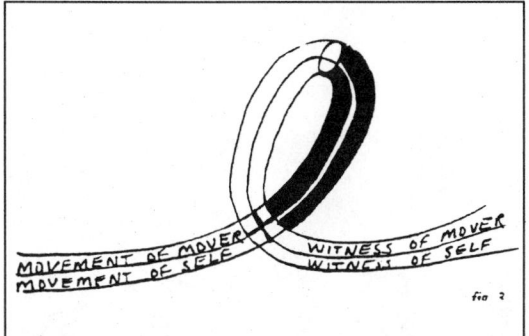

## Dancing
Ellen Jacob
1981; 350 pp.
**$11.95**
($13.20 postpaid) from:
Variety Arts
305 Riverside Drive
Suite 4A
New York, NY 10025
212/316-0399
or Whole Earth Access

*Dance may not be something to learn from a book, but this book serves as a great introduction to those of us who are beguiled and yet intimidated by the idea of dancing. Addressed both to the hesitant adult beginner who prances around the house when nobody's looking and to the young adult considering a career in dance,* **Dancing** *cuts through a lot of the mystique and mistaken glamour with practical, specific advice: choosing a*

*style of dance, finding a good teacher and getting the most out of a class, preventing injury, and even viewing dance.*

*A real aid for parents who want to get their youngsters started off on the right foot — both daughters and sons (plenty of photos of men dancing, though most of the pronouns are "she"). Competent directory of dance resources around the country, with special emphasis on New York.*

***Dancing** does what no elegant dance picture book can do: makes it plain that you can dance even if you don't look like a Capezio ad.*
*— Nancy E. Dunn*

◆

A good class has a thorough warm-up with adequate time to establish alignment and placement. The teacher should be constructive and inspiring, and should push you beyond your limits physically by increasing your range of movement and strength; and mentally, by breaking through barriers of fear. Avoid an inhibiting atmosphere in which too much discipline prevents you from making mistakes and learning from them; a frustrated, negative teacher; overcrowded classes, and rushed classes, especially the warm-up.

## The Dance Workshop
Robert Cohan
1986; 192 pp.
**$10.95**
($12.05 postpaid) from:
Simon & Schuster
Mail Order Sales
200 Old Tappan Road
Old Tappan, NJ 07675
201/767-5937
or Whole Earth Access

*I love to dance. Since the age of five I've been moving to music aided and encouraged by my mother, who shares my love. I was hesitant to review a book on dance because there is no music and you are sitting on your butt instead of moving about. But I remembered spending hours staring at my mother's book on ballet — copying over and over the different positions the stick figures were*

*doing.* **The Dance Workshop** *can be used in the same way. It starts off with warm-up exercises (very important if you want to spare yourself lots of pain) and progresses to positions, steps, and movements basic to all forms of dance. Instead of stick figures there are graceful drawings of people doing the movements step by step.*
*— Susan Erkel Ryan*

◆

The Basic Positions of Dance
In order to exercise well, it is important to know exactly where your body is in a given space. The body positions shown here are basic to dance all over the world, because they are basic to our body shape and function. It is important to learn them well since it is easier to execute any movement with care and precision if you have a formal position to start from and return to. The positions known as 1st and 2nd can be done either with the legs turned out or with the legs parallel.

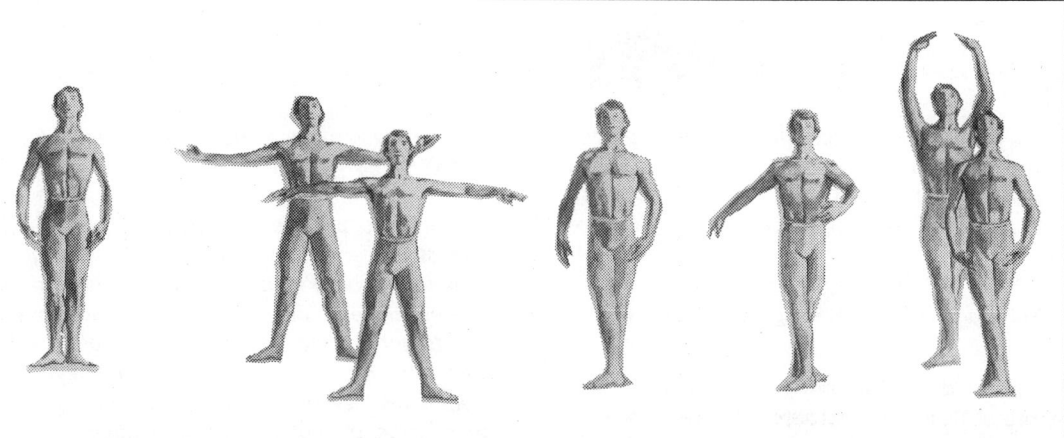

| 1st position turned out | 2nd position Turned out | 3rd position | 4th position | 5th position |

## Tattoo: Pigments of Imagination

Chris Wroblewski
1987; 128 pp.
**$15.95**
($17.45 postpaid) from:
Harper & Row
2350 Virginia Avenue
Hagerstown, MD 21740
or Whole Earth Access

Tattoos winding up backs, twisting around legs and arms, or curling up in some small curve of skin: dragons, eagles, cats, exotically dressed humans, and lots of other tattoo motifs writhe off the pages in Chris Wroblewski's book of dramatic color photographs.

American and English tattoo art is featured,

Bearclaw and bird by Cliff Raven, USA, 1981.

[ Far right] Tattoo by Dave Ross, U.K., 1985.

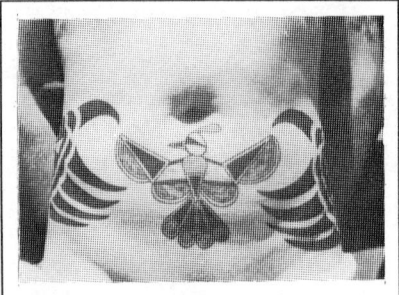

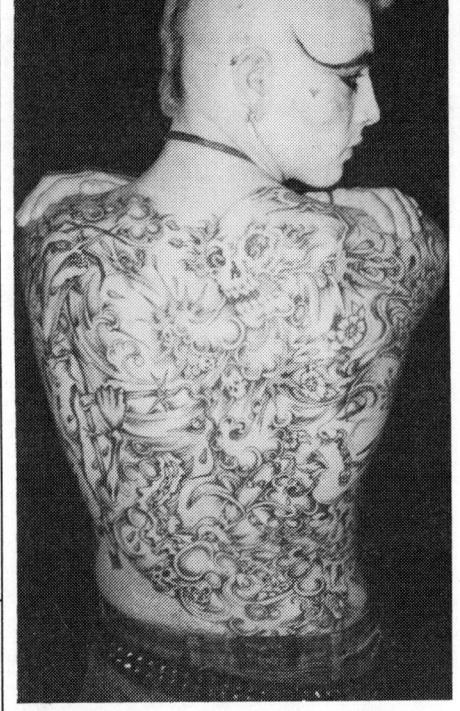

mainly examples of the more outrageous, abstract design of the '70s and '80s. Not too many anchors and "I love mom" tattoos, in other words. The introductory text is brief and perfunctory; look elsewhere for detailed history of the art. This is a fun visual introduction to the multicultural symbols of modern tattoo art and the various characters who choose to wear them.

*—Jeanne Carstensen*

## The Expression of the Emotions in Man and Animals

Charles Darwin
1873, 1965; 372 pp.
**$15**
($16.50 postpaid) from:
University of Chicago Press
11030 South Langley
Chicago, IL 60628
312/568-1550
or Whole Earth Access

Are we less joyful than gorillas? Less fearful than baboons? Does each species have its own repertoire of emotional possibilities? Do some (the dolphins) express emotions we have no name for? Darwin started it. His followers prefer "aggression" to anger; "submission" to affection. They copped out.

*—Peter Warshall*

As the sensation of disgust primarily arises in connection

with the act of eating or tasting, it is natural that its expression should consist chiefly in movements round the mouth. But as disgust also causes annoyance, it is

generally accompanied by a frown, and often by gestures as if to push away or to guard oneself against the offensive object.

Sneering, Defiance: Uncovering the canine tooth on one side. The upper lip is retracted in such a manner that the canine tooth on one

side of the face alone is shown; the face itself is generally a little upturned and half averted from the person causing offense. Mr. Rejlander has photographed for me a lady, who sometimes unintentionally displays the canine on one side, and who can do so voluntarily with unusual distinctness.

## Obsolete Body Suspensions

Stelarc
1984; 160 pp.
**$16.95**
($18.95 postpaid) from:
Contemporary Arts Press
P. O. Box 3123
Rincon Annex
San Francisco, CA 94119

I've never actually seen Stelarc perform a body suspension. I'm not sure I'd want to. The stretched landscape of his skin as he hangs from hooks through his flesh is difficult to look at even in a book.

Yet images of Stelarc hanging — above water,

surrounded by rocks, from granite slabs, or from wooden poles — have floated in my mind's eye ever since seeing his book. As I stare into my computer, delving into the mindspace of the networks and electronic drawers where I store and manipulate my ideas, Stelarc haunts me. Disembodiment has for me become one of the resounding themes of the information age; his images rehearns mind to body with the fierceness of a whip cracking in slow motion. And then slice them apart. The body is left suspended somewhere in mind, an obsolete carcass, empty, meaningless.

This book documents Stelarc's performances from his first suspension in 1976 through 1984. The large-format black-and-white photography makes you feel closer to the real events than you may care to get. Stelarc claims the subject of his work is not the hooks. It's worth looking at and beyond them to his bizarre, disturbing vision of physical submission to technology. And frightening.

*—Jeanne Carstensen*

Tamura Gallery, Tokyo — 11 May, 1980. The body was suspended in a sitting position encircled by 18 granite rocks, which counterbalanced its weight. Each rock weighed between 3.5 — 4.2 kgms. One rock for each insertion point. The rocks were first suspended from eye-bolts in the ceiling then connected to the body sitting on the floor. The rocks were then lowered, lifting the body into space. During the suspension time of approx. 17 minutes the body swayed, gently swinging all the rocks in different directions.

## The Body Electric

Robert O. Becker, M.D.,
and Gary Selden
1985; 364 pp.
**$8.95**
($10.45 postpaid) from:
William Morrow & Co.
Wilmor Warehouse
39 Plymouth Street
Fairfield, NJ 07006
201/227-7200
or Whole Earth Access

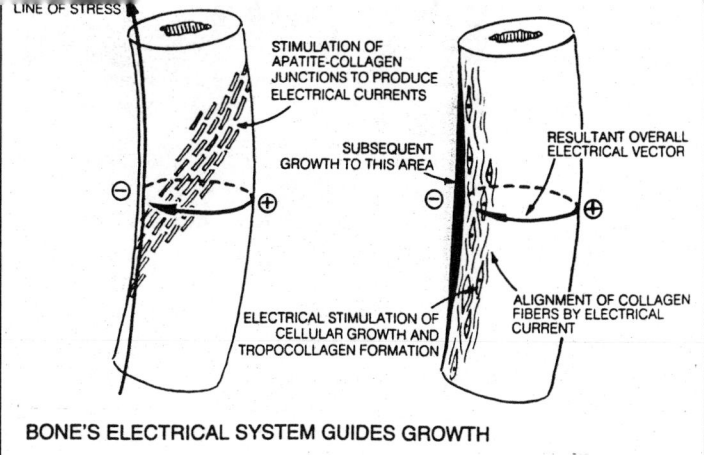

BONE'S ELECTRICAL SYSTEM GUIDES GROWTH

*This book is almost as annoying as it is astounding. Robert Becker is an orthopedic surgeon who spent most of his career studying bone-healing, tissue regeneration and the biological role of electromagnetic currents and fields. He wanted to find out how and why some animals could regenerate entire limbs and even vital organs and hoped that some of this resilience could be unlocked in the human body. Early on, he read reports from the Soviet Union about "currents of injury" — weak electrical flows in plants and animals that seemed to have something to do with tissue repair. In the West, bioelectricity was regarded as a subject unfit for serious research.*

*Becker's interest in the subject seemed quite subversive in the 1950s, and a subplot of this book is how the popularity or unpopularity of certain ideas affects the funding of medical research. To make a long story short, Becker's work produced many breakthroughs in our understanding of regeneration and led to the development of an implantable electrode charged solely by the electro-potential of the surrounding tissue that apparently accelerates bone-healing in humans. He also claims to have confirmed Albert Szent-Gyorgyi's hunch that certain types of living tissue are semiconductors — in particular, peripheral nerves and bone. When tissues with different electronic properties meet in the salty fluid of the body, a sort of "diode" is formed. The body as a whole, says Becker, not just the nervous system, is an active circuit.*

*For medical people, used to thinking of the body in chemical or mechanical terms, this is radical stuff. And the implications are more radical still: by analogy with solid-state semiconductors, where minute changes in the chemical structure of a chip drastically affect its electronic response, could minute chemical changes likewise alter the body's semiconduction? If, for example, we were immersed in an electromagnetic environment very different from the one in which our bodies evolved, might that not have subtle but significant repercussions on body chemistry?*

*When the book focuses on Becker's own research (as it does most of the time), it's quite detailed and convincing. In fact, it's a great detective story, as he probes the regenerative talents of salamanders, frogs and newts (when he cuts out half the heart of a newt, he discover it can regrow the missing half in less than a day!) He's careful to qualify his results and to discuss anomalous and contradictory evidence when his findings are inconclusive.*

*The book is less cautious in citing research by others, especially in fields beyond Becker's own expertise. And there's no bibliography — no way to go back to the original reports. Since so much in this book strains credulity, the lack of specific citations is very frustrating, even irresponsible.*

*But the most irritating flaws come toward the end of the book, where speculation starts to crowd out science. The long chapter on the hazards of man-made electromagnetic fields has a number of inaccuracies. However, there's nothing else like this book in print, and its content is much too important to ignore. The vistas it opens should keep researchers busy for decades — if they're not put off by the popularized presentation.*

—Robert Horvitz

◆

Szent-Gyorgyi pointed out that the molecular structure of many parts of the cell was regular enough to support semiconduction. This idea was almost completely ignored at the time. Even when Szent-Gyorgyi expanded the concept in his 1960 **Introduction to a Submolecular Biology**, most scientists (except in Russia!) dismissed it as evidence of his advancing age, but that little book was an inspiration to me. I think it may turn out to be the man's most important contribution to science. In it he conjectured that protein molecules, each having a sort of slot or way station for mobile electrons, might be joined together in long chains so that electrons could flow in a semiconducting current over long distances without losing energy, much as in a game of checkers one counter could jump along a row of other pieces across the entire board. Szent-Gyorgyi suggested that the electron flow would be similar to photosynthesis, another process he helped elucidate, in which a kind of waterfall of electrons cascaded step by step down a staircase of molecules, losing energy with each bounce. The main difference was that in protein semiconduction the electrons' energy would be conserved and stored in the chemical bonds of food.

◆

Most city dwellers continuously get more than a tenth of a microwatt from television microwaves alone. This may be especially significant, because of the human body's resonant frequency. This is the wavelength to which the body responds "as an antenna." Next to the ELF range, it's perhaps the region of the spectrum, in which the strongest bioeffects may be expected. The peak human resonant frequency lies right in the middle of the VHF television band.

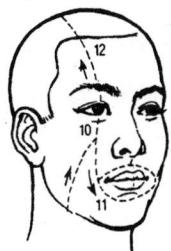

---

## The Web That Has No Weaver

Ted J. Kaptchuk, O.M.D.
1983; 402 pp.
**$12.95**
($15.45 postpaid) from:
Contemporary Books
180 North Michigan Avenue
Chicago, IL 60601
or Whole Earth Access

*The web connects distant parts of the body, so that they inform one another, communicating a wholeness we call health. Cybernetics of bodily information as the root of bodily unity is old hat in Eastern medicine. New to the West, the whole-system circuit approach needs a good explainer. Everyone working with acupuncture and oriental drugs says this articulate book is the best one.*

—Kevin Kelly

◆

All relevant information, including the symptom as well as the patient's other general characteristics, is gathered and woven together until it forms what Chinese medicine calls a "pattern of disharmony." This pattern of disharmony describes a situation of "imbalance" in a patient's body. Oriental diagnostic technique does not turn up a specific disease entity or a precise cause, but renders an almost poetic, yet workable, description of a whole person.

"The Liver rules the tendons and is manifest in the nails." The proper movement of all the tendons in the body is closely related to the Liver. To Chinese medicine, "tendons" is a broader category than it is in Western anatomy, for it includes ligaments and, to some extent, muscles. If the Liver Blood is insufficient and incapable of nourishing the tendons, symptoms such as spasms, numbness of the limbs, and difficulty in bending or stretching may result. Liver disharmonies may also cause the nails to be thin, brittle, and pale. When the Liver Blood is plentiful, however, the tendons are supple and the nails appear pink and moist.

## Communication Without Media

*by Kevin Kelly*

Performance art, as I see it, is communication through no media, or more accurately through a non-media. Rather than express via canvas, paper, video, dance, voice, or theater, performance artists live out their concepts. It gives them that weird, you-can't-be-serious color. A couple is tied together for a year by an eightfoot leash; they never touch one another, nor untie the rope even when they sleep. Doing becomes their media. When materials are crucial, as in the case of the techno-logical contraptions of Survival Research or the drapings of Christo, they are considered mere artifacts of the more important art of pure process. Exploration of process is a vital element in most great artists, past or present. But performance artists strip away the outward form of media, until they live in the naked doing itself.

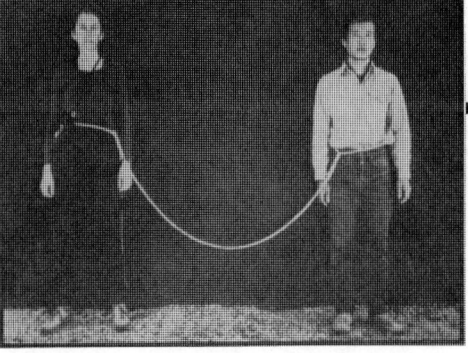

Linda Montano and Tehching Hsieh spent one year (1983-1984) attached at the waist by an eight-foot length of rope. They were not allowed to touch each other during that time.

SRL's Walking Machine with Flame Thrower. Look closely at the fuzzy black thing on top. That's Stu the guinea pig, controlling the machine's movements with his legs.

### Survival Research Laboratories

Information **free** from Target Video, 678 South Van Ness, San Francisco, CA 94110; 415/863-0118 or Re/Search, 20 Romolo Street, Suite B, San Francisco, CA 94133; 415/362-1465

*Defining Survival Research Laboratories is not easy. They are performance artists or, rather, the directors of a performance group. The actual performers are machines. Nightmare constructions; bits and pieces of scavenged industrial equipment, the flotsam of a post-industrial society. These found machines are stripped down, rebuilt, given new identities and personalities, then let loose on each other in parking lots and warehouse spaces in performances of mechanical savagery.*

*But the performances are not just sensational Bread and Circuses destruction. SRL's shows function as a sophisticated and sinister version of a Fun House mirror: a twisted mixture of familiar images (bizarre cars, destructive construction equipment, ludicrous mechanical men) and highly political satire.*

*Survival Research Laboratories are not to be read about, but experienced. If you can't get to one of their performances in San Francisco or New York, you can check out the numerous videos of their work. Whether you like them or not, you will be impressed.*

— Richard Kadrey

### Art Com

Catalog **$5** from Art Com/La Mamelle, Inc., P.O. Box 3123, Rincon Annex, San Francisco, CA 94119-3123; 415/431-7524, ext. 7672

*Your one-stop shopping source for performance art, on any medium you like: broadcast, closed circuit, and VHS videos; videodiscs; and computer software. Art Com also has an online magazine on the Art Com Electronic Network. It's accessible in the San Francisco Bay Area, through The WELL (415/332-6106 for modem), or, in the rest of the US, on PC PURSUIT (800/336-0437 for information) and TYMNET (800/336-0149 for information).*

— Sarah Vandershaf

### Pranks!

Andrea Juno and V. Vale
1987; 239 pp.
**$14.99**
($17 postpaid) from:
Re/Search publications
20 Romolo #B
San Francisco, CA 94133
415/362-1465
or Whole Earth Access

*Pranks!* is a hilarious book that had me laughing out loud. At the same time it is a manual of cultural subversion that administers a hot-foot to the archetypes of authority and robotic propriety. In a series of over 30 interviews, counterculture figures, performing artists, filmmakers, and other assorted provocateurs describe their favorite pranks and the philosophies that motivated them. From psychedelic revolutionary Tim Leary to raunch-film director John Waters (**Pink Flamingos**, **Hairspray**) to the Velvet Underground's John Cale, the lineup of interviewees is truly remarkable.

But **Pranks!** isn't just a recounting of naughty anecdotes. Many of those interviewed, such as Earth First! environmentalist Mike Roselle, perform their pranks as the most direct way of getting serious points across. And thanks to the intellectual style Andrea Juno and V. Vale, **Pranks!** comes off as a statement of avante-garde philosophy — a kind of

### High Performance

(A Quarterly Magazine for the New Arts Audience)
Steven Durland, Editor
**$20**/year
(4 issues) from:
High Performance
240 South Broadway, 5th Floor
Los Angeles, CA 90012

*Provocative quarterly examining the work of artists who, in making their lives their art, cut closer and closer to the bone while extending you the invitation to push your perceptual limits. Lots of photos and lucid, entertaining writing make even the most challenging contemporary art intriguing and accessible.*
—Sarah Satterlee

◆

On the bus, literally and figuratively, the 30 or so audience members proceeded through the busy Broadway area. At a bus stop, Dobrowolski and Slater came aboard as Louise and Rose, who began a bickering, mutually critical, melodramatic and rather stylized dialog, revealing a shared childhood memory of bus rides with their grandmothers. Their argument grew louder until the driver pulled over on a darkened side street, shut off the engine, said, "Jesus Christ, I can't take any more of this," and departed.

*cosmic wake-up call from an extended underground of surrealist artists.*
—Ted Schultz

◆

When you use the phone don't ever waste a wrong number. For instance, if someone calls up and says, "Is Jack there?" don't say, "I'm sorry, you have the wrong number." Say, "Hang on, I'll see. Who's calling?" Then wait a second. "I'm sorry, Jack doesn't want to talk to you. Jack is still very angry, and he doesn't want to discuss it."

Bob Zoell, a graphic designer and artist living in Los Angeles, infiltrated the wide world of parking signs with hundreds of lookalikes bearing quixotic messages.

# BUSKING — or How to Make Music on the Sidewalk
*by Ramón Sender Barayón*

USKING, or playing music for spare change, predates all types of formal musical performance. The Homeric bards, the minstrels and troubadours of the Middle Ages, all sang for their suppers or other favors. This ancient art still thrives in our urban centers.

For modern American buskers, the sidewalk or other thoroughfares must serve as the stage. Pedestrians vote with their feet by passing you by. Instant performance feedback — you don't have to toss and turn all night waiting to read your reviews.

How do you become a busker? Can you make a living? The following advice comes from my own experiences as an accordion-playing clown:

## DISCOVER YOUR "SPOT"

It must be right for you, and your act right for the area. Most obvious places are already crowded, and your added presence may not be appreciated by those already there. Also, your earnings will decrease in inverse proportion to the number of performers. Look for somewhere close to a traditional area for sidewalk performers but not in it. Join a tourist attraction (which may require an audition) or a shopping mall (which requires permission). Good money can be made playing outside occasional events such as conventions or queues outside a Woody Allen film. People already have their hands on their billfolds to buy tickets.

## CHOOSE YOUR PROPS & REPERTOIRE

*Your repertoire:* It should appeal to as broad a spectrum as possible, although obviously you are what you are. Playing an instrument may not be enough — maybe a little softshoe, maybe "whatever." Try to include some well-known songs. It's smart to have something that little children will find appealing —and nonthreatening. Every time a one-year-old bursts into wails, I tried to find something new. But finally I had to admit there are certain infants who find clowns terrifying.

*Your instrument:* Can it compete outdoors with city noise? Are you going to invest in a battery-operated amplifier? City codes on amplifiers may be a problem. Can you sing? That always personalizes an act, although in my case I just pumped the squeezebox. I only spoke with children, whom I encouraged to beep the bulb horn on my belt or, as a special favor, allowed to play on the black keys.

*Your clothes or costume:* I recommend a costume. After all, you are an entertainer and should look like one.

*Your props:* How about playing "to" something or someone? Love songs to a pretty doll? To a mannikin head on a stand?

## ANALYZE YOUR ACT

*The Long Shot:* How do you look from half a block away? Is there something about you that will draw a person's interest long distance? Or will it make him cross the street to avoid an interaction?

Ramón in action. Photo by Tom Nixon.

*The Approach:* As the potential audience approaches, try to establish eye contact and elicit a smile. This is tough work, although as a clown I found it fascinating and a constant challenge.

*The Stop:* Can you stop them in their tracks? You have them smiling, they slow down. Now what?

*The Performance:* Can your performance keep them riveted? Will it have a beginning and end or just be ongoing?

*The Donation/Collection:* If you have an act that draws to a close, end the song with a loud flourish and bow. Hope for applause while you or your assistant passes the hat. If it's ongoing (and I personally recommend this approach), then you must have some easy way people can drop some change. The open instrument case is traditional. I used a red plastic toy pot on wheels with a face. I added a microswitch and glued a basket on top with a quarter in the center. The addition of a few nickels was enough to trigger the switch and start it dancing around, puffing smoke from under its bouncing lid. In a few moments it would stall, and children, who found it irresistible, would run back to their parents for more change.

*The Exit:* Always have a way to escape, either around the corner to your car, a local comfort station, a friend's apartment. Remember, if you are in costume, you will be on stage all the time you are in public.

## MAKING MONEY

I used to average $4 to $8 an hour on a sunny day from donations. Some ideas for maximizing your potential:

*Photographers:* When a tourist aimed his camera, I turned my back long enough for the sign "Clone The Clown — $1.00" to be read.

*Advertisements:* Think about renting space on your costume. (Once when I was hired to promote a restaurant, I watched grey-haired ladies' frowns turn to smiles when they approached close enough to read the "Eat at So-and-So's" sign on my apron. That sign made me "legitimate" in their eyes.)

*Business cards:* Have some handy. People will hire you on the spot for parties or promotional ventures.

## HARRASSMENT

With the police, obviously be polite and innocent. With others, you can close up shop and move. I had very little trouble. Once at a street fair a passing drunk threw an insult, another time a passing carful of teenagers threw an empty milkshake carton. I picked it up and put it on my head. Instant laughter and good vibrations.

## GOOD HEALTH

Be prepared for a physical work-out. Being young is a definite asset. From my current vantage point in my midfifties, I don't think I'm up to the sashaying around in size sixty tennis shoes which I used to do. Even ten years ago I was weary at the end of a full day of clowning.

## LAST BUT NOT LEAST

Enjoy yourself! People are amazing and wonderful, and busking is a great way to increase your faith in the basic goodness of humankind.

## Words on Mime

Etienne Decroux
1985; 180 pp.
**$12**
($13 postpaid) from:
Mime Journal
Theatre Department
Pomona College
Claremont, CA 91711

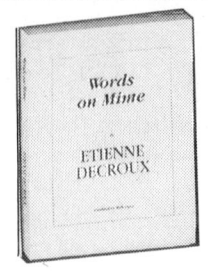

*I remember seeing Marcel Marceau when I was little and making my friends at recess the next day wriggle and shriek as I performed The Kiss.*

*Speaking on the art of mime, Decroux, Marceau's teacher, does with words what a mime does with body: makes manifest in you the reality of what his performance only suggests. Here, you are the mime, with his passion, intellect, spirit, grace.*

*Had I been a mime in 3rd grade, my friends would have swooned.   —Sarah Satterlee*

◆

I was born to love mime.

The body is a glove whose finger is thought. *"Pensée, pousée, pouce et pincée,"* which in French are almost homonyms, are also almost synonyms. ("Thought, pushed, thumb, pinched.") Our thought pushes our gestures in the same way that the thumb of the sculptor pushes forms; and our body, sculpted from the inside, stretches. Our thought, between its thumb and index-finger, pinches us along the reverse flap of our envelope and our body, sculpted from the inside, folds.

Mime is, at the same time, both sculptor and statue.

◆

1. When the part of the body has stopped so near the ideal line that the spectator guesses that the actor wanted to reach it; or sees that he should have wanted to.

For if we think of every ideal line as a magnet, the public demands that anything which approaches it should touch it.

2. Can one fix, equidistant between two ideal lines, a permissible route which would remain inside these lines because both of them would exercise an equal power of attraction?

—No, because the public would wonder what the actor was trying to do.

3. To begin is to promise to continue.
Any aberration is thus a mistake. It is possible to change direction, but it must be at such a clear angle that it is obvious it was done deliberately. To deviate is the act either of a cowardly hypocrite or of a groggy mind. The line has the right to commit suicide, but not the right to die.

◆

With us, gymnastics are reduced to beautiful movement for a long time. Beautiful movements are difficult. This perhaps arises from the fact that, since the beauty we have in mind is the corporeal expression of civilization, in order to achieve it, we must fight against our nature. Voltaire said: "To do good, you must climb upward; to do evil, you have only to let yourself slide."

Beauty is to the body as goodness is to the heart.

Sports.

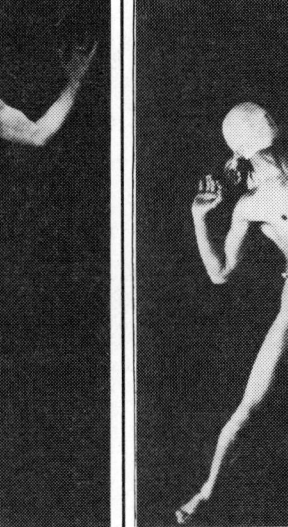

◆

Everybody is not a musician, or a sculptor, or a poet, or a doctor or a chauffeur. Those who practice these professions do not do so incessantly, whereas everybody does mime, even when asleep. If it is impossible to represent matter without form; it is also impossible to imagine a body without attitude. Being a mime or not being one, does not depend on you, for you are incurably one.

## Clown

(For Circus & Stage)
Mark Stolzenberg
1983; 160 pp.
**$8.95** postpaid from:
Sterling Publishing Co. Inc.
2 Park Avenue
New York, NY 10016
or Whole Earth Access

*This is the most accessible book I've found for the closet clown. It has sections on make-up, movements, and prop building, and sequence photos of six (count 'em) six classic routines that even a kid can comprehend. Time-tested at Camp Winna Rainbow. Yes, you too can learn to slap, take, slow burn, blow off, and add a little laughter to the sometimes weary world.*

*— Wavy Gravy*

◆

Remember: all your slaps and falls should have a comic feeling, and you always need to let the audience know that you haven't been hurt.

When you do a fall, always land facing the audience, if possible. If you want to land in profile, or at an angle to the audience, make sure you let the audience see your face and your reaction.

◆

Staying in Character: It's important to perform your slaps and falls as your character would do them. One character might get angry after a fall. Another might cry or laugh.

One clown might get up slowly; another might jump right back up to his feet. Your slapstick skills should not stand out awkwardly from your character.

The clown who is getting slapped should clap his hands and throw his head abruptly to the side in the upstage direction — or away from the hand that is slapping. This staccato movement of the head gives the illusion of impact. If you clap your hands exactly when the slapper's hand arrives, it will look and sound as though you've really been hit.

## Singing

(The Mechanism and
the Technic)
William Vennard
1949, 1967 rev.; 275 pp.
**$25**
($27 postpaid) from:
Carl Fischer, Inc.
Carl Fischer of Chicago
312 S. Wabash Avenue
Chicago, IL 60604
1-800-621-4496
1-800-572-3272 in Illinois
or Whole Earth Access

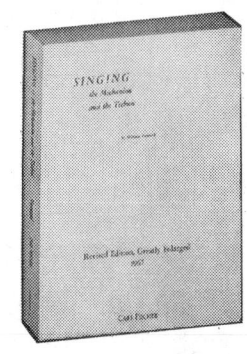

*Unusually comprehensive analysis and demonstration of the voice as an instrument. If you want to know how and why you sound as you do and don't mind somewhat technical explanations, Vennard is excellent. He includes detailed exercises on all the traditional subjects from breathing to articulation—to give one example, the chapter on Resonance tells you where and how to place your larynx, tongue, palate, jaw, lips and teeth (wow!).*
—Arlene Sagan

◆

The little pockets between the false and the true cords have fascinated many thinkers on the subject of voice. In howling monkeys, there are pouches connected with the

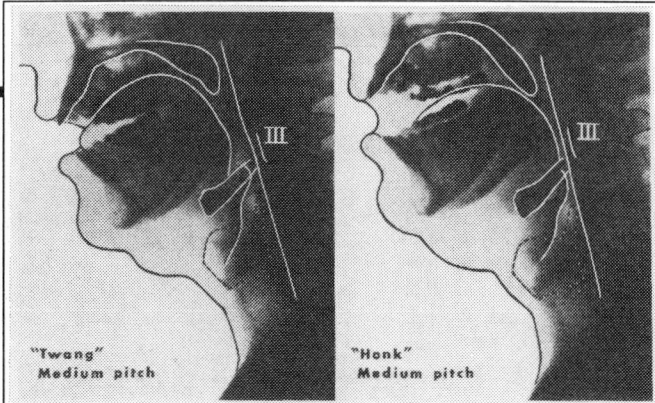

"Twang" Medium pitch     "Honk" Medium pitch

III, third cervical vertebra. In "twang" openings to mouth and throat appear equal, throat larger in diameter. In "honk" larynx is lower, but opening to mouth is almost closed.

ventricles which can be inflated with the breath, and when this impounded air is then forced back out it produces a sound. Vestiges of such pouches are found in some humans, and although no one has demonstrated any correlation between their presence and vocal talent, it is tempting to imagine them as resonators, (Kay).

◆

Long ago, Pythagoras, the famous mathematician, discovered that if one doubles the number of vibrations per second, the pitch is raised by the interval which we call an *octave*. He sounded a taut string, and then divided it in two, which raised the pitch an octave because it multiplied the frequency by two. Pythagoras used a string to demonstrate the principle, but, since the voice is a wind instrument, I should like to put it in terms of the

siren. Anyone can construct a simple siren by attaching a cardboard wheel to a motor and blowing air at it through a rubber tube. Make a series of ten holes at a given radius, and a series of only five in a smaller circle. When you blow through the five-series you will hear one pitch, and when you blow through the other you will hear a tone an octave higher, or with twice the frequency.

## Diction

John Moriarty
1975; 263 pp.
**$16.00** postpaid from:
E.C. Schirmer Music
Company, Inc.
138 Ipswich Street
Boston, MA 02215
1-800-777-1919
or Whole Earth Access

*Have you ever tried to pronounce a French "u" or perhaps even more difficult, knowing how so well, be unable to successfully demonstrate? If so, Moriarty is your guide to French, German, Italian and Latin, especially if you are an American who "practices bad diction in nearly every utterance." He tells you how to shape lips, tongue and jaw and includes plenty of very helpful examples and historical parallels. It may be ostensibly for singers but it's a vade mecum for any budding polyglot.*
—Arlene Sagan

◆

In English there are at least two sounds for the letter l. When it occurs before a vowel, we usually pronounce it with the tongue quite relaxed, the tip of the tongue against the hard gum ridge, the sides of the tongue turned down slightly to allow air to pass laterally. To test this, notice the position of the tongue as you are about to say **liquid.**

Now say **all,** and you will see that for a final **l** (and also for **l** before a consonant, as in **milk**), the tongue has quite a different position, and the **l** has a much darker sound. The tip of the tongue is still against the gum ridge, but now there is a deep depression down the center of the tongue, which is arched toward the back of the mouth. The root of the tongue is depressed.

◆

[r] is the symbol for the flipped **r.** American **r** is never used in Italian, French or German.

Sometimes Americans have difficulty in learning to flip or roll an **r.** There have been several ways suggested, such as trying to imitate a doorbell or a motorboat.

Italian words which have **r** occurring before a consonant will need a double flip. This takes more breath pressure.

Chart of Italian vowels, showing relative height, roundness, opening and closure.

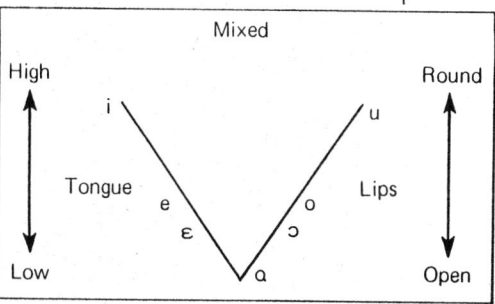

## Ventriloquism for Fun and Profit

Paul Winchell
1954; 190 pp.
**$3.98**
($5.49 postpaid) from:
Hollywood Magic Shop
6614 Hollywood Boulevard
Hollywood, CA 90028
213/464-5610

*Before Paul Winchell became the successful inventor of the artificial heart valve, he was very successful in a more "noble" profession — ventriloquism. Here Winchell explores every facet of this entertaining craft. He explains in detail how to create the ventriloquial voice through proper lip and mouth control as well as how to make and manipulate a dummy. (Pop quiz: what's the name of Winchell's wooden pal?) There's a section on performing in public, including several routines.*

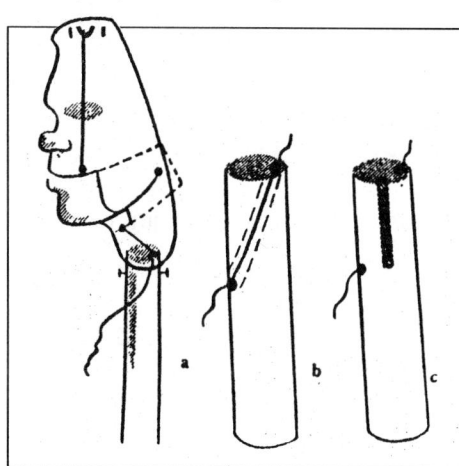

a. Route taken by string from mouth through the pole. b. Drill hole in pole for string. c. Make trough for eyes string.

*Most material you'll find in magic shops or book stores on ventriloquism are just pamphlets of 20 pages or so. This is by far the most comprehensive book I've seen and makes learning how fairly easy. (I tried it in a law class last week — the professor thought Duffy, a student who sits five seats down from me, had woken up and spoken for the first time all semester.)*      —Paul Chandler

◆

Ventriloquism is only an illusion; it's the art of using our keen sense of sight to deceive our often inaccurate sense of hearing.

◆

Close your jaw keeping the lips slightly apart, and the teeth touching lightly together. At no time let the teeth separate. This is vital to the illusion.

◆

You shouldn't have much trouble making the sound of "w" without moving your lips. But if you should have any trouble, just say the sound of "oo," as in moon, instead of the "w" sound. In that way "oo-air" would be where; "oo-ott" would be what; "oo-eye" would be why; and "oo-en" would be when.

◆

When you get into dialogue — with you and the dummy alternately doing the talking — you run smack into the first big mental problem confronting the ventriloquist. You are no longer one person. You are now two separate and distinct individuals and personalities. And you now have to think and act for two people.

## Louder & Funnier

(A Practical Guide for Overcoming Stagefright in Speechmaking)
Robert B. Nelson
1985; 115 pp.
**$5.95**
($6.95 postpaid) from:
Ten Speed Press
P.O. Box 7123
Berkeley, CA 94707
1-800-841-2665

*"Your heart is pounding, your breath is too short to catch, your mouth is full of cotton, your hands are so wet the papers you're clutching are curling, the voices around you are a numbing roar . . . ." Yep, that's me. I hate speaking publicly. I hate hating it. Although I haven't yet—phew!—the occasion to test its merits, the advice in this little book seems sound (and reassuring). It helps you identify what you're afraid of, analyze those fears and defuse them with specifics—checklists, exercises and suggestions. Maybe there's hope.*

*—Sarah Satterlee*

◆

Don't accept a topic for presentation unless you know approximately half of what you will say at the time of acceptance.

◆

Taking long, slow breaths prior to and during a presentation when you get a rush of anxiety will help to slow your heart down. In extreme cases, holding a long, deep breath will decrease the amount of oxygen available to your blood and slow down your pounding heart.

◆

Practice controlling your fright in situations where you know that there is no physical harm that can come to you. A good example is watching a scary movie. You know that the threat is imagined, yet the symptoms you experience are very real. It serves as an ideal situation to face your fear in order to be better able to work with it.

## The Overnight Guide to Public Speaking

Ed Wohlmuth
1983; 128 pp.
**$9.95**
($10.95 postpaid) from:
Running Press
125 South 22nd Street
Philadelphia, PA 19103
1-800-428-1111

*You can read this book overnight. Ed Wohlmuth's advice, delivered in a breezy, optimistic style, will help your speech. His approach is a bit "show biz," but you can modify that element to your own taste. When I had to give a three hour class recently I followed his suggestions, which included revising my remarks into a more informal style, consciously inserting some "signals" into the presentation and corraling a friend into letting me practice my talk on him the night before. Result: The class went well and everyone enjoyed themselves, including me. This book works.*

*—Jay Kinney*

◆

The Six Signals All Audiences Want to Hear
ONE: I will *not* waste your time.
TWO: I know who *you* are.
THREE: I am well *organized*.
FOUR: I *know* my subject.
FIVE: Here is my most *important* point.
SIX: I am *finished*.

◆

*"Thank you, Larry, and good afternoon everyone. I know you book pros have heard every overblown adjective in existence, but **The Overnight Guide to Public Speaking** is really a unique book—nothing like it is out there on the shelves at this moment. But before I give you a short tour of its contents, I need about a minute and a half to tell you about my background."*

Now, here's the actual note card for that portion of the talk:

```
THANK LARRY -- GOOD AFTERNOON

KNOW BOOK PROS  OVBL  ADJEC -- BUT OVERNIGHT GUIDE

   UNIQUE -- NOTHING LIKE IT ON SHELVES.

BEFORE SHORT TOUR  CONTENTS -- MINUTE & HALF

   TELL YOU MY BACKGROUND
```

## Interview

Shelley Wanger, Editor
$20/year; 12 issues
19 E. 32nd Street
New York, NY 10016
212/685-1800

*It's hard not to form opinions of public figures through the media. Yet when we chance to read an interview with these same people, they often seem surprisingly different from their media image. On a one-to-one basis they often come out more intelligent or decent or perceptive than the broad-brushed (and often preconceived) media portrayal. Conversely, others may appear dull and mundane compared to a dashing, intriguing media characterization.*

*My favorite place to look for famous-people interviews is **Interview** magazine, an oversize tabloid originally started by Andy Warhol in 1967. **Interview** has changed over the years yet has remained unique in its mix of excellent interviews and imaginative design. In addition to the interviews it often reproduces photos and paintings by contemporary artists good enough to cut out and hang on the wall. The ads alone are worth the price of admission.*     *—Lloyd Kahn*

◆

*Dan Yakir: Writing sometimes means editorializing instead of actually experiencing things. In that respect, perhaps it's less than a full life. Perhaps acting isn't all that different.*

*Jodie Foster: Maybe you're right. I guess it all depends on your compulsions. I'm someone who, if I like what I'm eating, will immediately tell myself, "God, I like what I'm eating!" I synthesize and analyze at the same time. I have to appreciate it somehow. At the same time, maybe it does stop you from having the actual experience, because you get out a lot of things on screen and you may think, Now I don't have to do it in life anymore.*

I feel that way about books I've read. The other day, I was telling a story about something that had happened to me when I stopped and realized, I read that in a book! But for me, I had done it somehow. Unlike writers, actors are middlemen. You can't just experience things as an actor. You have to interpret them and make them accessible to the audience.

# The Art of the Interview

*by Lloyd Kahn*

It's best if the person you're interviewing is as relaxed and natural as possible. Usually you'll go out to do the interview, start talking, everything going smoothly, and when you take out the tape recorder, things suddenly get stiff and formal. For a while I gave up the recorder for this reason and used a stenographer's hand book to take notes. This made for a more relaxed conversation, but unless you take shorthand, you'll obviously only be able to get the highlights. (If you do forego the tape recorder for this method be sure to go home right afterward and reconstruct the conversation while it's fresh in your mind.) I've since gone back to the machine and in doing more than a hundred interviews in recent years, have ended up with the following techniques.

It's good to get completely comfortable with your recorder so you're not fidgeting around with switches making someone even more nervous. With practice you'll be able to manipulate things without looking.

Even with the recorder I still use a steno notebook and take notes. I put the recorder under the notebook or place it as unobtrusively as possible. Taking notes focuses attention on your notebook and the conversation, rather than the machine. Also, in constructing the interview your notes point out highlights.

I generally have someone else type up the interview but I then go over it while listening to the tape and invariably make a lot of corrections that only I know about (because I was there and know the interviewee's accent or manner of speech).

If there is time to do a series of interviews, I will tell the person that I may use the recorder over the phone but won't say each time I call "I've just turned the recorder on." Some of my best material has come over the phone when the interviewee is at home (or workplace), comfortable and relaxed.

The more interviews I do, the less inclined I am to let the interviewee go over the finished product. They often fuss unnecessarily or try to make it into an essay or testament, or add in things they forgot and in so doing eliminate the spontaneity and candor. However, if they make a point of having final approval I will go over it with them prior to printing the interview.

## RECORDER

Microcassette recorders are small, unobtrusive and have been greatly improved in recent years. A good place to get these recorders, as well as mikes, earphones, transcribing equipment, etc. is Martel Electronics, Inc., in Anaheim, CA (mail order). A workhorse microcassette model is the Olympus Pearlcorder S911 ($65) which is voice activated, has two speeds, and a tape counter. Olympus also has a great new Pearlcorder, the model S810 ($209), that has extras like one finger slide control, tape end alarm, hi/lo microphone sensitivity, two tape speeds, and cue marking (you can put cue marks in between interviews and the tape will stop at each mark, or you can use this function like underlining paragraphs on a page—to emphasize good parts of the interview). Martel lists some 25 microcassette recorders, from Olympus, Sony, Sanyo, and Norelco. From what I understand, Olympus recorders are the best. They apparently invented the microcassette, their warranty and service departments are excellent and they do not change models often, as does Sony. (One thing the Olympus recorders do not have and that I like is a needle that moves in response to high volume. If you see the needle move, you know the conversation is being recorded.)

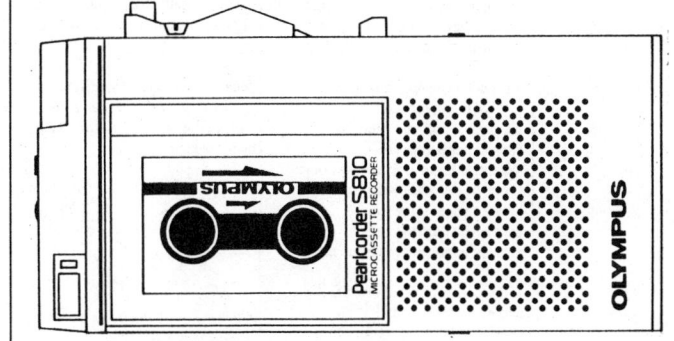

## MICROPHONE

All the recorders have a built-in mike, but I also have a small mike (Olympus Ultra Sensitive ME-7 — $39) for noisy places like restaurants; it will record either omni-directionally or can be set for a narrow band of reception. I also have a phone mike that fits over the telephone earpiece, but there's an intriguing new Sony miniature mike that you put inside your ear and it will not only record over the phone, but will also record your own voice—model MDR-E140C ($15).

## POWER

I have an A.C. adapter so I can run off an outlet when not using the 1.5-volt batteries. I always put in new or nearly new batteries when doing an interview or series of interviews. There's nothing like getting home and discovering I missed the good stuff because of low batteries.

## TRANSCRIBER

If you're doing a fair amount of recording you'll want a transcriber with a foot switch. I use a Sony BM-815T ($350) microtranscriber with a foot switch, so you can stop and back up either an automatic number of words or as far as you wish. Martel's catalog lists a variety of transcribers.

## TAPE

I like Sony tapes best (MC-60BM $3 — "for business use only"). The cases clip together conveniently and it's easy and clear to write in names and dates on the outsides.

**Martel Electronics**: catalog $2; 920-A East Orangethorpe, Anaheim, CA 92801; 1-8—0331-5231.

**Olympus** sells through authorized local dealers; alternatively, you can order directly from Olympus Corporation, 145 Crossways Park, Woodbury, NY 11797; 516/364-3000. Call for current prices.

---

## Interviews That Work
(A Practical Guide for Journalists)
Shirley Biagi
1986; 184 pp.
**$17.00**
($19 postpaid) from:
Wadsworth, Inc.
7625 Empire Drive
Florence, KY 41042
800/354-9706

*Simply, the most useful stuff ever written about interviewing others.*

*Biagi interviews famous interviewers and gets them to talk about how they do interviews. Not only do we hear professional conversationalists like Ted Koppel telling us what he's really doing when he's got someone on Nightline, we also pick up the techniques Biagi herself accumulated after finishing interviews with 40 other interviewing experts.*

*(Strategy for a great book: X-ray the familiar. Document the hidden structure in an overly visible process. Man, is that informative).*

*I've survived many flutters at both ends of an interview (more often in the interviewer's seat, frequently by phone). Yet I didn't turn a page in this remarkable book without learning a new trick or two, or three, or five.*

— Kevin Kelly

A question longer than three sentences is a speech, not a question. Your interviewee will lose interest by the fourth sentence, and by that time you will forget your first sentence.

To ask a difficult question, separate yourself from the interviewee's critics: "Some critics say that...," or "Your opponents claim that..." Quoting the opposition to the interviewee for a reaction puts you on the side of truth rather than on the side of the opposition.

Sam Donaldson says that one of the simplest questions is "Why do you say that?"

Set an agenda. Tell the interviewee generally why you want to know the information and what you want to know. ("I'm writing a profile of Mr. Walters at the Syntex Corporation [why] and I'd like to ask you about your friendship with him [what].") This focuses the interview and gives you and the interviewee a sense of shared purpose.

Some attorneys advise that you mention something about the tape recorder to the interviewee while the tape is running ("Is this tape recorder in your way?") so you have a record of the person's knowledge that the conversation is being recorded.

## Just Enough to Make a Story

(A Sourcebook for Storytelling)
Nancy Schimmel
1978, 1982; 56 pp.
**$9.75**
($10.75 postpaid) from:
Sisters' Choice Press
1450 6th Street
Berkeley, CA 94710
or Whole Earth Access

*This slim volume offers much more than sources, although there are these — story and song books; storytellers on record, book, and film; books about folklore and fairy tales. My favorite resource lists are the index to "active heroines" and "stories in service to peace."*

*Even more valuable is the insightful, experience-derived advice Schimmel offers. Never preachy, she speaks to the value of storytelling — motivating kids to read — with warmth and sagacious enthusiasm, and helps you choose, learn, and tell a story gratifying to teller and told.*

*—Sarah Satterlee*

◆

People tend to remember liking certain stories at a younger age than they actually did, and consequently try myths, fairy tales, and Alice in Wonderland on children too young for them. . . . The more complicated fairly tales require an audience much older than five, as do the myths, whose power and strangeness is lost in simplified versions intended for younger children.

Tell Me a Story
Words & music
© 1983 by Nancy Schimmel

Tell me a sto-ry, take me a-way, it's too soon to sleep and I'm too tired to play. When you were lit-tle, what did you do? Tell me a sto-ry that's all a-bout you.

Nancy Schimmel and assistant telling a tale.

◆

I usually warn the audience if I am going to tell a scary or bloody story; then they can brace themselves, and say "That wasn't so scary" afterwards. And it wasn't so scary, listening in a group, but it might be, thinking about it alone later. Kathryn Windham, who tells ghost stories most convincingly, also passes on a few beliefs about how to keep ghosts away at night; the simplest being to place your shoes with one pointing toward your bed and one pointing away.

◆

There is no rule that says a teller must meet the eye of each listener during the course of a story, but if you look mostly at the floor or ceiling, the audience could get the idea that you are afraid of them or not interested in them. I look around a lot at different faces, because I feel that looking at just a few people puts a burden on them to look interested.

◆

When I tell a story, I usually try to sound not like somebody else, but like me at my best, without the "uhs" and "you knows" that spatter everyday conversation, and without the bright cheerfulness that comes over even the most sensible people when they talk to the very young.

## The Family Storytelling Handbook

Anne Pellowski
1987; 150 pp.
**$15.95** postpaid from:
Macmillan Publishing Co.
Mail Order Department
Front and Brown Streets
Riverside, N.J. 08075
800/257-5755
or Whole Earth Access

*For years I've wanted a book about family story-telling to recommend to my storytelling audiences and classes. Now it's here and the right person has written it. Anne Pellowski knows a heap about storytelling around the world, and she also had lots of little nieces and nephews with big ears. She goes beyond bedtime to talk about storytelling for holidays, birthdays, family reunions, car trips. She gives hints for adapting folktales to particular kids and suggestions for holding interest with stories about family incidents, traditions, names, places. The stories included involve little tricks or props that work particularly well with intimate audiences. She ends with lists of books, stories, festivals, and even contacts for finding storytelling in England, France, Denmark, Australia, and Japan. A wise and useful book.*

*—Nancy Schimmel*

◆

I am convinced that the single most important story that each child hears is his or her birth story. The sense of being wanted or unwanted, of being an individual with interesting characteristics or just another statistic with no personality, of knowing who one is and one's place in the world or of feeling lost — all of this is conveyed most deeply in the way in which parents tell a child he or she arrived in the world (or the way in which they avoid the subject altogether).

◆

So many stories focus on the oldest or youngest child in a family. Since I was a middle child myself, I made sure, when telling stories to my nieces and nephews, that I concocted some tales in which it was the middle son, or the second or third daughter, not the youngest, who triumphed over difficult odds.

### THE PROFESSOR

Material needed: one handkerchief. any size. This story was remembered by many adults in my audiences, although it usually took some effort before they could recall the entire rhyme. I give it first in Dutch and then in English translation

Als heel de wereld stokvis was,
en elke boom een gas,
als zee en meer en waterplas,
eens louter haring was—
Waarmee lesten wij dan onze dorst?
Over dit gewichtig vraagstuk
hebben zeven professoren
zich zeven dagen lang
zitten te krabben achter hun oren.

If the whole world of dried fish was,
and every tree a gas,
if sea and lake and creek,
of only salted herring was—
With what could we quench our thirst?
About this important problem
seven professors have spent
seven long days
scratching behind their ears.

*Take a corner of the handkerchief and make a knot in it: leave about 1 inch of the corner tip sticking up over the knot.*

*Place the tip of the index finger inside the handkerchief, under the knot. While reciting the first lines. have the "professor" slowly nod his head.*

*At the final line, reach up with thumb and scratch behind knot.*

## National Association for the Preservation and Perpetuation of Storytelling

Membership $25/year for individuals, $30 for families libraries and institution. Information free.
NAPPS, P. O. Box 309, Jonesborough, TN 37659

*The best single resource for storytellers. Yearly $25 dues include subscriptions to the National Storytelling Journal, a quarterly magazine dealing with issues in the story-telling movement, and the Yarnspinner, a monthly national calendar of story-telling performances, workshops and festivals. You also get a national Directory of Storytelling which gives access to storytellers across the country, and a free Catalog of Storytelling which offers books and recordings. They also sponsor a festival, a conference, and an ongoing school of storytelling.*

*— Robin Moore*

◆

They were the first tales that I remember telling, and telling gratuitously, without practical exigency, without that sense of immediate necessity, of imminent danger, that motivated most of the ordinary, day-to-day fibs I remember inventing and which, I expect, all children with more imagination than courage have always invented to save their skins. *—The National Storytelling Journal*

## The Tape-Recorded Interview

(A Manual for Field Workers
in Folklore and Oral History)
Edward D. Ives
1980; 130 pp.
**$5.50**
($7 postpaid) from:
University of
Tennessee Press
740 Cascadilla Street
Ithaca, NY 14850
800/666-2211
or Whole Earth Access

*Some of your local history is in records, but a lot more of it is in minds. Here's how to ensure it's in both. When you're an old geezer, wouldn't you like to be asked what really happened back in 1988?*
—Stewart Brand

◆

I remember one young girl, interviewing an old woodsman, who asked what they cut down the trees with. "Well, girlie," he said with a kind of amused contempt, "we used an ax, that's what we used!" Girlie looked him right in the eye: "Poll or double-bit?" she said. You could feel his attitude change. "Well, mostly poll axes, but later. . . ." It comes down to this: The more you know about your informant's life, work, and times, the better equipped you will be to carry on the interviews — and the more you will enjoy your work!

◆

On-Site Interviewing: A man says, "Come on, hop in the car and I'll show you right where that was," or "I've got one of those out in the barn. Want to see it?" It sounds like a great idea, and it is, providing you keep in mind the same twin problems that exist for any "visual": identification and description. It may be necessary to include a careful map with your catalog, in order to make clear exactly where the informant took you, and you may find it helpful to "talk" the route right onto the tape as you move along ("We're heading down 178 toward Charlton. Now we're turning to the left three miles out of Wells, and there's a big white church on the corner . . .") Then you can retrace your path later, or you can check it on a state highway atlas or a "topo" map.

◆

That was the exciting part: going out and interviewing someone. What follows is far from exciting: making the resultant tape a useful and usable primary research document. That takes time and careful, systematic work, but if you skimp on it, you might just as well have stayed home in the first place.

◆

Write your catalog as a rather detailed summary of what is on the tape — a complete précis. Just as the tape should be as accurate a record as possible of what went on in the interview, the catalog should be an accurate description of what is on the tape.

◆

A number of circumstances will call for the inclusion of material that is not on the tape. All such material should be enclosed in brackets and underlined. You should explain all extraneous noises [clock strikes], account for all breaks [Tape turned off for five minutes while she goes to look for photograph album], identifying all photographs [looking at photo #11], and add anything you think will make listening to the tape more meaningful [His wife was shaking her head "no" to me from the kitchen door as he said this].

The proper set-up for a two-microphone interview. The mikes are placed close to both speakers; the recorder may be easily monitored; the interviewer may consult the question set without interfering with the microphone; eye-to-eye contact is easily made.

[Below] Labels for cassette copy.

## Voices

(A Guide to Oral History)
Derek Reimer, Editor
$7 (Canadian) postpaid from:
Crown Publications
546 Yates Street
Victoria, B.C.
V8W 1K8
or Whole Earth Access

*My favorite all-round guide to the history and intent of oral history. Very useful for the beginner as it addresses a lot of issues in a simple way: legal and ethical considerations, preservation of oral history, the interview itself, etc.*
—Cliff Martin

◆

In addition to the classic objective questions of who, what, when and where, questions which invite a more open-ended, descriptive or reflective answers, should also be used.... Interviewers have had great success with questions such as:

What would I have seen on my first day underground at that mine?

If you walked up one side and down the other of the main street of your town, what would you have seen and who would you have met?

◆

The arguments against transcription are two-fold. First, transcripts are only a poor reflection of the original recording and are devoid of a great deal of the meaning implicit in expression, accent and inflection. The transcript is like a musical notation, a kind of two-dimensional substitute for something much more complete and rich.... Second, and even more significant, is the expense of the process and the amount of time involved.

## Oral History Association

Membership: **$20** individual;
**$10** student/retired; **$40** library
P.O. Box 926, University Station
Lexington, KY 40506-0025

*The oldest (and only) national association for oral history. Great journal (annual—explores developments in oral history, reviews books, etc.) and newsletter (quarterly—news, bibliography, events, etc.). Also publishes pamphlets and books.*
—Cliff Martin

There may be considerable conflict of aims or opinion between you and the interviewee. Nevertheless, an experienced interviewer who is aware of the potential problem can direct an interview without leading or bullying the interviewee. The importance of understanding and empathizing with the interviewee's point of view cannot be overemphasized. This is not hypocrisy. In fact, some would argue that this understanding (or rethinking) is the real aim of historical study.

Interview Information Sheet.

## Listening

(It Can Change Your Life)
Steil, Summerfield & deMare
1983; 214 pp.
**$6.95** postpaid from:
McGraw-Hill Co.
P.O. Box 402
Heightstown, NJ 08520
800/262-4729
or Whole Earth Access

*I'm convinced we could relieve the majority of life's small problems by mutually improving our listening abilities. More than half of our waking hours are spent receiving message, and yet none are spent on doing it better. Listening matters. A few learn to do it skillfully. If a book would help you, attend to this one.*
—Kevin Kelly

◆

Actually, I had never thought about the listening aspects of my work. But now that I am aware of it, I realize listening is one of my principal jobs, that I spend almost 80 percent of my time either listening

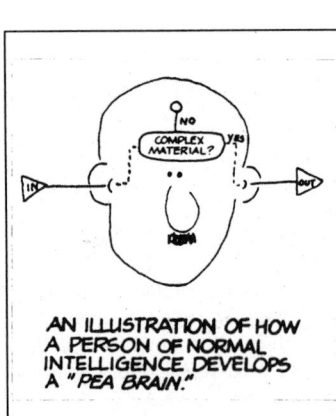

AN ILLUSTRATION OF HOW A PERSON OF NORMAL INTELLIGENCE DEVELOPS A "PEA BRAIN."

to someone or having someone listen to me.

◆

Eugene Raudsepp of Princeton Creative Research tells the story of a zoologist who is walking down a city street with a friend amid honking horns and screeching tires. He says to his friend: "Listen to that cricket!" The friend looks at him with astonishment. "You hear a cricket in the middle of all this noise?" The zoologist takes out a coin, flips it into the air, and it clinks to the sidewalk. A dozen heads turn in response. The zoologist says quitely: "We hear what we listen for."

◆

There is the attitude of making listening an active part of the total communicating process, which Dr. Steil terms "the 51% minimum responsibility," or taking the responsibility for at least 51 percent of the total communication process. To be this kind of active listener you must find areas of interest in any subject the speaker introduces, judge the content of the message rather than the delivery, listen for ideas rather than facts, put energy in your attention to the speaker, resist distractions, keep your mind open and flexible during the listening period, and be responsive in whatever form — that is, give the listener the feeling that you are enjoying or are interested in what he is saying.

The order in which the four basic communications skills are learned, the degree to which they are used and the extent to which they are taught. Listening is the communication skill used most but taught least.

|  | Listening | Speaking | Reading | Writing |
|---|---|---|---|---|
| **Learned** | 1st | 2nd | 3rd | 4th |
| **Used** | Most (45%) | Next Most (30%) | Next Least (16%) | Least (9%) |
| **Taught** | Least | Next Least | Next Most | Most |

## The Art of Asking Questions

Stanely L. Payne
1951,1979; 249 pp.
**$9.95** postpaid from:
Princeton University Press
Attn: Order Department
3175 Princeton Pike
Lawrenceville, NJ 08648
609/452-4900
or Whole Earth Access

Q: Do you need to research people's opinion?

A: 1) Sometimes, 2) Often, 3) Always.

*If you chose 1, 2, or 3, then you'll find this classic book (1951) indispensable. It will teach you how to avoid composing loaded questions like the one above, and how to make distinctions that make a difference. Without exception, every noble idea I have ever encountered began with a well put question.*
—Kevin Kelly

◆

If all the problems of question wording could be traced to a single source, their common origin would probably prove to be in taking too much for granted. The tendency to take things for granted is not easy to correct, simply because it is such a common characteristic of us all. It is a subtle fault, committed most, of course, when we are least aware of it. For this reason, some conscious safeguard is needed—self-discipline to stop and ask ourselves with each question, "Now, just what is being taken for granted here?"

◆

Words like "usually," "generally," and "most" are also helpful sometimes in avoiding the quibbling demand of, "What do you mean by that?"

◆

No interviewer should do more than 20% of the interviews. This should help reduce "interviewer bias" — the effect of deviations in responses due to the subtle influences of the interviewer.

## Public Opinion Polling

(A Handbook for Public Interest and Citizen Advocacy Groups)
Celinda C. Lake
1987; 166 pp.
**$19.95**
($22.70 postpaid) from:
Island Press
P.O. Box 7
Covelo, CA 95428
1-800-628-2828 x416
or Whole Earth Access

*The guy on the street, what does he really think about issue X, policy Y, or candidate Z? Maybe the mainstream media doesn't care enough about your concerns to have ever asked, or maybe they asked and you don't believe them. Here's how to use volunteers to do your own legitimate public opinion polling. Admirable book. Surprisingly effective.*

*(The publishers also sell POLLSTART, special software for IBM PCs to speed the polling.)*
— Kevin Kelly

◆

Sampling from the telephone directories is biased by unlisted numbers, duplicate listings, out-of-date listings, and nonworking numbers. People with unlisted numbers tend to be female, Republican, older, long-term residents, urban dwellers, and in some urban areas working-class members of ethnic groups.

◆

You should avoid a series of questions which differ only slightly in ways that seem important to you but which may be too subtle for the average respondent. If respondents think they are answering essentially the same question, they will be reluctant to continue the interview. Bear in mind that it is particularly difficult to communicate subtle differences between questions over the phone. Respondents tend to concentrate less in such interviews than they do in personal interviews.

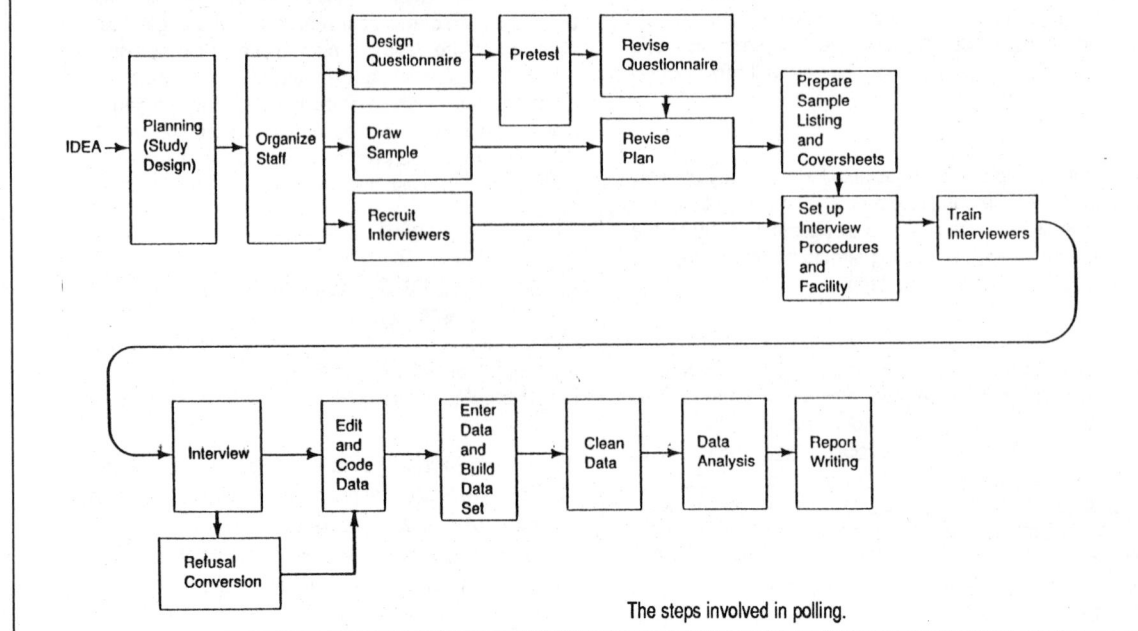

The steps involved in polling.

# CASSETTE CONSPIRACY
*by Robin James*

Cassette culture represents an increasing interest in complex and satisfying forms of expression and entertainment, outside the commercial studio-sponsored mainstream. "The biggest catalog of independent music is the network itself," observes Michael Chocholak, a cassette musician and distributor. "It's a fluid interchange of information where connections may be made and dissolved as interests and focuses change. By dropping down into this arterial flow you can become part of it and start mainlining information and resources. With a quarter or two you'll be amazed at what you can get to grow in your mailbox." Buying a cassette through the mail, making a cassette recording, writing a letter to a known cassette source for a catalogue, or sending a friend a cassette or an address: that's all part of cassette networking.

Cassettes can be taped anything: garage sessions of your kid sister's rock band, soothing meditation or difficult industrial noise, jams taken from record collections, trains in the distance, the gurgle of rivers, the pulse and jag of synthesizers. They can be practice tapes or finely laquered years-in-the-making treasures, very carefully produced and elaborately displayed.

Packaging is an important aspect of cassette production. Labeling is usually the J-sheet, a folded paper, often much-decorated, inserted into the plastic box, giving song titles, instruments, "Thanks, Mom" and the like. Wire mesh and gauze are favorite wrappers among the avante-hip fringe. Mostly cassettes seem to come in small simple envelopes, although they have been known to arrive in huge plastic toys.

If you want to jump into the network with your own cassette, first you need a tape recorder and some blank tape. What you do with that can vary. Then you take your cassette masterpiece and make copies of it. You send some copies to places/people doing interesting things (like radio shows, compilation projects, magazines, etc.) and see what happens.

Sending cassettes in the mail is very simple and generally inexpensive. Be sure the "where to" and "where from" addresses are prominant and easy to read. I usually send just the cassette itself in a reinforced envelope. If you use a plain envelope, mark it clearly CONTAINS CASSETTE (otherwise, it might go through the sorter at the post office

and hurt someone with shattered plastic) and pad the cassette itself. I like bubble sheets except people who fidget usually pop them.

"Tapping into the cassette scene requires activism," says David Ciaffardini, editor of Sound Choice. "You'll have to write letters if nothing else. Try to explain your interests or at least where you obtained their contact address and request more information about what they have to offer. Don't expect to get any thing for free, although some cassette artists will barter for their work. Include a stamped, self-addressed envelope or an international reply coupon. And be patient. Most of these people work for the love of it and don't have legions of office help to answer the mail. But when you do get your reply, it is liable to be thoughtful and personal."

So stick a stamp on an envelope, enclose an SASE, and send off a letter to one of the addresses listed below. You'll get back what are called "contact lists" — — or catalogs describing each cassette distributed and how to order.

**Cassette Mythos (P.O. Box 2391, Olympia, WA 98507).** The pioneer spirit of the indy cassette movement piloted by Robin James that currently includes the Audio Alchemy Digest cassette 'newsletter', a compilation of many artists' work all on one tape — an excellent introduction to what cassettes are about. Send $5 for a sample. —MC

**Sound Choice** (P.O. Box 1251, Ojai, CA 93023. **$10** for 4 issues). Quarterly (though often irregular) magazine of independent music that contains an incredible amount of audio reviews and is very supportive of the networking concept. —MC

**Sound of Pig** (c/o Al Margolis, 28 Bellingham Lane, Great Neck, NY 11023). Possibly the most prolific cassette label in the world, **SOP** releases approximately one new cassette a week from musicians throughout the world exploring the extreme reaches of musicality. —DC

**Floating World Distribution** (742 North Cherokee, Hollywood, CA 90038-3506). This is the most generous distribution outfit in the western world (maybe the world). They offer artists a place in their catalog with NO MARKUP so the stuff is very cheap. —RJ

**Insane Music Contact** (c/o Alain Neffe, 2 Grand Rue, B-6190 TRAZEGNES, Belgium). Very balanced compilations with a truly international focus put together under the energies of Alain Neffe. They have offered exclusive tracks by folks like Legendary Pink Dots, Merzbow,

Vox Populi, et al, and lots of other folks who may not be as well known but sound great. —MC

**CLEM** (c/o Alex Douglas, P.O. Box 86010, North Vancouver, BC Canada V7L4J5). Stands for Contact List of Electronic Musicians, — names and addresses of people and descriptions of their interests and what they do — and these days that leaves a lot of room for lots of eclecticism. This is updated semi-annually or so and is always thick with enthusiastic commentary. —DC

**Tellus** (c/o Harvest Works, 596 Broadway, #609, New York, NY 10012. **$40** for subscription of 6 issues/year). Each bimonthly **Tellus** cassette covers a particular audio theme — ranging from the Tango, to Radio, to Power Electronics — made up of submissions from a variety of contemporary new-music artists. —DC

## Cassette Mythos
Robin James, Editor
P.O. Box 2391
Olympia, WA 98507

*Here are some excerpts from a book-in-the-making on this electronic audio folk art — a collection of essays and letters by cassette artists, as well as reviews of hundreds of cassettes. Drop Robin a line; he'll let you know when the book is available.*

*—Sarah Satterlee*

◆

ERIK MUELLER: I have tapes that my father made of me before I was born (!), my first few days and first few years of life. When I was five my father gave me a tape recorder (open reel, this was before cassettes) and I've been taping ever since: WBIB shows (a fake radio and TV station I had from ages 6-12), film soundtracks, various rock groups, log tapes,

family trips, science fiction productions, musical compositions and experimentations, TV and radio snatches, interviews with people, environmental recordings. Being the methodical kid that I was I had all my tapes indexed by content material using 5 X 7 cards in a card box, so I could look up one of my friends and instantly access all the tapes that contained recordings of them. I haven't kept this up; I figure it will all be much easier in a few decades when I can just put it all on laser disc and have a speech understanding program do all the content cataloging.

◆

SANDY NYS: Visuals and music don't need words and translation. They show you things you can't explain but will understand. Even if you are not an artist or musician there is always something you can send to somebody, to communicate with somebody. And even if we all die in a big mushroom cloud or a polluted earth, at least we TRIED.

## Books on Tape

Catalog **$5** from:
Books on Tape  P.O. Box 7900
Newport Beach, CA 92660
800/626-3333

*The pioneer source is Books on Tape, now sporting over 1,000 titles. They issue 20 new ones a month. Their wide, pleasing selection is particularly strong in biographies, sea adventures, journals of early travelers, mysteries, contemporary non-fiction, and those acclaimed, long historical works by the likes of Churchill, Theodore White, etc. that you always wanted to get to. These books are read in their full length by trained, easy-to-hear narrators. For rent or sale.*

### SMILEY'S PEOPLE

*By John le Carré*
(1909) 12-1½ hour cassettes
Rental—$17.50   Purchase—$96.00
Read by Rupert Keenlyside

At some point George Smiley intends to retire. The problem is, his brain doesn't. So when the Circus asks him to play just one more round, his response is predictable.

Smiley's opponent in this final match is Karla, his opposite number in the Kremlin and top man in Soviet espionage. For years they have dualed at long range—now there is a chance to close.

What happens when they do is perfect le Carré—precise, inevitable, dispassionate. This treatment calls on the listener to supply the emotion, with the result, surely by design, that you finish the story as the author intended, a willing convert to the devoted legion, one of Smiley's life-long people.

Copy editor Ted Shultz embarks on his one-hour, twice a daily commute. He begins the review of 31 cassettes of "The Bigraphy of Peter the Great" [Books on Tape], about a month's work.

## Caedmon

Catalog **free** from:
Caedmon
1995 Broadway
New York, NY 10023
800/223-0420

SANDBURG, CARL: Carl Sandburg Reading Cool Tombs and Other Poems. *Performance by Carl Sandburg*
Carl Sandburg is the Johnny Appleseed of poetry in America. Poems such as ''Cool Tombs,'' ''Southern Pacific,'' and ''The Windy City'' are classics because they speak truths wrung from a new experience of life and because they speak them purely, simply and for that reason breathtakingly. 1 cassette. $12.95.
WILLIAMS, TENNESSEE: Tennessee Williams Reading. *Performance by Tennesse Williams.*
The wistful opening monologue and the tragic ending of *The Glass Menagerie* demonstrate Williams' gift as a playwright. Less well known are his light and charming poems and his uproariously wicked short story, *The Yellow Bird.* 1 cassette. $12.95.

**Claire Bloom reads Guy de Maupassant and Jane Austen; Conrad Aiken reads his own work on Caedmon recordings.**

*The fountainhead of poetry on tape. Originally founded 30 years ago to record modern poets on 78-RPM records. An illustrious pantheon of great poets and novelists perform their own masterpieces, or those of their mentors. Other great and fascinating literature is memorably recorded by spoken-word artists. Unfortunately most of the offerings are selections and abridgements. Tape quality varies due to the age of some of the recordings. For sale only.*

## On Cassette

Ernest Lee, Editor
1985; 655 pp.
**$59.95**
($63.45 postpaid) from:
R. R. Bowker
205 East 42nd Street
New York, NY 10017
800/521-8110

*Bingo! What a gold mine! This handy reference lists every nonmusic audio cassette known to be around (about 11,500 of them). In it you can find out if that wonderful book you wish they had on tape is made or not. It'll tell you its price and who to order it from. You can look it up by title, author, or subject. It covers plays and poetry, too. And interviews, radio shows, seminars, speeches, and language instruction. I'd be flabbergasted if you had trouble convincing your library to buy this book.*

—Kevin Kelly

## Listen for Pleasure

Catalog **free** from:
Listen for Pleasure
1 Columbia Dr.
Niagara Falls, NY 14305
716/298-5150

*About 100 popular (mostly recent) books read by famous British and American actors, some reading stories that became movies they starred in: for instance Tom Courtenay narrating **The Loneliness of the Long Distance Runner.** A couple of tapes feature famous authors reading their own: John Le Carre retelling his **Smiley's People,** which is outstanding. Every books is abridged Reader's Digest style to fit onto two cassettes — two or three hours' listening time. The voices are vigorous and of superb quality. For sale only ($14 each).*

—Kevin Kelly

## American Audio Prose Library

Catalog **free** from:
American Audio Prose Library
1015 E. Broadway
Columbia, MO 65205
314/443-0361

*Since 1980 the American Audio Prose Library has been dedicated to recording contemporary American prose artists reading and discussing their own works. Their current catalog has lists over 400 tapes, and reads like a Who's Who of contemporary American literature. Whether your interest runs to Vladimir Nabokov reading excerpts from **Lolita** or Toni Morrison reading and answering questions about **Tar Baby,** you're sure to find something surprising and exciting here.*

—Richard Kadrey

Josheph Chilton Pearce with Michael Toms. —New Dimentions

## National Public Radio Cassettes
Catalog **free** from:
National Public Radio Cassette Publishing
2025 M Street, NW
Washington, D.C. 20036
800/253-0808

*In 1967 Congress mandated a national alternative to mainstreet top-40 radio: a broad-based, independent, nonprofit National Public Radio. NPR usually lives between 88 and 93 on your FM dial. There you'll find intelligent discussions about difficult questions, marvelously creative interviews, original storytellers, and voices of the "other" America: Indians, feminists, blacks, the handicapped, farmers, teenagers, and a whole gold mine of fascinating veins and tributaries in American culture.*

*The most inspired of those hours are available on cassette tapes. That brings this daily audio magazine to those who can't pick up its signal, or never knew about it, or want to hear a certain program again. You can listen to them on your own schedule. There are 600 tapes ready, or you can request a custom cassette of any broadcasted show (except ones of music or drama) for $15 per half hour. A glance at their catalog will compel you to start tuning in.*
*— Kevin Kelly*

◆

GETTING INTO COLLEGE
For the first time on radio or television, a college admissions process is recorded. Listeners hear officials at Dartmouth College discussing and voting upon candidates.
OE-81-04-20 1 hr. $10.95

◆

HOW TO OPEN A RESTAURANT
Using one couple's experience, Robert Krulwich takes you step-by-step through the stages of starting a restaurant, and includes a list of "21 things everyone should know."
AT-80-06-23 40 min. $10.50

◆

BAG LADIES/WINOS
Bag ladies — destitute women who carry their belongings in a paper bag — and winos candidly talk about how they survive, the public assistance "runaround," and their daily existence. Caveat: Sensitive material.
OP-77-03-15 1 hr. $10.95

◆

IS IT FAIR WORK?
Professionals debate "workfare," a system where anyone on welfare must work in some capacity in order to receive benefits.
NJ-82-10-18 1/2 hour $9.95

### MAGIC WORDS with ROBERT BLY.
We take our title from an Eskimo poem recited by Bly during this extraordinary dialogue  with one of America's greatest contemporary poets. Bly brings us in touch with the deeper chords of consciousness residing in us all. He is the author of nine books, including *Light Around the Body* (Harper & Row 1967), which won the National Book Award.
(Tape #1678 1 hr. $9.95)

### "JUMPING" with KEITH JARRETT.
Among music lovers everywhere, Keith Jarrett is known as an artist of rare gifts. Here he brings those gifts to a captivating discus- sion of his work, especially the ineffable art of improvisation--or, as we termed it here, "jumping" (as in "jumping off the deep edge.") Jarrett is equally expressive with words as he is with music, and whether or not you're familiar with his work, you'll find this an engrossing exploration of the art of living.
(Tape #1828 1hr $9.95)

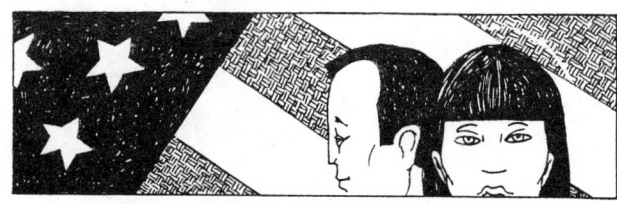

### ASIAN-AMERICANS
**BAMBOO RADIO — A DOCUMENTARY SERIES**
**Bamboo Radio Program #1: Almost Home: Violence Against Asian-Americans**
Focussing on three publicized incidents of harassment and violence agaist Asian-Americans, this segment provides insight and analysis into this rising racially-motivated hostility. Producers Julia Randall and Michael Yoshida look at historical and socio-economic implications for this situation, and what the Asian-American community is doing to counter it. Winner, National Federation of Community Broadcasters Award, 1986.
Catalogue No. SZ0300          29 minutes          $11

### U.S. INTELLIGENCE: DOMESTIC AND ABROAD
**The Secret Wars Of The CIA: John Stockwell**
Stockwell, the highest level CIA official ever to go public, exposes CIA covert operations around the globe, then narrows down to focus on operations in Central America. CIA manipulation of the press, and the nuclear war factor involved. A captivating program, which has brought producer Eric Schwartz several hundred letters daily following each broadcast. The Other Americas, 1986.
Catalogue No. SZ0337          120 minutes          $23

### SCIENCE AND HEALTH
**Fail-Safe: AIDS Public Policy Averting Disaster**
The 15th century had to face plague, the 20th century must confront AIDS. We look back in history and are amazed at the hysteria, excesses and ignorance that ran rampant 500 years ago. But how far have we really come in dealing with communicable diseases? KPFA's C.L. Moss, Carol Tucker, and Rebecca Ward look at who is making AIDS public policy decisions. Can we live with them or will they blow up in our faces? 1986.
Catalogue No. AZ0818          58 minutes          $13

### MIDDLE EAST
**Nairobi Women's Conference: A Palestinian Perspective**
Camelia Odeh describes her experience as one of the Palestinian delegates to the 1985 United Nations Women's Conference. She talks about conference presentations on the conditions of Palestinian women's lives in Israel, and the unity being developed between Palestinians and progressive Israeli Jews. She describes people working together for peace in South Africa, Central America, and the Middle East. Produced by Still Mad Collective. 1985.
Catalogue No. AZ0831          33 minutes          $13

## New Dimensions Radio
Sample issue/catalog **free** from:
New Dimensions Foundation
P. O. Box 410510
San Francisco, CA 94141
415/563-8899

*New Dimensions Radio bounces its programs off a satellite to 140 stations in 30 states, and features excellent interviews with everyone from Bucky Fuller and Paul Hawken to Wendell Berry and Ram Dass. For a counter-culture first, they've begun broadcasting on short-wave to the entire danged hemisphere via a transmitter in Costa Rica. A postcard will bring you programming info as well as a catalog of 1,000 cassettes that are available. For $35 a year you can become a member of the foundation and receive their bi-monthly magazine, Network News, full of stories about New Dimensions projects and upcoming events, as well as a 15% discount on all New Dimensions cassettes.*
*—Dick Fugett*

## Pacifica Radio Archive
Catalog **free;**
Microfiche **$26** postpaid from:
Pacifica Radio Archive
Educational Service
5316 Venice Blvd.
Los Angeles, CA 90019
213/931-1625

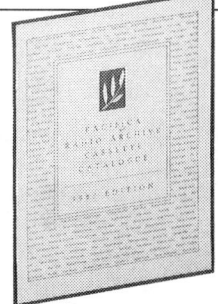

*Pacifica radio, a community-sponsored radio network based in Los Angeles,* brings us programs we'd never hear on commercial radio. Poetry, international issues, voices of minorities and live history confront us over the airwaves. If you missed the original broadcast, Pacifica National Archive probably has it on cassette. The current catalog lists over 300 recordings that date back to 1949. (A complete listing of material is available on microfiche, as well.)

Their recent affiliation with the National Federation of Community Broadcasters has *swelled their collection to 30,000* recordings. You can call or write Pacifica yourself to request a tape on a specific topic, and you can have them make custom cassettes from almost any anything in their archives. So if you're curious about what Marcel Duchamp has to say about Cubism, or would like to expand *your horizons with Dr. James* Pickering's history of Astrono*my, it's there for the hearing.*
*—Kathleen O'Neill*

Retail record stores stock is just the tip of the iceberg of the recorded music available through mail-order sources. Besides larger inventory, the great strength of mail-order suppliers is their catalogs.

The distributors covered tend to handle titles that are only sporadically covered by the mainstream music press. Listed are distributors who sell a wide range of styles and those who concentrate on one genre of music, all of whom make an extra effort to reach consumers with a mail-order service.
— *Jonathan E.*

## Wide Range

### Alcazar

Magazine **$8**/year (4 issues), Catalog **$2**, from: P.O. Box 429, Waterbury, VT 05676; 802/244-8657

*Alcazar is a 10-year-old company offering independent folk, Celtic, reggae, blues, Cajun, new age, gospel, international and classical recordings. They also have an especially strong selection for children, including videos. Books on folk music round out their catalog.*

### Down Home Music

Newsletter **$3**/year, Blues and Gospel catalog **$5**, Vintage Rock 'n' Roll Catalog **$5**, from: 10341 San Pablo Avenue, El Cerrito, CA 95430; 415/525-1494

*A wide range: vintage rock 'n' roll; country; blues and gospel; bluegrass; American folk; vintage jazz; ethnic music; British, Irish, and European folk; magazines and books. Honest descriptions of records offered along with track listings.*

### Ladyslipper

Catalog **free** from: P.O. Box 3130, Durham, NC 27705; 800/634-6044

*Women make an awful lot of music in as many genres as men and Ladyslipper has a large and diverse catalog to prove it. There are a lot of releases here that appear in no other catalogs. The descriptions are entertaining and educational. Nonsexist childrens' records and videos are well represented.*

### New Music Distribution Service

Catalog **free** from: NMDS, 500 Broadway, New York, NY 10012; 212/925-2121

*"The New Music Distribution Service distributes all independently produced recordings of new music, regardless of commercial potential or personal taste. A wealth of new music is being created in the areas of jazz, classical and rock as well as out of any clearly delineated experimental categories.*

*Because of its generally uncommercial nature, this music has had minimal representation in the music industry. Independent record production and distribution may be the only way for musicians to maintain artistic and economic control of their work."*

*All true. Their catalog is full of recordings from hundreds of independent labels, all with an informative description. NMDS is an extremely important resource in the alternative world.*

### Original Music

Catalog **free** from: R.D.1, Box 190, Lasher Road, Tivoli, NY 12583; 914/756-2767

*Their offerings are rapidly expanding and now include video. A good selection of African and Latin plus other music from around the world,*

*intelligently described. Their own label is the most concise and inclusive introduction to the range of African music. Also a great book selection.*

### Roundup Records

Catalog/Magazine **$5** from: P.O. Box 154, N. Cambridge, MA 02140

*Their mag, **The Record Roundup**, offers the latest releases with lengthy and unflinching reviews. Over 10,000 titles from 350 labels arranged by artists in their Artist Catalog. You can get the Artist Catalog alone for $2.*

## Specialists

### Andy's Front Hall

Catalog **$1** from: P.O. Box 307, Voorheesville, NY 12186; 518/765-4193

*Everything the folk fan needs: records, instruments (including bodhrans, bones and Celtic harps), tune books, instructional books and cassettes.*

### Eurock

Archie Patterson, Editor; **$8**/year (4 issues) from: P.O. Box 13718, Portland, OR 97213; 503/281-0247

*Eurock offers a fascinating array of mostly European, mostly unfamiliar and mostly (dread phrase) progressive rock. Catalog/magazine*

*editor Archie Patterson breathes life and style back into what had seemed a moribund musical field.*

### International Book & Record Distributors

Catalog **free** from: 40-11 24th Street, Long Island City, NY 11101; 800/435-7588

*Mostly classical recordings but IBR also carries quite a bit of jazz, nostalgia, and Brazilian music at good prices.*

### RAS Records

Catalog **free** from: P.O. Box 42517, Washington, D.C., 20015; 202/564-1295

*The most dedicated supplier of reggae music in the United States. Their catalog is a history of Jamaican music.*

### Seven Arrows Music

Catalog **free** from: P.O. Box 4904, Taos, NM 87571

*Seven Arrows has a large selection of Native American music in many different styles, traditional and contemporary. Informative descriptions encourage and educate the neophyte.*

### Shanachie Records

Catalog **free** from: Dalebrook Park, HoKo-Kus, NJ 07423; 201/445-5561

*As a label, Shanachie specializes in Celtic folk, reggae and increasingly in African music. As a mail-order service they specialize in the same styles, but they include releases from other labels. They offer practically all American-released LPs in those genres plus some traditional ethnic recordings from labels such as Folkways. Their reviews are enthusiastic if positive, but can be tart if the recording is ill-received and on another label.*

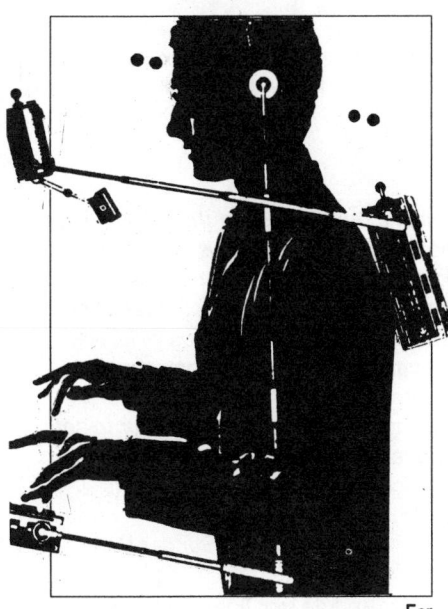

—Ear

## Ear
Carol E. Tuynman, Editor; **$20**/year (10 issues) from: Ear Magazine, 325 Spring Street, Room 208, New York, NY 10013; 212/807-7944

*Nothing even comes close to covering the progressive New Music scene the way Ear does. Whether it's the Hub's musical computer interface or Nicolas Collins's improvisational sabotage of found radio signals, Ear is there. Regular articles on early New Music pioneers round out this excellent magazine.*
— *Richard Kadrey*

## Electronic Musician
Craig Anderton, Editor; **$22**/year (12 issues) from: Electronic Musician, P.O. Box 3747, Escondido, CA 92025; in California call 800/255-3302; Outside California 800/334-8152

*You want to know what Prince wore to the Grammy's? Look somewhere else. The emphasis here is on equipment. What's new in MIDI. What's good; What's not. Lots of useful information on recording, performing and instrument modifications for the working musician.*
— *Richard Kadrey*

## JazzTimes
David Zych, Editor; **$10**/year (12 issues) from: JazzTimes, 8055-13th Street, Silver Spring, MD, 20910; 301/588-4114

*News and reviews from the jazz world. This is a magazine with a nice grass-roots feel. It's clearly put together by people who love and are committed to jazz.*
— *Jonathan E.*

## Living Blues
Jim O'Neal, Editor; **$18**/year (6 issues) from: Living Blues Magazine, University of Mississippi Center for the Study of Southern Culture, University, MS 38677; 601/232-5993

*Blues and nothing but the blues. Living Blues is published through the University of Mississippi and has the thoroughness of an academic journal, but with none of the stuffiness. Full of record reviews, interviews with blues pioneers and occasional obituaries.*
— *Jonathan E.*

## Maximum Rock'n'Roll
**$9**/year (6 issues) from: Maximum Rock'n'Roll, P.O. Box 288, Berkeley, CA 94701

*There's an enormous amount of energy in this magazine. Their coverage of the punk scene is thorough and enthusiastic, with encouragement in the front of each issue for readers to get involved by contributing articles and suggesting shops that might carry Maximum Rock'n'Roll. One of the few magazines around that lives and believes what it writes about.*
— *Richard Kadrey*

## Music Technology
Bob O'Donnell, Editor; **$34.50**/year (12 issues) from: Music Maker Publications, Inc., 7361 Topanga Canyon Blvd., Canoga Park, CA 91303; 818/704-8777

*Don't let the famous face on the cover of each issue fool you. This is a magazine about the theory and technologies that helped to create the music the face on the cover is famous for, whether it's Brian Eno talking about destabilizing his DX7 or Steve Reich talking about his new-found respect for samplers.*

—Jazz Times

*Informative product reviews and a lively letters column round out this fine magazine.*
— *Richard Kadrey*

## New Musical Express
**$97**/year (52 issues) from: NME, Publications Expediting Inc., 200 Meacham Avenue, Elmont, NY; 516-352-7300

*After all these years NME still rules as the essential weekly international guide to youth and pop culture. Music, music news, video, books, ideas, politics, gasbag letters, catty gossip, and blind enthusiasm for the latest thing just so long as it is the latest thing. Bring your hype detector but there's nothing else even close.*
— *Jonathan E.*

## Option
Scott Becker, Editor; **$12**/year (6 issues) from Sonic Options Network, 2345 Westwood Blvd. #2, Los Angeles, CA 90064

*No longer funky, Option's adventurousness in covering any music from anywhere but the mainstream is stimulating. A slight college radio rock bias is evident more in the ads than the editorial. Beefy features and many mid-length reviews of independent and major-label releases make Option the top all-round music mag in the States today.*
— *Jonathan E.*

## Pulse!
Mike Farrace, Editor; **$20**/year (12 issues) First Class, $10/year for Third Class from Tower Records Pulse!, 2500 Del Monte Street, Bldg 'C', West Sacramento, CA 95691

*Anything megastore Tower sells, Pulse! will cover. That means new releases in just about every genre, including country, opera, and schlock pop crooning. Reviews tend to be informational rather than critical. Also short news sections from towns and genres, and features on both well-established and up-and-coming artists.*
— *Jonathan E.*

## Reggae and African Beat
C.C. Smith, Editor; **$9.95**/year (6 issues) from: Bongo Productions, P.O. Box 29820, Los Angeles, CA 90029; 213/675-1134

*Committed to the spirit behind the music as well as to the form of the music. Heavy on features and comment, but erratic on reviews. Their recent airing of the problems behind reggae is a welcome and long-needed blast of truth in a genre often dominated by self-serving falsehoods.*
— *Jonathan E.*

—Reggae and African Beat

## Unsound
William Davenport, Editor
Back issues $1 and $3 from: Unsound P.O. Box 883202 San Francisco, CA 94188-3202 415/626-5017

*In their own words: "Unsound is focussed onto the hard edge of experimental art and music — the edge that most consider subversive." Unfortunately, this dangerous little magazine isn't publishing anymore, but you can get copies of individual back issues for $1 to $3 each, or a complete set for $60. Write for a list of available issues.*
— *Richard Kadrey*

—Unsound

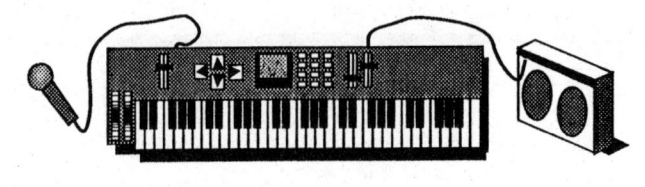

### Digital Samplers
Information **free** from: Casio Corporation, 15 Gardner Road, Fairfield, NJ 07006; 201/575-7400.

*One of the most astonishing musical innovations in decades is the digital sampler. A sampler records any sound — say, a clang of pots, or a cough, or a guitar strum on an old 78 — and lets you play that sound across a keyboard in several octaves. You probably wouldn't want to, but it's possible to play Bach on the cough. You can tweak the sound in the usual ways synthesizers do, by adding harmonics, distorting frequencies, until it's hardly recognizable. Anything — streetcars, insects, the whish of wind — can become an instrument, so that, in a sense, one can now play the whole Earth.*

*What's the best way to get into the fray? The cheapest route is the Casio SK-1 for $99. It has an adequate built-in microphone and tape input terminal. You can walk around the house recording found sounds, or tape stuff off TV commercials. It'll capture a second and a half's worth of noise at about AM-radio quality. Then you play the miniature keys up and down across two and a half octaves, and it squeaks out the "notes" through built-in speakers.*

*A more serious model like the Casio FZ-1 (about $1,800) is a 16-bit sampler. It will digitize and store up to 64 sounds on a built-in 3" floppy disk, and play them back over five octaves on a full-scale keyboard. Sound segments up to 14 seconds long can be captured. Most importantly, it sends the signals out in MIDI standard, which allows the sound to be reproduced by any piece of professional electronic recording or music-processing instrument.*

*Affordable music samplers like these are dismantling the boundaries of sound.* —Kevin Kelly

### The Sampling Book
Joe Scacciaferro
and Steve De Furia
1987; 150 pp.
**$17.95**
($19.95 postpaid)

### Casio FZ-1 &
### FZ-10M
Joe Scacciaferro
and Steve De Furia
1987; 143 pp.
**$14.95**
($16.95 postpaid)

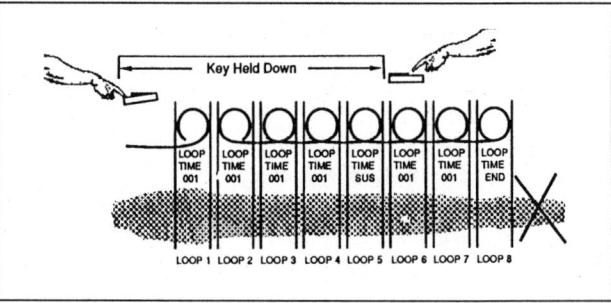

Both from:
Hal Leonard Books
P.O. Box 13810
Milwaukee, WI 53213
or Whole Earth Access

*You should consider buying one of these books before investing in an expensive sampling keyboard. The Sampling Book acquaints you with sampling techniques and demystifies arcane terminology. If the manual that comes with the sampler scares you, this will ease your learning curve. It helped me do some things I wanted to but couldn't figure out from the manual. A final chapter on test driving a sampler could be useful when you are ready to make a purchase.*

*If your sampler (to be) is a Casio FZ-1 or*

For most of the experiments in this book, all you need is your FZ, a mic, and an amp (or headphones). A tape recorder will also come in handy if you have one.

*FZ-10M (the rack-mount version of the FZ-1), then the second book has specific exercises for those machines. Both books explain how to splice sounds, loop sounds and mix them together. Producing your own studio-quality samples will always be a time-consuming, trial-and-error process, but the authors succeed in coaxing the determined user to keep trying. It took me about an hour to set levels, record a few takes and then play a cloned chorus of my voice on the keys. (These books need an index.)*

— Ramon Sender Barayon

Here's what you would hear with the Loop Time settings shown in this example. When a key is pressed, Loops 1 through 4 will each repeat three times. Next, Loop 5 (the Sustain Loop) will repeat for as long as the key is held. After the key is released, Loops 6 and 7 will each repeat three times. Finally, Loop 8 (the End Loop) will repeat continuously until the sound fades away. The portion of the sample after the end Loop will not be heard. (A Loop Time value of one causes a loop to repeat three times.)

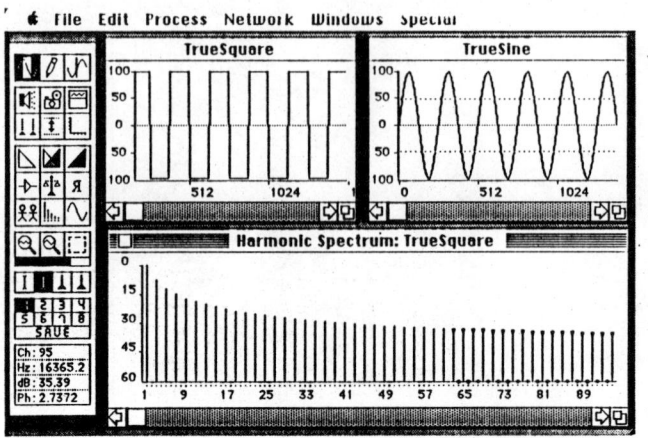

---

The FZ-1 features an 8-stage Loop function which allows the insertion of up to 8 loops in the sampled sound. These loops can be inserted at any point in the sampled sound's waveform, using loop "Start" and "End" parameters.

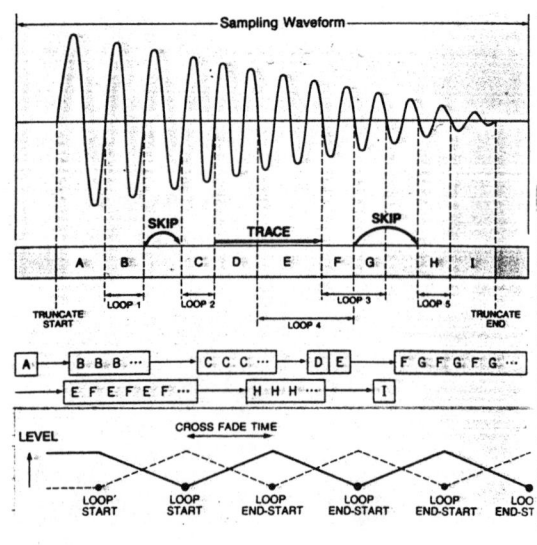

In addition, a Cross Fade Time parameter allows smooth transition from the end of one section into the beginning of another. Trace and Skip parameters allow tracing of one specified loop pattern or skipping to the next specified loop. . . .

### Alchemy
Copy-protected; Macintosh 512K, Plus, SE. **$495** from: Blank Software, 1477 Folsom St., San Francisco, CA 94103; 415/863-9224

*Alchemy allows your sampler to cut, copy, paste, insert, reverse, and mix samples and sample fragments, and its looping feature is more powerful and easier to use than any other piece of software I've worked with. Alchemy also allows you to edit waveforms by reducing samples to their harmonic components. Or you can start from scratch and synthesize a whole new sound by creating your own harmonic series. If you have more than one sampler, Alchemy can act as a central library for samples and allow you to play all of your sounds on all of the supported samplers. Another nice feature of this program is the ability to create stereo sound files, which may consist of either actual stereo sampled sounds, or hand-built stereo images.*

*Alchemy's power, combined with its fast and easy-to-use resynthesis features, makes it almost essential for anyone with a sampler and a Macintosh!*

— Paul Blankinship

An **Alchemy** screen used to analyze and "re-synthesize" sounds. This way, you can create a new sound by editing an existing waveform.

## Cheapest Synthesizers

Information **free** from: Yamaha Music Corporation, Digital Musical Instrument Division, P. O. Box 6600, Buena Park, CA 90622; 714/522-9011; Casio Corporation, 15 Gardner Road, Fairfield, NJ 07006; 201/575-7400. Prices are approximate.

*The standing rule of thumb in electronic music is that having many really cheap synthesizers is better than having a single expensive one. Richness and diversity in sound comes by the different ways in which each synthesizer computes a signal. Yamaha uses FM (as in the radio broadcast) for its synthesizing function. Casio uses a choppy digital process. Others use an "additive" algorithm. Take a multitude of sources, blend them together, and you'll get sound textured in the way real-life sounds are — impure, uneven, rich.*

*Combining sound generators, there's no reason to have a keyboard on each, so the cheapest synthesizer module doesn't. It is the Yamaha TX81Z (about $400), roughly the size of a hardback book. Some music stores that cater to electronic musicians have these keyboardless units stacked on the floor. Composers walk out with three or four of them. Each one they add is another layer of grain in their music fabric.*

*To use them you'll need at least one synth with a keyboard and the usual MIDI paraphernalia. The by-now-old standard at the low end is the Casio CZ-101 for around $300. It has a mini-keyboard which feels cramped, but you can link it to a hi-fi*

*tape deck and revel in a variety of built-in sounds. If touch sensitivity is important (the harder you hit the keys the louder the sound is) you'll have to get a velocity-sensitive keyboard. Currently the Casio CZ-1 ($600) is a good choice. The next step up from that is a used Yamaha DX-7 (about $1,000; used DX-7II's are still relatively rare and so a bit more expensive), the music industry workhorse. An alternative option for a professional tool is to combine the CZ-1 with the nifty TX81Z box. You get two flavors of sound generation (FM and digital) for better variety.*

—*Kevin Kelly and Ramon Sender Barayon*

## MIDI for Musicians

Craig Anderton
1986; 105 pp.
**$14.95**
($16.45 postpaid) from:
Music Sales Corp.
Distribution Center
P. O. Box 572
Chester, NY 10918
212/254-2100
or Whole Earth Access

*Electronic technology has recently given musicians several powerful tools: synthesizers, sound samplers, sequencers, and editors (devices which store sequences of sounds and give the musician the power to delete or add notes or parts, to play passages at various speeds, to change the order of parts, and write compositions in step time and play them back in real time. However, for many years each manufacturer had a different standard. A Yamaha sequencer, for example, might not work properly to sequence a part played on a Roland synthesizer. In order to allow various musical instruments and computers to work with each other regardless of the manufacturer, a standard format was developed called MIDI, Musical Instrument Digital Interface. This is a brand new technology (it's only been around since 1983). It gives musicians tremendous power to compose and record. This is the book that best explains what MIDI is and does.*

— *Rob Griffith*

◆

Due to the rapid rate of technological change, instruments often became obsolete within a few months after their introduction. Eventually keyboard players were almost afraid to buy anything because they felt that a newer, better version would be introduced soon. Although MIDI hasn't put an end to this problem, it has certainly helped extend the useful life of a piece of equipment by making it compatible with newer devices.

---

**Scanning Delays**

Some keyboard players can notice slight timing errors when they play a computer-controlled keyboard; in other words, the timing just isn't as "tight" as they would like. But as mentioned in the body of the text, the entire scan takes less than a millisecond . . . so what's the problem?

Delays can occur because of what the computer does *between* scans. During this time it is monitoring the MIDI data, perhaps calculating envelope shapes, sending messages to a display, and so on. As a result, successive scans may be separated by as much as 15 milliseconds. Most instruments seem to do a scan around every 10 ms or so, which is not an objectionable delay by any means.

---

## Roland D-50

Suggested retail **$2095** (but available for much less at many independent music stores); Catalog **free** from: RolandCorp US, 7200 Dominion Circle, Los Angeles, CA 90040; 213/685-5141

*Roland must have asked musicians exactly what they wanted in a synthesizer because the D-50 just about has it all: the ability to create new and different sounds, the realism of a sampler, built-in effects like Chorus, EQ and reverb, and a responsive keyboard. The D-50 uses an innovative Linear/Algorithmic (LA) synthesizer to produce warm, analog-type tones; the D-50 also carries 100 sampled sounds in its memory; you can combine these with your synthesized sounds, or use them to construct realistic-sounding samples. The D-50 is also easy to use (although you might not know it from*

*looking at the owner's manual). Unlike FM synthesis, as on Yamaha's DX-7, the D-50's LA synthesis allows you to create the sounds you have in mind, quickly and predictably. If you're looking for a performance synthesizer that sounds good, is easy to use, and offers a wealth of resources for programming new sounds, the D-50 may be just the right instrument for you.*

— *Paul Blankinship*

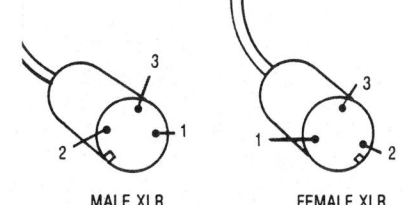

MALE XLR    FEMALE XLR

FRONT VIEW
XLR CONNECTOR PIN NUMBERING

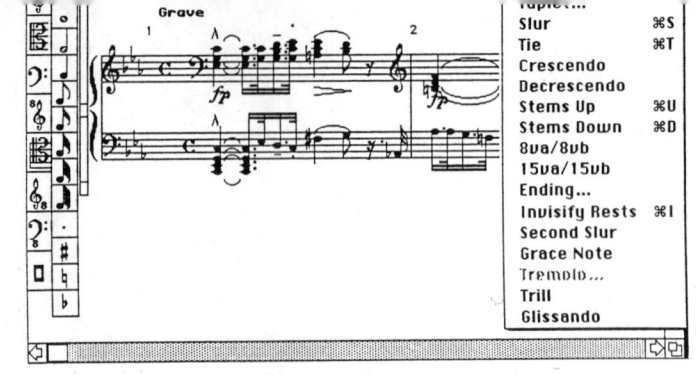

A section of a score entered into a Macintosh through **Composer**.

## Composer:
Version 2.0; copy-protected. $495

## Performer:
Version 2; copy-protected. $395. Both from: Mark of the Unicorn (call 617/576-2760 to find local dealer information)

*Wouldn't it be lovely to noodle around on a keyboard and, when you had a little tune you liked, capture it into a musical score which could be altered or printed out? Or maybe do it the other way around. Noodle around with notes on a score, and then have it played out in sound, perhaps with a full choir of instruments?*

*Two software pieces, working in tandem, make this a home job.*

*Composer lets you write out a score, modify it, store it, and print it out via your Macintosh. You can also "monitor" a piece you composed through the Mac's dinky speaker, which plays a simplified version of the melody.*

*Performer lets you capture the digital footprint of sounds from any MIDI-standard synthesizer and send it to Composer to be scored or*

*stored. Working in reverse, it takes a score from Composer and directs it through the MIDI inlets of any synthesizer module, to be played, amplified, or transfigured.*

*In short, if you're into serious music-making, this is simply the best music-processing software on any computer.*

—Ramon Sender Barayon

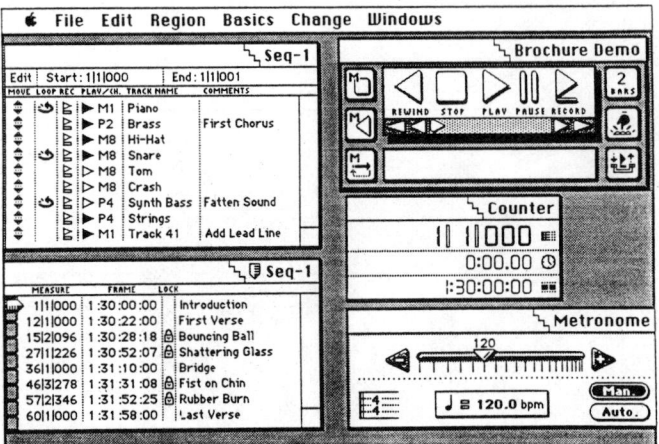

A **Performer** screen showing the structure and instruments used to record a song.

## Music, Computers & Software
Bill Stephen, Editor
$21/year (12 issues)
Music, Computers
& Software
P.O. Box 625
Northport, NY 11768
516/673-3241

*If you're interested in playing music with synthesizers or samplers, but still think that MIDI is just an ugly dress from the 60's, then you need this magazine. **Music, Computers & Software** is a glossy monthly (recently upgraded from their old bi-monthly schedule) devoted to exploring the interface of music and computers, concentrating on how "musicians have embraced technology and made it a very human thing."*

*Each issue of **Music, Computers & Software** contains practical information on using MIDI technology, as well as reviews of new electronic music software and hardware. Recent issues have featured detailed surveys of digital samplers, suggestions on how to select a PC-compatible music computer and the joys and sorrows of alternate MIDI controllers, such as electric violins and woodwinds. One new benefit to subscribing to **Music, Computers & Software** is a free membership to Compuserve's computer bulletin board, where the magazine sponsors an ongoing MIDI conference.*

—Richard Kadrey

### Example One

### Example One-A

| MSR | ST | EVNT | TIME | CH | TYP | NOTE | VEL | DUR |
|---|---|---|---|---|---|---|---|---|
| 1 | 1 | 1 | 0 | 10 | ON | C4 | 57 | 2 |
| 1 | 12 | 2 | 11 | 10 | ON | C4 | 55 | 3 |
| 1 | 24 | 3 | 12 | 10 | ON | D4 | 54 | 26 |
| 1 | 49 | 4 | 25 | 10 | ON | C4 | 64 | 3 |
| 1 | 63 | 5 | 14 | 10 | ON | E4 | 45 | 4 |
| 1 | 69 | 6 | 6 | 10 | ON | G4 | 40 | 5 |
| 1 | 74 | 7 | 5 | 10 | ON | C5 | 76 | 7 |
| 2 | 1 | 8 | 23 | 10 | ON | A#4 | 77 | 5 |
| 2 | 2 | 9 | 1 | 10 | ON | F5 | 63 | 3 |
| 2 | 2 | 10 | 0 | 10 | ON | D5 | 56 | 3 |
| 2 | 13 | 11 | 11 | 10 | ON | D5 | 70 | 4 |
| 2 | 13 | 12 | 0 | 10 | ON | A#4 | 76 | 4 |
| 2 | 14 | 13 | 1 | 10 | ON | F5 | 62 | 3 |
| 2 | 26 | 14 | 12 | 10 | ON | E5 | 63 | 62 |
| 2 | 26 | 15 | 0 | 10 | ON | C5 | 72 | 62 |
| 2 | 26 | 16 | 0 | 10 | ON | G4 | 64 | 62 |
| 3 | 1 | 17 | 71 | | DE | | | |

Two versions of J.R. Baker's "Homage To Lizst," the first in piano notation, the second as code for a sequencer.

All of the literature and hyperbole about sampling seems to center around bit resolution and there's a simple way to understand it. Imagine the screen of a television set. A close look at the screen will show that it's made up of small dots (pixels). If the dots were twice as big on the same screen, the picture would still be legible, but it's clarity would be greatly reduced. Conversely, twice the amount of dots as the original would result in a picture of stunning detail. In sampling, instead of pixels we are dealing with computer data; more specifically, bit words. One bit word of information can be 8, 12, 16, or 18 bits long, hence the higher the bit resolution, the more accurate the reproduction of the sound sampled.

## The Computers & Music Quarterly Report
Joe West, Editor
$20/year
(4 issues) from:
Computers & Music
1989 Junipero Serra Blvd.
Daly City, CA 94014
415/994-2909

*Software swallows music, read all about it! Follow the action in this homespun newsletter from a musician crazy about homespun music on personal computers. Use it to keep up in a field that is accelerating faster every second.*

— Kevin Kelly

◆

***System 1*** Price: $3,000
IBM Clone w/640K 2 disk drives
Voyetra OP-4001 interface
Sequencer Plus
Casio CZ-1 synthesizer
Yamaha FB-01 module
Roland TR505 drum machine

Comments
This system is awesome compared to what was available in our last issue. The CZ and FB give you 16 Multitimbral voices and they both sound great. The CZ keyboard has velocity and aftertouch to send to the FB and the Roland TR505 has both straight and Latin percussion. You have about 100 bucks left over to buy cables with. . . .

◆

***System 2*** Price: $5,000
Macintosh 512k w/Ext Drive
Performer
Austin Development interface
Oberheim Matrix 6 synthesizer
Yamaha TX-7 module
Roland JX8 module
Yamaha FB-01 module
Roland TR707 or Yamaha RX-11 drum machine
Casio TB-1 MIDI thru box

Comments
This is closer to $5500 but I couldn't help myself. This is designed for composition, but could be used quite effectively in a performance environment also. The whole system was selected for the ability to take care of just about all sonic requirements. You could scare most movies with this system easily.

## How to Make and Sell Your Own Record

Diane Sward Rapaport
1984; 183 pp.
**$12.95**
($15 postpaid) from:
The Headlands Press
P. O. Box 862
Tiburon, CA 94920
or Whole Earth Access

*Still the indispensable guide for those who wish to go vinyl on their own behalf. Gets in the groove of the independent recording business and stays there from early planning or promotion right through to tax returns. The work sheets will help you stay in the financial groove, as well. There's an appendix on cassette-only releases, a discussion on new technologies such as CD, and a bit on foreign licensing. Read it before you book your studio time.*
— Jonathan E.

A "master" and a "mother." The master (left) is a negative metal impression of the lacquer produced by the disk-cutting machine. It is then converted into a thicker, positive metal impression — the mother (right). The mother is then converted into a negative metal stamper, which presses the records.

◆

Selling in stores: Placing your record for sale in record stores should be one of your main sales goals. Once you have persuaded an audience that your record is worth buying, it will be important that stores in the area carry it. . . . You will probably find the most receptive stores are small, individually owned ones, especially those specializing in particular kinds of music, such as jazz, blue-grass, or reggae. The owners of these stores are often sympathetic to individual business efforts, which in many ways resemble their own. Like independent labels, they are attempting to provide customers with records they might not find in the larger chain stores.

◆

We chose to do an EP in accordance with our budget ($2000, which ended up $2500 plus) — not wishing to have such an important step to us result in only a two-song single, but not being able to afford an LP. Also, the record was an experiment to see whether our established audience would come through for record sales, as well as the already proven aspect of ticket sales. Fortunately, we found success.

## How To Build A Small Budget Recording Studio From Scratch

F. Alton Everest
1979; 335 pp.
**$14.95**
postpaid from:
Tab Books
P. O. Box 40
Blue Ridge Summit,
PA 17214; 717/794-2191
or Whole Earth Access

*Frequently a home-based composer forgets to consider the environmental impact of his art until the neighbors begin pounding on the walls. If you need complete acoustical isolation, this detailed manual covers everything you need to construct a recording studio. Good discussion of preferred acoustical characteristics, although the writing style is that of a stiff, elderly English gent. Designs for a home studio, garage multitrack, control room servicing two studios, and many more. Even if you live in a rented space, this information could prove useful for isolating your studio from the neighbors' ears.*
— Ramon Sender Barayon

◆

After seeing and hearing of numerous horror stories concerning attempts to treat studios acoustically at minimum cost (egg cartons come to mind), the importance of truly budget absorbing modules is emphasized.

The molded plastic trays nurseries use for small bedding plants offer some promise. . . . These could be fitted with pads of glass fiber of 3 pounds per cubic foot density, $1\frac{1}{2}$ inches thick and mounted to wall or ceiling surface with a few screws in the lip. The high perforation percentage means that this 1.7 square foot module would give the same absorption as $1\frac{1}{2}$ inches of glass fiber without the plastic support.

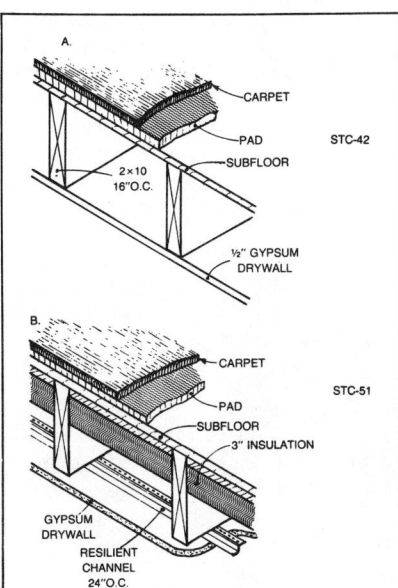

Two methods of protecting a studio from noise from the floor above with frame construction: (A) with normal gypsum board ceiling and (B) with resiliently mounted ceiling and insulation in the air space.

## Tascam Porta One

Information **free** from: TEAC, 7733 Telegraph Road, Montebello, CA 90640; 213/726-0303.

*The heart of home recording is an inexpensive editing setup. There is an increasing number of mixers for sale that are based on cassettes. Fostex has a popular one called a "portastudio." I recommend another brand, the TEAC Tascam Porta One for **$450** (street price; $549 list). It's easy for a beginner to use. you can record 4-tracks onto one normal cassette tape. By carefully sweeping three tracks onto one, you can get a poor man's 7-track mix in only two generations. Perfect for adding orchestration to a one-person band. All micro-multitrack equipment is more awkward to operate than the large pro machines, but, hey, you can do it all with cassettes.*
—Ramon Sender Barayon

## Mix Bookshelf

Catalog **free** from: Mix Bookshelf, 2608 9th Street, Berkeley, CA 94710;800/233-9604 (in California: 800/641-3349)

*A wide-ranging mail-order source for every aspect of electronic music that's in print. They have an unbelievable selection, and are really on top of the whole field. Pick your level, from professional to experimental hobbyist.*
— Ramon Sender Barayon

**5150C) MELODY WRITING** One of America's top songwriting teams, Al Kasha and Joel Hirschhorn, discuss why people remember tunes, rhythmic prosody and melodic prosody, comparisons made of bridge and verse, compounding the melody, the importance of intros, hooks, sub-hooks, range, intervals, the different ethnic flavors in melodies, minor and major chords, bass figures, progressions and more. 90 minutes $10.00

**DX DROID from Hybrid Arts** *Electronic Musician* praised this program for DX/TX series synthesizers as "the vanguard of a new generation of software." It's one of the first to use a form of artificial intelligence for random patch generation—a brand-new tool for today's musicians, and one that's packed with creative possibilities. Why not have your computer do some of the busywork necessary to create new sounds? Why not let it surprise you? Simply select one of the Droid options, and every click of the mouse will send a new patch (or bank of patches) to your synthesizer. Listen to it, fine-tune it, save it or trash it; the choice is yours. The Droid feature is only one of five useful programs that come with this package. The Patch Librarian buffers 18 groups of sounds with 32 voices per group for a total of 576 patches in memory (with the 520 ST) and more as memory is expanded. The Numeric Editor lists all parameters and offers six-window editing (one window per operator). The Graphic Editor displays all DX7 parameters and shows keyboard scaling on the graphic on-screen keyboard. The Automated Patch Loader loads any combination of patches and groups of patches over any or all of the 16 MIDI channels with a single keystroke. It's a workhorse of a program, and it *thinks*. **13031) for Atari, $245.00**
*What you need to run it:* any Atari ST computer. *Optional:* printer.

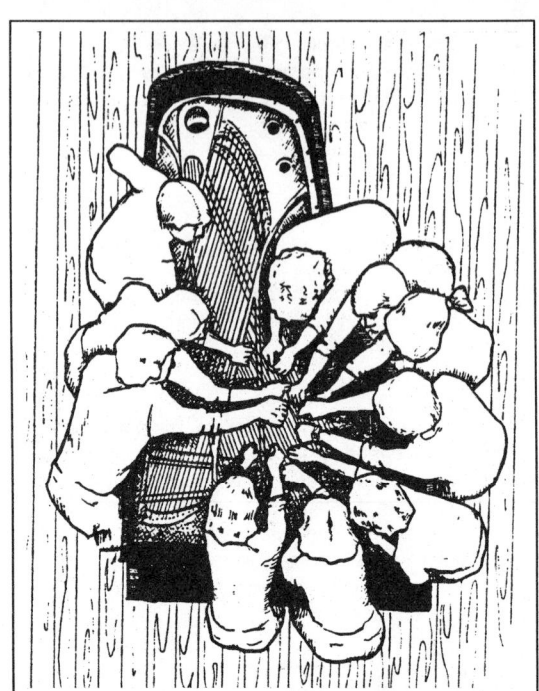

Stephen Scott's Bowed Piano Ensemble seen from the rafters.

## Experimental Musical Instruments

Bart Hopkin, Editor
$20/year
(6 year) from:
Experimental Musical
Instruments
P.O. Box 784
Nicasio, CA 94946
415/662-2182

The second step following a successful revolution is to build new kinds of tools to overthrow the next success. After the acceptance of far-out music, here come radically insurgent instruments — harps 50 feet long, steel cellos, drums that float on water, and devices that amplify the natural micro-sounds of a fly heartbeat or a seedling sprouting. All are discussed in this fascinating newsletter with great emphasis on trying out newly invented apparati that make musical sounds.

— Kevin Kelly

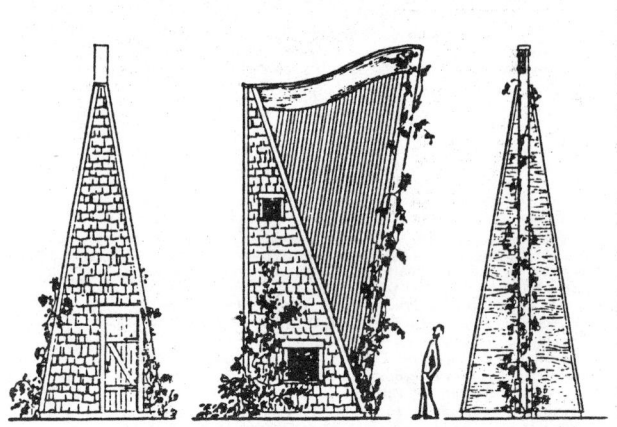

THE PUGET SOUND WIND HARP

proposed building/instrument on Puget Sound

Tony Levin on tour with the Stick

## The Stick

Suggested retail **$1041**.
The new hybrid system
with 5 MIDI'd strings is
**$1891**; 10 MIDI string version
**$2491**. Catalog **free** from:
Stick Enterprises, 8320 Yucca
Trail, Los Angeles, CA 90046;
213/656-6878

*Imagine an electric guitar; now, lose the body; widen the neck to accommodate a set of bass strings, and stretch the whole thing out to 5 1/2 octaves. What you have is The Stick, the brainchild of jazz musician and inventor Emmett Chapman. You play the Stick by tapping the strings against the instrument's neck, piano-style, to produce an amazing variety of tones and sound textures. A great advantage of the Stick's two-handed playing technique is that it gives you complete freedom to play both the melody and bass parts simultaneously. Chapman's most recent innovations are 2 MIDI-compatible versions of the Stick, a 5 MIDI'd string model, and a full 10 MIDI string verion. Older models can be retrofit by Stick Enterprises with MIDI pick-ups.*

*— Richard Kadrey*

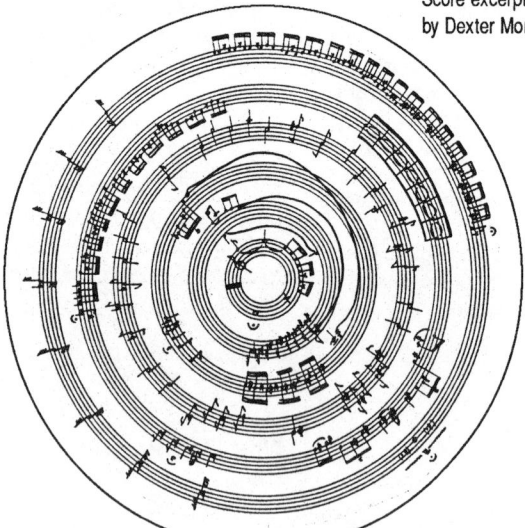

Score excerpt from Studies (1975) by Dexter Morrill.

## Computer Music Journal

Curtis Roads, Editor
$26/year
(4 issues) from:
MIT Press Journals Dept.
28 Carleton Street
Cambridge, MA 02142
617/253-2866

*The international experts cover everything about computer music in this quarterly. Upcoming symposiums and scholarly dialogue on the latest sys-tems and techniques. Good reviews of the newest products and publications. Sometimes includes a special soundsheet or flexi-disc with examples of some wonderful music. There is no more authoritative place to get information on the subject.*

*— Tim Ennis*

◆

The robot is designed to track a human singer who sings into a micophone connected to the system. The robot plays the organ along with the human, with tempo regulated in part by the vocalist. For pitch analysis, a system of five narrowly tuned bandpass filters is used to derive a fundamental frequency every 30 msec. If the singer is out of tune, the organ player can adjust the tuning of the organ for a more euphonious ensemble effect. Ironically, the robot musician cannot hear its own perfomance.

The Wabot, designed by Ichiro Kato

## Musics of Many Cultures

Elizabeth May, Editor
1980; 434 pp.
**$19.95**
($21.45 postpaid) from:
University of California
Press
2120 Berkeley Way
Berkeley, CA 94720
800/822-6657
or Whole Earth Access

*As much as can be put down on paper, here is the music springing from human life on Earth. This book speaks about structure, role in culture, and history of ethnic musics around the world, and gives a thoroughly handy film bibliography and album discography so you can dip into one corner of the world, get comfortable, and become lost in the stirring songs others make. Comes with three floppy records to get you started.*

— Kevin Kelly

◆

*Ghost Dance Music: A Special Song Style*

The Ghost Dance religion arose among the Paiute Indians of Nevada in 1870 and again in 1890, at which time it had a phenomenal spread among the Plains Indians who sought religious help now that their military resistance was at an end. A prophet name Wovoka dreamed that dance and prayer would make the European invaders disappear. The Ghost Dance was performed in a large circle to the music of plaintive songs of suffering and pleas for help. Many of the participants went into a state of trance in which they saw visions of their dead relatives restored to life and of a happier time ahead when the buffalo would return and the white man would be gone forever.

## New Sounds

A Listener's Guide to
New Music
John Schaefer
1987; 296 pp.
**$10.95**
($14.45 postpaid) from:
Harper & Row
Keystone Industrial Park
Scranton, PA 18512
800/242-7737
or Whole Earth Access

*Not new as in this week's Top Forty mega-single, but new as in new ideas, from Glenn Branca's thrash guitar symphonies to Brian Eno's "Ambient Music;" from the pointillism of Philip Glass to the vocal experiments of Meredith Monk and David Hykes.* **New Sounds** *also thoroughly explains the contributions of early sonic pioneers such as John Cage and Harry Partch, as well as providing excellent introductions to the traditional musics of the U.S., Europe, India, Indonesian and West African. The extensive record and tape guides at the end of each chapter make navigating through this world of new sounds exciting and fun.*

— Richard Kadrey

A bonang barung of a gamelan.

## Basic Concepts in Music

Gary M. Martin
1980; 288 pp.
**$21.75** postpaid from:
Wadsworth Publishing Co.
7625 Empire Drive
Florence, KY 41042
415/595-2350
or Whole Earth Access

*An interesting and useful programmed text designed to accommodate both the absolute ignoramus and the person with any degree of musical experience. Covers basic components of music notation; notational components of rhythm and melody; harmonic structure of basic intervals and chords; major and minor scales, chords and keys; and the basic structure of music. The child who can read can progress through the book at his own rate; the parent with a piano or a penny-whistle and some sheet music at his disposal can learn much to pass on to the children.*

— Carol Van Strum

Even if two white keys do not have a black key between them, the two keys are still a half step apart.

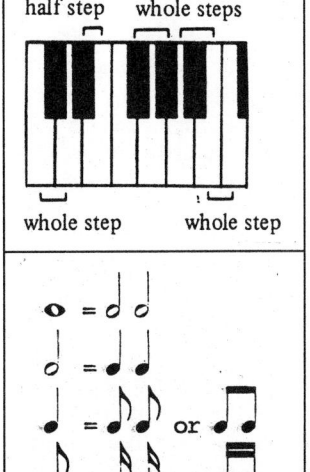

The mathematical relationship of music notes is illustrated at right. Observe the two ways of writing eighth and sixteenth notes shown on the chart — with flags or connecting beams. There is absolutely no difference in time value between the two ways of writing eighth notes.

## Listen!

Version 2.0; copy-protected. **$99** from:
Resonate, P.O. Box 996, Menlo Park, CA
94026; 415/323-5022

*One of the hardest things about learning to read and play music is to take ideas like "F Sharp" or "Flatted Fifth" and turn them into sounds in your head. Listen! software is designed to help you do just that with a series of simple exercises that help you learn to recognize basic chords, intervals and melodies. To keep from getting bored, you can change the level of difficulty on any of the exercises at any time. Listen! will play through the sound chip built into your Macintosh, and since it's MIDI-compatible you can use it to trigger an external sound-source to create a terrific music learning lab.*

— Richard Kadrey

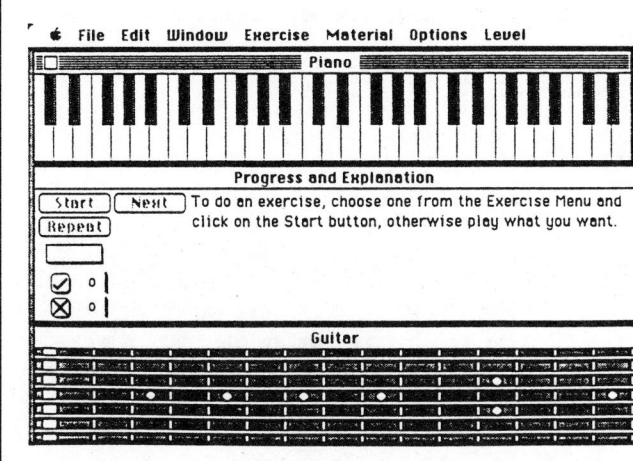

Listen! uses a variety of pull-down menus on screen windows you can handle primarily with the mouse. At startup, the Listen! screen displays three windows: the Piano, Guitar, and Progress windows.

Believe it or not, you can record a whole lot of sound with equipment that costs as little as $110. But before you get in your car and head to Radio Shack, consider these questions:

1. What do I want to record? Specific animals? General ambience?

2. Where do I want to record? Weather conditions? Land-based environments? Marine environments?

3. To what use will these recordings be put?

Now, back to the first statement. $59.95 buys you a perfectly good mono standard cassette recorder at Radio Shack. It's called the Minissette 15 and it's voice-activated which means that it starts when a signal is loud enough to activate the "record" electronics and stops when there is silence for a certain period of time. This allows you to sleep in your tent knowing full well that you won't miss much vocal creature activity, at least for the duration of the tape length and the life of your batteries. Radio Shack also sells a PZM (Pressure Zone Microphone) for $44.95 that makes up a perfectly functional system for recording evening and dawn choruses and a few specific animals (if loud enough). I've used this system to record penguins at the California Academy of Sciences and gorillas at the San Francisco Zoo. I couldn't wait around for the animals to decide it was time to vocalize and simply taped the mike and recorder to a nearby wall. The quality of the recordings was not the greatest because there is a short time lag (40-50 ms.) between the time the recorder detects a sound and when it gets fully up to speed. So you lose the onset of the activating vocalization. However, you will get the ones that follow. With a little editing and signal processing (filtering and gating) when you get the tapes home, the recordings will be perfectly functional.

If you're going to seriously record birds or whales, however, you'll need better equipment that won't have as much of a tendency to distort at higher frequencies. Sony makes two viable stereo recorders: the Walkman Pro and the TCD5M. For evening or dawn choruses and ambient sound in general, couple either of these recorders with a pair of Sony ECM 155 microphones, small wind screens to cut out puffs of ubiquitous wind, clip them to your shoulders and you're in business. The ECM 155s are omnidirectional, meaning that they pick up signal from all directions. The last five minutes of *Nature* (an album of mine released by The Nature Company) were recorded with my TCD5M and two ECM 155s clipped to the windshield wipers of my rental car on a mountaintop in a St. Maarten, VI, rain forest. For me, the TCD5M has a slight edge in that it has a combination of Dolby B, switchable limiter, a little more dynamic and frequency range, more accessible metering, and, in general, offers better human-engineering for field work.

If you're going to record specific creatures in a fairly noisy ambient field, you might want to use a parabolic dish. It looks like a plastic bowl and, when pointed in the direction of a vocalizing bird or other animal, tends to sharply focus and gather in the sound picked up only in that narrow field. The microphone is mounted on the dish facing into the center. And the Schoeps 541 works just fine for this purpose. The dish is primarily successful in mono and tends to "color" the sound slightly in addition to severely limiting frequency response. Sony's Model PBR330 sells for around $80. It is 13.625" in diameter, which means it will only respond well to frequencies of about 1000Hz and above. Perfect for white-crowned sparrows (3.8kHz — 4.2kHz). However, if you're not keen about approaching a lion too closely, you'll need a dish 6 to 8 ft. in diameter! With parabolics, the lower the vocal frequency of your subject, the greater-diameter dish you will require.

## Tools for Environmental Recording

*by Bernard L. Krause, Ph.D.*

For recording underwater, you'll need a special mike called a hydrophone. Generally, they come in two parts: the hydrophone and cable, and a pre-amplifier. For the industrious, buy the basic hydrophone element (a little capsule with two wire leads) for $9.95 from Edmund Scientific of Barrington, N.J. Then you'll have to attach a long enough cable to go from the capsule underwater to your recorder, seal the cable and capsule, add a connector to the end of the wire, build a pre-amp and plug it in to a tape machine. It has a frequency response of from 10Hz. to 6kHz. Spartan Electronics (2400 E. Ganson Street, Jackson, MI 49202; 517/787-8600) sells the complete package (stock 110-8158-002) for about $500 each, and the same item in quantities of 1000 for less than $30 each! Go figure that one! But the best is B&K (Bruel & Kjaer) Instruments, Inc. Their 8103 sells (without pre-amp) for a little over $1,000 and it's worth every penny. The frequency response is well beyond 100kHz. and you can use it as a regular mike under certain circumstances.

Over the years there has been considerable discussion about the kinds of tape to use for analog recording. The folks at the Library of Natural Sounds, Laboratory of Ornithology, Cornell University, did some investigation and found that, for their reel-to-reel purposes, Scotch 806, 807, 808, and 809 was superior in that it offered less print through (a phenomenon whereby the signal is transferred from layer to layer at some detectable level when audio tape is wound onto a reel). For audiophile uses, however, more in line with the kinds of results I'm after, I prefer Ampex 456 or 457 Grand Master (or the Scotch counterpart 226). While there is some print-through problem with certain kinds of signal (the trade-off), in general the tape gives more extended frequency and dynamic range, less tape hiss and distortion. When combined with Dolby SR noise reduction systems, the recorded signal on Ampex 456-7 or Scotch 226 stock will often equal or surpass the dynamic range of current digital equipment. Cornell and I agree, however, that Maxell UDS-2 and Maxell XLI-S are the cassette tapes to use.

There has been no intent here to be comprehensive or greatly detailed about the vast range of available equipment. Several other kinds of very fine cassette recorders and a whole host of microphones will do the job. Don't worry too much about whether or not you have exactly the right machine. Keep your equipment serviced properly and keep your field components light and compact. Just go do it and you will quickly discover what works and what doesn't. Everyone I know claims to have a secret methodology down pat. Don't believe it. Nature recording is full of surprises. Your ingenuity will be tested every time you go out into the field. And let us know what you find.

Minissette 15 and PZM: **$59.95** and **$44.95** from Radio Shack (all hamlet-size and larger communities)

Nature and The Equator: **$9.95** each (plus $3.25 postage and handling for one or both tapes) from The Nature Company, P. O. Box 2310, Berkeley, CA 94702

Sony Walkman Pro **$379**; TCD5M approx. **$550** (discontinued; superceded by TCD5 Pro 2 — $870); ECM 155 **$79.95**; PBR330 approx. **$80** (discontinued; see below)

A parabolic dish comparable to the Sony PBR330 (which is still in stock at some dealers) is the Dan Gibson Parabola: **$150** from Geleco Electronics, 2 Thorncliffe Park Drive/Unit 28, Toronto, Ontario M4 H1 H2; 416/421-5631

Hydrophone Element (41759): no longer listed in catalog, still in stock. **$10** from Edmund Scientific, 101 East Gloucester Pike, Barrington, NJ 08007; 609/573-6260

Hydrophone (8103): **$1,144** from Bruel & Kjaer Instruments, Inc., 185 Forest Street, Marlborough, MA 01752; 617/481-7000

# A Lack of Communication

*by Sarah Vandershaf*

The study of interspecies communication has suffered setbacks in recent years, partly because of the overall reduction of government funding for (nonmilitary) science research, partly because the field is viewed as being somewhat flaky, if not quite comparable to Kirlian photography and spontaneous combustion. Ironically, the more mainstream science neglects interspecies communication research, the more the field is left to people whose devotion to the scientific method may be less than total, but who are willing to invest their own time and energy to investigate animal (even plant) language. Some, more traditional, scientists such as Penny Patterson (of Koko, the gorilla, fame) and John Lilly's dolphin researchers perisist regardless of the present climate. So the study of interspecies communication is far from dead. The idea of finding new creatures to talk with is just too compelling for researchers to ever give up. If it also sounds compelling to you, this page may give you a place to start.

## Interspecies Communication

**$25/year**
(4 issues) from:
IC, Inc.
273 Hidden Meadow Lane
Friday Harbor, WA 98250

*Interspecies Communication, Inc. was founded to promote relations between humans and animals the way civic groups promote relations between sister cities — with meetings between representatives, full of warm smiles and good intentions. IC's newsletter reports on these meetings, which have recently involved U.S., Soviet, and cetacean musicians in one case, and psychics and orcas in another.*

*You can't call this pseudoscience, though; IC doesn't claim that this is any sort of science at all. The idea, rather, is to interact with other species in whatever way — scientific, artistic, shamanistic — seems most appropriate to the situation. This is certainly a broader definition of "communication" than most researchers would accept. But the approach does give the animals a greater opportunity to shape the exchange to their liking than a purely scientific approach would allow.* —SV

◆

In Nome, we found much local interest in our project, and intimations of several other Soviet/American "bridgings" also in the planning stage. Flying to an outlying Eskimo village located directly across from Siberia, a place still locked by the sea ice in late June, we were received quite cordially. One elder, a lifelong whale hunter, seemed keen to learn all we could tell him about the joy of communicating with various whale species via music. "I'd like to hear that," he answered, but then added, "You know, of course, that we still need to hunt the whales. For us, it's a matter of survival." When we gave him a copy of *Orcas Greatest Hits* he responded warmly, and assured us that he and his friends would give it a close listen.

## Silent Partners

(The Legacy of the Ape Language Experiments)
Eugene Linden
1986; 247 pp.
**$3.95**
($4.95 postpaid) from:
Random House
400 Hahn Road
Westminster MD 21157
800/638-6460
or Whole Earth Access

*This is a book about territoriality, about aggressive posturing for dominance, about love and hate and jealousy within the tightly-knit tribes of a highly intelligent yet sometimes volatile species — scientists. Specifically, the animal-language researchers in the mid-70s who attempted to teach sign language to chimps (and one gorilla), with apparent success.*

*But this golden age was as brief as it was brilliant. Divisiveness between labs and the controversial nature of the experiments themselves nearly destroyed the research's credibility; government funds soon dried up. Then, many of the apes were dispersed to various laboratories, some for medical experimentation.*

*To Eugene Linden, an observer of the ape-language studies almost from the beginning, these apes were friends. As Linden explains the reasons why such promising research collapsed, his devotion is apparent — a devotion that transcends the usual journalistic desire to uncover the truth.*
—SV

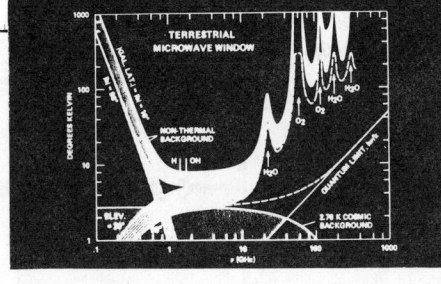

## The Search for Extraterrestrial Intelligence

(A Slide Set and
Introductory Booklet)
ASP Catalog #AS 304
Dr. Frank Drake
1988; 19 pp. & 20 color slides
$20.50 postpaid from:
ASP
SETI Slides Department
390 Ashton Avenue
San Francisco, CA 94112
415/661-8660

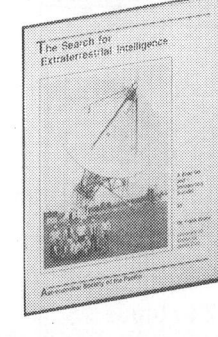

*No review of interspecies communication would be complete without a word from the little green men. They haven't been found yet, but there are plenty of big pink men working on the problem. The Astronomical Society of the Pacific has compiled a concise, readable update (complete with a set of 20 slides) on efforts to contact extraterrestrial*

◆

That first day my attention was on Washoe, and, a little nervous about meeting a full-grown chimp for the first time, I was grateful for whatever relationship Roger might have with the animal. Washoe gave Roger a big hug when she came out, and then we went for a walk.

During the walk, Roger picked up an apple and offered it to Washoe, signing, "What's this?" Washoe knuckle-walked over to us from the tree in which she had been playing and made the sign for "fruit" by placing her fist against the side of her mouth. Roger asked her, "Who fruit?" to which she replied, "Washoe fruit." Roger said, "What Washoe fruit?" and Washoe dutifully said, "Please Washoe fruit."

Depending on who you talk to, this was either a conversation, or, on Washoe's part at least, a rote response triggered by the opportunity to get a reward, or a rote behavior cued either consciously or unconsciously by Roger, or a series of hand movements only vaguely associated in Washoe's mind with the symbols and sentences Roger thought he was eliciting. It is also a dead ringer for innumerable conversations Madelaine and I have recently had with our daughter, Gillian.

◆

. . . I left with the feeling that sign language was an important means of contact with humanity for these chimps. It must be somewhat mystifying to them that no one seems to care about communicating with them in this way anymore. Even though virtually all sign contact with any of the chimps ceased long ago, the chimps themselves have not given up signing. What do the signs mean to these chimps? Why did they enter into signing again with such alacrity? At the time of my visit, no one was really interested in finding out the answers to these questions. Roger Fouts was gone, sign-language experiments were out of favor, and little funding was available, even if people had been interested in these questions. Only the chimps had not gotten the news.

Because interstellar space travel would take far too long, the best way to communicate with extraterrestrials would be to send a signal over radio waves. It is important that the channel we select be as free from noise (static) as possible and that our means of communication be as cost-effective as we can make it. For both these reasons, the microwave region of the radio spectrum seems to be the best bet.

A message to space, broadcast from the Arecibo transmitter in Puerto Rico on November 16, 1974. The top row of the message gives binary notation for the numbers 1-10, to explain the encoding method to the message's recipients. The second row shows the numbers 1, 6, 7, 8, and 15 — the atomic numbers of the key elements that make up life on earth. The next four rows contain molecules composed of these elements that form the DNA molecule. Below that is the spiral of the DNA molecule itself, and a cartoon of a human, with the human population of earth coded to the left, and human height coded to the right. Last is a representation of the solar system, with the third planet from the Sun directly over a diagram of the Arecibo dish.

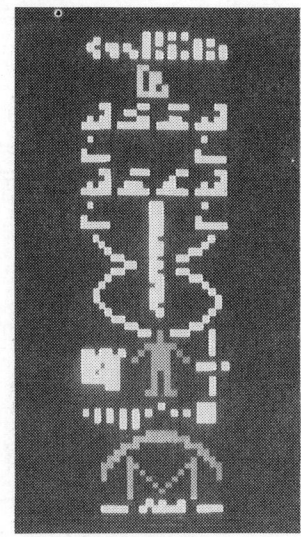

*intelligence, including current projects that will set the stage for research into the 21st Century.*
—SV

SERIES 2000    SERIES 1000

## Sound Idea Sound Effects Library

Series 1000 Library (28 analog CDs)
**$1250**
Series 2000 Library (22 digital CDs)
**$975** from:
Sound Ideas 86 McGill Street, Toronto, Ontario
Canada M5B 1H2; 800/387-3030

*Rocking chair creaks. Dentist drilling. Bottle smashes. Whooshes. Giggles. Children screaming. Windshield wipers. Booms, barrack bugles, and butcher knives sharpening. Harps, applause, and my favorite: Dog, terrier — sneezing. Three thousand human-life-on-earth sounds trapped into a tidy set of 28 compact discs (or 22 discs in digital).*

*To find a sound, you look it up in the accompanying 431 page catalog. For instance: "207-21-01 Weather, TV Broadcast — Generic Summer Fore-*

*cast, Wet." The set is expensive, complete, and the ultimate sound effects source. Perfect for a musician's or filmmaker's co-op.*

*— Kevin Kelly*

| SOUND IDEAS SOUND EFFECTS LIBRARY | | | | |
|---|---|---|---|---|
| CD#-Track-Index | Title | Description | Time | Code |
| 1016-49-01 | LAUNDRY, WASHING | -GENERAL b/g:VOICES,MACHINES,ETC. | 01:33 | AAD |
| 1029-39-01 | LAUNDRY, WASHING | -WATER RUNNING | 00:32 | AAD |
| 1011-07-01 | LAVA BUBBLING, COSMIC | -EARTH QUAKE | 02:41 | AAD |
| 1015-18-01 | LAVATORY, TOILET | -FLUSH Version # 1 | 00:08 | AAD |
| 1015-18-02 | LAVATORY, TOILET | -FLUSH Version # 2 | 00:11 | AAD |
| 1015-18-03 | LAVATORY, TOILET | -FLUSH Version # 3 | 00:19 | AAD |
| 1015-18-04 | LAVATORY, TOILET | -FLUSH Version # 4 | 00:08 | AAD |
| 1015-18-05 | LAVATORY, TOILET | -FLUSH:LEFT-WATER TANK:RIGHT-TOILET BOWL | 00:32 | AAD |
| 2014-67-01 | LAVATORY, TOILET | -FLUSH AND FILL Version # 1 | 01:02 | DDD |
| 2014-68-01 | LAVATORY, TOILET | -FLUSH AND FILL Version # 2 | 01:06 | DDD |
| 1015-19-01 | LAVATORY, URINAL | -FLUSH Version # 1 | 00:14 | AAD |
| 1015-19-02 | LAVATORY, URINAL | -FLUSH Version # 2 | 00:05 | AAD |
| 1016-50-01 | LAWN MOWER | -GAS POWERED:FOUR PULLS,START,REV | 00:19 | AAD |
| 1016-51-01 | LAWN MOWER | -GAS POWERED:PULL,START,REV,IDLE | 00:42 | AAD |
| 1016-52-01 | LAWN MOWER | -GAS POWERED:THREE PULLS,START,CUT GRASS,TURN OFF | 00:36 | AAD |
| 1016-53-01 | LAWN MOWER | -GAS POWERED:CUTTING GRASS | 00:40 | AAD |
| 2015-86-01 | LAWN MOWER | -ELECTRIC:START,RUN,STOP | 00:43 | DDD |
| 2015-87-01 | LAWN MOWER | -ELECTRIC:START,CUT,STOP Version # 1 | 01:28 | DDD |
| 2015-88-01 | LAWN MOWER | -ELECTRIC:START,CUT,STOP Version # 2 | 02:42 | DDD |
| 2015-89-01 | LAWN MOWER | -GAS:START,CUT,STOP | 00:49 | DDD |
| 2015-90-01 | LAWN MOWER | -GAS:CUTTING LAWN Version # 1 | 01:40 | DDD |
| 2015-91-01 | LAWN MOWER | -GAS:CUTTING LAWN Version # 2 | 01:20 | DDD |
| 2015-92-01 | LAWN MOWER | -GAS:CUTTING,STOPS | 00:33 | DDD |
| 2015-84-01 | LAWN TRIMMER | -ELECTRIC:START,TRIM,STOP | 01:40 | DDD |
| 2015-85-01 | LAWN TRIMMER | -GAS:START,RUN | 01:56 | DDD |
| 1013-23-01 | LEAVES, FOOTSTEPS | -ONE PERSON WALKING THROUGH LEAVES Version # 1 | 00:15 | AAD |
| 1013-24-01 | LEAVES, FOOTSTEPS | -ONE PERSON WALKING THROUGH LEAVES Version # 2 | 00:37 | AAD |
| 1013-25-01 | LEAVES, FOOTSTEPS | -ONE PERSON WALKING THROUGH LEAVES Version # 3 | 00:09 | AAD |
| 2011-19-01 | LEAVES, FOOTSTEPS | -FOOTSTEPS:SHOES, SLOW | 00:30 | DDD |
| 2011-19-02 | LEAVES, FOOTSTEPS | -FOOTSTEPS:SHOES, MEDIUM SPEED | 00:30 | DDD |
| 2011-19-03 | LEAVES, FOOTSTEPS | -FOOTSTEPS:SHOES, FAST | 00:30 | DDD |
| 2011-19-04 | LEAVES, FOOTSTEPS | -FOOTSTEPS:SHOES, JOGGING | 00:30 | DDD |
| 2011-19-05 | LEAVES, FOOTSTEPS | -FOOTSTEPS:SHOES, RUNNING | 00:30 | DDD |
| 1023-30-01 | LEAVES, RAKING | -RAKING INTO PILE | 00:32 | AAD |
| 1018-47-01 | LETTER BOX | -OPEN AND CLOSE | 00:03 | AAD |
| 1014-53-02 | LETTER SLOT | -LETTER COMING THROUGH THE SLOT | 00:01 | AAD |
| 1014-53-03 | LETTER SLOT | -LETTER COMING THROUGH THE SLOT | 00:01 | AAD |
| 1011-37-01 | LIFT, ELEVATOR | -GENERAL ATMOSPHERE:WAITING FOR ELEVATOR,BELL RING | 00:20 | AAD |
| 1011-38-01 | LIFT, ELEVATOR | -GENERAL ATMOSPHERE:BELL RINGS AND DOOR OPENS | 00:10 | AAD |
| 1011-39-01 | LIFT, ELEVATOR | -OPEN AND CLOSE DOOR:BELL | 00:15 | AAD |
| 1011-40-01 | LIFT, ELEVATOR | -CLOSE DOOR,OPERATE,OPEN AND CLOSE DOOR Version # 1 | 00:15 | AAD |
| 1011-40-02 | LIFT, ELEVATOR | -OPEN AND CLOSE DOOR,OPERATE,OPEN DOOR Version # 2 | 00:27 | AAD |
| 1011-41-01 | LIFT, ELEVATOR | -DOOR:OPEN AND CLOSE Version # 1 | 00:14 | AAD |
| 1011-41-02 | LIFT, ELEVATOR | -DOOR:OPEN AND CLOSE Version # 2 | 00:11 | AAD |
| 1011-42-01 | LIFT, ELEVATOR | -GOING UP,MACHINERY | 00:43 | AAD |
| 1011-43-01 | LIFT, ELEVATOR | -START,RUN,STOP | 00:15 | AAD |
| 1014-27-01 | LIFT, ELEVATOR | -GEN.ATM.:VOICES,FOOTSTEPS,ELEVATOR BELL | 01:58 | AAD |
| 1009-36-01 | LIGHT BULB, CRASH | -GLASS,LIGHT BULB CRASH Version # 1 | 00:02 | AAD |
| 1009-36-02 | LIGHT BULB, CRASH | -GLASS,LIGHT BULB CRASH Version # 2 | 00:01 | AAD |
| 1014-54-01 | LIGHT SWITCH | -Version # 1 | 00:01 | AAD |
| 1014-54-02 | LIGHT SWITCH | -Version # 2 | 00:01 | AAD |
| 1014-54-03 | LIGHT SWITCH | -Version # 3 | 00:01 | AAD |
| 1014-54-04 | LIGHT SWITCH | -Version # 4 | 00:01 | AAD |
| 1014-55-01 | LIGHTER | -Version # 1 | 00:05 | AAD |
| 1014-55-02 | LIGHTER | :ion # 2 | 00:02 | AAD |

180

## The New CBS "Audio-File" Sound Effects Library

Volumes I & II each
**$18.98** postpaid from:
The Collectors' Series 51 West 52nd Street, Room 861
New York, NY 10019; 212/975-5073

*Killer noise for the sound effects freak on a budget. Volume I contains 90 separate sounds on three*

*discs; Volume II holds another 90, from airport lobbies to artillery fire, tropical birds to a NASA countdown. These are all analog recordings and the quality of the individual sounds varies greatly. Many sounds you can pull straight off the discs, but some you're going to have to modify with a graphic equalizer. Still, for the money, these sets can't be beat.*

*— Richard Kadrey*

## MacRecorder

**$199** retail at most computer software stores; information free from: Farallon Computing, Inc., 2150 Kittredge Street, Berkeley, CA 94704; 415/849-2331

*Snag a fleeting sound and compress it into digits. Handy Macintosh flavored digits. The advantages of capturing sounds on the Mac is the ease with which they can be edited and shuffled into sound tracks.*

*MacRecorder is a little gizmo that lets you take a sound from a tape and put it into a Macintosh file to fiddle with. The software part displays what you've captured as a soundgram. You edit by manipulating the visual pattern, which is easy to learn, accurate to control, and tremendously satisfying to do. What's hard to hear, you can see. It's one way to own your own digital sound archive.*

*— Kevin Kelly*

If you want to add a tremolo to a sound, set up the line like this:

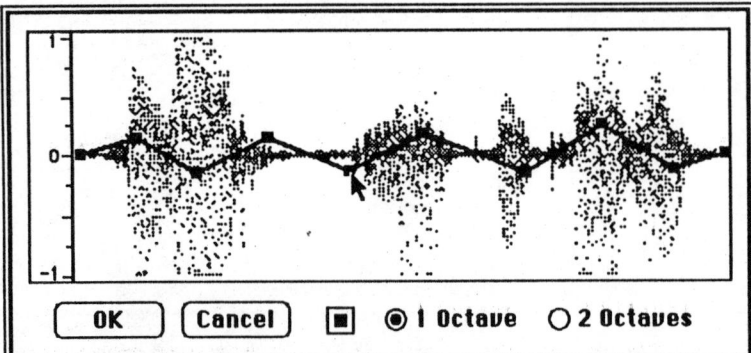

**Bender:** Use the Bender effect to adjust the pitch of a sound by an amount that can vary along the length of the sound. The waveform is shown in grey. The dark line indicates how the pitch will be altered at each point along the waveform. In this example, the first part of the wave will have its pitch lowered by an octave (with everything in between adjusted proportionally). The radio buttons located at the bottom of the box adjust the scale to the left of the waveform. If you check the radio button labelled "2 Octaves," you can raise or lower the pitch by as much as two octaves instead of only one.

## THE SOUNDEDIT WINDOW

When you record a new sound or open an existing sound, the sound is displayed graphically as a waveform in the SoundEdit window. This is how a monaural sound appears:

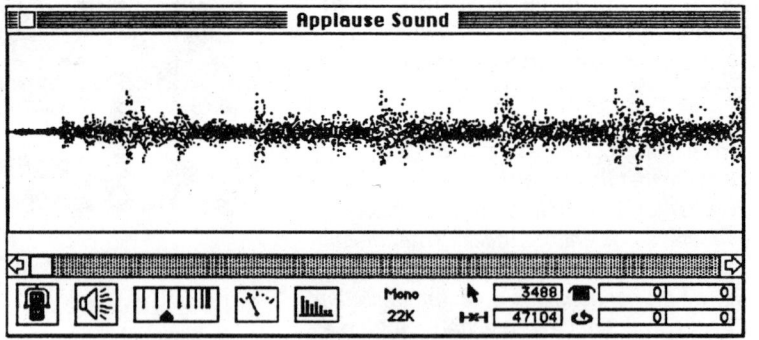

If you are recording in stereo, SoundEdit displays the waveform for both channels. The left channel is displayed in the top half of the window and the right channel is displayed in the bottom. Here is how stereo sound appears:

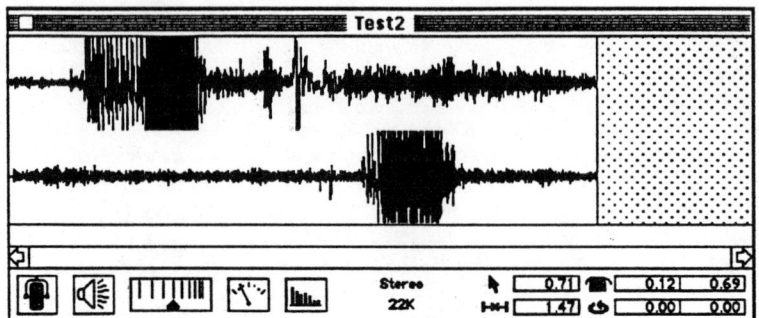

## The Art of Noises

Luigi Russolo
1986; 87 pp.
**$24** postpaid
from:
Pendragon Press
R. R. 1, Box 159
Stuyvesant, NY
12173-9720
518/828-3008

*Noise as art. Noise as music. Music as the art of noises.*

*From 1916 comes this essential work of modern music and sound theory,*

The noise instrument laboratory in Milan. Luigi Russolo on the left.

*the first work that asks the question "if music is sound, why not use all the sounds available?" Italian Futurist, Luigi Russolo wanted to create music that would incorporate the full spectrum of the twentieth century soundscape — cars, trains, animal sounds, industrial machinery, the roar of crowds. His ideas, dismissed at the time, anticipated the work of composers such as John Cage, Karlheinz Stockhausen, and Pierre Boulez by decades. Russolo was also active in designing some of the first musical "synthesizers," instruments that could reproduce the sounds of the machinery and street noises that he loved. After reading **The Art of Noises** you may never hear the world in the same way again.*

*— Richard Kadrey*

## African Rhythm and African Sensibility

John Miller Chernoff
1979; 261 pp.
**$12**
($13.20 postpaid) from:
University of Chicago Press
11030 South Langley
Chicago, IL 60628
312/568-1550
or Whole Earth Access

*J. M. Chernoff spent more than a decade as a drum student in West Africa. This is his masterwork, part Yorubaland adventure story, part sociological dissertation. Its obsession with drumming as history and its passion for rhythm as style is credited with pushing Western pop musicians like Brian Eno and David Byrne to introduce Africanisms to Anglo-American pop (Talking Heads member Byrne claims to have read the thing twice). As a writer, Chernoff is obsessed with getting every nuance on the page, and the descriptions of polyrhythmic structures occasionally read like watchmaking manuals. It's that precise. For an additional $15, a 90-minute cassette illustrating the various rhythms is also available, and very worthwhile.*

*— Stephen Davis*

◆

Whether or not one is looking from the point of view of a social scientist, one of the most noticeable things about African culture is that many activities — paddling a canoe, chopping a tree, pounding grain, smashing up yams for dinner, or simply moving — seem set within a rhythmic framework which can and often does serve as the basis for music and songs. On one of my first afternoons in Accra I went to the airport to fill out the many forms I needed to clear my tape recorder, which had been sent as unaccompanied baggage. . . . The clerk began typing. I flipped. Using the capitalization shift key with his little fingers to pop in accents between words, he beat out fantastic rhythms. Even when he looked at the rough copies to find his next sentence, he continued his rhythms on the shift key. He finished up each form with a splendid flourish on the date

## The Tuning of the World

R. Murray Schafer
1977; 301 pp.
**$13.95**
postpaid from:
University of
Pennsylvania Press
Blockley Hall
418 Service Dr., Floor 13
Philadelphia, PA 19104
800/242-7737
or Whole Earth Access

*One of the most remarkable books on sound around. The author charts the geography and history of our sonic environment — our soundscape. No type of noise, roar, clatter, hiss, twang, vibration, or audible rhythm escapes his notice. For instance, he discovered that European towns hum at G sharp (50 hertz power supply), while America drones at B natural (60 hertz). He divides our surroundings into dominant tonal patterns, mapping out the evolution of sound on Earth. Other topics discussed: Sacred sounds, the concert hall as a substitute for outdoor life, the intent of Muzak, sounds of water creatures, sound imperialism, ceremonies about silence, and taboo sounds. A marvelous, awakening book.*

*— Charlie Bremer*

◆

The rhythms of all poetry and recited literature bear a relationship to breathing patterns. When the sentence is long and natural, a relaxed breathing style is expected; when irregular or jumpy, an erratic breath pattern is suggested. Compare the jabbing style of twentieth-century verse with the more relaxed lines of that which preceded it. Something has happened between Pope and Pound, and that very likely is the

accumulation of syncopations and offbeats in the soundscape. And the perceptible jitteriness in Pound's verse begins after he has moved from rural life in America to the big city of London. Just as human conversational style is abbreviated by the telephone bell, contemporary verse bears the marks of having dodged the acoustic shrapnel of modern life. Car horns punctuate modern verse, not bubbling brooks.

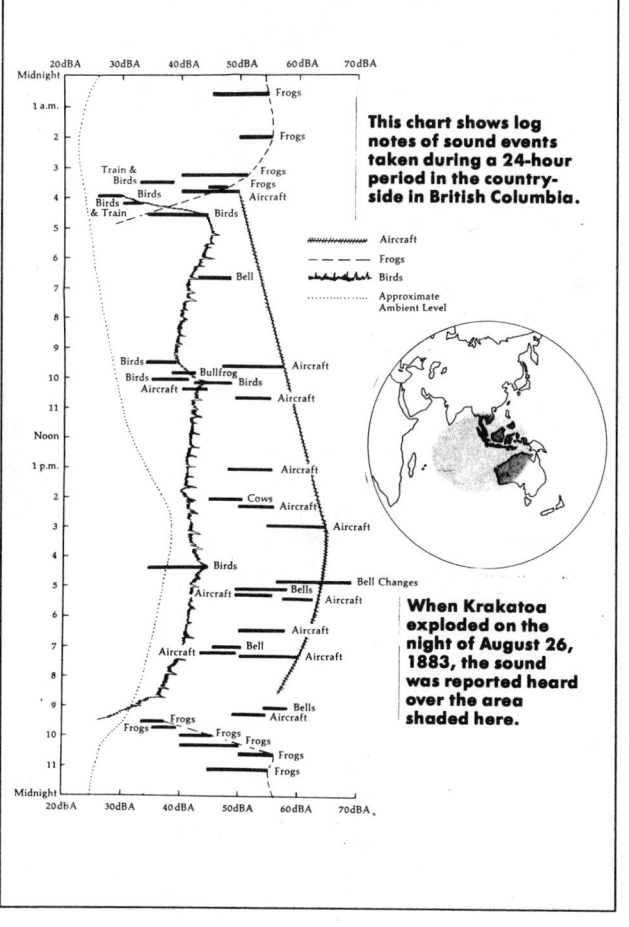

This chart shows log notes of sound events taken during a 24-hour period in the countryside in British Columbia.

When Krakatoa exploded on the night of August 26, 1883, the sound was reported heard over the area shaded here.

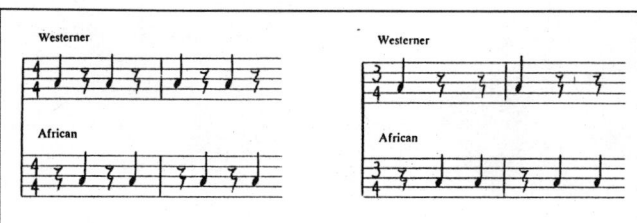

and port of entry. I thanked him for his display, and though I regretted having to leave the customs office, I was eager to go out and begin my work, for I realized that I was in a good country to study drumming.

Asked to supply a second rhythm to a piece on either 3/4 or 4/4 time, a Westerner and an African would respond in quite different manners.

## Art & Camouflage

Roy R. Behrens
1981; 89 pp.
OUT OF PRINT
North American Review

*Camouflage: to bewitch the visual landscape. This out-of-print book is the only one that addresses the power of camouflage in both organic and manufactured environments.*

*According to author Behrens, the leap from nature to military was spearheaded by modern artists.*
*— Kevin Kelly*

◆

Recalling her trips to the war zone, Getrude Stein would later remark: "Another thing that interested us enormously was how different the camouflage of the french was from the camouflage of the germans, and then once we came across some very very neat camouflage and it was american. The idea was the same but as after all it was different nationalities who did it the difference was inevitable. The colour schemes were different, the way of placing them was different, it made plain the whole theory of art and its inevitability.

In what Hugh B. Cott calls "coincident disruptive patterning," strongly contrasting patterns cut across the surface of the figure, then coincide with similar patterns on other parts of the body. Thus, in this example, the top wing appears to be a continuation of the lower wing.

During World War I, convoys of dazzle-painted merchant ships were sometimes referred to as a "floating art museum," "a flock of sea-going Easter Eggs," and "cubist painting on a collosal scale." Depicted here are four hypothetical camouflaged ships, based on actual World War I naval camouflage measures. Such razzle-dazzle was intended to confuse German submarine torpedo gunners in their critical estimates of the speed, direction and anticipated location of ships.

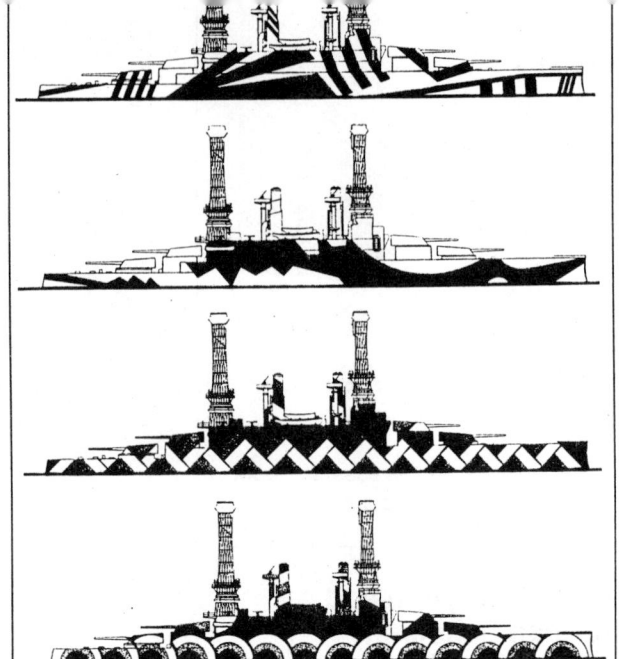

## How To See

(A Guide to Reading Our Manmade Environment)
George Nelson
1977; 233 pp.
**$14.95**
($16.45 postpaid) from:
Little, Brown and Company
200 West Street
Waltham, MA 02254
800/343-9204
or Whole Earth Access

*How many of us actually see our environment? For the most part, we've trained ourselves to screen out much of the world around us: the pollution, the billboards, homeless people, etc.* **How To See** *is a book about rediscovering the world right in front of our noses. In dozens of beautiful, and occasionally disturbing, photos of manmade landscapes (which is where most of live nowadays) we are able to rediscover the images and form of our everyday lives, from neon signs to church ceilings, from billboards to coins, from abstract expressionist sculpture to fire hydrants. If we are going to live in this world, it makes sense that we should be able to see it. If we are going to change the world for the better, it is essential. This book is a step in that direction.*

*— Richard Kadrey*

[Suggested by Scott Kim]

Three different views of man-made landscapes: Left) Very big spaces became attainable in the mid-1800's, when the use of iron and steel, often combined with glass, suddenly made superspans possible. Take the great old Galleria in Milan, Italy: why would anyone build it? Well, it is right alongside the big cathedral square. It rains quite a lot in Milan. It also gets very hot in the summer. If you make two streets in the form of a cross, pave the floor with mosaics, fill the buildings with shops and cafes at ground level, and throw two glass vaults over the streets, pleasant things happen. Below left) Junk is not just the disorder of discards. It, like everything else, can be read on a variety of levels. At the most immediate and superficial, it is unsightly waste which immobilizes land that could be put to better use; at another level, junk is a resource that becomes more valuable as prime mineral sources are depleted. At still another level, junk can be seen as an unexpected source of accidental beauty. Below) One really does a double take when confronted by Hans Hollein's photomontage of a Rolls Royce radiator growing in the financial district of New York. Do we see a natural affinity between the Rolls and Wall Street? Is the radiator, with its vertical metal fins, virtually indistinguishable from the new buildings, telling us something about modern buildings and modern products, both equally devoid of character?

## SPOT 1

Information **free** from: SPOT Image Corporation, 1897 Preston White Drive, Reston, VA 22091; 703/620-2200

*On February 21, 1986, the French space agency launched the first satellite specifically designed for remote sensing on a commercial basis: SPOT 1. Its high-resolution images are marketed through an international network of subsidiaries and affiliates. Because of SPOT's sidelooking capability, it can view a site without passing directly overhead. Thus, it can review ground areas more often than Landsat — every few days, if necessary.*

*Prices for a scene showing 60 x 60 km of surface range from $500 for a 9" x 9" color transparency (from their new digital photo facility), to $1700 for a computer-compatible tape with geometric corrections. "Panchromatic" images can attain a ground resolution of ten meters — three times better than Landsat's best — with prices starting at $550 for a photoprint on paper. But the boost in clarity comes*

The SPOT1 image that gave the civilian world one of the first glimpses of the damaged Russian reactor at Chernobyl in 1986. Arrow points toward a dark squiggly diagonal line — thought to be scorched ground resulting from an explosion.

Deforestation and agriculture in the Rift Valley, Kenya — one of the many scenes available in SPOT's educational slide sets.

*with a loss of color: panchromatic images are only available in black and white. They also carry sets of educational images in slide, transparency and digital form. The slide sets start at $60.*

*Thus, the two system's have different strengths that make them suited to somewhat different purposes. SPOT's shaper images make it more useful for investigation where human activity and constructions are the focus, while Landsat's superior spectral filtering gives it an advantage in resource identification and surveys.*

— *Robert Horvitz*

## EOSAT Satellite Images

Information **free** from: EOSAT, 4300 Forbes Boulevard, Lanham, MD 20706; 301/552-0500

*In 1984, the U.S. Congress decided to turn the Landsat program over to the private sector. The still-functioning Landst 4 and 5 satellites, and the huge archive of data accumulated since 1972, have been transferred to the Earth Observation Satellite Company (EOSAT).*

*Prices range from $50 for a black and white photo on paper with 80-meter ground resolution (image size 7.3 inches on an edge, showing approximately 115 miles square), up to $3,300 for a computer-compatible tape of a scene from the Thematic Mapper (TM) on Landsat 5. TM scenes have a ground resolution of 30 meters — less than SPOT (see review above) provides, but the TM's primary sensor has seven spectral filters, compared with SPOT's three. This finer spectral discrimination makes it possible to identify different*

*plant species or types of rock by detecting subtle differences in the color of the sunlight they reflect, even when they're not identifiable by shape or texture.*

— *Robert Horvitz*

EOSAT/Landsat view of center-pivot irriogated cropland south of Garden City, Kansas.

## The Photogrammetric Coyote

Marilyn M. O'Cuilian, Editor
**Free** from:
E. Coyote Enterprises
P. O. Box 1119
Mineral Wells, TX 76067
817/325-0757

*Your one-stop aerial surveying shop. **The Photogrammetric Coyote** has it all: new and used aerial photography and remote sensing equipment, profiles of famous pilots, and news from the world of aerial surveying. Before I read the Coyote, I didn't even know what a photo interpretation instrument was, and now I want one.*

— *Richard Kadrey*

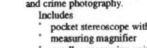

# Mapmaking

*by Don Ryan*

A measure of the difficulty of progress in cartography is the out-of-printness of two of these texts. Their market is limited to academe and a small interface with commerce and government. The costs of production are disproportionate: High quality reproduction of already printed maps is technically difficult, therefore costly; the generation of hundreds of entirely new illustrations is even more so.

Slow, conservative evolution within a proven market had kept the third book alive. What has suffered is the growth of knowledge and advancement of the art.

Find these books in a large public or university library.

## Semiology of Graphics
University of Wisconsin Press
OUT OF PRINT

*"Semiology" means the "language of signs," and it's significant that semiology originated within the same circle of french sociologists to which this book's author, Jacques Bertin, belongs.*

*This book is mother-lode of the theory of technical graphics. But it is written in the tone of one artist speaking to another. That is, technical graphics are treated as a legitimate art-form, to which standards of clarity, form, and balance are to be applied. Every mapmaker and computer graphics jockey will find useful material in this book.*
*— Robert G. Flower*

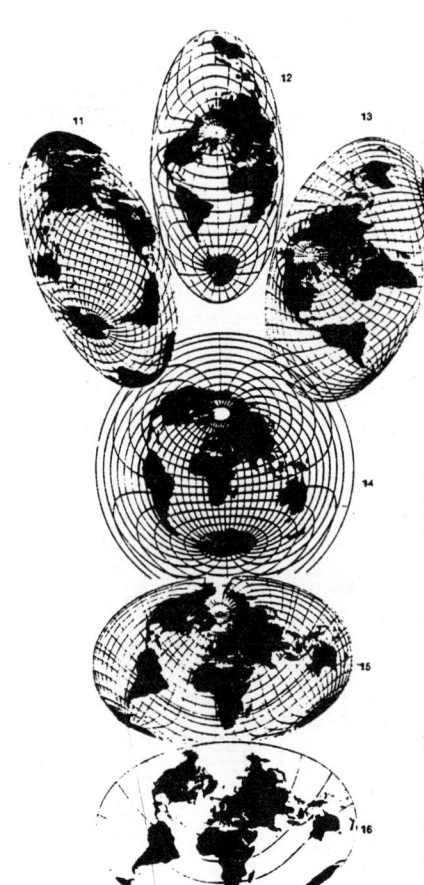

**Examples of Several Oblique Planispheres**
Along with Brisemeister's equivalent projection (figure 12, page 293), several oblique projections are given in the following figures:
11—Guillaume Postel's compromise projection. This is similar to the projection in figure 6, with the axis through the Pacific Ocean (J. Strohl);
12—"Atlantis" projection. Mollweide's equivalent projection, where the main axis corresponds to the meridian 30° west;
13—projection with regional compromise (J. Bertin, 1953), in which the compromise is no longer homogeneous, but is modified for a larger deformation of the oceans, to give a lesser deformation of the continents;
14—azimuthal equidistant projection, centered on Khartoum; this is like the projection in figure 10, centered to group the set of the continents, including the South Pole, in the zone of least deformation;
15—split projection with regional compromise (J. Bertin, 1952);
16—projection with regional compromise achieved by juxtaposition of azimuthals (J. Bertin, 1954).

## Mapping Information
Abt Books
OUT OF PRINT

*This is the book for one entering thematic cartography in a serious way (this subset of the field excludes maps of general interest such as topographic maps or road maps, to deal with special subjects such as economic or scientific data, including non-physical events and totally abstract or hypothetical matters).*

*By assuming that the beginning cartographer already knows several ways to make a mark on a piece of paper — including via computer, if his or her pencil is broken (Fisher founded the pioneering Harvard Laboratory of Computer Graphics) the author frees the book of the necessity of describing penpoints and typesetters and reproduction technology which will be obsolete by the time the book enters its second printing. In essence, the book becomes timeless.*

*The chapter on using color is the only case I have ever seen where the verbal and diagrammatic description — in black and white — is sufficiently lucid that color is not needed on the pages. The rest of the book is as clear.*

*A monumental work, essential in its theory. A visual feast, full of transparent layers of beautifully-defined content. Ultimately desirable. No wonder it's out of print.*
*— Don Ryan*

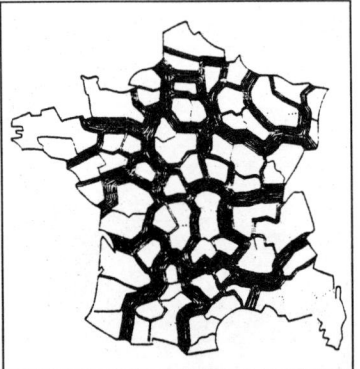

Consider the problem of superimposing eleven administrative systems (economic regions, social security, work inspection, postal regions, military regions, regional planning areas, etc.) that were obtained from a preparatory survey for the determination of administrative regions. The various departmental boundaries can thus include from one to eleven regional boundaries.

*An engagingly written and clearly illustrated, very valuable book. A companion volume, covering general reference maps would make a world-beating set. I want them both. Please?*
*— Don Ryan*

## Elements of Cartography
(Fifth Edition)
Arthur Robinson
1984; 448 pp.
**$45.45**
($47.40 postpaid) from:
John Wiley & Sons
1 Wiley Drive
Somerset, NJ 08875
201/469-4400
or Whole Earth Access

*The great, grey tome of my college years has grown greater through many editions but is still not the single sufficient source I'd like it to be.*

*The book first appeared in 1953, concentrating on history, design, and time-proven technique. Since then it has grown by accretion — like a hailstone — picking up layers here and there: remote sensing in the 60's and layers of computer applications in the 70's and early 1980's. Unfortunately, the busy layout of the book emphasizes the diversity of its origins rather than the cohesiveness of its theme. It is, frankly, uninspiring. A book about a visual craft or science just ought to look better.*

*Too much space has been devoted to ephemeral technology. Large sections have been made obsolete by evolution in the printing industry or the ongoing revolution in micro-computing. This coverage should have been left to the books and magazines in those areas (see pages 140-150) to which, by the way, no reference is made.*

*Despite the shortness of art and deficiencies of organization, however, the core of academic cartography is adequately served. I would wish for some influence from outside that circle and eventually a total revision of illustration and layout.*
*— Don Ryan*

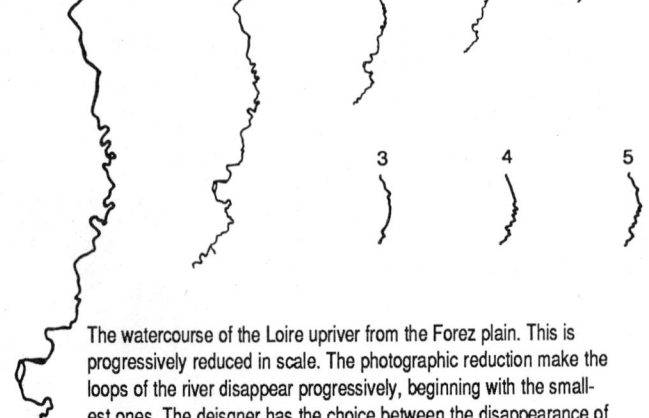

The watercourse of the Loire upriver from the Forez plain. This is progressively reduced in scale. The photographic reduction make the loops of the river disappear progressively, beginning with the smallest ones. The deisgner has the choice between the disappearance of the smallest loops or their preservation by amplification.

Top: Land-use and land-cover, 1972.
Bottom: Census county subdivisions, 1970.

## Map Data Catalog

1984; 30pp., U.S. Government Printing Office

*Between the covers of this thin booklet from the National Cartographic Information Center is everything you need to know about how to order a topographic map, geological survey map, aerial photograph, or any other kind of cartographic information from the vast archives of the U.S. Government. It gives explicit step by step instructions for identifying and ordering the particular part of the world you want, including procedures for securing copies of out-of-print maps for historical research. You can also order the components of U.S. Topo maps in order to construct your own maps, and even get advance "proofs" of maps in the making. For instance you can get the latest street maps of an area by requesting only the "cultural" overlay for the chosen area, which may be completed years before the rest of the map is. These are hard-to-find secrets; since it is currently out of print from*

### Uses

The land-use and land-cover and associated maps will help to satisfy a longstanding need voiced by land-use planners, land managers, and resource-management planners. In answer to the needs of these and other users, they will provide a consistent level of detail and a standardization of categories mapped at scales well suited for planners and managers.

When the bench-mark series of maps is completed, updating of the maps will provide a much-needed tool for analyzing trends, changes in land-use patterns, and problems in local and regional areas throughout the United States.

### How to order

1. From any Mapping Center NCIC office, request a free copy of the *Index of Land-Use and Land-Cover and Associated Maps.*

2. To order a copy of *Professional Paper 964*, write to: Branch of Distribution, U.S. Geological Survey, 1200 South Eads Street, Arlington, VA 22202 and with your order send a money order or check for 75¢ for each copy desired.

3. If enlargements, composites, or other special processing is desired, request assistance from the nearest Mapping Center NCIC office.

4. Based on the information you have received, place your order with any Mapping Center NCIC office. List the maps you want:
(a) Land-Use and Land-Cover Maps.
(b) Associated Maps (Political units; Hydrologic units; Census county subdivisions; Federal land ownership). For each map, specify whether you want:
(a) Stable-base film positive, clear or matte;
(b) Semi-stable diazo foil, matte; or
(c) Paper diazo.
Specify requirements, if any, for enlargements, composites, or other special processing.

5. With your order, enclose a money order or check payable to the Geological Survey.

### Price

Prices are for stable-base film positive, semi-stable diazo foil, and paper diazo. Prices are contained in a separate list available upon request from NCIC.

*the government, it's worth tracking down this booklet at a library and photocopying it.* — Kevin Kelly

## The Map Catalog

(Every kind of Map and Chart on Earth and Even Some Above It)
Joel Makower, Editor
1986; 252 pp.
**$14.95**
($15.95 postpaid) from:
Random House
400 Hahn Road
Westminster, MD 21157
800/638-6460

*A guide to over 50 kinds of maps and atlases from commercial sources and governments, both foreign and domestic, of land, sky, and water. Appendixed with addresses of agencies, map libraries, and selected map stores; glossaried and copiously indexed.*

— Don Ryan
[Suggested by Bill Belmont]

◆

**U.S. Geological Survey.** USGS has several world maps available, most popular being the "International Map of the World" ($3.60), a basic multicolored reference map showing borders, capital cities, and other key features to delineate the nations of the world. Another popular USGS world map is the "Relief Edition of the International Map of the World," which has been created in three scales: the 1:20,000,000-scale map ($3.90), a single sheet measuring 42" x 56"; the 1:22,000,000-scale map ($9.90), consisting of three sheets, each measuring 34" x 57"; and the 1:14,000,000-scale map ($33.30), consisting of six sheets, each measuring 42" x 56".

Portion of a 1:25,000-scale from the Swiss Federal Office of Topography's National Map Series, illustrating the basic features of the Swiss countryside, including roads, railroads, cities, towns, and bodies of water.

## Electronic Map Cabinet

$200 from Highlighted Data, P. O. Box 17229, Washington Dulles International Airport, Washington, D.C. 20041; 703/533-1939

*The outline of a country (or state or city) doesn't change much from year to year. No need then to redraw its profile each time you need a base map if you could pull out a blank one to the size you wanted. Stockpiling all the thousands of blank ones into a tidy and manageable place has been the obstacle to this great idea. Even most map libraries don't have that kind of room.*

*The Electronic Map Cabinet solves this problem by storing a continuous map of the U. S. on a Macintosh-readable CD-ROM disc. You can then enlarge the lines to the scale you desire. It will zoom in from an overview of the United States down to the level of counties and further down to a close up of city streets in all the SMSA (Standard Metropolitan Statistical Areas — fair size cities*

*and environs). It does this in "vector graphics" which means that it will hold its resolution sufficiently to be printed out in clean crisp ink-like lines on a laserprinter. The image can be manipulated later by the usual Mac paint tools — words, tints, or additional lines added — and filled out into a real custom made map.*

*The underlying cartography is based on public domain government data. The maps you see now in newspapers and weekly magazines are almost all constructed in this manner. You'll need a Mac, HyperCard, CD-ROM driver, and a Laserwriter to make this work. It's not a toy.*

— Kevin Kelly

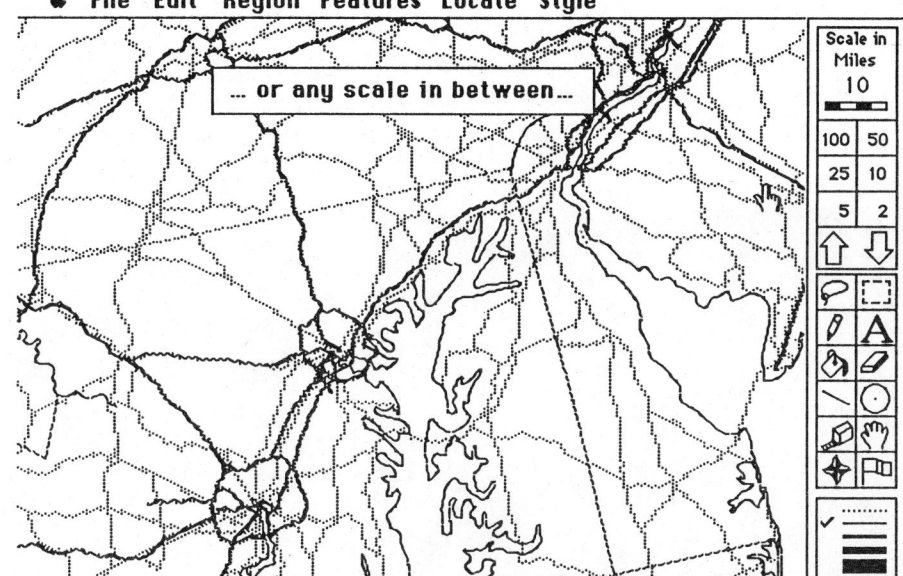

## MapMaster

$395 from: Ashton-Tate, 25 Sylvan Road South, Westport, CT 0680; 203/222-1974

*MapMaster is a mass-market mapping program from Ashton-Tate (formerly Decision Resources). For a mapping program, it is easy to learn and use (all menu-driven) and produces good-looking maps. It lacks some of the sophistication that hardcore cartographers like, but outputs nicely to both dot-matrix printers and plotters, something the others don't do.*

*The software comes with boundaries for the U.S. by state and some population data items.*

— Diane Crispell

## The Visual Display of Quantitative Information

Edward R. Tufte
1983; 197 pp.
**$34** postpaid from:
Graphics Press
Box 430
Cheshire, CT 06410

*THE visual style book. Turn a page in this finely printed volume and you'll be treated to another ingenious chart that is at once simple, telling, and beautiful. Flamboyant graphs, particularly those dressing up insensible data, are bad craft: "If the statistics are boring, then you've got the wrong numbers." The rules are like writing well—do it honest and clear. Tufte gives memorable, handsome examples of how to display information with integrity and clarity. The book is a good example. It's one that you return to dip into before you pick up graph paper.*

—Kevin Kelly

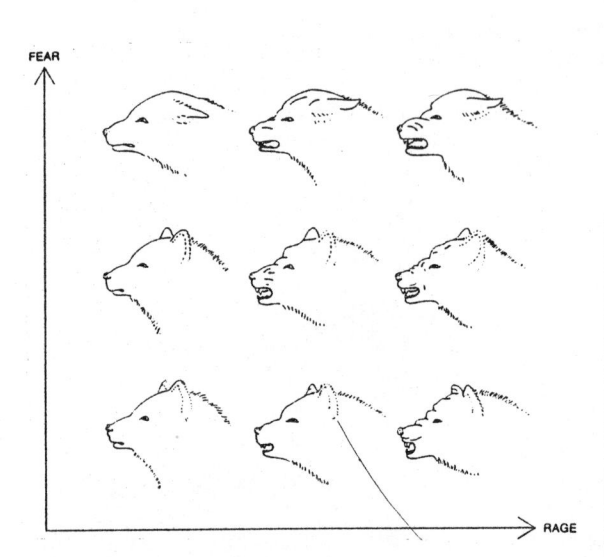

The effect of religion, taking into account party affiliations, on a person's vote for president in 1960 (when a Catholic ran for president). Reading the slope in the other direction shows the persistent effect of party:

◆

The theory of the visual display of quantitative information consists of principles that generate design options and that guide choices among options. The principles should not be applied rigidly or in a peevish spirit; they are not logically or mathematically certain; and it is better to violate any principle than to place graceless or inelegant marks on paper.

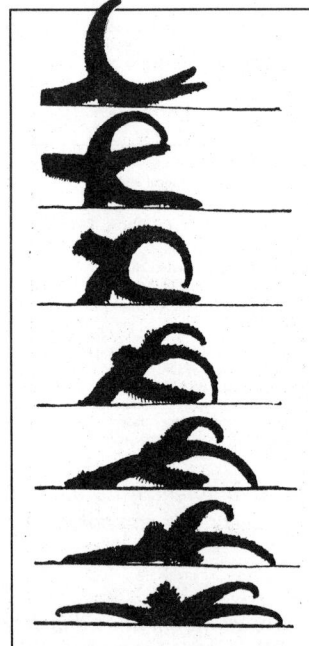

The movement of a starfish turning itself over (read images from the bottom upwards).

[Left] Here the effect of two variables interacting is portrayed by the faces on the plotting field:

The data graphical arithmetic looks like this—the original design equals the erased part plus the good part:

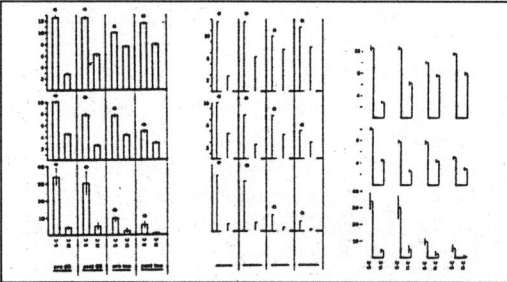

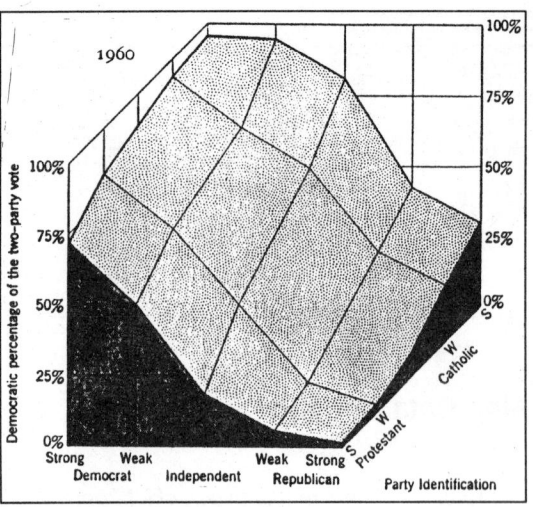

## Designer's Guide to Creating Charts & Diagrams

Nigel Holmes
1984; 192 pp.
**$32.50**
($34.50 postpaid) from:
Watson-Guptill Publications
1695 Oak Street
Lakewood, NJ 08701
212/764-7300
or Whole Earth Access

*Advance chart making. Charts that dwell on the bland pages of a scholarly report need only to be clear and accurate. Charts that live in newspapers and magazines must compete with the flash of advertisements across the page. Here's some tips by the famous diagram maker who creates all those striking ones in* **Time** *magazine.*

— Kevin Kelly

◆

When to Avoid Using a Chart?

Do not be afraid to suggest this as a solution to the problem presented to you. You will save everyone a lot of time if after studying the raw data you can see that it is (1) too simple to even bother with, (2) so complicated that even splitting it up into more than one image will still not explain the material, or (3) you can encapsulate the essence of the information more easily in a sentence than in a graphic translation. . . . Avoid doing a chart when it is really only fulfilling the role of decoration or of making a page or presentation look more authoritative, factual, or important.

Figures of speech can be literally illustrated. The phrase itself usually makes the best title for the chart, especially if it is changed slightly to fit exactly the sense of the idea, in this case "over a barrel."

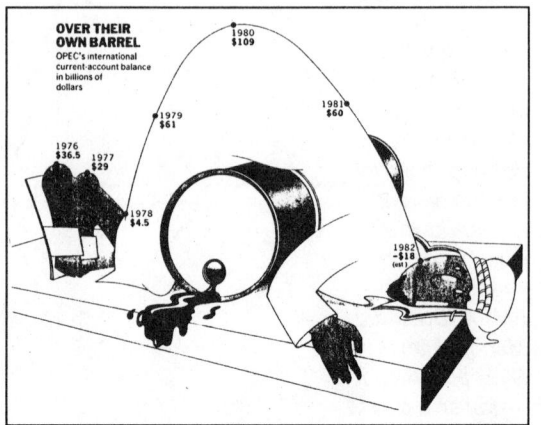

## Boeing Graph

Version 4.0; IBM compatible, 512K required. Will run on B/W or CGA monitors or with Hercules or EGA graphics adaptor. **$395** from Boeing Computer Service, P. O. Box 24346/Mail Stop 7A-32, Seattle, WA 98124-0346; 800/ 368-4555

*Numbers stun; pictures illuminate. If you have ever tried to present numerical information visually, you know how difficult it can be.*

*This program turns tables of data into exquisite three-dimensional graphs. You can choose among 32 different types of three-dimensional graphs, 15 types of two-dimensional graphs, and almost endless points of view. Graphs can be rotated, moved vertically and horizontally, repainted, and labeled as you choose. The program drives plotters and will use dot-matrix and laser printers.*

*If you present scientific or financial information to people, this is an exquisite tool. It's also a lot of fun to play with.*

—Birrell Walsh

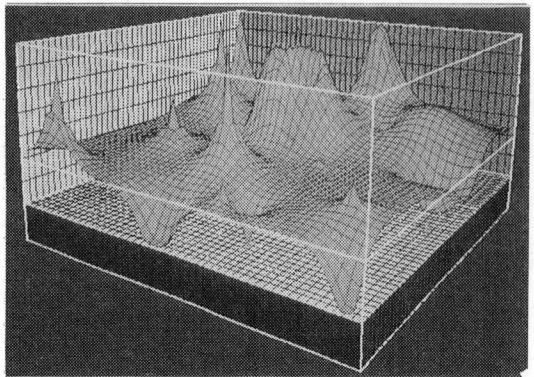

## Forget All the Rules . . .

Bob Gill
1981; 168 pp.
**$17.95**
($19.95 postpaid) from:
Watson Guptill Publishers
1695 Oak Street
Lakewood, NJ 08701
or Whole Earth Access

*As he was being taken away by the police, acrobat Philippe Petit explained why he had walked a rope between two of the world's tallest buildings: "I see three oranges, I have to juggle. I see two towers, I have to walk."*

*Seeing unique aspects in commonplace things is also what makes for original graphic design. In this inspiring book, John Gill showcases a hundred of his toughest design problems with his wittiest solutions. According to Gill, to arrive at a unique solution you need to define a unique problem. However, the complete title of the book is: **Forget all the rules you ever learned about graphic design. Including the ones in this book.***

*— David Jouris*

# Dancin'

◆

I wanted to do something that was original. But I kept thinking of ideas based on images I had already seen. Then I realized that it was inevitable that my ideas had to be based on previous experiences. What else could possibly be in my consciousness but previous experiences?

I would have to go outside of my head to look for an original idea. I decided that getting involved with the new problem was the most likely way of going outside. Of having a new experience.

If I could express the uniqueness of what the problem was trying to communicate with an image which was valid only for that problem, then I would have invented a unique image.

In other words, defining a unique problem would inspire a unique solution.

Original problem:  Logo for the Broadway musical Dancin'. It has no plot but many styles of dancing.

Redefined:  How can one image give the impression of many styles of dancing?

---

## Step-By-Step Graphics

Nancy Aldrich-Ruenzel, Editor
$42/6 issues from:
Step-by-Step Graphics
6000 N. Forest Park Drive
P.O. Box 1901
Peoria, IL 61656-9979
800/255-8800

## How . . .

Philip Smith, Editor
$27/6 issues from:
R.C. Publications
6400 Goldsboro Road
Bethesda, MD 20817
800/229-6700

*The current trend in graphics magazines is the how-to genre, indicating a growing hunger for nitty-gritty studio tips on tools and techniques.*

***Step-By-Step Graphics** is a good entry-level introduction, offering solid advice on such basics as copy-fitting, trouble-shooting the airbrush, or simple techniques for adding color to black and white line art. The emphasis is on the creative process rather than the finished result, with lots of large, clear photos showing each stage of a project. Readers are encouraged to participate by sharing short cuts and case studies of their own. Though a bit pricey at $7.50 a copy, the information is often worth it.*

***How . . .** is geared more for the graphic arts professional, focusing as much on business tips as studio techniques. Each issue offers advice from top-level art buyers on developing and presenting your portfolio. The how-to features include the evolution of concepts as well as the steps involved*

*in their execution. Close-up articles feature graphics heavyweights such as Milton Glaser. The magazine itself is quite attractively designed.*

*— Rebecca Wilson*

Instead of using coins and other heavy objects to weight down the acetate, Yi prefers magnets. "It's a neat trick that I've developed. First, I tape the drawing board to a metal plate; then I put magnets down to keep the frisket in place; the magnets stay in place even if I prop the board up," he says.

*—How . . .*

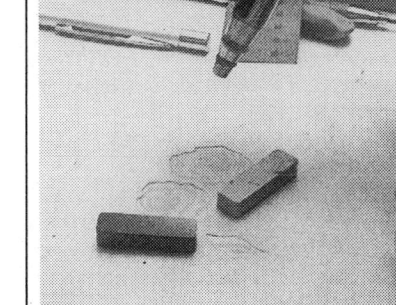

If you do not have a large paper cutter, but do have to trim oversize material on occasion, you can still use your small cutter to make straight and accurate trims. First, establish and mark your trim lines. Cut a "wedge" halfway down the length of the trim side. Place the board on the paper cutter and proceed to trim the upper half, making sure the upper trim line corresponds with that same line which is showing through the "wedge." Turn the board around and cut the bottom part, aligning the previous cut with the lower trim line. If your paper cutter is very small, simply cut as many "wedges" as needed.

*—Step-By-Step Grahpics*

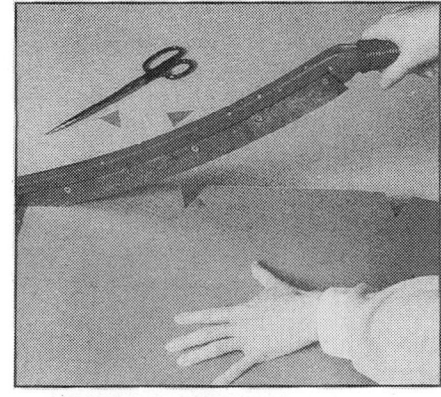

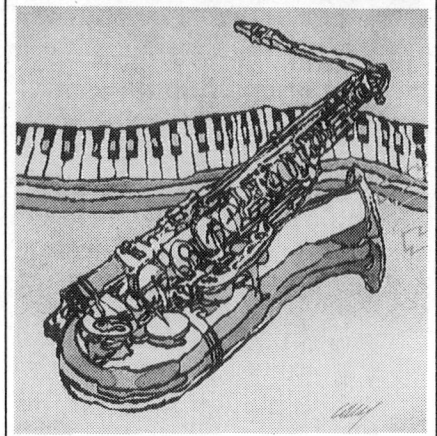

To get a distorted effect on a line drawing or line art, you can "wigglify" it by using a piece of rippled shower glass. Lay the shower glass over the drawing under a repro camera. The farther you separate the glass from the drawing, the more distortion. Shoot with bottom lights as well as top lights to knock out any refractions that occur in the glass.

*—Step-By-Step Graphics*

## Patterns in Nature

Peter S. Stevens
1974; 240 pp.

**$21.95** postpaid from:
Whole Earth Access
2950 Seventh Street
Berkeley, CA 94710
415/845-3000 in CA
800/845-2000

*This is a book in which, with a bunch of photographs, some clear uncomplicated text and an occasional number, you are plunged into nature's mysteries. I suspect that the route to the frontier need never be more complicated than this, but there are so few guides who can show you the way.*

*I wish the book were five times as long as it is*

because reading it is such a pleasure. There are eight chapters:

1. Space and Size
2. Basic Patterns
3. All Things Flow
4. Spirals, Meanders and Explosives
5. Models of Branching
6. Trees
7. Soap Bubbles
8. Packing and Cracking

—Steve Baer

◆

Shrinkage of surfaces allows us to understand the dramatic coincidence of form: why the shell of the box turtle looks like a regular cluster of bubbles. We know that the films between the bubbles minimize their area so as to join one another at 120°. The same holds for the lines between the plates of the shell. New cells grow along those lines and gravitate outward to join the edges of the plates. Consequently, as the plates increase in size, the lines between them keep to a minimum.

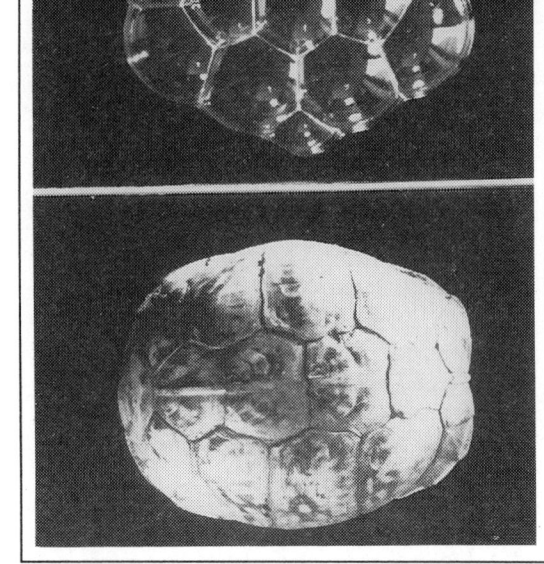

## Visual Thinking

Rudolf Arnheim
1969; 345 pp.

**$12.95**
($14.45 postpaid) from:
University of California Press
2120 Berkeley Way
Berkeley, CA 94720
1-800-822-6657
or Whole Earth Access

*Eyeballs are precisely where minds meet the world. Our perceptions, particularly our visual perceptions, structure the way we think about the world. Rudolf Arnheim's classic **Visual Thinking** uses examples from art and psychology to demonstrate that we derive our ideas and our language itself from how we see.*

*— Howard Rheingold*

◆

My earlier work had taught me that artistic activity is a form of reasoning, in which perceiving and thinking are indivisibly intertwined. A person who paints, writes,

composes, dances, I felt compelled to say, thinks with his senses. This union of perception and thought turned out to be not merely a specialty of the arts. A review of what is known about perception, and especially about sight, made me realize that the remarkable mechanisms by which the senses understand the environment are all but identical with the operations described by the psychology of thinking. Inversely, there was much evidence that truly productive thinking in whatever area of cognition takes place in the realm of imagery. This similarity of what the mind does in the arts and what it does elsewhere suggested taking a new look at the long-standing complaint about the isolation and

neglect of the arts in society and education. Perhaps the real problem was more fundamental: a split between sense and thought, which caused various deficiency diseases in modern man.

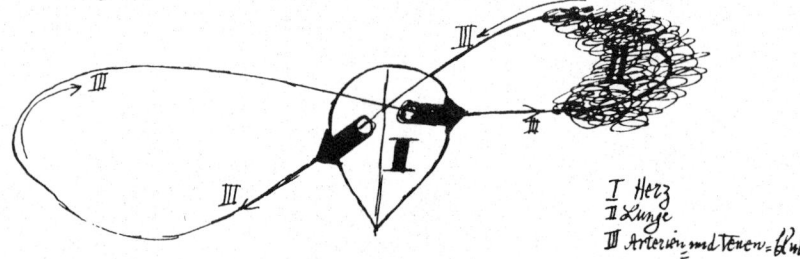

Figure 78. Paul Klee: Drawing of the human heart. With permission of the Paul Klee-Stiftung, Kunstmuseum, Bern; and SPADEM, 12 rue Henner, Paris.

◆

The fundamental fact about seeing is that it is learned. Seeing is believing, but the beliefs are the creation of the viewer.

## Inversions

Scott Kim
1981; 122 pp.

**$9.95**
($11.45 postpaid) from:
MIT Press
55 Hayward Street
Cambridge, MA 02142
800/356-0343
or Whole Earth Access

*Shape inverts into meaning. Meaning folds back into shape. A name becomes geometry, then swallows itself. Language put into symmetrical meaning, the same upsidedown, left to right. Playing a fugue of words, Scott Kim dances with visual double-jointedness.*

—Kevin Kelly

The job (1980)

## Suterisms
David Suter
1986; 97 pp.
**$4.95**
($5.95 postpaid) from:
Ballantine/Random House
400 Hahn Road
Westminster, MD 21157
800/638-6460
or Whole Earth Access

Selectovision (1985)

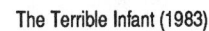

*David Suter's visual mind-benders appear regularly in national publications such as **The New York Times, Harper's,** and **The Progressive.** Like the famous optical illusionist M.C. Escher, Suter melds foreground and background in drawings that inherently express contradictions in our political unconscious.*
— Jeanne Carstensen

The Terrible Infant (1983)

## Thinking Visually
(A Strategy Manual
for Problem Solving)
Robert H. McKim
1980; 210 pp.
**$14.95**
($16.95 postpaid) from:
Dale Seymour Publications
P.O. Box 10888
Palo Alto, CA 94303
800/872-1100
800/222-0766 in California
or Whole Earth Access

*If you're a poor visualizer, you're working without one of the most important mental tools. Fortunately, visual thinking is an ability one can develop and improve, and Bob McKim has provided a manual for doing just that. The book is both informative — good background information on creativity and problem-solving — and experiential, full of excellent exercises structured to develop specific aspects of visual thinking. A fine balance of about and how to. It's one of the very few books with exercises to do that I've actually managed to work my way through.*

— Linda Williams

◆

Because thinking flows quickly, graphic ideation is usually freehand, impressionistic, and rapid. Because communication to others demands clarity, graphic communication is necessarily more formal, explicit, and time-consuming. Education that stresses graphic communication and fails to consider graphic ideation can unwillingly hamper visual thinking.

Take the following abstract words one by one and experience the abstract inner image elicited by the word. Make an abstract sketch of each image.

1. Nouns: chair / tree / house / car / animal.
2. Verbs: thrust / shut / penetrate / collapse / swing.
3. Adjectives: turbulent / sharp / voluptuous / decayed / lively.

The two designs in the first row of Figure 3-15 are related to each other and also to one of the designs in the second row. Which of the four lettered designs below fits into the empty space?

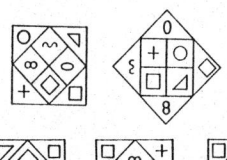
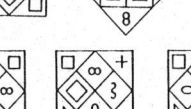

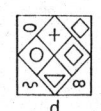

a     b     c     d

## Pictionary
**$25.** For nearest retail outlet:
The Game Gang, Ltd., 1107 Broadway, Suite 1603, New York, NY 10010. 212/929-0470.
or Whole Earth Access

*If you want to play a game that will stretch your visual thinking capacity and generate merriment in a group, try Pictionary, a board game for children and adults. It is like charades, in that each team tries to guess what one of their members is trying to communicate. But the communication does not involve words or gestures. The team member whose task is to communicate the key word or phrase must do it by sketching. You'll be astonished at the near-telepathic results you can get — guessing a complex phrase by three hastily scribbled lines, for example.*

— Howard Rheingold

## Dale Seymour Publications
P.O. Box 10888, Palo Alto, CA 94303.
800/872-1100; 800/222-0766 in California.

*Call or write for one of their catalogs — Educational Materials K-8, Secondary Mathematics, and Secondary Language Arts — of above-average educational stuff. They seem intent on providing stimulating, innovative books and classroom aids, many of them expressly chosen to develop both creative and visual thinking.*
— Sarah Satterlee
[Suggested by Scott Kim]

**Tensegritoy** *(Grades 7–12)*
R. Buckminster Fuller coined the term *tensegrity*, a contraction of the words *tension* and *integrity*, to describe structures whose shapes are maintained by tensile forces. Tensegrity lets your students see these principles at work as they build a tetrahedron, octahedron, and icosahedron—the three basic building blocks of natural structures—as well as other polyhedra. They'll also learn how to turn other shapes into tensegrity structures. Complete directions included.

| | | |
|---|---|---|
| RS16804 | Basic kit | $25.00 |
| RS16805 | Extender kit | $35.00 |

**Googolplex** *(All ages)*
An excellent set of manipulatives for understanding polygons and polyhedra. The colorful plastic shapes and connectors can be used to make up to 92 geometrical shapes—from simple squares, triangles, and pentagons to pyramids, Archimedean polyhedra, and more. Available in two sets: **Googolplex 5** has 240 pieces; **Googolplex 9** has 342 pieces. Both sets include two colorful instructional posters. Also available: two teaching guides, one for grades K–6 and the other for grades 7–12.

| | | |
|---|---|---|
| RS16868 | Googolplex 5 | $33.95 |
| RS16869 | Googolplex 9 | $44.95 |
| RS16870 | TG, grades K–6 (48 pp.) | $ 6.95 |
| RS16871 | TG, grades 7–12 (96 pp.) | $ 9.95 |

TOUPEE

## Leonardo
(Journal of the International
Society for the Arts,
Sciences and Technology)
Roger F. Malina, Editor
**$40**/year
(4 issues) from:
Leonardo
P.O. Box 75
1442A Walnut
Berkeley, CA 94709
415/845-8298

*Artists, as mythmakers,
are the first to explain new frontiers. Technological
publications tell the "what." **Leonardo,** the journal
for the union of art, science and technology, tells
the "so what." The authors are artists colonizing
technology. They paint and storytell with lasers,
hybrid materials, computers,
holograms, scanners, experimental musical instruments,
indeed with the whole developing communication tissue.
There is more of tomorrow here
than in any **Futurist** magazine.*
*— Kevin Kelly*

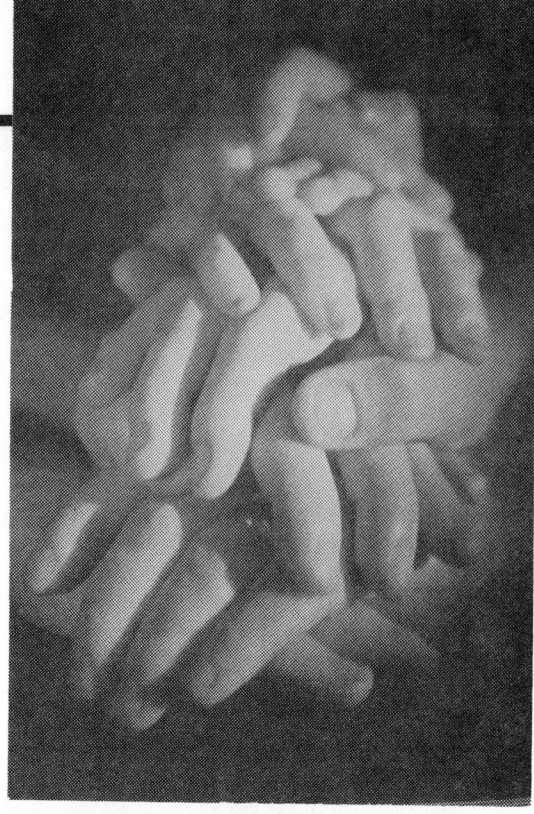

From *Conjugal Series: Pile of Hands*, reflection hologram, silver
halide on glass, 8 x 10", 1983. A pyramid of the generations is
formed of male and female hands with a child's hands on top.

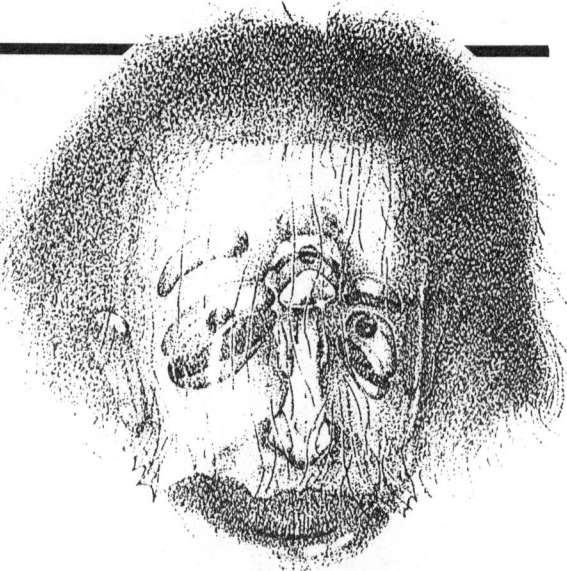

Using his mathematical method for visualizing the 4-dimensional
analogue of a 3-dimensional object, Koji Miyazaki renders a 4-
dimensional Einstein, having three eyes, three eyebrows, three ears,
a nose and a mouth.

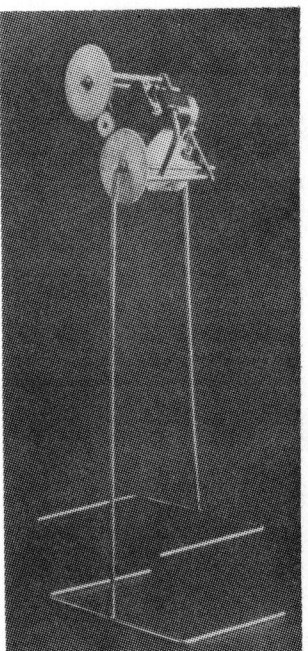

Martin Riches,
*Rotater*, walking
machine con-
structed of
mixed media, 35
cm high, 1978.
Riches, an
Englishman
living in Berlin,
is a maker of
machines that
walk, paint, play
music and provide bursts of percussion.
This walking machine moves with gentle,
delicate steps.

## Lightworks
Charlton Burch, Editor
**$20**/4 issues
(about one per year) from:
Lightworks
P.O. Box 1202
Birmingham, MI 48012
313/626-8026

The wooden Sonny
Eliot hitching in
downtown Detroit.

*Most experimental art
is so unsatisfying and pretentious to be
around that the last thing in the world I want
to do is read about it. **Lightworks,** an annual labor of love, is the opposite. Here they
round up far-ranging explorations of art and
communications that make it all great FUN. I
like the wooden cut-outs of hitchhikers that
are propped up along the road with an address scribbled on their backs, and space to
document their journey as they are passed
around the country. A whole issue was
devoted to Sky Art — from kites, to skywrit-
ing, to fireworks and helium balloon sculp-
tures. An upcoming issue is called "Available Resources" and is dedicated to art
made from recycled materials and found
media. Some of it is weird and strange, but
in an invigorating way. This magazine is
about the art of possibilities.*
*— Kevin Kelly*

◆

Don't step over the fence.

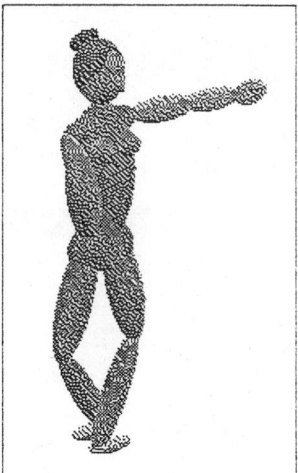

Fig. 3. A computer dancer figure, such as can be
used in a computerised interpreter for Benesh
Movement Notation at the University of
Waterloo. The interpreter can be used to aid in
visualising the movements described in a dance
score written in Benesh Movement Notation.

Don't Step Over The Fence:
The exhibition space is divided by a corrugated fence approximately 6 to 7
inches tall. On one side are the camera, tripod, and monitors. On the other
side are the paintings on the wall with corrugated animals, houses, and
landscape paraphernalia on the floor. The paintings are related to the
landscape. The audience is not allowed to step over the fence but can look
at the paintings by pointing the camera at the desired art-object, then
viewing the painting on the monitors. If the viewer wishes, the colors can
be changes by adjusting the controls on the monitor.

Order forms are made available for potential purchasers
of a painting(s). The purchaser points the camera at the
painting, changes the color on the monitor and writes in
the appropriate information on the order form. This is
then sent with a check or money order, to Mr.
Rutkovsky's studio, Paper Mache Video Institute, where
the custom painting is completed and forwarded to the
art patron.

## Daniel Smith Inc.

Catalog **$4** from Daniel Smith Inc., 4130 1st Avenue South, Seattle, WA 98134; 800/426-6740; 800/228-0458 in WA

*Here is an immense selection of absolutely first rate art supplies, as well as a wonderfully prompt and efficient mail order house. Their goods are discounted, generally 20-30 percent off retail, and are interestingly and informatively laid out in the illustrated (photos) yearly catalog, supplemented by intermittent special sale catalogs. In terms of sheer care and knowledgeability, no other art supplier I have found even comes close.*

*The fine artist is at home here. Unlike most of the other large art supply houses like Flax, Pearl, etc., they focus on fine arts and secondarily on graphic arts.*

*Daniel Smith has grown from a small manufacturer of fine etching and lithographic inks to their present just described stature, without sacrificing one bit of integrity; one couldn't ask for more.*

*And they still make those wonderful inks.* — *Garta Hodge*

### Fantasy Paper #1

Handmade in Japan from kozo and sulphite pulp, Fantasy Paper represents one of the great decorative achievements in Japanese papermaking. It is a tissue weight white paper with real maple leaves embedded in the sheet. Silky fibers also decorate the sheet.

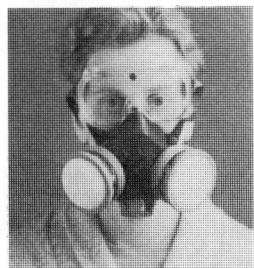

### Respirator

This professional quality tool is made by American Optical Corporation, and is recommended for use with solvents, dry pigments or in any artistic environment where high dust levels are present. It has also been approved for organic vapors, paint, lacquer and enamel mists. The mask is made of soft rubber, and although it is sized to fit all adult faces it does run big. Extra replacement cartridges and pre-filters (order one each for replacement) are available below. Remember, in respirators and safety equipment, you get the protection you pay for.

| Product Number | | Our Price |
|---|---|---|
| 9894003 | RESPIRATOR | 32.05 |
| 9894004 | Replacement Cartridge (Package of 2) | 7.87 |
| 9894005 | Replacement Filters (Package of 2) | 2.47 |

### Caran D'Ache Supracolor II

These thick-lead colored pencils are water soluble! When a drawing is complete and an aquarelle effect, or a softening is desired, the artist can brush an area with water (or the whole drawing) and colors dissolve into beautiful, soft watercolors. Besides sets, we offer open stock.

**SUPRACOLOR II**

| Product Number | List Price | Our Price |
|---|---|---|
| 6879412 12 Color Set | 8.80 | 7.95 |
| 6879418 18 Color Set | 13.20 | 12.55 |
| 6879430 30 Color Set | 21.50 | 19.35 |
| 6879440 40 Color Set | 31.00 | 27.90 |

### Daniel Smith Series 33 "Exquisite" Jumbo Hog Bristle Brushes

**SERIES 33-91 JUMBO ROUNDS**

| Product Number | Size | Our Price |
|---|---|---|
| 4630442 | 12 | 14.75 |
| 4630446 | 16 | 23.19 |
| 4630450 | 20 | 33.57 |

## Charrette

Catalog **$5** from Charrette, 31 Olympia Avenue, Woburn, MA 01888; 617/935-6010

*This is an excellent catalog for browsing — it's the most complete graphic supplier I've seen. The prices are not discounted, but Charrette carries items that are difficult to find or are simply not found in this country. My favorite items are the metal stencils from France with letters that Le Corbusier used and the Caran'd Ache Fixpencil from Switzerland that has fat leads for sketching (6B).*
— *Lawrence Kasparowitz*

▲ **Dahle Double Pocket Sharpener** Lightweight, rustproof metal block sharpener has two openings for up to 8mm and 10.5mm pencils with normal or colored leads. Silver. Mfr. No. 53485.
Item 27-0075 **$1.59**

Charrette MC-150 Scale Model Camera with Quartz Halogen Light for architects, designers, and model-makers who need to photograph scale models to aid in visualizing, rendering, and presenting design concepts. Simple-to-operate automatic camera takes instant, distortion-free photographs — in true perspective — of architectural, engineering, and other scale models, from the interior or the exterior. Small lense aperture causes everything in the scene — from 2 1/2" to infinity — to be in focus.

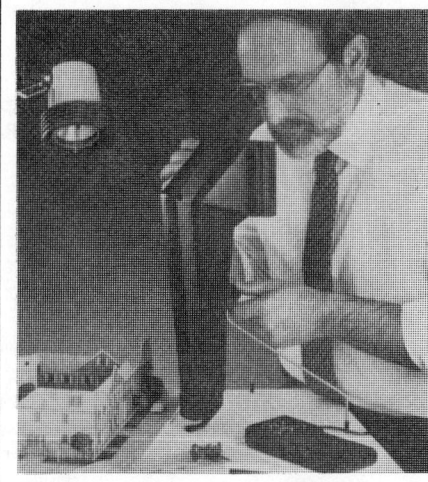

## Art Hardware

(The Definitive Guide to Artist's Materials)
Steven L. Saitzyk
1987; 326 pp.
**$19.95**
($21.95 postpaid) from:
Watson-Guptill Publications
1695 Oak Street
Lakewood, NJ 08701
201/363-4511

*Van Gogh's yellows are fading. But at the same time many other paintings in the Museum of Modern Art which were painted on cheap masonite from the lumberyard are doing okay. What materials should you use? This guy knows a lot of possibilities, and knows a lot about them.* — *KK*

◆

Artists occasionally complain about many brands [of crayons] that claim light-fastness yet seem to have a few

*Types of Hair and Bristle*

1. KOLINSKY SABLE
2. SABLE
3. NYLON
4. OX
5. SQUIRREL
6. SHEEP
7. MONGOOSE
8. HORSE
9. BADGER
10. BRISTLE

ARRANGEMENT OF HAIRS

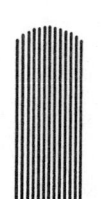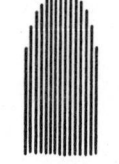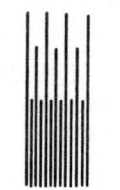

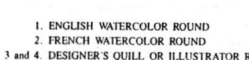

1. ENGLISH WATERCOLOR ROUND
2. FRENCH WATERCOLOR ROUND
3 and 4. DESIGNER'S QUILL OR ILLUSTRATOR ROUND
5. SPOTTING BRUSH

colors that do not hold up well over time. Consequently, I recommend that when you buy a set of crayons, you do your own test. Simply take a piece of drawing paper, preferably bristol, and apply each color so that when the paper is cut in half each sample of color will also be cut in half. Place one half in direct sunlight for several weeks and store the other half in the dark. At the end of the test put each half together and compare them. This simple test will indicate the colors to avoid.

◆

Three grades of paint seem to have developed in the United States: artist (finest, extra-fine, super-fine), amateur (fine, professional), and student. The European products that are available in the United States are often of two grades: artist and student. Many of the European student-grade paints are equivalent in quality to American amateur-grade paint.

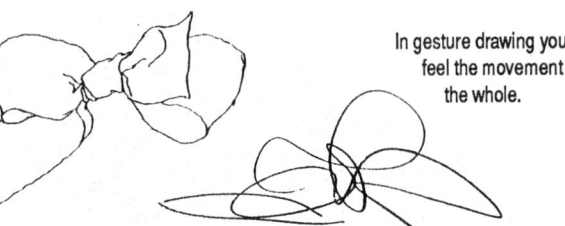

## The Natural Way to Draw

Kimon Nicolaides
1941, 1969; 221 pp.
**$8.95**
($9.95 postpaid) from:
Houghton Mifflin Co.
Mail Order Dept.
Wayside Road
Burlington, MA 01803
617/272-1500
or Whole Earth Access

*This classic work by an outstanding art teacher is not only the best how-to book on drawing, it is one of the best how-to books we've seen on any subject.*
— Stewart Brand

A gesture drawing is like scribbling rather than like printing carefully — think more of the meaning than of the way the thing looks.

◆

The sooner you make your first five thousand mistakes, the sooner you will be able to correct them.

In gesture drawing you feel the movement of the whole.

In contour drawing you touch the edge of the form.

## Drawing

(Second Edition)
Philip Rawson
1969, 1987; 322 pp.
**$17.95**
($19.90 postpaid) from:
University of Pennsylvania Press
418 Service Drive
Blockley Hall
Thirteenth Floor, Philadelphia, PA 19104-6097
215/898-6261
or Whole Earth Access

*About 15 years ago when I was a student at the Boston Museum School, I took an art history class for which this book was required reading. I was thoroughly impressed with this $5.95 book at the time. Unfortunately, I had the hots for this girl who wanted to borrow the book and swore that she'd return it. I've been looking to purchase the book ever since, but it's been out of print. The second edition is now available for $19.90 and I still think it's a good deal for the money. What Rawson does is to define a grammar of drawing, using terms which are unambiguous, and then to discuss drawing in terms of that grammar. I recommend this book because for me as an artist, the book is both an inspiration to do and an elucidation of what it is that I do. In a time when most discussion about art and the meaning thereof is mumbo jumbo at best, Drawing by Philip Rawson is a breath of fresh air.*
— Jonathan Herbert

◆

We know that Rembrandt used to teach his pupils by getting them to copy, stroke for stroke, his own drawings. In this excellent fashion they would absorb the master's own way of scanning the world and his own vocabulary of graphic forms. Raphael and Primaticcio copied drawings by Leonardo. On the whole, however, this kind of drawing has not been done nearly so extensively in Europe as in the Far East. In the Far East, however, a greater conscious emphasis was laid on capturing the "spirit of the forms." Good copies of masterpieces, either close or free, were very highly valued, even when the copyists were not themselves major masters — so long as they captured something of the spirit of the original. It is still very much an open question how many of the much admired drawings attributed to major artists of the Southern Sung dynasty are "originals" or inspired copies.

## Drawing on the Right Side of the Brain

Betty Edwards
1979; 207 pp.
**$9.95**
($11.20 postpaid) from:
St. Martin's Press
175 5th Avenue
New York, NY 10010
212/674-5151
or Whole Earth Access

## Drawing on the Artist Within

Betty Edwards
1986; 240 pp.
**$18.95** postpaid from:
Simon and Schuster
Mail Order Sales
200 Old Tappan Road, Old Tappan, NJ 07675
800/223-2336
or Whole Earth Access

If you've always wanted to draw, but lacked the "talent," Betty Edwards' simple exercises can help you turn your stick figures into real drawings. **Drawing on the Right Side of the Brain** gives the basics on how to see and how to put what you see onto paper.

Once you've learned to draw what you can see you'll want to draw what you can imagine. Edwards' second book, **Drawing on the Artist Within,** helps you add expressiveness and innovation, turning your drawing into art.
— Kathleen O'Neill

A casual observer viewing R.F.'s three drawings might conclude that he had "learned to draw" in the three weeks. But that wasn't it at all: R.F. had learned to *see* "differently" — that is, to "see" information which was out there all the time, but which was at first simply rejected because of quick closure and premature, preprogrammed conclusions.
— *Drawing on the Artist Within*

Fig. 7-17.

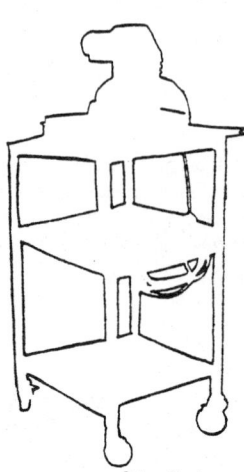

Robert Dominguez

In the first drawing, the student had great difficulty reconciling his stored knowledge of what the objects were "supposed to look like" with what he saw. Notice in the drawing that the legs of the cart are all the same length, and a symbol is used for the wheels. When he switched to R-mode drawing, using a viewfinder and drawing only the shapes of the negative spaces, he was far more successful. The visual information apparently came through clearly; the drawing looks confident and as though it were done with ease. And, in fact, it was done with ease, because the left hemisphere had been tricked into keeping quiet.
— *Drawing on the Right Side of the Brain*

Inverted drawing. Forcing the cognitive shift from the dominant left-hemisphere mode to the subdominant right-hemisphere mode.

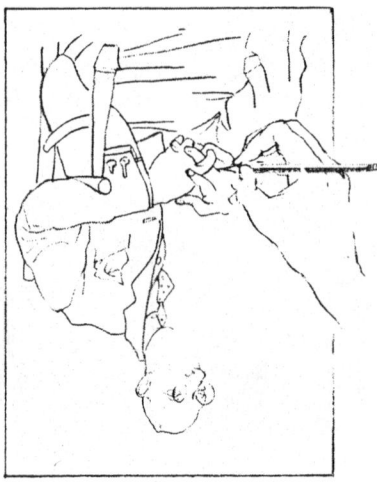

— *Drawing on the Right Side of the Brain*

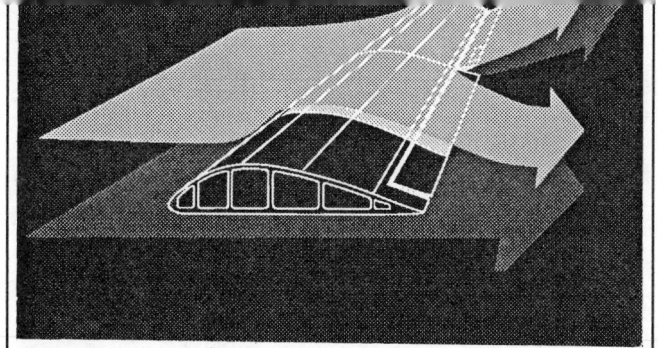

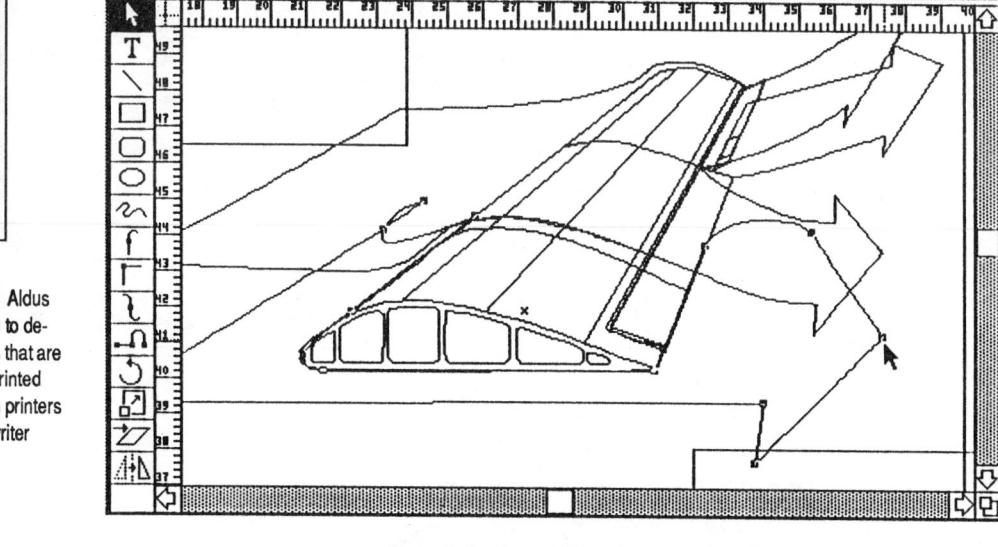

## Canvas

Version 1.0; not copy-protected. Macintosh 512K required. Laserwriter suggested. $195 (list price) from Deneba Software, 7855 NW 12th Street, Suite 202, Miami, FL 33126; 305/594-6965

## Aldus FreeHand

Version 1.0; not copy-protected, Macintosh Plus and external drive recommended. Laserwriter suggested. $495 (list price) from Aldus Corporation, 411 First Avenue South, Suite 200, Seattle, WA 98104; 206/622-5500

[Above and to the right] Aldus Free-Hand enables you to develop complex graphics that are tightly rendered when printed out on Postscript-driven printers such as Apple's Laserwriter series.

*As in most areas of software, computer drawing programs are constantly being made obsolete by competitors or by later updates of themselves. Thus Fullpaint fulfilled MacPaint's potential, only to be aced out by Superpaint's wider abilities. All these Macintosh drawing programs have, in turn, been quietly topped by Canvas from Deneba Software. This painting program lets you combine both bit-mapped and object-based art in the same drawing, with able access to laser fonts as well. Because its drawing tools are extensive and basic Bezier curves are included in its repertoire, I've often turned to Canvas to crank out simple designs that would take more sweat and tears to produce in Postscript-based drawing programs like Adobe Illustrator or Aldus FreeHand.*

*On the other hand, if you are a design professional utilizing the Mac for high-level design, Canvas is not going to do all the tricks you require. Aldus FreeHand provides sophisticated control over Bezier curves and type manipulation (including kerning), up to 200 drawing layers, plus "graduated" and "radial" fills and other special effects, and can save the art produced as an encapsulated Postscript file for use in other programs like PageMaker. Perhaps most notable, it has a "freehand" drawing tool which lets you draw shapes and lines that are then rendered into maneuverable bezier curves, a boon if you are drawing on screen from scratch. Truth to tell, bezier curves are one of the more maddening inventions around — rather like trying to use french curves made out of writhing snakes. Since Bezier curves lie at the heart of the Postscript language's high-resolution capabilities, there's no escaping them in Mac graphics programs like this. FreeHand has a set of drawing tools that embody a relatively smooth approach to the problem, although they are not as much of an advance in ease of use over those of its closest rival Adobe Illustrator as I had originally hoped.*

*Of course, as I write, a new upgrade of Illustrator has just appeared with some features that top FreeHand, while a powerful new version of Canvas was due to appear in July 1988. In the world of software only one thing is certain: No one stays ahead of the pack for long. As this week's Mac graphics powerhouses, Canvas and FreeHand are excellent programs. Tomorrow may hold new surprises.*

— *Jay Kinney*

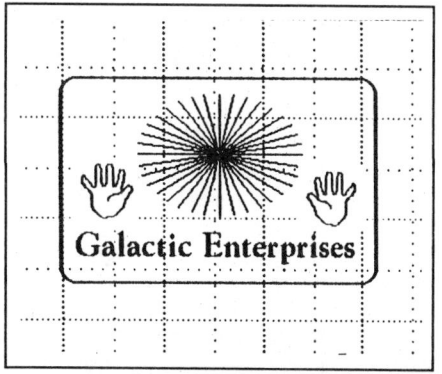

Canvas's forte is combining bitmapped and object-oriented graphic elements in the same drawing or design. Bitmapped graphics take what you draw on the screen and reproduce the image dot by dot (actually square by square) on the print-out. There's no limit to the form, but it can print out with rough, stair-stepped edges. Object-oriented graphics are produced by constructing images with mathematical curves or forms produced by complex algorithms, somewhat like beginning the sketch of a mouse with three circles. This more troublesome method produces seamless, fine-edged print-outs. In the exercise pictured, left the hands are bitmapped, while the star burst and rectangle are object-oriented. In other programs these two kinds could not be merged onto one graphic plane. Grids on the background don't print out; you can set up guidelines and then have your image lines "snap" to the nearest ones if you want to create a regular pattern. The Arabic border was produced using Canvas's smooth Bezier curves and then replicated easily.

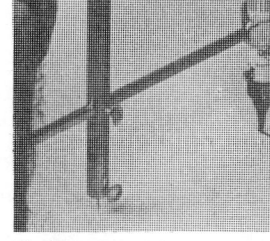

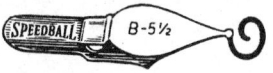
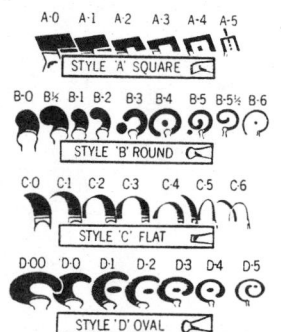
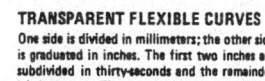

## The Algorithmic Image

(Graphic Visions of
the Computer Age)
Robert Rivlin
1986; 284 pp.
**$24.95**
($27.45 postpaid) from:
Microsoft Press
P.O. Box 1532
Hagerstown, MD 21741
800/638-3030
or Whole Earth Access

*The first (and only) book about computer graphics, in its myriad marvelous forms, which non-technical people can follow — not just to look awestruck at the pictures, but to understand the conceptual underpinnings behind them. Books like this, **Programmers at Work,** and **Computer Lib/Dream Machines** are making Microsoft Press the pre-eminent quality computer book publisher.*

*— Art Kleiner*

## Fundamentals of Interactive Computer Graphics

J.D. Foley & A. Van Dam
1982; 6664 pp.
**$48.50** postpaid from:
Addison-Wesley
Publishing Co. Inc.
1 Jacob Way
Reading, MA 01867
800/447-2226
or Whole Earth Access

*The art of making other people's tools is a high calling. This textbook is for those with the craving to not merely use computer graphic programs, but to create better ones. The fundamental software concepts and examples of code are laid out in abundance.*

*—Kevin Kelly*

◆

**Stylized tricycle with three coordinate systems.** As the bike moves forward, the front wheel rotates about the $z$ axis of the wheel coordinate system, while simultaneously the wheel and tricycle coordinate systems move relative to the world coordinate system. The wheel and tricycle coordinate systems are related to the world coordinate system by time-varying translations in $x$ and $y$ plus a rotation about $y$. The tricycle and wheel coordinate systems are related to each other by a time-varying rotation about $y$ as the handlebars are turned. (The tricycle coordinate system is fixed to the frame, not to the handlebars.)

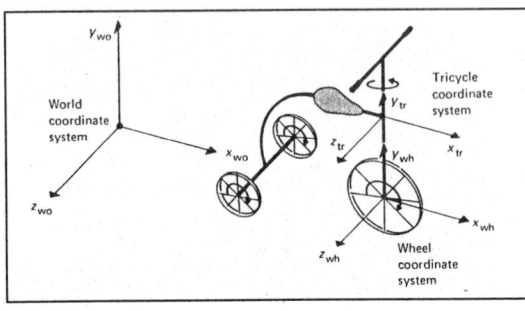

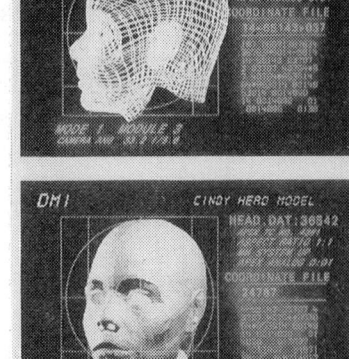
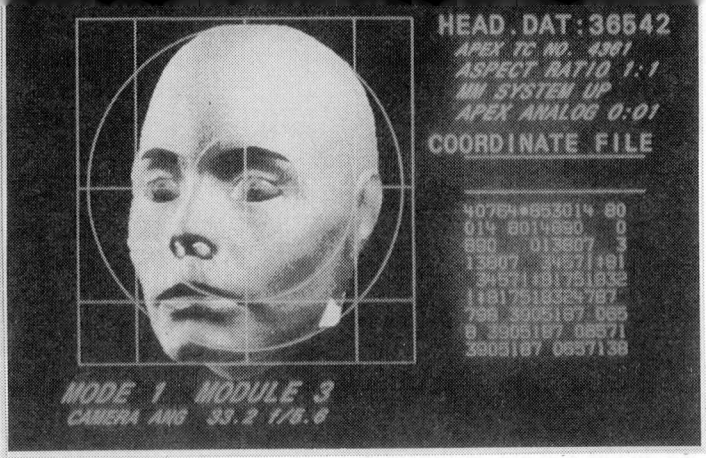

Information International Inc. (Triple-I) produced some digital effects for the movie Futureworld, which led to the job of creating extensive effects sequences for Michael Crichton's film *Looker*. In the movie, the actress Susan Dey is digitized and transformed into a computer database that can be used to simulate her form for use in political-campaign commercials. The process of creating the computer simulations for the movie were remarkably similar to the fictional digitizing process in the movie script. The actress was painted with a grid of lines and then photographed. The grid lines were traced into the computer, and then used as a guide to construct a polygon mesh. The mesh was then rendered using conventional polygon techniques, including smooth shading.

◆

For the artist, a three-dimensional object or landscape portrayed on a two-dimensional surface merely has to look real. But a model in the computer database must, for all intents and purposes, actually simulate the properties of a three-dimensional object in nature. The single view of an object in a painting or drawing is not enough for an interactive three-dimensional computer-graphics display, which must allow a view of any part of the object, front or back, top or bottom, from any viewing angle in a 360-degree sphere around the object.

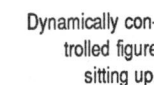

Norm Badler and Stephen Platt produced this series of wire-frame faces, which illustrate the analysis and synthesis of human facial expressions.

## Computer Graphics World

$30/12 issues from Computer Graphics World, P.O. Box 122, Tulsa, OK 74101; 800/331-4463.

*A cozy spot to watch the future erupt. Non-technical, out-in-front, colorful, especially of interest to those in the business (you are in the business of alternative realities, aren't you?), this trade magazine gives good vibes to computers. I'm in it for the pictures.*

*— Kevin Kelly*

By controlling the mix of chaos and order in noisy images, artists can create textures resembling wood grains, rug weavings, and even watermelons.

Dynamically con-
trolled figure
sitting up.

## IEEE Computer Graphics and Applications

$58/12 issues
(includes
membership in
the Computer
Society of the
Institute of
Electrical and
Electronics
Engineers, Inc.)
from:
Computer Society
of the IEEE,
10662 Los
Vaqueros Circle,
Los Alamitos, CA
90720-2578; 714/
821-8380.

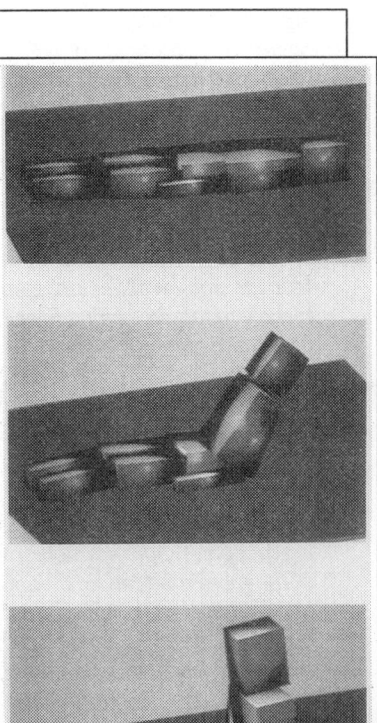

*The on-going technical bulletin where the graphic hackers hang out and show off their latest demos.*

*—Kevin Kelly*
*[Suggested by Eric Haines]*

## Desktop Special Effects

### by Kevin Kelly

THERE ARE SEVERAL low-rent computer graphic special effects methods. The rough and ready way is to hook up a personal computer to VCR. Create the graphics on the computer and have the VCR tape it. The only personal computer that will do that hassle-free is the Amiga computer (about $700). Its claim to fame (otherwise it's an okay computer without much software to run on it) is that it is a low-price color computer that generates signals that are NTSC compatible, which means that you can plug it directly into TV equipment.

Because of this unique clean connection, the Amiga is used by small community TV stations to produce very simple special effects and captions on the TV screen. The quality of the effects is not up to "network broadcast" but will certainly suffice for many needs. It's perfect for do-it-yourself documentaries, and such things as corporate and industrial training videos where information rather than style counts. Its roughness can also be used creatively. The Amiga was employed extensively in the production of *Max Headroom*, and a few syndicated TV series like *Secrets and Mysteries of the Universe*, and *Amazing Stories*.

A main component in this setup is some nifty software from Electronic Arts called Deluxe Video. It provides elemental animating functions. The results are nothing to marvel at, but are adequate for basic projects.

Another way to get computer graphics onto video is by purchasing an add-on

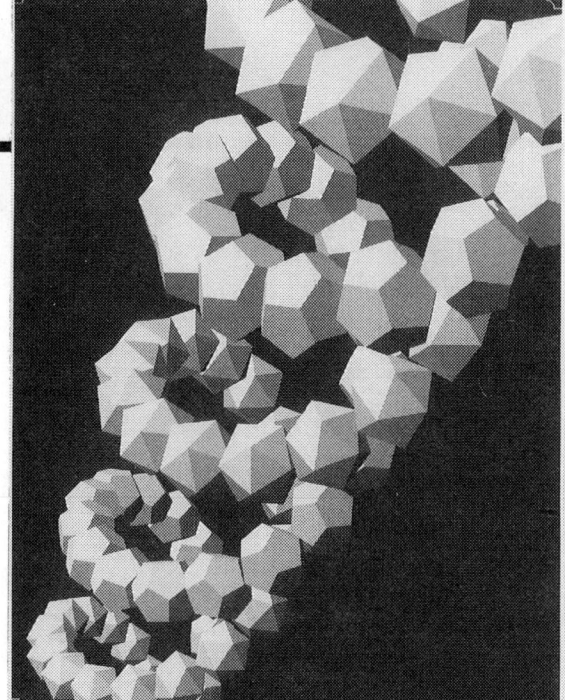

Helix (Tony Smith)

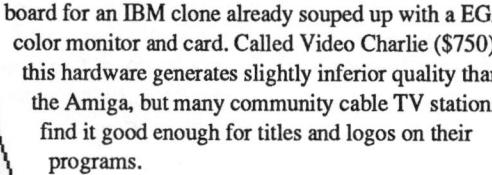

Max Headroom on an Amiga.

board for an IBM clone already souped up with a EGA color monitor and card. Called Video Charlie ($750), this hardware generates slightly inferior quality than the Amiga, but many community cable TV stations find it good enough for titles and logos on their programs.

**Amiga 500, $700.** For a dealer near you, call: Commodore Business Machines; 800/436-4200.

**Deluxe Video**, version 1.2 for the Amiga, $130 ($133 postpaid) from: Electronic Arts, P. O. Box 7530, San Mateo, CA 94403; 800/245-4525.

**Video Charlie, $750** ($760 postpaid) from: Progressive Image Technologies, 322 E. Bidwell, Folsom, CA 95630; 916/985-7501.

### VERBUM

Michael Gosney, Editor
$28/4 issues from:
Verbum Subscriptions
P. O. Box 15439
San Diego, CA 92115
619/463-9977

*Remember the sort of graphics you fantasized would be possible when you first heard of personal computers? They can finally be done. Artists are grabbing the cursor and spawning a distinct design sense, which this classy journal explores. "It looks like computer art" is the first thing you are cured of.* —Kevin Kelly

Easter 5 (David Brunn).

---

## Zen & The Art of the Macintosh

(Discoveries on the Path to Computer Enlightenment)
Michael Green
1986; 236 pp.
**$16.95**
($18.30 postpaid) from:
Running Press
125 S. 22nd Street
Philadelphia, PA 19102
800/428-1111
or Whole Earth Access

CLEARLY, A BOOK ABOUT THE CREATIVE POSSIBILITIES OF THE MAC...
A KIND OF EXTENDED GRAPHIC SAFARI EXPLORING THE FURTHEST REACHES OF MACPAINT, AND ITS POTENTIAL TO OPEN UP NEW TERRITORY.

*When Gutenberg invented moveable type, he found strong resistance to it among the current publishing experts— medieval monks transcribing the Bible. It seemed that what the monks most objected to was that his innovation removed the cursive strokes that connected letters within one word, breaking up the calligraphy and also separating writing from illustration. What Michael Green has done in this picture book is to pioneer the return to a unified graphic in which the artist creates both the typography and the illustration. The meditating Macintosh is the pen for this electronic manifesto. It promises a change in publication design.* — Kevin Kelly

## AutoCAD

**$300-$2,750** from: Autodesk, Inc., 2320 Marinship Way, Sausalito, CA 94965; 415/331-0356

*Ideal uses for computer graphics: jobs that demand constant alterations, pictures constructed with numerical precision, and designs that make use of repeating patterns.*

*The best computer aided design (CAD) program for personal computers: AutoCAD.*

*One typical application for this well-proven program would be to render a manufacturing sketch of windmill, down to the thousandths of a inch. Or draw a project assembled out of standard components. Then when you are just about finished, amend the whole drawing, re-sizing it where needed, to fit a substituted smaller part. Ughhh. Get me my computer slave.*

*Or computer genii. The newest increment of AutoCAD (Release10) elevates it to the status of Master Draftsman. Fully powered with 3D rotation, it can draw with bewitched perspective. It lets you rapidly depict convoluted objects from various angles at engineer precision, a chore that is torturous punishment with pencils. Weird machine parts,*

*ornate architecture, complexly layered floor plans. CAD programs in general, and AutoCAD in particular, are so uncannily articulate that I would use them as an imagining tool alone.*

*AutoCAD has endeared itself to legions of professional engineers and architects because it can be clothed in one of thousands of specialized templates. These guild templates tailor AutoCAD's talents to a specific task, say plotting the layout of the electrical system in a factory, or designing toothed gears. Techies love these "vertical applications" because they short-cut a lot of the grunt work of design, redesign, redesign.*

*This program ain't cheap. It's $3,000 for the Macin-*

A client's residence drawn by a Chicago architecture firm, using AutoCAD.

*tosh II, or IBM PC versions (you'll need a hard disk and supercharging). But it is a true tool. It moves you from can't to can.*

*— Kevin Kelly*

## CADENCE

Dave Baceski, ed., **$34.95**/yr. (12 issues) from Ariel Communications, 12710 Research Blvd.,Suite 250, Austin, TX 78759; 512/250-1700

## The CAD/CAM Journal

Shawn Hopwood, ed., **$20**/yr. (6 issues) from Koncepts Graphic Images Inc., 16 Beaver Street, New York, NY 10004; 212/425-4441

*Periodicals, not books, are where you keep up with stones rolling downhill as fast as computer assisted design is. As is often the case in truly vanguard fields, the advertisements can be more useful than whimpy editorial filler, which is mostly what is in these two.*

*CAD/CAM is "For The Macintosh Professional". That last word will give you an idea of where their heart is— corporations. But the Mac is where you want to be as it takes over the design field, particu-*

*larly in the small shop. CADENCE is for "Using AutoCAD in the Professional Environment". There's that word again. This is the best rendezvous point to meet up with hundreds of specialized AutoCAD applications and user groups thereof. The real power of AutoCAD is in these user-developed templates, and in the practical stories of how "professionals" converted to the true-belief of small computer CAD.*
*— Kevin Kelly*

Douglas Electronic's new package *Professional Layout* assists electrical engineers design the ever-increasingly complex layouts of printed circuit boards. Wiring the connections is mind-boggling complicated. *Professional Layout* implements an autorouting procedure. This example shows a file that is 85% complete. The autoroute pass will stop when it is 91% complete, about the best a machine can do. The engineer will have to figure out the rest. **— The CAD/CAM Journal**

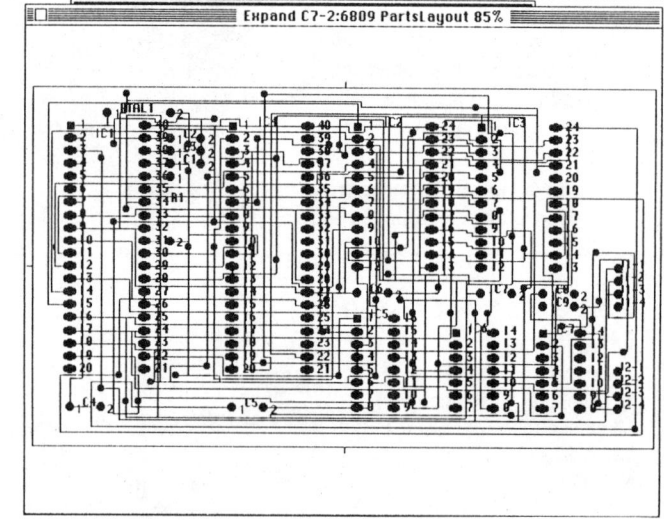

## Generic CADD

**$99.95** to **$345.95** for IBM or compatibles, 512K, graphics card, mouse needed. Hard disk, color monitor, math coprocessor recommended. From Generic Software, 8763 148th Ave. N.E., Redmond, WA 98052; 206/885-5307

*The brown paper bag version of CAD. While its abbreviated capabilities are impressive, and cheap, it still needs the expensive add ons (graphic card and mouse) high price spreads need. Generic CADD comes in ascending grades. The plainest ($100) is not much more than a fancy drafting program. Level 3 ($200) will get you through respectably complicated*

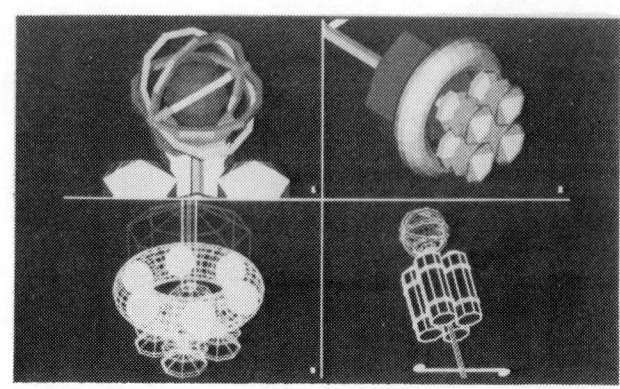

*floor plans. Generic CADD 3•D ($350) brings you three dimensional modelling and surface shading if you try extra hard (the manual doesn't help much). It's price doesn't seem low-rent until you compare it to $3,000. What you get is your basic peanut butter and jelly CADD — no frills, no promises, take it or leave it.*
*— Kevin Kelly*

Generic 3.D Solids is a true 3-Dimensional modeler which defines solids through faces, vertices, and edges. This method is inherently more powerful than other approaches. Even if you are new to 3.D drawing, you can produce intricate solid or wireframe models.

# Digital Retouching

*by Stewart Brand*

**Time** magazine does it. **USA Today** does it. **National Geographic** does it and has caught some flak about it. Very soon nearly everyone will do it, and the culture will be different as a result.

They all use high-tech page makeup processes that involve turning photographs into computer data, where it is so easy to fiddle with the images that the temptation is overwhelming. This new capability comes from the merging of laser technology, used to scan the original photographs and convert them into digital data, and computer technology, whose increasing power at decreasing cost allows sophisticated manipulation of the no-longer-photographic image.

**National Geographic** moved one of the pyramids of Giza to suit their cover design. **Popular Science** put an airplane from one photo onto the background of another photo on one of their covers and then bragged about how they did it inside the magazine. In a book of photographs of France, the photographer moved unsightly telephone poles from the picture of a Basque shepherd. The **Whole Earth Review**, in questionable taste, appealed to mass credulity with a completely phony "photograph" of flying saucers on its cover.

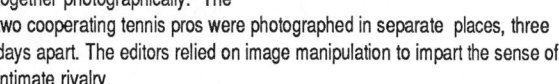

NOW YOU SEE THEM.

NOW YOU DON'T.

Two things not apparent in this promotional demonstration for Pacific Lithographic: First, this set is one photograph, not two in sequence; and second, the magic is not a disappearing show, but a reappearing act. The camera's film captured the intricate grain of the scene: four hikers against distant mountains. It was then digitized. Clicking on the cloning option on the Chromacom machine, two cursors appear in the picture about an inch apart. The operator can vary that distance, and slide the duo anywhere on the photograph. One cursor will copy the color of the point it rests on over to the nearby cursor. Waving the cursor copies a patch of color. Identical in color and brightness, the texture of the adjacent area is replicated point by point in a new spot. Distinctive patterns are copied exactly. Thus the people standing in the picture were not beamed out of the scene; rather they were washed over with sky and mountain paint, stolen nearby. Closing the distance between cursors results in ever-finer degrees of seamlessness. Done with skill (it is almost a routine operation; the main thing to watch for is incestuously cloning what has already been cloned once), the phoniness is completely convincing.

This is a total fake. This particular can of Comet was never photographed. It was never in a studio. It never existed. Taking digital retouching to the extreme, Alan Green and C. Robert Hoffman III, two animators for Digital Effects in New York City, added tinselly gleams and reflections to a computer-generated image fabricated from equations. Retouching a phantom, starting from nothing.

These two famous athletes didn't really meet back to back. To convey the competition between tennis champions Bjorn Borg and John McEnroe, **World Tennis** magazine arranged to portray them in an eighteenth-century duel on the magazine's March 1981 cover. Susan B. Adams, explaining on the editor's page of that issue how the cover was shot, said, "Finding a simultaneous hour in the hectic lives of the world's best tennis players. . . proved the most frustrating detail. As it turned out, we failed. With deadlines staring us bleakly in the face, we'd have to put them together photographically." The two cooperating tennis pros were photographed in separate places, three days apart. The editors relied on image manipulation to impart the sense of intimate rivalry.

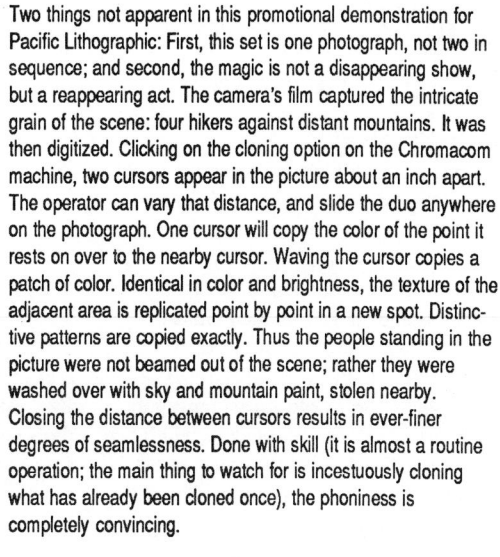

It's advertising that has paid for computer digitizing machines. Color catalogs use them all the time to alter a product's color, enhance its shininess, tone down its shininess, remove blemishes. Art directors use them to accomplish what photographers couldn't or didn't do. And, according to an operator of the Chromacom, who has sat through more than one quarrel, ad agencies use the imaging computers as arenas for battling out their visual fantasies. Bausch & Lomb Sunglasses used the Scitex to insert models into an old WWII photo and alter a few other details to their liking.

---

# HANDS - ON DIGITAL RETOUCHING

*by Barbara Robertson*

In 1985, AT&T's EPICenter (Electronic Picture and Imaging Center) introduced the first graphics board in its price range for a microcomputer that 1) captures and digitizes video images in real time; 2) displays images with enough colors to simulate a video picture in video resolution; 3) generates a standard NTSC video signal (which means TARGA pictures can be transferred to videotape and broadcast on American television); and 4) allows an incoming analog signal to be mixed onscreen with the digital picture (genlock).

AT&T also sells a painting package, TIPS, developed by Island Graphics specifically for ths board. Although other software companies offer painting packages for the TARGA 16, TIPS, is still the lowest priced and the best value.

With the TARGA 16 and TIPS system, live video can be mixed with an onscreen digital image and the composite digitized; brushes can paint with any pattern selected from the screen; selected areas on the screen can be instantly filled with color and patterns, cut and pasted, or flipped and rotated. Yet the system is remarkably easy to use.

Artists who can afford the system would find it a good conceptual tool and may find the images acceptable for some purposes. But the system's primary, application is for people who want to quickly modify reality to show how things would look "if" — architects, landscapers, interior designers, plastic surgeons, etc. The output is not photographic quality, but to create the same altered, yet nearly photographic, view of reality using any other means would be tedious if not impossible.

**Targa 16:** 512 x 512 resolution, 32,768 simultaneous colors, frame grabber and buffer, captures video in 1/60th second, NTSC and Analog RGB output, **$1995**; TIPS software, **$795**. Requires IBM PC/XT/AT or compatible; TV set, composite video or analog RGB monitor; TIPS requires Summagraphic digitizing tablet, MS-DOS 2.0 or higher; both from: AT&T's EPICenter, 2002 Wellesley Boulevard, Indianapolis, IN 46219; 800/858-8783

# Caution: Adults Reading Comics

*by Richard Kadrey*

Orange juice isn't just for breakfast anymore, and comics aren't just for kids. Actually, they haven't been for some time, but most adults still seem to regard books with word balloons as a vaguely embarrassing habit from their childhoods, like picking their noses and socking girls in the arm. The comics on this page will probably appeal mostly to adults (which doesn't mean kids won't like them; they'll just like them differently). What's different about an "adult" comic, as opposed to a "kid's"? The ideas are often a little more complex; sex and moral ambiguity are often present. Themes are resolved in a more open-ended manner. In other words, comics aren't just escapism anymore, either. Real life has settled in quite nicely with the wholesome hippies in **Omaha,** and **Love and Rockets'** punk chicanas. About time, too.

— American Splendor

AND THE STRUGGLE CONTINUES...

— Itchy Planet

## Fantagraphics Books
Catalog **free**: 1800 Bridgegate, Suite #101, Westlake Village, CA 91361

## Love and Rockets
From Fantagraphics
*Arguably the finest regular comic now being published. Written and drawn by the Hernandez brothers, **Love and Rockets** combines classic comic art with scripts worthy of Gabriel Garcia Marquez. Plus it has the best female characters in comics today. Seek this one out!* — Jay Kinney

## Itchy Planet
From Fantagraphics
*Serious and funny at the same time. Cartoonists like Larry Gonick, Norman Dog, Michael Dougan, and Leonard Rifas examine nuclear war, AIDS, electoral horrors, etc.* — Richard Kadrey

## Comics Journal
$35/year; 12 issues from Fantagraphics
*The only essential journal of news and criticism for the comics industry. Good coverage of both mainstream and alternative comics and creators.*
— Jay Kinney

## "Omaha" The Cat Dancer
Information **free** from: Kitchen Sink Comix, 2 Swamp Road, Princeton, WI 54968
*Funny animal comics for adults. The stories of Omaha and her friends day-to-day healthy-hippie lives. Entertaining and frequently erotic.* — Richard Kadrey

## Lone Wolf and Cub
Information **free** from: First Comics, 435 N. LaSalle, Chicago, IL 60610
*The continuing adventures of the ronin, Lone Wolf, and his infant son, Cub, in medieval Japan. Well drawn and written, and the stories sometimes provide unexpected insights into Japanese mores.* — Richard Kadrey

## The Phoenix Restaurant
$4.50 postpaid from: Fandom House, P. O. Box 1348, Denver, CO 80201
*The sequel to Ferret's **Neo-Canton Legacy** is another of his surreal tales starring the Neo-Canton Guy; this time the story concerns giant insects, annoying mutations, suicide and the problems of running a really high-class restaurant after a nuclear war.*
— Richard Kadrey

## Eddy Current
Information **free** from: Mad Dog Graphics, P. O. Box 931686, Hollywood, CA 90093
*One night in the life of Eddy Current, mental patient and, with the aid of his mail-order "Dynamic Fusion" suit, super hero. A limited series that should be out as a graphic novel by the time you're reading this.* — Richard Kadrey

## American Splendor
Information **free** with SASE from: Harvey Pekar, P. O. Box 18471, Cleveland Heights, OH 44118
*Harvey has been chronicling his "ordinary" life in Cleveland for years now. He writes the strips and hires a variety of cartoonists to illustrate them. All true, all deadpan, always entertaining.*
— Jay Kinney

## Raw Magazine
Flyer **free** from: Raw Books, 27 Greene Street, New York, NY 10013
*Giant-format comics-as-art magazine, edited by Art Spiegelman and Francoise Mouly. Exquisitely designed.*
— Jay Kinney

## Maus (A Survivor's Tale)
*A personal tale of the Holocaust uses animals to represent people, but don't be fooled. This is serious, adult material. Although, parts of the comic appeared in* **Raw** *magazine, this beautiful trade paperback is published by Pantheon Books ($8.95).* — Richard Kadrey

## Those Annoying Post Brothers
Information **free** with SASE from: Vortex Comics, 367 Queen Street West, Toronto, Ontario, Canada M5V 2A4
*Ron and Russ Post are existential bad boys with the ability to shift into alternate universes. If Sartre had written **Batman,** this is what it might have looked like.*
— Richard Kadrey

— Maus

"Omaha" The Cat Dancer

— The Phoenix Restaurant

— Eddy Current

— Love and Rockets

— Raw Magazine

## The Santa Cruz Comic News

Thom Zajac, Publisher
$12/year (24 issues) from:
Comic News Subs, P. O. Box 8543, Santa Cruz, CA 95061; 408/426-0113

*If you're one of those people who buys the paper everyday just check out the comics and then feels guilty because you only skim the front page, take heart.* **The Santa Cruz Comics Journal** *gives you all the funnies and none of the guilt. No*

news here, just funny drawings and jokes, from the political cartoons of Conrad and Oliphant to Jules Feiffer's social satire to **The Far Side** and **Calvin and Hobbes**. The rest of the paper is ads for businesses in Santa Cruz, California. These are easily ignored, even if you live in Santa Cruz. 　　　　　— Richard Kadrey

Another unsubstantiated photograph of the Loch Ness monster (taken by Reuben Hicks, 5/24/84, Chicago).

— Lone Wolf and Cub

— Those Annoying Post Brothers

## Target

(The Political Cartoon Quarterly)
Richard Samuel West, Editor
$15/year (4 issues) from:
Target, 461 Sharon Drive, Wayne, PA 19087

*One of the most effective political tools is the cartoon. This quarterly promotes the art of graphic comment by shining a small spotlight on the greats of the past and on younger newspaper cartoonists. However, by focussing on those in traditional newspapers, those working in smaller-circulation papers, and mags — where there's more innovation and idiosyncrasy — are slighted.*
　　　　　— Robert Horvitz

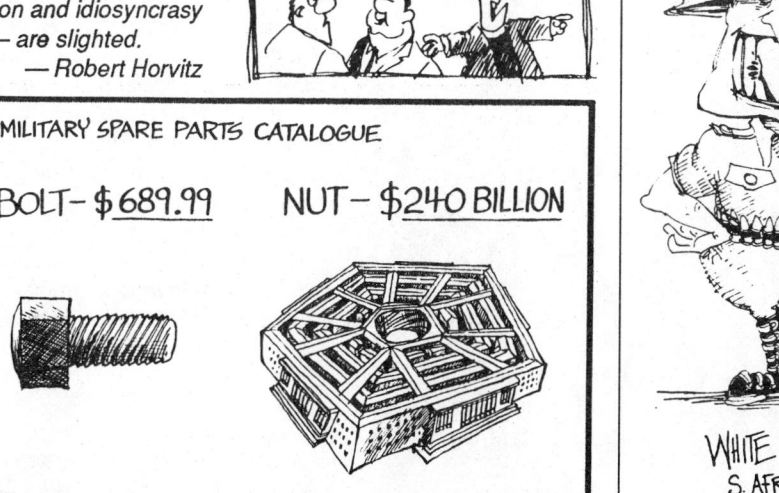

WHITE MAN
S. AFRICA

## Visual Anthropology

(Photography as
a Research Method)
John Collier, Jr.
and Malcolm Collier
1986; 248 pp.
**$14.95**
($15.95 postpaid) from:
University of
New Mexico Press
220 Journalism Building
Albuquerque, NM 87131
505/277-4810

The great 19th-century American photographer Matthew Brady felt he was morally obligated to record for the future the events, places, and people of his time. Since Brady's time, with the exception of the Roosevelt administration's documentation of the Great Depression, the public face of photography has shown more consistent attention to aesthetic achievement.

Brady's plea for recording has been answered by the Colliers, who show how. For the anthropologist, geographer, or sociologist, the authors present the photograph (film and video are also thoroughly discussed) as a rich source of both qualitative and quantitative information about human behavior and culture.

As a photographer, I was struck by the methodology of "interviewing with photographs," in which photographs are cycled back to their subjects, who are asked to interpret and expand on what is going on in the picture.

Surely broadening for the photographer as well as a valuable tool for the social scientist.
—Don Ryan

◆

When Siegel carried out interviews using the photographs, to our amazement, only cursory comments were made on the deer dance; "We just do that for the Spanish people. . . ." But when the photographs showed the crowd moving down the hill to the foot race the interview tone changed; "Now the solemn time begins. . ." and intense commentary followed. Running was more of a central ceremonial mystique than the elaborate deer dance. This revelation suggested changes in classical beliefs regarding ceremonialism at both Picuris and its larger neighbor, Taos Pueblo. Both had excelled, historically, in long-distance running, but it was the drama and pageantry of the deer dance that had always captivated the attention of outside observers in the past.

◆

Photographer Jim Goldberg urged people to write comments on their photographs in a unique form of informal feedback and interview. His initial work . . . was with poverty-stricken people in San Francisco's Tenderloin district whose comments often produced profound viewpoints on their lives.

Goldberg extended his photographic efforts to more affluent subjects. The wealthy were as responsive as the poor in projectively revealing the aspirations, joys, and psychological hardships of their lives.

This picture says that WE ARE a VERY Emotional & tight family, like the three Musketeers.

Poverty sucks, but it brings us closer together. *Linda Banks*

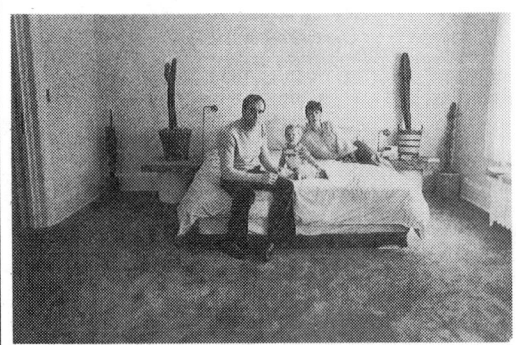

We are a contemporary family. We don't want to be part of the masses. We want to live with style! *JoAnn Roberts*

---

## Second View

(The Rephotographic
Survey Project)
Mark Klett,
Chief Photographer
1984; 221 pp.
**$65** ($66.50 postpaid)
from University of
New Mexico Press
220 Journalism
Building Albuquerque,
NM 87131; 505/277-4810

A book that justifies having a coffee table, a book that will grow in value with the decades. The subject is time. The method is "rephotography" — the exact reshooting of historic photographs with modern research and camera work. The effect: you learn to feel and observe like a mountainside.

At first I was disappointed that the modern photographers chose 120 government survey photographs of the 1870s and 1880s to work with — Timothy O'Sullivan, William Henry Jackson, etc. — since their images were so dominantly, and magnificently, geological. I though more ephemeral subjects would be more revealing — cityscapes, farmland, and such. But in a century obsessed with change, it is lovely to see change put in its place. **Second View** teaches respect for rocks, disrespect for human projects.

And it introduces rephotography as an astonishing technique for insight into place. Try it in your place.
—Stewart Brand

William Henry Jackson, ca. 1880. Devil's Slide, Weber Canyon, Utah (Amon Carter Museum). (Right) Mark Klett for the Rephotographic Survey Project 1978, Devil's Slide, Weber Canyon, Utah.

A mathematical technique for checking the accuracy of a new vantage point.

(Above) Timothy O'Sullivan, 1867. Rock formations, Pyramid Lake, Nev. (M.I.T.) (Below) Mark Klett for the Rephotographic Survey Project, 1979. Pyramid Isle, Pyramid Lake, Nev.

38. woman of Nuremberg [ca. 1500]
39. shoulder cape
40. Burgundian [15th Cent.]
41. short doublet
42. piked shoes (peaked shoes, copped shoes crackowes, poulaines)

### The Oxford-Duden Pictorial English Dictionary
John Pheby, Editor
1984; 820 pp.
**$14.95**
($18.95 postpaid) from:
Oxford University Press
Attn: Order Department
16-00 Pollitt Drive
Fairlawn, NJ 07410
201/796-8000
or Whole Earth Access

*A useful book that proceeds from the premise that you may not know the name of something but you can certainly know*

*what it looks like. If you are wondering what to call those pointy shoes Renaissance men wore, you look up a page illustrating costumes and find that the name is crackowes. That a hat with brim turned up to form three sides is a tricorn. That an aglet is the plastic tip of a shoelace.*

—Joseph Hold

*This is a* British *visual dictionary with British terminology. Americans may find* **Facts on File Visual Dictionary** *and* **What's What** *more useful.*

—Sarah Vandershaf

### What's What
Reginald Bragonier, Jr. and David Fisher, Editors
1981; 565 pp.
**$9.95**
($10.95 postpaid) from:
Random House
400 Hahn Road
Westminster, MD 21157
800/638-6460
or Whole Earth Access

*In 1981, the* **Oxford-Duden Pictorial English Dictionary** *created a new type of reference book. If you couldn't think of the name of a commonplace or technical object, but knew what it looked like,*

### Facts on File Visual Dictionary
Jean-Claude Corbeil
1986; 797 pp.
**$29.95**
($31.45 postpaid) from:
Facts on File
460 Park Avenue South
New York, NY 10016
212/683-2244
or Whole Earth Access

*you could look up its picture and get its name — sort of like a field guide to modern life. Now there are two superior predators in this literary niche. Where the original* **Oxford-Duden** *uses an un-*

*wieldy numbering system to link its words and pictures, these two,* **Facts on File** *and* **What's What**, *use direct pointer-type labels.*

*Which to get?* **Facts on File** *is the most inviting overall, with a great index and broad range (about 800 pages that cover science and technology well), but it's expensive ($30, or three times more than* **What's What**). *Have your library order this heavy-duty version. If you find yourself constantly needing words you can't think of, I'd buy* **What's What**. *It's glib, cheaper, and focuses more on the things of contemporary everyday life.*

—Art Kleiner

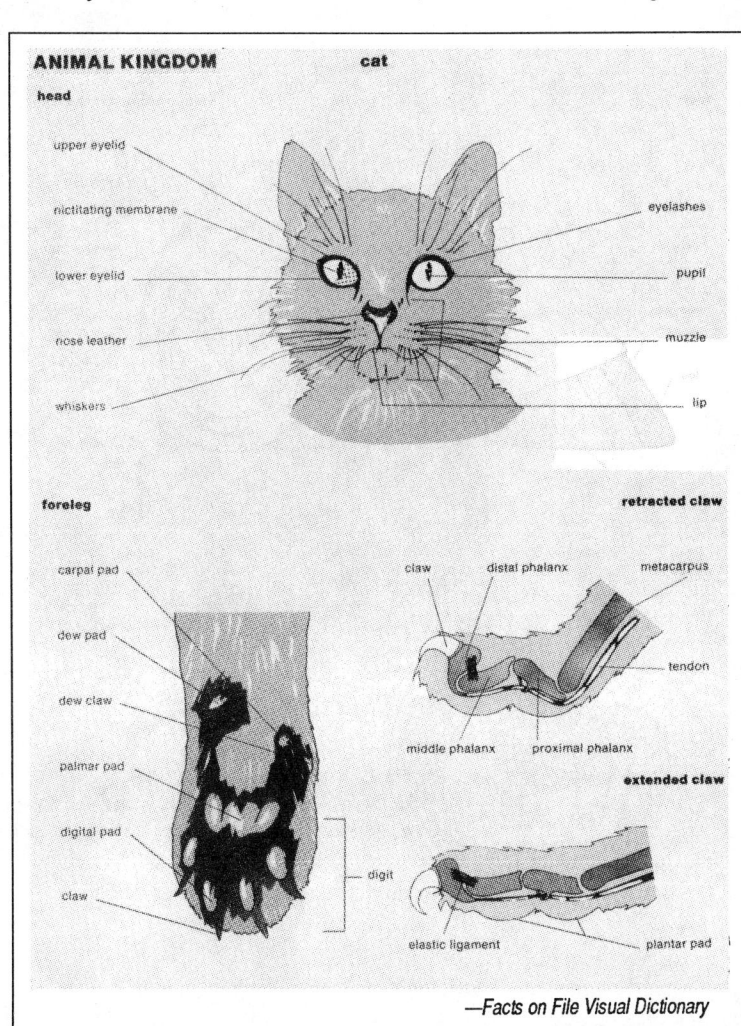

—Facts on File Visual Dictionary

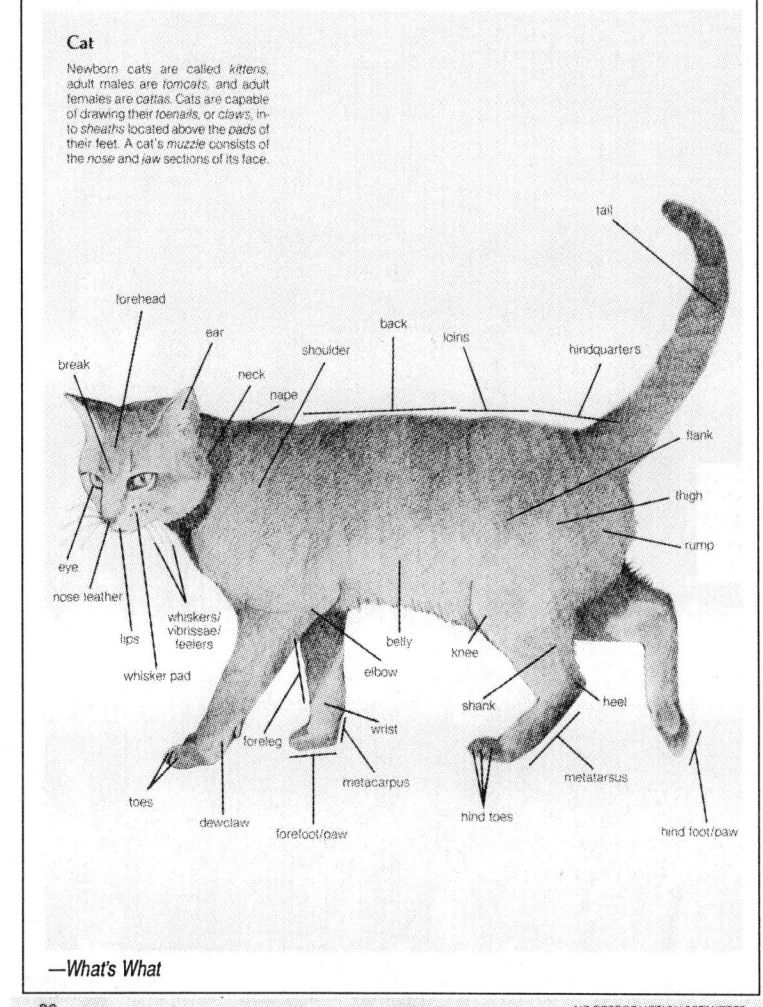

—What's What

# Art Reference

*by David Wills*

"What do you do when you run out of ideas?" my civil servant Dad asked when he worried about me working as an artist. Use picture archives, that's what.

A working artist needs pictorial reference as a tool for inspiration, for seeing visual connections not made before, or for models to draw from. Inventing images, drawing constructions out of the blue, is helped if you've got a few aids.

My bookshelves are lined with field-tested books that I crib from while working in the studio. I use them as creative inspiration. Small books will do. Like any postage stamp book. Mine cost me 25 cents at a street sale. Stamps in general give good art-ref; they're very graphic and basic, these vignettes and symbols of the world.

Big picture books, encyclopedias, and reference tomes are expensive and often out of print. Since art reference is often used as found art, this is reflected in their purchase— a bit of an old encyclopedia is quite useful in a found-art context. So I buy my books at street sales, the flea market, and jumble sales when I can. This means that much of my collection is quite fortuitous — a random lot. Keep looking around the stalls and you'll find them cheap.

## The Complete Dover Art Catalogs

Catalogs **free** from: Dover Publications, Inc., 31 East 2nd Street, Mineola, NY 11501; 516/294-7000

*By far the most useful source for in-print copyright-free material is the fascinating collection from Dover pictorial archives — very cheap books crammed with old, odd, wonderful reference pictures, weird typefaces, classy etchings, vintage photographs, and off-beat scientific treatises. Their free catalogs (**Fine Art, Art Instruction,** and **Pictorial Archive**) are a trip in themselves.*
*—David Wills*

**SPECIAL-EFFECTS AND TOPICAL ALPHABETS, Edited by Dan X. Solo.** Advertise or identify any product or service in lettering that reinforces your product. Use letters aflame, made with chopsticks, frozen with ice, in lights, in computer type, etc. Wide range of 100 copyright-free fonts from sophisticated to naive, plus many lower case and/or numerals. 100 plates. 100pp. 8⅛ x 11.                 23657-9 Pa. **$4.95**

### TIBETAN AND HIMALAYAN WOODBLOCK PRINTS
**Douglas Weiner    $7.95**

Fascinating in their own right and for the religious feelings they embody, the 65 prints convey the traditional images of Buddhist deities, Bodhisattvas, saints and spirits, as well as mandalas, prayer flags, talismans, charms, snow lions, dragons, demons and many other elements. Carved by contemporary craftsmen, these illustrations comprise some of the finest examples of woodblock prints from the Tibetan and Himalayan region.

Original Dover publication. 65 prints. Captions. Introduction. ix + 66pp. 11 x 16
                22988-2 Paperbound **$7.95**

## The Electronic Clip Art Digest

**$105.95** postpaid from:
The Electronic Clip
Art Company
6376 Quail Run
Kalamazoo, MI 49009
616/375-8996

*We use found-art a lot for illustrating articles in our magazine, the **Whole Earth Review**. Over the years we have accumulated 20 feet of bookshelf space of illustration sources. Occasionally we manipulate an illustration we discover in a book by taking it into the Macintosh. We Xerox the illo, then scan the Xerox on an Abaton Scanner, and then stretch or reverse the image on the Mac.*

*Electronic clip art is for those who don't have a library of print images, or a nearby quality Xerox machine, or a digitizing scanner, but who do want an image in a Mac paint file. This **Digest** catalogs by picture, and indexes by subject, all the 15,000 black and white digital images available from 30 commercial sources. The "art" ranges from the cutsie to the olde to the exotic. You'll then need to purchase the disks directly from the various manufacturers.    — Kevin Kelly*

Tower of Pisa

Pelican

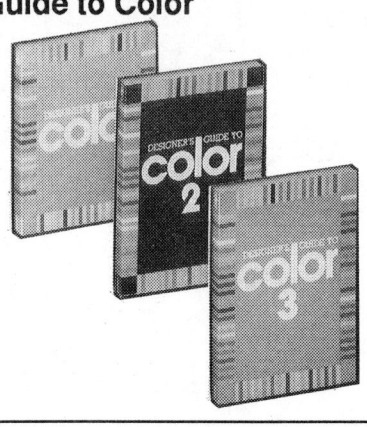

## Designer's Guide to Color

Volume One
1984; 135 pp.
**$9.95**
($12.20 postpaid)

Volume Two
1984; 128 pp.
**$12.95**
($15.20 postpaid)

Volume Three
1986; 119 pp.
**$12.95**
($15.20 postpaid)

All from: Chronicle Books, One Hallidie Plaza, Suite 806 San Francisco, CA; or Whole Earth Access

*Anybody who designs with color — house painters, knitters, graphic types, etc. — will find at least the first two of these volumes useful. All three volumes show the effect of thousands of color combinations, and how perceived colors change in relation to their neighbors. The charts will lead you to thoughtful and often surprising color combinations.*

*Volume One shows mostly dual color combinations, with one hue constant per page. Volume Two deals with pastels and brights, and includes* more three-color combos. Volume Three is specifically for fabric design, showing a variety of prints, plaids and stripes in many colors. Each color is broken down into percentages of stock printing tints: yellow, magenta, cyan, and black, for graphic-arts folks.

*Most color books costs hundreds; these have gobs of color, few words, and are very affordable.*
*—Kathleen O'Neill*

## Stock Workbook

Information **free** from Scott & Daughters Publishing, 940 North Highland Avenue, Los Angeles, CA 90038; 800/547-2688

*Pro photographers out and about on assignment usually return with more images than their client ordered. The photographers deposit the extra pictures in a joint repository called a stock agency. When you need a photograph, instead of hiring a commercial photographer to shoot it, you can check a stock agency to see if they already have one in stock. Rates vary depending on what you are going to use it for — color advertising being the most expensive and black and white editorial being the least (probably $50 minimum). Unfortunately there is no central index yet to tell you which of the hundreds of agencies has what pictures, so it can be quite frustrating to research.*

*Stock agencies print gorgeous full-color publicity material to advertise their holdings, a source that is often ideal for artistic reference. A large edited collection, like the Stock Workbook, a free 215 page representation of a dozen major agencies, is a perfect reference for digitizing images from, or for xerox art, or for backgrounds ideas. It also has a long appendix of other agencies that would probably send you more printed sample booklets.*
— Kevin Kelly

Photo credits clockwise, from top: Jonathan Blair, Woodfin Camp; P.L. Raota, Shostal Associates; Viesti Associates; Viesti Associates; Viesti Associates.

## The Bettmann Archive

Information **free** from The Bettmann Archive, 136 East 57th Street, New York, NY 10022; 212/758-0362

*Bettmann is the Taj Mahal of picture files. It's a cornucopia of visual images comprised of historical portraits from all ages, a lifetime of movie stills, and news photographs since the turn of the century — a total of 25 million images. The archive is both expensive and efficient to use, and many times the only source. We occasionally rent from them when we can't find a particular picture any other way. We call them with a query of what we're after, and they'll send photocopies of some candidates. If we pick one, they charge us about $75 for non-profit publication of the print they send.* — Kevin Kelly

Clockwise, from upper left: Michelangelo's David; Montgolfier balloon; President Ronald Reagan; Dante.

## Picture Sources Four

Ernest H. Robl, Editor
1983; 200 pp.
**$35**
($36.50 postpaid) from:
Special Libraries Association
1700 18th Street NW
Washington, DC 20009
202/234-4700
or Whole Earth Access

*I haven't found a better resource for locating pictures than this. As editorial assistant for the Whole Earth Review, the job of locating illustrations for articles often falls to me. This book eliminates a lot of the frustration in tracking down a particular type of photo — which makes it well worth the $35 price tag.*

*Easy to use, Picture Sources Four lists major and minor sources for pictures — archives, libraries, businesses, special collections — with all the information you'll need to do business (except price). The best part is the hefty index section. The geographic index helped me locate nearby archives; the subject index is the most comprehensive I've seen. The biggest drawback is the date of publication — 1983. Some of the material has to be dated.*
— Corinne Cullen Hawkins

# Mail Order Suppliers

*by Kevin Kelly*

My experience in ordering photo equipment by mail leans toward satisfaction. The favored procedure: Know exactly what you want, down to the minutiae of model numbers; know what you don't want; call in on the 800 number; confirm that they have it in stock right then; and order with a credit card (do NOT pay by check). I've tried other ways, but this one is the most successful.

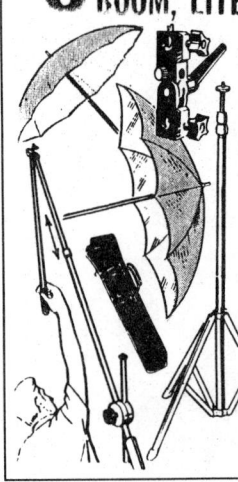

— Spiratone

## Spiratone

135-06 Northen Blvd., Flushing, NY 11354; 800/221-9695. Catalog **$1.50**.

*Full of gizmos, most useful, some frivolous, all inexpensive. We use them for photo gadgets needed in putting this book together. Good source for make-your-own gear.*

## Competitive Camera

363 Seventh Avenue, New York, NY 10001;
800/544-5442. Catalog **$2.**

*The best rock-bottomest discount prices on the full spectrum of popular 35mm photo stuff. Far surpasses prices at your local camera shop. Usually, but not always, beats the discount competition (which you should check anyway; see 47th Street Photo, p. 175, and the listings in the photo magazines). They operate in "New York mind" so you need have your act together when you shop this way — their prices change weekly.*

*Competitive also stocks other optical and electronic goods at cheap*

prices: binoculars, video camcorders, telephones and such. Good buys if you know what you're doing.

## Maine Photographic Resource

2 Central Street, Rockport, ME 04856; 800-227-1541. Catalog **free**.

*Materials and supplies for the creative process of Photography, with a capital "P". Their specialty is large format field photography, a la the old masters.*

## Zone VI

Newfane, VT 05345; 802/257-5161. Catalog **free**.

*Strictly for the followers of Ansel Adams and Edward Weston. High priced, highly-refined apparatus and accessories for big-negative landscape photography.*

## Calumet

890 Supreme Drive, Bensenville, IL 60106; 800/225-8638. Catalog **$5.**

*Has everything for the hardware world of commercial and professional photographers. They service medium and large cameras, anything beyond the ordinary 35mm format. You probably couldn't build a pro studio without consulting this catalog. Prices range from moderate to sky high.*

## Light Impressions

439 Monroe Ave., P.O. Box 940, Rochester, NY 14603; 800/828-6216. Catalog free.

*Dedicated to displaying and archiving photographs. Holding off Time and holding onto Value. Books, specialized papers and paraphernalia that you'd find museums and galleries using.*

## Shutterbug

Christi Ashby, ed.,**$15**/year (12 issues) from:
5211 S. Washington Ave., P.O. Box F, Titusville, FL 32781; 305/269-1663.

*Not a catalog, but a pudgy, oversized tabloid monthly crammed with*

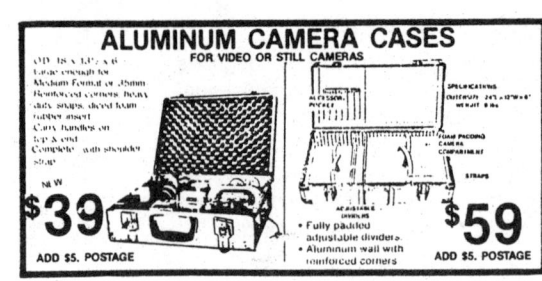

*tiny dense ads for used and new cameras, camera parts, repair manuals, and a bewildering display of camera accessories. Some articles on how-to build it yourself. Photo scavanger's paradise.*

## Clark Color Labs

Information **free** from: P.O. Box 96300, Washington, DC 20090.

*For ten years I've been sending my film by mail to Clark Color Labs to get it developed. They're fast, cheap and good. They give you credit for unprintable negatives, offer you two prints for just slightly more than one, have labs all over the country, and print on Kodak paper. Their prices are the cheapest I've ever found. If you like to see your pictures the same day you finish a roll, this isn't for you. But if, like mine, your roll of film has been in your camera a few months anyway, what's one more week?*

— Cindy Fugett

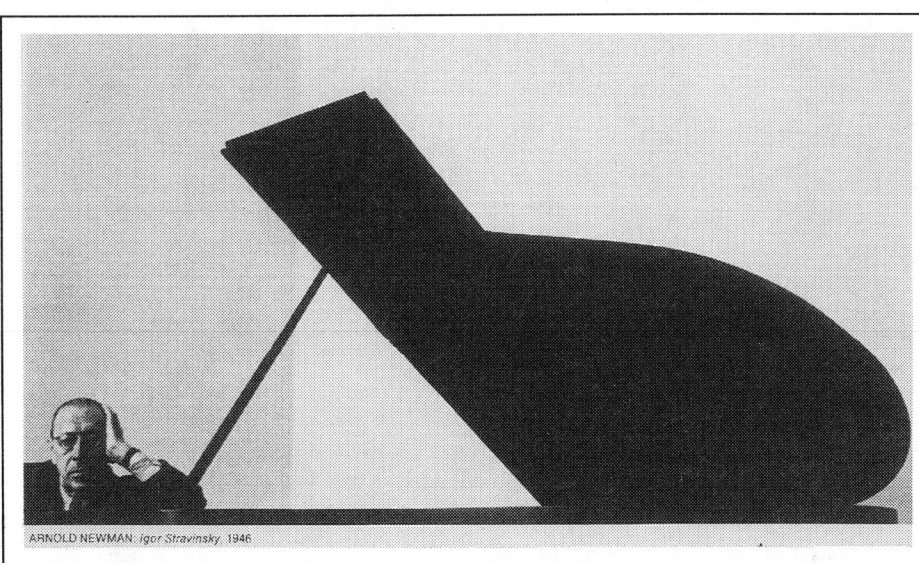

ARNOLD NEWMAN: Igor Stravinsky, 1946

Arnold Newman is famous for portraits that use graphic and symbolic elements to suggest what a person does. One of his best-known photographs is of the composer Igor Stravinsky, a portrait that Newman cropped to its essentials. Newman knew what he wanted to do, but, just starting out at the time, he didn't have the focal length lens he needed. He moved back until he had what he wanted in the frame, then cropped the photograph later. Newman says that the image "echoed my feelings about Stravinsky's music: strong, harsh, but with a stark beauty of its own."

## Photography

Barbara London Upton
1985; 426 pp.
**$25.95**
($26.95 postpaid) from:
Little, Brown & Co.
200 West Street
Waltham, MA 02254
800/343-9204
or Whole Earth Access

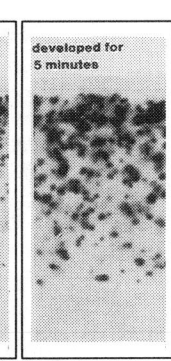

developed for 2 minutes

developed for 5 minutes

*The old **Life** magazine wrote the book on the experience called photography. Every week it conjured up new possibilities of using the silver eye. The editors of **Life** have taken a half century of this talent, put it into a 15-volume set last decade, and recently distilled the whole spirit down to an hearty, eye-popping, mind-stuffing single tome.*

*It's an education in one volume, the text-book of choice in most college photography courses. I learned easily three-quarters of my technical skills as a professional photographer from the step-by-step pictures outlined here.*
*— Kevin Kelly*

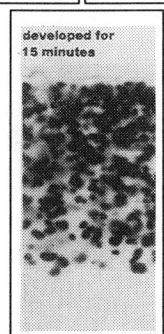

developed for 15 minutes

Grains of silver, enlarged about 2,500 x in this cross section of film emulsion, get denser as development is extended.
Grains near the surface (top) form first and grow in size. As developer soaks down, subsurface grains form.

## Photo Art Processes

Nancy Howell-Koehler
1980; 127 pp.
**$18.95** postpaid from:
Davis Publications
50 Portland Street
Worcester, MA 01608
800/533-2847
or Whole Earth Access

*How to put an image made with light on pumpkins, t-shirts, glass, old wood, decals, pottery, paper-mache, wallpaper, painted over with colors, pasted into collages, mixed with other media, on anything other than a boring square piece of white paper.*
*— Kevin Kelly*

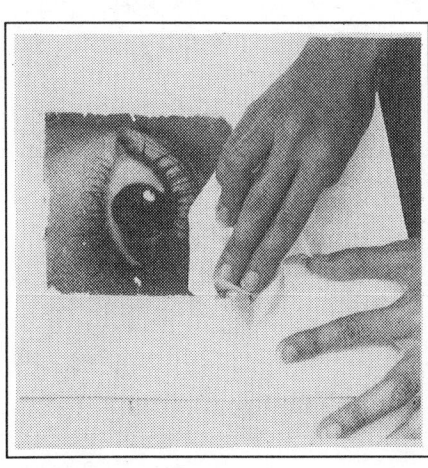

A free-form image area, produced by brushing on sensitizer, is used as a background for the printed portrait of Victorian ladies.

The clay-base papers that hold printed magazine images act as an intermediate support form which the image, coated with polymer gel, can be transferred. Images suspended on an acrylic "skin" can be removed from their paper backing and applied to any surface that will bond with an acrylic medium.

## Photography for Student Publications

Carl Vandermeulen
1979; 159 pp.
**$12.95** postpaid from:
Middleburg Press
Box 166
Orange City, IA 51041
712/737-4198
or Whole Earth Access

*The essential foundations of conveying an editorial message through photographs. Put together to cure the dreadful look of most high school yearbooks, this friendly book is also the best introduction there is for anyone shooting, printing, or selecting photographs for publication. Unintimidating straight-talk about how to inform the reader with a camera.*
*— Kevin Kelly*

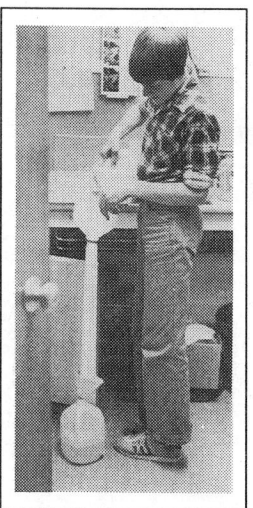

One budget-stretcher is distilled water from home dehumidifiers, but it has to be filtered before you can use it.

When you photograph people in their natural surroundings watch for ways that you can include something in the background to add information about the subject.

## Zoom

Joel Laroche, Editor
$35/year
(5 issues) from:
Charles Treves
European Publishers
P. O. Box 2000
Long Island City,
NY 11101
718/937-4606

One of Don Weinstein's "recomposed and treated" movie poster series, where he tries to bring a new awareness of the images that surround us by altering familiar movie images.

*Zoom* calls itself "The Image Magazine," and easily lives up to that claim. Printed in an oversized format with an interior design that is simultaneously functional and flashy, it features an enormous variety of black & white and color photos, ranging from nudes to portraits, from fashion layouts to photojournalism, from archival material to travel shots. Produced in France, the magazine has the semi-familiar feel of many European cities, where people and places seem ordinary, but are just different enough that you are forced to pay attention to things you might have overlooked before. *Zoom* is a loud magazine, and not always subtle, but its contents are a constant reminder of why good photography is so exciting.

— Richard Kadrey

## Pinhole Journal

Eric Renner, Editor
$32.50/year
(3 issues) from:
Pinhole Resource
Star Route 15, Box 1655
San Lorenzo, NM 88057
505/536-9942

## The Hole Thing

(A Manual of Pinhole Fotografy)
Jim Shull
1974; 64 pp.
**$9.95**
($11.45 postpaid) from:
Morgan & Morgan
145 Palisades Street
Dobbs Ferry, NY 10522; 914/693-0023
or Whole Earth Access

*Photography minus equipment. Sounds Like fun.*
— Stewart Brand

★ **VARIOUS PINHOLE CAMERAS** ★

BASIC BOX TAKES "NORMAL FOTOS" · FLAT BOX "WIDE ANGLE" · COFFEE CAN · LONG BOX "TELEPHOTO"

—The Hole Thing

—The Hole Thing

David Pugh "Pig on Manhole Cover," November 1982 PinZip photo f/110, 4 sec. Newark, Del. of a 3" high brass piggy bank standing on a manhole cover which is on a 4 foot high concrete structure on the edge of a swamp. The PinZip was placed directly on the manhole cover. The raised letters (part of the word "SALISBURY") are about 1/8" high; the square bumps are about 1/4" high.
— Pinhole Journal

## Visual Symphony

Bruce Barnbaum
1986; 128 pp.
**$50**
($52.50 postpaid) from:
Alfred van der Marck
Editions
1133 Broadway
Suite 1301
New York, NY 10010
800/999-BOOK
or Whole Earth Access

For me, this is the best photo book in over 20 years. I haven't been so excited by a collection of photographs since 1960's **This Is the American Earth,** which launched Sierra Club's exhibit-format series of books that became an engine of the ecology movement.

Bruce Barnbaum's photos imprint themselves instantly on your mind and become part of your memory, and yet they reward constant return and reinspection. The book is organized into four "movements" — following a musical metaphor that works throughout the volume — The Landscape; The Cathedrals of England; Urban Geometrics; The Slit Canyons. The slit canyons are little-known geological marvels of the American west, sometimes only an arm's length wide; Barnbaum now owns them photographically. Likewise no one has ever photographed cathedrals better; he restores their original soaring impulse perfectly. And his mad-math views of urban highrise buildings and his intense psychoanalysis of rural landscapes can change how you see both.

Barnbaum has matched or surpassed Edward Weston's extraordinary novelty of composition and Ansel Adams's technical perfectionism (lucidly carried by the jewel-like quality of reproduction in the book). And he has an eye for full-field complexity that is uniquely his own. I add him to my short list of photographers who can show me something new every time I let them: Eugene Atget, Edward Weston, and now Barnbaum. — Stewart Brand

## Holography Handbook

Fred Unterseher, Jeanne Hansen, and
Bob Schlesinger
1982; 408 pp.
**$16.95**
($18.95 postpaid) from:
Ross Books
P.O. Box 4340
Berkeley, CA 94704
415/841-2474
or Whole Earth Access

*How to make holograms in
your basement. You'll need a
basement to hold the one-ton
plywood sandbox that serves
as a vibration-free table. It's got
to be dark, too. The sand allows you stick in and adjust
optical components glued to
sharpened plastic pipes. About
as low-rent high-tech as you'll
ever see. Making holograms
is modern alchemy. Use the
formulas in this great, mas-
terful book.*

— Kevin Kelly

[Right] Sand/Slab Table for keeping
equipment stable

[Left] Here I am making an innertube
sandwich using plenty of carpet
pieces for bread. There is carpet between the concrete floor
and the concrete blocks, between the blocks and the wood
base, between the wood and the inner tubes, and the top of
the tubes. I used 6 inch size inner tubes, the type used in
forklift tires.

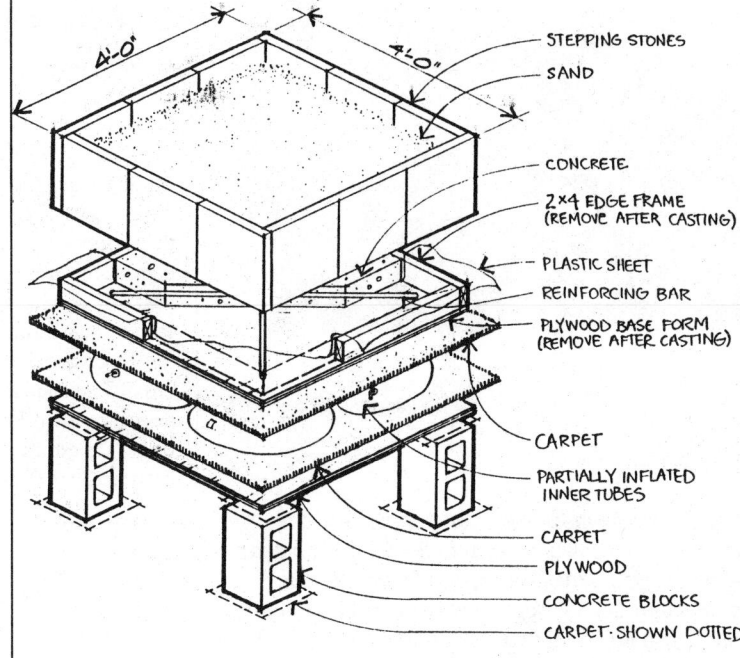

## Laser Holography

(Experiments You Can Do . . .
From Edison)
Tung H. Jeong And
Albert B. Dick
1987; 32 pp.
**$2** postpaid from:
Thomas Alva Edison
Foundation
21000 West Ten Mile Road
Southfield, MI 48075
313/354-3003

*Written originally for students from junior high
through college level, this slim booklet tells you,
with a minimum of technical language, how to
make 7 types of holograms. Helpful diagrams and
a straight-forward writing style make this an excellent book for the beginning holographer.*

— Richard Kadrey

◆

Below is a list of essential equipment:
* helium-neon laser with output of 1-5 mW
* small concave mirror, glued to a rod
* front surface mirror (10 cm by 12.5 cm approximately)
* double concave lens, 5 cm diameter
* smallest automobile inner tube available
* steel plate (or wood board with sheet steel top)
* steel paper clamps (3)
* black cardboard
* white cardboard
* glass trays (3)
* 1 liter glass bottles (3)
* 100 cc beakers (2)
* rubber gloves
* night light (green color preferred)
* windshield wiper (or photographic squeegee)
* box of holographic plates (or a roll of film)
* developing chemicals

[Figure1] White Light Reflection Hologram set up
from **Laser Holography**

## The Holo-Gram

Frank DeFreitas, Publisher
**Free** from:
The Holo-Gram
P. O. Box 9035
Allentown, PA 18105
215/434-8236

## L.A.S.E.R. News

Louis M. Brill, Editor
**$15**/year
(4 issues) from:
L.A.S.E.R. News
P. O. Box 42083
San Francisco, CA 94101
415/664-0694

*Two magazines that will keep you in touch with
what's most exciting in holography today.* **The
Holo-Gram** *is a free quarterly with the no-frills look
and energy of the best fanzines. It features news
on the international holo scene, as well as information on books and magazines that write about and
use holograms.* **L.A.S.E.R.** *is published by the
non-profit Laser Arts Society for Education & Research. This is more of a hands-on journal featuring articles on hologram-making and interviews
with holographers. Whether you're an experienced
laser jock or just getting started, both of these
magazines will have something to excite you.*

— Richard Kadrey

Figure 1

## The Holography Information Center

P. O. Box 586, Lake Forest, IL
60045; 312/234-4244

*For general information on
sources and prices for holographic film, plates, chemicals
and how-to instructions, send
the Holography Information
Center a self-addressed
stamped envelope.*

—Robert Horvitz

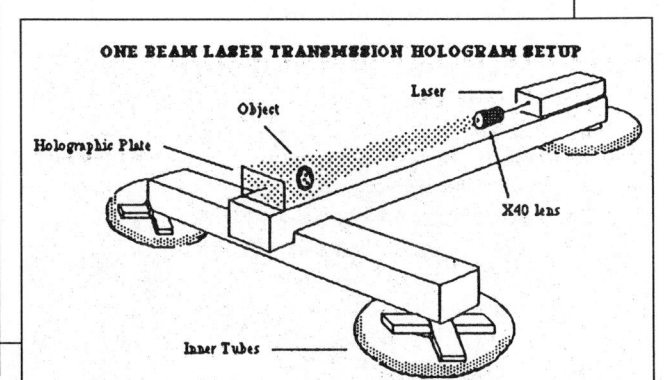

ONE BEAM LASER TRANSMISSION HOLOGRAM SETUP

The Panasonic fax model 115.

# Fax

*Fax (facsimile machines) send copies of documents across town, or around the world, the same way you would make a regular phone call. Because they send a copy of whatever is on the page (including text, graphics, and signatures), fax machines have replaced much of the worldwide Telex and some of the overnight express traffic. Fax has become increasingly common and is now a reasonable product for most businesses (large and small) to consider.*

*To meet this need, several manufacturers are making desktop fax machines for under $2000 which include telephones, autodialers, and auto-answer features. These machines are capable of sending a page in 20 seconds to a compatible machine on the other end. There are many available, including the FAX 110 from Canon (about $2000 list price, under $1700 from discounters).*
*—Michael J. Kleeman*

*In Hong Kong, fax machines are so hot they are putting bicycle messenger services out of business. Hong Kong Telephone says there is more fax traffic between Hong Kong and the USA than voice traffic. Wave of the future? I'm so tired of trying to figure out problems with my computer modem, fax may be the answer. Good resolution, and some of the machines can even be used as copiers!*
*—Dave Brook*

## Freedom to Fax

*by Rob Horn*

RECENT EVENTS in Panama have shown that facsimile equipment (fax) has become an important part of the free press. When the Panamanian government closed the opposition press, the local and international business community organized an independent free press. Overseas offices will fax important news clippings to a list of Panamanian businesses. The overseas offices are coordinated to avoid duplication so that within minutes dozens of Panamanian offices get each article. The local offices then use office copiers and distribute the news locally. The estimated equivalent print run is somewhere between 30,000 and 50,000 issues.

The government cannot disable fax equipment and copiers without effectively severing their ties to the Western economy. This would destroy the country, too high a price for the government to pay. Since virtually all international businesses have the needed equipment, selective confiscation or monitoring is also impossible.

Printing presses and copiers have long been restricted by totalitarian dictatorships. Now facsimile machines must be added to their lists. People have conjectured in the past about the impact of computer communications, but have not mentioned facsimile. With an estimated 500,000 machines installed in the United States, they are significantly less common than computers. But fax can handle both computer generated and handwritten, printed or photographic material. Most importantly, they can distribute international news.

*A corporate chairman I know refuses to deal with computers, yet enjoys the benefits of computer telecommunications. Whenever he travels he carries a portable fax machine. To communicate he writes his notes on legal pads, flops the notes down on his fax machine and lets it dial headquarters. They'll get his handwritten messages and send back whatever documents he needs to his machine in a matter of hours. It's like putting a telephone into the heart of a Xerox machine, which is almost what faxes are.*

*I talked to Whole Earth Access, who keep up with*

## Public Fax Directory

**$40**/year (4 issues) from Public Fax, 2811 East Katella Avenue, Suite 200, Orange, CA 92667; 714/532-5330

*Fax for plain folks. Like copy machines before them, fax machines are now flourishing in quick-print shops, mailbox rental outlets and other such places. When you want to send a document, and either you or the receiver doesn't have access to a fax machine, this quarterly directory will tell you the location of the public fax nearest to you.*
*—Sarah Vandershaf*

*practical electronic gear at discount prices. Here are what they are selling:*

**Northwestern Bell Fax** — has built-in phone with speed dialing, stores five documents, has autoreceiving. **$1399**, plus UPS shipping.

**Panasonic Fax** — Superlative quality, also has a built-in answering machine for voice messages. The one Whole Earth Access uses between their stores. **$1699**, plus UPS shipping.

(See p. 2 for Whole Earth Access ordering information.)
*—Kevin Kelly*

Above left is the original document, a page from the Table of Contents of the **Whole Earth Review** #56 (Fall 1987). On the right is the transmitted fax document, warts and all. In this case, we used a PacTel machine set on the "Fine" setting. You can see that it duplicates text faithfully, but smudges pictures into blackness. Overall the quality is comparable to a low-grade copier. The same test, below, using a Northwestern Bell machine to transmit that issue's cover, shows you CAN send graphics by choosing settings and machines. The Northwestern sent the clearest graphics; the Panasonic the sharpest text.

## CD ROM: The New Papyrus (Vol. 1)
Steve Lambert and Suzanne Ropiequet, Editors
1986; 619 pp.
**$21.95** ($23.95 postpaid)

## Optical Publishing (Vol. 2)
Suzanne Ropiequet, Editor
1987; 358 pp.
**$22.95**
($26.42 postpaid)

## Interactive Multimedia (Vol. 3)
Sueann Ambron and Kristina Hooper, Editors
1988; 352 pp.
**$24.95**
($28.42 postpaid)

All from:
Harper & Row
Route 3
P.O. Box 20-B
Hagerstown, MD 21741
800/638-3030

*Here comes privileged advance warning of new techniques for storing everything — pictures, text, video, programs — on the same kinds of compact discs (CDs) that have reshaped the audio industry during the last few years. You'll be able to fit a library into a shoebox and to summon any part of it instantly. Whether or not the world wants this new medium is uncertain, but it threatens to go ahead and reshape publishing and libraries anyway. These three high-quality anthologies tell how.*
*—Art Kleiner*

*The third volume in this series is the most revolutionary. It's goal is not merely to reshape how we store books, films, and music, but to reshape how we think of them. How do you scan a movie? What happens if it doesn't have just a single ending? Can you make a book that learns as quickly as you do? Recent experiments are reported here.*
*— Kevin Kelly*

◆

If you have a lot of text to distribute, such as a law library, one CD ROM disc, costing $10 or less from the disc maker, stores as much material as microfiche costing $150 to make or books costing $1000 to print.
*—The New Papyrus*

---

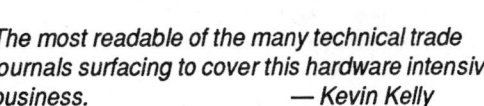
The Director's Kit. The student has chosen the desired costume and will transfer it to the stage area. When all the design elements are selected, the students can animate the scene.—*Interactive Multimedia*

◆

Data Base Search Keys from Life

Well, Hillary had certainly caught one this time. It was a large bug, over an inch long, with yellow and orange stripes around its body, and two pairs of wings. Unfortunately for it, one of its wings was broken, which is how Hillary had caught up with it on the windowsill.

"What is it, Mom?"

"I don't know, dear, but please don't wave it in my face. You should go look it up in the encyclopedia."

"OK," said Hillary, and she ran to the family room and inserted the encyclopedia disc into the reader. Holding her prize tightly in one hand, she zipped through the index until she came to the "I" section, and then slowly homed in, first on "insects," then on the "insect identification" section. She had been there many times before to use the "build-an-insect" classification table.

Hillary selected parts from the table that matched her new prey, and as she did so, the encyclopedia assembled, on screen, a reasonable likeness of the creature in her hand. "This is a member of the sawfly family." the encyclopedia said, just as the assembled illustration of the creature began to crawl around on a green, leafy background. "A primitive relative to the ant, bee, and wasp. Some species are considered pests because their larvae bore into the trunks of weakened or dead deciduous tree."

"Oh-oh, better tell Dad about that," Hillary thought, and paused long enough to print out a picture of the sawfly and its caterpillar-like larva and a paragraph about its feeding habits. Her father had been wondering lately about the elm in the backyard. —*Interactive Multimedia*

### CD-ROM Review
Roger Strukhoff, Editor
**$34.97**/year
(12 issues) from:
IDG Communications/
Peterborough
80 Elm Street
Peterborough, NH 03458
603/924-9471

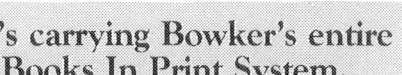

*The most readable of the many technical trade journals surfacing to cover this hardware intensive business.*
*— Kevin Kelly*

---

## The Electronic Whole Earth Catalog
List price not fixed yet; probably under **$150**, certainly less than that at street price. Needs Macintosh and new Apple CD-ROM driver. From Brøderbund Software, 17 Paul Drive, San Rafael, CA 94903; 415/492-3200

*Our latest publishing experiment. Better than the book in several ways. It plays music, for starters. The best music-by-mail sources are rounded up, reviewed and classified in **Whole Earth Catalog** fashion. The user then navigates to a musical territory through a series of menus, until she arrives at samples of particular albums. Near the picture of the album cover is a note symbol, which if struck, unleashes a sample cut from the album. Ghanaian drums. Yemenite folk songs. Old jazz. About 20 seconds each. A mini-**Whole Earth Music Catalog**.*

*This compact disc incarnation of the **Catalog** also has an active index allowing you to search for specifics a little better than in the book, which though it excelled for browsing was not constructed for intense research. **The Electronic Catalog**'s index is hot-wired to the actual items so going from one to the other is like turning the next page — it's right there.*

*Like all the **Catalogs**, this one has fresh, accurate (read: expensive to do) ordering and access information. The bulk of text derives from the **Essential Whole Earth Catalog**, with additional material from our on-going periodical **Whole Earth Review**, and some from this book.*

*Ways it's not better than a book: It's expensive, and runs on expensive equipment (due to get cheaper someday). And it's desk bound. You can't read it on the john, at least not gracefully.*

*We think of it as the first of a co-evolving species. Your feedback, alterations, tinkering and modifications are an essential half of its advancement.*
*—Kevin Kelly*

Tim Oren (of Apple Computer, co-developer for the CD) holds the first pressing of the Electronic Whole Earth Catalog. Like a top-40 hit, this disc is gold. Ordinarily a compact disc is coated with aluminum. Since there is a suspicion that aluminum may only last decades, this one was gold-plated for posterity

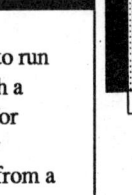

What the Author Sees

What the Browser Sees

# HyperCard

*by Kevin Kelly*

The model for HyperCard is the 3-by-5 card. A card is represented by a Macintosh screen. As you flip through screens (cards), you read them one after another, as if they were in a stack. Cards can hold any kind of information you want, in any format you designed, including pictures. Rather than rest inertly, as on a Rolodex, information on a HyperCard can be actively linked to any other point on any other card. Those linking spots can be a word, a bunch of words, or a picture. When your cursor touches that spot, it brings forth the card (screen) that it is linked to. The links form a thread through a "stack" of cards. You weave through a stack, jumping from card to card, idea to idea, choosing your own path by touching on the items you are interested in, endlessly discovering new levels, or deliberately aiming toward a desired card.

Your HyperCard Rolodex, for instance, might have one card for every individual. You could link their telephone number so that it dials the number. You could link their address to a small map on another card to show how to get to their house. And that map of the town might be linked to several other names as well. You would then have an interactive Rolodex giving you as much information as you wanted each time.

HyperCard will be a medium of communication. Within a week after it was introduced in 1986, the WELL had a raging conference on the topic. A prime function there is the Stackware Exchange where user written stacks of cards are swapped, showcased, and improved upon. Early stackware will have some of the untamed innovation that early BASIC computer programs had. The WELL confronts the possibilities with a topic called "What can you do with HyperCard?"

Some of the things I imagine are: incredibly complex adventure games, self-directed classroom courseware, interactive shopping catalogs, pictorial spreadsheets, and ultimate clip art files. Enough, anyway, to get going.

Skinny Macs, even Fat Macs, won't quite do for this muscle-bound program. You'll need a Hunk Mac (a Plus or better), with at least 1 meg RAM to run things smoothly. Very best is a set up with a hard disc. There are two official sources for HyperCard. It's bundled free with all new Macintoshes, or it can be bought for $49 from a local Apple dealer.

## HyperAge

Jan Lewis, Editor
$19.95/year
(6 issues) from:
HyperAge
5793 Tyndall Avenue
Riverdale, NY 10471
800/682-2000

*I like this magazine because it avoids the creepy mystique and glamour that usually shrouds technical expertise. The premier issue (the only one we've seen) ran lots of good stuff by prominent innovators in the HyperCard field, such as a special feature on interactive sound and Hyper-Card by Tim Oren at Apple, who did the lion's share of development for the Electronic Whole Earth Catalog.* —Ramón Sender Barayón

## Windoid/AHUG

Sample copy for **SASE** from Apple Computer, M/S 27AQ, 20525 Mariani Boulevard, Cupertino, CA 95014

## Open Stack

Sample copy for **SASE** from Walking Shadow Press, P.O. Box 2092, Saratoga, CA 95071

*Two useful newsletters from Silicon Valley, both with roots in the Apple community and local user groups. Each carries essential information, hot tips, and chatty gossip about HyperCard mania. A courteous SASE will get you a copy of either. **Windoid** Nos. 1-5 are available in stack form with all the scripts implemented by Team Hackinslash. Amusing and well thought-out! Ask for BMUG Disk Hyper 32, $3 postpaid from BMUG, Inc. 1442A Walnut Street, Berkeley, CA 94709.*
—Ramón Sender Barayón

HyperCard is uniquely suited for activist causes. It goes without saying that its great ease of use and flexibility favors the underdog. Activist groups have often relied on people power an maneuverability to counteract the brute economic and political force of various Powers-That-Be; HyperCard can enhance both of these advantages.

Aside from its inherent qualities, the way in which Hyper-Card made its entrance marked it as a paradigm of practical idealism. Bill Atkinson wanted to to give Hyper-Card away because he wanted to make the world a better place. Apple is consenting because they want to sell more computers. The result: free application that may eventually empower millions of people to use computers who may never have done so otherwise.

The near future will no doubt bring everything Ted Nelson has described, at least as far as education is concerned. It will probably bring much more. Media labs around the world are experimenting with new ways to "connect" people to computers. For instance, tactile gloves are being developed that allow a person to "feel" objects that appear on CRT's. Masks are being developed that enable a person to see a computer-generated environment. When combined, these new developments point to an age not far off when a person will be able to submerge into an entirely computerized environment and "commune" with information.

You may ask what all this has to do with hypertext, but it is obvious that to drive these new "environments," information will have to be organized in highly interconnected, non-hierarchical, and versatile ways. The databases of the future will all be "hypertext" or "hypermedia," or what have you. In fact, information of the future will have to be so connected and layered that it will have a fractal-like quality. It will be viewable on many levels, deep or shallow, each seeming to have as much content as the next. Future databases will reflect reality, and they will share the physical and mathematical characteristics of the real world.
—Open Stack

## The Complete HyperCard Handbook

Danny Goodman
1987; 695 pp.
**$29.95**
($31.95 postpaid) from:
Bantam Books
414 East Golf Road
Des Plaines, IL 60016
800/223-6834

*Some software programs have all the luck. On the day HyperCard was released, an equally ground-breaking guidebook to it was published in tandem. Like HyperCard itself, it is thorough and deep. It's a massive, hefty tome of 700 pages, completely fluff-free.*

*It exhaustively treats the mechanics of making cards; assembling them into "stackware;" creating links; and writing instructions in HyperTalk. Even if you don't usually use paint programs, you'll find yourself creating graphics in HyperCard regularly. The paint options are therefore covered in depth. As we worked on the Electronic Whole Earth Catalog, we picked up a number of tips from the **Handbook** we hadn't known about. Not a reference book per se, the **Handbook** does its best job illustrating the conceptual innovations introduced by HyperCard. Notions like "stackware" (stacks of cards that are exchanged), "buttons" (linking hot spots), and "backgrounds" (the layers of information on a card) are all illuminated into clarity.*

*I primarily use those Macintosh programs which stick with me if I don't ever open the manual. But HyperCard, with its tools-for-making-tools structure, is simply one Macintosh program that you won't be able to unfold fully without a supplemental help book. For the immediate future, this is the book to get.*
—Kevin Kelly

## Heizer Software

Catalog and sample disk **$4** from Heizer Software, 1941 Oak Park Boulevard, Pleasant Hill, CA 94523; 415/943-7667 or (outside CA) 800/225-6755

*There are two sources for low cost non-commercial stackware: informal regional Macintosh user groups and Heizer Software. The former have them for nearly free and in overwhelming quantity; the latter for modest cost with more selectivity and annotation of content. They deal by mail and have a sensible catalog. Also, their authors offer phone support during certain hours.*
—Ramón Sender Barayón

## Traffic 4

BMUG Disk Hyper 9 freeware **$3** postpaid from BMUG, Inc., 1442A Walnut Street #62, Berkeley, CA 94709

*Neat graphics in an embryonic hypertext comic strip. As the brief strip grows in length and complexity (the author is sharing his work as he proceeds), multiple branchings will weave the story into an appropriately bizarre science fiction tale. For information on further versions, send SASE to John Laney, Desktop Graphics, 85 South Washington #308, Seattle, WA 98104.* —RSB

## HyperMacinTalk

BMUG Disk Hyper 5.2 freeware **$3** postpaid from BMUG, Inc., 1442A Walnut Street #62, Berkeley, CA 94709 or The WELL in the library of the Macintosh Conference

*Want to drive your relatives crazy? Teach your Mac to recite in English whatever you type in as a message. Sounding like a robot from the 21st Century, this utility provides everything you need to give voice to your HyperCard stacks. You can improve its pronunciation by incrementally tweaking the phonetic translation for each message. It is powered by the MacinTalk speech engine, which must be placed in your system folder.* —RSB

## Focal Point

**$99.95** postpaid from HyperWare Direct, Activision, P.O. Box T, Gilroy, CA 95021-2249

*Perhaps the most useful HyperCard product to date. Pulls together many functions you might find in small, incompatible HyperCard utilities, such as a phone rolodex that is linked to a daily datebook. I prefer to pin paper notes on my wall, but this program gives you a happily compatible core of organizational aids with which you can build your own computerized termite mound. One fine trick it does is to carry over the undone items on your today To Do list to tomorrow. Those who use their computer to schedule (or bill) their work will be in hog heaven.* —RSB

## AmandaStories

Catalog **free** from AmandaStories, 1025 Martin Road, Santa Cruz, CA 95060-9721; 408/423-0565

*"Inigo Gets Out," a story halfway between an inter-active cartoon and an adventure game, was one of the first HyperCard stacks created. It lights up the most "Ah, isn't that neat!" comments from an audience. Those who remember Alicia Bay Laurel's laid-back drawings of life in the sixties and who find **The Little Prince** charming will enjoy Amanda Goodenough's childlike animations of the adventures of Inigo the Cat and Your Faithful Camel.* —RSB

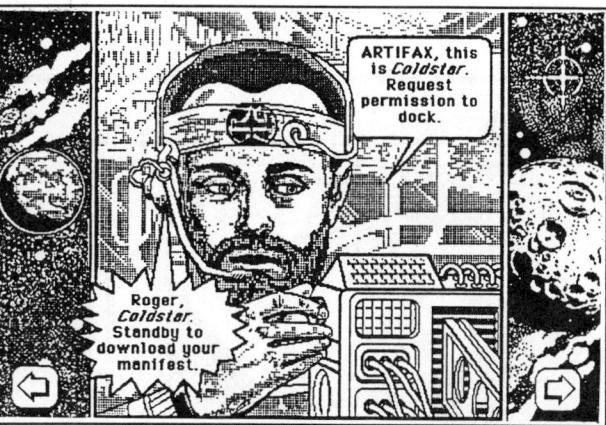

— Traffic 4

Stackware is what you make with HyperCard. For a vague idea, imagine a stack of cards pertaining to one topic, every card interlinked in many directions. Stackware offered everyone an easy way to make neat custom-tailored programs, or an easy way to make complicated junk. Within months of HyperCard's release, there was an avalanche of programs that no one other than the maker would ever want to look at. Ramón Sender Barayón volunteered for the toilet-cleaning job of sifting through this widening tidepool of flimsy programs to find a few worth writing home about. Here's his selection, as of spring 1988.     —Kevin Kelly

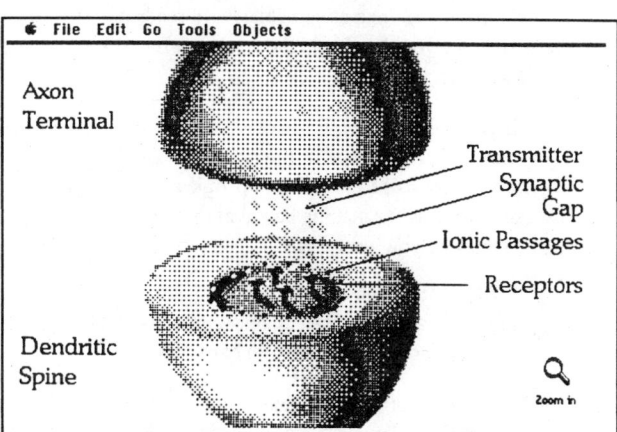

— NeuroTour

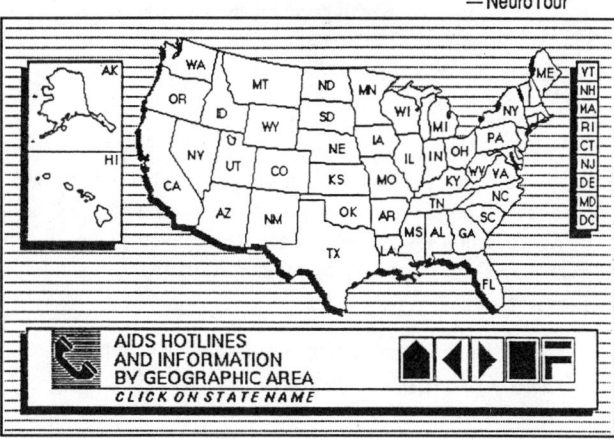

— The AIDS Stack

"Inigo Takes a Bath" from AmandaStories.

## Port Authority 1.0

**$25** postpaid from Heizer Software, 1941 Oak Park Boulevard, Suite 30, Pleasant Hill, CA 94523; 415/943-7667 or (outside CA) 800/225-6755

*An elementary, but essential, servant. It moves information from HyperCard into an ordinary database or word processor file, or vice versa. Uses the well-known Font/DA Mover dashboard.* —RSB

## HyperCard Developer's Toolkit

APDA membership **$20**/year from APDA, 290 SW 43rd Street, Renton, WA 98055; 206/251-6548

*For the upper-end, technically oriented script writer. Consists of the HyperCard Script Language Guide (**$18.50**) and The HyperCard Developer's Toolkit, which contains The Design Guidelines (**$10**). To purchase these you need to be a member of APDA (Apple Programmer's and Developer's Association). You also receive a quarterly newsletter.* —RSB

## NeuroTour

BMUG Disk Hyper 6 freeware **$3** postpaid from BMUG, Inc., 1442A Walnut Street #62, Berkeley, CA 94709 or The WELL in the library of the Macintosh Conference

*A voyage similar to the **Powers of Ten** journey, descending into the structure of the brain by successive leaps downward in scale. Nothing more than an inspirational sketch of what might be accomplished with serious scientific illustrations.* —RSB

## The AIDS Stack

Shareware **$20** postpaid from Michael Tidmus, Being Alive, P.O. Box 69532, West Hollywood, CA 90069

*More inviting than a sheaf of papers for someone searching for AIDS information. Very artistic introduction shows some of the imaginative use of visual effects. Ideal way to keep a lot of quick-changing information updated and organized.* —RSB

## Developer Stack 1.1

BMUG Disk Hyper 29 freeware **$3** postpaid from BMUG, Inc., 1442A Walnut Street #62, Berkeley, CA 94709 or The WELL in the library of the Macintosh Conference

*A handy collection of tools that allows a HyperCard builder to employ short programs written in other computer languages. These utilities allow you to call a routine constructed outside of HyperCard, execute its function, and return its result into HyperCard. For instance, if you want to have a menu "pop up" when a word is selected, use the Pop Up Menu XCMD.* —RSB

# Ten Paths to Computer Purchases

*by Art Kleiner*

THE NEWS ABOUT personal computers begins with shopping news. For between $1,500 and $2,500, including software, you can buy an "XT Clone" or "AT Clone" — imitations of IBM computers which provide many — but far from all — of the clerical, creative, and communicative tools that a personal computer can offer. You can use such a clone to automate the drudgery of routine clerical work; to manipulate the fine-grained grids of probabilities and statistics; to write in a facile, intuitively correct way; and to seek out computer-based information and textual conversations on a broad variety of topics through the phone lines. But you can't use this sort of clone without devoting a few months to learning its arcane peculiarities, and it can't (without difficulty) deal with such niceties as typefaces and graphics.

To get a more "intuitively correct" system that meets you halfway, you'll need between $2,500 and $3,500; that gets you a Macintosh, with the ability to manipulate sounds and black-and-white images, and investigate the burgeoning arena of "information navigating" via Apple's HyperCard program. For $5,000 or more, you can "desktop publish." In other words, you can produce publishable-quality page layouts and typesetting on your own laser printer, which is a photocopier body controlled by a computer brain. Beyond $6,000 and you're in the realm of intensely fast, intensely capable personal computers that can store, say, complexly interwoven data banks of text, numbers, and pictures, which even room-sized computers couldn't have handled a decade ago.

But no matter what you use them for, at root personal computers are tools for understanding the self. Even the most straightforwardly businesslike program conducts you into a miniature world, which is not physically real, but which you often experience as if it were. A word processor, for instance, starts as someone's idealized idea of a typewriter, but eventually becomes what computer people call a "virtual" typewriting universe — with extra capabilities that couldn't exist in the real world, and hidden shortcuts that you continue learning about long after you begin using it. "Playing" the word processor effectively, and customizing it to your own taste, is often a matter of figuring out the right strategies within the oh-so-complex, but nonetheless finite and controllable, rules of the game.

Apple's Macintosh family of computers has lately gained enough popularity (among corporations, at least, which are the largest and thus most influential computer purchasers) to inspire a host of new software and add-ons. Apple itself keeps upgrading and improving its computer line; most recently with an operating system called MultiFinder which allows you to work in several programs at once, switching back and forth between them.

Then there's the advent of laser printers, which raised many people's standards of what a computer-printed page should look like (this page was made on a laser printer), and of compact disks feeding into computers (called CD-ROMs in the trade), which may make pos-

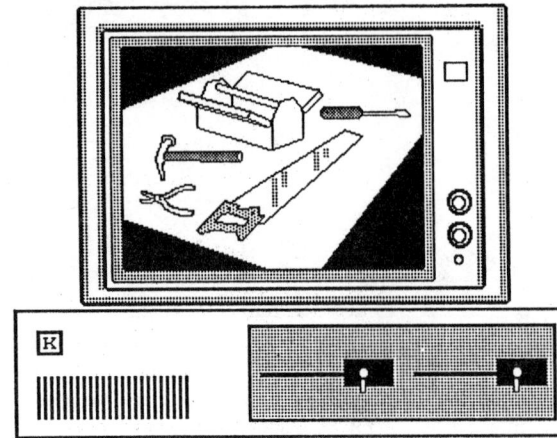

sible the decades-old dream of keeping an entire library in a shoebox.

Macintoshes are easier than most other computers to learn to use, but even on the Mac, data management and desktop publishing are prodigious endeavors. As for IBM, it is indeed easy to send electronic mail on their new computers, as long as someone has already set up the system for you. Lord help the novices who set it up for themselves.

Even if you don't give your life over to learning to use a computer, it will change your life irrevocably. Here, organized along paths for different people and different uses, are the tools for making sure that those changes happen the way you want them to.

### Path #1: For independent work (writing, small-scale organizing, telecommunicating, research, etc.) at minimum cost: XT Clone with hard disk.

The XT "clone" is the Gallo wine of computers. Its major advantages: low cost and high adaptability. So many people own the things that there's a wide range of available software and accessories that work together. (This is also true of the far-less-capable Apple II and Commodore 64 computers.)

The clone's main disadvantage is its operating system, MS-DOS; it's too hard to learn and use, much too hard to set up, too prone to crisis points where different programs don't work together and freeze the machine, and too easy to make typing errors that destroy your work.

Several hundred manufacturers — including Compaq, Tandy, Leading Edge, and Hyundai — make XT clones, but there is no need to buy a brand-name computer unless you get a good deal. The best approach is to find, by word of mouth, a local computer retailer who is trustworthy and offers good prices. Shop locally; computer chips and disk drives often develop flaws, and local dealers are quicker to reach (and often more responsible).

Buying a clone means confronting an overwhelming array of choices. I recommend 640 kilobytes ("640K") of "Random Access Memory (RAM)" — the computer's internal "attention span" for programs and documents that it is working on at the moment. You should also have a built-in clock, printer ("parallel") port, communications ("serial") port, and at least one

20-megabyte (or larger) hard disk drive, for storing programs and documents.

### Path #2: For the same kind of independent work (writing, small-scale organizing, telecommunicating, research, etc.) without having to think too much about the computer, or for anyone who needs black-and-white graphics, at minimum cost: Macintosh SE with built-in hard disk and Imagewriter.

The Mac operating system employs a "desktop" metaphor where every program and document is represented by a small image (an "icon") superimposed on a rectangle (the "desk"). You use the mouse (it comes with the Mac), to point at different parts of the screen, to click on different onscreen "buttons" with commands attached, and to grab hold of an onscreen image and move it somewhere else. To delete a file, for instance, you don't type DELETE; you grab its onscreen icon and move it over to a little picture of a trashcan.

Even the Mac's floppy disks are better. Small enough to fit in a shirt pocket and encased in a plastic covering, they're far less fragile and hold more than twice as much as an IBM floppy.

But consistency is the real Macintosh boon. No matter what type of program you use, you know that its menus will appear at the top of the screen, and that the first menu, invariably marked File, will open and close documents. Moving text from one part of a document to another works the same way in nearly every program. Desk accessories, which conflict chaotically on XTs, work together on the Mac. Even printers, the traditional gremlin of compatibility, fall into line; if one program works with a printer, so does every program. Thus, not only are most Mac programs easier to learn, but Mac users avoid most of the setup hassles endemic to XT clones.

Is all this worth the extra $1000 or so to get equivalent computing power on a Mac? If you use black-and-white graphics regularly, at this moment you have no choice: graphics programs exist for XTs and ATs, but they either require thousands of dollars worth of special hardware, or dozens of hours of special setup. If you're new to personal computing, or employ novices, you could save $1000 in training and setup costs (though not for Desktop Publishing or Data Base Management).

Macs also have a more intangible appeal: they represent the future. Interesting new software seems to show up there first.

### Path #3: For independent work (particularly writing and number-shuffling) with high-quality printing: XT Clone with hard disk and HP-compatible laser printer.

Unlike the abominable "tractor feeds" of regular printers, laser printers feed paper like photocopiers; you dunk a bunch of paper in a paper tray and the printer handles it. But the main difference is the text of your printed page. It's as readable as the page of a book, far more readable than even the best typewriter.

This path contains everything in path #1 except the need for a superior word processor. Only a few writing programs can master the niceties of laser printing. Those that do include MICROSOFT WORD (if you like using a mouse) and XYWRITE III (if you telecommunicate your text as well as laser-print it).

**Path #4: For desktop publishing and black-and-white graphics: Macintosh with Postscript compatible Laser Printer.**

This path includes everything in path #2 plus page layout programs that take text from word processing programs, graphics from graphic programs, and additional graphic elements which you type in yourself, and arrange them all on the screen. Then the laser prints out a (more-or-less accurate) replica of your screen. (See *Desktop Publishing*, p. 58-59.)

Postscript-compatable laser printers cost $4,000 and up. For that price, you get images of 300 dots per inch — not comparable to a professional typesetting shop, but fairly professional-looking to the untrained eye. Several graphics and typesetting shops accept Macintosh-based files for running out on their higher-quality 1200-dot-per-inch Linotronic laser printers.

**Path #5: For playing with color graphics, animation, sound, and programming at the lowest possible cost: an Amiga 500.**

In strictly technical terms, the Amiga is one of the most advanced personal computers available. Its operating system, called Workbench, combines the Mac's icons with the shortcut commands of MS-DOS. Not only that, but the Amiga has the lowest-cost rich color graphics available, terrific sound generation, and video compatibility unequalled in other computers. You can hook this machine to your TV and superimpose images you've created yourself over **Dallas** or the evening news.

The video compatibility makes it hard to look closely at details on the full-resolution screen, however. There's also something clunky about the Amiga's general ambiance. And because it never gained wide popularity, there's still a shortage of software.

**Path #6: For heavy-duty dealing with text: an AT-compatible with extra memory and Framework II software.**

People are just beginning to realize the potentials of manipulating text on microcomputers. It goes far beyond writing as most people think of it now. The computer-based writer to come is really a text navigator, pulling reams of incoming material off telecommunica-

tions networks, sorting and sifting them so that they make thematic sense, and then using those as grist for his or her own writing. This sort of writing requires the ability to mix and match hundreds of text files at once and sort between them. That capability is available right now on FRAMEWORK II, a masterpiece of programming, combining an extremely-easy-to-use spreadsheet, a data manager, a word processor, and an adept telecommunications program in one package.

Framework requires extra memory; otherwise, after you call up two or three frames' worth of text, you'll be told you hit your limit. You need to add a $750-$1000 accessory to your computer — the Intel Above Board (or equivalent "L.I.M. 4.0-compatible extended/expanded memory" cards made by other manufacturers).

**Path #7: Heavy-duty bookkeeping and small-business use: an AT-compatible with extra memory and Lotus 1-2-3.**

The AT-compatible is a minimum; you might be better off with a 386-based computer, because you'll probably want to migrate to path #9 later on, when your data bases overflow your current work. And if you're adapting a small business on personal computers, it's probably worthwhile to ask a reliable consultant about choosing software.

So many people have grown to use the spreadsheet Lotus 1-2-3 that it has, for some people, replaced the operating system. You can now buy writing, accounting, spelling, graph-making, and data managing programs that fit within 1-2-3's confines. To use them, you cordon off a section of the spreadsheet's grid, bring up the "Add-In," as these programs are called, and use it.

**Path #8: For keeping up with the Joneses: OS/2 machines and 386 machines.**

Released in December 1987, OS/2 is an infant operating system. It only runs MS-DOS software, so far. None of the new OS/2 software really exists yet, except for a few cobbled-together versions of existing programs.

OS/2 has intriguing advantages against MS-DOS and even the Mac. Like the Mac, it uses the better 3 1/2" disks and permits virtually unlimited memory (meaning more complex programs and bigger documents). Like

the Mac, it can run several programs at one time, switching back and forth between them. It also can run several parts of one program at one time, a first in personal computing. This means that while waiting for a data manager to print out a list of everyone in your college graduating class, you could add names to the same list, and have those names show up at the end of the same printout.

OS/2's disadvantages: It's expensive — both the program itself and (more importantly) the hardware required to use it (2 megabytes of memory for starters, about four times as much as an MS-DOS computer). It's cumbersome, retaining a few of MS-DOS' most irritating features (like file names that can be no longer than 11 characters long). Finally, perhaps most importantly, not many people who aren't programmers *need* all that heavy-duty power or can understand it yet.

**Path #9: For keeping up with the Joneses' Joneses: The Macintosh II.**

A wonderful, speedy, intuitively correct, large-screened, incredibly adaptable, fully-featured — $9,000 — computer (if you count the cost of the laser printer which would logically go with it). Because it's "open" — compatible with a variety of monitors and other accessories — it's more complex to set up.

**Path #10: The simplest, cheapest path: Apple IIe with Swyftcard or Canon Cat.**

If all this seems unnecessarily expensive and Byzantinely overcomplicated to you, there's at least one plain, inexpensive solution. Buy an Apple IIe, an otherwise antiquated and frustrating computer (in my opinion) and fit it with Swyftcard/Swyftdisk, a $39.95 writing, calculating, and telecommunications tool of unusual simplicity.

The Canon Cat is an extended adaptation of the Swyftcard, with a box and monitor. You can set up the Cat easily as a bulletin board for other people to call, but the Swyftcard has the advantage of allowing you to use that cumbersome, old-fashioned Apple IIe for other things — like exploring the many games and educational programs still available for it.

---

## Computer Lib/ Dream Machines

Ted Nelson
1987; 330 pp.
**$18.95**
($20.95 postpaid) from:
Microsoft Press
Attn.: Consumer Sales
16011 36th Way
P.O. Box 97017
Redmond, WA 98073-9717
800/426-9400
or Whole Earth Access

*Ted Nelson started the entire genre of mainstream computer books in 1974 with a **Whole Earth Catalog**-sized polemic called **Computer Lib/Dream Machines**. Like an Ace pulp science-fiction novel, it came in two halves, bound upside-down together. The "Lib" side was a tourist guide to available*

computers and the corporate policies behind them; the "Dream" side showed up evanescent innovations that (Nelson knew) would reshape everyone's lives. (One of these nascent innovations was "Hypertext" — in which text or pictures contain "links," or passages through which people can metaphorically leap to other information important to them. Nelson is the most prominent populizer of this idea, which he has devoted much of his working life to developing, and which is now itself linked with various suddenly prominent programs like HyperCard and Lotus Agenda.)

Now Nelson has voraciously updated both halves of his old book. The format is (a bit too much) old stuff updated copiously with brilliant new stuff. Amidst viciously well-targeted assessments of

> The problem is not software "friendliness." It is conceptual clarity. A globe does not say "good morning." It is simple and clear, not "friendly."

machines, metaphors, and manufacturers, you will be guided through hacker in-jokes and skilled pithy judgements. Nelson is sometimes justly criticized for quirkiness and self-indulgence; but he has an innate ability to judge the significance of particular technologies, shared by few other writers. He has, in this edition, also recreated what was then and is still the most fun-to-read computer book of all time.

—Art Kleiner

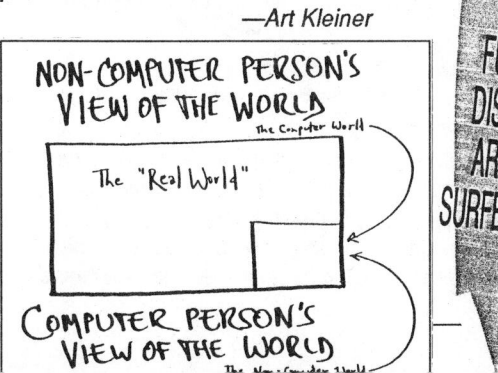

IF COMPUTERS ARE THE WAVE OF THE FUTURE, DISPLAYS ARE THE SURFBOARDS.

## How to Buy Software

Alfred Glossbrenner
1984; 648 pp.
**$14.95**
($16.20 postpaid) from:
St. Martin's Press
Attn.: Cash Sales
175 Fifth Avenue
New York, NY 10010
800/221-7945

*Glossbrenner's amazing book has the best explanation I've seen anywhere of how personal computers work, put strictly in term's of a shopper's perspective. Dense with good information, the book is big and comprehensive but never heavy. Its rich sprinkling of tidbits and tips keeps you turning the pages looking for more. The book is divided into chapters on each kind of software. The shopping advice is sound enough and general enough that it's surprisingly up to date for an early 1984 book.* —Stewart Brand

There is no clean solution to getting a copy-protected program onto a hard disk, though in the computer industry, few things are truly impossible. The question is always whether the game is worth the candle. If you have a good relationship with the retailer who sold you the hard disk or the hard-disk-equipped computer, and if you are purchasing the applications program from him, then he may be able to arrange to install the program for you.

In addition, it is not unheard of for a customer to ship a hard disk unit to a software house, along with a purchase order for the program. The software company can then install the program and then send back the disk unit. Obviously, detailed arrangements must be made beforehand. And, since hard disk units are rather delicate, they must be carefully packed and insured.

Most mail order houses will sell the same products at prices that are within about $10 of each other. You can take a nickel and dime approach if you like and always order from the firm with the absolute lowest price, but once you have found a mail order firm that you like, it is much more sensible to stay with it, as long as its prices are generally in line.

## Software Digest Ratings Report

Michael D. Stern, Editor/Publisher
**$295**/year
(12 issues) from:
Software Digest
One Winding Drive
Philadelphia, PA 19131
800/223-7093

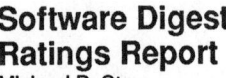

*The closest thing to* **Consumer Reports** *that exists for software. If you buy software at all professionally, it's certain to be worth the substantial price. Nobody does as thorough a job of comparing programs feature by feature, virtue by virtue, in painstaking fashion. Each major application program for MS-DOS (only) machines is tested by new users, bench-tested*

The Personal Writer Pen allows you to write on a pad with the pen and have your writing keyed into a word processor.

## MacGuide

Patricia Bensky, Editor
**$14.85**/year
(4 issues) from:
The Delta Group, Inc.
818 17th Street
Suite 210
Denver, CO 80202
303/825-8166

*We're big on Macintoshes around here. Computer virgins love 'em because the Mac is gentle and understanding. Computer veterans love 'em because the Mac is ambitious and elegant. We use 'em because the Mac is a graphic beast and takes kindly to the tremendous visual component of our work. It's become a chore to keep up with all the programs written for it, a chore blessedly relieved by this weighty directory. It catalogs all 3100 Macintosh programs and accessories together with specifications, ordering info, and in some cases, a "reader rating" from* **MacGuide Magazine** *for the more popular programs. We find it handy.*
— Kevin Kelly

## Software by Mail

Catalogs **free** from: **800-SOFTWARE**: 800/225-9273; **Logicsoft**: 800/645-3491; **Computer Mail Order**: 800/233-8950

*Substantial deals here. 800-SOFTWARE offers free help after the sale — sometimes better than what you get from the software manufacturer. They have a crack team of advisors, and a really good newsletter. Logicsoft discounts software deeply — I and others have had good luck with them. Computer Mail Order has the widest range. At reasonable prices, they sell software for just about any type of computer.* —Saul Feldman

*(for speed primarily), compared to its competition, and rated.* —Stewart Brand

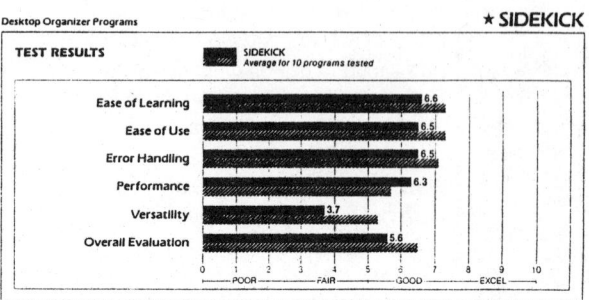

Desktop Organizer Programs

| TEST RESULTS | SIDEKICK | Average for 10 programs tested | ★ SIDEKICK |
| --- | --- | --- | --- |

| | | |
| --- | --- | --- |
| Ease of Learning | 6.6 | |
| Ease of Use | 6.5 | |
| Error Handling | 6.5 | |
| Performance | 6.3 | |
| Versatility | 3.7 | |
| Overall Evaluation | 5.6 | |

POOR — FAIR — GOOD — EXCEL

## Apple Programmers and Developers Association

Membership **$20** from APDA, 290 SW 43rd Street, Renton, WA 98055; 206/251-6548

*This is Apple's back door — the way it distributes all those Macintosh and Apple II development tools and technical documents that your local dealer has never heard of and can barely pronounce. The APDA was formed by the Apple Puget Sound Program Library Exchange with Apple's cooperation and, for a modest annual membership fee, gives cut rate mail-order access to essential and powerful tools such as the Mac Programmer's Workshop. APDA also distributes some Apple developer's kits and programmer's tools as works in progress. Be warned that this means exactly what it says — beta versions of documentation may arrive Xeroxed and without figures, and prerelease software is prone to annoying and occasionally damaging bugs. But if you want or need to be up on the latest, this is the place.* —Tim Oren

## CP/M Times

Catalog **$3** from Central Computer Products, 330 Central Avenue, Fillmore, CA 93015; 800/533-8049 or 800/624-5628 (in CA)

*CP/M may be "dead," but there are 2 million orphans out there, doggedly clinging to their Kaypros. One of the last sources of CP/M software (and hardware) is CP/M Times, a newsletter/catalog lifeline-by-mail.* —Sarah Vandershaf

## Computer Shopper

Stan Veit, Editor
**$21**/year
(12 issues) from:
Patch Publishing Co., Inc.
P.O. Box 1209
Titusville, FL 32781
800/327-9926

*The heart of this newsprint tabloid is classifieds — used computers, mail-order software — and listings — user's groups, bulletin boards, and meetings. Range, nationwide. Features are uneven, but they cover each major type of micro and pick up on low-cost and public domain news that most other magazines miss. I've come to feel affection for it in a gritty, technical kind of way.*

*I was just talking with a small software developer who commented that* **Computer Shopper** *reviewed his product long before any other magazine did.* —Art Kleiner

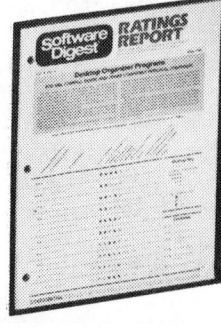

◆

Family Roots is an extensive, full-featured $185 genealogy database system, with a 150-page looseleaf manual, for anyone who has a great deal of family data, and who wants to set it up so it can be referenced in a variety of ways, printed out neatly, and be easily read and understood.

## How to Get Free Software

Alfred Glossbrenner
1984; 432 pp.
**$14.95**
($16.45 postpaid) from:
St. Martin's Press
Attn.: Cash Sales
175 Fifth Avenue
New York, NY 10010
212/674-5151
or Whole Earth Access

*No one we know of has a more comprehensive knowledge of software then Alfred Glossbrenner. His book, **How to Get Free Software**, has chapter and verse on the subject. The major problem with public domain programs is finding out about them and finding where to get them. He takes care of both.*

*(The minor problems are dealing with the sheer volume of choices and working without manuals.)*
*—Stewart Brand*

◆

Some of the free software available for nearly every machine is unquestionably of professional quality and can more than hold its own with any commercial product in the same category.

Admittedly, this runs contrary to everything one would assume about a high quality product: "If the stuff's so good, why didn't the author try to sell it?" In point of fact, some of them have. More than a few free programs started out as commercial products. But many more of them were written by computer professionals or skilled hobbyists in their spare time. For philosophical reasons, or simply because they did not want the hassle of "going commercial," many of these individuals have contributed their work to the public domain instead.

◆

Indeed, if you are interested in programming, free software can provide a wonderful learning experience. Unlike most commercial software, the vast majority of public domain programs are "listable." That means you can print out and review the program itself and see how its author accomplished (or failed to accomplish) a particular goal. This can alert you to interesting techniques or save you from making similar mistakes. And in some cases it can teach you more about BASIC, Pascal, assembler, and other languages than many textbooks can.

◆

Once you get "plugged in," you'll discover that there is an informal network of users groups across the continent. Many groups regularly exchange newsletters and information, and many share their member-contributed free software.

In almost all users groups there will be a "software librarian" who has taken the responsibility for organizing, building, and maintaining the group's free software collection. Frequently, the librarian and assisting members will bring the entire library to the group's monthly meeting. And either before, after, or during the meeting, members will be free to pick up any programs they want. If you bring your own blank disks, there will usually be a copying charge of about $1 to help maintain the library. But often a club will be able to provide you with a disk at a discounted price. (If you do bring your own floppies, try to format them beforehand.)

## The PC-SIG Library

(Public Domain and User-Supported Software for the IBM-PC, PCjr, and Compatibles.) 1987; 424 pp., **$12.95** ($16.95 postpaid) from PC-SIG, Inc., 1030 East Duane Avenue, Suite D, Sunnyvale, CA 94086; 800/245-6717 (800/222-2996 in CA) or Whole Earth Access

## The PC-SIG Library on CD-ROM

IBM PC/XT/AT or compatible computer and CD-ROM player with Microsoft MS-DOS extensions. **$295** ($300 postpaid) from PC-SIG, Inc., 1030 East Duane Avenue, Suite D, Sunnyvale, CA 94086; 408/730-9291

*For years PC-SIG, largest shareware vendor in the known universe, has published **The PC-SIG Library**, a catalog of hundreds of IBM-PC programs to be had for free or for a "suggested donation" to the program's author. The 750 programs reviewed in the latest edition are available directly from PC-SIG, Inc. (order forms are printed in the back of the book). Or you can skip this step and get thousands*

The entire PG-SIG library to date of public domain and user-supported programs is now on CD-ROM.

## User Groups

*One of the best ways to get your hands on shareware is to find other people who use your type of computer. User groups often have shareware libraries for members to browse through. To find out about user groups in your area, you can call 800/538-9696 for Apple or Macintosh computers; 800/IBM-3333 for IBM PCs; and 408/745-2367 or 408/745-5759 if you have an Atari.*

*Even if the nearest user group is too far away for regular visits, some groups offer shareware by mail. The Berkeley Macintosh User Group maintains a fine collection of Mac shareware for members near or far. Or you can join The Boston Computer Society, which has shareware compatible with many computer types — Mac, Apple, IBM PC, Atari, Amiga, CP/M.*

**Berkeley Macintosh User Group:** Membership $40/year. 1442A Walnut Street, #62, Berkeley, CA 94709; 415/849-BMUG.

**The Boston Computer Society:** Membership $35/year. One Center Plaza, Boston, MA 02108; 617/367-8080.
*—Sarah Vandershaf*

*of shareware and public domain programs on **The PC-SIG Library on CD-ROM**.*
*—Sarah Vandershaf*

◆

Is it Shareware, User-Supported or Public Domain?

Public domain software is created by authors who choose not to seek formal rights or royalties. Such work is free to be used by all with few or no restrictions.

This type of software can be found on the numerous electronic Bulletin Boards around the country and in the PC-SIG library.

Shareware and User-Supported software paint a slightly different picture. Some of these programs are copyrighted, some are not. . . . You are purchasing your software directly from the author, thereby eliminating costly marketing, promotion and packaging — allowing you to obtain sophisticated software at a fraction of the cost.
*—The PC-SIG Library on CD-ROM User Manual*

## Shareware Magazine

M. Palmer Barnes, Editor
**$20**/year
(6 issues) from:
PC-SIG, Inc.
1030 East Duane Avenue
Suite D
Sunnyvale, CA 94086
800/245-6717
or 800/222-2996 (in CA)

*This magazine reviews new shareware/public domain/user-supported programs and reports on the shareware industry. Use it to update **The PC-SIG Library**.*

*—Sarah Vandershaf*

◆

A number of software companies and individual programmers have been marketing PC versions of the popular MONOPOLY® game, claiming that the game is public domain.

Parker Brothers wants to set the record straight. The MONOPOLY® game, including board graphics, instructions, playing cards, Title Deed cards, and all other distinctive elements of the MONOPOLY® game are fully protected under the Federal Copyright Act and the Federal Trademark Act. . . .

Parker Brothers has licensed the MONOPOLY® property to Sega for the Sega Master Systems and Virgin Games for home computers.

Other than these two licensees, *none* of the software versions of MONOPOLY® now on the market have been authorized by Parker Brothers.

## Personal Computing
Fred Abatemarco, Editor
$18/year
(12 issues) from:
Hayden Publishing
10 Mulholland Drive
Hasbrouck Heights, NJ 07604
800/525-0643

*Only a couple of years ago this was a contemptible piece of advertising-driven fluff. Now it's a reliable and (mirabile!) interestingly written general-interest computer magazine. The only one left, in fact, that covers Apple, IBM, and other computers together without getting lost in trivia, vagueness, or industry in-groupiness. To find that such a magazine could still exist after the Balkanization of computerdom was downright refreshing — and I find myself WANTING to read **Personal Computing** more than any other computer magazine.*

—Art Kleiner

◆

## PC Week
Sam Whitmore, Editor. $160/year or **free** to qualified subscribers (51 issues) from PC Week, P.O. 5970, Cherry Hill, NJ, 08034; 609/428-5000

## MacWEEK
(The Workstation Weekly)
Daniel J. Ruby, Editor
$75/year
or **free** to qualified subscribers
(50 issues) from:
MacWEEK
Circulation Department, 5211 South Washington Avenue
Titusville, FL 32780; 305/269-2687

*Yeah, sure, you want to learn about personal computers, but everything changes so fast, how will you ever keep up? These two sources are free (as long as you fill in the proper qualification cards), up-to-date, and comprehensive — between them, you get a weekly education in what's available in*

Electronic-mail gateways sort and send messages from one electronic-mail network to another. Gateways on local-area networks can send messages created with LAN E-Mail products to wide-area networks like MCI Mail or CompuServe using modems and communications software.

—MacWEEK

*Personal Computing.* **PC Week's** *extra bonus is corporate iconoclast Jim Seymour, probably the most cogent computer writer in print.*

*I have found these far superior to their competitors — including* **InfoWorld** *and* **Macintosh Today.**
—Art Kleiner

---

## 10 Hidden Costs Of Personal Computing

1) Disks
2) Software upgrades
3) Technical support
4) Printer ribbons
5) Laser-printer toner cartridges/consumables
6) Training
7) Cables
8) Hardware upgrades with add-in boards
9) Equipment repair/maintenance
10) Time

How can a manager know if fax, and PC fax specifically, is appropriate technology for his office? "If they send out three or four overnight mail packages every day, they probably should look at fax," says Stanley R. Greenburg, a New York publisher who has compiled a directory of fax telephone numbers, "The Official Facsimile Users' Directory," (published by F.D.P. Associates).

◆

Q: What can I do about an employee who has become so enamored with his personal computer that he neglects his assigned duties in favor of helping others in the department with their personal computer problems?

A: Cherish him! In addition, change his assignment from whatever it was before so he only has to do half of that, but add on top of that the formal duty to help the other klutzes who work for you. You may pull your supervisory rank and put helping *you* out on top of his priority list.

## 5 Best Tips For Taking Your Computer On The Road

1) If it's a transportable desktop model with a hard disk, park the hard disk heads.
2) Be sure to take along the original distribution disks.
3) Back up software and check to see that the machine is working before you leave.
4) If you're going overseas, be prepared to buy a step-down transformer to run your computer on 220-volt current.
5) Carry your computer onto the airplane.

---

## Release 1.0
Esther Dyson, Editor
$395/year
(12 issues) from:
EDventure Holdings Inc.
375 Park Avenue, Suite 2503
New York, NY 10152
212/758-3434

*The most literate and informed writing on the technology of thinking comes on the gray, typewritten pages of this very expensive newsletter. For many of its subscribers, it's an unbelievable bargain. Instead of tramping to the computer industry's most tantalizing conferences, they can read Esther Dyson's personable reports and soak up more than they would by being there. Dyson deciphers esoteric technical issues into oh-I-get-it! language, further refined by an impenetrable filter against PR hype. Moreover, she has an unerring nose for the significant consequence. Talk a library into subscribing.*
—Kevin Kelly

*My favorite computer read is* **Release 1.0,** *a pricey monthly from Esther Dyson, who writes with more*

*intelligence per column than anyone else in the business — and with a high quaint humor. This sharp-eyed daughter of physicist Freeman Dyson treats the biz like a good field biologist might. She observes acutely, notes trends early, predicts boldly, and retains a wicked remote fondness for her obligingly complex subject.*
—Stewart Brand

◆

Ed Tufte teaches at Yale, where he is Professor of Political Science and Statistics, Senior Critic in Graphic Design, and Lecturer in Law. Despite all that, he is best known as the creator of **The Visual Display of Quantitative Information,** a stunning book that explains with illustrations how graphics can be used to elucidate rather than merely decorate or, at worst, obfuscate, quantitative data. Tufte is an ardent foe of "chart junk, simple data tricked up with three dimensions and six colors." Asked to comment on **USA Today,** he says politely that the weather map's not bad and then points out, "People think it's so successful, but what's the best-selling paper in the country? The **Wall Street Journal**. It's absolutely full of information, and no chart junk."

He is currently working for IBM as the corporate consultant on information design. "If you want the right skills to design a computer interface, don't go to a programmer,

or a psychologist, or a graphic designer. Go to a mapmaker! Mapmakers are a magnificent combination of engineer and designer. They have a 5000-year history of visual craft. The map is an ideal model for interface design."

## PC
(The Independent Guide of IBM Personal Computers)
Bill Machrone, Editor
$39.97/year
(22 issues) from:
PC Magazine
P.O. Box 2886
Boulder, CO 80322
800/525-0643

*The pre-eminent magazine for understanding MS-DOS and OS/2 computers (the cheapest and the most corporate-heavy) keeps getting better and better. Most effective are their focus sections which adopt a topic, consider it from all angles, and comparatively, skeptically review all appropriate software. Biweekly and ad-crammed, back issues require reinforced shelving.*     —Art Kleiner

## The Plain English Repair and Maintenance Guide for Home Computers

Henry F. Beechhold
1984; 265 pp.

## The Plain English Maintenance and Repair Guide for IBM Personal Computers

(IBM PC, PC XT, PC*jr* and Compatibles)
Henry F. Beechhold
1985; 259 pp.

**$14.95** each
($18.95 postpaid) from:
Simon & Schuster
Mail Order Sales
200 Old Tappan
Old Tappan, NJ
07675; 800/223-2336
or Whole Earth Access

Beware of static electricity. You can generate enough of the stuff to lose all your data just by taking off your sweater!!

—*Home Computers*

— *IBM Personal Computers*

*Great books to own even if your computer never breaks down. The technical jargon of electronics and computer repair is translated into something we non-techies can grasp, a sort of folk-wisdom shop sense that explains "the why and wherefores below the surface." Step-by-step tutorials walk you through what you need to know for simple repairs and maintenance as well as how to modify your home computer and build some add-on gadgets, like a null modem for hooking two com-*puters together, or an audio monitor.*

—*Levi Thomas*

*IBM PC-compatible owners should get the special edition targeted for them.*

—*Art Kleiner*

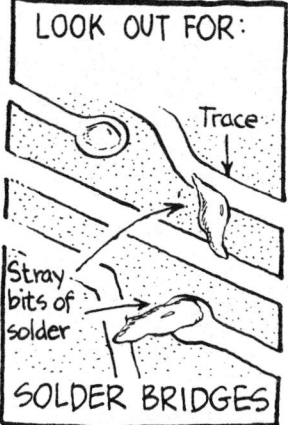

— *Home Computers*

— *Home Computers*

◆

Substitution of ICs without removing originals.

INSIDE A FLOPPY DISKETTE DRIVE

Disk hub....
Index emitter (works with index detector below disk.)
Write-protect switch
Disk spindle
D.C. Stepper motor
D.C. Drive motor
Head assembly and band drive
Index detector

—*IBM Personal Computers*

One sick chip can infect all others that are logically connected to it "downstream."

If you suspect that a chip is defective, you can simply press another of the same type over it. This is called "piggybacking" (big surprise!) and is a handy trouble-shooting technique if you have a stock of chips on hand. Here's how to do it:

a. Turn off power.

b. Carefully bend the new chip leads in slightly so that each will contact its mate on the original chip.

c. Orient the chip with pin 1 to match pin 1 on the original.

d. Press the chip down over the original, making absolutely certain that all pins are "mated" and that none is touching any other.

e. Power up the computer and test for proper functioning.

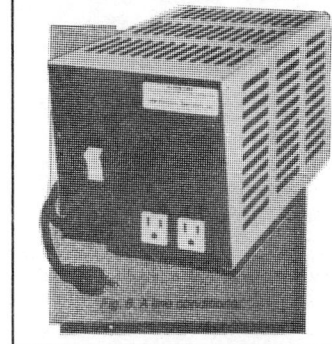

"PIGGYBACKING"

— *Home Computers*

## Protecting Your Computer From Power Line Disturbances

Francis J. Stifter. Reprint **free** from Electronic Specialists, Inc., P.O. Box 389, 171 South Main Street, Natick, MA 01760; 800/225-4876

*Power surges are thieves in the night, robbing you of precious information stored on your computer. There are ways, though, to protect your work — such as by shutting off the machine whenever you're not using it and pulling the plug. More elegant solutions to power fluctuations (including safeguards that work while the computer is in use) are listed in this article, reprinted from **Computers and Electronics** magazine and free for the asking.*

—*Sarah Vandershaf*

◆

On a hot day, even with an air conditioner running, your computer "acts up." Heat sensitive equipment? Unlikely. Heavy air conditioning loads accompanying summer heat often give rise to brownouts — evidenced by temporary low voltage conditions and increased power-line disturbances.

◆

Ideally, interference should be eliminated at the source. Unfortunately, many sources are inaccessible — lightning comes to mind! — or not readily identifiable as a culprit (perhaps an innocent little postage meter located in the back office of a factory).

Fortunately, most power line interference can be controlled directly at the computer installation. Noise-isolation transformers, power line conditioners, and line filters will generally reduce noise levels to the point where they no longer interfere with satisfactory computer operation.

A commercial line-conditioner will protect a computer from virtually all electrical calamities except a direct lightning strike or total power failure.

## Cheap IBM Clones

Whole Earth Turbo XT-20: IBM compatible; 640K; 20MB hard disk plus single floppy disk drive; B/W monitor. $895 postpaid from Whole Earth Electronics, 2990 Seventh Street, Berkeley, CA 94710; 415/653-7758 or 800/323-8080.

*The best approach for procuring a clone is to find, by word of mouth, a local retailer who is trustworthy and offers good prices. Many of these shops are too small to advertise in the Yellow Pages; check ads in your local newspaper with the best computer section (in New York, that means the Tuesday* **New York Times***; in California, it means two small tabloids called* **MicroTimes** *and* **Computer Currents***). To help you shop, the* **IBM/ XT Clone Buyer's Guide** *(see review below) is invaluable.*

*Buy a PC clone locally if at all possible, so you benefit from local servicing on problems. If you need to shop by mail, one of the best buys is from the burgeoning computer company, Whole Earth Access (there's no financial tie to us). They assemble their own line of clones from cut-rate parts and guarantee the result. Their XT clone, with built-in 20-meg hard disk and monitor, goes for $895(!) postage paid. This is a small-business bargain. Edwin Rutsch, author of* **The IBM XT Clone Buyer's Guide***, examined Whole Earth's IBM AT clone, which is a generation better and about twice as expensive as their XT. His comments follow.*

*—Kevin Kelly*

*The Whole Earth Computer Systems 286 (AT clone) is a close copy of the IBM AT, mimicking not only its power, but also its plainness. A lot of the other clones sport "bells and whistles" which this lacks. However, it is reliable and operates 30*

percent faster than IBM's newest computer, the Personal System 2 (PS/2), Models 50 and 60. It is a good-quality product for a clone, at a reasonable, competitive price. A main advantage is that unlike some clone packagers, the company will probably be around for a while to honor their one-year parts and labor warranty.

*—Edwin Rutsch*

## IBM XT Clone Buyer's Guide

Edwin Rutsch
1988; 79 pp.
**$19.95**
($23.45 postpaid)

## IBM AT Clone Buyer's Guide and Handbook

Edwin Rutsch
1988; 406 pp.
**$24.95**
($28.45 postpaid)

both from:
Modular Information Systems
431 Ashbury Street
San Francisco, CA 94117
415/552-8648
or Whole Earth Access

*The cheapest computers you can buy are half-witted numskulls for sale in bargain discount stores for under $100. They're bimbos. The cheapest computers that you can buy which might help you get some work done are instruments known as IBM clones. They are manufactured by the largest corporations in the country and by some of the very smallest. The clones vary widely in reliability and cost. The cheapest method to find a clone that won't become expensive in the long run is to immerse oneself in one of these remarkably clear, remarkably current self-published books.*

*The XT is the minimum machine, the AT is the preferred muscle-bound workhorse, and the 386 is the coming "must have." These guidebooks have a similar layered structure. The AT book tells how to upgrade an XT clone, and the forthcoming 386 book (**$33.45** postpaid, also from Modular Information Systems) shows how to upgrade an AT. Any of them will tell you all you need to know on what to purchase, and why.*

*Beyond buying advice, these books are the most crystalline introduction to MS-DOS computers you can find. You should probably read one of them (I'd choose the AT book) before you buy any kind of computer.* *—Kevin Kelly*

## Build Your Own IBM Compatible

(And Save a Bundle)
Aubrey Pilgrim
1987; 208 pp.
**$14.95**
postpaid from:
TAB Books, Inc.
P.O. Box 40
Blue Ridge Summit, PA 17214
717/794-2191
or Whole Earth Access

*You may be ready to save a bundle, but are you ready for an adventure? The scheme is to take cheap parts from Asian manufacturers which are advertised in the backs of computer magazines and assemble them into an IBM knockoff. A lot can go wrong in an instant. I recommend that you read*

*this book first. It'll either convince you that you don't have the needed electronic common sense, or else if you do, it will provide you the key tips for successful construction. Besides becoming the proud owner/builder of a cheap, versatile machine, you'll probably use it more effectively since you know how it works. Your warranty, though, is your fix-it abilities.*

*An equally wise (though less exciting) choice is to consider the ever-blossoming varieties of already assembled clones for sale at very cheap prices. They are often sold by hobbyists who successfully put together an IBM compatible for themselves and then, seeing a market, charge a minimal amount to assemble another. You pay for the few tricks that they learned the painful way. That's the way I'd go.*

*—Kevin Kelly*

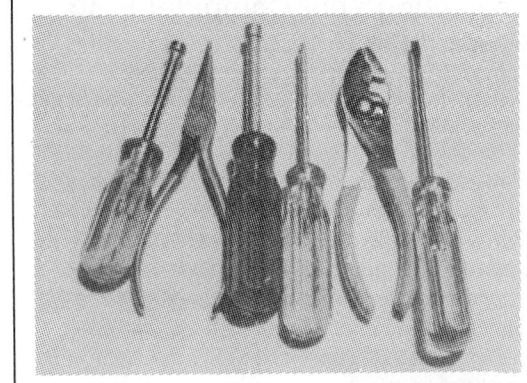

A.                B.

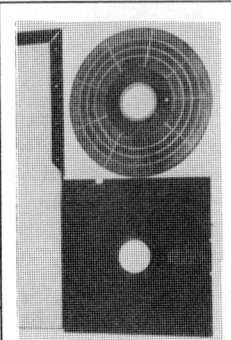

A. Parts and components needed to build an XT:
1. A case, flip top or slide on.
2. A mother board with components installed (would recommend a turbo board with 640 K of memory).
3. A power supply, 130 watt minimum.
4. A floppy disk drive controller card (or board).
5. One or two floppy disk drives.
6. A monitor card (or adaptor), should be monochrome or color, depending on the type of monitor you buy.

7. A monitor.
8. A keyboard.

B. Tools needed to build an XT.

A floppy diskette that has been taken apart. Lines representing tracks and sectors have been drawn on the surface.

## The Skeptical Consumer's Guide to Used Computers

Ed Kahn and Charles Seiter
1985; 306 pp.
**$9.95**
($10.95 postpaid) from:
Ten Speed Press
P. O. Box 7123
Berkeley, CA 94707
415/845-8414

## Before You Buy a Used Computer

Dona Z. Meilach
1985; 150 pp.
**$1.98**
($4.98 postpaid) from:
Crown Publishers
225 Park Avenue South
New York, NY 10003
800/526-4264

*Computers don't wear out or break easily. They obsolesce. Thus, though it may not run the latest techno-status software, a used 1983 machine will still process your words fine and could be the best way to break into computering. After all, prices drop fast, and someone else has already gone through the grief of setting the thing up. Anyone buying a used computer will have three basic questions: What should I get? What should I avoid? Where do I look?*

*To answer the first two questions, read **The Skeptical Consumer's Guide**. It walks you down the list of computer companies as if they were dealers on auto row and interprets each one's carnival spiel for you. A beginner could avoid some serious errors here — the CompuPro or the Workslate, for instance (for different reasons). This is that rare beast, a charming computer book, but it unfortunately skimps on the section on where to look after you narrow your list.*

*Hence you need **Before You Buy a Used Computer**. Skip to page 55 ("Finding Sources for Used Merchandise") and read to the back. It's all search*

A computer "bargain" may not be such a bargain if you have to buy a printer, disk drive, and software as well. The best overall bet is to buy a computer that has all the features you need in the first place.
—*The Skeptical Consumer's Guide to Used Computers*

*strategies. The chapter on auctions alone could save you hundreds of dollars. This is obviously a much more hurried, less painstaking book.*

*Sorry, I must recommend both. But once you buy your used computer, you can always sell these books to someone else, right? As a used-computer owner, you'll need Henry Beechhold's **Plain English Repair and Maintenance Guide for Home Computers** (page 171), since you won't be getting a warranty.*

—*Art Kleiner*

*If you think that $1.98 price for **Before You Buy a Used Computer** is a misprint, rest assured that it's not — the book has been remaindered but is still available from the publisher. It's a fantastic bargain, even for a book that's somewhat old by computer industry standards. Computers may change, but basic methods of buying and selling them remain.*

—*Sarah Vandershaf*

◆

The biggest fear of the first-time computer buyer is really the one most easily set aside. The usual service problems don't concern chips — which are easily replaced, not repaired — but mechanical parts (the physical cabinet and housing for the computer, disk drives, and peripherals). It is much like the situation with older cars. If you set out to restore a rare automobile, you will find that it is not the engine that will give you grief so much as the accessories like the cigarette lighter knob.
—*The Skeptical Consumer's Guide to Used Computers*

◆

Don't think that every swap meet has only good buys. Many dealers discover they can sell new merchandise at the regular price; sometimes over regular price because people are conditioned to think that swap meets spell bargains.

◆

At a computer auction, the items may not be plugged in and working, especially if this poses electrical connection and potential power problems. Neither should you expect people on the auctioneer's staff to know about or offer advice on the merchandise. If you persist, and bring along your own electric cord, you can usually get permission to plug in an item and try it. (Take along compatible software, too.) If it performs as it is supposed to, you are within safe boundaries. On large equipment, some provisions may be available for testing.
—*Before You Buy a Used Computer*

Used magazines for sale at a swap meet may give you an idea of the price range on an older item.
—*Before You Buy a Used Computer*

[Below]Computer swap meets are growing in popularity and sophistication. Merchandise will be varied and include anything from back copies of magazines to complete computer systems.
—*Before You Buy a Used Computer*

We heard that IBM is terminating a few members of their family. We're ready to move in on their AT/XT territory!

## Godfather's Used Computer Syndicate

Catalog **free** from Godfather's Used Computer Syndicate, P.O. Box 3037, 851 West State Road 436, Suite 1015, Altamonte Springs, FL 32714; 305/774-1111.

*Their name sounds like they should be selling pizzas, but really this outfit sells used IBM PCs and peripherals at (naturally) a price you can't refuse.*
—*Sarah Vandershaf*

## Working From Home

Paul and Sarah Edwards
1985; 420 pp.
**$11.95**
($13.20 postpaid) from:
St. Martin's Press
Cash Sales
175 Fifth Avenue
New York, NY 10010
800/221-7945

*Best of the books we've seen on this subject, but there's not enough detail. For instance, the authors mention health insurance, a major knot to untangle, but don't really point you toward sources. But the table of contents lists almost everything you need to think about if you are going to work from home.*

*— Art Kleiner*

◆

*Tips for Keeping Your Home and Work Separate:*
1. Clearly define your workspace.
2. Set definite work hours.
3. Have a way to signal that you're working; for example, keeping the office door closed or putting up a Do Not Disturb sign.
4. Learn how to firmly, but nicely, say, "No, I'm working now."

Room dividers

5. Use a separate business telephone line and an answering machine or answering service.
6. Soundproof your office.
7. Dress in a certain way when you're working.
8. Keep work materials, paper, and equipment in your office space.
9. Have a door or other barrier to your office. Close it while you're working and after you've finished working.

## Home Business Advisor

Charlie and Jan
Fletcher, Editors
**$16/year**
(6 issues) from:
Home Business Advisor
P.O. Box 41108
Fayetteville, NC 28309
919/867-2128

*The quote on the front page says it all: "Helping parents work at home." Each issue has helpful articles on how to arrange your schedule and workspace with a toddler around, how to deal with the stress of being a work-at-home-parent, and the good and bad points of bringing children along on business trips. Good general articles on selecting a computer and establishing small business networks makes this a valuable tool for anyone thinking about starting a home business.*

*— Richard Kadrey*

◆

No matter how small your living space, set boundaries between home and work, and keep them. Whether you have a room, closet, or a drawer, you need to have a place where your business things can remain undisturbed. In addition, you'll escape the stresses of the business more easily if you can put the traces away and turn your attention fully to home life. Your family also needs room to maintain a normal family life. Your kids will be more supportive of your work if they are not constantly confronting and adapting to it.

The bottom line to a home business isn't just financial. Pursuing a home business allows you to do what's really important to you as both a parent and an individual. A home business can help you live the way you think you should, while letting you follow your dreams... and isn't that what success is all about?

## NEBS
## Computer Forms
## NEBS
## Business Forms

Catalogs **free** from: NEBS, 500 Main Street, Groton, MA 01471; 800/225-9550

## The Reliable Corp.

Catalog **free** from: The Reliable Corporation, 1001 West Van Buren Street, Chicago, IL 60607; 800/621-4344

## Quill

Catalog **free** from: Quill, P.O. Box 4700, Lincolnshire, IL 60197-4700; 312/634-4800

*Good cheap office gear — cardboard filing drawers, inexpensive business forms, address labels, and discounted prices on tape, pens, etc. We used to use Quill. They are fast, and easy to work with. Now we use Reliable because their prices are often a tad cheaper. Nicely serving all one-person-one-computer businesses is NEBS, supplier of every conceivable kind of tractor-fed stationery and microcomputer need (daisy wheels, ribbons, disks and so on). All three provide excellent quick service and allow you to order by phone, toll free.*

*— Kevin Kelly*

— Nebs

**Product W9694-1 Continuous Envelope**
**20 lb. Ripple Finish bond**
**Size: 4¹/₈" × 9", 10 carrier**
**For pin feed printers that are adjustable up to 10"**

| Product | 2,000 | 1,000 | 500 |
|---------|-------|-------|-----|
| W9687-1 | $163.00 | $ 94.95 | $59.95 |
| W9694-1 | 189.95 | 107.50 | 72.50 |

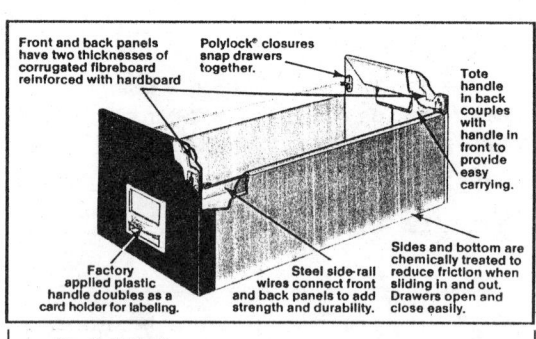

— The Reliable Corp.

**Available in paper weight to meet your needs**

MINI-PACK CARBONLESS
*As Low As*
**$18⁰⁰**
Per 500 Sheet Ctn.

— The Reliable Corp.

## Personal Electronics Book

Peter McWilliams
1987; 331 pp.
**$10.95**
($11.95 postpaid) from:
Prentice Hall Press
200 Old Tappan Rd.
Old Tappan, NJ 07675
800/223-2336
or Whole Earth Access

*This is one of those rarest of books — one that is informative and well written. The **Personal Electronics Book** is a comprehensive primer on not just what electronics to buy, but how to buy just about anything electrical that costs more than a light bulb. One cautionary note though: with the dollar bobbing around world markets like a demented jellyfish, some of the prices quoted in the book may be incorrect.*

— *Richard Kadrey*

◆

Microwaves work by speeding up the movement of water molecules within foods. The friction of the speeding molecules heats the water, which in turn cooks the food. Everything cooked in the microwave is essentially "steamed in its own juices."

◆

The power of an amplifier is measured in watts — the more watts, the more volume the amplifier can produce. Actually, you can create ear-damaging volume levels with just a few watts, but the double- and even triple-digit wattage ratings are sometimes necessary for peak power demands.

Let's say you're playing a violin solo. Your amplifier might be (depending on your speakers) consuming only four or five watts. Then suddenly, the cymbals crash and the timpani booms. That demands a lot more power, and *fast*. The total wattage consumption might jump to thirty watts, or more. If you have, say, a twenty-watt amplifier, the violin will sound great, but at the peak of the timpani's power demand, you will hear distortion.

The first television image: Felix the Cat, 1930 (NBC).

## J & R Music World

Catalog **free** from:
J & R Music World Department BSO388
59-50 Queens-Midtown Expressway
Maspeth, NY 11378-9896
800/221-8180

## 47th Street Photo, Inc.

Catalog **free** from:
47th Street Photo, Inc. Mail Order
Department 36 East 19th Street
New York, NY 10003
800/221-7774

*Mail order can offer major savings over local retail. Unlike most mail order consumer electronics stores, J & R offers three comprehensive catalogs — on computers, stereos, and videotapes. Between them you'll find home security devices, musical keyboards, telephones, blank tapes, copiers, watches, and shavers. 47th Street Photo has one enormous catalog with a full-range of consumer electronics. While they're prices are about on par with J&R's, some people have been put off by the New York brusqueness of 47th Street's sales people. Before you order anything, first visit a store near you and get familiar with the features — then compare prices and shop mail order via their 800 numbers.*

— *Saul Feldman*

**Sony CCD-V3 HandyCam**
**Auto Focus 8mm Camcorder**
• Compact • Auto focus zoom lens • Electronic viewfinder • Package comes complete with AC adaptor/charger and battery

Sale Price **$799**⁹⁵ List $1499 (SON CCDV3)
— J & R Music World

**Panasonic RX-SA66**
**Am/Fm Cassette Stereo To Go**
• Auto reverse convenience plays both sides of your favorite cassette • Ultra phonic mode switch for deep bass sound • Fm sensitivity control

Sale Price **$54**⁹⁵ List $69 (PAN RXSA66)

— 47st. Photo

**Portable CD Player**
• Ultra-compact size • Supplied rechargeable battery and built-in battery compartment • Automatic Music Sensor (AMS) • Shuffle play plus disc repeat modes • Auto Tracking recovery • Unilinear Converter with digital filter.

**Model D-3**

**$199**⁹⁵

— J & R Music World

**Sony SRS-50B**
**Self Powered Portable Speakers**
• Built-in amplifiers • Unique flat speakers with passive radiator design for realistic distortion free sound at high or low volumes • Auto power on/off

Sale Price **$74**⁹⁵ List $99 (SON SRS50)

— 47st. Photo

**PhoneMate 7050**
**Performance Series Phone System**
• Beeperless remote answering machine • 9 number auto dial telephone • Remote turn on • Call screening • Toll saver feature • Black

Sale Price **$99**⁹⁵ List $159 (PM 7050)

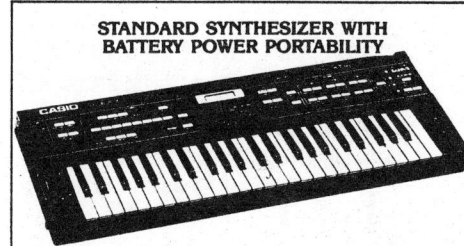

**STANDARD SYNTHESIZER WITH BATTERY POWER PORTABILITY**

49 full size key keyboard • 32 preset voices to provide realistic original effects • Modify these and create your own sounds for storage on an optional RAM cartridge • Battery powered for outdoor play and unlimited portability • Dimension: 3⅞"(H) x 32"(W) x 12¼"(D) • Weight: 12.1 lbs. • Accessories/6 size D dry batteries, plug cord set.
CZ-1000 **$289**⁹⁵

## Consumer Reports Guide to Electronics in The Home

Editors of Consumer Reports Books
1988; 224 pp.
**$7**
($10 postpaid) from:
Consumer Reports Books
540 Barnum Avenue
Bridgeport, CT 06608
914/667-9400
or Whole Earth Access

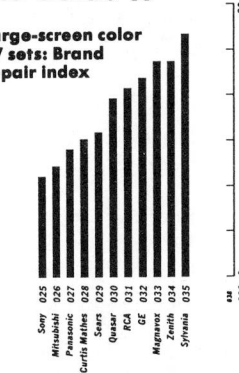

Large-screen color TV sets: Brand repair index

*The more antiquated among us sometimes find it difficult to deal with things electronic. Which devices are useful? The second in Consumer Reports annual review of consumer electronic items explains it all as it reviews home computers, TVs, hifis, radios, tape decks, phones, and alarms. As is their custom, the Consumers Union folks don't comment on every model of every brand. They make up for this by educating you in the* basics so you can, for instance, make sense out of specification sheets and salesman hype. This is the best general introduction to electronic gadgetry this side of the nearest teenage hacker.

— *J. Baldwin*

◆

The graph compares the reliability of eleven brands of large-screen TV sets, as reported by some 50,000 readers who had bought TV sets between 1980 and 1985. The bars in the graph represent an index showing the frequency with which the sets in each brand have needed repairs; the longer the bar, the more frequent the need for repair.

◆

There's no extra benefit in using expensive tapes in a portable cassette recorder. It lacks the electronic refinements necessary for getting the best out of a tape. Bargain-priced tapes, however, could increase the risk of an exasperating tape tangle or cassette misfit. You probably won't go wrong if you follow a middle course and buy the lowest-priced brand-name Type I (ferric) tape available.

## Computers & Nonprofits: Easing the Transition

*by Steve Johnson*

FIVE YEARS AGO fewer than 10 percent of nonprofit organizations owned computers; now it is estimated that over 50 percent of the organizations have access to small computers. Small computers have brought on a new era for nonprofit work in this country.

The computerization of the nonprofit sector has not come without some disappointments and disasters. People have learned the hard way that computer technology — unlike the other office technology of typewriters and copier machines — doesn't always come easy or cheap.

### BUDGETING FOR COMPUTERS

It is estimated that a $5,000 computer investment will, in five years, represent as much as a $30,000 investment: there are many hidden costs in buying a computer, including insurance (theft, transit, medical/ liability), depreciation, supplies, software, hardware and software upgrades, security, repair, and staff training.

Before you buy, you might want to try a needs assessment or requirement analysis. The Information Technology Resource Center in Chicago (below) has developed a good model for this with their 300 nonprofit member organizations.

### PRINT RESOURCES

**Computer Resource Guide for Nonprofits** (Volume I: Software Directory; Volume II: Funding Source Directory). **$95** each ($175/set) from Public Management Institute, 358 Brannan Street, San Francisco, CA 94107; 415/896-1900

*Volume II describes computer related-giving programs of 200 corporations, foundations, and government agencies. Volume I describes client-services software for tracking client costs, client demographics, client history; events software, food services, job matching, library management, public housing management, and survey software. There is extensive coverage of fund accounting and membership management software.*

**Computerization Needs Analysis.** Elizabeth Mandell and Morgan Lyons 1986; 41 pp. **$10** postpaid from Southern California Center for Nonprofit Management, 315 West 9th Street/ Suite 1100, Los Angeles, CA 90015; 213/623-7080

*Provides the information one needs to conduct a needs analysis — a systematic examination of the functions an organization wishes to computerize, and the identification of needs within each function. Plenty of worksheets make the book more than worth the price.*

**The Women's Computer Literacy Handbook.** Deborah L. Brecher, 1985; 254 pp. **$9.95** ($11.45 postpaid) from Plume/ New American Library, P. O. Box 999, Bergenfield, NJ 07621; 201/387 0600

*This excellent handbook covers history, basic computer concepts, ethical choices, and much more.*

**Computer Use in Social Services Network Newsletter.** $10/year from Dick Schoech, UTA, P. O. Box 19129, Arlington, TX 76019

*I always look forward to the CUSS Newsletter: with its reader-based contribution format one can find out about unusual and useful applications of computer technology to the social services.*

**RE:SET.** **$1**/issue from 90 East 7th Street/ 3A, New York, NY 10009

*A real gem, full of information about grass-roots and public-interest computing that you can't find out about anywhere else.*

**Managing With Computers.** $24/year (6 issues) from Lodestar Management/ Research, Inc., 1052 West 6th Street/ Suite 714, Los Angeles, CA 90017

*Each issue of this small but handy newsletter for nonprofit managers covers a special topic such as desktop publishing, nonprofit fund accounting, etc.*

**Communicating in the '80s:** New Options for the Nonprofit Communty; **Communicating Today:** Serving Nonprofit Needs with Technology. $3 each, postpaid from: The Benton Foundation, 1776 K Street, N.W., Suite 605, Washington, D.C. 20006

*These are reports summarizing the activities of the Benton Foundation in exploring how nonprofit organizations are using new electronic communication and information technology.*

### TECHNOLOGICAL SUPPORT

In 1983, nonprofit information technology resource centers began to appear in response to the education and technical assistance needs of nonprofits. Currently there are centers in Washington, D.C., Chicago, Los Angeles, Dallas, Portland, Oregon, and New York City. Together they form the Technology Resources Consortium. Their primary services are education, a wide range of classes, and training opportunities; access, availability of a computer-lab environment for testing and using computer equipment; and technical assistance, providing inexpensive assistance for nonprofits in purchasing equipment or further developing their computer systems. Recently the TRC evaluated membership management software; the compiled reviews are available from the Public Interest Computer Association for $25 (address below).

**Public Interest Computer Association.** 2001 O Street N.W., Washington, D.C. 20036; 202/775-1588

**Members of the Technology Resources Consortium. Computer Help and Information Program.** Southern California Center for Nonprofit Management, 315 W. 9th Street/Suite 1100, Los Angeles, CA 90015; 213/623-7080

**Information Technology Institute.** Center for Urban Education, 1135 S.E. Salmon, Portland, OR 97214; 503/231-1285

**Information Technology Resource Center.** 57th Street and S. Lake Shore Drive, Chicago, IL 60637; 312/684-1050

**Nonprofit Computer Exchange.** 419 Park Avenue S., 16th Floor, New York, NY 10016; 212/481-1799

**Technology Learning Center.** Center for Nonprofit Management, 2820 Swiss Avenue, Dallas, TX 75204; 214/826-3470

### CORPORATE SUPPORT

Apple has done more than any other corporation to support the automation of nonprofit work, providing grants to nonprofit organizations with an emphasis on using computer communication to build networks; support to the nonprofit computer resource centers; computers to larger nonprofits to distribute to their constituencies; computer grants to schools and colleges; and assistance to the disabled and groups which support the disabled.

**Apple Computer Co., Corporate Grants Program.** 20525 Mariani Avenue, Cupertino, CA 95014; 408/973-4475

With the exception of Apple, the computer industry has not gone out of its way to provide assistance to nonprofit organizations. However, the following companies have provided some support. Write for information.

**Digital Equipment Corporation**, Corporate Contributions, 111 Powdermill Road, Maynard, MA 01754; 617/493-7161

**Kaypro**, Dept. of Public Relations, 533 Stevens Avenue, Solana Beach, CA 92075; 619/259-4509, has been fairly generous in its support of nonprofit organizations and has a strong interest in international development uses of computers.

**Lotus Corporation**, The Philanthropic Committee, 55 Cambridge Parkway, Cambridge, MA 02142; 617/577-8500, has a loaned executive program and other support for nonprofit organizations (currently, Boston area only).

For more information on corporate support, see: **Computer Resource Guide for Nonprofits** (Printed Resources, above).

### NONPROFIT SOFTWARE

If you want to find out more about nonprofit software, contact the nonprofit computer resource center in your area, get hold of one of the periodicals or books reviewed in this section, or write to one of the following:

**Directory of Fund Accounting Software.** Donald Will, 1984. **$24.95** postpaid from Center for Local and Community Research, P. O. Box 5309, Elmwood Station, Berkeley, CA 94705; 415/654-9036

**Directory of Microcomputer Software in the Human Services.** Joseph A. Doucette. **$26.50** postpaid from Computer Consulting and Programming Associates, 7553 Canal Plaza, Portland, ME 04112; 207/774-8242

**Donor & Membership Software Review.** $25 postpaid from Technology Resources Consortium, 2001 O Street N.W., Washington, D.C. 20036; 202/775-1588

**Guide to Software for Nonprofits.** $79 postpaid from NPO Resource Review, Box A-6 Cathedral Station, New York, NY 10025

**Fund Accounting Software Review.** 1031 3rd Street, Santa Rosa, CA 95405 (conducting review of fund accounting software; distributes its own package)

The LOCT (light operated computer terminal) system uses a low powered infrared light source mounted on the nose bridge of spectacle frames to activate a receiver terminal (or keyboard). The user looks directly at the receiver and by small head movements can direct the light beam to activate whichever key or function they choose.

## Personal Computers and the Disabled

Peter McWilliams
1984; 416 pp.
**$9.95**
($11.95 postpaid) from:
Doubleday Cash Sales
P.O. Box 5071
Des Plaines, IL 60017-5071

***Personal Computers for the Disabled*** has lots of technical information, including detailed critiques of every personal computer, printer, and electronic typewriter I've ever heard of (and many I haven't heard of). McWilliams is learning-disabled (he never mastered multiplication tables), so he sympathizes with disabled people while avoiding sentimentality.           —*Mark O'Brien*

◆

People with the use of neither arms nor legs — but who have full use of head and neck — have several options for computer input. One is the sip and puff straw or the head switch. Others are spoken input and joysticks that operate by tongue or head movement.

## The Rehab/ Education Technology ResourceBook Series

(Communication, Control, and Computer Acces for Disabled and Elderly Individuals)
Brandenburg & Vanderheiden, Editors
University of Wisconsin
Trace R & D Center,
Reprint Service
S-151 Waisman Center
1500 Highland Avenue
Madison, WS 53705-2280

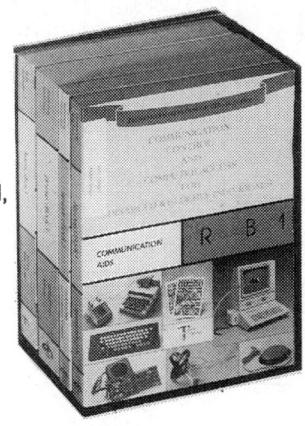

**ResourceBook 1 — Communication Aids,** 1987, 239 pp. **$24.50** postpaid. *Services and equipment for vocally impaired people.*

**ResourceBook 2 — Switches and Environmental Controls,** 1987, 227 pp. **$24.50** postpaid. *Also includes section on call, monitoring and memory systems. (I found this volume to be the most intriguing and informative of the scope of needs and abilities of disabled people.)*

**ResourceBook 3 — Hardware and Software,** 1987, 491 pp. **$29.50** postpaid. *Sources of hardware and software to make computers useful to disabled people.*

Set of 1, 2, and 3 **$69.50** postpaid.

**ResourceBook 4 — Update,** Borden & Vanderheiden, Editors, 1988, 380 pp. **$18.50** postpaid. *Update to ResourceBooks 1, 2, and 3.*

Believing you'd rather spend your time and energy in using or learning something rather than trying to find it or determine if it even exists, the editors have designed a many-tentacled tool for therapists, educators, parents, and disabled consumers to deal with a rapidly expanding technological sea of augmentative and rehab products and devices.

The bulk of these books are product descriptions and access information. Although you don't get told what's more hype than performance — descriptions are supplied by producers — you do get led to newsletters, databases, and service organizations who evaluate and make public their reviews.

Particularly impressive are the cross-referencing indexes, allowing you to match up particular needs and capabilities with specific availability.
—*Sarah Satterlee*
*[Suggested by Mark O'Brien]*

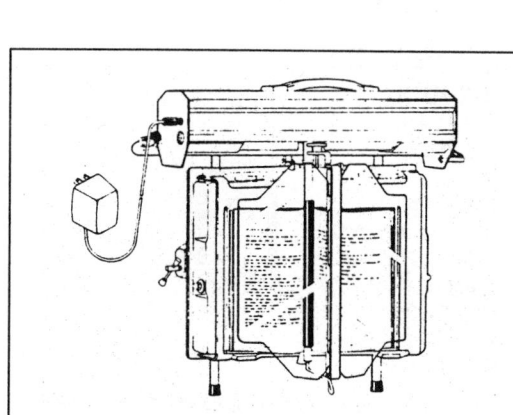

Gewa Page Turner is an automatic page turning system that can accommodate most textbooks, paperbacks, magazines, and smaller newspapers. A rubber roller manipulates pages forward and backward, singly or continuously, with no adjustments necessary for size, texture or style of document.

## Communication Outlook

(Focusing on Communication Aids and Techniques)
Luis Wassman, Editor
$15/4 issues per year
Artificial Language Laboratory
Michigan State University
405 Computer Center
East Lansing, MI 48824-1042
517/353-0870

## Closing the Gap

$21/6 issues
per year
(One of these issues
is the annual **Resource Directory** available separately for **$14.95** postpaid) from:
Closing the Gap
P.O. Box 68
Henderson, MN 56044
612/341-8299

*For special education and rehabilitation professionals, a comprehensive newsletter offering evaluations of new products, listings of service organizations, synopses of pending legislation, and a calendar of conferences and events. This year's resource directory focuses on microcomputer products that can assist people with disabilities.*

*When I asked two people, 2000 miles apart, for their recommendations, they both said, "Of course, there's Closing the Gap."*          —*Sarah Satterlee*
*[Suggested by Jim Vagnoni and Luis Wassman]*

◆

LD children do not necessarily need "special" software. They can use virtually any well designed program that contains specific characteristics suited to their needs. Here are some things to look for when choosing software for LD children:

1. Clear, uncluttered screen display with easy to read text and clearly drawn graphics — this is vital

2. Ease of use

3. Clear instructions on screen

4. Incorrect answers result in:

   —less interesting responses than given to correct answers

   —respectful responses — no harsh buzzers, x-ed out answers, etc.

   —helpful feedback leading to correct answers

5. Incorrect answers stay on the screen until users choose to remove them —this allows children and teachers to analyze mistakes and try to correct them.

6. Users control of as many options as possible — ability to control speed, content, sound, exit and entry points, amount of repetition, length of presentations, etc. . . .

12. And most important of all . . . programs that intrigue children and motivate them to want to learn — look for programs that provide novelty, humor, suspense, variety, a means of creating products of which they can be proud (pictures, stories, printed copies of problems they have solved), etc.

*Enabling the disabled must be a personal computer's proudest moment. Read this capable newsletter for reports on sophisticated and home-brewed experiments to extend the body's senses into hardware for the benefit of the disabled. The whole domain is more pragmatic and service oriented, and therefore more successful, than similar robotic research.*          —*Kevin Kelly*

## Inside the Robot Kingdom

(Japan, Mechatronics, and the Coming Robotopia)
Frederik L. Schodt
1988; 256 pp.

**$19.95**
($21.45 postpaid) from:
Harper & Row
2350 Virginia Avenue
Hagerstown, MD 21740
800/638-3030
or Whole Earth Access

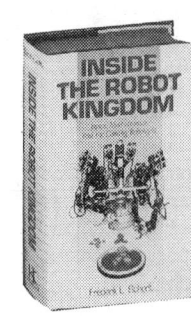

*The robots are coming, and they are Japanese. About 50% of the world's population of robots live on the island of Japan, and a large share of the rest living outside have been exported from there. Japan manufactures the mythic image of robot*

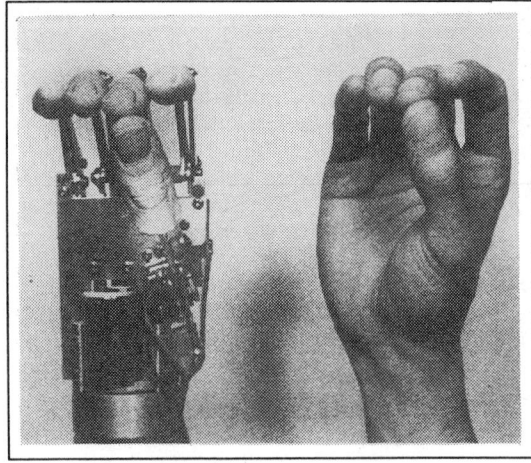

A 1979 forearm prosthesis, WH-11E2, could pinch and grip.

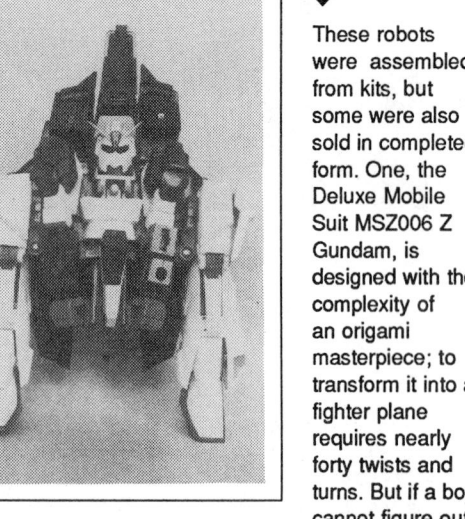

These robots were assembled from kits, but some were also sold in completed form. One, the Deluxe Mobile Suit MSZ006 Z Gundam, is designed with the complexity of an origami masterpiece; to transform it into a fighter plane requires nearly forty twists and turns. But if a boy cannot figure out the complex movements, all is not lost. Bandai was one of the first Japanese toy makers to guarantee its wares in 1958 and like most major toy companies today has a national network of walk-in service centers where specially trained staff answer questions and complaints from customers — and demonstrate how to properly transform the robots.

## Robotics

Marvin Minsky, Editor
1985; 317 pp.
**$19.95**
postpaid from:
Doubleday and Company
Direct Mail Order
501 Franklin Avenue
Garden City, NY 11530
800/223-5780
or Whole Earth Access

*Edited by an artificial intelligence pioneer, this anthology covers all the bases: the history of automatons, artificial common sense, sensors, human-machine partnerships (cyborgs), industrial robots, and the effects of robots on society. Here is the best starting point for a non-tinkerer who wants to know what robotics is about, and how it might change the world.*

— *Art Kleiner*

At some point in the future someone would go to work by slipping on a comfortable jacket lined with a myriad of sensors and musclelike motors. Each motion of his arm and fingers would then be reproduced at another place by mobile, mechanical hands. Light, dexterous, and strong, these remote mechanical hands have their own sensors, which will transmit what's happening back to the worker so that he will seem to feel whatever the remote hands may touch. The same will be done for the motions of the head and eyes, so that the operator will seem to see and sense what's happening in the other workplace. Once we can do such things, it will be another simple step to give those remote presences different strengths and scale of size. These remote bodies can have the brute capacity of a giant or the delicacy of a surgeon. And, using these information channels, an operator could be anyplace — in another room, another city, another country, even out on a space station orbiting the Earth.

A 1980 census of robots, taken by Bache Halsey Stuart Shields, Inc., showed that United States had 3,000 of them. . . . The entire Soviet Union had only 25, and these were evidently experimental devices, but Poland had 360. . . . The true homeland of the robot appears to be Japan, with 10,000 in the census, more than the rest of the world combined.

*plural, of comprising a countless, advancing army; it is the source of nearly all the millions of robot toys and epic Saturday morning robot cartoons. This book surveys life in* robotto okuku, *the Japanese nickname for their own Robot Kingdom, and illuminates the way a culture aspires to, eventually accommodates, the ways and metaphors of robots.*

— *Kevin Kelly*

Shobe-e Tamaya with a spring-driven karakuri doll made by his ancestors over 250 years ago and still used in religious festivalstoday.

## Basic Robotic Concepts

John M. Holland
1983; 270 pp.
**$19.95**
($22.45 postpaid) from:
Howard W. Sams & Co.
4300 West 62nd Street
Indianapolis, IN 46268
317/298-5400
or Whole Earth Access

*Generally agreed upon as the best overall technical book. It's designed to educate people about the various problems of robotics — balancing the machine, vision systems, motors, torque curves,* wheels versus legs, and programming the intelligence.

— *Art Kleiner*

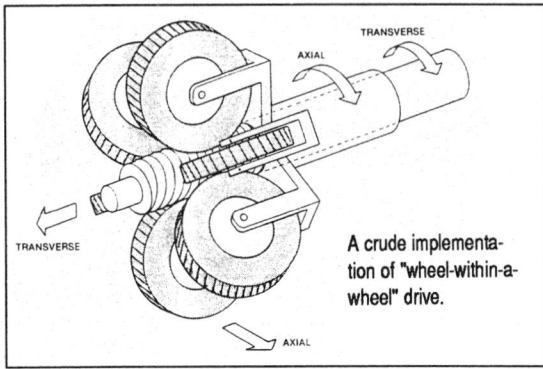

A crude implementation of "wheel-within-a-wheel" drive.

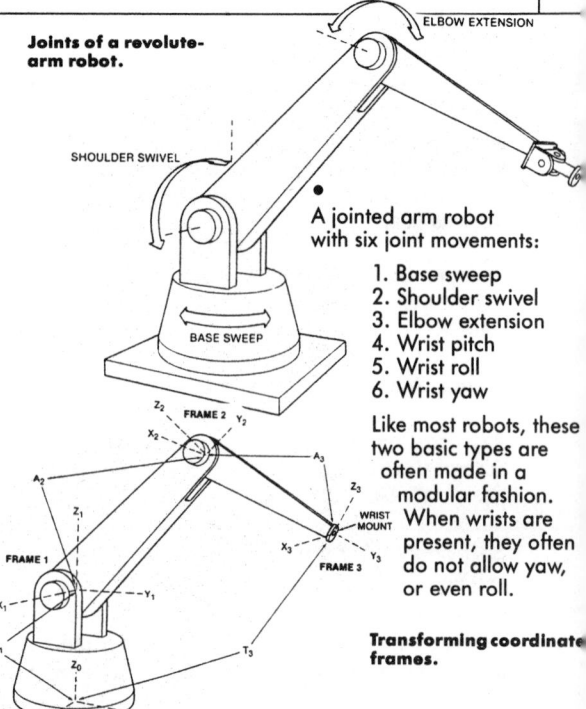

Joints of a revolute-arm robot.

ELBOW EXTENSION

SHOULDER SWIVEL

BASE SWEEP

A jointed arm robot with six joint movements:

1. Base sweep
2. Shoulder swivel
3. Elbow extension
4. Wrist pitch
5. Wrist roll
6. Wrist yaw

Like most robots, these two basic types are often made in a modular fashion. When wrists are present, they often do not allow yaw, or even roll.

**Transforming coordinate frames.**

ROBOT experimenters are like hackers waiting to happen. Twenty years ago, people interested in computers had to work with clumsy analog equipment, throwing switches by hand and writing reams of code in low-level languages, all to tell the machine how to add a few lousy integers. Today, computer jocks are starting their own multi-million dollar companies and hacking their way into corporate databases. Not so with robot freaks. They're still dealing with enormous programming and mechanical problems. Think about it — how do you explain to a near-blind contraption that looks like a stripped down cash register on roller skates that it has just bumped into a wall and that it shouldn't do it again? What about the dozens of tiny movements and corrections you make unconsciously when picking up a glass of water? All of that information must be programmed into a robot. Then you have to hope that the mechanics all work right. On top of that, finding parts for your robot can be very difficult. And expensive. Finding people who share your interest in robots can be even harder.

The following lists of robot clubs and suppliers is not meant to be comprehensive, but to give someone who is interested in robots a place to start. Robot experimenting is not easy, but it is a wide open field, where you can let your intelligence and imagination run wild. With patience and some luck you can be out overturning the world in no time.

— *Richard Kadrey*

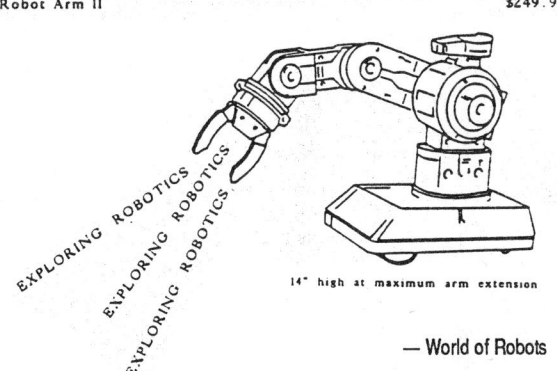

— Heathkit

Electronic Voice Synthesizer

Temperature and Sound Sensors

Optional on-board 5¼" DSDD Disk Drive

Rechargeable Gelled Electrolyte Battery

Optional Autodock System

Two-wheel Dual Servomotor Drive System

360° Sonar and Light Scanner

16-bit Master Processor and Eleven 8-bit Slave Microprocessors

Articulated Arm

Gripper with Sense of Touch

Radio Remote Control Console with Keyboard, Display, and Teaching Pendant Mode

**HERO® 2000**

## Robotics Groups

### Connecticut Robotics Society
Al Vitello, President. 15 Abbey Road, East Hampton, CT 06424; 203/267-7485

### Homebrew Robotics Club
91 Roosevelt Circle, Palo Alto, CA 94306; 415/494-8499

### National Service Robotics Association
P.O. Box 3724, Ann Arbor, MI 48106; 313/994-6088

### Robotics Society of America
36 Newell Street, San Francisco, CA 94133; 415/673-2376

## Sources

### Edmund Scientific
Catalog $5 from: Edmund Scientific Company, 101 E. Gloucester Pike, Barrington, NJ 08007; 609/573-6250

### Heathkit
Catalog free from: Heath Company, P.O. Box 1288, Benton Harbor, MI 49022; 800/253-0570

### Herbach & Rademan
Catalog free from: H & R Corporation, 401 E. Erie Avenue, Philadelphia, PA 19134; 215/426-1708

### World of Robots
Catalog $6.25 (includes $5 gift certificate) from: World of Robots, 55 Earle Street, Milford, CT 06460; 203/877-4400

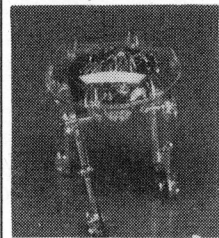

— Edmund Scientific

**D) Medusa Robot Has Electronic Brain**
At your command, Medusa starts to hobble on its four legs. Stops automatically after a preset time. You register your command through a sound sensor, including a condensor microphone and transistor. Two crankshaft legs on each side. Powered by two 1.5V N size batteries (not included). Clear plastic body.
**P36,633 $37.95**

— Herbach & Rademan

### MOTORIZED WHEEL ASSEMBLY

Perfect for motorizing numerous devices such as carts, wagons, turntables and robots. *"The Wheel" is similar to the one featured in "How to Build a Computer Controlled Robot" by Ted Loofbourrow.* The low voltage DC PM field reversible motor is geared down to drive the 4¾ dia. x 1⅜" W rubber wheel. Motor operates on 6 or 12 VDC & can be rheostat speed controlled. Shipping Weight each, 4 lbs.

|  | 12 VDC | 6 VDC |
|---|---|---|
| Speed approx. (no load) | 200 RPM | 90 RPM |
| Current (no load) | 2 Amps | 1.75 A |
| Pulling force approx. | 20 lbs. | 8 lbs. |
| Stall current | 10 Amps | 8 Amps |

Mounting post, heavy wall steel tubing 5" long, ¾" dia. Heavy duty plastic gears drive the tire which is enclosed in a metal shroud. New.
H&R# **TM21K460____ $29.95 EA.**

— Herbach & Rademan

**5 to 6 VDC RELAY FOR ROBOTIC APPLICATIONS**
**4 PDT** Relay with low power consumption. *Ideal for use with our* **TM22K638, 6 V Dual Motor Drive for reversing or for other robotic applications.** Can be interfaced with 5 V solid state devices. Coil resistance 60 Ω, 415 mW, 80 mA @ 5 V, 600 mW, 100 mA @ 6 V. Contacts rated 2 A, 28 VDC or 120 VAC non-inductive. Wrap type connections tinned for soldering. Plastic encased, 1¼ H x ¾ x 1¼"; 2 tapped mtg holes in metal base, or cement in place. New. Wt, 3 ozs. **$2.95 EA.**
MFR. FUJITSU
H&R# **TM22K751____4 @ $2.50 EA.**

*Even if you live in a big city, finding just the right motor to operate that servo arm for your robot can be a problem. That's why mail order suppliers are so helpful. Herbach & Rademan's catalog is for the real "hands-on" type; they sell everything for the experimenter, from EPROMs to rubber wheels, from stepping motors to rechargeable batteries. World of Robots catalog is geared more toward robot kits and educational products, including videos. They also offer enabling robots for the handicapped and a robot rental service. Besides general electronic products, both Edmund Scientific and Heathkit offer several kit robots, with Heathkit's HERO 2000 earning the reputation as one of the most popular and versatile personal robots available. The key to selecting a catalog is knowing what you want. Are you designing a robot from the ground up, or do you want to try a kit to get started?*

— *Richard Kadrey*

**ROBOT ARM II** - affordable robotics for your Apple II and IIe computer. The Robot Arm II proves that learning can be fun!

The Robot Arm II movements are: Forward, Reverse, Right, Left, Hand rotate, Jaw open/close, Wrist up/down & Arm up/down.

Robot Arm II                    $249.95

EXPLORING ROBOTICS

14" high at maximum arm extension

— World of Robots

### Robot Resources
(The International Robotics Newsletter)
Jacob Mendelssohn, Editor
$12/year
(eight issues) from:
Robot Review
c/o Science Museum of Connecticut
950 Trout Brook Drive
West Hartford, CT 06119
203/236-2961

*Under the editorial direction of Ray Cote (editor of the now defunct Robot Experimenter), **Robot Resources** is the only magazine dedicated to people interested in working with and building robots. The first issues contain reports on the robot experiments of a group of third graders, as well as an explanation of strategic arm torques with enough details that you can apply the information to your own robot experiments.*

— *Richard Kadrey*

## The Media Lab
(Inventing the Future at MIT)
Stewart Brand
1987; 285 pp.
**$10**
($12 postpaid) from:
Viking Penguin Books, Inc.
299 Murray Hill Parkway
E. Rutherford, NJ 07073
800/631-3577
or Whole Earth Access

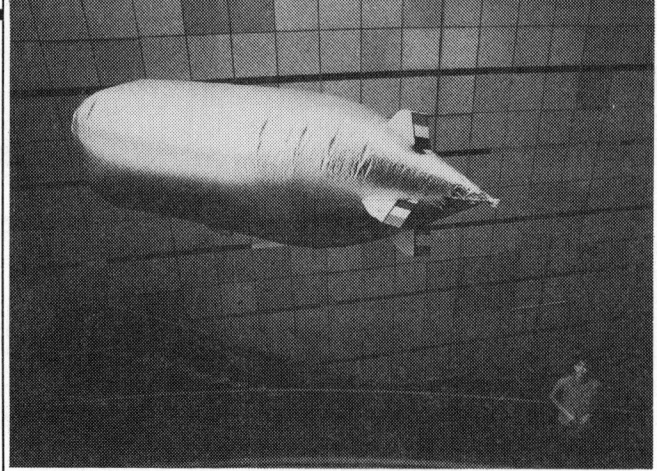

The first creatures created for the Vivarium were radio- and computer-controlled blimps that pretended to be fish, swimming around in the Media Lab's atrium. The blimps had rudimentary sensors that helped them orient in relation to walls, each other, and "food" (electricity). With the help of some blue light a classroom was spectacularly transformed into an ocean where child and "fish" become collaborators in a shared experiment.

*As we speak, the once-separate galaxies of computers, publishing, and broadcasting are melding into each other with a great deal of muttering, armwaving, and hustling of new hardware. At the confluence is MIT's radical technology department, the Media Lab, which is betting multimillions that it can steer the collision into a cohesive whole: perhaps a mega-combo of telephone/video/audio/ simulation/newspaper that is uniquely tailored to each individual. The goal, as the Media Lab sees it, is to let the audience take over. At stake is the major source of wealth in the future — entertainment/news.*

*Sounds like an exciting place to visit. Trouble is, the Media Lab's work is spread vexingly thin since its range is so wide. When I was there I came away with unfocussed glimmers of vague, halfunderstood somethings. Stewart Brand, founder of the **Whole Earth Catalog**, spent a year hanging out there, writing the ultimate tour of the Lab that everyone would like, but can never get. As you might expect from Stewart, there is a meta-level to the book: the media laboratory that our world has become. He envisions supremely individualized connections with appliances that would "know the user so intimately that the dialogue between machine and human would bring about ideas unrealizable by either partner alone." Stewart's astute and rigorously researched insights are the only aerial view of this uncertain landscape so far. I view this book as philosophical documentation for the practical examples paraded in **Signal**.*
— Kevin Kelly

◆

Students and professors at the Media Laboratory write papers and books and publish them, but the byword of this grove of academe is not "Publish or Perish." In Lab parlance it's "Demo or Die" — make the case for your idea with an unfaked performance of it working at least once, or let somebody else at the equipment.

◆

Want to know where the action in a culture is? Watch where new language is turning up and where lawyers collect, usually in that sequence.

◆

Me: "Do you have a standard timeline for when machine intelligence catches up with human intelligence and goes rolling past?"

Minsky: "Yeah. Between 100 and 300 years. Intelligent evolution is unprecedented. Nobody's ever seen one. So in a few hundred years it could do trillions of years of ordinary slow evolution."

Me: "And make enormous mistakes."

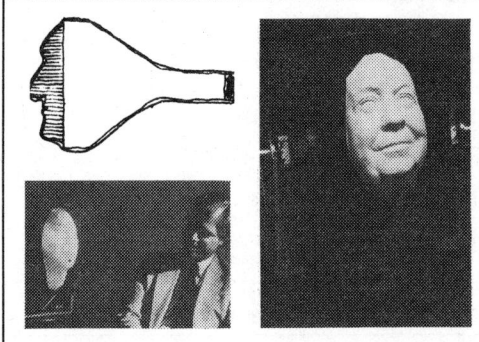

The original "Talking Head," circa 1979, had gimbals to replicate head movement. It would enable five people, in widely separated locations, to meet around a highly intimate "virtual" conference table. At each of the five locations there would be one real person and four video faces representing real people, glancing at each other, nodding or shaking their head, able to converse with a high degree of nuance.

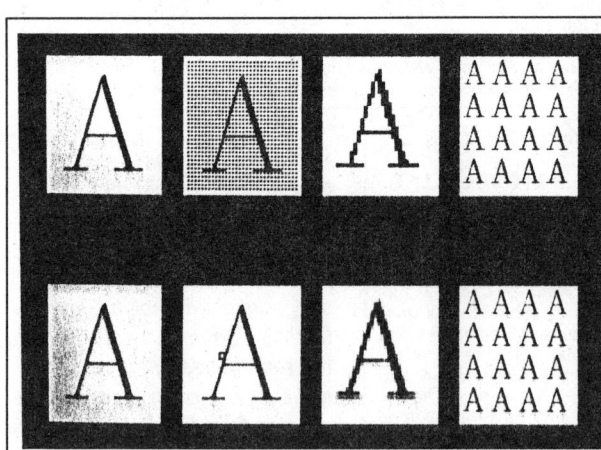

Minsky: "That's the trouble. There's no time to iron out the bugs. It might fill up the universe with styrofoam or something because it had some wrong theory about how the cosmos needs a shock absorber." Suddenly I saw a Vivarium as a swell place to work out some of these problems, rather than in the world.

◆

If, as alleged, the only real freedom of the press is to own one, the fullest realization of the First Amendment is being accomplished by technology, not politics.

◆

While computers probe and imitate the "society of mind," they are also shaping the mind of society. Computers and communications have already blended so far that they are one activity, still without a verb to express what it does. We don't even have a word for nervous activity in the body — it's not "thinking," "sensing," or "talking." All the chemical and energy activities in a body (or a society) have a word for their sum action — "metabolism" — but there is no equivalent word for the sum of communi-cations in a system. The lack of a word signals a deeper ignorance. We don't know what constitutes healthy communications.

◆

When I mentioned to Jerome Wiesner that I was shifting my work environment from one kind of personal computer to another, he commiserated, "I think that nobody should have to learn a new machine after the age of twenty-seven." It's not just what you have to learn, it's what you have to teach the machine. More powerful machines require more teaching. That's something the Media Lab would like to reverse: more powerful machines should be able to learn from you on their own.

The counter-intuitive use of blurring, called anti-aliasing or Fuzzy Fonts, makes text more readable on computer screens. The technique was pioneered in 1972 at the Architecture Machine Group (a predecessor of the Media Lab) but ignored by industry until 1987. You lose sharpness by introducing shades of grey instead of sticking with strict black & white, but you gain resolution. It is dramatically less tiring to read Fuzzy Font text.

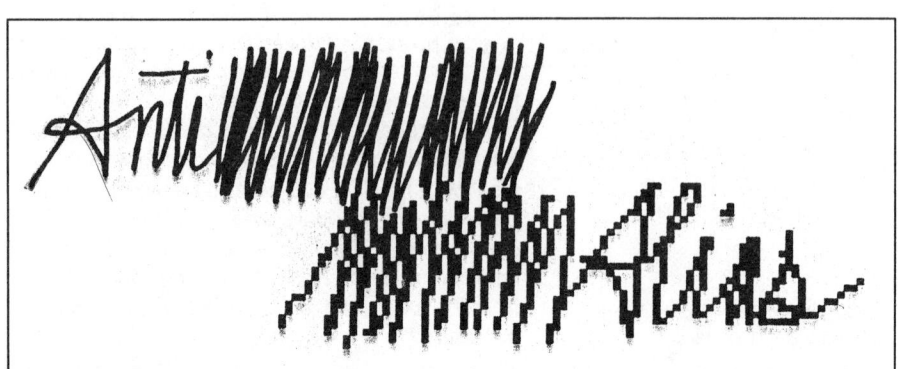

## Mirrorshades

(The Cyberpunk Anthology)
Bruce Sterling, Editor
1986, 256 pp.
**$3.50**
($4.50 postpaid) from:
Warner Publications Service
75 Rockefeller Plaza
New York, NY 10019
212/686-9820
or Whole Earth Access

*Cyberpunk is a form of science fiction steeped in the philosophy of the Information Age, the age of the global village, the personal computer, Chernobyl, and SDI. Cyberpunk is important because it accepts the technological changes of the last quarter-century and attempts to put them into some kind of perspective. Cyberpunk isn't interested in predicting the future; it's an attempt to find out how we can live there. Mirrorshades offers a few fine examples of what living there might be like.*

*—Richard Kadrey*

◆

Science fiction — at least according to its official dogma — has always been about the impact of technology. But times have changed since the comfortable era of Hugo Gernsback, when Science was safely enshrined — and confined — in an ivory tower. The careless technophilia of those days belongs to a vanished, sluggish era, when authority still had a comfortable margin of control.

For the cyberpunks, by stark contrast, technology is visceral. It is not the genie of remote Big Science boffins; it is pervasive, utterly intimate. Not outside us, but next to us. Under our skin; often, inside our minds.

Technology itself has changed. Not for us the giant steam-snorting wonders of the past: the Hoover Dam, the Empire State building, the nuclear power plant. Eighties tech sticks to the skin, responds to the touch: the personal computer, the Sony Walkman, the portable telephone, the soft contact lens.

Certain central themes spring up repeatedly in cyberpunk. The theme of body invasion: prosthetic limbs, implanted circuitry, cosmetic surgery, genetic alteration. The even more powerful theme of mind invasion: brain-computer interfaces, artificial intelligence, neurochemistry — techniques radically redefining the nature of humanity, the nature of the self.

*—From the Introduction*

## Science Fiction Magazines

*by Richard Kadrey*

Science fiction is changing fast in the Eighties. The following publications will keep you up on all that's interesting and important in the field. **Science Fiction Eye** specializes in fine features and exhaustive interviews with authors; **Locus** gives you the latest publishing news from New York; and **Science Fiction Guide** provides an outlet for authors and editors to critque the field themselves.

### Science Fiction Eye

Stephen P. Brown and Daniel J. Steffan, Editors; **$7**/year (3 issues) from: Science Fiction Eye, P.O. Box 43244, Washington, D.C. 20010-9244

### Science Fiction Guide

Charles Platt, Editor; **$6**/year (4 issues) from: Science Fiction Guide, 594 Broadway, Rm. 1208, New York, NY 10012

### Locus

Charles Brown, Editor; **$28**/year (12 issues) from: Locus Publications, P. O. Box 13305, Oakland, CA 94661

## Cyberpunk 101

*by Pat Murphy*

For a quick intro to cyberpunk, read the **Mirrorshades** anthology. If you're willing to invest more time, check the novels listed here. Cyberpunk, like most successful art movements, has spawned a second generation of practitioners. This list includes many of the folks who helped create and define the movement, as well as some relative newcomers.

### Neuromancer

William Gibson; 1984; 271 pp., **$2.95**; Ace Books

### Count Zero

William Gibson; 1984; 246 pp., **$2.95**; Ace Books

### Mona Lisa Overdrive

William Gibson; 1988; 260 pp., **$18.95**; Bantam Books
*Highly recommended.* **Neuromancer**, *Gibson's first novel captured the attention of the science fiction community, winning the Hugo, Nebula, and Philip K. Dick awards. In it, Gibson introduces the Matrix, a graphic representation of data culled from all the computer banks in the human system. Every user who jacks into this "consensual hallucination" projects his disembodied consciousness into an abstract world of data where battles of life and death are fought. Gibson's second and third books, linked to* **Neuromancer** *but capable of standing alone, have fulfilled the promise of the first book and continue the story of the evolution of the Matrix and how it affects those who enter it. Read any one or read them all.*

### Mindplayers

Pat Cadigan; 1987; 288 pp., **$2.95**; Bantam Books
*A first novel by one of the hottest new science fiction short story writers.* **Mindplayers** *follows the training of "Deadpan" Allie, a mindplayer who goes "mind to mind" with her clients, exploring the inner reaches of their delusions.*

### When Gravity Fails

George Alec Effinger; 1987; 256 pp., **$2.95**, Bantam
*A fast-paced novel of murder and intrigue set in the decadent Arab ghetto known as the Budayeen. An interesting example of second-generation cyberpunk.*

### Metrophage

Richard Kadrey; 1988; 240 pp., **$2.95**; Ace Books
*Vivid, imaginative writing with flashes of brilliance. A gutter-level view of the future city of Los Angeles — which authorities have abandoned to smugglers, gangs and a new plague. For reasons he does not understand, Jonny Qabbala is pursued by an anarchist-surrealist gang, by smuggler lords, by the paramilitary, and even by the extraterrestrials who have a base on the moon.*

### Wetware

Rudy Rucker;1988; 183 pp., **$2.95**; Avon Books
*More ideas per chapter than most authors use in an entire novel. Sentient robots (called "boppers") find a way to incorporate their software with human DNA, creating Manchile, the first "meatbop" combination.*

### Eclipse / Eclipse Penumbra Total Eclipse

John Shirley; 1988; **$2.95** each; Warner Books
*The most political cyberpunk yet. In the not too distant future, a neo-fascist movement sweeps across Europe, threatening the world with all-out war.*

### Islands in the Net

Bruce Sterling; 1988; 352 pp., **$17.95**; Arbor House
*A thoughtful extrapolation of a future in which nuclear weapons have been banned and information is the most valuable commodity.*

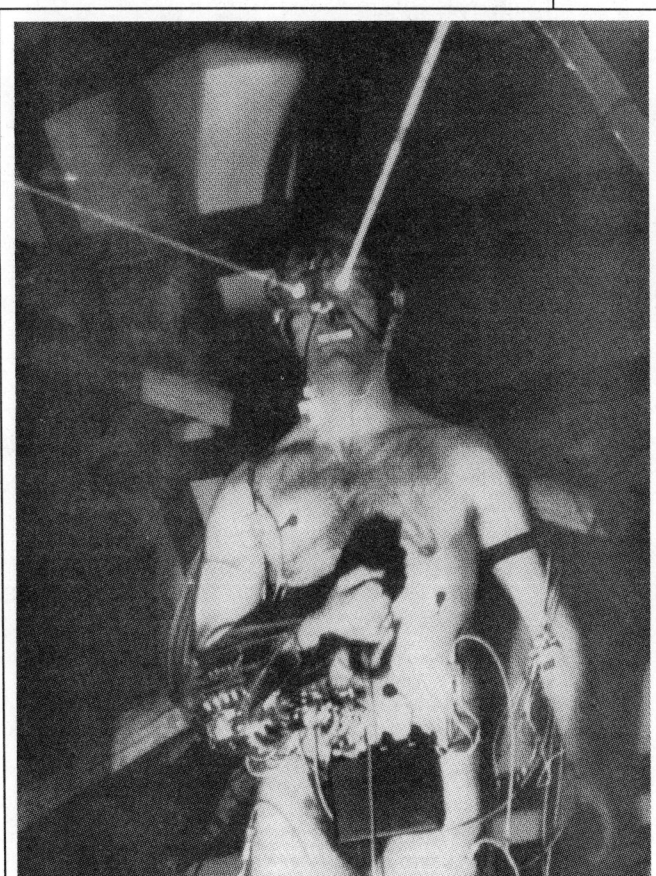

Stelarc's "Event For Amplified Body, Laser Eyes And Third Hand" from **Science Fiction Eye**

## Mark V. Ziesing, Bookseller

All of the books mentioned in **Cyberpunk 101**, plus many other science fiction, fantasy, and small press books, are available by mail order. Catalog **free** from: Mark V. Ziesing, Bookseller, P. O. Box 806, 762 Main Street (2nd Level), Willimantic, CT 06226; 203/423-5836

*Y*OU MAY *reproduce this material if your recipients may also reproduce it.*

Sometime in the last year or so, announcements like the one above were being attached to computer network messages. Unlike communication in the public domain, which anyone can use for whatever commercial purpose, share-right limits its benefits to those willing to share the bounty in the same way they received it. Users can take it only if they pass it on with the same promise. As Jack Powers, one of the network riders, says, "I like this idea of rights which travel together with the merchandise." Although share-right was born on the networks, I envision it taking root in other decentralized, highly replicating communications, like Xerox publishing, or tape duplicating. Howard Rheingold, a host on The Well, calls it "a self-reproducing word virus that eats intellectual property."

As far as I know, the share-right concept first appeared at the junction of USENET and Stargate, two network systems of different politics. USENET, one of the most libertarian networks running, distributes and redistributes messages in an ad hoc style of complete non-ownership. You don't post something in USENET without expecting it to be copied all over the country, or the world. Stargate is a privately run network which beams netnews into space by hitching the messages to an unused area of information transmission in the "blink" between screens on cable TV broadcasts. It would bounce news off a satellite, down to distant pickup sites, and into local computers again. I'll let Erik Fair, a USENET engineer, tell the rest of the story:

"Stargate as originally envisioned was a cheap way to send USENET news everywhere by true broadcast.

at the junction of USENET and Stargate, two network systems of different politics. USENET, one of the most libertarian networks running, distributes and redistributes messages in an ad hoc style of complete non-ownership. You don't post something in USENET without expecting it to be copied all over the country, or the world. Stargate is a privately run network which beams netnews into space by hitching the messages to an unused area of information transmission in the "blink" between screens on cable TV broadcasts. It would bounce news off a satellite, down to distant pickup sites, and into local computers again. I'll let Erik Fair, a USENET engineer, tell the rest of the story:

"Stargate as originally envisioned was a cheap way to send USENET news everywhere by true broadcast.

Unfortunately, the communication legalities were such that they could not claim to be a common carrier (like telephone companies), and this led directly into Stargate becoming a subscriber service instead (like a publisher). Stargate has an agreement that prohibits their subscribers from redistributing the articles they get from Stargate because, of course, it would erode Stargate's subscriber base if they did.

"Naturally, this caused a bit of a stink on the net, and the result was the copyright notices which you see on some people's articles. ('You can redistribute only if your recipients can'), preventing Stargate from transmitting those articles unless their subscribers can."

You, reader, are encouraged to duplicate this message, but only if your readers may also duplicate it.

---

### How to Copyright Software

(Everything You Need to Copyright All Types of Computer Programs and Output)
M.J. Salone
1984; 232 pp.
**$24.95**
($27.45 postpaid) from:
Nolo Press
950 Parker Street
Berkeley, CA 94710
415/549-1976
or Whole Earth Access

*Laid out in the structured logic of a computer program, this expert how-to knowledge will unfailingly lead you through the current copyright maze, a hall of mirrors in large part created by the paradoxical nature of software (I can give away a thousand dollar item and still have it). With engineer precision it even covers an all too common error: "Correcting a Defective Copyright Notice." This manual is a smart investment.* —KK

If your code makes perfect sense when separated from the existing work, it may qualify as an independent work which you can copyright, even if you don't own the original program. This is particularly likely to be true if you treat it as an independent work. However, in some circumstances, it might still be a derivative work and thus not entitled to independent protection. This is because the Copyright Act says that one work is derivative of another if it is "based" on it. What the term "based on" means has been left to the courts to define, and they have done so case by case, without establishing any clear guidelines.

◆

Place a copyright notice on your work and register it, depositing object code. Object code is probably immune from reverse engineering at the Copyright Office because that office only allows the examination, not the copying, of deposits. In other words, to reverse engineer your object code, a pirate would have to be able to do it in his head while standing in the Copyright Office.

---

### The Copyright Book

(A Practical Guide)
William S. Strong
1981, 1984; 223 pp.
**$6.95**
($9.45 postpaid) from:
MIT Press
28 Carleton Street
Cambridge, MA 02142
617/253-5251
or Whole Earth Access

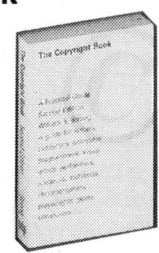

*Not a mere legalistic regurgitation of rules and regulations, this is the best book on copyright principles for my money. With clear insight, imaginative examples, and hardly a Latin word in sight, the author pierces the thicket of riddles we call copyright. He's the only one I've read willing to tackle thorny issues like parody, private copying, and "librarying" — archiving copies for research.* —KK

◆

If copyright is like property in land, infringement is like moving onto someone's land without permission, chopping down trees, mining coal, and stealing water from the well. But, unlike boundaries in land, the boundaries of a copyright are never clearly defined and frequently are not known until the end of a lawsuit.

◆

Where lies the boundary between copyright and freedom of speech, both of which derive from the Constitution? One's first answer is to say that although a citizen may be free to speak, he is not entitled to speak his mind in the same words as his neighbor. He is free to speak the idea, if you will, but not the expression. However, when you consider that "expression" can mean an arrangement of ideas this answer wears a bit thin. In the end, discussions on this subject are generally reduced to "Well, we know what we mean by free speech, even if we can't put it into words."

◆

So, in full knowledge of the risks, I will undertake to put into words a rule for drawing the line between the First Amendment and copyright. My suggestion is this: use of copyright work is fair to the extent that the user could not otherwise convey or demonstrate his ideas in exercise of his freedom of speech.

---

### How to Register a Copyright © and Protect Your Creative Work

Robert B. Chickering and
Susan Hartman
1980, 1987; 230 pp.
**$10.95** postpaid from:
Macmillan Publishing Co.
Attn.: Mail Order Department
Front & Brown Streets
Riverside, NJ 08075
800/257-5755
or Whole Earth Access

*Which hoops to jump through in the great paper-chase. All the forms are covered, steps one, two, three, four. . . .* —KK

◆

When you convert your idea into a fixed form, it is your form of expression — not your concept — that is protected. If it seems unfair that someone can use your ideas, a simple explanation of the reasoning behind the law is that copyright is designed to stimulate, not limit, the development of original works.

◆

Your work is automatically protected by the copyright law from the moment it is created — fixed in a tangible medium — even though you have not registered it with the Copyright Office. You do not have to register a claim to copyright in your work in order to reproduce, distribute, market, transfer ownership, or license your work.

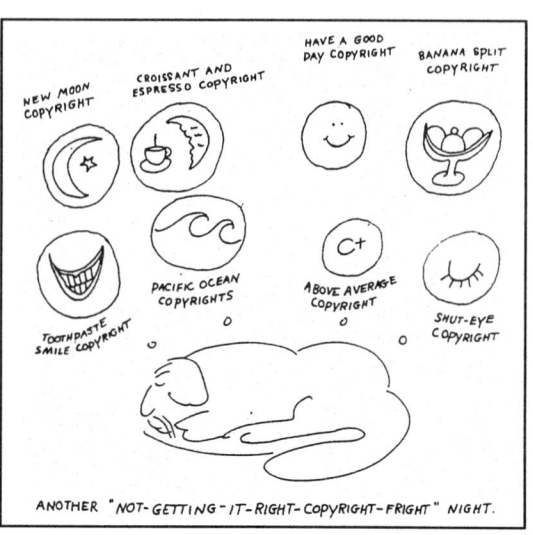

ANOTHER "NOT-GETTING-IT-RIGHT-COPYRIGHT-FRIGHT" NIGHT.

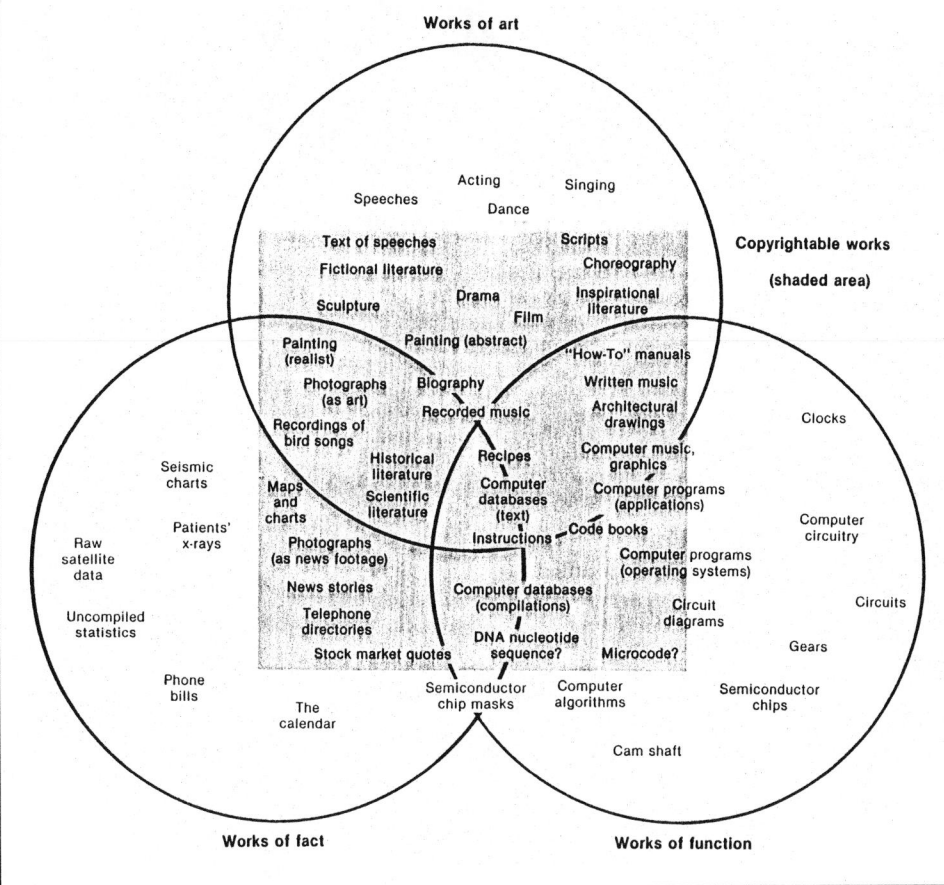

**Works of art**

Acting · Singing
Speeches · Dance

Text of speeches · Scripts
Fictional literature · Choreography
Drama · Inspirational literature
Sculpture · Film
Painting (realist) · Painting (abstract)
Photographs (as art) · Biography · "How-To" manuals
Recordings of bird songs · Recorded music · Written music
Historical literature · Recipes · Architectural drawings
Maps and charts · Computer databases (text) · Computer music, graphics
Scientific literature · Code books · Computer programs (applications)
Instructions · Computer programs (operating systems)
Photographs (as news footage) · Computer databases (compilations)
News stories · Circuit diagrams
Telephone directories · DNA nucleotide sequence? · Microcode?
Stock market quotes · Semiconductor chip masks · Computer algorithms · Semiconductor chips

Seismic charts
Patients' x-rays
Raw satellite data
Uncompiled statistics
Phone bills
The calendar

Clocks
Computer circuitry
Circuits
Gears
Cam shaft

**Copyrightable works** (shaded area)

**Works of fact**          **Works of function**

---

# Intellectual Property Rights

(In an Age of Electronics and Information)
NTIS Stock #PB87-100301
1986; 299 pp.
**$32.95**
($35.95 postpaid) from:
NTIS
5285 Port Royal Road
Springfield, VA 22161
703/487-4600

*A prime document of the revolution now in progress. What is property and therefore due government protection? This report tips the balance of the arguments toward the commonwealth side by virtue that the report itself, a GPO publication, is copyright free.*

*(It is published by that rare entity, a government agency that works: the noble Office of Technology Assessment. Check out their other remarkably well-researched reports too.)*
—Kevin Kelly

◆

The emergence of new information and communication technologies is placing new demands on governmental institutions responsible for the administration of intellectual property rights. The question arises, therefore, of whether existing Federal institutional arrangements for administering intellectual property rights, as initially designed, can adequately cope with the new technological developments and the new responsibilities that may be placed on them.

---

# Intellectual Property

(Patents, Trademarks, and Copyright in a Nutshell)
Arthur R. Miller and
Michael H. Davis
1983; 428 pp.
**$10.95** postpaid from:
Telemarketing Department
West Publishing
P.O. Box 64833
St. Paul, MN 55164-1804
612/228-2500
or Whole Earth Access

# Intellectual Property Law Dictionary

Stephen R. Elias
1985; 222 pp.
**$17.95**
($20.45 postpaid) from:
Nolo Press
950 Parker Street
Berkeley, CA 94710
415/549-1976
or Whole Earth Access

*For amateur lawyer types. Succinct expositions of the current law in compact books. It's helpful to have the **Intellectual Property Law Dictionary** at your side while burrowing into **Intellectual Property Law**.*

—Kevin Kelly

—Intellectual Property
Law Dictionary

◆

A process is a way of doing something. If it is a patentable process, it must be a new, useful, and nonobvious way of doing something. If the process is patentable, the result of that process — the something getting done — need not of itself be new, useful, or nonobvious. . . .

Thus, the patentability of the result or product of a process is not relevant to the patentability of the process. Clearly, pressed pants, the product of the process, could not be patented. Pressed pants, though useful, are neither novel nor nonobvious. But an ingenious way of producing creases certainly might qualify if it were novel, useful, and nonobvious.

—Intellectual Property

◆

One rule beyond dispute is that a law of nature, including its mathematical manifestations, is not patentable. This

prohibition proceeds from the notion that such laws are the fundamental building blocks of science and should not be monopolized. The recent proliferation of computer software has forced the courts to define more precisely which inventions involving the use of computers or mathematical formulas (or "algorithms") are disqualified under section 101 of the Patent Act.

—Intellectual Property

**senior users and junior users**

**senior users and junior users** When a dispute exists over ownership of a mark, the person (or entity) who first used the mark is called the "senior user" and the second person or entity to use the mark is termed the "junior user". Although the senior user is generally considered the **owner of the mark** in dispute, this may not be so in situations where the junior user did not know of the senior user's use, and is first to register the mark under the **Lanham Act** , or under state laws. Related terms: **exclusive right to use mark** and **ownership of a mark**.

—Intellectual Property Law Dictionary

**head start rule** A type of judicial relief sometimes granted in **trade secret infringement actions** wherein the infringer is prevented from using a **trade secret** for as long a period of time as it would have taken him independently to develop the information that comprise the secret. In other words, the rightful trade secret owner is provided with a commercial "head start" in the information's use. This "head start" remedy shows recognition that the essential value of a trade secret is the **competitive advantage** it affords its owner. Related terms: **trade secret infringement action**.

## The Next Hurrah

(The Communications Revolution in American Politics)
Richard Armstrong
1988; 300 pp.
**$18.95**
($20.45 postpaid) from:
William Morrow & Co.
WILMOR
39 Plymouth Street
P.O. Box 1219
Fairfield, N.J. 07007

*There's an art to writing junk-mail seductive enough to get a wary reader to pull out his or her checkbook. Richard Armstrong's mastery of that mode is put to much better use in this engrossing, wide-ranging look at political applications of new information technologies.*

*He starts with what he knows best — direct mail fund-raising — then shows how this ties in with voter databases, campaign software, telephone banks, opinion polling, electronic news-releases, broadcast production, cable TV, satellite relays, and computer communications. Neither a utopian nor a cynic, at one point he asserts that the new political technology (particularly computers) is "amateurizing" campaigns — giving newcomers capabilities that only entrenched "party machines" had in the past. But the bulk of the book suggests otherwise, as telemarketing specialists increasingly replace grassroots volunteers, manipulating candidates' positions to fit statistical models and "geodemographic" game-plans.*

*Recognizing how rapidly campaign technology is evolving, and how unexpected the synergies have been, Armstrong doesn't try to peer very far into*

*the future. He doesn't really have to: just pulling together what's already happening produces some future shock. But he does predict a splintering of the two-party system soon, as well as growing difficulty in balancing personal privacy with political involvement.*

*While not meant as a how-to manual, there are enough tips, models and pointers to set you thinking how you can adapt some of these already-available techniques to the elections and issues you care about.*

—Robert Horvitz

◆

It's been estimated there are approximately five hundred thousand electoral offices in the United States, with roughly 750,000 candidates vying for them. These candidates spend about 1.25 *billion* dollars more in donated services in their effort to get elected. Congressional, gubernatorial, and senatorial campaigns make up only a tiny fraction of this market. The bulk of it is comprised of local politicians who spend five, ten, or fifteen thousand dollars to get elected to city councils, state legislatures, school boards, and county commissions. In the past, only big campaigns could afford to use computers. In the future, 90 percent of the use of computers in politics will be in the smaller campaigns.

◆

Nowadays, candidates in effect "cover" their own campaign. Staffers are hired to follow the candidate around with cassette recorders and minicams, taping anything that resembles news. These tapes are then delivered to radio stations, television stations, and cable systems by telephone, by satellite, or by hand, where they will find their way on to the air — often without much editorial comment. In the print media it's very rare for a press release to be published intact. But with radio and television actualities, it happens all the time. And, for the most part, the press regards it as a service!

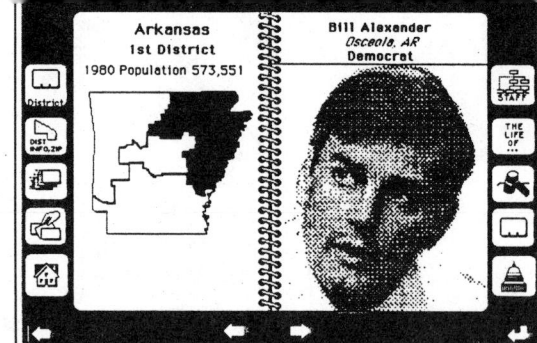

Card in the House stack.

## Congress Stack

**$159.95** from Highlighted Data, Inc., P.O. Box 17229, Washington, DC 20041; 703/241-1180.

*This electronic database is ideal for anyone who wants or needs to "work" Congress. In fact, lobbyists and public-interest groups will soon probably wonder how they ever got along without it.*

*Built on the versatile HyperCard program, it pulls together information about every member of Congress, their biographies, home districts (including maps and zip-codes), office staff (names, roles, and phone numbers), and committee assignments. This information is all available on paper, but not from one source, not so conveniently cross-linked and customizable, and not in a form where it can be so quickly searched and output to other applications. You can, for example, take a zip code and quickly find what Congressional District it's in and who represents it. Or take a subcommittee and compile a list of all the zip codes of the members' constituents.*

*Hardware requirements for Congress Stack are a Macintosh Plus, SE or II, with a hard disk and 800K drive. The current edition is about 10 megabytes: 17,000+ "cards" organized into 19 "stacks." It's now being shipped as a set of ten 3.5" floppies with user-removable copy protection (to prevent accidental data loss while learning how to use and customize it). Updated editions of Congress Stack will be released every two years. Between editions, you can add and delete notes and graphics on your copy as you wish. The one obvious problem is transferring your additions and customizations to a new edition — but that's a problem with any timebound reference.*

—Robert Horvitz

## Campaigns & Elections

James M. Dwinell, Editor
$48/year (7 issues)
or $4.50 per issue from:
C&E, Inc. Suite 1200-E
1331 Pennsylvania Ave., N.W.
Washington, D.C. 20004r
800/237-7842

*A slick trade journal for professional campaigners, political consultants, and those running (or interested in running) for public office.*

*Unabashedly committed to candidate-packaging and -marketing, most of the articles are how-to pieces and interviews with successful practitioners. The ads are intriguing, and each issue's "directory of resources" (paid listings for PR firms, mailing-list brokers, fundraisers, computer specialists, etc.) seems like an essential tool. My favorite column is "Politics Across America": local campaign stories rarely picked up by reporters outside the immediate locale.*

*C&E has an odd pricing policy: subscriptions cost 50% more than the per-issue cover price. Since*

*Washington, DC, is about the only place you can find this publication on newsstands, they appear to be discriminating against the rest of the country — at least in cost. The content, on the other hand, is geographically diverse. They're particularly attentive to races at the state and district levels.*

—Robert Horvitz

◆

. . . The race remained close until the campaign's final week, when Moore's opponent, three-term Jackson Mayor Dale Danks, aired a controversial TV spot showing Moore in 1975 with long hair. . . with a voice-over: "Who has the experience to be attorney general? Well, when Mike Moore was a law student, Dale Danks was a prosecutor winning 90 percent of his cases. . . ."

A second spot depicted Danks in college with his closely cropped wethead, circa 1963, while the voice-over intoned ". . . Dale Danks worked for the city sanitation department while earning his degree from the Jackson School of Law."

Danks found himself on the defensive for what many voters described as "a low blow." He tried to explain the ads as an insight into his opponent's background and character. . . . Most voters did not agree. As he continued campaigning, Moore sensed the tide turning in his favor. "Everybody's mad about that hair thing. . . .

People walked up to me and said, 'Boy, I was for Danks, but when he came out with that hair ad I decided to be for you.'"

In fact, the entire experience-versus-inexperience approach taken by Danks helped Moore ride the tide of youthful reformers, such as gubernatorial candidate Ray Mabus, who were sweeping the state. By Election Day, Moore's come-from-behind victory was complete. He won by more than 100,000 votes, and defeated Danks in the Mayor's home base of Hinds, Madison, and Rankin counties.

## Understanding Media

(The Extensions of Man)
Marshall McLuhan
1964; 318 pp.
**$4.95**
($5.95 postpaid) from:
New American Library
P.O. Box 999
Bergenfield, NJ 07621
or Whole Earth Access

*That media are extensions of our senses — telephones for ears, computers for mind — and that these new media are forces in themselves, the main event, regardless of what they bother to say ("the medium is the message"), are insights originating from McLuhan. That the media immediately engulfed McLuhan's ideas, and made them at once obvious and degrees more consequential, is part of his message.*

*— Kevin Kelly*

*Everybody talks about McLuhan, and everybody does something about him, and that makes it subjectively harder to get at him. He's got other insights than what you hear about, so it's worth the trouble to track him down. The primest McLuhan is* **Understanding Media.**

*— Stewart Brand*

◆

The electric light ended the regime of night and day, of indoors and out-of-doors. But it is when the light encounters already existing patterns of human organization that the hybrid energy is released. Cars can travel all night, ball players can play all night, and windows can be left out of buildings. In a word, the message of the electric light is total change. It is pure information without any content to restrict its transforming and informing power.

◆

Man the food-gatherer reappears incongruously as information-gatherer. In this role, electronic man is no less a nomad than his paleolithic ancestors.

◆

Everybody experiences far more than he understands. Yet it is experience, rather than understanding, that influences behavior, especially in collective matters of media and technology, where the individual is almost inevitably unaware of their effect upon him.

◆

It is a principal aspect of the electric age that it establishes a global network that has much of the character of our central nervous system. Our central nervous system is not merely an electric network, but it constitutes a single unified field of experience. As biologists point out, the brain is the interacting place where all kinds of impressions and experiences can be exchanged and translated, enabling us to react to the world as a whole.

## No Sense of Place

Joshua Meyrowitz
1985; 416 pp.
**$9.95**
postpaid from:
Oxford University Press
16-00 Pollitt Drive
Fair Lawn, NJ 07410
800/451-7556
or Whole Earth Access

*TV, telephones, and movies explode. The Earth shrinks. Social behavior alters. Childhood, a recent invention, disappears again. All heroes die. Places become events. The rest of this show, hinted at early by McLuhan, is rehearsed here in this analytical book. The news is not new; the comprehensible and comprehensive evidence is.*

*— Kevin Kelly*

◆

In contrast to print, television does not allow control over what is "expressed" along with what is "communicated." Television news programs, for example, cannot escape presenting a wide range of personal expressions in addition to "objective facts." Rather than attempting to fight this aspect of television news, producers have taken the parts of the back region that are difficult to hide and thrust them into the show itself. This is especially true of local news programs. Backstage expressiveness, personal feelings, informal interaction, and ad-libbed jokes have become an important aspect of the performance. Similarly, many television quiz and talk shows have abandoned attempts to hide microphones, camera operators, "applause" signs, and cue cards.

◆

We cannot select uses for new media that advance old goals without often altering the social systems out of which the goals developed. We cannot, for example, "buy the wife" a television set to ease her boredom with housework without changing her sense of place in the world. We cannot use television to "educate" our children without simultaneously altering the functions of reading and the structure of the family and the school. . . .We cannot have mediated intimacy with our political leaders, in the hope of getting closer to greatness, without losing a belief in heroes. And if we use media to teach many different groups about each other, we also change the lines of social association and the perimeters of group identities.

## Turing's Man

(Western Culture in
the Computer Age)
J. David Bolter
1984; 264 pp.
**$8.95**
($10.45 postpaid) from:
The University of
North Carolina Press
P.O. Box 2288
Chapel Hill, NC 27514
919/966-3561

*Bolter is a professor of classics and his book is about how technology effects the way people think about themselves and their society. He notes that the Greeks lived with a technology based on craft and they likened man to a clay vessel. The advent of mechanical clocks brought in the idea of the mind as a clock work and the body as an engine. This is beginning to be supplanted by the idea of human beings as computers. We talk blithely about burn out, about information overload, and about the system crashing as ways that our minds and bodies work. His subject is therefore not artificial machine intelligence but artificialized humans. The book is a little uneven and to my mind doesn't go far enough in its exploration of the modern metaphors. For example he makes no note that the metaphors of the computer are largely drawn from usages which were originally military—systems crashing, commands, core dumps, etc. Nor does he address the effects of the structure of computer logics and linguistics which I believe will profoundly affect the way we think about how people think. Still he has made a start.*

*—Elin Whitney Smith*

◆

Turing set out the nature and theoretical limitations of

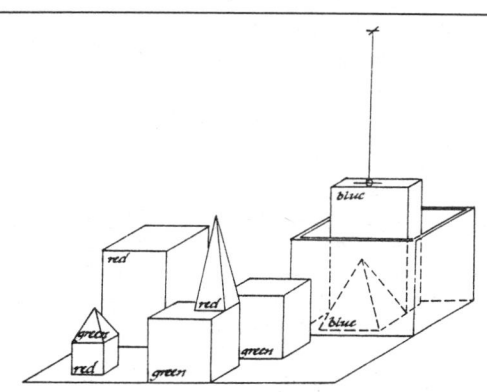

1. Pick up a big red block.
   OK. (The system answers "OK" when it carries out a command.)

2. Find a block which is taller than the one you are holding and put it into box.
   BY "IT", I ASSUME YOU MEAN THE BLOCK WHICH IS TALLER THAN THE ONE I AM HOLDING.
   OK.

3. What does the box contain?
   THE BLUE PYRAMID AND THE BLUE BLOCK.

4. How many blocks are not in the box?
   FOUR OF THEM.

5. Can a pyramid be supported by a block?
   YES.

6. Can a pyramid support a pyramid?
   I DON'T KNOW.

7. Stack up two pyramids.
   I CAN'T. (The robot tries and fails.)

8. I own blocks which are not red, but I don't own anything which supports a pyramid.
   I UNDERSTAND.

9. Do I own a box?
   NO.

10. Do I own anything in the box?
    YES, TWO THINGS: THE BLUE BLOCK AND THE BLUE PYRAMID.

logic machines before a single fully programmable computer had been built. What Turing provided was a symbolic description, revealing only the logical structure and saying nothing about the realization of that structure (in relays, vacuum tubes, or transistors). A Turing machine, as his description came to be called, exists only on paper as a set of specifications, but no computer built in the intervening half century has surpassed these specifications; all have at most the computing power of Turing Machines.

◆

By promising (or threatening) to replace man, the computer is giving us a new definition of man, as an "information processor," and of nature, as "information to be processed."

The world of toy blocks manipulated by the program SHRDLU, more an expression of faith in what artificial intelligence may someday achieve than a practical result in itself.

## American Demographics

Cheryl Russell, Editor
$48/year
(12 issues) from:
Circulation Department
American Demographics
P.O. Box 6543
Syracuse, NY 13217
800/828-1133

*Considering that demographics provides the mass culture with its self-knowledge, most of us are demographically illiterate. I didn't realize how much this industry had evolved until I was introduced to this slick trade journal for seekers and users of statistics. Demographic question-askers are usually politicians and advertisers, so the answers are weighted with manipulative purpose, and real news of economic change or neighborhood growth often gets lost.* **American Demographics** *keeps track of that news. It covers the latest raw data and reveals how the data was gathered, how it will be used, and occasionally how little to trust it. I wish the magazine was more cynical and investigative, but I find it nonetheless as fascinating as a funhouse mirror.* —Art Kleiner

Thinking about expanding your household? Before you do, consider how much it costs to feed that extra mouth.

The weekly cost of feeding an additional person for the average household of 2.6 people ranges from $2.61 for a child under age 5 to $20.98 for an adult aged 30 to 44, according to Bureau of Labor Statistics researchers Raymond W. Giesman and Brent R. Moulton. Spending on bakery products increases directly with age, rising from $.73 a week for children under age 5 to a high of $1.84 a week for people aged 65 and older. Spending on fresh fruit, on the other hand, starts out at $.42 for a child under age 5, drops even lower for teenagers, then picks up in middle-age before reaching a high of $.96 a week for people aged 65 and older.

## Census Catalog and Guide

U.S. Bureau of the Census
1987; 450 pp.
$21
postpaid from:
Superintendent of Documents
Government Printing Office
Washington, D.C. 20402
202/783-3238
or Whole Earth Access

*Here it is in one place: access to Census Bureau documents. Data on topics ranging from women-owned businesses to soybean production are available on various media —computer disks, microfiche, maps, machine-readable files, and plain old paper pamphlets. To order the 1987 edition of this invaluable compendium, ask for GPO stock #003-024-06637-8. The number changes with each year's updated catalog, so call to ask for the new number if you want the 1988 edition.*
—Sarah Vandershaf
[Suggested by Brad Edmondson]

---

**Percent of Americans who enjoy spending money, by age:**

| | |
|---|---|
| under 35 | 77% |
| 35–49 | 72% |
| 50–64 | 62% |
| 65+ | 47% |

*Americans & Their Money 5, The Fifth National Survey from Money Magazine, 1987*

## D E M O M E M O

**Percent of Americans who can remember the stock market crash of 1929: 10%**

*Based on current age structure of U.S. population, and assuming those who remember the crash were aged 10 or older in 1929*

Over 27,000 of the 50,441 foreign-born children adopted from 1980 to 1986 are from South Korea. Many South Korean married couples don't have the space or money for more than two children. And in a country with ancestral worship and a strong emphasis on racial purity, illegitimate children and children of mixed race have little chance of getting a good education or a good job. Although not without regret, adoption has become a workable solution to South Korea's rapid urbanization and overpopulation.

## Federal Census on Microfilm

$20 (each county) from National Archives Trust Fund, P.O. Box 100793, Atlanta, GA 30384; 202/523-3164

*To protect personal privacy, data from the Federal census on specific individuals is kept closed for 72 years. That means the 1910 and earlier censuses are open to the public — a wealth of historical or genealogical information. Specify year, state, and county of choice.*

*(For general information on all Federal censuses, contact Data User Services Division, U.S. Bureau of the Census, Washington, DC 20233; 301/763-2074.)*
—Sarah Vandershaf

---

Who will borrow tomorrow? The pool of prime borrowers — the 25 to 54 age group — is larger now than ever before, but it will be shrinking fast in about 12 years.

## CENDATA

$36/hour (plus phone charges) from Dialog Information Services, 3460 Hillview Avenue, Palo Alto CA 94304; 800/334-2564

*The best and simplest way to access Census Bureau data with a microcomputer is — lo and behold — through the Bureau's own database on Dialog Information Services. The database is necessarily an extremely small subset of the Bureau's massive data holdings, but has the most current stuff. It's also convenient if you happen to already have an account with Dialog.*

*CENDATA — Dialog file 580 — has Census Bureau press releases up within a day of their release, and a bunch of summary population and economic data reports. You can download the data and import them to Lotus 1-2-3 worksheets.*

*Since they're government data, they're cheap to access, and there are no restrictions on using them.*
—Diane Crispell

## Directory of Microcomputer Data and Software for Demographic Analysis

Diane Crispell, Editor. $20 from American Demographics, P.O. Box 68, Ithaca, NY 14851; 607/273-6343

**American Demographics** *publishes a little directory which covers just what the lengthy but apt title says it does. It's a specialized sort of field, but the demographic data industry had grown tremendously in the past decade, and the data vendors (people who sell population estimates and projections, as well as other services) keep up with high-tech developments. This directory is* **American Demographics'** *attempt to keep up with the vendors, and we think it's the only one of its kind (and I don't say that just because I edited it).*
—Diane Crispell

## Secrets of Successful Direct Mail

Richard V. Benson
1987; 182 pp.
**$19.95**
($21.45 postpaid) from:
The Benson Organization, Inc.
4 Baywood Lane
The Landings, Skidaway Island
Savannah, GA 31411

*The modern day Horatio Alger would be selling his apples by mail. That's the message from the countless workshops and books peddling useless "formulas for success" designed to make you think you could be the next millionaire on your block by selling your brilliant idea/product through direct (read: junk) mail. Benson is not one of these; he's actually an expert, one of the early pioneers of direct mail, one of a handful who, for better or worse, opened the Pandora's box of junk mail for the American public. In this book, Benson recounts his successes and failures in his uniquely anecdotal, abrasive and opinionated style. And why not? Benson has sold everything from the Admiral Byrd Society's first public trip around the world from north to south ($10,000 per person, please, for a total profit of $600,000 on a $5,000 direct mail budget) to Ruby Red grapefruit through the mail. Naturally, he didn't always succeed, but he learned*

*from both his successes and failures, and it's these lessons and stories you'll find in this book. Although he unabashedly distills these lessons into thirty-one "Benson's Rules of Thumb," the essential lesson of the book is that, rules or no rules, you have to think about what you're doing. Then you realize that what it takes to succeed with direct mail is knowledge of some basic principles, a little math, common sense, and luck. Sounds simple, doesn't it? Read on.*

—Richard Schauffler

◆

Benson's Rules of Thumb

In defense of these prejudices: I have a lot of scar tissue backing up these principles. I offer them to you with this qualifier: They work for me.

1. A two-time buyer is twice as likely to buy as a one time buyer. . . .

2. The same product sold at different prices will result in the same net income per thousand mailed.

3. Sweepstakes will improve results by 50% or more.

4. A credit or bill-me offer will improve results by 50% or more.

5. Tokens or stickers always improve results.

6. Memberships renew better than plain subscriptions by 10% or more.

7. "Department store" pricing always pays except for membership offers.

8. You can never sell two things at once. . . .

Nothing works all the time, but ignore any of these rules at your own peril.

## DM News

(The Newspaper of Direct Marketing)
Ray Schultz, Editor
**$36/year**
or **free** to qualified
subscribers
(26 issues) from:
DM News
19 West 21st Street
New York, NY 10010
212/741-2095

*The tabloid of choice for junk mail professionals throughout the country.* **DM News** *is everything you want to know about this way of thinking and selling, and more. Here in lurid detail you'll find out just how the contras describe themselves in their direct mail letters. You'll find yourself siding with the knights of the junk mail roundtable in their epic attempts to slay the US Postmaster. You'll never sleep soundly again or mail another letter after you read the the horror stories about the post office you always imagined but could never prove: "Temporary Postal Carrier Canned After Dumping Mail in the Garbage." And, for the junk mail professional: how-to articles, updates on postal rate increases, classifieds and the latest mailing list wars ("Owner: Sex Had Nothing to Do with Market Removal of Swaggart File"). Just when you thought it was safe to go back to your mailbox. . . .*

—Richard Schauffler

## Successful Direct Marketing Methods

Bob Stone
1984, 1988; 496 pp.
**$29.95**
($32.35 postpaid) from:
National Textbook Company
4255 West Touhy Avenue
Lincolnwood, IL 60646
800/323-4900
or Whole Earth Access

*Here is your standard reference textbook written by one of the captains of the industry on the entire field of direct marketing, which is that system of marketing techniques whereby businesses sell directly to you the customer and you the customer respond directly to the business without a middleman. These techniques include direct mail (junk mail), telemarketing (those unsolicited phone calls asking you to buy things), mail order catalogs, advertising in print media ("Send one penny plus shipping and handling and choose any six hit records or tapes!") and on radio and TV ("Call 800-123-4567 now to order your subscription to* **Whizgig Illustrated**; *our operators are standing by . . ."). Here you'll find definitions of standard concepts and terms, along with self-quizzes and hypothetical marketing projects which require you to apply the concepts you're learning at the end of each chapter. A useful book for beginners who want to gain an overview of the field. Don't expect to find much that's very critical or sophisticated here — that's where you'll need* **Secrets of Successful Direct Mail** *(see review this page). But*

*failure to master the basics is the root of most beginners' direct marketing failures, and the basics are all here, well-illustrated and indexed. The chapter on "Mathematics of Direct Marketing" alone will save the novice the cost of the book many times over.*

—Richard Schauffler

◆

Creativity in direct marketing brings recognition, awards, and applause. Unfortunately, profitability and success do not always accompany the recognition and the awards. Some of the attributes of direct marketing that appeal most to those who engage in it are the accuracy with which profitability can be evaluated and the careful ways that a program can be expanded with predetermined financial risk. Accountability and analysis lie at the heart of successful direct marketing.

◆

Pilot Project

You are the advertising manager of a mail order operation selling collectibles. You have been successful in magazines offering a series of historic plates. You have never used newspapers, but now you have a $75,000 budget to test the medium.

Outline a newspaper test plan.

1. Select your test cities.
2. Will your tests run in the Sunday edition or the weekday edition, or both?
3. What formats will you test — preprints, supplements, comics, local TV books, ROP?
4. What size preprints or ads will you test?
5. At what time of year will you run your tests?

A continuity newsletter series advising teenage girls how to look better and be more popular and a magazine consisting mostly of advertisements for sweetened food, which will be mailed free to households with children, are two of five new products introduced by Field Publications. The magazine is a joint venture with General Foods Corp.

## The Unabashed Self-Promoter's Guide

Dr. Jeffrey Lant
1983; 366 pp.
**$30**
($32.50 postpaid) from:
Jeffrey Lant Associates, Inc.
50 Follen Street, Suite 507
Cambridge, MA 02138
617/547-6372
or Whole Earth Access

*The value of your product, service, or cause will communicate furthest when wrapped around the image of a person. In many cases that will be YOU, and self-promotion will be necessary. Self-promotion dispensed at the levels recommended by this mildly cranky book will be self-destroying for most people. But taken in small doses, the strategies herein will clear up the mystery of fame.*
—Kevin Kelly

As you develop your image you must keep in mind the following critical facts:

—Subtlety is beyond the power of the public. When dealing with the public, you must always present yourself in the least complicated fashion and with no more than one leading idea. To do more is to risk accomplishing nothing.

—Likewise, the media cannot comprehend complexity. Thus all those dealing with the media must present themselves in the most simple, uncomplicated, direct fashion possible. In the media all ideas, all images are weakened if they deviate from the necessary standard of profound simplicity.

—You cannot afford either to worry or despair about the fact that your image is not the whole you. It can never be, never will be.

Never, never fail to inform media people — or anyone else, for that matter — what your image is if they have not figured it out for themselves.

Most organizations, whether the local Kiwanis, Knights of Columbus or PTA, are hard up for good speakers. Members constantly lament the tedium of the speeches they are forced to hear. Most lavish excessive praise on efforts which by any standard are mediocre. Thus, take heart! If you are bad, with thin content and abject delivery, you will be no worse than what they've already heard, and will quickly be dumped into the grateful darkness of oblivion. If you are anything other than bad, you will be remembered as the closest thing to silver-tongued Cicero who has ever graced their podium.

---

Always remember, "the sexiest item for local press is a local name." That rule holds with one minor qualification: the more you can relate the local name to the issue, the better. Mr. & Mrs. Middle America want desperately to be reassured that people THEY know, people who live in THEIR town, actively support your issue.

## P.R.

Michelle Cauble
1977, 1986; 22 pp.
**$1.50**
(Send 5" X 7" SASE with $.39 postage) to: Do It Now Foundation, P.O. Box 21126 Phoenix, AZ 85036
602/257-0797

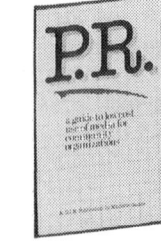

*What people haven't heard about they can't take action about. Uncommunicated issues DON'T EXIST. For local promotion on the quick and dirty and cheap, here's a quick, dirty, and cheap pamphlet of how-to.*

—Stewart Brand

*This was written for community organizations, but*

---

## The Publicity Manual

Kate Kelly
1979, 1988; 234 pp.
**$29.95**
postpaid from:
Visibility Enterprises
11 Rockwood Drive
Larchmont, NY 10538
914/834-0602
or Whole Earth Access

*Exploiting the media is not just for the big boys. Even if the business or organization you are responsible for promoting is just a small one, you can learn how to get free publicity through newspapers, radio and TV by using the techniques outlined in this manual. You'll learn how to write a press release, how to develop a good relationship with media people, how to tell when you need outside public relations help, and much, much more!*

*All this free advertising can be even better than paid advertising: potential customers often see news stories, even those engendered by promotion, as 'friends' advice" (consider the power of movie critics and restaurant reviewers). The media, then, can become an extension of the word-of-mouth publicity that small businesses rely on to keep a steady stream of good customers flowing through their doors.*
—Sarah Vandershaf

One of the special benefits of publicity is that, in effect, it

---

Our McLuhanesque world has imbued the media with a mystique which sometimes interferes with our ability to perceive them as they are: simply modern mechanisms for reaching vast numbers of people.

*the tricks work for community businesses as well.*
—Kevin Kelly

◆

In the beginning at least, one person, preferably with previous experience in media relations, should be the MAIN MEDIA CONTACT, rather than different people contacting the media on different occasions. This allows a personal relationship to develop, rather than haphazard or impersonal — "just another group trying to get publicity" — relations.

---

is an *editorial recommendation* — an unbiased opinion — saying that you are good: "I found this worthy of notice," is what the reporter is saying. Obviously, a recommendation from a member of the press whom the reader or viewer trusts can often carry more weight than an ad which was paid for and written by the company itself.

◆

A news hook or a news angle to the story is almost always essential when trying to get publicity, and it will add zest to you background press release. Members of the press are often so busy that they may not have time to think of the news angle themselves. If you are able to give them a "hook" and present them with interesting facts, then you'll be way ahead of the game in getting publicity.

```
Contact:   Name                )   SOURCE INFO
           Company
           Address                              RELEASE
           Phone Number )                       DATE

                        FOR IMMEDIATE RELEASE  )

SUMMARY HEADLINE TYPED IN CAPS    )   HEADLINE
GIVING STRAIGHT FACTS OF STORY    )

Dateline -- Press release follows in short, straightforward  )
paragraphs in the inverted pyramid style.        BODY
                                                  OF
                                               RELEASE

                        -0-
```

Press release format.

◆

[Some restaurant] critics prefer to arrive unannounced, so they may be vague as to how they select restaurants for review and when they might choose to do so. Many restaurant owners keep photographs of local reviewers posted in the kitchen so that the personnel will have the opportunity to recognize a critic who arrives unannounced.

## Marketing Without Advertising

Michael Phillips and
Salli Raspberry
1986, 1987; 200 pp.
**$14**
($16.50 postpaid) from:
Nolo Press
950 Parker Street
Berkeley, CA 94710
415/549-1976
or Whole Earth Access

*The first two chapters of this startling book argue convincingly, and with documented proof, that almost all advertising is totally ineffective and an utter waste of money; and that most business owners, including top executives of large corporations, have been successfully duped into believing advertising is both necessary and productive in spite of obvious evidence to the contrary. The evidence presented — the at-times hilarious ads themselves, the statistics, the quotes from advertising executives, the **Wall Street Journal** articles — will actually make you laugh, or if you're a buyer*

With a little creative thinking, every small businessperson can use discounts, small gifts or extra services to make good customers feel appreciated. We know a nice little Japanese restaurant in San Francisco that gives customers a Japanese coin good for a free order of sake at the next visit.

*of advertising, maybe make you cry. Next time you see or hear an advertisement, think about it a minute. Would you buy what they're trying to sell you? When was the last time an ad convinced you to buy anything? If you run a business, how successful have your ads been? Read the beginning of this book, and I guarantee you'll have an entirely new perspective on advertising.*

*The rest of the book, the bulk of the writing, explains clearly and in detail how you can promote*

*your business without advertising, primarily by encouraging personal recommendations. The ideas are useful and well presented, of a value to any business. But it's those first two chapters. . . .*
—*Bernard Kamoroff*

◆

There are four main reasons why advertising is inappropriate for a small business:

● First, advertising is simply not cost-effective. Claims that it produces even marginal financial returns are usually fallacious.

● Second, even when advertising produces enough paying customers to justify itself, customers lured by the ads tend to be disloyal. In other words, advertising does not provide a solid customer base for future business.

● Third, dependence on advertising to get new customers is often actually debilitating to a business, making it more vulnerable to changes in volatile consumer taste and thus more likely to fail.

● Fourth, because a significant percentage of advertising is deceptive, advertisers are increasingly seen by the public (both consciously and unconsciously) as dishonest and manipulative. Businesses that advertise heavily are often suspected of offering poor quality goods and services.

## Guerrilla Marketing

Jay Conrad Levinson
1981, 1984; 226 pp.
**$8.95**
($10.45 postpaid) from:
Houghton Mifflin Co.
Mail Order Dept.
Wayside Road
Burlington, MA 01803
800/225-3362
or Whole Earth Access

*It's a rare business that will survive without successful, ongoing marketing. Marketing means promotion, and **Guerrilla Marketing** offers up a couple of dozen creative, inexpensive promotion ideas. I'm still not sure what "guerrilla" means except that it is a good example of what's in the book: the title is a marketing device itself — it catches your eye, makes you a little curious about it, costs nothing. The bulk of the book deals with advertising, which I view with great skepticism since reading **Marketing Without Advertising** (above). But I personally got several good ideas from the book, a couple of very good ideas, and one business-saving idea. What more could you want for nine dollars?*
—*Bernard Kamoroff*

◆

George then distributed his circulars by several methods: He mailed 1000; he placed 1000 on auto windshields (he had a high school student do some of this for him); he distributed 1000 more at a home show in his area; he handed out 1000 more at a local flea market; and he held on to 1000 to give to satisfied customers to pass on to their friends and neighbors. Being bright as a penny when it comes to saving money, the enterprising George also asked each of his customers where they had heard of him. When they said, "I saw your flier," George asked where they got it. This way, he learned which of the five methods of circular distribution were most effective.

## Positioning

(The Battle for Your Mind)
Jack Trout and Al Reis
1981, 1986; 213 pp.
**$4.95**
($6.45 postpaid) from:
Warner Books
P.O. Box 690
New York, NY 10019
212/484-2900
or Whole Earth Access

## Marketing Warfare

Jack Trout and Al Reis
1986; 215 pp.
**$8.95**
($10.45 postpaid) from:
New American Library
P.O. Box 999 Bergenfield, NJ 07621; 201/387-0600
or Whole Earth Access

*Howls from the wolves of the marketplace.*

*"Positioning" caught on about 13 years ago as a marketing trend. To make your (probably undistinguished) product seem more distinct and unique, you aim at your competitor, not at your public. The classic positioning campaign was from Avis: "We're only #2, we try harder." But that campaign had substance — it forced Avis to shape up its service. More often, positioning is an image game in which the business competitors seek the chinks in each other's armor, while the public is the turf they trample on. In mainstream advertising,* 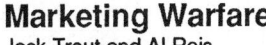 *the positioning trend seems about to decline, but not before it influenced the methods of all types of business — and the way business is seen. You could accuse Smith and Hawken of positioning, for instance; by importing a small line of garden tools, they created an image "position" as the highest-quality importers of their kind. By contrast, you could say that the **Whole Earth Catalog** has ad-*

*vanced despite a lack of positioning — the catalogs have consistently refused to hone in on one particular audience or point of view (to their credit, in my opinion).*

***Marketing Warfare**, by the same authors, is partly a disguised rehash of **Positioning** and partly an extended analogy between marketing and war.*
—*Art Kleiner*

◆

The classic mistake made by the leader is the illusion that the power of the product is derived from the power of the organization.

It's just the reverse. The power of the organization is derived from the power of the product. The position that the product owns is in the prospect's mind.

Coca-Cola has power. The Coca-Cola Company is merely a reflection of that power.
—*Positioning*

**Principles of guerrilla marketing warfare.**

1. Find a segment of the market small enough to defend.

2. No matter how successful you become, never act like the leader.

3. Be prepared to bugout at a moment's notice.

—*Marketing Warfare*

by Salli Raspberry

Advertising is offensive, expensive, and takes advantage of the vulnerable members of our society. Advertising in America is more intrusive than in any other industrialized country. Yet, in spite of the fact that most Americans are exposed to an estimated 1,000 advertising messages every day, the majority of us are hardly influenced, at least not in the sense that it induces us to buy anything.

Advertising as a means to sell a product or service is simply not effective. People know that advertising is propaganda and don't trust it, nor do they remember it. According to market research studies, only 9 percent of television viewers can name the brand or even the product category they saw advertised a moment before.

If we as consumers have personal experience and a network of friends and relatives whom we can trust to

Macy's ad found in the **San Francisco Chronicle**.

[Right.] This is no joke. Nearly all surveys on why people buy a particular product show advertising has much less influence than does word of mouth.

recommend products and services, this is most likely to influence us. When survey research studies of the final sales influence are conducted, rarely is advertising credited by the survey respondents as a reason for choosing a product or service.

We seem politically and morally blind to the fact that so many ads are dishonest. The victims of this self-serving industry are children, the economically poor, tourists, the elderly, and the educationally disadvantaged. Pre-school children, for instance, have not yet learned to be defensive and wary of commercials as have their older siblings and cannot distinguish between television programming and advertisements.

This is not to imply that the majority of advertising agencies or their employees are evil and calculating, attempting to make our lives miserable for a profit. Ad agencies exist to serve their clients and are extremely vulnerable to their every whim. There is little loyalty in this industry. And we, the buying public, are equally guilty, as to a large extent we use advertisers to support our media. Regardless of how tasteless an ad or how corrupt the business supporting that ad might be, by our silence we give them the power over our media.

Those of us who would prefer to use our dollars wisely might consider more actively supporting public television and radio as well as journals and general-interest magazines without advertising. They can stay in business only if their community wants the information they have to offer badly enough to pay for it.

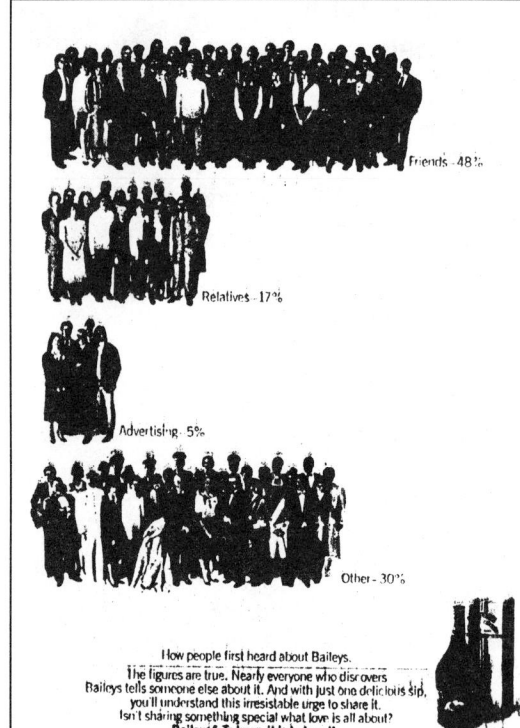

How people first heard about Baileys.
The figures are true. Nearly everyone who discovers Baileys tells someone else about it. And with just one delicious sip, you'll understand this irresistable urge to share it. Isn't sharing something special what love is all about? Baileys? To know it is to love it.

## Advertising Pure and Simple
Hank Seiden
1976; 197 pp.
**$9.95** postpaid from:
American Management
Association
P.O. Box 1026
Saranac Lake, NY 12983
518/891-1500
or Whole Earth Access

First, read "Advertising Doesn't Work." Then, if you decide you still must write ads for your own small business, start here. Written by "one of the few ad men who enjoys helping young people get started in advertising," this is also recommended for people seeking jobs as copywriters. Author Hank Seiden began his ad career before television, and implies that advertising should have stayed there. That print-oriented approach makes this a good book for learning how to persuade in writing with taste and skill. Seiden pretty much leaves the ethnical dilemmas for you to resolve for yourself, except for two: he says cigarette and liquor

companies should be allowed to advertise on television, but political candidates should not.

If you like to read advertising "confessions" by insiders (as I do), the annotated bibliography is worth the price of this book.
—Art Kleiner

◆

The first step, when creating any ad or commercial, is the most critical: Jot down, as two guidepoints, what you're trying to say and the audience you're trying to say it to. If you can't compose one or at most two sentences summing up the key point of your ad, then you're simply not going to be an ad writer. Go to bartender school.

◆

At one time all commercial tuna fish was pink. A new company came on the scene with a white tuna — a tremendous disadvantage, wouldn't you say? — in a market used to pink tuna. The white tuna people didn't think so, and advertised their tuna as guaranteed not to turn pink, thereby implying that something was wrong with pink tuna. They made all the other guys see red. How's that for turning a disadvantage into an advantage? They did it so well that all tuna marketed since then is white.

## Advertising, The Uneasy Persuasion
(Its Dubious Impact on
American Society)
Michael Schudson
1984, 1986; 288 pp.
**$8.95**
($10.95 postpaid) from:
Basic Books
10 East 53rd Street
New York, NY 10022
800/242-7737
or Whole Earth Access

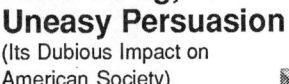

Many people passionately hate advertising and marketing, without really knowing why. They should read **Advertising, The Uneasy Persuasion**. It subtly debunks all the foofaraw about advertisers as conspiratorial manipulators of the public — and then it tells what's really going on: "Advertising is capitalism's way of saying 'I love you' to itself." No wonder advertising feels so icky to those of us who aren't similarly infatuated.
—Art Kleiner

◆

To the extent that there is an answer to the problem of whether, in the aggregate, advertising causes sales, the answer seems to be no, sales cause advertising. And business practice ensures that this will be so. Field experiments varying the amount of advertising and measuring the results on sales have been relatively rare. Especially rare are experiments that dare to lower advertising expenditures below current rates. In a number of these cases, including a celebrated set of experiments at Anheuser-Busch for Budweiser beer, reducing advertising expenses actually led to increases in sales. It is very likely that many firms spend more on advertising than, for their own best interests, they should.

## Propaganda
*by Dick Fugett*

Remember when you were a kid, and you first saw the puppeteer's hands? After that, puppets were never quite the same. There's a similar discovery about Authorized Truth, the reality presentation we're given by the major media. Here are two new publications offering a refreshing dissection of how information choices are made for us, as well as investigating the slant, the curveball delivery, the deception that too often becomes the public perception of reality.

Reading these journals could produce a healthy cynicism towards the mainstream media anywhere from the USA to the USSR. Healthy because that mainstream mouthpiece and its output, Authorized Truth, reflects the interests of the people in charge, and those interests may not be the same as yours.

### Propaganda Review
Marcy Darnovsky, Editor
$20/year
(4 issues) from:
Media Alliance
Fort Mason, Building D
San Francisco, CA 94123
415/441-2557

*Watching a 1984 Reagan TV pitch called "Morning in America" so impressed a group of journalists that they began investigating how the media is used for political goals. The propagandizing of US nationalism had surpassed even Orwell's predictions in its use of language, picture and symbol.*

*The group's initial research was published in the **Media Alliance Newsletter**, the San Francisco journalism review. Response was excellent and the project has now advanced to a slick quarterly magazine. It doesn't stress the media watchdog aspect as much as **Extra!** does, but looks more closely at the foundations of propaganda in politics, advertising, and entertainment, with stories that are longer and more reflective.*

*Like FAIR, the group plans to go beyond publishing and host public forums that will encourage the general population to respond to egregious media deeds. Consider the endless letters that outraged citizens write to Congresspeople's computers. That same effort directed towards a local newspaper editor who reprinted without comment the latest government disinformation might be far more energy effective.*

*Good new ideas come from lean, hungry organizations. The **Propaganda Review** crew is in their fourth year now, and no one draws a salary yet. Besides qualifying for lean and hungry, they're demonstrably dedicated.*

—D.F.

◆

Many terms in political discourse are used in a technical sense that's very much divorced from their actual meaning, sometimes even the opposite of it.

Take the "national interest." The term is commonly used as if it's something good for all of us. If a political leader says, "I'm doing this in the national interest," you're supposed to feel good because that's for you.

But if you look closely, it turns out that the national interest is not defined as the interest of the entire population. It's really the interests of small, dominant elites who command the resources that enable them to control the state — basically, corporate-based elites. Correspondingly, the "special interests," of whom we're all supposed to be suspicious, really refer to the general population. . . .

In both the 1980 and 1984 election, Reagan and his handlers identified the Democrats as the "party of special interests." That's bad, because we're all against the special interests. But if you asked who the special interests were, they listed women, poor people, workers, young people, old people, ethnic minorities — in fact, the vast majority of the population.

One group was not listed among the special interests — the corporations. In the campaign rhetoric, that was never a *special* interest, and in their terms that's right — because that's the *national* interest.

Photographer Richard Cross said, "I think photographers sometimes very short-sighted in looking at causes. They are interested in the more dramatic symptoms of the problem rather than the cause of the problem. There's this sort of refusal to look at pattern. I would opt much more for telling the story with lots of images and text that tries to relate what has been going on in El Salvador with what has been going on in the last fifty years in the world — things like the decline of neo-colonialism and the rise of independent nation-states." Cross called this picture — of a Salvadoran National Guard sergeant and his platoon — "Authority."

### Extra!
Martin A. Lee, Editor
$24/year
(9 issues) from:
FAIR
666 Broadway
Suite 400
New York, NY 10012
212/475-4640

*Fairness and Accuracy in Reporting (FAIR) came about when founder Jeff Cohen, a former ACLU lawyer, decided it was time to quit grumbling about media bias and do something instead. What he and a few friends created was an organization that not only scrutinizes the information we're given as "news," but also responds when gross errors are detected.*

*Their journal **Extra!** slices through the baloney in commendable fashion. With quotes, pictures, and excerpts, it shows exactly how the mass media presented a story, then offers its own scrupulously documented commentary. Insights and conclusions are left to the reader. Topics have ranged from the Moonie-owned **Washington Times** to Soviet TV coverage of Afghanistan. Compared to **Propaganda Review** this is more immediate stuff, analyzing headline stories as opposed to investigating background and theoretics. Taken together, they're not only complementary, but salutary.*

*FAIR also puts on conferences, organizes phone tree campaigns, and focuses public attention on specific issues, such as Contra aid. This is a creative group encouraging new ideas, and I've been sufficiently impressed to fork over my own $24 to watch them develop.*

—D. F.

Gorbachev: snake or charmer?

◆

The principal media obsession during summit week was Gorbachev's public relations acumen, as though the Kremlin had somehow cracked a prized American code. . . . A frontpage **New York Times** (12-10-87) headline chimed: "Soviet Visitor is Turning On All His Charm."

Curiously, a later **Times** edition changed this headline to "Soviet Visitor Mixes Charm With Venom." The byline changed as well, from Joel Brinkley to Andrew Rosenthal. But the text changed only slightly, with the addition of several paragraphs describing Gorbachev's meeting with news executives. **Extra!** contacted **The Times** writers for an explanation. When asked about the venom, Rosenthal said that Gorbachev took a hardline position at the meeting. "You might think this is a cop-out," he added, "but headlines are written by editors not reporters . . . I didn't use the word 'venom' in my story."

## The Vanishing Hitchhiker
Jan Harold Brunvand
1981; 223 pp.
**$8.95**
($9.85 postpaid)

## The Choking Doberman
Jan Harold Brunvand
1984; 254 pp.
**$6.95**
($7.85 postpaid)

Both from:
W.W. Norton
500 Fifth Avenue
New York, NY 10110
800/223-2588
or Whole Earth Access

*This lady came in from the rain, and her miniature poodle was wet and shivering. So she put him into the microwave oven to dry him off. He exploded. She was so horrified she had a heart attack and died.*

*I've told that one. I thought it was true. It is, but a different kind of true. It's a modern urban legend, a gripping, bizarre, often moralistic tale that goes the rounds as a factual account — "It happened to a friend of a friend of mine"; "I read it in the newspaper." Hundreds are in circulation at any time, and many do get picked up in newspapers. Vanishingly few have factual origins.*

*But they are wonderful stories, living for decades. A major collector of these modern folk talkes is Jan Harold Brunvand, in two riveting books, **The Vanishing Hitchhiker** (1981) and **The Choking Doberman** (1984). He collects, tells, compares versions, tests factuality, and interprets.*
— *Stewart Brand*

## The Mexican Pet
Jan Harold Brunvand
1986; 221 pp.
**$6.95**
($7.85 postpaid) from:
W.W. Norton
500 Fifth Ave.
New York, NY 10110
800/223-2588
or Whole Earth Access

*Brunvand introduces 50 new legends in his latest title, third in what looks to be a never-ending series of books on urban lore.*
— *Sarah Vandershaf*

◆

There was some kind of problem with the dam at a reservoir in the Midwest or South, and a couple of divers were hired to go down and check into it. They had only been underwater a short time before they came rushing back up to the surface, and they were really upset about something — absolutely pale as death and shaking all over. It seems that they had seen some giant catfish [or carp] down there in the deepest part of the lake, right up next to the dam. These catfish were so huge that they could easily swallow a man ! The divers refused to go back down, or even to dive again anywhere, and both of them had their hair turn white overnight from the scare they had suffered in those murky waters. . . .

Jon M. Graznak of Columbia, Missouri, a fisheries biologist, had heard giant catfish stories since his childhood in Alabama. In about the mid-1970s he began to keep closer records of them. He reported to me in November 1985, after talking to thirty-eight powerhouse superintendents (most of whom had heard the stories), that "None claimed to have firsthand knowledge, and

only two had ever been in a powerhouse where any type of underwater maintenance was even required." Graznak also wrote, "I have met only one person who claims to have been one of the divers. However, the individual was remarkably drunk at the time, and I believe that if I had continued the conversation, he might well have claimed to be the fish."

◆

Some baggage handlers for an international airline flying out of Chicago . . . find a dead poodle in a crate they are loading on a flight to Rome. Fearing they might be sued for letting the dog die, they secure a similar one from a kennel and substitute it. When the owner comes to recover her crate at the terminal in Rome, she faints in terror when the dog bounds out of its crate and licks her face, because she was shipping her dead pet home to Italy for burial.

# MYTH MANNERS
## by ALAN DUMAS

Credit: Alan Dumas and Peter Hoey

## Rumor!
Hal Morgan and Kerry Tucker
1984; 159 pp.
**$3.50**
($6.50 postpaid) from:
Penguin Books
299 Murray Hill Parkway
East Rutherford, NJ 07073
800/631-3577
or Whole Earth Access

*For a somewhat more trivial perspective — "here's a popular wild story; is it true or false?" — **Rumor!** is an enjoyable exercise. Did Roy Rogers really stuff his horse, Trigger? (Yes.) Do green M & Ms really make you horny? (No.) Is the stuff in the middle of golf balls really explosive (No.) Was President Cleveland's upper jaw secretly removed while he was in office? (Yes.) With details. Fun, brief.*
— *Stewart Brand*

◆

Orange Fiesta Ware is radioactive. (1940s)

Partly true. Fiesta Ware, a line of brightly colored dishes first produced in 1936 by the Homer-Laughlin China Company, originally came in five colors, one of them a

vivid orange. The color was taken off the market in the forties, and a rumor spread that the orange dishes were radioactive.

In 1981 that rumor was substantiated when the New York State Department of Health warned against eating regularly from the orange dishes because the glaze contains lead and uranium compounds, both of which tend to be absorbed by acidic foods. Ingested lead may, over a long period of time, cause stomach disorders and worse, and ingested uranium may cause kidney dysfunction. The uranium also emits low levels of radiation. However, it is not dangerous to use the dishes as decorative objects.

◆

There are full-grown alligators in the sewers of New York City. They were pets brought back from vacations in Florida, then flushed down toilets when their owners grew tired of keeping them. (1960s)

Possibly true. . . . Between 1932 and 1938 the **New York Times** printed several reports of alligators caught around the city — in the Bronx River, in New Jersey, in the East River, and even in a Brooklyn subway station. On August 16, 1938, the paper told of a sudden bonanza in alligator fishing in Huguenot Lake in New Rochelle, just to the north of the city. Five of the reptiles had been

A UFO crashed during the Eisenhower administration, and the bodies of the occupants are on ice at Wright-Patterson Air force Base in Ohio. (1955) Unsubstatiated.

caught by fishermen over the weekend. Major Elvin L. Barr managed to land two, using ordinary bass flies. He theorized that the creatures "had been put there by some resident who had bought them in Florida as pets and then tired of them." Did we see those wondering eyebrows go up? But wait. A story even more crucial to the rumor appeared on February 10, 1935, under the headline "Alligator Found in Uptown Sewer." According to the **Times** reporter, several boys on East 123rd Street were shoveling snow into a manhole when they spotted an alligator in the sewer below. They lassoed it with a clothesline and dragged it out onto the street, where it was found to be "seven and a half or eight feet" long. . . . In May 1982, the **New York Times** quoted John Flaherty, Chief of Design for the New York City Bureau of Sewers, as stating that "there are no alligators in the New York City sewer system." We don't believe him. Do you?

## Processed World

Group Edited
$10/year
(4 issues) from:
Processed World
41 Sutter Street #1829
San Francisco, CA 94104
415/495-6823

*Sick & tired of living a life of quiet desperation? Try some noisy desperation instead — from **Processed World**, the unofficial mouthpiece of disgruntled and alienated employees everywhere! Each issue contains devilishly entertaining articles on ways low-level white-collar workers can jazz up their work life — for instance, by diverting corporate information channels to their own use. Stuffing envelopes today? Add copies of radical leaflets (preferably Xeroxed at the boss' expense) to the mailings! Emulating such manoeuvres is sure to get you fired eventually — but if you share **Processed World**'s opinion of wage slavery, you'll be glad to shuck that crummy job, anyway.*

*—Sarah Vandershaf*

◆

My stint at the Downtown Community College at 4th and Mission in San Francisco lasted a mere three months. But it was a turning point for a couple of reasons. For one thing I learned word processing there, which catapulted me from $5-$6/hr. jobs up to $10-$12/hr. ones. It also made me aware that most people worked in offices, especially in SF, and I wanted to address this fact, since I too was suddenly an "information handler." As an information clerk I sat right inside the front door and spent seven hours a day telling people where the bathroom was, when and where classes met, and about English as a second language. The school provided two basic services, both primarily for the benefit of the downtown office world: basic training in office skills and English classes for newly arrived immigrants and refugees that prepared them for rudimentary data entry jobs at very low wages. . . .

I had never planned to stay long, despite the two-year minimum I promised in the interview. Instead I was going east for a nice, long, summer vacation. About six weeks before I planned to quit, I composed a fake advertisement for the DCCC and had it printed up. This ad summarized all my jaded views of the purpose of this

graphic by R.B.

"training institute for the clerical working-class" after a few months of being there 40 hours a week. About ten days before I had planned to quit, I began surreptitiously placing them inside the Fall schedules of SF City College, which I distributed at the front desk. A few days later the shit hit the fan. A coworker came running up to me when I came to work in the morning and asked if I had done a yellow leaflet that had the entire school in an uproar. Apparently a Bechtel executive had turned it in to the administration the night before. I smiled and told her "No, never heard of it." It was nonetheless obvious to my coworkers, who knew of my bad attitude, that I was the culprit.

I was absent from my work station when the snooty director, Dr. B, came in, oblivious to my "crime." She gave me a dark look as I scurried back to my position. Five minutes later the phone rang, and I was told to come to her office. She looked rather pale as I entered.

She was boiling but tried to act calm. From beneath a 16-inch pile of papers she pulled out a copy of the leaflet — she had only seen it moments ago and had already hidden it — and thrust it at me, saying "What can you tell me about this?!"

I said, "Oh, is that the yellow leaflet I was told about? Can I see it?" I took it and sat down and slowly read it as if I had never seen it before. I chuckled at the funny parts, dragging out my feigned surprise until she finally exploded:

"You are SICK! You must be deranged to do something like this; it's damaging to our institute, YOU'RE FIRED!!" I denied responsibility just in case some kind of lawsuit resulted (I had put her name and the school's actual logo on it) and protested that I wanted to complete my final week, but she told me to go. I left feeling quite satisfied with the extra days off before my vacation. . .

## Loompanics

Information **free** from: Loompanics Unlimited
P.O. Box 1197 Port Townsend, WA 98368

*The endless trail of information (consisting of medical and tax records, bank statements, credit card accounts) an individual lays down during the course of a life is braided with everyone else's trails into the engulfing web of an information Black Widow. A few fugitives dare snip the threads to escape. They have compiled a fat catalog of anarchist books that thumb their noses at all authority and any bureaucracy.*

*Some of these books are at the edge of legality and sanity: how to make bombs, or tap phones. A few you may want to know about for your own defense: how credit card scams work, or tricks for procuring false ID. Others deal with the simple matter of information outlawry. Approach with prudence.*

*—Kevin Kelly*

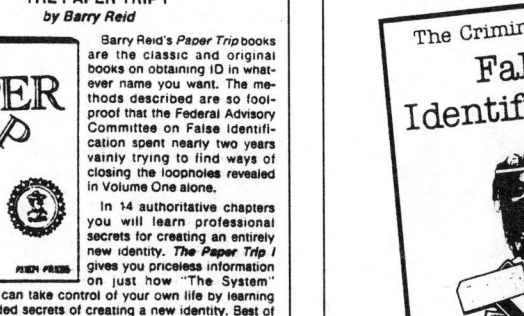

**THE PAPER TRIP I**
by Barry Reid

Barry Reid's *Paper Trip* books are the classic and original books on obtaining ID in whatever name you want. The methods described are so foolproof that the Federal Advisory Committee on False Identification spent nearly two years vainly trying to find ways of closing the loopholes revealed in Volume One alone.

In 14 authoritative chapters you will learn professional secrets for creating an entirely new identity. *The Paper Trip I* gives you priceless information on just how "The System" works. Now you can take control of your own life by learning the closely guarded secrets of creating a new identity. Best of all, your next ID will be *undetectable* because it will be issued by the government itself!

Topics covered include: ★ A step-by-step method for assembling a complete package of alternate ID, based on an original birth certificate ★ All the information you need to obtain your documents directly from the government itself ★ How to make or obtain any kind of supporting card you need ★ Where to obtain commercial ID forms and stock ★ And much, much more!

Too good to be true? Read *The Paper Trip I* and you will be a believer! Even if you don't need to change your identity now or use some of the more radical techniques, this information is absolutely priceless. Some day you may be very glad indeed that you took time for The Paper Trip I...

1984, 8½ x 11, 82 pp, illustrated, soft cover.
**THE PAPER TRIP I: $15.95**

The Criminal Use of
**False Identification**

**THE CRIMINAL USE OF FALSE IDENTIFICATION**
A Summary Report on the Nature, Scope and Impact of False ID Use in the United States
*The Report of the Federal Advisory Committee*

**NEW I.D. IN AMERICA**

BY ANONYMOUS

## Index on Censorship

George Theiner, Editor
$27.50/year
(10 issues) from:
The Fund for Free
Expression
36 West 44th Street
Room 911
New York, NY 10036
212/840-9460

*The Star*, Johannesburg, 10 October 1987

*Even if you're sure the news is being censored, you're a prisoner of your own particular brand of paranoid speculation unless you know exactly what is being left out. This magazine reports on stories not covered and why they weren't from all parts of the world and political spectrum. The style is calm, careful, well-researched, and horrifying.*
—Anne Herbert.

◆

Soviet scholarship is being seriously inhibited by a policy which treats photocopiers as a "class enemy," Dr. Pyotr Fedoseyev, Vice-President of the Soviet Academy of Sciences told the Academy's 1987 Annual Assembly. He is not the only one to complain; among leading Soviet scholars who have accused the bureaucracy of trying to "shield" academics from the information they need for their work are sociologist Igor Kon and chemist Vitaly Goldansky. (The latter made his views clear in intellec-

tual journals such as **Argumenty i fakty** and in the mass circulation weekly **Ogonyok**.)

Photocopiers are in short supply in the Soviet Union. About 1,000 are produced a year, almost all from a single factory, and a few hundred more imported (according to the information bulletin **NTR — Nauchno-teknicheskaya Revolutsiya** —produced by the **Znaniye** "Knowledge" society). **NTR** noted that Japan produces between 1.5 and 2 million photocopiers a year.

◆

Dr. Gillian Cardy, a 50 year old community medical officer was suspended on 16 December after telling a newspaper that she thought a 30% cut in family planning services in Bath [U.K.] would lead to more unwanted pregnancies. Her remarks appeared in the **Bath and West Evening Chronicle**. She was reprimanded by the

In 1982 South Korean journalist Kim Hyong-jang was charged with arson and Communism (both of which he denies) and was sentenced to death. The only evidence against him was a confession extracted by torture. His sentence has been commuted to life imprisonment.

health authority which employs her and wrote a letter warning her not to speak to the press again. When journalists subsequently asked for her comments after a healthy authority meeting about savings in family planning services, she told them she was not allowed to speak. After her reasons for not speaking appeared in print she was suspended. The British Medical Association, which says that her contract states that she can speak to the press on matters of public health, will defend her.

## Readers International

Catalog **free** from:
Readers International
P.O. Box 959
Columbia, LA 71418
318/649-7288

*Sherman Carroll was working in the world head-quarters of Amnesty International in London and Dorothy Connell was on the staff of the magazine* **Index on Censorship**. *They knew firsthand that there were many extraordinary writers out there who couldn't get published in their own countries. Knowing that they couldn't help get these books published in their writers' home countries, Carroll*

"Many's the husband who goes off in search of work, only to come back alone and penniless. The place for the farmer is on the farm."

—*The Land* by Antonio Torres

*and Connell decided to publish them instead for the English-speaking world.*

*Thus was born* **Readers International**, *a unique enterprise which is half publisher and half book club. RI publishes six books a year in hardbound editions on a subscription basis for its members. They also make most of their titles available to bookstores in paperback editions. In its first three years RI has published works for their first time in English from Latin America and the Caribbean, the Middle East, Asia, Africa, and Eastern Europe.*

*Though* **RI** *features writers who have suffered political censorship, this is only occasionally the direct subject of their works. RI's titles bear the ponderous (and unfortunate) label of being "important" books because of the censorship of their authors, but I have found them to be of very high literary quality (as has the* **New York Times**, *which at my last check has reviewed nearly all of RI's titles). I greatly look forward to each new book's arrival.*
—Keith Jordan

◆

It so passed that I chanced upon this mullah with a questionnaire in his hand. He gave it to me to fill in for him, excusing himself that he did not have his glasses with him. Or perhaps it was that he did not have his mastery of words with him.

I seized a plume and asked his name. "Hassan, Pilgrim of Blessed Mecca, Exalted Kerbela and Holy Meshed," said he. "Surname?" asked I. "Ever praying," replied he. "Religion?" I enquired. "Muslim," he answered. "Profession?" I queried. He shuffled about and then whispered in my ear: "Write 'Muslim' against that too."
—*The Ayatollah and I* by Hadi Khorsandi

## Censorship News

Leanne Katz, Editor
$25/year
(4 issues) from:
National Coalition
Against Censorship
132 West 43rd Street
New York, NY 10036
212/944-9899

*Big censorship — of international news, of stories on the actions of U.S. and foreign governments — makes you mad. But little censorship — of your local library, of your children's school texts — affects you much more directly. The National Coalition Against Censorship keeps track of attempts at censorship by high school officials, Christian fundamentalists, and other neighbors of yours. The $25 membership gets you the coalition's newsletter,* **Censorship News**, *and* **Books On Trial**, *a survey of recent legal cases involving attempts to ban school books (available to nonmembers for $5).*
—Sarah Vandershaf

◆

A group of parents have filed suit against the Columbia County, Florida school board which banned works by Chaucer and Aristophanes. . . . "The Miller's Tale," written in the fourteenth century, and **Lysistrata**, written about 400 B.C., were in a state-approved humanities textbook; the books were confiscated from students and placed under lock and key. The superintendent had told the school board that "any literature in which God's name is used in vain is not appropriate for use in the classroom." The attack on the book began when a local minister, filing a complaint, described **Lysistrata** as "pornography and women's lib." He said Chaucer's "Miller's Tale" was "crass humor," "inappropriate reading for anyone."

*Ever wondered if Big Brother has you in his files? Why not find out? The procedure is simple. Fill out some basic forms and mail them to the government agency of your choice. They should notify you within a month whether or not you exist in their files. If you do they'll give you a number, and you start waiting. My dealings with the National Security Agency, for example, went on for 7 months before I got a definitive response.*

*More interesting is the FBI response. After telling me that no new material had been added to my file* since my last FOI search, they added coyly that *"new references identified during our search were documents that originated with another agency."* Hmm, what does that mean?

*FOIA, Inc. is a volunteer crew assisting people in their uphill struggle with The State, whether you're looking for your own files, researching a book, or pressuring OSHA to release environmental records. If you're not sure where to start, try the FBI first: they're the all-purpose receptacle for subversion. If you've worked with the Sanctuary movement, add Customs, Treasury, and INS to your list. If you misbehaved overseas, try State and the CIA, though the latter is a reticent outfit. In general, I was alternately impressed by the depth of the agencies' information and astonished by some of their blunders.*

*The Fund survives on your help. They'll send you the necessary forms for $2, but if you enclosed more, it would go towards a good cause.*

—Dick Fugett

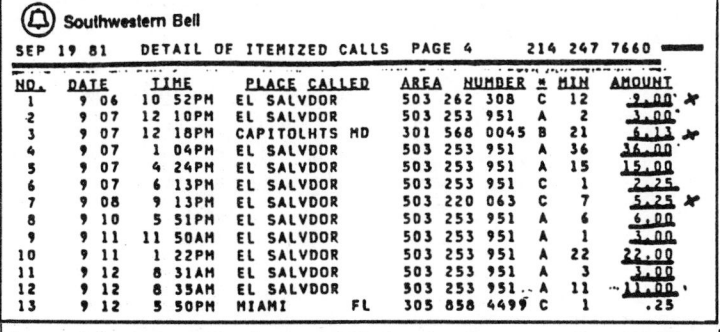

**Page of Frank Varelli's telephone bill, showing frequent calls to El Salvador National Police, as he provided names of returning Salvadoreans and visiting Americans.**

*Your bad self has gotten you in trouble. You've gone straight. Can your name be cleared? Maybe. If it's possible to do so in California, this book will tell you how in minute detail. Even shows the forms you must fill out and what to say on them. Though specifically for California folks, the basic steps will work in other states after a bit of imaginative snooping and adapting. If you're contemplating a life of crime, this peek at the bureaucratic hassles involved might serve as a deterrent!*
—J. Baldwin

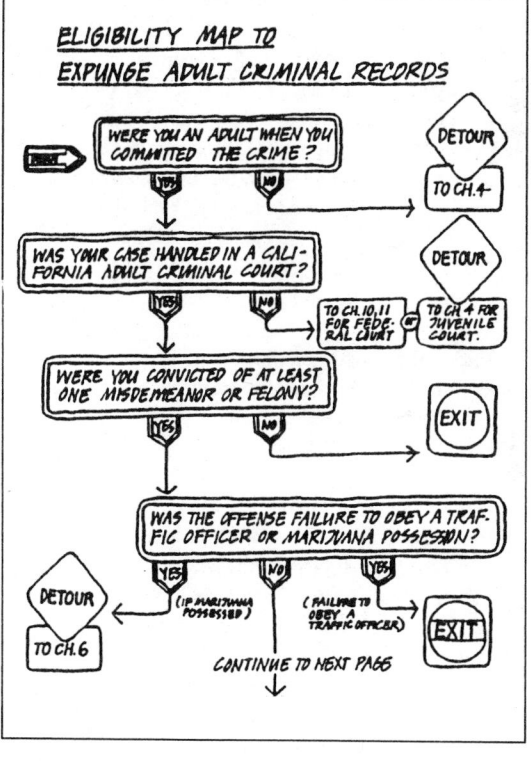

## A Citizen's Guide On Using the Freedom of Information Act

*The horse's mouth. This compact little pamphlet tells you how to request government documents through the Freedom of Information Act and the 1974 Privacy Act (which allows you to see what the government has on you in its records), and also warns you which types of documents you can't get.*

—Sarah Vandershaf

◆

The FOIA requires agencies to publish or make available some types of information. This includes: (1) Descriptions of agency organization and office addresses; (2) statements of the general course and method of agency operation; (3) rules of procedure and descriptions of forms; (4) substantive rules of general applicability and general policy statements; (5) final opinions made in the adjudication of cases; and (6) administrative staff manuals that affect the public. This information must either be published or made available for inspection and copying without the formality of an FOIA request.

All other "agency records" may be requested under the FOIA. However, the FOIA does not define "agency record." Material that is in the possession, custody, or control of an agency is usually considered to be an agency record under the FOIA. Personal notes of agency employees may not be agency records. A record that is not an "agency record" will not be available under the FOIA.

◆

An agency may refuse to disclose an agency record that falls within any of the FOIA's nine statutory exemptions. The exemptions protect against the disclosure of information that would harm national defense or foreign policy, privacy of individuals, proprietary interests of business, functioning of the government, and other important interests.

◆

The Privacy Act of 1974 provides safeguards against an invasion of privacy through the misuse of records by federal agencies. In general, the Act allows citizens to learn how records are collected, maintained, used, and disseminated by the federal government. The Act also permits individuals to gain access to most personal information maintained by federal agencies and to seek amendment of any incorrect or incomplete information.

◆

At many agencies, FOIA and Privacy Act requests are processed by the same personnel. When there is a backlog of requests, it takes longer to receive a response. As a practical matter, there is little that a requester can do when an agency response is delayed. Requesters should be patient.

*by Robert Horvitz*

There's a growing number of periodicals available to the public reporting on intelligence work. They run the gamut from rabidly hostile to sycophantic, from thoroughly researched to merely polemical to just plain fluff. When the stance is critical and the focus is on agencies of the country where the publication is based, an intelligence magazine may be operating at the edge of that society's tolerance for journalism.

Among the better critical journals, **Intelligence/Parapolitics** provides a concise monthly overview of recent press reports about covert activities worldwide. Most articles are summarized, others are reprinted whole. Emphasis is always on facts rather than polemics. Published in Paris, it comes in "full" and "summary" editions, both available in either French or English. By all means get the "full" version.

Philip Agee and Norman Mailer helped the **Covert Action Information Bulletin** get started in 1978. CAIB used to make a point of revealing the names and covers of currently active CIA agents. Since passage of the Intelligence Identities Protection Act in 1982, they've shied away from naming names, concentrating instead on more general detective work, piecing together incidents and relationships to adduce U.S.-backed covert operations or disinformation campaigns. Often assembled into theme issues, CAIB articles are opinionated but based on substantial research.

**The National Reporter** has similar preoccupations (it used to be called **Counterspy**), but is not as slick or as well-documented as CAIB.

Germany has a history of state-sponsored domestic surveillance, and is now a major arena for East-West spy-sparring. The West German magazine Geheim (Secret) boldly spotlights this murky business. It seems especially intent on breaking the covers of American and Soviet agents (they have a "Naming Names" column almost every issue), and is very critical of its own government. (All articles in German.)

**Lobster** is a British newsletter on intelligence, "parapolitics" and "state research," published somewhat irregularly, with no love for British intelligence, the right wing, or international conspiracies. (Content varies quite a bit from issue to issue, so it's not easy to characterize.)

**Big SISter** is a little newsletter published by OASIS (Organisation to Abolish the Security Intelligence Service), which reports on domestic spying and foreign involvements of New Zealand's SIS.

The British newsletter **Counterpoint** and the U.S.-based **Nightwatch** are likewise specific in their focus: Soviet propaganda and disinformation. But where **Counterpoint** is analyti-cal, trying to deduce the goals of specific propaganda projects by close study of the products (or suspected products), Nightwatch indulges in a lot more free-floating paranoia and Cold War speculation.

Military Intelligence may be the only periodical published by an intelligence agency about their work that offers subscriptions to the public. **MI** occasionally has interesting articles, but its main purpose seems to be to disseminate innocuous bureaucratic news and promote careers in Army intelligence. Published by a school that trains soldiers in tactical intelligence for the battlefield, the feature articles tend either to be very general, or case-studies with parable value.

**The International Journal of Intelligence and Counterintelligence** reads a bit like an academic journal whose reason for existence is to help its authors inch closer to tenure. In this instance, the authors are mostly either retired from or aspiring to intelligence agency employment. We can only hope the CIA's classified journal, **Studies in Intelligence**, is more trenchant.

Somewhat livelier, though no less academic, is **Intelligence and National Security**, published in England. It emphasizes historical scholarship rather than current

From Big SISter, March 1987.

events, and while many articles concern British activities, its scope is worldwide. Not as rabidly critical as, say, **Geheim** or **CAIB**, the editor nonetheless hopes "to lift some of the official veils which still pointlessly conceal the past history of intelligence."

Livelier still, though much thinner, is the **Intelligence Quarterly**, edited by Michael Speers and Rupert Allason (a.k.a. Nigel West). Mostly book reviews by writers who are themselves well-known authors in the field, it includes a set-the-fur-flying column which reviews the reviews of intelligence books in other publications — "a new artform which might make some small contribution to keeping such reviewers more honest — or at least forcing them to read the book in question all the way through."

**IQ**'s chief competitor is the **Foreign Intelligence Literary Scene**, which, with a change of editorship in 1986, seems to have lost whatever independence it may have had from those running the U.S. agencies. Book reviews fill most of the pagespace; there's also a regular listing of recent intelligence-related articles in the establishment press.

**First Principles** fights the impulse to use the legitimate need for secrecy in intelligence work to conceal illegal activities and thwart public oversight. Published by the Center for National Security studies, an active FOIA litigator, it features "op-ed" type opinion essays, policy analyses, and condensed coverage of recent court cases and news articles.

The biweekly **Access Reports/FYI** may not be affordable by most people, but its detailed coverage of legislative activity, federal regulations and court cases concerning privacy, freedom of information, and security classification, is without peer.

Last and least, we have **Espionage**, a relatively new Guccione-backed publication. According to one of their subscription adds, it's "the only international espionage magazine in existence!" Which should give you an idea of the quality of journalism it offers. Actually, it's mainly short fiction pieces and reviews of spy novels, with rehashes of last year's newspaper spy sensations mixed in for "realism." Definitely NOT recommended.

---

**Access Reports/FYI:** Harry Hammitt, editor. **$250**/year (24 issues) from Monitor Publishing Co., 1301 Pennsylvania Ave./Ste. 1000, Washington, D.C. 20004.

**Big SISter: $5**/4 issues from OASIS, Box 1666, Wellington, Aotearoa NZ.

**Counterpoint:** Stanislav Levchenko and Peter Deriabin, editors. **$35**/year (12 issues) from Ickham Publications Ltd., Westonhanger, Ickham, Canterbury CT3 1QN, England.

**Covert Action Information Bulletin: $15**/year (3 issues) from Covert Action Information Bulletin, P. O. Box 50272, Washington, D.C. 20004.

**Espionage:** Jackie Lewis, editor/publisher. **$21**/year (6 issues) from Leo 11 Publications, P. O. Box 1184, Teaneck, NJ 07666.

**First Principles:** Sally Berman, editor. **$15**/year (6 issues; $10/year for students) from Center for National Security Studies, 122 Maryland Ave. NE, Washington, D.C. 20002.

**Foreign Intelligence Literary Scene:** Marjorie W. Cline and David L. Thomas, editors. **$25**/year (6 issues) from National Intelligence Study Center, 1800 K Street NW, Washington, D.C. 20006.

**Geheim: DM 90**/year (4 issues) from: Lutticher Strasse 14, 5000 Koln 1, Federal Republic of Germany.

**Intelligence and National Security:** Christopher Andrew, editor. **£ 22**/year (3 issues) from Frank Cass & Co. Ltd., Gainsborough House, 11 Gainsborough Road, London E11 1RS, England.

**Intelligence/Parapolitics:** Olivier Schmidt, editor. **$40**/year (12 issues) from Association pour la Droite a l'Information, 16 rue des Ecoles, 75005 Paris, France.

**Intelligence Quarterly:** Michael Speers and Nigel West, editors. **$30**/year (4 issues) from Michael Speers, P. O. Box 232, Weston, VT 05161.

**International Journal of Intelligence and Counterintelligence:** F. Reese Brown, editor-in-chief. **$10**/issue (quarterly) from Intel Publishing Group, P. O. Box 188, Stroudsburg, PA 18360.

**Lobster:** Robin Ramsay, editor. **$14**/year (4 issues) from Lobster, 17C Pearson Avenue, Hull HU5 2SX, England.

**Military Intelligence:** Capt. William A. Purciello, editor. **$14**/year (4 issues) from Superintendent of Documents, U.S. Government Printing Office, Washington, D.C. 20402.

**The National Reporter:** John Kelly, editor. **$13**/year (4 issues) from The National Reporter, P. O. Box 21279, Washington, D.C. 20009.

**Nightwatch: free** (12 issues/year) from Security and Intelligence Foundation, 1010 Vermont Avenue/Ste. 1020, Washington, D.C. 20005.

# Counterintelligence Tools

*by Robert Horvitz*

## Tom Davis Books
Catalog **free** from: P. O. Box 1107, Aptos, CA 95001

*Mail-order specialist in muckraking political and conspiracy books, many concerning intelligence agencies, bankers, royal families, Masons, organized crime, etc. All points of view, all shades of credibility. Stuff not generally found in bookstores — not even in the National Intelligence Book Center.*

◆

[Some unusual catalog listings:]
Applied Surveillance Photography, by Raymond P. Siljander (C. C. Thomas, 1975), 120 pp. hardback, $14.50

Find'em Fast: A Private Investigator's Workbook, by John D. McCann (Palladin, 1984), 168 pp. paperback, $12

Low Profile: How to Avoid the Privacy Invaders, by William Petrocelli (McGraw-Hill, 1982), 261 pp., $5.95

## National Intelligence Book Center
Catalog $6 from N.I.B.C., 1700 K Street NW/Ste. 1007, Washington, D.C. 20006; 800/624-2232 ext. 350

*A bookstore and mail-order service for unclassified books and videotapes, apparently aimed at intelligence professionals and amateurs with a yen to know. Many manuals, case studies and histories; extensive selection of books on cryptography, investigative techniques and "comsec" (communications security). Stock is mainly from commercial publishers, but a few government documents are sprinkled in. They also buy and sell out-of-print books. Their current catalog doubles as a 115-page bibliography that's a pretty good introduction to unclassified intelligence literature, with an emphasis on anti-KGB material and "tradecraft." "Due to the hectic hours of many of our customers, the Center has a 24-hour, 7-day-a-week electronic order line at 202-797-1234."*

## U.S. Military Radio Communications
Michiel Schaay, editor, 1985; 259 pp. (3 volumes), $33.95 postpaid from: Universal Shortwave Radio, 1280 Aida Drive, Reynoldsburg, OH 43068

*The most comprehensive, unclassified monitoring guide to U.S. military radio communications, in three softbound volumes. If trouble starts anywhere in the world, and you have a shortwave receiver, a decent antenna, and these books, there's a chance you won't have to wait until the evening news to find out what's happening.*

*Focusing mainly on voice and radioteletype channels, Volume 1 is organized by both region and service, covering Air Force, Army, and Navy bases*

*worldwide. Volume 2 looks at affiliated agencies, like the Coast Guard, Federal Emergency Management Agency and NASA. A composite frequency-order list of stations starts in Volume 2 and concludes in Volume 3.*

*Note that in the U.S. as well as many other countries, it is legal to monitor these channels, so long*

 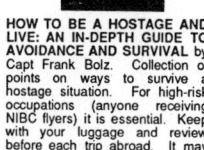

PROTECTING YOUR BUSINESS SECRETS by Michael Saunders. Industrial espionage gains new practitioners everyday. The author outlines the techniques used by professionals and how these risks can be managed through airtight policies, protective measures, the latest equipment and, careful staffing. 128 pp $25.00 HB + Shipping.

HOW TO BE A HOSTAGE AND LIVE: AN IN-DEPTH GUIDE TO AVOIDANCE AND SURVIVAL by Capt Frank Bolz. Collection of points on ways to survive a hostage situation. For high-risk occupations (anyone receiving NIBC flyers) it is essential. Keep with your luggage and review before each trip abroad. It may save your life. 128 pp. $5.95 PB + Shipping.

*as you don't divulge or economically benefit from what you hear. The military is perfectly able to protect any transmissions it needs to, and even on unscrambled channels, they make extensive use of codes and jargon to conceal content. An AWACS plane might radio to ground control, "I'm painting bogeys at 5 o'clock," when he means his radar is showing unidentified aircraft coming from the east-southeast. Such verbal camouflage is, for some people, part of the allure.*

## Search For Security
1985; 281 pp., $45 postpaid from: Access, 1755 Massachusetts Avenue SW/Ste. 501, Washington, D.C. 20036

*This fat, spiral-bound guide is designed to help projects on war prevention and improving national security find and get grants. Over 70 foundations are profiled, including their funding criteria, deadlines and contact addresses, plus lists of grants awarded. Also includes a survey and analysis of groups that succeeded in getting these grants. A well-done, time-saving reference. Nothing else quite like it; compiled in 1985, the people who distribute it believe most of the information is still reliable.*

# A Short List of Recommended Intelligence Books

## Intelligence and Espionage (An Analytical Bibliography)
1983; 559 pp., George C. Constantides, **$71** from: Westview Press, 5500 Central Avenue, Boulder, CO 80301; 303/444/3541

## The U.S. Intelligence Community
Jeffrey T. Richelson, 1985; 381 pp., **$16.95**

## Sword and Shield
Jeffrey T. Richelson, 1986; 297 pp., **$16.95.**
Both from: Ballinger Publishing Co., 54 Church Street, Cambridge, MA 02138

## KGB Today (The Hidden Hand)
John Barron, 1983; 257 pp., **$4.95** ($5.95 postpaid) from: Berkley Books/Order Dept., P. O. Box 506, East Rutherford, NJ 07073

## Bibliography on Soviet Intelligence and Security Services
Raymond G. Rocca and John J. Dziak, 1985; 203 pp., **$19.50** from: Westview Press, 5500 Central Avenue, Boulder, CO 80301; 303/444/3541

Vasili Averyanov, a Soviet employed by the United Nations Secretariat in New York City, clears a drop in Westchester County, in September, 1977.
—KGB Today

## Inside the Company (CIA Diary)
Philip Agee, 1975; 640 pp. OUT OF PRINT. Penguin Books, 299 Murray Hill Pkwy., East Rutherford, NJ 07073

## The Clandestine Service of the Central Intelligence Agency
Hans Moses, 1983; 24 pp. **$1.25** postpaid from: the Association of Former Intelligence Officers, 6723 Whittier Ave./Ste. 303A, McLean, VA 22101

## Intelligence Requirements for the 1980s
Roy Godson, editor. Seven volumes; **$7.50-$11.95** ($55/set) postpaid from: the National Strategy Information Center Washington, D.C. Call for titles and individual prices: 212/838-2912

## The Puzzle Palace
James Bamford, 1982; 655 pp. **$7.95** ($8.95 postpaid) from: Viking Penguin Books, 299 Murray Hill Parkway East Rutherford, NJ 07073; 201/933-1460

## Defending Secrets, Sharing Data

(New Locks and Keys for Electronic Information)
Charles K. Wilk,
Project Director
1987; 187 pp.
**$8.50** postpaid

## Electronic Record Systems and Individual Privacy

Fred B. Wood, Project Director
1986; 152 pp.
**$7.50** postpaid
Both from: Superintendent of
Documents, Government Printing Office, Washington,
D.C. 20402-9325; 202/783-3238

*Privacy is becoming a more important issue than ever as computers take over data storage for the government. By linking databases, it would be possible to trace virtually all of the movements of anybody in the country. These two books, written in a clear, non-technical style, give you the government's own words on topics such as the*

*vulnerability of communications systems, federal interpretations of the Privacy Act of 1974, as well as trends in policy relating to data protection. If you're interested in how the government looks at information, these books are a good place to start.*

— Richard Kadrey
[Suggested by
Howard Rheingold]

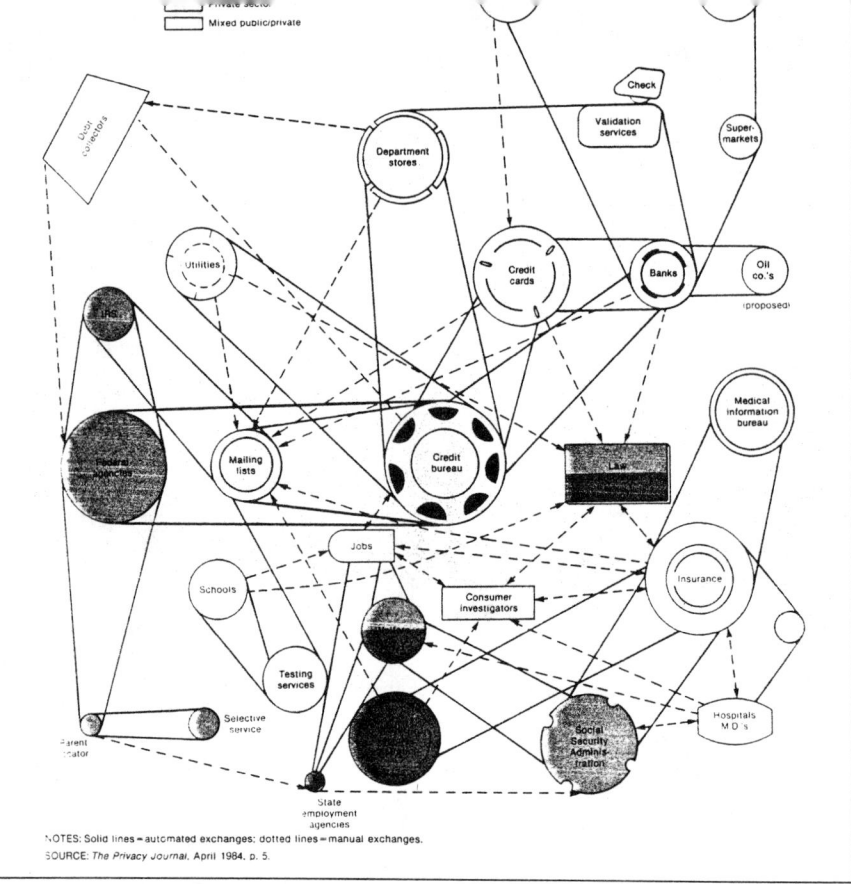

Current Database
Linkages.

NOTES: Solid lines = automated exchanges; dotted lines = manual exchanges.
SOURCE: *The Privacy Journal*, April 1984, p. 5.

## Privacy Journal

(An Independent Monthly on Privacy in a Computer Age)
Robert Ellis Smith, Publisher
$98/year (12 issues)
Special discount rates for students
From:
Privacy Journal
P. O. Box 15300
Washington, D.C. 20003
202/547-2865

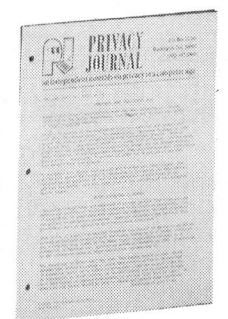

*From Washington, DC, the **Privacy Journal** tracks issues like confidentiality of records, lie detector testing, electronic surveillance, inaccurate credit reporting, invasion of privacy suits, and suppression of free speech. This is the only newsletter on privacy issues, and it's as thoughtful and comprehensive as a newsletter can be. There is a question column, too; if you feel you've been harassed or spied on, you can raise your case. The only drawback is its absurdly high price, annoying in any newsletter but downright distressing here since Smith is a champion of privacy rights for the poor. Maybe a local college library would go for it.*

— Art Kleiner

◆

"Mailing lists don't hurt anyone. No one gets hurt by mailing lists!" says Robert Sherman, attorney for the Direct Marketing Association, reflecting the position of his association that mail advertising does not create an invasion of privacy.

The American public had evidence to the contrary this month, with the national circulation of a story by **The New York Times'** David Burnham that the Internal Revenue Service plans to experiment with "lifestyle" demographic mailing lists to detect persons paying inadequate taxes.

## The Rise of the Computer State

David Burnham
1984; 282 pp.
**$6.95**
($7.95 postpaid) from:
Random House
Attn.: Mail Order Dept.
400 Hahn Road
Westminster, MD 21157
301/848-1900
or Whole Earth Access

***New York Times*** *reporter David Burnham has written a very scary book about the surveillance potentials of a computerized society. Computers make possible what the author says is likely, in fact, already underway: a very high degree of Orwellian tracking of each of us. Justified as effective for fighting criminals and terrorists, the FBI, CIA, NSA, local police and private security agencies have already created vast interlocked computer networks. You and your organization are probably to be found somewhere in them. What's more, these networks are only half a step (and one or two remaining laws) from being able to interlock their data with your social security file, your telephone, your zip code, your IRS records, your employer, your bank accounts, your insurance company, your charge cards and someday, perhaps, your own dear home computer, the one that makes you "free." Thus far, as the author describes, civil libertarians have held the line against the meshing of all identification into one all-knowing central computer. But technology has a way of fulfilling itself.*
— Jerry Mander

◆

Consider the small but sophisticated computer General

Motors has installed in the V8-6-4 model Cadillac automobile. "Your Cadillac," the 181 owner's manual boasts, "is equipped with a digital fuel injection system which monitors the exhaust stream with an oxygen sensor. The oxygen sensor signals the control unit to adjust the air-fuel ratio as necessary."

The manual further notes that the "check Engine" light in the instrument panel "is designed to warn you if the system has detected any faults. If the light comes on and stays on while driving, the car should be taken to a Cadillac Dealer as soon as possible for system inspection and maintenance. If the light comes on and goes off, it is an indication that a temporary problem has cleared itself. While it is not as critical that the vehicle be brought in to a dealer for inspection immediately, the dealer may at a later date be able to determine what trouble had occurred and if any maintenance is necessary."

But **Electronics Engineering News**, a trade publication, discerned another possible motive in the tiny onboard electronic spy: to ascertain owner negligence over warranty claims. The publication noted that the computer allowed the dealer to determine how many times the car has been driven faster than 85 miles an hour and also how many times the engine was started after the "Check Engine" message first lit up on the dashboard.

◆

The 1980 Office of Technology Assessment sent a questionnaire to the fifty states about how they managed their criminal- history records. One question was whether they checked the accuracy of the records in their files. Four out of five of the forty-nine states answering this question responded that they had never conducted record quality audits. . . .

The astounding finding that only one out of five of the states has ever sought to audit and purge information in their criminal-history files may explain why so many of the records are inaccurate or incomplete.

## CCS Communication Control, Inc.

Brochure **free**; Comprehensive catalog **$25** from: 160 Midland Avenue, Port Chester, NY 10573; 914/934-8093

*If you've ever watched a spy movie and wondered whether all those odd little gadgets the actors were using were real, this catalog is the place to find out. CCS Communications is a company that keeps a low profile. They deal in surveillance and countersurveillance equipment, essentials in the Lifestyles of the Rich and Paranoid. Their clients range from private individuals to multinational corporations to embassies that want to keep tabs on their rivals without their rivals keeping tabs on them. If you're in the market for a terrorist-proof limousine, a tear gas pen, a voice scrambler, or a new night vision scope, you need look no further.*

*— Richard Kadrey*

### HAVE A FEW (UNINTELLIGIBLE) WORDS WITH PARIS.

The pocket-sized SX-12 brings data encryption into the computer age. Have a formula or business proposal that must be sent to Paris immediately? The keyboard and internal memory will store up to 5 pages of information and, at your command, send it over the phone lines . . . anywhere in the world. Or, with a simple plug-in, SX-12 will transcribe directly from your tape recorder. Its built-in scrambler means that all messages are safe from prying eyes and ears no matter if you are using your own desk, the airport pay-phone, international telex network or worldwide electronic mail.

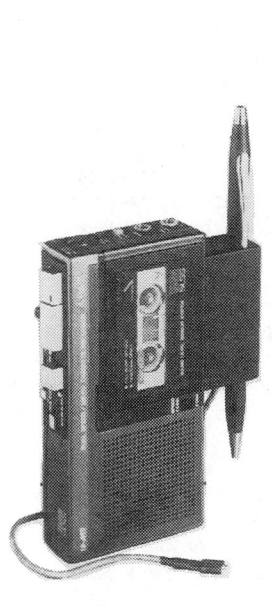

When you reach into your pocket, all anyone sees is an ordinary pen. But when you remove the pen from its holder, you are actually activating this incredible taping system. Pick up the pen . . . the tape recorder starts. Put the pen back . . . and the tape recorder stops. Because of its compact size, the Executive Investigator's Kit can be carried easily and discreetly in your pocket. It includes the tiniest "seed" microphone that can be worn under the collar or necktie. Even the faintest conversation can be clearly recorded.

### LET A COMPUTER PROTECT YOUR CONVERSATIONS.

Not all telephone scramblers are created equal. When your conversation requires maximum security, the computer-based CC-7000RC is always several steps ahead of any eavesdropper.

Program in your individualized code and this state-of-the-art scrambler automatically begins its computer-controlled "random rolling code" process that continually encodes and scrambles your conversation every 1/10th second. Eavesdroppers are thoroughly defeated and only the intended receiver can unscramble the message. Designed for simple operation and portability, the CC-7000RC even allows you to go back and forth from scrambler to "clear" mode by simply pushing a button.

### BATTLE THE COMMON BUG.

It is quite possible — in fact, quite likely — that sometime today your conversation will be bugged. That is why the micro-Bug Alert EJ-7 was created. If you have any suspicions, simply flick on the switch. Any eavesdropping device will automatically activate the tiny light in silent warning. What better way to eliminate the guesswork than to let EJ-7 battle the bug for you?

## Sherwood Communications Associates Ltd.

Catalog **free** from: P. O. Box 535, Southampton, PA 18966; 215/357-9065

*The Loompanics catalog (page 193), a source for books on the quasi-legal activities of the "lunatic fringe of the libertarian movement," and the Sherwood Communications book catalog have something in common. Both feature books on how to break the law, survival readiness, and "protecting" yourself; the difference is that Sherwood, founded, it says in the introduction to their catalog, by "Security Professionals," takes a more upscale approach to the subject. Printed on slick paper to give it the look of an oh-so-respectable security reference guide, Sherwood's catalog contains an exhaustive list of how-to books on lockpicking, wiretapping, car theft, torture, lip reading, poison extraction, fuel theft, fake ID and many other subjects for the do-it-yourselfer. If the books aren't enough, Sherwood also sells a complete line of surveillance and countersurveillance equipment, similar to CCS's products, but not quite as flashy.*

*— Richard Kadrey*

## Technologies of Freedom

Ithiel de Sola Pool
1983; 299 pp.
**$8.95**
($10.45 postpaid) from:
Belknap Press (Harvard University Press)
79 Garden Street
Cambridge, MA 02138
617/495-2600
or Whole Earth Access

*This book sums up a lifetime of reflection on the impact of electronic media. Until his death, author Pool was head of the MIT Program on Communications Policy Research. The focus of this book is easy to state: our tradition of free speech and free press has not been fully extended to electronic media for a variety of reasons, some still convincing, others not. As the center of cultural "gravity" shifts toward electronic publishing and electronic speech, will we lose that pre-electronic First Amendment tradition?*

*Pool answers the question by media: broadcasting publishing, mail, cable television, telephony, etc. For each he reviews its evolution from the perspective of conflicts between freedom of expression and regulation of access and use. The language is simple, clear and largely non-technical. Since I am a believer in the need for some kinds of regulation of electronic media, I was all set to hate this book, but it won me over completely. There is a good case for minimizing regulation, and this is its strongest presentation to date.*

*— Robert Horvitz*

◆

The paperless office or paperless society is probably a fantasy. Though for both storage and transmission, paper is likely to become a rarity because of its cost, the use of paper for display, reading, and current work may grow, partly because it will not be economical to retain the paper copies. The paper industry has cause for optimism. Experience shows that when word processors are introduced into offices, paper consumption increases, since with a word processor it is easier, when minor corrections are made, to run a whole new version of a document than tediously to correct old copies.

## In the Age of the Smart Machine
(The Future of Work and Power)
Shoshanna Zuboff
1988; 468 pp.
**$19.45**
($20.43 postpaid) from:
Basic Books
10 East 53rd Street
New York, NY 10022
800/242-7737
or Whole Earth Access

*This book is a truly comprehensive look at the emergence of the information economy, from its origins in the 19th Century to its infiltration of modern American industry. Zuboff, a Harvard Business School professor and industry consultant, focuses on several computerized firms — pulp mills, a telecommunications company, a pharmaceutical business, a bank — for a preview of the problems and solutions that are likely to arise in this next economy.*
— Sarah Vandershaf
[Suggested by Howard Rheingold]

◆

In one area of Piney Wood, where a computer system automatically controlled the pulp-drying process, operators had taken to calling the computer Otto (for automatic). They spoke about Otto according to their mood and estimation of its current level of performance. "Otto is the person who does all the thinking." "Otto won't speed up fast enough." "Otto just isn't making any sense." In another control room, a large axe was mounted on a wall, and underneath it was a sign that read,"IN CASE OF COMPUTER FAILURE, USE FIRE AXE." The crew leader told me that the axe had been presented to him by his co-workers — a sympathetic gesture toward his frequent frustration with the automatic controls.

◆

The most striking feature of the operators' behavior was the dependency they had developed on the computer system. Because of the relative simplicity of automating this part of the pulping process, the digesting module was the first in the plant to have a high level of computer control in the early 1970s. By 1982, there was wide agreement that it had become impossible to achieve a high-quality cook without the computer system. Management purchased an expensive backup computer when a

Insurance benefits analyst's self-portrait, after computerization of her office: "No talking, no looking, no walking. I have a cork in my mouth, blinders for my eyes, chains on my arms. With the radiation I have lost my hair. The only way you can make your production goals is give up your freedom."

systems failure revealed that the operators had lost their manual cooking skills. The operators freely admitted their dependency:

"We would be lost without the screen. Sometimes when it goes down, we sit and stare at it; we don't know what to do, we just sit and stare. Our job now really is to observe the screen. You may not be thinking exactly, but you sure have to pay attention."

"Before I started working in the control room, I would walk through here and think that everyone was crazy because they were just sitting in here all day long staring up at the screen. Now I do the same."

◆

When the plant manager asks, "Are we all going to be working for a smart machine, or will we have smart people around the machine?" he portrays two divergent scenarios. In the former, the line that separates worker from managers is sharply drawn. Workers are treated as laboring bodies, though in fact there is less that their bodies can contribute in effort or skill. As workers become more resentful and dependent, managers react by sinking more resources into automation. In the alternative scenario, both groups work together to forge the terms of a new covenant, one that recasts the sources and purposes of managerial authority. The choice to automate will strike many as the easier and more expedient of the two.

## The Second Self
(Computers and
the Human Spirit)
Sherry Turkle
Simon and Schuster

OUT OF PRINT

*Get this book back in print!*

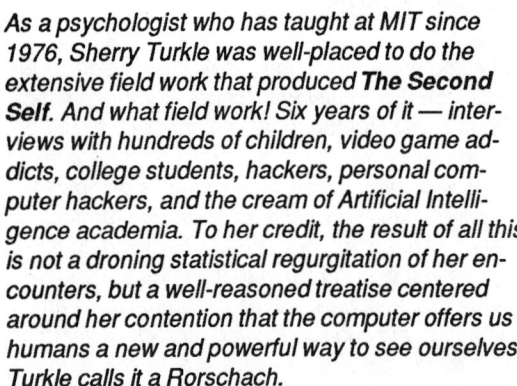

*As a psychologist who has taught at MIT since 1976, Sherry Turkle was well-placed to do the extensive field work that produced **The Second Self**. And what field work! Six years of it — interviews with hundreds of children, video game addicts, college students, hackers, personal computer hackers, and the cream of Artificial Intelligence academia. To her credit, the result of all this is not a droning statistical regurgitation of her encounters, but a well-reasoned treatise centered around her contention that the computer offers us humans a new and powerful way to see ourselves. Turkle calls it a Rorschach.*

*She starts by showing us that the computer stimulates little kids to talk philosophy and ends with a non-alarmist view of how Artificial Intelligence advances will bring a human-as-machine metaphor into common usage. Her perceptions, backed with long chunks of speech from her subjects (first names only given here), are provocative, reasonable, and sometimes witty. I was particularly pleased with her chapter on hackers, because her classical ethnographic approach led her to some conclusions that I had reached through a classical journalistic approach while researching my own book, **Hackers**.*
—Steven Levy

◆

The hackers illustrate another facet of our emerging relationships with machines. Their response to the computer is artistic, even romantic. They want their programs to be beautiful and elegant expressions of

their uniqueness and genius. They recognize one another not because they belong to the same "profession," but because they share an urgency to create in their medium. They relate to one another not just as technical experts, but as creative artists. The Romantics wanted to escape rationalist egoism by becoming one with nature. The hackers find soul in the machine — they lose themselves in the idea of mind building mind and in the sense of merging their minds with a universal system. When nineteenth-century Romantics looked for an alternative to the mechanism and competition of society, they looked to a perfect society of two, "perfect friendship," or "perfect love." This desire for fusion has its echo today, although in a new and troubling form. Instead of a quest for an idealized person, now there is the computer as second self.

## Smart Cards
(The Ultimate Personal
Computer)
Jerome Svigals
1985; 204 pp.
**$24.95** postpaid from:
Macmillan Publishing Company
Front and Brown Streets
Riverside, NJ 08075
609/461-6500

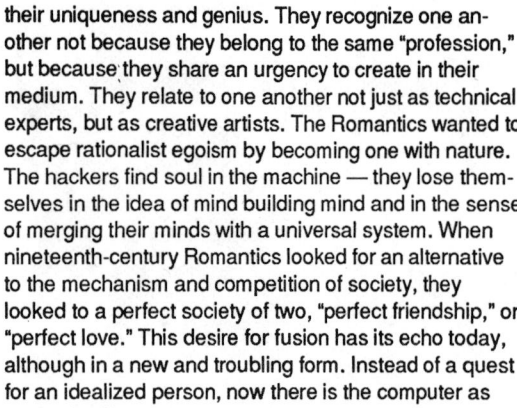

*Automated teller machine cards are only a first step. Combine those with card-sized calculators and computer network connections, and you get — what? At the very least, electronic i.d. cards that pay your bills, punch your time clocks, and keep track of your daily progress through the world. At the most, pocket-sized windows for you to know about the world — and the world to know about you.*

*The author, apparently an electronics engineer, considers smart cards A) a good thing and B) inevitable. I look at this book as you might look at a new power-plant proposal for your city. It's a necessary document, but what we need to see —*

*before these things are instituted, please — is an independent environmental impact report.*
— Art Kleiner

◆

Tomorrow's ultimate personal computer is a hand-held package. The package has been prepared so that each one provides a specific application result. We will carry a set of these ultimate personal computers. There will be a library at home, in the office, and at our work location. Like a pocketbook, the cover will be immediately identifiable as to its application area and expected results. In more complex applications, several Smart Cards will be used.

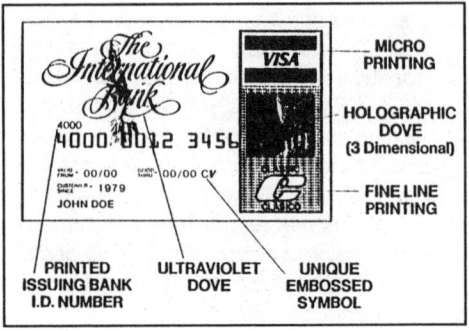

The VISA electron card anti-crime features.

MICRO PRINTING

HOLOGRAPHIC DOVE (3 Dimensional)

FINE LINE PRINTING

PRINTED ISSUING BANK I.D. NUMBER

ULTRAVIOLET DOVE

UNIQUE EMBOSSED SYMBOL

15,000 White House Pickets Denounce Vietnam War

## The Media Monopoly
Ben H. Bagdikian
1983; 282 pp.
**$10.95**
($11.83 postpaid) from:
Harper & Row
Keystone Industrial Park
Scranton, PA 18512
800/242-7737
or Whole Earth Access

*Why is local news coverage so poor? Because it's expensive (especially for chain newspapers), because advertisers prefer the lifestyle-type coverage that's taken over most papers, and because many newspapers have monopolies and don't need local reporting to hook readers. Living with a lousy newspaper is like sleeping in a room with a cat litter box; after a while you don't notice. This book tells how newspapers got so bad, and why magazines take so few chances. Like other professional gadflies, Ben Bagdikian oversimplifies his case somewhat, but the stories he tells are themselves fascinating. It's not a book to read unless you care passionately about periodicals, in which case it may spur you to create your own. There's no other remedy in most places. Good luck.      —Art Kleiner*

◆

An important element is missing in the standard newspaper histories of the late nineteenth century. Most stories of "yellow journalism" and the wild circulation wars of Hearst and Pulitzer in New York and the newspaper gangs in Chicago are true. But they are mistakenly presented as the main reason newspapers became popular with ordinary citizens. Before mass advertising, however, papers succeeded solely because they pleased their readers. Readers were clustered in terms of their serious political and social ideas — some were conservative, some liberal, some radical — and they had religious or regional loyalties. Each paper tended to focus a great deal of its information on the preferences of its readers. Because papers were physically smaller, lacking mass advertising, they were cheaper to print. And because they appealed to the strong interests of their readers, subscribers paid more for newspapers as a percentage of average wages than they otherwise might have done. Because newspapers were cheaper to print, newspaper businesses could be started more easily, either when new communities arose or when existing papers did not satisfy the interests of some significant group in the community. The result was a wider spectrum of political and social ideas than the public gets from contemporary newspapers. The frequent excess among adversarial papers of the past is a normal social cost of rigorous debate in a democracy.

[Left] From the **New York Times**, Sunday, April 18, 1965, page 1.

[Above] One of the April 17, 1965, photos sent out by United Press International and not chosen by the **New York Times**. Note the visible proportion between the antiwar demonstrators in the foreground and the few counterdemonstrators in the background, across Pennsylvania Avenue.

antiwar and right-wing demonstrations, and to give the impression — since the photographed segment of the two picket lines were identical in length — that they were equally large.

## The Geopolitics of Information
(How Western Culture Dominates the World), Anthony Smith, 1980; 192 pp., **$7.95** ($9.45 postpaid) from Oxford University Press, 16-00 Pollitt Drive, Fairlawn, NJ 07410; 800/451-7556 or Whole Earth Access

*News stories about Africa, Asia, or South America rarely match what filters back through friends and acquaintances who have been there. It's not so much deliberate censorship as it is the Western way of noticing and reporting, which makes non-Western cultures seem to disappear — even to themselves. The already slim chance for a developing nation to evolve its own identity in media is further complicated by new computer and broadcast technologies which by their nature ignore national and cultural boundaries. Even getting trained in programming or radio production usually means going to a developed country and picking up methods which clash with many of the world's diverse communication customs. Here's a well-written book of political analysis, spurred by recent U.N. debates about ownership and control of the world airwaves and data links. While tackling the problems of the Third World in the information age, the author also made me look freshly at my Western assumptions about what media should be like here.      — Art Kleiner*

◆

When a European or American reporter goes to Asia or Africa and discovers "shortages," "instability," "corruption," "crisis," he is often *seeing* the society in the light of the prior images of his own society. A shortage of spare parts which prevents the Westerner from driving about is not necessarily an *abnormal* deficiency in a society which is used to having to walk for twenty miles. A different aspect of this process can be discerned in the famous agency reporter who always counts the Mercedes-Benzes at meetings of African political leaders as a *per se* sign of corruption; if, however, he were at a gathering called by the World Bank, the same reporter would probably not consider the numbers of Rolls-Royces or Mercedes a significant fact worthy of mention. The same

## The Whole World Is Watching
(Mass Media in the Making & Unmaking of the New Left)
Todd Gitlin
1980; 327 pp.
**$10.95**
($12.45 postpaid) from:
University of California Press
2120 Berkeley Way
Berkeley, CA 94720
415/642-4247
or Whole Earth Access

*Todd Gitlin is probably the country's second-best observer (after Abbie Hoffman) of how media manipulates, shapes, defines, and creates popular movements — and how those movements can turn the relationship around. Nobody involved with politics at any level should be without this book.*
*—Tim Redmond*

◆

An opposition movement is caught in a fundamental and inescapable dilemma. If it stands outside the dominant realm of discourse, it is liable to be consigned to marginality and political irrelevance; its issues are domesticated, its deeper challenge to the social order sealed off, trivialized, and contained. If, on the other hand, it plays by conventional political rules in order to acquire an image of credibility — if, that is, its leaders are well-mannered, its actions well-ordered, and its slogans specific and "reasonable" — it is liable to be assimilated into the hegemonic political world view; it comes to be identified with narrow (if important) reform issues, and its oppositional edge is blunted. This is the condition of movements in all the institutions of liberal capitalism; one major site of the difficulty lies within the mass media.

◆

A look at the other photos UPI sent out that day to its subscribers, including the **Times**, throws the **Times'** choice into especially sharp relief. I retrieved the five other April 17 photos from UPI's archives. Two show a mass of antiwar pickets carrying signs bearing readable slogans . . . ; one shows a large mass at the antiwar rally at the Washington monument; and the other two give an accurate sense of the degree to which the antiwar people outnumbered the counterdemonstrators. All five were, in formal terms, printable; the pictures of the picketers with their signs were elegantly composed, with high contrast and good formal balance. But the effect of the photo the **Times** chose was visually to equate the

conflicts of perception work in the reporting of politics. Any African country is vulnerable to a coup d'état committed by a small number of armed men; does this in itself constitute "instability," or is it rather the common condition of governments which are attempting to construct new national entities out of territories which have been crudely carved from the geography of a defunct empire? When does a government become merely a "regime," and by what criteria may it earn reclassification by Western journalists? What commodities have to be subject to scarcity — and in what geographical regions of a society — before they constitute a famine or economic dislocation? Scotch whisky? Chanel No. 5? Petrol? Bread? Rice? Bananas?

## The Society of Mind

Marvin Minsky
1986; 339 pp.
**$9.95**
($10.95 postpaid) from:
Simon & Schuster
1230 Avenue of the
Americas
New York, NY 10020
201/767-5937
or Whole Earth Access

*This seminal work from the foremost pioneer in artificial intelligence is a metalogue on the mind. (A metalogue is a message whose form is echoed by its content — a conversation about conversations, for example). Minsky's landmark book is about, and at the same time is, a community of thoughts on thinking.*

*His thesis, that the mind is a muddling bureaucracy composed of different departments of calculation, from dumb machine logic to elegant consciousness, has become the most workable metaphor for cognition research. Taken as a whole, there is nothing that penetrates the zen of mind as boldly as this society of witty ideas does.*

*— Kevin Kelly*

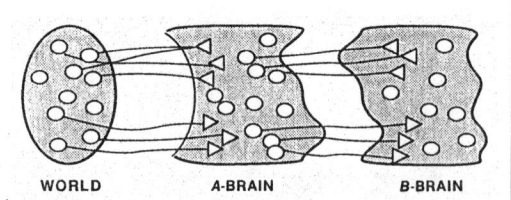

WORLD    A-BRAIN    B-BRAIN

There is one way for a mind to watch itself and still keep track of what's happening. Divide the brain into two parts, A and B. Connect the A-brain's inputs and outputs to the real world — so it can sense what happens there. But don't connect the B-brain to the outer world at all; instead connect it so that the A-brain is the B-brain's world! Now A can see and act upon what happens in the outside world — while B can "see" and influence what happens insides.

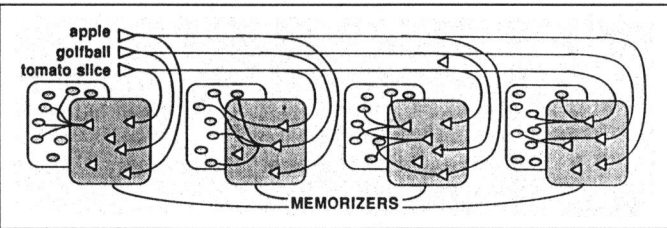

apple
golfball
tomato slice

MEMORIZERS

Can any simple scheme like this give rise to all the richness of the meaning of a real language-word? The answer is that all ideas about the meaning will seem inadequate by themselves, since nothing can mean anything except within some larger context of ideas.

◆

Minds are simply what brains do.

◆

Why can't we grow by steady, smooth development?

I'll argue that nothing so complex as a human mind can grow, except in separate steps. One reason is that it is always dangerous to change a system that already works. Suppose you discover a new idea or way to think that seems useful enough to justify building more skills that depend on it. What happens if, later, it should turn out that this idea has a serious flaw? How would you restore your previous abilities? One way might be to maintain such complete records that you could "undo" all the changes that were made — but that wouldn't work if those changes had already made your quality of thought so poor that you couldn't recognize how poor it had become. A safer way would be to keep some older version of your previous mind intact as you constructed each new version. Then you could "regress" to a previous stage in case the new one failed, and you could also use it to evaluate the performance of the new stage.

---

## The Minds of Billy Milligan

Daniel Keyes
1982; 443 pp.
**$4.50**
($6.50 postpaid) from:
Bantam Books
414 East Golf Road
Des Plaines, IL 60016
800/323-9872
or Whole Earth Access

*Sometimes you can't understand how something works until it's broken; the repair process then becomes a time to explore the constituent parts of the system, trying to figure out how they all go together. When Billy Milligan's mind broke it came apart in twenty-four separate pieces, or personalities. His personas ranged in ages from three to twenty-three, were male and female (one was a lesbian), had different IQs, spoke with different accents (one was fluent in Arabic), behaved with different mannerisms, and even looked different. This is the true story of how Billy came to know and understand the hidden parts of his own mind, how his lawyers and doctors fought to keep him in a safe environment within the Ohio State medical system, and how he became the first person in U.S. history to be judged not guilty of felonies because he was found to have multiple personalities.*

*— Richard Kadrey*

In her testing, Dorothy Turner discovered significant IQ variation among the different personalities: Allen, 120; Ragen 119; David, 69; Danny, 71; Tommy, 87; and Christopher, 102. Christene was too young to be tested, Andalana would not come out and Arthur declined to take the IQ portion of the tests, saying it was beneath his dignity.

◆

Ragen knew some of the other people who shared his body. He knew Billy, whom he had know from the beginning of his own consciousness; David, who accepted the pain; Danny, who lived in constant fear; and three-year old Christene, whom he adored. But he knew there were others as well — many others he hadn't met. The voices and things that happened couldn't be explained by just the five of them.

◆

"Think of it," he said, "as if all of us — a lot of people, including many you have never met — are in a dark room. In the center of this room is a bright spot of light on the floor. Whoever steps into this light, onto the spot, is out in the real world and holds the consciousness. That's the person other people see and hear and react to. The rest of us can go about our regular interests, study or sleep or talk or play. But whoever is out

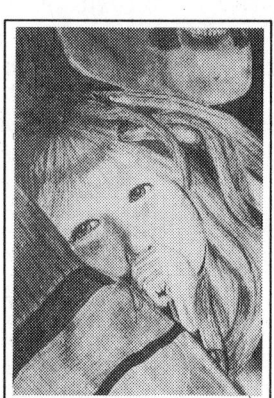

From Christene

Christine's note to attorney Judy Stevenson

"Ragen Holding Christine." Pencil sketch by Allen. Christine spells her own name with an "e" — Christene — whereas the other personalities spell it as usual, with an "i."

must be very careful he or she doesn't reveal the existence of the others. It is a family secret."

---

## When Rabbit Howls

The Troops for Truddi Chase
1987; 350 pp.
**$18.95**
($20.45 postpaid) from:
New American Library
P. O. Box 120
Bergenfield, NJ 07621
800/526-0275
or Whole Earth Access

*If you've ever had deep searching questions about the relationship between the mind and the sense of self, this book's for you. I'm not sure I believe the*

*basic premise: that it was written by the "Troops," a cooperative of at least 90 personalities nesting in one woman, Trudi Chase; the style is a little too homogenized, though the clash of competing voices gets confusing at times. If you buy the basic premise, then maybe this is what it's like to be inside Trudi's head. However, whether* **When Rabbit Howls** *is 100 percent true or not, it's a fascinating tale of the human spirit and raises questions about the origins of personality and the survival capabilities of the human mind.*

*— Pamela Winfrey*

## AI Expert

(The Magazine of Artificial
Intelligence in Practice)
Philip Chapnick, Editor
**$37/year**
(12 issues) from:
AI Expert
P.O. Box 11328
Des Moines, IA 50340-1328
800/341-SERV

*In current computer patois, an "expert system" is
one that can perform complex tasks in a single-
minded and efficient manner. All of the system's
actions are predictable because they have been
pre-programmed; in other words, the system's
knowledge of any given task is deep, but its understanding is shallow. That's why you need other
expert systems that can perform other specific
tasks. The current theory in AI circles is that if you
hook up enough expert systems, you might be able
to create something that is able to model human
intelligence. AI Expert is not a magazine devoted
to the theory of AI, but to its business and commercial applications. Mostly this takes the forms of
various expert systems. While I'm not a programmer and have only a passing interest in big business, I find the magazine interesting precisely
because it reports on how AI is being used in the
real world. With all the fascination and banality that
that implies.*

*— Richard Kadrey*

## Artificial Intelligence Using C

Herbert Schildt
1987; 360 pp.
**$21.95**
($25.95 postpaid) from:
McGraw Hill, Inc.
13955 Manchester Road
Manchester, MO 63011
800/722-4726
or Whole Earth Access

*This could serve as a base for a home-brew expert
system — an AI system that mimics the complex
knowledge of an expert. These simple programs,
written in a very clear coding style, include such
sophisticated features as heuristic search strategies, natural language processing, pattern recognition, backtracking, and machine learning. Schildt
shows how to build the programs step-by-step,
each part gradually adding to the techniques
just developed.*

*If you're a programmer and won-
der how people can imple-
ment uncertainty and
"fuzzy logic" in
clean, tight C code,
read this book. And
order the diskette
with the program
listings. Not a bad
way to learn C, either.*

*— Matthew McClure*

## The Tomorrow Makers

Grant Fjermedal
1986; 272 pp.
**$8.95**
($11.45 postpaid) from:
Microsoft Press
Attn.: Consumer Sales
16011 NE 36th Way,
Box 97017
Redmond, WA 98073-9717
206/882-8080
or Whole Earth Access

*Deep robotics, deep shivers.*

*Fjermedal has done the formidable footwork of
staying up countless nights working, scheming and
speculating with most of the cutting-edge robot
fanatics in the labs at Carnegie-Mellon, MIT, Stanford, Thinking Machines Corp., and on and on — a
fine comprehensive sweep. His report on work in
Japan is a scoop and fittingly closes the book,
since it proves that some of the wilder speculation
he begins with is already stalking about in Japan,
like some ominous, humorous Transformer toy,
just barely still a plaything.*

*For grasping what technology is rapidly bringing by
way of exploding human bodies and minds into
new configurations,* **The Tomorrow Makers**
*blends nicely with Eric Drexler's* **Engines of
Creation** *and my own* **The Media Lab**. *This stuff is
even more interesting than gene-splicing, and
more thrilling, both for promise and menace. For
example: serious immortality, soon.*

*—Stewart Brand*

◆

Will the robots recall that we were their creators?

And if they do, how much will we be able to trade on
this? Will there be a sentimentality about this sense of
origin? Initially we could program this in, but later, as the
robots begin propelling their own evolution, will this be a
memory deemed worthy of retention? Will they not
remember who taught them to play, who blessed them
with the need to frolic?

◆

Tachi has succeeded with his vision system. It truly
gives you the feeling that you are inside the robot, looking at the world from within its body, not your own. This
is possible because the operator isn't just looking at a
television monitor; his head is encased in a black-velvet-
lined box. Within this box are two television receivers,
one for each eye. The receivers are gauged so that the
image that is reflected against the retina of each eye is
exactly the same as if you were looking at the world
unaided. Further, every movement of your head is dupli-
cated on the robot, where two precisely placed video
cameras transmit a human range of what is seen.

The result of this is that when I went into the laboratory
and strapped my head inside the black box, it was as if I
were seeing with my own eyes. The depth and scope of
human vision was so completely reproduced, and the
color was so clear, that it was at first unsettling and then
a wild visual delight. . . .

Someone in the laboratory went over to the robot-
mounted cameras and swung them around so that they
focused on me. The walls spun during the maneuver,
and then when the motion stopped and I was looking at
myself, the out-of-body experience began. It was as if I
were standing a few feet away in another body looking at
myself. I moved my head to look up and down and even
to look away. And when I looked away from that person
who was me, it was as if that body were just another
passerby. . . .

"Are you here?" Tachi laughed. "Or are you there?
Where is your body?"

Example of a way a computer can find a route from New York to Los
Angeles using artificial intelligence: This "depth-first " solution explores all possible paths to their conclusions before trying other
paths. The computer's solution is good, but depth-first for complex
problems is a slow process. Another technique, breadth-first searching is the opposite of depth-first searching. Breadth-first searching
checks each node at the same level before it proceeds to the next
deeper level. A disadvantage to breadth-first searching when you're
looking for an answer that is several layers deep. Generally, the
programmer chooses between depth-first and breadth-first searching
by making an educated guess as to where the goal is most likely to
be. Another search technique is a hill-climbing search, which attempts to find as a first solution one that uses the heuristic that states
that the longer the distance
covered, the greater the
likelihood that you will be
placed closer to the destination — thereby reducing the
number of connection. The
opposite of the hill-climbing
search is the low cost
search. Think of this strategy
as being similar to standing in
the middle of a street on a big hill while
wearing roller skates: you have the definite feeling that it is
much easier to go down, rather than up. Thus, least-cost takes
the path of least effort.

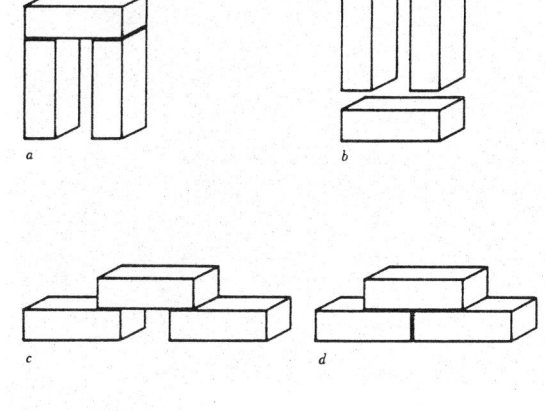

Computers can "learn" by rote (a program
that tells them what to do), or by the much
more difficult method of cognitive learning
(recognizing classes of objects and ideas and drawing conclusions).
The Hit-and-Near- Miss Method is one way to teach a computer (or
human) about objects. Here we see correct arches (a, c, d, e) and a
near-miss (b). By creating an algorithm that teaches class descriptions, a computer can learn, for instance, the difference between a
correctly built arch and a near-miss.

## Brain/Mind Bulletin

Marilyn Ferguson, Editor
$35/year
(12 issues) from:
Brain/Mind Bulletin
P. O. Box 70457
Pasadena, CA 91107
818/577-7233

*Easily the handiest way to stay current with news and gossip on the soft psychology frontier. Despite success and a burgeoning of the subject matter, editor Marilyn Ferguson has admirably kept the bulletin's format to a terse, packed six pages.*
— Stewart Brand

A startling new finding: Not only do the brain hemispheres switch dominance every 90 to 120 minutes throughout the day, but the sides of the body switch regularly in their dominance of sympathetic tone.

Researchers sampled nervous-system transmitters by taking blood from both arms every 7.5 minutes for periods of three to six hours. They found that the catecholamines — dopamine, norepinephrine, epinephrine (adrenaline) — were more concentrated on one side or the other every two to three hours.

Pickering showed Persian real words and nonsense anagrams to English-speaking undergraduates who later drew them from memory. Neither subjects nor experimenters knew which Persian character strings were real words until after the data had been collected and analyzed.

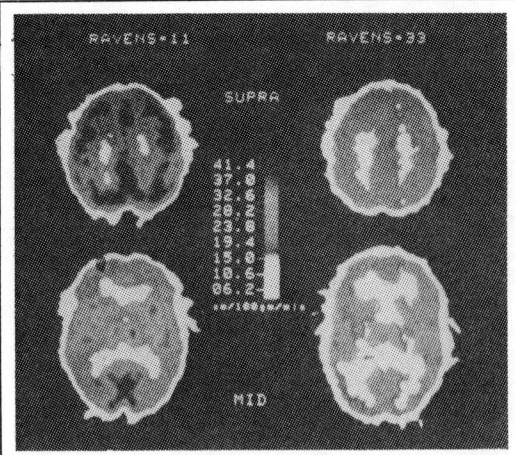

This composite photograph of computer images shows the contrasting glucose uptake of individuals who scored well and poorly on a test of abstract reasoning. The brighter images correlate with poorer test scores.

Subjects guessed the meaning of each word and rated their confidence in each guess. They reported feeling more confident in their guesses when they were viewing the true words, and their confidence ratings were twice as strong for high-frequency as compared to low-frequency words.

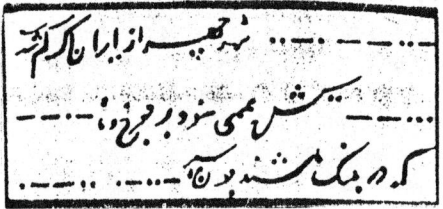

## Psychological and Behavioral Treatments

(Vol. 1: For Disorders of the Heart and Blood Vessels)
Mady Horning-Rohan
and Steve E. Locke
1985; 179 pp.
$45
($47.50 postpaid)

(Vol. II: For Disorders Associated with the Immune System)
Steven E. Locke
1986; 306 pp.
$65
($67.50 postpaid)

## Advances

Harris Diensfrey, Editor
$35/year
(4 issues)

All three from:
The Institute for the Advancement of Health
16 E. 53rd Street/5th Floor New York, NY 10022;
212/832-8282

*Those who criticize Western medicine for neglecting the psychological aspects of illness will welcome this excellent series of annotated bibliographies. By compiling well-written summaries of hundreds of journal articles in the fields covered,* the editors provide the best available overview of our current knowledge of how thoughts and emotions can contribute to disease.

*Volume I reviews the contributions of the psyche to high blood pressure, heart disease, and vascular disorders. Volume II covers asthma and other allergic disorders, hemophilia and other blood disorders, diseases of the skin, and cancer. Volumes I and II contain 916 and 1,479 entries, respectively. One quibble: good as these books are, the prices seem high. You may wish to pass this review on to your favorite librarian.*

*As these excellent volumes make clear, the psychosomatic approach means not that you consider the body less, but that you study the psyche more. The editors and Institute for the Advancement of Health deserve our thanks for making this important information available in such a readable and useful form.*

*The Institute's scholarly magazine, Advances, has established a fine reputation for publishing many of the freshest and most exciting pieces on the mind-body connection. One of my favorite sections, "Second Reading," reprints classic papers of the past. Another, "Abstracts," provides an extensive listing of recently-published studies in related fields.*
— Tom Ferguson, M.D.

## The Omni Whole Mind Newsletter

Judith Hooper, Editor
$24/year
(12 issues) from:
Whole Mind
P. O. Box 11208
Des Moines, IA 50347
800/341-7378

*I am of two minds about this one. On the downside, it's pricey, and published by **Omni** in hip sci-fi romanticism. On the upside, it's concise, broad (though seldom deep), and stimulating. Covering the same territory which the venerable **Brain/Mind Bulletin** has been prospecting for years, this one digs into the wide darkness we call the mind with more exuberance and gusto. They typically point me to something to follow up on, and bless 'em, they provide access to information.*
— Kevin Kelly

Using themselves as guinea pigs, a handful of neuroscientists at the State University of New York's Health Science Center have been bravely exposing their brains to strong magnetic fields and observing what happens.

In one experiment, the scientists placed a magnetic coil, shaped like a flat, palm-sized donut, over the backs of their heads when the occipital lobes interpret visual information. As the magnetic pulse beamed into the underlying brain tissue, it causes transient electrical changes in the scientists' neurons. But what did it feel like?

"It's very hard to describe," says Paul Maccabee. In this experiment the pulse was applied about a tenth of a second after the scientists saw letters flash on a computer screen. "You're essentially blind," Maccabee notes. Others described a strange confusion or perceptual blank. Essentially, the electromagnetic field had interrupted a brain process — in this case, visual processing — for a fraction of a second.

On October 30, at the Kennedy Center in Washington, D.C., The National Symphony Orchestra will present a concert of music composed entirely by manic-depressives.

The program, not yet set at this writing, will have many composers to choose from, including Berlioz, Tchaikovsky, Handel (so unpredictable he was said to have a "head full of maggots"), Schumann (who during a manic four-day period once wrote 130 songs), and songwriter Hugh Wolf (who avowed he "led the existence of an oyster" for years at a time).

In a glass dish in a National Institutes of Health laboratory in Washington lies what may be a harbinger of 21st-century brain repair. Saturated in a nutrient solution, a clump of living brain cells from a rat fetus grows directly onto an electronic computer chip.

The idea, says NIH neurobiologist Richard Wyatt, is to use the computer chip to "eavesdrop" on the electrical conversations that take place among the brain cells — to learn "the electric language of the brain." Once that language is learned, the chip could also act as a bridge between brain cells, passing electrical signals back and forth like a sort of switchboard.

## Steps to an Ecology of Mind

Gregory Bateson
1972; 541 pp.
**$4.95**
($5.95 postpaid) from:
Random House Inc.
Westminster, MD 21157
1-800-638-6460

## Mind and Nature

(A Necessary Unity)
**Out of print**
Bantam Books

*Gregory Bateson is responsible for a number of formal discoveries, most notably the "Double Bind" theory of schizophrenia. As an anthropologist he did pioneer work in New Guinea and (with Margaret Mead) in Bali. He participated in the Macy Foundation meetings that founded the science of cybernetics but kept a healthy distance from computers. He wandered thornily in and out of various disciplines—biology, ethnology, linguistics, epistemology, psychotherapy—and left each of them altered with his passage.*

***Steps to an Ecology of Mind*** *chronicles that journey. It is a collection of all his major papers, 1935-1971. In recommending the book I've learned to suggest that it be read backwards. Read the broad analyses of mind and ecology at the end of the book and then work back to see where the premises come from.*

*Bateson has informed everything I've attempted since I read Steps in 1972. Through him I became convinced that much more of whole systems could be understood than I had thought, and that much more existed wholesomely beyond understanding than I thought— that mysticism, mood, ignorance and paradox could be rigorous, for instance, and that the most potent tool for grasping these essences— these influence nets—is cybernetics.*

***Mind and Nature: A Necessary Unity*** *addresses the hidden, though unoccult, dynamics of life—the misapprehension of which threatens to unhorse our civilization. Bateson doesn't have all the answers, he just has better questions—elegant, mature, embarrassing questions that tweak the quick of things.*

*One of the themes that emerges is the near identity between the process of evolving and the process of learning, and the ongoing responsibility they have for each other which includes our responsibility, which we have shirked. We shirked it through ignorance.* ***Mind and Nature*** *dispels that.*

*Bateson's previous writing—**Naven; Communications; The Social Matrix of Psychiatry; Balinese Character** and **Steps to an Ecology of Mind**— has been addressed to various audiences of specialists.* ***Mind and Nature*** *is addressed to a general readership. It is new thought in an old virtue—the use of fine original writing to express ideas whose excellence is embedded in the clarity of their expression.* —Stewart Brand

When you narrow down your epistemology and act on the premise "what interests me is me, or my organization, or my species," you chop off consideration of other loops of the loop structure. You decide that you want to get rid of the by-products of human life and that Lake Erie will be a good place to put them. You forget that the eco-mental system called Lake Erie is part of your wider eco-mental system and that if Lake Erie is driven insane, its insanity is incorporated in the larger system of your thought and experience.

◆

Mere purposive rationality unaided by such phenomena as art, religion, dream, and the like, is necessarily pathogenic and destructive of life; its virulence springs specifically from the circumstance that life depends upon interlocking circuits of contingency, while conciousness can only see such short arcs as human purpose may direct.

◆

In no system which shows mental characteristics can any part have unilateral control over the whole. In other words, the mental characteristics of the system are immanent, not in some part, but in the system as a whole.
— Steps to an Ecology of Mind

◆

It is a nontrivial matter that we are almost always unaware of trends in our changes of state. There is a quasi-scientific fable that if you can get a frog to sit quietly in a saucepan of cold water, and if you then raise the temperature of the water very slowly and smoothly so that there is no moment marked to be the moment at which the frog should jump, he will never jump. He will get boiled. Is the human species changing its own environment with slowly increasing pollution and rotting its mind with slowly deteriorating religion and education in such a saucepan?

◆

Ross Ashby long ago pointed out that no system (neither computer nor organism) can produce anything new unless the system contains some source of the random. In the computer, this will be a random-number generator which will ensure that the "seeking," trial-and-error moves of the machine will ultimately cover all the possibilities of the set to be explored.

◆

I do not believe that the original purpose of the rain dance was to make "it" rain. I suspect that that is a degenerate misunderstanding of a much more profound religious need: to affirm membership in what we may call the ecological tautology, the eternal verities of life and environment. There's always a tendency — almost a need — to vulgarize religion, to turn it into entertainment or politics or magic or "power."

◆

It seems to puzzle psychologists that the exploring tendencies of a rat cannot be simply extinguished by having the rat encounter boxes containing small electric shocks.

A little empathy will show that from the rat's point of view, it is not desirable that he learn the general lesson. His experience of a shock upon putting his nose into a box indicates to him that he did well to put his nose into that box in order to gain the information that it contained a shock. In fact, the "purpose" of exploration is, not to discover whether exploration is a good thing, but to discover information about the explored. The larger case is of a totally different nature from that of the particular.
— Mind and Nature

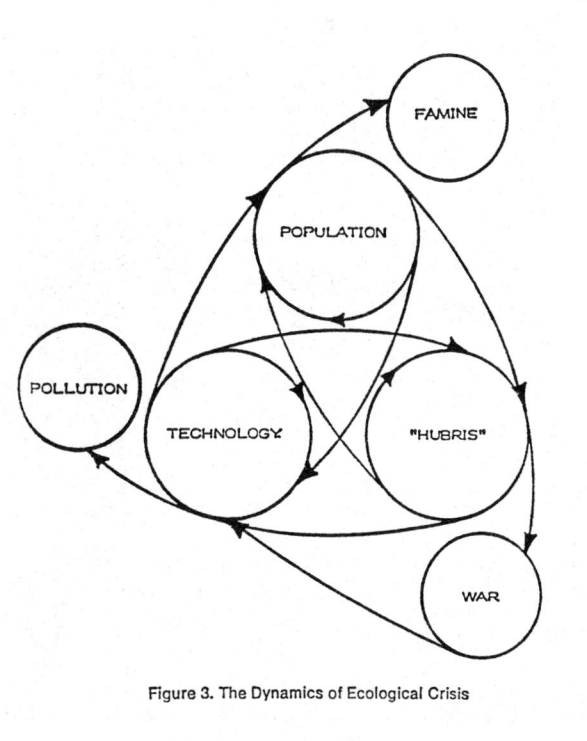

Figure 3. The Dynamics of Ecological Crisis

— From "Steps to an Ecology of Mind"

---

## Angels Fear

(Towards an Epistemology of the Sacred)
Gregory Bateson
and Mary C. Bateson
1987; 224 pp.
**$18.95** postpaid from:
Macmillan Publishing
Company
Front & Brown Streets
Riverside, NJ 08370
609/461-6500

*In **Angels Fear**, Gregory Bateson repeatedly reframes his attempts to understand the ecological groundings of and constraints on religion and aesthetics by stepping back to view the next "level" of abstraction, then stepping again, and yet again, until he eventually backs right off the edge of the cliff of hypostatization. Humbled by the abyss preventing him from telling too much about the holy (which would be made unholy by the telling), Gregory begins telling stories about telling stories about telling too much. So don't expect an overt resolution of The Mysteries here (even with Mary Catherine Bateson's persistent attempts to gather up loose ends). To pursue your own resolution, read the stories — they communicate the sacred, instead of trying to nail it down.*
— Greg Williams

## Megabrain

Michael Hutchison
1986; 347 pp.

**$4.95**
($5.95 postpaid) from:
Ballantine/Random House
400 Hahn Road
Westminster, MD 21157
800/638-6460
or Whole Earth Access

*A gee-whiz reporter for* **Omni** *magazine travels around the country trying out various gizmos claimed to elicit altered states of awareness, looking for action beyond biofeedback. Most of the inventions he examines apply weak electrical currents to the skull. One machine is reputed to emit "love waves" — frequencies that would churn up cheery hormones in the user's cortex. Do they work? Well, they do induce changes in the brain's activity, and the literature he digs up on each device indicates they produce some kind of mind molecules (the appropriate ones?). His own direct experiences suggest that the contraptions, in general, tend toward instilling "alert relaxation." Some would call that simply daydreaming or meditation.*

*Too bad his reporting is so uncritical. On the other hand, he deserves attention for his heads-on experimentation. He also supplies manufacturers'*

The opaque goggles of the Tranquilite give the user a stylish "human fly" look appropriate for all occasions. Indirectly lit from within, the goggles present a featureless visual field called a ganzfeld, while the compact pink noise generator provides a steady auditory stimulus that drowns out external sounds. The device thus serves as a sort of portable sensory isolation chamber.

*references for second opinions. It's the only comprehensive foray into the flaky world of do-your-own brain tuning, and so may be worth a look.*
— *Kevin Kelly*

◆

The ancient Egyptians apparently used natural electrical stimulation quite frequently, zinging themselves with the Nile electric catfish, which can be seen on Egyptian tomb reliefs. Some two thousand years ago a Greek physician, Scribonius Largus, was known for his "seashore treatment," which he prescribed for sufferers

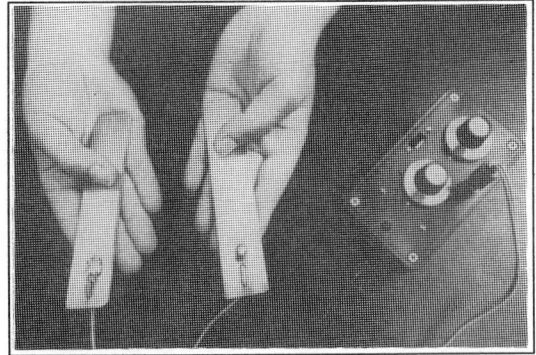

Joseph Light's simple TENS (Transcutaneous Electrical Nerve Stimulator) device is made from "about nineteen dollars' worth of parts from Radio Shack." Many users report that at certain frequency settings, the instrument can increase alertness and concentration, and produce mild euphoria

of pain (particularly gout). The patient was advised to put one foot on an electrical torpedo ray and the other foot on wet sand: the electrical circuit was completed, the patient got zapped, the pain was alleviated.

◆

Monroe found that by dropping the body into a state of profound sleep and then triggering a wakeful awareness with a combination of extremely rapid beta signals, he was able to induce the body vibrations and other sensations that led, for many of his subjects, to those mysterious mental events known as out-of-body experiences.

---

# Brain Tuners

In his book, **MegaBrain,** Michael Hutchison describes in depth a number of devices that relax or stimulate the brain in various ways. The following is a list of some of the devices he explores.

## Tens

Joseph Light, Biomedical Instruments Co., Inc., 315 Mountain Road, Glastonbury, CT, 06033; 203/643-8193

## Alpha Stim

Philip Brotman, Biofeedback Instrument Co., 255 West 98th Street, New York, NY 10025; 212/222-5665

## Alphapacer

Keith Simons, Alphatronics, P. O. Box 42006, Portland, OR 97242; 503/238-0448

## Cap Scan

Dr. Charles Stroebel, Institute for Advanced Studies in Behavioral Medicine, Ten Jefferson Street at Jefferson Court, Hartford, CT 06106; 203/527-8835

## Mind Mirror

Coherent Communications, 13756

Glenoaks Boulevard, Sylmar, CA 91342; 818/362-2566

## Hemi-Sync

Robert Monroe, Monroe Institute of Applied Sciences, Route 1, Box 175, Faber, VA 22938; 804/361-1252

## Synchro-Energizer

Synchro-Tech, 4392 State Road, Cleveland, OH 44109; 216/749-1133

## Graham Potentializer

David Graham, 2823 E. Malapai, Phoenix, AZ 85028; 602/971-9034

## Tranquilite

Montbray Inc., 26 Elwyn Lane, Woodstock, NY 12498; 914/679-2711

## Flotation Tanks

Flotation Tank Association, P. O. Box 30648, Los Angeles, CA 90030; 213-264-7960

## Sensory Deprivation Research

International REST Investigators Society, c/o Thomas Fine, Medical College of Ohio, CS# 10008, Toledo, OH 43699; 419/381-4106

---

## High Frontiers/ Reality Hackers

R. U. Sirius, Editor
$30/year (4 newsletters, 2 magazines) from:
Haile Unlikely Communications
P. O. Box 40271
Berkeley, CA 94704
415/861-5825

*Frontiers as in: life extension, cryogenics, hallucinogenics, bio-feedback, new age consciousness, artificial intelligence and anything else on the brink of understanding. These are the most electrifying periodicals I read. Funky, home-brewed, refreshingly unpredictable in content and format, they'll try out anything.* — *Kevin Kelly*

◆

I'm very nervous right now because I have no backups of myself. I back up my disks quite often but I've never once had a backup of myself. So I'm very interested in any technologies that might emerge in the future that will allow backing up the essence of a human. Therefore, I'm

interested in life extension and computer-human interface.
— Reality Hackers Newsletter

◆

I know that many people who have shared the chemical mind experiences of the past may be surprised or even shocked when I suggest that electrons are the next evolutionary step in turning yourself on, booting up your mind, activating new circuits in your mind. I don't see how you can use psychedelic drugs and not want to talk in electrons. Anyone who's had profound LSD experiences knows that the brain operates in clusters of flash on/offs, the so-called vapor trails. The clarity of atomic vision you get when you're very high on LSD or peyote or psilocybin is a sheer tuning in to the way the brain actually operates. . .
— Timothy Leary, High Frontiers

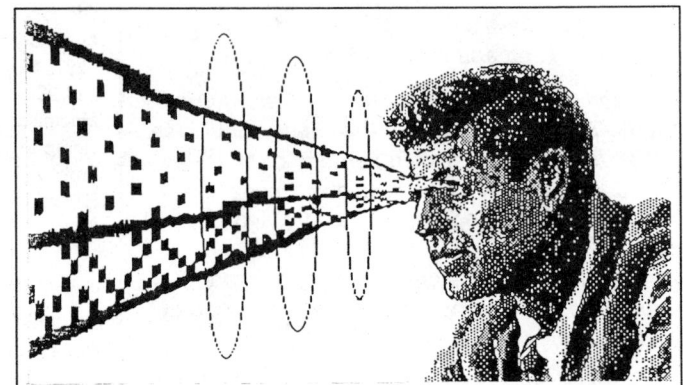

JFK: America's first psychedelic president?

## Foresight Update

Chris Peterson, Editor
$25/year from:
Foresight Institute
Box 61058, Department S
Palo Alto, CA 94306
415/364-8609

*Imagine molecule-sized machines that can alter or repair any organ in your body.*

*Imagine biologically-based machines that can enter and repair your defective cells and, so, extend your life indefinitely.*

*Imagine a molecule-sized weapon that is undetectable and able to enter an organism and "re-program" its genetic code.*

*This isn't science fiction, but a relatively new field of research called "nanotechnology" ("nano" for nanometers, the measurement standard for*

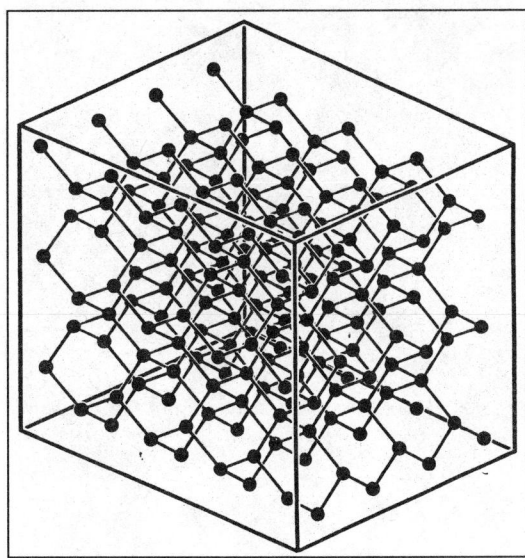

One cubic nanometer of diamond, containing 176 atoms. A cube 100 nm on a side would contain 176 million atoms.

*molecules), first described in K. Eric Drexler's excellent book, Engines of Creation. While still in its infancy, biologically-based nanotechnology promises to change (and challenge) us on the internal level as profoundly as the personal computer has on the external.*

*The Foresight Institute is a non-profit group dedicated to the study and promotion of nanotechnology research. When you subscribe to their feature-oriented newsletter, the Foresight Update, you will also receive the Foresight Background, a forum for on-going discussions about the possible benefits and dangers of nanotech. Frankly, a bit more objectivity in both publications would have been welcome. There's a "gee-whiz" tone to some of their articles that's unsettling, considering the potential dangers of nanotechnology. But if you're interested in keeping up with what's going on in this important new field, this is the place to do it.*

*— Richard Kadrey*

## Mind Children

Hans Moravec, 1988; 196 pp., **$20** ($21.25 postpaid)
from: Harvard University Press, 79 Garden Street, Cambridge, MA, 02138; 617/495-2600

*The ideas are heretical, and if they weren't coming out of the Robotics Institute of Carnegie-Mellon University, slightly lunatic, too. What is proposed is the end of biology, and the birth of a new cybernetic race, more machine than human. More efficient, more intelligent and more likely to survive their indefinite lifespans. Moravec also lays out the methods these autonomous machines might use to think: program in a little piece of a person into each unit. The human conciousness would be the wide-eyed innocent, the one who would keep things interesting, the one who, in the end, would be responsible for furthering evolution; the machine would keep the unit running smoothly, repair*

*damage, and sort the information the human part absorbs.*

*Like many visionaries, Moravec tends to be somewhat myopic. How many people do you know that would willingly take a backseat to a robot, no matter how elegant its design or function? But the future Moravec presents is truly mindbending, one where intelligent machines explore distant planets for us, and can not only repair themselves, but design and build improved descendents. Mind Children is by turns inspiring and disturbing; read it and it will leave you thinking about yourself, your body, and your humanity, in a whole new way.* — Richard Kadrey

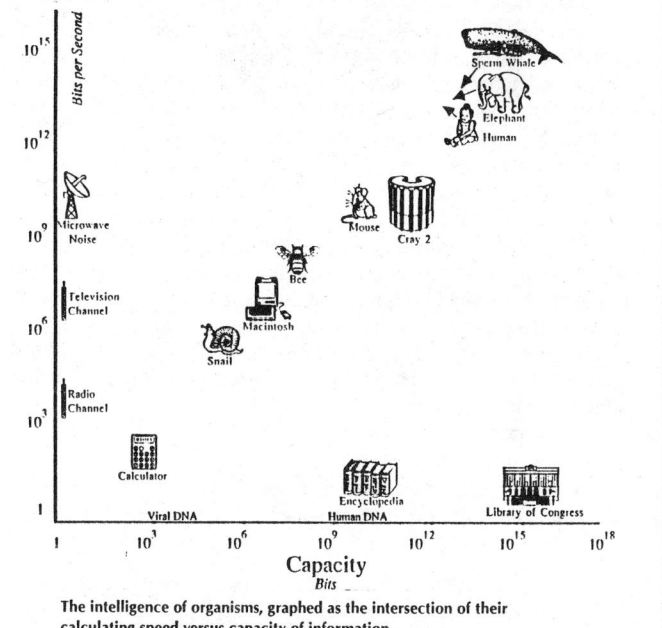

The intelligence of organisms, graphed as the intersection of their calculating speed versus capacity of information.

## DNA Suite

Dr. David Deamer
& Riley McLaughlin
**$9.99**
($11.99 postpaid)

## DNA Music

Riley McLaughlin
**$9.99**
($11.99 postpaid)

both from:
Science and the Arts
144 Mayhew Way
Walnut Creek, CA 94596; 415/943-7255
or Whole Earth Access

## DNA Music Articles

by Susumu Ohno ; Reprints **free** from: Dr. S. Ohno, Beckman Research Institute of the City of Hope, 1450 East Duarte Road, Duarte, CA 91010; 818/359-8111, extension 2820

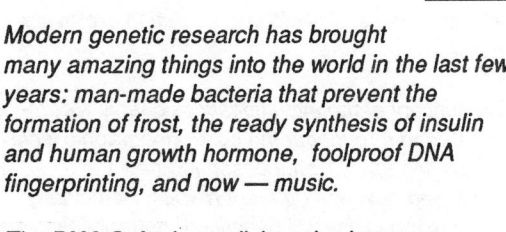

*Modern genetic research has brought many amazing things into the world in the last few years: man-made bacteria that prevent the formation of frost, the ready synthesis of insulin and human growth hormone, foolproof DNA fingerprinting, and now — music.*

*The DNA Suite is a collaboration between molecular cell biologist Dr. David Deamer and synthesist Riley McLaughlin. Originally designed as a teaching aid, side one of the tape features melodies inspired by assigning musical values to the repeating 4 letter codes that describe bases (A, C, G, and T) in DNA, and on side two, a brief, but thorough explanation of the music and basic genetics. DNA Music is a solo tape by McLaughlin. The slow, meandering melodies on both of these tapes are disappointing, relying on soupy New Age cliches. But the existence of the music points out exciting connections between the repetition of form in nature and the man-made*

*repetition in music. If you think of the notes and dynamics of music as something like computer code, instructingthe performer what to play and how to play it, you can imagine the human biocomputer reacting to and appreciating good, tight code.*

*Dr. Susumu Ohno explores ideas similar to Deamer's, but in "The All Pervasive Principle of Repetitious Recurrence Governs Not Only Coding Sequence Construction But Also Human Endeavor in Musical Composition," he compares the repetition of bases in DNA to a Chopin Nocturne, which gives his music a classical feel. As of this writing, there are no recordings of Dr. Ohno's music, but some of his articles contain transcriptions of his DNA-inspired pieces with such romantic titles as "Last Exon of the Largest Subunit of Mouse RNA Polymerase (Part 2)" and "Chicken Lens Alpha-A Crystallin."* — Richard Kadrey

## The Three-Pound Universe

Judith Hooper
and Dick Teresi
1986; 410 pp.
**$12.95**
($13.70 postpaid) from:
Dell Publishing Co.
6 Regent Street
Livingston, NJ 07039
800/626-3355
or Whole Earth Access

*Man, with arm around graduating son-in-law, pointing to the future. "I have one word for you, son: Brain-juices."*

*This lucid book constitutes the necessary orientation to the flow of neurotransmitters from the mind to the soul.*

—Kevin Kelly

Back in the mid-1950s Robert Heath, chairman of the psychiatry department at Tulane Medical Center in New Orleans, found a mysterious protein in the blood serum of schizophrenics, which he baptized taraxein (from the Greek for "madness"). After experimenting with monkeys to make sure the procedure was safe, Heath injected the taraxein fraction into nonpsychotic prisoner-volunteers (using a comparable serum fraction from normal people for controls). Like characters in a mad-scientist horror movie — and, as a matter of fact, these experiments were filmed, like a kind of neuro-psychiatric film noir — the men who received the taraxein injections were plunged into instant psychosis. "Some hallucinated and had delusions and thought disorders," Heath recalls. "Some became severely anxious and paranoid. Some were withdrawn and catatonic. An hour or so later, they went back to being entirely normal."

In the 1940s MacLean became fascinated with the "limbic storms" suffered by patients with temporal-lobe

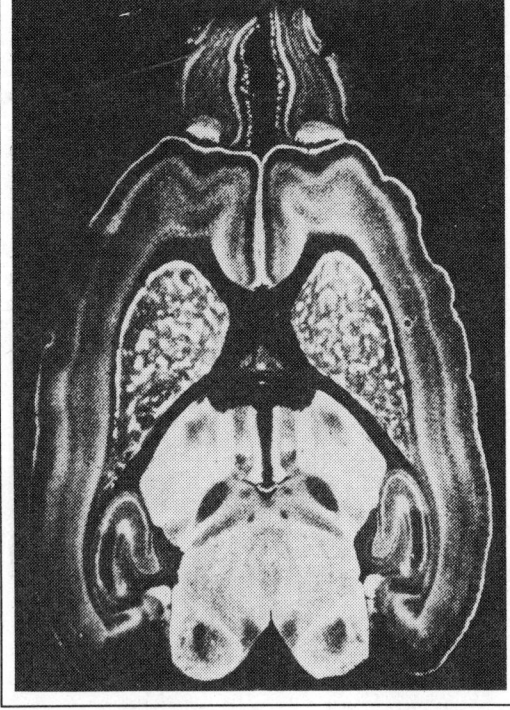

The face of pleasure: Candace Pert's autoradiographic map of opiate receptor sites on a rat brain. The receptors, activated with an injected opiate drug "labeled" with radioactivity, glow in this cross-section of brain as shades of white and gray aganist the unactivated black background. The complex pattern of receptor density and distribution provides hints about the way the brain "filters" reality. (Courtesy of Dr. Candace Pert, NIMH.)

epilepsy. "During seizures," he recalls, "they'd have this Eureka feeling all out of context — feelings of revelation, that this is the truth, the absolute truth, and nothing but the truth." All on its own, without the reality check of the neocortex, the limbic system seemed to produce sensations of deja-vu or jamais-vu, sudden memories, waking dreams, messages from God, even religious conversions.

"You know what bugs me most about the brain?" MacLean says suddenly. "It's that the limbic system, this primitive brain that can neither read nor write, provides us with the feeling of what is real, true, and important."

## The Oxford Companion to the Mind

Richard L. Gregory, Editor
1987, 450 pp.
**$45**
($49.95 postpaid) from:
Oxford University Press
16-00 Pollitt Drive
Fair Lawn, NJ 07410
201/796-8000
or Whole Earth Access

*Of all the professors who write on brains and psychology for general readers, Richard Gregory is surely one of the most articulate. A founder of the cognitive cognoscenti and the artificial intelligentsia (except the British more reasonable call it "machine intelligence"), he is remarkably knowledgeable about nuts-and-bolts neurophysiology and clinical matters as well. So when I heard that he was putting together this not-quite-encyclopedia of 1001 entries, I was delighted with the prospect.*

*Most contributors are British, but the subjects selected are of universal interest. Noam Chomsky writes on his own theory of language; the late Norman Geschwind on language areas in the brain; and the late Alexander Luria on neurolinguistics. All are disappointingly "basic," containing little of the exciting 1980s language contributions from brain stimulation and PET scans. But the sections on brain imaging (CT, NMR-MRI, and PET) are up-to-date and perfectly pitched for the general reader. Many entries have some bibliographic leads.*

*This isn't a book you read seriatim; there are many cross-references to other entries. And since many read like accessible essays, it is a book that I find myself sampling constantly for pleasure. You might buy it as a dictionary-encyclopedia reference work, but you'll read it like a magazine.*

— W. H. Calvin

## The River That Flows Uphill

William H. Calvin
1986; 528 pp.
**$12.95**
($15.95 postpaid) from:
Sierra Club Store Orders
730 Polk Street
San Francisco, CA 94109
800/638-6460
or Whole Earth Access

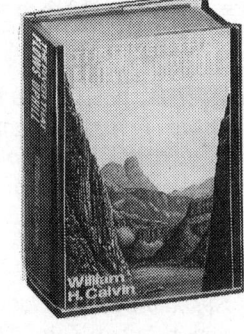

*This is good science, well presented. Most importantly, it illuminates that peculiar function of the human brain: to be conscious of consciousness.*

*Neurobiologist William Calvin was part of several rafts full of scientists on a boat trip down the Colorado River through the Grand Canyon. Their conversations — relaxed, witty, skillfully rendered — teach as much about river rafting, Southwest anthropology, and respect for Nature as about neurophysiology, biology and evolution. The Grand*

Canyon almost forces a broad, long-term point of view: the marks of geological evolution are everywhere.

*The concept of the evolutionary ratchet is a common thread throughout the book: geographic isolation causes speciation, conserving new traits. Something new and different results. Particularly tasty are the incidental benefits of natural selection that survival traits have made possible. Feathers let birds fly, though the feather's warmth would have been sufficient to give them an evolutionary edge. In people, the evolution of the brain (learning sequencing operations to hunt and throw, for example) lets us laugh, make music, and produce complex arguments — of which this book is a fine example.*

— Matthew McClure

"We neurobiologists want to know not only what the 'brain programs' are, but how the brain machinery operates them. The Artificial Intelligence folk figure that if they can postulate a program that seems to do the trick,

then they can build a hardware computer that will mimic the actions of the mind, running the same program using silicon chips rather than wet and unreliable nerve cells," I replied, pausing for a drink from my canteen.

"We neurobiologists work up from the bottom much of the time, trying to fathom the computation processes of the building blocks. We're constantly coping with parallel processing, a notion which is still novel in AI. I happen to think that the AI types are missing the boat, by trying to ignore the unreliable nature of the individual cells, the real brain's computing elements. Instead of trying to work around jittery cells by using reliable pigeonhole computers, unreliable cells should be seen as the essence of the brain's way of doing things, just as sex's institutionalized randomness is the essence of how evolution has done more and more elaborate things. But philosophically, both neurobiologists and the AI folk start from the premise that the mind can be explained, that it isn't beyond understanding. And most of us would assume that mind is going to emerge from a lucky combination of more elementary 'dumb' processes."

# Cognition Enhancing Drugs
### by R. U. Sirius

INTELLIGENCE-INCREASING drugs might be labelled "Cognitive Enhancers," "Memory Enhancers," or, in some cases, "Psychic Energizers." What many of these drugs and nutrients have in common is that they produce effects similar to the effects people are seeking from popular stimulants such as caffeine, amphetamines and cocaine. These popular drugs temporarily enhance cognition and memory, and amp up the user's energy levels only to leave the user depleted. However, the drugs and nutrients discussed in this review are all believed to create long-term improvements in memory and cognition. Some of them also provide the short-term high-energy states associated with the stimulant drugs. Also, there is virtually no tendency towards the kind of weirdness and darkness of the spirit which so often accompanies even the occasional speed or cocaine high. It seems that while the illicit stimulants cause short-term release but long-term depletion of norepinephrin, many of the memory-enhancing drugs and nutrients work on the noradrenergic nervous system in a different way, apparently modulating nerve cell control mechanisms so that the cellular response is neither too great nor too little.

This survey deals primarily with the short-term experiential effects of these compounds, since I only have the experience of a relative and imprecise ongoing use of one drug, Pemoline, and no scientific proof of any intelligence increase on my part.

In consideration of all this, I hereby present a review of intelligence-increasing drugs. May you never sleep.

*Vasopressin* — Definitely the most euphoric of the memory-enhancing intelligence-increase drugs outside of the one being called "Euphoria" (more on Euphoria later), Vasopressin is marketed as Diapid, a prescription drug made by our old friends at Sandoz. It can also be ordered as Vasopressin through chemical supply houses by those who know the ropes. I had five squirts of Vasopressin out of a nasal inhaler. I was surprised by how strong the effects were. I had that charged-up hyperconfident rush that one experiences with cocaine, but combined with much clearer ideation and without the numbing and discomfort or the strange and disquieting hard edges which often accompany even the more euphoric coke highs. It didn't last very long, about two hours. I did not have an opportunity to experience Vasopressin as a work/writing drug. It was clear, however, simply from reading (I was re-reading **Gravity's Rainbow** at the time and I consider that a fairly challenging test of comprehension) that Vasopressin is an excellent tool for rapid learning and comprehension of complex systems of thought.

Cys-Tyr-Phe-Gln-Asn-Cys-Pro-Arg-GlyNH$_2$

**VASOPRESSIN**
Other names: beta-hypophamine; Leiormone; Pitressin; Tonephin; Vasophysin. An anti-diuretic hormone.

*Hydergine* — The invention of one Dr. Albert Hofmann of Sandoz laboratories. I know of many people who got their hands on buckets of this stuff and I know of nobody who continues to take it. The effects are said to be cumulative rather than immediate and everybody seems to lose interest. "I forgot to take my Hydergine" is a term which one often hears from chagrined "intelligence agents," fully cognizant (even without Hydergine) of the ironies involved. This probably says more about the people that I hang out with than about Hydergine as an intelligence increase agent.

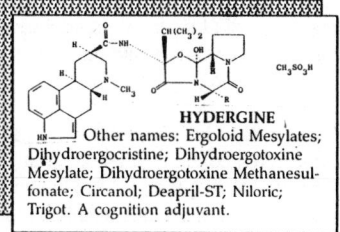

**HYDERGINE**
Other names: Ergoloid Mesylates; Dihydroergocristine; Dihydroergotoxine Mesylate; Dihydroergotoxine Methanesulfonate; Circanol; Deapril-ST; Niloric; Trigot. A cognition adjuvant.

*Lecithin, Choline with Inositol, Phenylalanine (with vitamin C and B6)* — While perhaps less intriguing and glamorous to technophilic reality hackers, most of these easily available cognitive enhancers have a substantially perceptible effect. Lecithin seems to be the exception. Even at minute dosage levels there was no noticeable enhancement of focus, recall, etc. Choline and Inositol, at about three grams each, produce mild but definite results with no discomfort and can be used daily. I did this once for about a month and found myself losing my sense of humor. However, if you're already humorless you might just as well give this a go. Phenylalanine is quite speedy. While it can be used for creativity and focus it tends to make one irritable. For emergeny use only.

CH$_2$OCOR
|
CHOCOR
|                    O$^-$
|                    |
CH$_2$O—P—OCH$_2$CH$_2$N$^+$(CH$_3$)$_3$

**LECITHIN**
Other names: Phosphatidylcholine; Lecithol; Vitellin; Kelecin; Granulestin. Often used as an emulsifying agent.

PHENYLALANINE structure

**PHENYLALANINE**
Other names: alpha-aninohydrocinnamic acid. An essential amino acid for humans.

*Deaner* — This is getting really popular with the "health food set." Experientially, the effect is very subtle but noticeable. I've tried this a few times and what I've found is that if I already have a task to do, I will do it and, in retrospect, I will realize that I sustained my attention for an unusually long time without flagging or needing a break. However, if I use this (as I often do with other cognitive enhancers) without a precise sense of what the task at hand is, it doesn't clarify and help to motivate activity.

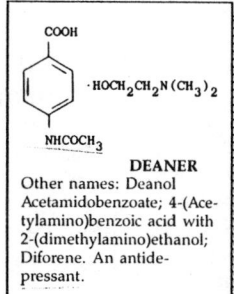

**DEANER**
Other names: Deanol Acetamidobenzoate; 4-(Acetylamino)benzoic acid with 2-(dimethylamino)ethanol; Diforene. An antidepressant.

*Pemoline (usually combined with Magnesium)* — In the 20-30 milligram range, I've found that this can be used twice weekly with excellent results. The lift is very substantial and noticeable. I, and several of my friends, find it particularly good for writing, both creative and functional. For rapid-fire associations and grand synthesis just combine it with moderate amounts of cannabis (Sativa if possible). It lasts about twelve

**PEMOLINE**
Other names: 2-Amino-5-phenyl-4(5H)-oxazolone; phenoxazole; phenyliso-hydanoin; azoxodone; Azoksodon; Cylert; Dantromin; Deltamine; Endolin; Hyton; Kethamed; Nitan; Notair; Pioxol; Pondex; Ronyl; Sigmadyn; Sisral; Sofro; Tradon; Votital. A stimulant.

hours, coming on slowly and having its greatest effect at around the fifth through the tenth hours. Clarity and verbal acuity are the strong points here. WARNING: From my observations, approximately one in every ten people get nothin' but headaches from even small doses of Pemoline.

*Euphoria* — Well, someone took Pemoline, twisted it around a little bit and put a whole lot of pleasure into the equation. This might be a dangerous drug! There are a lot of different things that seem to happen with Euphoria. The first time I took it (40 milligrams — I've learned since that 25 mg. is considered your basic dose) I got really charged up. This is definitely a high and it comes on suddenly (about 45 minutes after ingestion).

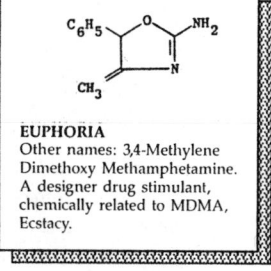

**EUPHORIA**
Other names: 3,4-Methylene Dimethoxy Methamphetamine. A designer drug stimulant, chemically related to MDMA, Ecstasy.

Subsequent experiments have shown Euphoria to be predictable as an effective tool for organizing binges, brainstorming sessions, and radio talk-show appearances. It also seems to induce ongoing personal growth in terms of clarity of personal will. (I've received three other testimonies in this same direction.) As a writing tool, I've found Euphoria to be variable. It seems that verbal acuity comes on strong but the verbal circuits burn out quickly from intensity of use and one has to move on to less verbally oriented tasks.

**CHOLINE WITH INOSITOL**
Other names (Choline): Bilineurine. A constituent of lecithin. (Inositol): Hexahydroxycyclohexane; cyclohexanehexol; cyclohexitol; phaseomannite; dambose; meso-inosite. A vitamin.

My only complaint about Euphoria is that it lasts 16 hours, which feels about four hours too long. In two of my five experiences, the last four hours were spent feeling slightly "headachy" and weary, although there was still no burnout following sleep. I would say, at this point, that Euphoria should not be used more often than once a week since it is so powerful and so much energy is expended in the experience. This is easily the most fun of the intelligence increasers and, as such, is probably most likely to be abused.

*PRL-8-53* — Untried by your reviewer at this time. However, Durk Pearson is quoted in **High Frontiers** as saying that "PRL-8-53 is a terrific memory enhancer. Normally you can memorize about seven or eight digits just by looking at them for a second. PRL-8-53 gives the average person a memory span of about 21 to 22 digits." He also reported that one amnesia victim was cured with one dose.

*THA* — Untried by your reviewer at this time. Again, Durk Pearson, this time in High Frontiers' **Reality Hackers Newsletter:** "In combination with arecoline, THA has been found to be remarkably effective as a memory improver . . . it's important that the dosage be individualized. . . too much will actually impair memory and produce sweating, excessive muscle tone and mouthwatering." The standard dosage is "1 to 2 mg." However, Durk recommends that you start with a quarter of that every two to four hours and work up — if you get those side effects, back off.

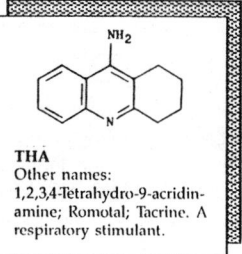

**THA**
Other names: 1,2,3,4-Tetrahydro-9-acridin-amine; Romotal; Tacrine. A respiratory stimulant.

## Mind Food and Smart Pills

Ross Pelton
1986; 207 pp.
**$9.95**
($11.45 postpaid) from:
T & R Publishers
12922 Cree Drive
Poway, CA 92064
800/255-2665
or Whole Earth Access

*Could be another crackpot vitamin book, but looks to me like there is enough intriguing studies cited here to be worth a glance. Subtitled "Nutrients and Drugs that Increase Intelligence and Prevent Brain Aging," it parallels the information presented by R. U. Serious on the previous page. Needless to say, this is outlaw territory.*

— *Kevin Kelly*

◆

Lucidril is one of the most promising new drugs in the areas of brain research and anti-aging. It was widely used throughout Europe to prevent biological aging and reverse the aging process (Kent, 1982a). Studies have shown that it removes age pigment deposits from brain cells (Nandy, 1968). This is actually reversing the aging process. Human clinical trials with Lucidril have demonstrated improvements in memory and mental functioning (Gedye, 1972; Marcer, 1977).

They designed a study to look at the effects of Lucidril on synaptic deterioration. This study was published in 1980 in Mechanisms of Aging and Development. The results of this study are extremely exciting. They found that treatment with Lucidril restored the synaptic contact zones in brain cells of old rats to the values found in young animals (Guili, 1980).

The effects of Lucidril on memory performance was studied in a double-blind study with 76 elderly subjects who were all in good physical health but suffered from a measurable amount of intellectual deterioration. The tests revealed that centrophenoxine appears to increase the storage of new information into long term memory. Many of the subjects also reported an increased level of mental alertness (Marcer, 1977).

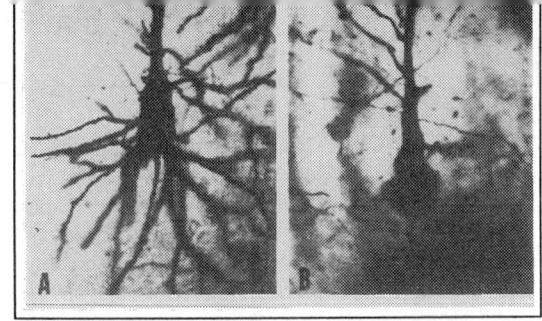

Figure A - Normal large cortical motor neuron in a young adult. Note the healthy dendritic system. Figure B - The same type of cell in a 75 year old individual. The massive change in the dendritic system is obvious. (Stained by Golgi method, X450)

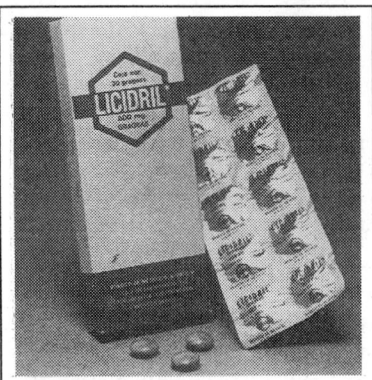

The usual dosage of Lucidril administered in both animal and human clinical trials has been 80 mg/kg of body weight. That translates to 9 tablets per day for a 120-lb. person up to 16 tablets per day for a 220-lb. person.

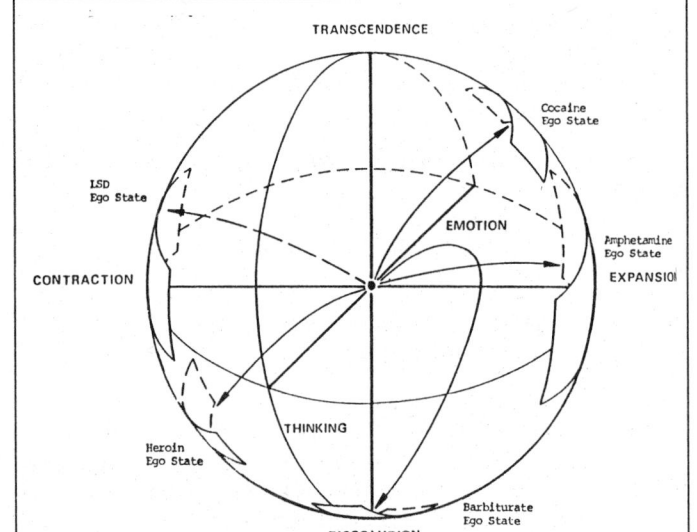

## Psychedelic Monographs and Essays

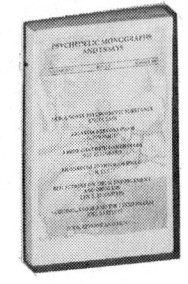

Thomas Lyttle,
Editor/Publisher
$20/year
(2 issues) from:
Psychedelic Monographs and Essays
624 NE 12th Avenue #1
Fort Lauderdale, FL 33304

*This young periodical attempts to referee the underground investigation into psychedelic drugs, now in a revival after a decade's lull. It flunks the measure for science journals, but passes the electric kool-aid acid test. Delivers hard-to-collect data if you can put up with interviews from old drug gurus.*

—*Kevin Kelly*

◆

In 5 years there were only 8 emergency room visits and one death reported to DEA involving MDMA, out of about 750,000 drug incidents. The few MDMA incidents probably involved overdoses. It's dangerous to take more than a standard dose or to mix drugs, and the results may show up quickly or only after several years or decades. So many drug deaths involved 2 or 3 drugs that it is CLEARLY DANGEROUS to take two drugs within 24 hours (unless both are prescribed by a physician together) or

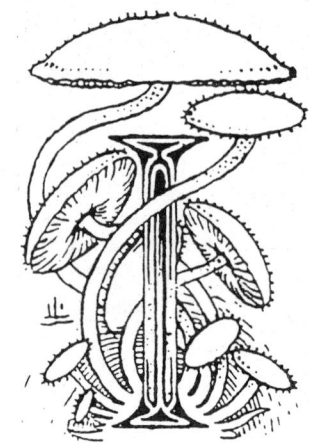

to take any drug and drink alcohol (which vastly intensifies drug absorption into the brain). There is no evidence at all of addiction to MDMA or dependency on it. However, when MDMA became popular in San Francisco and Texas, there were reports of people taking many doses in one day, and that MDMA's good effects reversed at high doses and could cause bad trips (as well as permanent brain damage).

◆

Chemical investigations have confirmed lysergic acid amides are produced in several plants of the bindweed family including Baby Hawaiian Woodroses, which contain up to ten times the concentration of psychoactives as Morning Glories. Lysergic acid amides including chanclavine, ergine, isoergine and ergonovine are present in the psychoactive *Argyriea* species which include *speciosa*, *acuta*, *bernesii*, *capituata*, *osyrensis*, *wallichii*, *splendens*, *hainanensis*, *obtusifolia*, and *pseudorubicunda*, mainly concentrated in the seeds. The larger Hawaiian Woodrose, *Merrimia tuberosa*, also produces such amides, but unlike the others it is not nearly as potent as the Baby Hawaiian Woodrose.

## Social Pharmacology

S. Einstein, Editor
$65/year
(four issues) from:
S.P./D.I.A., Inc.
122 Carol Street
Danbury, CT 06810

Schematic Representation of the Ego States Induced by Five Major Drugs of Abuse.

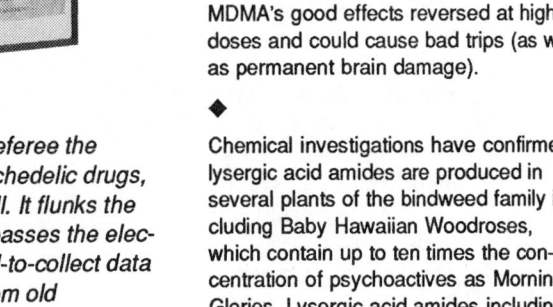

*The white-lab-coat approach to mind-altering drugs. Scholarly papers about the broad issues of self-medication, the psychosocial aspects of drug taking behavior, and "the creation of knowledge, its transmission and utilization, about drugs, medicines and social substances."*

*They're right: it's more than chemicals.* — *Kevin Kelly*

◆

DRUG INDUCED EGO STATES: A TRAJECTORY THEORY OF DRUG EXPERIENCE

(Abstract). This first of two reports describes the ego states induced by five substances of abuse: cocaine, heroin, amphetamine, barbituates and LSD. Descriptions of drug induced ego states are based on reports from 45 heavy, chronic drug users each of whom had experimented with a variety of substances before becoming personally committed to a particular drug or class of drugs. A three-dimensional theoretical diagram, in the shape of a sphere, is presented and utilized to characterized the various ego states.

## The Mind of a Mnemonist

(A Little Book About a
Vast Memory)
A.R. Luria
1986, 1987; 160 pp.
**$7.95**
($9.45 postpaid) from:
Harvard University Press
79 Garden Street
Cambridge, MA 02138
617/495-2600
or Whole Earth Access

*In pre-Revolutionary Russia there lived a boy with an ability that made him unique among his peers: he had a perfect memory. As he grew up, he found that he couldn't forget anything — any conversation, any experience — unless he made a conscious effort to erase it from his mind.*

*But his gift was also a curse. Since he remembered everything as concrete, visual images, it was difficult for him to comprehend abstractions, such as the meaning of a Pasternak poem. Unable to hold down his job as a journalist, he became a professional mnemonist, amazing audiences with feats of memory.*

***Mind of a Mnemonist** is Soviet psychologist A.R. Luria's account of how this man's amazing memory affected his life. Luria initially planned simply to measure the memory capacity of his subject, who the psychologist refers to only as "S." After it became apparent that S.'s memory had no limit, Luria switched to studying his psychological makeup instead. The result is a sensitive, insightful account of a man who never grew up emotionally, simply because he retained a child's visual way of reasoning for his entire life.*

*—Sarah Vandershaf*

◆

His problem is familiar to us now: each word he read produced images that distracted him and blocked the meaning of a sentence. When it came to texts that contained descriptions of complex relationships, formulations of rules, or explanations of causal connections, S. fared even worse.

For example, I read him a simple rule such as the following, which any schoolboy could easily understand: "If carbon dioxide is present above a vessel, the greater its pressure, the faster it dissolves in water."

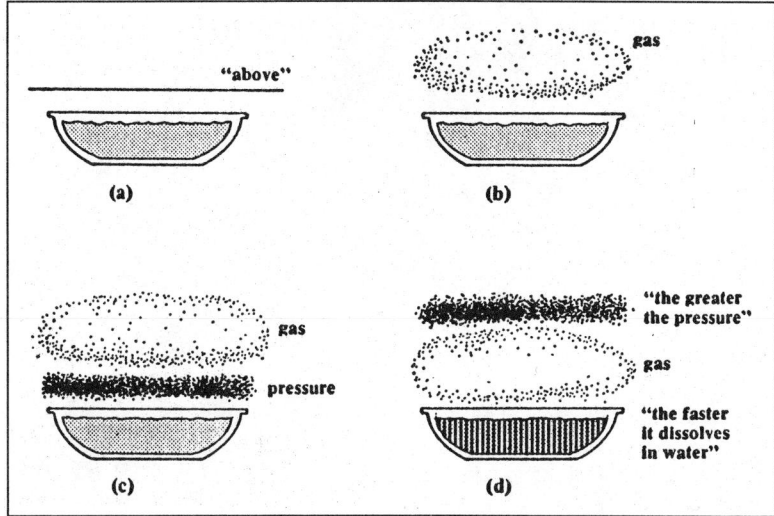

What S. visualized: His overly literal interpretation blocks S.'s ability to comprehend a simple rule of physics

| | | TABLE 2 | | | |
|---|---|---|---|---|---|
| ZH* | CH* | SH* | T | I | P | R |
| K | P | O | S | M | K | SH* |
| L | T | O | A | L | KH* | T |
| M | T | ZH* | S | K | R | CH* |
| etc. | | | | | | |

* In Russian, single letters: ZH = Ж, CH = Ч, SH = Ш, KH = X.

Number and letter tables memorized by S.

Consider the obstacles this abstract, yet nonetheless uncomplicated, statement presented.

"When you gave me this sentence I immediately saw the vessel. As for that *above* that is mentioned, it's here . . . I see a line (a). Above the vessel a small cloud that's moving in an upward direction. That's the gas (b). I read further: 'the greater the pressure' — so the gas rises . . . Then there's something dense here — the

| TABLE 1 | | | |
|---|---|---|---|
| 6 | 6 | 8 | 0 |
| 5 | 4 | 3 | 2 |
| 1 | 6 | 8 | 4 |
| 7 | 9 | 3 | 5 |
| 4 | 2 | 3 | 7 |
| 3 | 8 | 9 | 1 |
| 1 | 0 | 0 | 2 |
| 3 | 4 | 5 | 1 |
| 2 | 7 | 6 | 8 |
| 1 | 9 | 2 | 6 |
| 2 | 9 | 6 | 7 |
| 5 | 5 | 2 | 0 |
| x | 0 | 1 | x |

pressure (c). But the pressure is greater — it rises higher . . . As for the phrase 'the faster it dissolves in water' — the water has become heavy (d) . . . And the gas — you say 'the higher the pressure' — it's moved steadily higher . . . So what does it all mean? If the pressure is higher, how can it dissolve in water?"

◆

We presented S. with a table of letters written either on a blackboard or on a sheet of paper. . . . He told us that he continued *to see* the table . . . that he merely had to "read it off," successively enumerating the numbers or letters it contained. Hence, it generally made no difference to him whether he "read" the table from the beginning or the end, whether he listed the elements that formed the vertical or the diagonal groups, or "read off" numbers that formed the horizontal rows. The task of converting the individual numbers into a single, multidigit number appeared to be no more difficult for him than it would be for others of us were we asked to perform this operation visually and given a considerably longer time to study the table.

◆

It appeared that there was no limit either to the *capacity* of S.'s memory or to the *durability of the traces he retained*. Experiments indicated that he had no difficulty reproducing any lengthy series of words whatever, even though these had originally been presented to him a week, a month, a year, or even many years earlier. In fact, some of these experiments designed to test his retention were performed (without his being given any warning) fifteen or sixteen years after the session in which he had originally recalled the words. Yet invariably they were successful. During these test sessions S. would sit with his eyes closed, pause, then comment: "Yes, yes . . . This was a series you gave me once when we were in your apartment . . . You were sitting at the table and I in the rocking chair . . . You were wearing a gray suit and you looked at me like this . . . Now, then, I can see you saying . . ." And with that he would reel off the series precisely as I had given it to him at the earlier session.

## The Memory Book

Harry Lorayne and
Jerry Lucas
1974, 1986; 206 pp.
**$3.95**
($4.95 postpaid) from:
Random House
Order Department
400 Hahn Road
Westminster, MD 21157
800/638-6460
or Whole Earth Access

*I almost forgot to mention this compact paperback which concisely outlines methods to improve your recall. They truly work. My dad taught me these when I was a kid and I still rely on them. At first the methods seem to be gimmicky, but soon become habit. One of the authors is the guy who memorizes phone book listings as a stunt on late night talk shows. The techniques are well proven (a couple are thousands of years old) and will benefit anyone. Imagine how much more efficient you'd be if your memory was just five percent better, and how much easier your life would be if everyone else's improved.*

*—Kevin Kelly*

◆

Here's a basic memory rule: You Can Remember Any New Piece of Information if It Is Associated to Something You Already Know or Remember. . . .

Very few people can easily remember the shape of Russia, or Greece, or any other country — except Italy, that is. That's because most people have been told, or have read, that Italy's shaped like a boot. There's that rule again — the shape of a boot was the something already known, and the shape of Italy could not be forgotten once that association was made.

◆

As you reach for the phone, you place the pencil behind your ear, or in your hair. The phone call is finished — that took only a few minutes — but now you waste time searching for the pencil that's perched behind your ear. Would you like to avoid that aggravation? All right, then; the next time the phone rings and you start to place the pencil behind your ear, make a fast mental picture in your mind. Actually "see" the pencil going into your ear — all the way.

The idea may make you shudder, but when you think of that pencil, you'll know where it is. That silly association of seeing the pencil go into your ear forced you to think of two things in a fraction of a second: 1) the pencil, and 2) where you were putting it. Problem solved!

## C.G. Jung: Word and Image

Aniela Jaffe, Editor
1979; 238 pp.
**$16.50** postpaid from:
Princeton
University Press
3175 Princeton Pike
Lawrenceville,
NJ 08648
201/932-2280
or Whole Earth Access

*If not nothing, then Jung is surely image. This collection by an old collaborator of his takes his lifelong caterpillar-crawl of thought and gives it colorful flight and new life. Jung's biography is visible, as well as the things he saw that moved him, the archetypal images he recognized, and his own bizarre beautiful paintings, carvings, buildings. He lived with beautiful care. The book is bright and clear and not the slightest bit slick.* —Stewart Brand

Symbol of the sacred in a ring of flames floating above the world of war and technology. Painted in 1920, it was inspired by a dream Jung had had on 22 January 1914, anticipating the outbreak of war in August 1914.

Tree-man, by a thirty-five-year-old woman. Image of neurotically delayed development caused by psychic disturbances in childhood. Difficulties centered around developing a will of her own.

## The Man Who Mistook His Wife for a Hat

Oliver Sacks
1970,1985; 233 pp.
**$16.95**
($18.95) postpaid from:
Simon & Schuster
Mail Order Sales
200 Old Tappan Rd.
Old Tappan, NJ 07675
800/223-2336
or Whole Earth Access

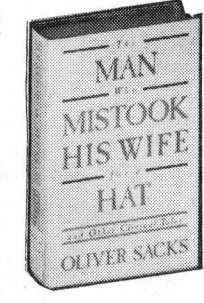

*Oftentimes you can't learn how something works until part of it goes wrong. Neurologist Oliver Sacks has written a book of compassionate, true stories about people whose brains have short-circuited through disease, injury, or failure to develop. For every reader, one or two stories latch on to the heart and don't let go. Two gripped me: The horrible story of a woman athlete who suddenly lost all feeling of inhabiting her body, and the story of a man with no context, a sweet-natured man who cannot remember anything that happened to him during the last 35 years (including what happened a minute ago). This is an important book, I suspect, for anyone researching the brain — or designing such brain-oriented tools as computer software. It's as close as we'll get to a cutaway view of our neurological lives.* —Art Kleiner

◆

I showed him the cover, and unbroken expanse of Sahara dunes. 'What do you see here?' I asked.

'I see a river,' he said. 'And a little guest-house with its terrace on the water. People are dining out on the terrace. I see coloured parasols here and there.' He was looking, if it was 'looking,' right off the cover, into mid-air and confabulating non-existent features, as if the absence of features in the actual picture had driven him to imagine the river and the terrace and the coloured parasols.

I must have looked aghast, but he seemed to think he had done rather well. There was a hint of a smile on his face. He also appeared to have decided that the examination was over, and started to look round for his hat. He reached out his hand, and took hold of his wife's head, tried to lift it off, to put it on. He had apparently mistaken his wife for a hat! His wife looked as if she was used to such things.

I could make no sense of what had occurred, in terms of conventional neurology (or neuropsychology). In some ways he seemed perfectly preserved, and in others absolutely, incomprehensibly devastated. How could he, on the one hand, mistake his wife for a hat and, on the other, function, as apparently he still did, as a teacher at the Music School?

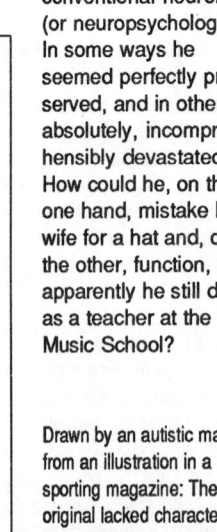

Drawn by an autistic man from an illustration in a sporting magazine: The original lacked character, had looked lifeless, two-dimensional, even stuffed. José's fish, by contrast, tilted and poised, was richly three-dimensional, far more like a real fish than the original.

## The Throwing Madonna

(Essays on the Brain)
William H. Calvin
1983; 253 pp.
**$7.95**
($10.95 postpaid) from:
McGraw-Hill
P.O. Box 400
Hightstown, NJ 08520
800/262-4729
or Whole Earth Access

*In this collection of essays reminiscent of Lewis Thomas, neurobiologist William Calvin explores some of the evolutionary steps that led to the development of the human brain, and how this development affects the modern possessors of those brains. Calvin touches on a wide range of topics — Why do people like cats? Is there a link between schizophrenia and Parkinson's disease? Each answer is one more piece in the immense mosaic of human intelligence.* —Sarah Vandershaf

◆

Infants cry and fuss much less if they are allowed to listen to a tape recording of a heart beating . . . . So it is hardly surprising that three out of every four mothers observed in shopping centers are carrying their infant with their left arm. This has been going on for centuries before shopping centers: a survey of madonna-with-child paintings in European art galleries (indeed, of over 400 such artworks from four cultures) showed left-armed infant carrying in 80 percent of the cases. And it may be a very, very old practice indeed. . . .

Who would be the most successful hunters, the left- or the right-handed throwers? For hominid men not encumbered with infants, there might be no consistent side preference when averaging across the population. But mothers with left-brain sequencers should be better hunters (faster throws and quieter infants) than those mothers who had to hold their infants on the right side in order to use their best throwing arm. More of the infants carried by the right-handed mothers (and in turn often carrying their right-handed genes) would survive than those of left-handed mothers.

The cat's eyes were bigger than saucers, a 19th century engraving. Artist unknown.

## Ballast

Roy R. Behrens, Editor
**eight 25¢ stamps/year**
or 2 stamps/single
issue from:
Ballast
Art Academy of Cincinnati
Eden Park
Cincinnati, OH 45202

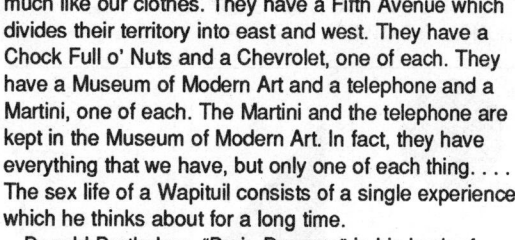

*In exchange for a few stamps per year, you'll receive this idiosyncratic dispatch of verbal illusions and visual anecdotes. Works like conceptual anti-freeze — keeps your inspiration unclogged. May it live long.*

—Kevin Kelly

◆

When artists are living and working as closely together as we were in those years, they are all obviously influenced in some degree by one another. I remember one day when Juan Gris told me about a bunch of grapes he had seen in a painting by Picasso. The next day these grapes appeared in a painting by Gris, this time in a bowl; and the day after, the bowl appeared in a painting by Picasso.
—Jacques Lipchitz, with H.H. Arnason, *My Life in Sculpture* (New York: Viking Press, 1972), P. 40.

◆

The Wapituil are like us to an extraordinary degree. They have a kinship system which is very similar to our kinship system. They address each other as "Mister," "Mistress," and "Miss." They wear clothes which look very much like our clothes. They have a Fifth Avenue which divides their territory into east and west. They have a Chock Full o' Nuts and a Chevrolet, one of each. They have a Museum of Modern Art and a telephone and a Martini, one of each. The Martini and the telephone are kept in the Museum of Modern Art. In fact, they have everything that we have, but only one of each thing. . . . The sex life of a Wapituil consists of a single experience, which he thinks about for a long time.
—Donald Barthelme, "Brain Damage" in his book of short stories, *City Life* (NY: Bantam, 1971)

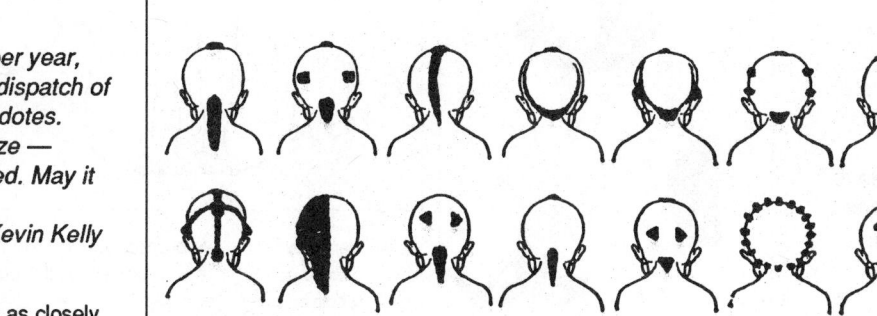

Haircuts of young Native American males of the Osage and Omaha nations were indications of the plant or animal clan with which they were associated. For example, the first haircut from the left on the top row was analogous to the head and tail of an elk, while the second from the right on the bottom row was emblematic of the teeth of a reptile. See F. La Flesche, "The Osage Child-Naming Rite" in *43rd Annual Report of the Bureau of American Ethnology 1925-1926* (Washington, D.C., 1928).

The evolution of the piano, according to Darwin, a cartoon first published in Berlin in 1872. Artist unknown.

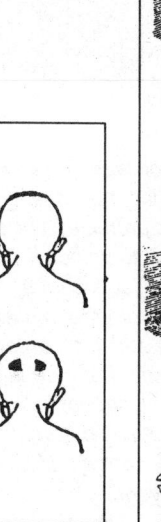

## Seeing the Light

James Broughton
1977; 80 pp.
**$3.50**
($5 postpaid) from:
City Lights Books
261 Columbus
San Francisco, CA 94133
415/362-8193

*I wish everyone would do a book like this, made of the things they say to themselves to keep themselves doing what they do well. Embarrassing stuff — bombastic, personal, and wholly invaluable to anyone else trying to do something well. The revelant here is avant-garde filmmaker James Broughton.*
—Stewart Brand

◆

You may be reeking of talent, but real art comes from knowledge. No work can be greater than the man who made it.

◆

Oz is run by witches and little girls. Its queen is a 10-year-old named Ozma. No one in Oz can get sick or grow old or die. No one earns a living, puts on weight, or thinks deeply. In short, Oz is everything the U.S. would secretly like to be. The surest way of getting there: go to the very heart of America. That should be Kansas. There get yourself into the cockpit of a cyclone. Off you go! However, the landing fields in Oz are unpredictable. Sensibly there is no airport near the capitol. You are bound to come down in the middle of an adventure, not a predicament.

◆

Unless you have some Oz in you, you will go along with President Holdfast and General Apathy. You will believe in doctors, insurance companies, statistics, national defense, pensions, retirement communities, and a thoroughly safe dwindle. You will garner some fringe benefits but miss out on the central Benefit.

◆

I love going to the editing table. It is an altar of mysteries. Dust it off devotedly. Let us consecrate. At any moment a temporal ecstasy may occur.

Making a film is a more hazardous act than looking at one. For you will create a dream. Whereas dreams themselves are natural events which happen to us. You will create a dream for others to dream and to be dreamed by.

An example of visual metamorphosis by the 19th century caricaturist and illustrator, Jean Ignace Isidore Gerard, more commonly known by his pen name, Grandville.

## A Whack on the Side of the Head

(How to Unlock Your Mind for Innovation)
Roger von Oech, Ph.D.
1983; 141 pp.
**$10.95**
($11.95 postpaid) from:
Random House, Inc.
400 Hahn Road
Westminster, MD 21157
800/638-6460

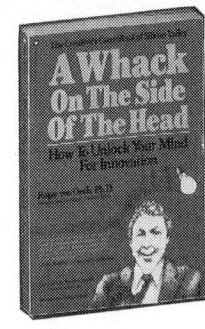

*What I liked most about this book was that it was peppered with anecdotes, puzzles, fascinating facts, silliness, and science. Its premise: "Here's this mental lock; now here's how to unlock it." Its method: a whole raft of pinpricks, seductions, strategies, and whacks ranging from the minute to the mystic to engage your mind and set it on any course than its usual one. It's aimed at men in suits and ties, judging from the illustrations, but what it teaches — to think something different than you would ordinarily and take advantage of that new thinking — is a boon to anyone.*

*—Sarah Satterlee*

*Exercise:* Are you creative? (Check the appropriate box.)

☐ YES ☐ NO

SELECT THE ONE THAT IS DIFFERENT FROM ALL THE OTHERS.

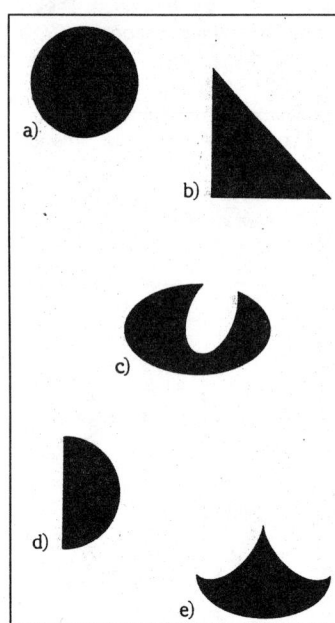

a)
b)
c)
d)
e)

Each selection is correct, depending on your point of view.

◆

An aerospace manager told me that several years ago he took up the hobby of designing and constructing backyard waterfalls for himself and his friends. "I don't know why," he said, "but designing waterfalls has made me a better manager. It has brought me a lot closer in touch with ideas such as 'flow,' 'movement,' and

Soft thinker: They both have a place to put fish; they both have tails. Hard thinker: Members of two different sets.

'vibration' which are difficult to put into words, but which are important in the communication between two people."

◆

I think one of life's great thrills is falling out of love with a previously cherished idea. When that happens, you're free to look for new ones.

◆

Soft thinking is metaphorical, approximate, diffuse, humorous, playful, and capable of dealing with contradiction. Hard thinking tends to be more logical, precise, exact, specific, and consistent.

## Playful Perception

(Choosing How to Experience Your World)
Herbert L. Leff, Ph.D.
1984; 161 pp.
**$9.95**
($11.95 postpaid) from:
Waterfront Books
98 Brookes Avenue
Burlington, VT 05401
800/456-7500

*Here are the tools you'll need to see in new ways — the essence of creative thinking. No more dead time waiting for water to boil, the bus to come, Godot to show up. Instead, make your mind a kaleidoscope, jar loose your mental constructs, and shift around the patterns of reality. Perceptual play changes routine into adventure.*

*The photographs poked me visually and the exercises (ugly word) pushed my mind down an infinite progression of new possibilities — into channels,*

*tunnels, streams, corridors I'd never explored before. The old mind-set will never be the same.*
*—Corinne Cullen Hawkins*

◆

So often in our culture we seem to think of arguing as if it were a kind of war. What if we shifted to viewing disagreements as if they were celebrations or parties of idea? What if we thought of ourselves as living in a shared pool of thoughts rather than as "possessing" or originating ideas? What if we also thought of error or being wrong as simply an opportunity to learn rather than as a weakness to be attacked? And, most of all, what if we could think of our own goals or proposals as invitations to explore for even better ideas?

Regard whatever you're doing, thinking, or feeling as if it were your hobby. Can you do that — imagine that washing dishes is really a hobby, something you look forward to, take pride in, savor, know the fine points of, do for recreation, and so on?

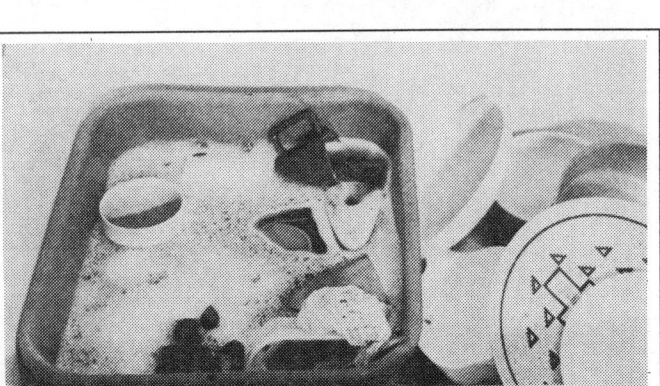

## The Act of Creation

Arthur Koestler: 1964; 750 pp.
OUT OF PRINT
Macmillan Publishing Company
*Get this book back in print!!!*

*Koestler takes his notion of bisociation to be the root of humor, discovery, and art. I take it to be one of the roots of learning, subject to applications of method (on yourself or whomever).*

*Koestler is a scientist of some reputation by now. He's made contributions beyond the work of others that he's generalized from. This is the book — on how discovery of every kind really occurs in the mind — that gave him the reputation. His most lasting contribution.*   *—Stewart Brand*

◆

When two independent matrices of perception or reasoning interact with each other the result (as I hope to show) is either a collision ending in laughter, or their fusion in a new intellectual synthesis, or their confrontation in an aesthetic experience. The bisociative patterns found in any domain of creative activity are tri-valent: that is to say, the same pair of matrices can produce comic, tragic, or intellectually challenging effects.

◆

In the popular imagination men of science appear as ice-cold logicians, electronic brains mounted on dry sticks. But if one were shown an anthology of typical extracts from their letters and autobiographies with no names mentioned, and then asked to guess their profession, the likeliest answer would be: a bunch of poets or musicians of a rather romantically naive kind.

◆

I have coined the term "bisociation" in order to make a distinction between the routine skills of thinking on a single "plane," as it were, and the creative act, which, as I shall try to show, always operates on more than one plane. The former may be called single-minded, the latter a double-minded, transitory state of unstable equilibrium where the balance of both emotion and thought is disturbed.

## Serious Games

Clark C. Abt
1970, 1987; 176 pp.
**$9.95**
($11.70 postpaid) from:
University Press of America
4720 Boston Way
Lanham, MD 20706
or Whole Earth Access

*Serious games are games designed to teach a skill, or to accomplish a complicated goal. Military war games are serious games. So are the management games played in university business schools. Serious games can be fun.*

*At the same time, games designed entirely for fun can be used for serious purposes, such as helping kids learn how to survive and thrive in real life. Games are often the best way to teach them strategy, cooperation, and intellectual skills. For the past ten years I have been devising new games that really work in schools.*

*Serious Games is a classic book about games which simulate life's complex rules. The author was inspired by games as a doctoral student in Henry Kissinger's Harvard class on arms control. Long out of print, it's back again. I wish every teacher would read it.* —Bob Albrecht

◆

Players often become so involved in their specific roles and in the game play itself that they do not consciously concern themselves with the wider, more universal consequences of a set of decisions. For this reason it is useful to have a postgame discussion to analyze and evaluate the forces which interacted, the over-all consequences of the game play, and the specific decisions which led to the consequences. In games where the outcome differs from historical reality, the reasons for the differences can then be considered; in games "rigged" to produce a particular result, the reasons for the rigging and the eliminated factors can be analyzed. The scope of learning, then, extends beyond the game itself and includes the analysis of the game, its components, and the context for which it was designed.

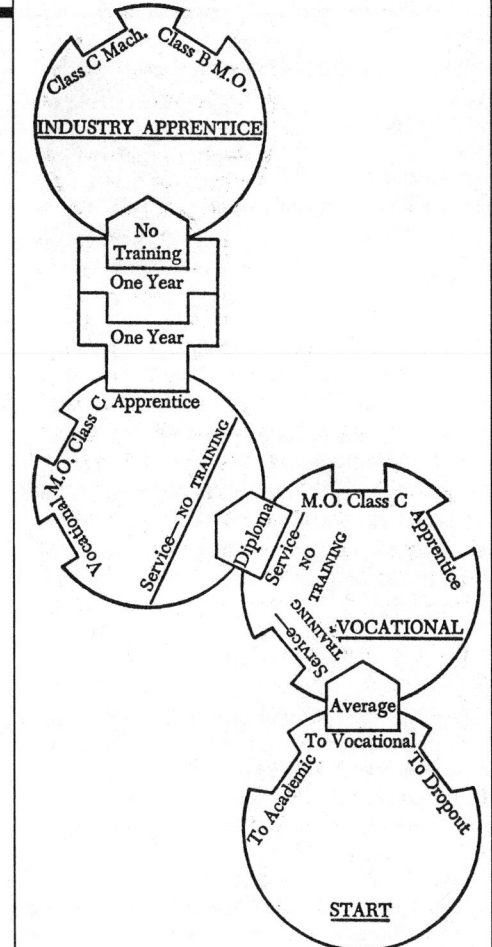

Sample Moves: From Start position to Apprenticeship.

## Homo Ludens

(A Study of the Play Element in Culture)
Johan Huizinga
1950, 220 pp.
**$4.95** postpaid from:
Beacon Press
Harper and Row
Keystone Industrial Park
Scranton, PA 18512
or Whole Earth Access

*Huizinga contends that civilization owes its existence to the play element—to special rituals apart from the daily grind which are joyful, contained in time, space, and rule structure, uncertain in outcome, requiring of fair play, participated in by all. To the roster of convivial tools that Ivan Illich fosters I would add widespread renewal of convivial gaming—play rituals at every level from family to planet. The more frivolous, the more essential to homo ludens.*

—Stewart Brand

◆

The hazy border-line between play and seriousness is illustrated very tellingly by the use of the words "playing" or "gambling" for the machinations on the Stock Exchange. The gambler at the roulette table will readily concede that he is playing; the stock-jobber will not. He will maintain that buying and selling on the off-chance of prices rising or falling is part of the serious business of life, at least of business life, and that it is an economic function of society. In both cases the operative factor is the hope of gain; but whereas in the former the pure fortuitousness of the thing is generally admitted (all "systems" notwithstanding), in the latter the player deludes himself with the fancy that he can calculate the future trends of the market. At any rate the difference of mentality is exceedingly small.

## The Evolution of Cooperation

Robert Axelrod
1984; 241 pp.
**$17.95** postpaid from:
Basic Books, Inc.
10 East 53rd Street
New York, NY 10022
or Whole Earth Access

*The "Prisoner's Dilemma" is a situation where two individuals can choose to cooperate with each other or not cooperate (defect). If they both cooperate they each get three points. If they both defect they each get one point. If one cooperates and one defects, the cooperator gets zero and the defector gets five. Axelrod uses this non-zero-sum game to explain the arms race, international relations and the interaction of regulatory agencies with those they regulate.*

*First the good news: In a population of individuals interested in their own welfare, where no central authority exists, it pays to cooperate. Cooperative rules "won" over noncooperative ones in simulated iterations.*

*Now the bad: In the same situations it also pays to be provokable (to defect in retaliation). Rules that were totally cooperative without retaliation did not win.*

*There is little value for complexity here. The best strategy is simple enough to be readily recognized by another player. No strategy is a winning strategy by itself. It can only be judged by its interaction with other strategies.*

—Judith Brophy

*The universe in a grain of sand. The grain is a mathematical/sociological paradox, much studied, call "Prisoner's Dilemma." The universe is the one we might survive into if these lessons are believed and applied. Scholarly tour-de-force.*

—Stewart Brand

◆

A wonderful illustration of this principle is provided in the memoirs of Ron Luciano, a baseball umpire who sometimes had his "bad days."

Over a period of time I learned to trust certain catchers so much that I actually let them umpire for me on the bad days. The bad days usually followed the good nights. . . . On those days there wasn't much I could do but take two aspirins and call as little as possible. If someone I trusted was catching . . . I'd tell them, "Look, it's a bad day. You'd better take it for me. If it's a strike, hold your glove in place for an extra second. If it's a ball, throw it right back. And please, don't yell."

This reliance on the catcher could work because if Luciano ever suspected that he was being taken advantage of, he would have many opportunities to retaliate.

### The Prisoner's Dilemma

|  |  | Column Player | |
|---|---|---|---|
|  |  | *Cooperate* | *Defect* |
| **Row Player** | Cooperate | $R=3$, $R=3$ <br> Reward for <br> mutual cooperation | $S=0$, $T=5$ <br> Sucker's payoff, and <br> temptation to defect |
|  | Defect | $T=5$, $S=0$ <br> Temptation to defect <br> and sucker's payoff | $P=1$, $P=1$ <br> Punishment for <br> mutual defection |

NOTE: The payoffs to the row chooser are listed first.

# Dreamwork

*by Howard Rheingold*

Dreamwork consists of remembering your dreams and seeking to understand them. There's nothing esoteric or psychologically dangerous about it. It's simply a matter of taking a look at what's right in front of your mind's eye, and using what you see to improve your life. We all know how to turn on televisions, ride elevators, and open pop-top cans, but nobody teaches us how to dream. This situation is changing rapidly, however, because the most important "secret" of dreamwork is becoming more and more well-known: anyone who has tried to remember their dreams and understand their meaning has discovered that the ability to obtain valuable knowledge is not a gift or talent but a skill, like tying your shoelaces, reading a book, or driving a car.

Your basic tools for dreamwork are a pad of paper and a pen with a small flashlight taped to it, or a tape recorder, to record dream impressions, images, plots, and keywords in the middle of the night; a larger sketchbook or notebook to expand, amplify, and interpret those midnight jottings; and some knowledge of what to do with your dreams once you've learned to recall and record them. Fortunately, the secrets of the ages are now out in paperback.

## Living Your Dreams

Gayle Delany
1979; 242 pp.
**$8.95**
($9.45 postpaid) from:
Harper & Row
2350 Virginia Avenue
Hagerstown, MD 21740
800/638-3030

*Learn the "mind movie" approach: dreams are internal scenarios, and we are the producers, directors, and audiences of our own nightly shows. We can learn how to interpret and even consciously direct the action. The author's orientation toward the more mundane but personally important aspects of dreamwork—what we can learn about our personal and business relationships, for example—can prove the value of dreamwork to people who aren't interested in creativity or spiritual growth but are very interested in why they aren't getting along with their spouse or boss.*

*—HR*

## Creative Dreaming

Patricia Garfield
1976; 256 pp.
**$2.95**
($4.95 postpaid) from:
Ballantine Books/Random House
400 Hahn Road
Westminster, MD 21157
800/638-6460

*My first and still one of my favorite introductions to the hows and whys of dreamwork. It gives a compelling, lucid history of dreamwork throughout the centuries and around the world, introduces several different approaches to self-analysis, touches on the highest aspects of dreamwork— lucid dreaming and other methods of altering dreams as they happen—and offers practical advice on keeping dream diaries and developing dream control.*

*—HR*

◆

The best time to begin developing skill in dream recall is during an unpressured time in the morning when you awaken naturally (it will be from a REM period). If you have trouble recalling your dreams, plan a time when you can spontaneously awaken and be unhurried.

When you awaken from a dream, lie still and allow the dream images to flow back into your mind. If no images come, let yourself run through the important people in your life; visualizing them may trigger association to your recent dream.

When dream recall is complete in one body position, move gently into other sleeping positions to see whether you have additional dream recall in these positions. Always move gently into any recording position.

Record your dreams whenever they come to you, immediately, later in the day, or several days later.

## Lucidity Letter

Jayne Gackenbach, Editor
**$10**/year
(2 issues) from:
Lucidity Letter
Department of Psychology
University of Northern Iowa
Cedar Falls, Iowa 50614

*Awareness within dreams is not an easy state to achieve, but the experience can be worth the effort. This newsletter (actually a scholarly journal in pamphlet guise) tells you why. In it, researchers, psychotherapists, physicians and other scientists report on their progress uncovering the role lucid dreams can play in physical and mental healing, as well as in everyday problem-solving. Other articles discuss the nature of the lucid dream itself. For the lucidity connoisseur.*

*—Sarah Vandershaf*

◆

The concept of lucid dream healing is not a new one, and anecdotal reports abound. In my own experience, I have had one lucid dream opportunity to practice adjunctive physical healing. I had some minor surgery and the bleeding would not stop. I decided that this would be an opportunity to try a lucid dream imaged healing. I made the suggestion while awake and in the

## Lucid Dreaming

Stephen LaBerge
1986; 304 pp.
**$3.95**
($4.95 postpaid) from:
Ballantine Books/Random House
400 Hahn Road
Westminster, MD 21157
800/638-6460

*An account of the most exciting realm of dreamwork — the ability to awaken in your dreams and control their outcomes as you participate in them! Author Stephen LaBerge is a scientist, long associated with Stanford's Sleep Laboratory, and an accomplished "oneironaut" (his word for those of us who explore the dream realm).*

*—HR*

◆

Non-lucid dreamers perceive themselves as being contained within the experiential world of their dreams. Whether they play starring roles or are only pawns in the dream game, they are still contained in a dream that they take for external reality. As long as they perceive themselves contained in this world, they are sentenced to a virtual prison with walls no less impenetrable for the fact that they are made of delusion.

In contrast, lucid dreamers realize that they themselves contain, and thus transcend, the entire dream world and all of its contents, because they know that their imaginations have created the dream. So the transition to lucidity turns dreamers' worlds upside down. Rather than seeing themselves as a mere part of the whole, they see themselves as the *container* rather than the *contents*. Thus they freely pass through dream prison walls that only seemed impenetrable, and venture forth into the larger world of the mind.

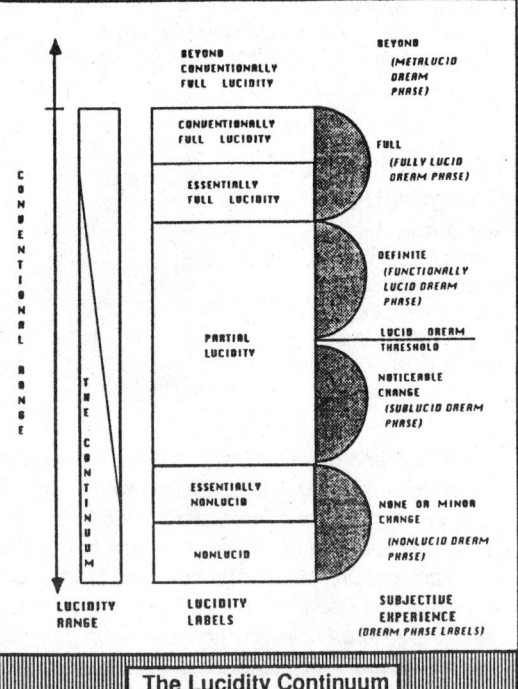

The Lucidity Continuum

dream state that I would affirm that area of the body finally heal. In a complex lucid dream I was able to lay my hands on that area and essentially affirm my intention for healing. I awakened with the oozing continuing, but it stopped approximately 10 to 14 hours later. Whether this would have happened without the lucid dream I don't know.

## Dreams, Visions of the Night

David Coxhead and
Susan Hiller
1976; 96 pp.
**$9.95**
($10.95 postpaid) from:
Harper & Row
Keystone Industrial Park
Scranton, NJ 18512
800/638-3030

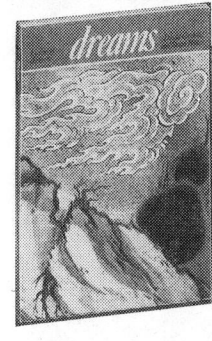

*Besides containing marvelous information about the ancient and esoteric history of oneirology, this book has marvelous illustrations, gathered from the art of every culture, illustrating key points about dreams.*

*—HR*

◆

The dream mediates between the worlds of matter and spirit, time and eternity. In Jacob's dream the ladder with angels ascending and descending it symbolizes the ease of transition between these levels of reality in the mind of the dreamer. Time is abolished, and analogous incidents of past and future are perceived simultaneously as the dream opens the way from one world to

Jacob's Dream, from the Lambeth Bible, England, 12th c.

another, establishing a relationship between mundane and spiritual realities.

◆

The entire world may be understood as the dream of an awakened dreamer. In dreams of this order there is, literally, no distinction between levels of reality.

The creative principle of the world grows out of the navel of the dreaming god in the mythical instant of the creation of the universe. This concept is present in the shamanic tradition, perhaps as old as human history, in which the individual adept assumes the role of conscious creator.

Krishna acting out the role of Vishnu in his sleep, gouache, India, 18th c.

## Dreams and Spiritual Growth

Louis M. Savary, Patricia H.
Berne and Strephon
Kaplan Williams
1984; 252 pp.
**$9.95**
($11.70 postpaid) from:
Paulist Press
997 MacArthur Boulevard
Mahwah, NJ 07430
201/825-7300

*The authors take a Christian approach to dreamwork, but the book is a resource for anyone who is interested in the spiritual aspects of dreamwork. One of the nice ecumenical aspects of dreamwork is the fact that you can find it endorsed by the scriptures of the Jewish, Christian, Moslem, Hindu, Buddhist, Pagan, and Animist religions! The authors include 37 dreamwork techniques for spiritual growth.*

*—HR*

◆

Establishing relationship to God is a keynote of the Western spiritual tradition. In doing dreamwork we are acknowledging the Source of our healing and wholeness, and we are also building a relationship to that Source. In dreamwork, as in meditation and contemplation, we are strengthening our relationship to God.

◆

Who is willing and able to look God straight in the eye, and for how long? And yet to be seen by God is to begin really to see ourselves. We must be seen in order to see. We are invited to look into the dark night and remember what we have seen. The dream is the potential, the beginning. In our devotion, we can make the eyes of God more real for ourselves and the world.

And still all is mystery!

## Dreams, Illusion and Other Realities

Wendy Doniger O'Flaherty
1984; 382 pp.
**$13.95**
($15.20 postpaid) from:
University of Chicago Press
11030 S. Langley Avenue
Chicago, IL 60628
312/702-7740

*A thick book, quite readable, about the central role of dreams in the mythology, epistemology, and theology of the Hindu and Buddhist religions. Since both the Hindu and Buddhist doctrines contend that the waking conscious state is an illusion, and that the goal of life is to awaken from the illusion, the idea of learning to control your dreams has particular importance in these spiritual disciplines.*

*—HR*

◆

Do all cultures make the same radical distinction between "appearance" and "reality" which ours has inherited from Plato? Are their hierarchies the same? In other words, do they necessarily accept the demand that contradictions must be ironed out and that all perceptions that clash with beliefs must force us either to change our views of the "objective world" or declare the perception to have been a subjective experience — an illusion? Even in our rationalist culture we don't often live up to this logical precept. We try to evade it, especially when our emotions are involved.

*—Sir Ernst Gombrich*

## Dream Network Bulletin

Linda Magallon, Editor
**$18/year**
(6 issues) from:
Dream Network Bulletin
1083 Harvest Meadow Court
San Jose, CA 95136

*This newsletter has a folksier, broader approach to dreaming than does* **Lucidity Letter** *(see page 216). It covers dream interpretation, dream poetry, even the role dreams play in maintaining proper nutrition! Weak on scientific rigor, strong on fascinating first-person accounts.*

*—Sarah Vandershaf*

## Symbols of Transformation in Dreams

Jean Dalby Clift and
Wallace B. Clift
1986; 159 pp.
**$9.95**
($10.95 postpaid) from:
Harper & Row
Keystone Industrial Park
Scranton, NJ 18512
800/638-3030

*The best short, nontechnical account of Jungian ideas about dream symbols as harbingers of psychological and spiritual transformation. Jung saw dreams as snapshots of the psyches, and he and his followers have combined knowledge from the world's collection of mystical symbology (such as alchemical texts) with the experiences of thousands of analysands, and have shown how those people who don't have gurus or who aren't initiates of one spiritual tradition or another can use their dreams as a guide to inner growth.*

*—HR*

*T*HE GENESIS OF THIS BOOK lies in a low-rent, high-yield Critical Information Service begun twenty years ago by Stewart Brand. Conceived as a mobile truck store, the idea survived as a portable store printed on newsprint. The store, the *Whole Earth Catalog*, was a moveable education for Stewart's friends who were reconsidering the structure of modern life and building their own version of it on communes in the backwoods. The *Catalog* evaluated knowledge needed for these tasks, the kind of information which schools never taught: how to start a farm, run local politics, teach kids, build a house, make a business. It was a short course in innovation.

It started as a cheaply printed quarterly publication, fed by suggestions and recommendations of users until it became a series of accumulated books (*The Last Whole Earth Catalog*, 1971; *The Whole Earth Epilog*, 1974; *The Next Whole Earth Catalog*, 1980; *The Whole Earth Software Catalog*, 1984; *The Essential Whole Earth Catalog*, 1986) not ending with the most recent one, *The Electronic Whole Earth Catalog* (1988, see page 163).

Along the way Stewart birthed a quarterly magazine more modest in its expectations than the *Catalog*, and more successful in churning up innovation. Called the *CoEvolution Quarterly* from 1974 to 1984, the journal changed its name to the *Whole Earth Review* during a mild spell of schizophrenia in the midst of the personal computer revolution. In that computer craziness, Stewart saw something deep brewing and set off to investigate. I remained as editor of the magazine in his absence.

His poking about brought Stewart to the busy labs of a man whom he had encountered many years before in a pioneer book called *The Architecture Machine*. The author, Nicholas Negroponte, was now heading a world renowned research center, the MIT Media Lab, at MIT in Cambridge, Massachusetts. Negroponte was "inventing the future" by asking the simple question, "what happens if TV, computers, and books all merge into one media?" He presented his answers as small do-able experiments, or demos. Stewart was hanging out writing a book about this den of invention (see page 180), asking a simple question himself, "how do you hook up the human nervous system to the global information network?"

In parallel, I was exploring my own question, "what is the natural history of information?" in *Whole Earth Review*. All three questions spawned this book, *Signal*.

In reporting this esoterica, I began to hunger for a practical manual. If this is the information age — a time ruled by the adroit wielding of information, rather than of materials like gold or oil — what are useful information tools? How does information work? It proliferates so rapidly, can you have too much of it? What utilities do you use to keep it under control?

I envisioned a small, quickly produced book similar to the original *Catalog* in its use of immediate processes. The book should employ the same tools it reported: electronic networks, personal computers, affordable laserprinters, Polaroid film, and copy machines. Ideally it should be done rapidly with a short cycle from user experience to editorial filter to transmission by desktop publishing. It should give an overview to frontiers that are still isolated,

informing other pioneers of the breadth of their territory. Ideally, it should speak to (and be produced by) the new inhabitants — young mavericks. It should promote trying stuff.

I had a hard time selling the idea to publishers. (Point Foundation, the fiscal agent for Whole Earth ceased to be a publisher of books after the *Epilog*, 1974.) There was no classification for what I had in mind; there were no books already like it, a terrible pair of no-nos from a marketeer's viewpoint. The concept was as difficult to describe as information itself. It was very expensive to research which made it more unappealing. It was a good idea.

The solution was to try the notion as a special issue of *Whole Earth Review*. Jeanne Carstensen and I waded into the swamps of communication technology and came back with 288 pages of news which Jeanne edited into 144. We mailed that issue, *SIGNAL*, in the fall of 87, soliciting feedback and suggestions of where to search for more. Reader response in both forms (yeas and more suggestions of tools) persuaded me that this was marketable news.

By winter New York was beginning to think the same. I issued our proposal again. We cut our projected expenses further by relying more on the Macintosh for such chores as proofreading (we cut several of the usual many proofs by sending the copy through a spellchecking program) and layout. Finally in December, 1987, we got an offer from Harmony/Crown Books which we accepted after negotiation.

The book began in earnest about the first of the year, 1988. First hire was Richard Kadrey, an upcoming cyberpunk science fiction author. His first novel had just hit the bookstores, unbeknownst to me. Everyone I bumped into, including my brother, seemed to be reading his *Metrophage* (Ace Special, see page 181). It's gone around the office, its plot gabbed about during lunch, so I've hardly needed to read it. I would guess that there is plenty in the research Richard did for *Signal* to be grist for his next novel.

Second hire was Sally (Sarah) Vandershaf who had a suitable background as a researcher for Time-Life Book's series on computers. Sally went from a complete Macintosh innocent to a desperate Macintosh computer game junkie in the span of five months. She figured out it was very easy to score free review copies of the games. She devoured every one she could locate and disappeared into them for hours every day while trying to locate the Seventh Mirror in the dungeon of Trantor or some such. Her productivity skyrocketed. She turned in every page ahead

Holy smoke! After interminable hours before the Mac screen, the face of Kevin is sucked into his computer via the Apple Scanner.

of time. When she finished her section first, she helped work on the others. Long live the dragons of Shadowgate!

Sarah Satterlee was the third editor hired to create *Signal*. More than anyone else, Sarah took to the Macintosh like it was her native habitat. I took my "I wonder if we can do this?" questions to her, and she usually had it already figured out. Relying on her experience as co-producer of the *Goodfellow Catalog of Wonderful Things*, a catalog of neat handmade crafts from around the country, Sarah cast

## Business

*Investigative journalists are taught to follow the money to get the real story. Here's what happens to the $16.95 you paid for this book.*

> *7.20 to Harmony Books*
> *7.12 to the bookseller*
> *1.36 to book wholesaler*
> *.19 to John Brockman Assoc.*
> <u>*1.08 to Whole Earth*</u>
> *16.95 Signal*

*John Brockman is Whole Earth's literary agent. He takes the industry standard 15% of our royalties for negotiating the nit-picks in the contract. The wholesaler's deal is considerably more straightforward. He buys a crate full of the books, inventories them, and hopes to divvy them up among the booksellers. As middleman he'll siphon off more than we'll get. At the end of the line is the bookseller who takes a fair chunk of the change for the worrisome toil of persuading ordinary folk to come in and actually pay for information. Booksellers hedge their reasonable risk with the option to return unsold books to the publisher.*

*The publisher reaps the most because they have the most to lose. If this book bores the browsers in the stores, Harmony is out the $152,000 they have probably invested into it. Beside the cost of printing an initial lot of 35,000 books (which costs them 15% of the cover price, or $87,500) they would also lose the $65,000 advance they paid us. On the other hand they need only sell 21,100 copies of **Signal** to break even on the printing and advance expenses. That doesn't count what they'll spend on promotion (usually figured as 10% of the net*

her net far and wide and fished in many of the most nifty tools and contacts we found.

Many of the other principals in putting this catalog together have been making *Whole Earth Catalogs* long before I arrived. Don Ryan, who has been photographing the book covers and pictures since before the *Next Catalog*, has the science of it down to formula. Twenty one sheets of film for twenty shots, the extra one his low error rate at this point. Kathleen O'Neill, here since she designed the *Next Catalog* with scissors and tape, says that she is absolutely corrupted by the absolute power of being able to change type fonts and size whenever she wants to on the Mac, without having to ask the typesetter politely to do it. Of her elegant design on these pages, I'd say "more corruption, please." The difference between a system that veers toward chaos and one that crystalizes into self-organization (see page 8) is, in human institutions, usually one overworked, underappreciated, indespensible woman who mothers the details into wholeness. The Organizing Intelligence in *Signal* was Susan Erkel Ryan, veteran production manager.

A host of other Whole Earth Regulars were on the scene and behind the scene. David Burnor, our index guru, dutifully compiled the index, a weird art if there ever was one. Few people consider how intuitive indexing is, and how much you don't want it to be computer created (computer assisted, certainly). David provided an index a little more thorough than the most unusual query expected, which is exactly what you want. Hank Roberts proofread (faster, friendlier, and more accurate than a computer spellchecker), and Lori Woolpert did all the thankless jobs that one forgets to assign to anyone in particular. (Thank you, Lori.) John Chan and Laura Benne, who arrived to paste up the pages, finished them so fast that we hardly had time to get to know one another.

The book, like any project, wore its own routine. Mail in everyday at noon, sorted for goodies by Susan Rosberg. Make calls to the east coast before one o'clock, Pacific time. (Don't bother calling a New York publisher on Friday in the summer. They won't answer.) Check the WELL for messages from our far-flung correspondents. Scout for books in the mountain of review copies collected on David Burnor's desk. About three times a week, Susan Ryan would holler the call to volleyball. We'd play two great games, balancing players between sides to even it up and stretch the games out. Have lunch in Kathleen's horticultural flower garden in the courtyard just outside her window. Grumble at the computer. Try out some software that would actually work. Discover an amazing newsletter to tell readers about. Write a book, about the future. Bury inside the book the seed of what is next.

Okay, book, what's next?

— Kevin Kelly

*receipts for the first printing, or about $20,000 for **Signal**), or their overhead. I'd guess they'll hit real breakeven at 35,000 — the first printing sellout.*

*Our $65,000 advance is part advance payment against our projected royalty payments— 7.5% of the retail price of each book, and part out-right payment for production costs. Since we provided Harmony with camera-ready everything , they had to do none of the work they would usually do on a book, typesetting , proofreading, and all that. They agreed to allot $25,000 toward that, although it cost us more. The remaining $40,000 is our modest royalty advance. We don't receive any more income until the book earns us more than $40,000 in royalties. We'll pass $40,000 in royalties after 31,000 copies are sold. Deducting our agent's 15% cut, that raises our threshold to more than 37,000 copies of **Signal** sold before we see any payola. (Actually the deal is more complicated than this. **Signal** is joint-accounted with another book we are making for Harmony, called **The Fringes of Reason**, about ec-*

Cindy, keeper of the financial books.

*centric science and weird beliefs. Sales must exceed about 80,000 copies in total for either book, or in combination, before we earn any royalties for either book.)*

*So where did the $65,000 advance go? Very little went to equipment. We bought one new Macintosh SE for another project which freed one we already had,to be used for **Signal**. It joined five other Macs, and one Laser-Writer on the premises. We consumed 100 floppy discs, 3 laser toner cartridges, and 600 sheets of Polaroid film. We made a lot of phone calls, $900 or so. Cindy Fugett kept track of everything. Her full report appears to the right.*

*Of the $65,000 we pocketed in advance, we spent $63,709. That leaves a sure and certain $1,291 gain, even if we sell less than 37,000 copies. Sell more than that, and we're on a roll.*

— Kevin Kelly

## SIGNAL FINANCIAL REPORT

| | |
|---|---:|
| Editorial | $21418 |
| Design | 5753 |
| Proofreading | 3509 |
| Paste-up | 2840 |
| Production | 2271 |
| Photography | 2135 |
| Indexing | 1061 |
| Film | 1022 |
| Phones | 860 |
| Miscellaneous (supplies, etc) | 1865 |
| Contributors | 4000 |
| Overhead (rent, utilities) | 10975 |
| **Total** | **57709** |

## PROFIT/LOSS

| | |
|---|---:|
| Harmony advance | 65000 |
| Literary agent | -6000 |
| Signal costs | -57709 |
| **Net Gain** | **$1291** |

Book and software items are indicated by *italics*. Articles and surveys are in "quotes."

Compiled by David Burnor

[Left] Sifting through early drafts of these pages to squeeze out an index, David Burnor set up a Compaq Plus (IBM compatible) using the intergrated database, Smart, which has been custom programmed to collate this book's index. He was unexpectedly invited to join the Indexer's Association on the strength of his indices for Whole Earth Review, which one of their members had spotted.

[Right] Buckets keep each pair of pages intact as they travel around the offices. A bucket ferries the items, as well as the writing, for each spread. Lori hustles up some empties.

# A

# B

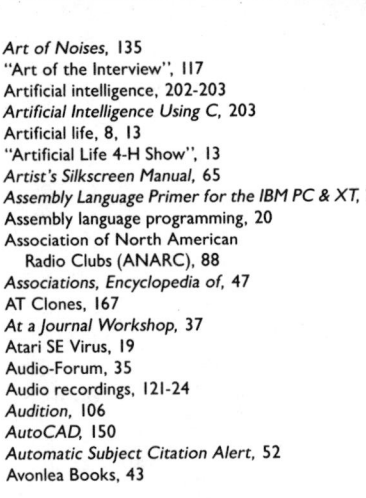

# C

Maniacal laughter, thunder, gunshots, bellowing dragons, and death screams periodically emanated from Sally's office. We knew Sally was caught up in another one of her computer games. Here she emerges after defeating the Evil Entities in Uninvited (see page 72) with a certificate of honor.

Serious hang-gliderist, accomplished mobile artist, Macintosh wizard, and part-time proofreader, Hank Roberts.

# E

# F

[Above left] Using the latest hi-tech editiing tool, Richard scissors text for Signal.

[Left] Jeanne Carstensen with handy Sony Camcorder.

[Below left] Sarah takes over the kitchen table, the last clear tablespace available, to arrange a spread.

[Above] Don adjusts his contorted 4 x 5 view camera for its unique perspective of book covers.

[Right] Susan trying to proofread newly printed page while Richard tells a joke.

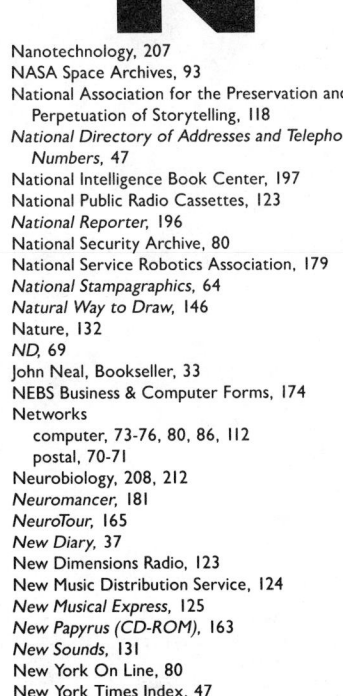

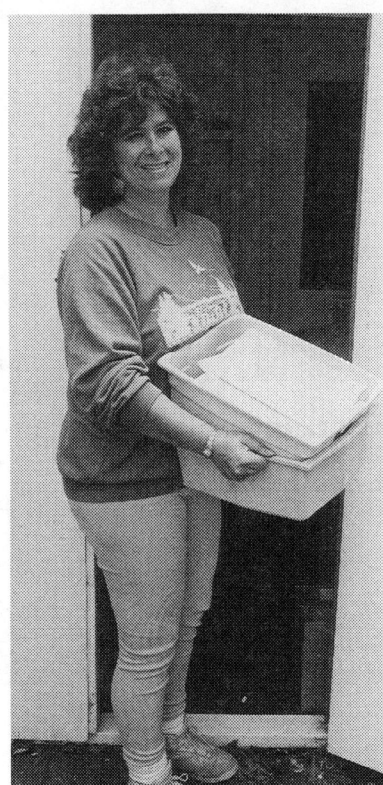

To accommodate extra staff, we put up the "dog house," a rough'n'ready shed with paste up tables inside. Laura heads in with a bucket load of undone work.

The black and white illustrations throughout this book were pasted up straight off the Japanese made Mita (model 2055) copier by John Chan. We found the quality nearly equal to a photographic stat camera, and infinitely more convenient.

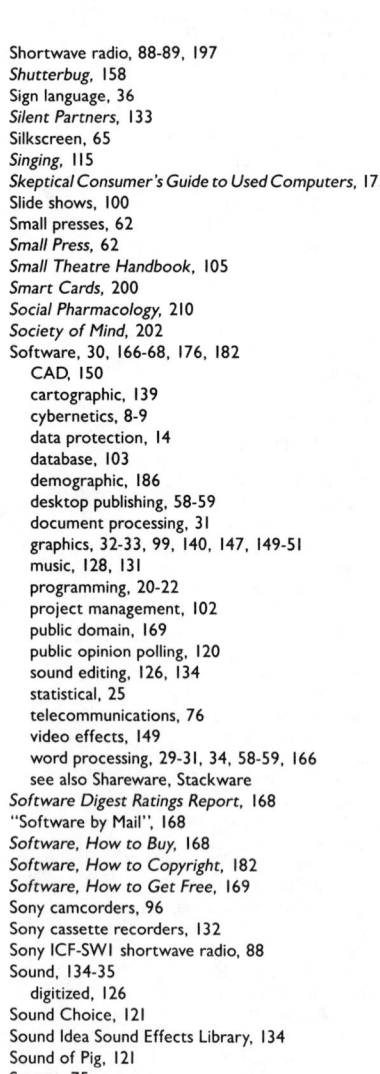

[Left] Without volleyball in the afternoons most of us would meld into blobs of disembodied computer ghosts. Volleyball gets us out of our heads and loosens up limbs and friendships. We play on a side court adjacent to the main office.

[Right] Wish this one was in color. Kathleen tends her magnificent garden of delights outside the production annex.

# How to Contribute to Future Updates of Signal

**T**HE EVALUATIONS IN *SIGNAL* ARE IN some cases inadequate. In every case they will date at the usual rate — fast. When you are sure that something you know is better than what we've run, have at us. We depend on far-flung expertise to keep our recommendations sharp. Contributing what you know is how we can be more comprehensively accurate in pointing at excellence.

When will there be an update to *Signal*? Don't know. Do know that when (if) it happens, feedback from readers will be a paramount part of its content and cause. Here's our standard advice for suggesting and reviewing items:

• Send them. We don't know about things unless someone tells us. Address your communications to Assistant Editor, 27 Gate 5 Road, Sausalito, CA 94965. We often print things that everyone, including the author, thought were too odd to be printed anywhere.

• Give the kind of information you would like to get. This should include what the item is good for, how it compares to others, where to get it, and some clue to how competent you are to judge. Avoid comments like "This is a good book." Prove it.

• Think of yourself as writing a letter to an intelligent,

uninformed friend. That's us. Be succinct. A paragraph is frequently enough. You don't have to analyze it, just tell us why you love it and why we should run it.

• Keep a copy. We are careful but not perfect. Be patient too. We are busy and want to carefully consider each submission. We'll let you know if we are going to use it. If you don't hear from us, it means we aren't.

• We pay for everything we print, including complaint letters. You get $20 for a review and $20 for first suggestion ($40 if we use both). Articles get more, depending on wonderfulness, clarity, ease of handling, and profusion of illustrations.

• Suppliers are invited to suggest their own goods. Samples or review copies are welcomed; response not predictable. We ask for no payment and will accept none. We serve as an information exchange and owe only accuracy to suppliers.

Samples, suggestions, and surveys should be sent to:

**Whole Earth Catalog**
**27 Gate 5 Road**
**Sausalito, CA 94965**
**415/332-1716**

# How To Receive Future Updates of Signal

**S**IGNAL WAS INCREMENTALLY GROWN. The knowledge gathered here is built upon 20 years of highly selective filtering. Both the content and process have evolved.

Key parts of this book began as embryonic ideas in our ongoing research tool, the *Whole Earth Review*, a quarterly magazine. There we freely try out new products, test promising books, and incubate half-baked ideas. A few survive. They are tested again against competitors during the assembly of each accumulated publication. All along we print our reports in the pages of *Whole Earth Review*. The best place to keep up with our continued investigation into *Signal* frontiers, is to subscribe to *Whole Earth Review*.

Each issue is 144 pages long, with merely two pages of advertising (entirely consisting of small unclassifieds available to subscribers only). The other 142 pages flaunt unorthodox technical news, first-hand reports of personal experiments, art, cartoons, excerpts from hard-to-find books, and anything else that might qualify as conceptual news.

Some recent articles in the last year:

• The rights of robots

• Voodoo and the origins of rock'n'roll

• Rental tools no one has ever told you about

• The information-wants-to-be-free business strategy

• Software to run a country with

• Access to World Beat music

• The cryonic suspension of a human head

• Interactive history

• Opiate chemicals as the information of emotions

• Evolutionary sidestep theory

The economic structure of *Whole Earth Review* is of a non-profit reader-driven service. We carry almost no advertising (except reader ads) and do almost no advertising ourselves. Carrying no advertising means we have the freedom to serve readers unusual topics that a more commercial magazine would have difficulty persuading

advertisers to support. No ads means our income is almost exclusively from readers who renew loyally. Those readers in turn pass on word of the magazine to friends, which helps us avoid having to advertise ourselves, except as we are doing now. We are reader-supported in another, equally important way. About half of the material in each issue is reader-suggested, or reader-written.

With such a notoriously vague self-definition, *Whole Earth Review* manages to wander a wide conceptual landscape and still remain true to itself and its readers. We have no idea where the magazine is going because the future isn't predictable. We'll go where issues are murky, the crosscurrents are swift, and the risk substantial and rewarding. It's $20 per year for four seasonal issues of the best ideas we can find.

Sign up by sending your check or credit card info to:

**Whole Earth Review**
**Box 38**
**Sausalito, CA 94965**
**415/332-1716**

Subscriptions: $20/year (4 issues) for U.S. Surface mail; foreign subscribers add $4/yr. for surface delivery, and $8/yr. for airmail.

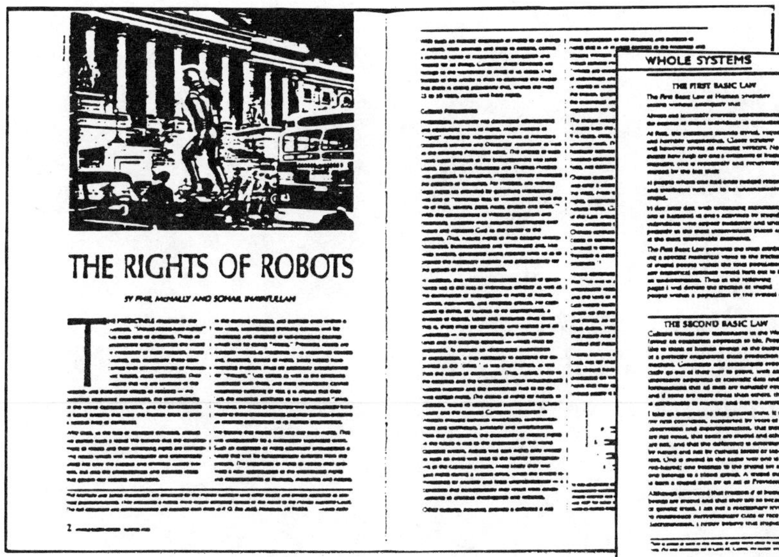

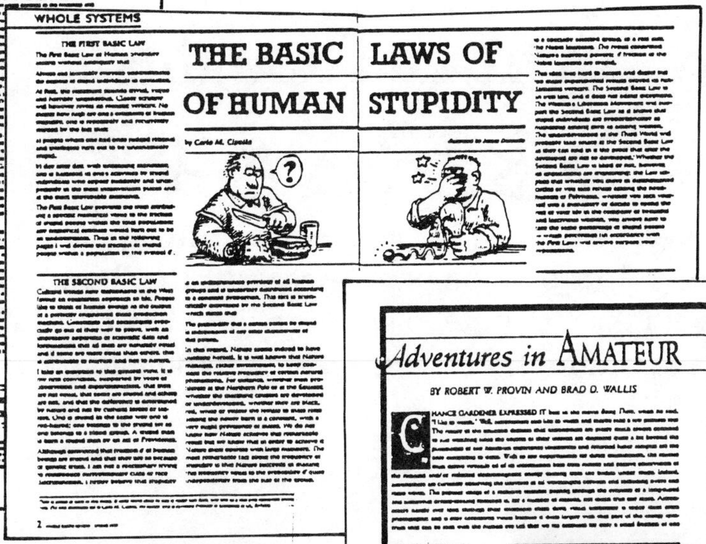

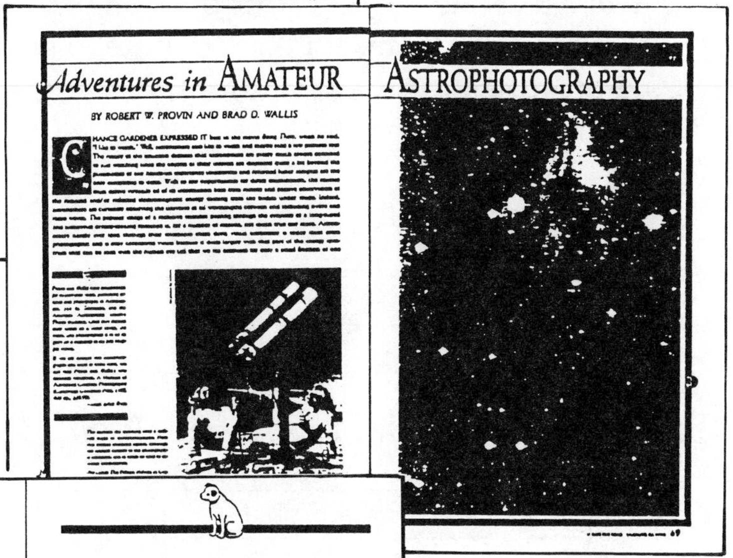

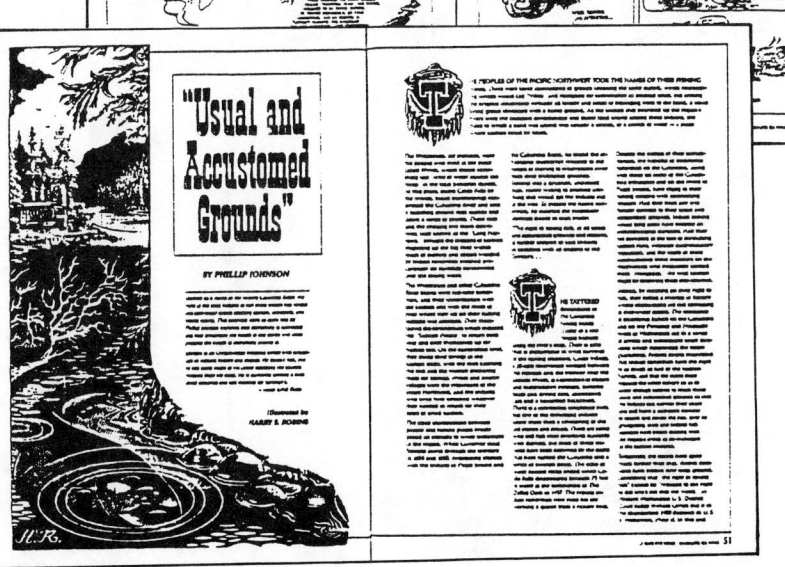

**In contrast to the collection of crystallized** nuggets of information found in this catalog, the *Whole Earth Review* could be thought of as the mother lode. As these sample pages from recent issues show, the magazine acts as a watershed of large ideas, in-depth stories, and unconventional wisdom finely illustrated. Where *Signal* is telegraphic and pithy, *Whole Earth Review* is journalistic and deep. Original thinkers hang out here. Recent issues have included: Ken Kesey, Ralph Nader, Joseph Campbell, Ursula LeGuin, Marvin Minsky, Eric Drexler, Hazel Henderson, Ed Abbey, Annie Dillard, Tim Leary, Jerry Brown, Brian Eno, Ted Nelson, Richard Dawkins, Jim Lovelock, Marilyn Ferguson, Wendell Berry, Bruce Sterling, Gary Snyder, Robert Bly, Paul Hawken, Lynn Margulis, Ram Dass, Lyall Watson, Allen Ginsberg, Ivan Illich, and R. Crumb.

# A Penny For Your Thoughts . . .

**DEAR READER,** *FREE MAGAZINE!*

We hope you've enjoyed *SIGNAL*. In the event that we update the book, we'd appreciate having your opinion of it — in particular, how it might be improved. If you'll take a minute to give us a little feedback, we'll be happy to send you a recent issue of our magazine, *Whole Earth Review*, at no cost.

**W**hat did you like best about *SIGNAL*?

_____

_____

_____

**W**hat did you like least about *SIGNAL*?

_____

_____

_____

_____

**W**hat wasn't in *SIGNAL* that should have been?

_____

_____

_____

**I**f this were a traditional questionnaire, we'd start asking about how many cars and VCRs you're going to buy this year for the benefit of our advertisers. But since *Whole Earth Review* doesn't carry any advertisements, we can skip that. All we'd like to get is an idea of who's talking to us, so please tell us your age and occupation. Feel free to make any other comments. ★ If you're reluctant to mutilate your copy of *SIGNAL*, send us a photocopy of this page (these pages).

Many thanks for helping.

Name _____

Address _____

_____

Age _____ Occupation _____

**S**end your valuable thoughts to:

*SIGNAL/Whole Earth Review,*
27 Gate Five Road, Sausalito, CA 94965.

# Xerox These Pages

# ORDER FORM

*WHOLE EARTH REVIEW:* Why stop with *SIGNAL?* Order now and receive *Whole Earth Review* for one year (four issues).

☐ Enter My Own Subscription (**$20**/year). . . . . . . . . . . . . . . . . . . . . . . . . . . . . . $ _____

☐ Send a Gift Subscription to the following person. I'll pay the $20. . . . . . . . . . . $ _____

**GIFT TO:**

Name _____

Address _____

City _____ State _____ Zip _____

**CARD:** *To* _____ *From* _____

**Fine Print:** Add **$4** for subscriptions outside the U.S. Add **$8** if you want it sent airmail — anywhere in the world.

*SIGNAL:* Order more from us, it's cheaper. **$15** each. . . . . . . . . . . . . . . . . . . . . $ _____

Send *SIGNAL* as a gift. We'll include a card. Just fill in the blanks below:

**GIFT TO:**

Name _____

Address _____

City _____ State _____ Zip _____

**CARD:** *To* _____ *From* _____ . . . . . . . $ _____

*The Electronic Whole Earth Catalog on CD-ROM* (**$149.95** each) * . . . . . . . $ _____
(See p. 163 for a complete description of the CD and what hardware you need to run it.) * *Available* **after** *January 1, 1989.*

**TOTAL: $** _____

**M**Y NAME: _____

Address _____

City _____ State _____ Zip _____

☐ Payment Enclosed   ☐ MC   ☐ VISA

Card # _____ Expiration Date _____

**S**end your order to:                                                    **SIG**

*Whole Earth Review*
27 Gate Five Road, Sausalito, CA 94965

# Xerox These Pages

# "Only connect."

— E. M. Forster, 1924